Principles behind the Agile Manifesto

We follow these principles:

- Our highest priority is to satisfy the customer through early and continuous delivery of valuable software.

- Welcome changing requirements, even late in development. Agile processes harness change for the customer's competitive advantage.

- Deliver working software frequently, from a couple of weeks to a couple of months, with a preference to the shorter timescale.

- Business people and developers must work together daily throughout the project.

- Build projects around motivated individuals. Give them the environment and support they need, and trust them to get the job done.

- The most efficient and effective method of conveying information to and within a development team is face-to-face conversation.

- Working software is the primary measure of progress.

- Agile processes promote sustainable development. The sponsors, developers, and users should be able to maintain a constant pace indefinitely.

- Continuous attention to technical excellence and good design enhances agility.

- Simplicity—the art of maximizing the amount of work not done— is essential.

- The best architectures, requirements, and designs emerge from self-organizing teams.

- At regular intervals, the team reflects on how to become more effective, then tunes and adjusts its behavior accordingly.

Agile
Principles, Patterns, and
Practices in
C#

Robert C. Martin Series

The mission of this series is to improve the state of the art of software craftsmanship. The books in this series are technical, pragmatic, and substantial. The authors are highly experienced craftsmen and professionals dedicated to writing about what actually works in practice, as opposed to what might work in theory. You will read about what the author has done, not what he thinks you should do. If the book is about programming, there will be lots of code. If the book is about managing, there will be lots of case studies from real projects.

These are the books that all serious practitioners will have on their bookshelves. These are the books that will be remembered for making a difference and for guiding professionals to become true craftsman.

Managing Agile Projects
Sanjiv Augustine

Agile Estimating and Planning
Mike Cohn

Working Effectively with Legacy Code
Michael C. Feathers

Agile Java™: Crafting Code with Test-Driven Development
Jeff Langr

Agile Principles, Patterns, and Practices in C#
Robert C. Martin and Micah Martin

Agile Software Development: Principles, Patterns, and Practices
Robert C. Martin

UML For Java™ Programmers
Robert C. Martin

Fit for Developing Software: Framework for Integrated Tests
Rick Mugridge and Ward Cunningham

Agile Software Development with SCRUM
Ken Schwaber and Mike Beedle

Extreme Software Engineering: A Hands on Approach
Daniel H. Steinberg and Daniel W. Palmer

For more information, visit http://www.prenhallpofessional.com/martinseries

Agile
Principles, Patterns, and
Practices in
C#

Robert C. Martin
Micah Martin

PRENTICE
HALL

Upper Saddle River, NJ • Boston • Indianapolis • San Francisco
New York • Toronto • Montreal • London • Munich • Paris • Madrid
Capetown • Sydney • Tokyo • Singapore • Mexico City

Many of the designations used by manufacturers and sellers to distinguish their products are claimed as trademarks. Where those designations appear in this book, and the publisher was aware of a trademark claim, the designations have been printed with initial capital letters or in all capitals.

The authors and publisher have taken care in the preparation of this book, but make no expressed or implied warranty of any kind and assume no responsibility for errors or omissions. No liability is assumed for incidental or consequential damages in connection with or arising out of the use of the information or programs contained herein.

The publisher offers excellent discounts on this book when ordered in quantity for bulk purchases or special sales, which may include electronic versions and/or custom covers and content particular to your business, training goals, marketing focus, and branding interests. For more information, please contact:

U.S. Corporate and Government Sales, (800) 382-3419
corpsales@pearsontechgroup.com

For sales outside the United States, please contact:

International Sales
international@pearsoned.com

This Book Is Safari Enabled

 The Safari® Enabled icon on the cover of your favorite technology book means the book is available through Safari Bookshelf. When you buy this book, you get free access to the online edition for 45 days.

Safari Bookshelf is an electronic reference library that lets you easily search thousands of technical books, find code samples, download chapters, and access technical information whenever and wherever you need it.

To gain 45-day Safari Enabled access to this book:

- Go to http://www.prenhallprofessional.com/safarienabled
- Complete the brief registration form
- Enter the coupon code RMI2-9AVK-NIU1-A8KM-RPMJ

If you have difficulty registering on Safari Bookshelf or accessing the online edition, please e-mail customer-service@safaribooksonline.com.

Visit us on the Web: www.prenhallprofessional.com

Library of Congress Cataloging-in-Publication Data

Martin, Robert C.
    Agile principles, patterns, and practices in C# / Robert C. Martin, Micah Martin.
        p. cm.
    Includes bibliographical references and index.
    ISBN 0-13-185725-8 (hardcover : alk. paper)
    1. Object-oriented programming (Computer science) 2. C# (Computer program language)
    3. Computer software--Development. I. Martin, Micah. II. Title.

    QA76.64.M383 2006
    005.1'17—dc22   2006013350

ISBN 0-13-185725-8
Text printed in the United States on recycled paper at Courier in Westford, Massachusetts.
2nd   Printing   April 2007

Contents

Foreword

In my first professional programming gig, I was hired to add features to a bug database. This was for the Plant Pathology Department of the University of Minnesota farm campus, so by "bug" I mean actual bugs, for example, aphids, grasshoppers, and caterpillars. The code had been written by an entomologist who'd learned just enough dBase to write his first form and then duplicated it throughout the rest of the application. As I added features, I consolidated as much of the functionality as possible so that bug fixes (code bug fixes) could be applied in a single place, enhancements could be applied in a single place, and so on. It took me all summer, but by the end, I'd doubled the functionality while halving the size of the code.

Many, many years later, a friend of mine and I were hanging out with nothing pressing to do, so we decided to program something together (it was either an implementation of IDispatch or IMoniker, both of which weighed heavily on our minds at the time). I'd type for a while with him watching over my shoulder, telling me where I got it wrong. Then he'd take over the keyboard while I kibitzed until he relinquished control back to me. It went on for hours and was one of the most satisfying coding experiences I've ever had.

Not long after that, my friend hired me as the chief architect for the newly formed software division of his company. On many occasions, as part of my architecture work, I'd write the client code for objects that I wished would exist, which I'd pass along to the engineers, who would keep implementing until the client worked.

Like many kids who learned applied techniques in the back seat of a '57 Chevy before sex education became a normal part of the curriculum, I'm guessing that my experiences experimenting with various aspects of agile development methodologies is not unique. In general, my experimenting with agile methods, like refactoring, pair programming, and test-driven development were successful, even though I didn't quite know what I was doing. Of course, there have been agile materials available to me before this, but just as I'm unwilling to learn how to ask Suzy to the sock-hop from back issues of National Geographic, I'd like my agile technologies served up as appropriate for my peer-group, that is, .NET. By using .NET (even though he's clear to say that .NET is no better than Java in many cases), Robert is speaking my language, just like those high school teachers that bothered to learn your slang, knowing that the message was more important than the medium.

But not just .NET; I'd like my first time to be gentle, to start slowly without scaring me, but to also make sure I get a grounding in all of the good stuff. And that's just what Robert "Uncle Bob" Martin has done with this book. His introductory chapters lay out the basics of the agile movement without pushing the reader towards SCRUM or Extreme Programming or any of the other agile methodologies, allowing the reader to join the atoms into the molecules that pleases them. Even better (and easily my favorite part of Robert's style) is when he shows these techniques in action, starting with a problem as it would be presented in a real-world environment and walks through it, showing the mistakes and missteps and how applying the techniques he advocates leads him back to safe ground.

I don't know if the world that Robert describes in this book really exists; I've only seen glimpses of it in my own life. However, it's clear that all of the "cool" kids are doing it. Consider "Uncle Bob" your own personal Dr. Ruth of the agile world whose only goal is that if you're going to do it, you do it well and make sure that everyone enjoys themselves.

Chris Sells

Foreword

From *Agile Software Development: Principles, Patterns and Practices*

I'm writing this foreword right after having shipped a major release of the Eclipse open source project. I'm still in recovery mode, and my mind is bleary. But one thing remains clearer than ever: that people, not processes, are the key to shipping a product. Our recipe for success is simple: work with individuals obsessed with shipping software, develop with lightweight processes that are tuned to each team, and adapt constantly.

Double-clicking on developers from our teams reveals individuals who consider programming the focus of development. Not only do they write code; they digest it constantly to maintain an understanding of the system. Validating designs with code provides feedback that's crucial for getting confidence in a design. At the same time, our developers understand the importance of patterns, refactoring, testing, incremental delivery, frequent builds, and other best-practices of XP that have altered the way we view methodologies today.

Skill in this style of development is a prerequisite for success in projects with high technical risk and changing requirements. Agile development is low-key on ceremony and project documentation, but it's intense when it comes to the day-to-day development practices that count. Putting these practices to work is the focus of this book.

Robert is a longtime activist in the object-oriented community, with contributions to C++ practice, design patterns, and object-oriented design principles in general. He was an early and vocal advocate of XP and agile methods. This book builds on these contributions, covering the full spectrum of agile development practice. It's an ambitious effort. Robert makes it more so by demonstrating everything through case studies and lots of code, as befits agile practice. He explains programming and design by actually doing it.

This book is crammed with sensible advice for software development. It's equally good whether you want to become an agile developer or improve the skills you already have. I was looking forward to this book, and I wasn't disappointed.

Erich Gamma
Object Technology International

Preface

But Bob, you said you'd be done with the book last *year.*

—Claudia Frers, *UML World*, 1999

Bob's Introduction

It's been seven years since Claudia's justifiable complaint, but I think I have made up for it. Publishing *three* books—one book every other year while running a consulting company and doing a lot of coding, training, mentoring, speaking, and writing articles, columns, and blogs—not to mention raising a family and enjoying a grandfamily can be quite a challenge. But I love it.

Agile development is the ability to develop software quickly, in the face of rapidly changing requirements. In order to achieve this agility, we need to use practices that provide the necessary discipline and feedback. We need to employ design principles that keep our software flexible and maintainable, and we need to know the design patterns that have been shown to balance those principles for specific problems. This book is an attempt to knit all three of these concepts together into a functioning whole.

This book describes those principles, patterns, and practices and then demonstrates how they are applied by walking through dozens of different case studies. More important, the case studies are not presented as complete works. Rather, they are designs *in progress*. You will see the designers make mistakes and observe how they identify them as mistakes and eventually correct them. You will see the designers puzzle over conundrums and worry over ambiguities and trade-offs. You will see the *act* of design.

Micah's Introduction

In early 2005, I was on a small development team that began work on a .NET application to be written in C#. Using agile development practices was mandatory, which is one of the reasons I was involved. Although I had used C# before, most of my programming experience was in Java and C++. I didn't think that working in .NET would make much difference; in the end it didn't.

Two months into the project, we made our first release. It was a partial release containing only a fraction of all the intended features, but it was enough to be usable. And use it they did. After only two months, the organization was reaping the benefits of our development. Management was so thrilled that it asked to hire more people so we could start more projects.

Having participated in the agile community for years, I knew a good many agile developers who could help us. I called them all and asked them to join us. Not one of my agile colleagues ended up joining our team. Why not? Perhaps the most overwhelming reason was the fact that we were developing in .NET.

Almost all agile developers have a background in Java, C++, or Smalltalk. But agile .NET programmers are almost unheard of. Perhaps my friends didn't take me seriously when I said we were doing agile software development with .NET, or maybe they were avoiding association with .NET. This was a significant problem. It was not the first evidence I'd seen of this problem, either.

Teaching week-long courses on various software topics allows me to meet a wide cross-section of developers from around the world. Many of the students I've instructed were .NET programmers, and many were Java or C++ programmers. There's no gentle way to put this: In my experience, .NET programmers are often weaker than Java and C++ programmers. Obviously, this is not always the case. However, after observing it over and over in my classes, I can come to no other conclusion: .NET programmers tend to be weaker in agile software practices, design patterns, design principles, and so on. Often in my classes, the .NET programmers had never heard of these fundamental concepts. *This has to change.*

The first edition of this book, *Agile Software Development: Principles, Patterns, and Practices*, by Robert C. Martin, my father, was published in late 2002 and won the 2003 Jolt Award. It is a great book, celebrated by many developers. Unfortunately, it had little impact on the .NET community. Despite the fact that the content of the book is equally relevant to .NET, few .NET programmers have read it.

It is my hope that this .NET edition acts as a bridge between .NET and the rest of the developer community. I hope that programmers will read it and see that there are better ways to build software. I hope that they will begin using better software practices, creating better designs, and raising the bar for quality in .NET applications. I hope that .NET programmers will not be weaker than other programmers. I hope that .NET programmers achieve a new status in the software community such that Java developers are proud to join a .NET team.

Throughout the process of putting this book together, I struggled many times with the concept of my name being on the cover of a .NET book. I questioned whether I wanted my name associated with .NET and all the negative connotations that seemed to come with it. Yet I can no longer deny it. I am a .NET programmer. No! An agile .NET programmer. And I'm proud of it.

About This Book

A Little History

In the early 1990s I (Bob) wrote *Designing Object-Oriented C++ Applications Using the Booch Method*. That book was something of a magnum opus for me, and I was very pleased with the result and the sales.

The book you are reading started out as a second edition to *Designing*, but that's not how it turned out. Very little remains of the original book in these pages. Little more than three chapters have been carried through, and those have been massively changed. The intent, spirit, and many of the lessons of the book are the same. In the decade since *Designing* came out, I've learned a tremendous amount about software design and development. This book reflects that learning.

What a decade! *Designing* came out just before the Internet collided with the planet. Since then, the number of acronyms we have to deal with has doubled. We have EJB, RMI, J2EE, XML, XSLT, HTML, ASP, JSP, ZOPE, SOAP, C#, and .NET, as well as Design Patterns, Java, Servlets, and Application Servers. Let me tell you, it's been difficult to keep the chapters of this book current.

The Booch connection In 1997, I was approached by Grady Booch to help write the third edition of his amazingly successful *Object-Oriented Analysis and Design with Applications*. I had worked with Grady before on some projects and had been an avid reader and contributor to his various works, including UML. So I accepted with glee and asked my good friend Jim Newkirk to help out with the project.

Over the next two years, Jim and I wrote a number of chapters for the Booch book. Of course, that effort meant that I could not put as much effort into this book as I would have liked, but I felt that the Booch book was worth contributing to. Besides, at the time, this book was simply a second edition of *Designing*, and my heart wasn't in it. If I was going to say something, I wanted to say something new and different.

Unfortunately, the Booch book was not to be. It is difficult to find the time to write a book during normal times. During the heady days of the dot-com bubble, it was nearly impossible. Grady got ever busier with Rational and with new ventures such as Catapulse. So the project stalled. Eventually, I asked Grady and Addison-Wesley whether I could have the chapters that Jim and I wrote to include in *this* book. They graciously agreed. So several of the case study and UML chapters came from that source.

The impact of Extreme Programming In late 1998, XP reared its head and challenged our cherished beliefs about software development. Should we create lots of UML diagrams prior to writing any code? Or should we eschew any kind of diagrams and simply write lots of code? Should we write lots of narrative documents that describe our design? Or should we try to make the *code* narrative and expressive so that ancillary documents aren't necessary? Should we program in pairs? Should we write tests before we write production code? What should we do?

This revolution came at an opportune time. During the middle to late 1990s, Object Mentor was helping quite a few companies with OO design and project management issues. We were helping companies get their projects *done*. As part of that help, we instilled into the teams our own attitudes and practices. Unfortunately, these attitudes and practices were not written down. Rather, they were an oral tradition that was passed from us to our customers.

By 1998, I realized that we needed to write down our process and practices so that we could better articulate them to our customers. So I wrote many articles about process in the *C++ Report*.[1] These articles missed the mark. They were informative and in some cases entertaining, but instead of codifying the practices and attitudes that we used in our projects, they were an unwitting compromise to values that had been imposed on me for decades. It took Kent Beck to show me that.

The Beck connection In late 1998, at the same time I was fretting over codifying the Object Mentor process, I ran into Kent's work on Extreme Programming (XP). The work was scattered through Ward Cunningham's *wiki*[2] and was mixed with the writings of many others. Still, with some work and diligence, I was able to get the gist of what Kent was

---

1. These articles are available in the *publications* section of www.objectmentor.com. There are four articles. The first three are entitled "Iterative and Incremental Development" (I, II, III). The last is entitled "C.O.D.E Culled Object Development process."

2. The website http://c2.com/cgi/wiki. contains a vast number of articles on an immense variety of subjects. Its authors number in the hundreds or thousands. It has been said that only Ward Cunningham could instigate a social revolution using only a few lines of Perl.

talking about. I was intrigued but skeptical. Some of the things that XP talked about were exactly on target for my concept of a development process. Other things, however, such as the lack of an articulated design step, left me puzzled.

Kent and I could not have come from more disparate software circumstances. He was a recognized Smalltalk consultant, and I was a recognized C++ consultant. Those two worlds found it difficult to communicate with each other. There was an almost Kuhnian[3] paradigm gulf between them.

Under other circumstances, I would never have asked Kent to write an article for the *C++ Report*. But the congruence of our thinking about process was able to breech the language gulf. In February 1999, I met Kent in Munich at the OOP conference. He was giving a talk on XP in the room across from where I was giving a talk on principles of OOD. Being unable to hear that talk, I sought Kent out at lunch. We talked about XP, and I asked him to write an article for the *C++ Report*. It was a great article about an incident in which Kent and a coworker had been able to make a sweeping design change in a live system in a matter of an hour or so.

Over the next several months, I went through the slow process of sorting out my own fears about XP. My greatest fear was in adopting a process in which there is no explicit upfront design step. I found myself balking at that. Didn't I have an obligation to my clients, and to the industry as a whole, to teach them that design is important enough to spend time on?

Eventually, I realized that I did not really practice such a step myself. Even in all the article and books I had written about design, Booch diagrams, and UML diagrams, I had always used code as a way to verify that the diagrams were meaningful. In all my customer consulting, I would spend an hour or two helping them to draw diagrams and then direct them to explore those diagrams with code. I came to understand that though XP's words about design were foreign, in a Kuhnian[4] sense, the practices behind the words were familiar to me.

My other fears about XP were easier to deal with. I had always been a closet pair programmer. XP gave me a way to come out of the closet and revel in my desire to program with a partner. Refactoring, continuous integration, customer onsite: All were very easy for me to accept. They were very close to the way I already advised my customers to work.

One practice of XP was a revelation for me. Test-driven development (TDD[5]) sounds innocuous when you first hear it: Write test cases before you write production code. All production code is written to make failing test cases pass. I was not prepared for the profound ramifications that writing code this way would have. This practice has completely transformed the way I write software: transformed it for the better.

---

3. Any credible intellectual work written between 1995 and 2001 must use the term *Kuhnian*. It refers to the book *The Structure of Scientific Revolutions,* by Thomas S. Kuhn, University of Chicago Press, 1962.

4. If you mention Kuhn twice in paper, you get extra credit.

5. Kent Beck, *Test-Driven Development by Example*, Addison-Wesley, 2003.

So by fall of 1999, I was convinced that Object Mentor should adopt XP as its process of choice and that I should let go of my desire to write my own process. Kent had done an excellent job of articulating the practices and process of XP; my own feeble attempts paled in comparison.

.NET A war is going on among major corporations. These corporations are fighting to gain *your* allegiance. These corporations believe that if they own the language, they'll own the programmers and the companies that employ those programmers.

The first volley of this war was Java. Java was the first language created by a major corporpation for the purpose of gaining programmer mindshare. This turned out to be wildly successful. Java has indeed penetrated very deeply into the software community and is largely the de facto standard for modern multilayer IT applications.

One responding volley comes from IBM, which via the Eclipse environment is capturing a large segment of the Java market. The other significant barrage comes from those consumate elaborators at Microsoft who have given us .NET in general and C# in particular.

Amazingly, it is very difficult to differentiate between Java and C#. The languages are semantically equivalent and syntactically so similar that many code snippets are indistiguishable. What Microsoft lacks in technical innovation, it more than makes up for in its remarkable ability to play catch-up and win.

The first edition of this book was written using Java and C++ as the coding language. This book is written using C# and the .NET platform. This should not be viewed as an endorsement. We are not taking sides in this war. Indeed, I think that the war itself will burn itself out when a better language surfaces in the next few years and captures the mindshare of the programmers that the warring corporations have spent so much to secure.

The reason for a .NET version of this book is to reach the .NET audience. Although the principles, patterns, and practices in this book are language agnostic, the case studies are not. Just as .NET programmers are more comfortable reading .NET case studies, Java progarmmers are more comfortable reading Java examples.

The Devil Is in the Details

This book contains a *lot* of .NET code. We hope that you will carefully read that code, since to a large degree, the code is the *point* of the book. The code is the actualization of what this book has to say.

This book has a repeating pattern: a series of case studies of varying sizes. Some are very small, and some require several chapters to describe. Each case study is preceded by material that is meant to prepare you for it by describing the object-oriented design principles and patterns used in that case study.

The book begins with a discussion on development practices and processes. That discussion is punctuated by a number of small case studies and examples. From there, the book moves on to the topic of design and design principles and then to some design patterns, more design principles that govern packages, and more patterns. All these topics are attended by case studies.

So prepare yourself to read some code and to pore over some UML diagrams. The book you are about to read is *very* technical, and its lessons, like the devil, are in the details.

Organization

This book is organized into four sections and two appendixes.

Section I, Agile Development, describes the concept of agile development. It starts with the *Manifesto of the Agile Alliance*, provides an overview of Extreme Programming (XP), and then goes to many small case studies that illuminate some of the individual XP practices, especially those that have an impact on the way we design and write code.

Section II, Agile Design, talks about object-oriented software design: what it is, the problem of and techniques for managing complexity, and the principles of object-oriented class design. The section concludes with several chapters that describe a pragmatic subset of UML.

Section III, The Payroll Case Study, describes the object-oriented design and C++ implementation of a simple batch payroll system. The first few chapters in this section describe the design patterns that the case study encounters. The final chapter is the full case study, the largest and most complete one in the book.

Section IV, Packaging the Payroll System, begins by describing the *principles of object-oriented package design* and then goes on to illustrate those principles by incrementally packaging the classes from the previous section. The section concludes with chapters that describe the database and UI design of the Payroll application.

Two appendixes follow: Appendix A, A Satire of Two Companies, and Appendix B, Jack Reeves' article, "What Is Software?"

How to Use This Book

If you are a developer, read the book cover to cover. This book was written primarily for developers and contains the information needed to develop software in an agile manner. Reading the book cover to cover introduces practices, and then principles then patterns, and then provides case studies that tie them all together. Integrating all this knowledge will help you get your projects *done*.

If you are a manager or business analyst, read Section I, Agile Development. Chapters 1–6 provide an in-depth discussion of agile principles and practices, taking you from requirements to planning to testing, refactoring, and programming. Section I will give you guidance on how to build teams and manage projects. It'll help you get your projects *done*.

If you want to learn UML, first read Chapters 13–19. Then read all the chapters in Section III, The Payroll Case Study. This course of reading will give you a good grounding in both the syntax and the use of UML and will also help you translate between UML and C#.

If you want to learn about design patterns, read Section II, Agile Design, to first learn about design principles. Then read Section III, The Payroll Case Study, and Section IV, Packaging the Payroll System. These sections define all the patterns and show how to use them in typical situations.

If you want to learn about object-oriented design principles, read Section II, Agile Design, Section III, The Payroll Case Study, and Section IV, Packaging the Payroll System. The chapters in those sections describe the principles of object-oriented design and show you how to use them.

If you want to learn about agile development methods, read Section I, Agile Development. This section describes agile development from requirements to planning testing, refactoring, and programming.

If you want a chuckle or two, read Appendix A, A Satire of Two Companies.

Acknowledgments

Lowell Lindstrom, Brian Button, Erik Meade, Mike Hill, Michael Feathers, Jim Newkirk, Micah Martin, Angelique Martin, Susan Rosso, Talisha Jefferson, Ron Jeffries, Kent Beck, Jeff Langr, David Farber, Bob Koss, James Grenning, Lance Welter, Pascal Roy, Martin Fowler, John Goodsen, Alan Apt, Paul Hodgetts, Phil Markgraf, Pete McBreen, H. S. Lahman, Dave Harris, James Kanze, Mark Webster, Chris Biegay, Alan Francis, Jessica D'Amico, Chris Guzikowski, Paul Petralia, Michelle Housley, David Chelimsky, Paul Pagel, Tim Ottinger, Christoffer Hedgate, and Neil Roodyn.

A very special thanks to Grady Booch and Paul Becker for allowing me to include chapters that were originally slated for Grady's third edition of *Object-Oriented Analysis and Design with Applications*. A special thanks to Jack Reeves for graciously allowing me to reproduce his "What Is Software Design?" article.

The wonderful and sometimes dazzling illustrations were drawn by Jennifer Kohnke and my daughter, Angela Brooks.

About the Authors

Robert C. Martin ("Uncle Bob") is founder and president of Object Mentor Inc., in Gurnee, Illinois, an international firm that offers process improvement consulting, object-oriented software design consulting, training, and skill development services to major corporations worldwide. He is also the author of *Designing Object Oriented C++ Applications Using the Booch Method* and *Agile Software Development Principles, Patterns, and Practices* (both Prentice Hall), *UML for Java Programming* (Addison-Wesley), and was the editor-in-chief of *C++ Journal* from 1996 to 1999. He is a featured speaker at international conferences and trade shows.

Micah Martin works with Object Mentor as a developer, consultant, and mentor on topics ranging from object-oriented principles and patterns to agile software development practices. Micah is the cocreator and lead developer of the open source FitNesse project. He is also a published author and speaks regularly at conferences.

Section I

Agile Development

© Jennifer M. Kohnke

Human interactions are complicated and never very crisp and clean in their effects, but they matter more than any other aspect of the work.

—Tom DeMarco and Timothy Lister, *Peopleware*

Principles, patterns, and practices are important, but it's the people who make them work. As Alistair Cockburn says: "Process and technology are a second-order effect on the outcome of a project. The first-order effect is the people."[1]

---

1. Private communication

We cannot manage teams of programmers as if they were systems made up of components driven by a process. To use Alistair Cockburn's phrase, people are not "plug-replaceable programming units." If our projects are to succeed, we are going to have to build collaborative and self-organizing teams.

Those companies that encourage the formation of such teams will have a *huge* competitive advantage over those that hold the view that a software development organization is nothing more than a pile of twisty little people all alike. A gelled software team is the most powerful software development force there is.

1

Agile Practices

The weather-cock on the church spire, though made of iron, would soon be broken by the storm-wind if it did not understand the noble art of turning to every wind.

—Heinrich Heine

Many of us have lived through the nightmare of a project with no practices to guide it. The lack of effective practices leads to unpredictability, repeated error, and wasted effort. Customers are disappointed by slipping schedules, growing budgets, and poor quality. Developers are disheartened by working ever-longer hours to produce ever-poorer software.

Once we have experienced such a fiasco, we become afraid of repeating the experience. Our fears motivate us to create a process that constrains our activities and demands certain outputs and artifacts. We draw these constraints and outputs from past experience, choosing things that appeared to work well in previous projects. Our hope is that they will work again and take away our fears.

But projects are not so simple that a few constraints and artifacts can reliably prevent error. As errors continue to be made, we diagnose those errors and put in place even more constraints and artifacts in order to prevent those errors in the future. After many projects, we may find ourselves overloaded with a huge, cumbersome process that greatly impedes our ability to get projects done.

A big, cumbersome process can create the very problems that it is designed to prevent. It can slow the team to the extent that schedules slip and budgets bloat. It can reduce the responsiveness of the team to the point of always creating the wrong product. Unfortunately, this leads many teams to believe that they don't have enough process. So, in a kind of runaway process inflation, they make their process ever larger.

Runaway process inflation is a good description of the state of affairs in many software companies circa 2000. Although many teams were still operating without a process, the adoption of very large, heavyweight processes was rapidly growing, especially in large corporations.

The Agile Alliance

Motivated by the observation that software teams in many corporations were stuck in a quagmire of ever-increasing process, a group of industry experts calling themselves the *Agile Alliance* met in early 2001 to outline the values and principles that would allow software teams to develop quickly and respond to change. Over the next several months, this group worked to create a statement of values. The result was *The Manifesto of the Agile Alliance*.

Manifesto for Agile Software Development

We are uncovering better ways of developing
software by doing it and helping others do it.
Through this work we have come to value:

Individuals and interactions over processes and tools
Working software over comprehensive documentation
Customer collaboration over contract negotiation
Responding to change over following a plan

That is, while there is value in the items on
the right, we value the items on the left more.

Kent Beck	Mike Beedle	Arie van Bennekum	Alistair Cockburn
Ward Cunningham	Martin Fowler	James Grenning	Jim Highsmith
Andrew Hunt	Ron Jeffries	Jon Kern	Brian Marick
Robert C. Martin	Steve Mellor	Ken Schwaber	Jeff Sutherland
Dave Thomas			

Individuals and Interactions over Processes and Tools

People are the most important ingredient of success. A good process will not save a project from failure if the team doesn't have strong players, but a bad process can make even the strongest of players ineffective. Even a group of strong players can fail badly if they don't work as a team.

A strong player is not necessarily an ace programmer. A strong player may be an average programmer but someone who works well with others. Working well with others—communicating and interacting—is more important than raw programming talent. A team of average programmers who communicate well are more likely to succeed than is a group of superstars who fail to interact as a team.

The right tools can be very important to success. Compilers, interactive development environments (IDEs), source code control systems, and so on, are all vital to the proper functioning of a team of developers. However, tools can be overemphasized. An overabundance of big, unwieldy tools is just as bad as a lack of tools.

Our advice is to start small. Don't assume that you've outgrown a tool until you've tried it and found that you can't use it. Instead of buying the top-of-the-line, megaexpensive source code control system, find a free one and use it until you can demonstrate that you've outgrown it. Before you buy team licenses for the best of all computer-aided software engineering (CASE) tools, use whiteboards and graph paper until you can unambiguously show that you need more. Before you commit to the top-shelf behemoth database system, try flat files. Don't assume that bigger and better tools will automatically help you do better. Often, they hinder more than they help.

Remember, building the team is more important that building the environment. Many teams and managers make the mistake of building the environment first and expecting the team to gel automatically. Instead, work to create the team, and then let the team configure the environment on the basis of need.

Working Software over Comprehensive Documentation

Software without documentation is a disaster. Code is not the ideal medium for communicating the rationale and structure of a system. Rather, the team needs to produce human-readable documents that describe the system and the rationale for design decisions.

However, too much documentation is worse than too little. Huge software documents take a great deal of time to produce and even more time to keep in sync with the code. If they are not kept in sync, they turn into large, complicated lies and become a significant source of misdirection.

It is always a good idea for the team to write and maintain a short rationale and structure document. But that document needs to be short and salient. By *short*, I mean one or two dozen pages at most. By *salient*, I mean that it should discuss the overall design rationale and only the highest-level structures in the system.

If all we have is a short rationale and structure document, how do we train new team members about the system? We work closely with them. We transfer our knowledge to them by sitting next to them and helping them. We make them part of the team through close training and interaction.

The two documents that are the best at transferring information to new team members are the code and the team. The code does not lie about what it does. It may be difficult to extract rationale and intent from the code, but the code is the only unambiguous source of information. The team holds the ever-changing roadmap of the system in its members' heads. The fastest and most efficient way to put that roadmap down on paper and transfer it to others is through human-to-human interaction.

Many teams have gotten hung up in pursuit of documentation instead of software. This is often a fatal flaw. There is a simple rule that prevents it:

> **Martin's First Law of Documentation**
> *Produce no document unless its need is immediate and significant.*

Customer Collaboration over Contract Negotiation

Software cannot be ordered like a commodity. You cannot write a description of the software you want and then have someone develop it on a fixed schedule for a fixed price. Time and time again, attempts to treat software projects in this manner have failed. Sometimes, the failures are spectacular.

It is tempting for company managers to tell their development staff what their needs are and then expect that staff to go away for a while and return with a system that satisfies those needs. But this mode of operation leads to poor quality and failure.

Successful projects involve customer feedback on a regular and frequent basis. Rather than depending on a contract, or a statement of work, the customer of the software works closely with the development team, providing frequent feedback on its efforts.

A contract that specifies the requirements, schedule, and cost of a project is fundamentally flawed. In most cases, the terms it specifies become meaningless long before the project is complete, sometimes even long before the contract is signed! The best contracts are those that govern the way the development team and the customer will work together.

An example of a successful contract is one I negotiated for a large, multiyear, half-million-line project in 1994. We, the development team, were paid a relatively low monthly rate. Large payouts were made to us when we delivered certain large blocks of functionality. Those blocks were not specified in detail by the contract. Rather, the contract stated that the payout would be made for a block when the block passed the customer's acceptance test. The details of those acceptance tests were not specified in the contract.

During the course of this project, we worked very closely with the customer. We released the software to him almost every Friday. By Monday or Tuesday of the following week, he had a list of changes for us to put into the software. We prioritized those changes together and then scheduled them into subsequent weeks. The customer worked so closely with us that acceptance tests were never an issue. He knew when a block of functionality satisfied his needs, because he watched it evolve from week to week.

The requirements for this project were in a continual state of flux. Major changes were not uncommon. Whole blocks of functionality were removed and others inserted. And yet the contract, and the project, survived and succeeded. The key to this success was the intense collaboration with the customer and a contract that governed that collaboration rather than trying to specify the details of scope and schedule for a fixed cost.

Responding to Change over Following a Plan

The ability to respond to change often determines the success or failure of a software project. When we build plans, we need to make sure that they are flexible and ready to adapt to changes in the business and technology.

The course of a software project cannot be planned very far into the future. First, the business environment is likely to change, causing the requirements to shift. Second, once they see the system start to function, customers are likely to alter the requirements. Finally, even if we know what the requirements are and are sure that they won't change, we are not very good at estimating how long it will take to develop them.

It is tempting for novice managers to create and tape to the wall a nice PERT or Gantt chart of the whole project. They may feel that this chart gives them control over the project. They can track the individual tasks and cross them off the chart as they are completed. They can compare the actual dates with the planned dates on the chart and react to any discrepancies.

But what *really* happens is that the structure of the chart degrades. As the team gains knowledge about the system and as the customer gains knowledge about the team's needs, certain tasks on the chart will become unnecessary. Other tasks will be discovered and will need to be added. In short, the plan will undergo changes in *shape*, not only in dates.

A better planning strategy is to make detailed plans for the next week, rough plans for the next 3 months, and extremely crude plans beyond that. We should know the individual tasks we will be working on for the next week. We should roughly know the requirements we will be working on for the next 3 months. And we should have only a vague idea what the system will do after a year.

This decreasing resolution of the plan means that we are investing in a detailed plan only for those tasks that are immediate. Once the detailed plan is made, it is difficult to change, since the team will have a lot of momentum and commitment. But since that plan governs only a week's worth of time, the rest of the plan remains flexible.

Principles

The preceding values inspired the following 12 principles. These principles are the characteristics that differentiate a set of agile practices from a heavyweight process.

1. *Our highest priority is to satisfy the customer through early and continuous delivery of valuable software.* The *MIT Sloan Management Review* published an analysis of software development practices that help companies build high-quality products.[1] The article found a number of practices that had a significant impact on the quality of the final system. One was a strong correlation between quality and the early delivery of a partially functioning system. The article reported that *the less functional the initial delivery, the higher the quality in the final delivery.* The article also found a strong correlation between final quality and frequent deliveries of increasing functionality. *The more frequent the deliveries, the higher the final quality.*

   An agile set of practices delivers early and often. We strive to deliver a rudimentary system within the first few weeks of the start of the project. Thereafter, we strive to continue to deliver systems of increasing functionality every few weeks. Customers may choose to put these systems into production if they think that they are functional enough. Or, they may choose simply to review the existing functionality and report on changes they want made.

---

1. "Product-Development Practices That Work: How Internet Companies Build Software," *MIT Sloan Management Review,* Winter 2001, reprint number 4226.

2. *Welcome changing requirements, even late in development. Agile processes harness change for the customer's competitive advantage.* This is a statement of attitude. The participants in an agile process are not afraid of change. They view changes to the requirements as *good* things, because those changes mean that the team has learned more about what it will take to satisfy the customer.

   An agile team works very hard to keep the structure of its software flexible, so that when requirements change, the impact to the system is minimal. Later in this book, we discuss the object-oriented design principles, patterns, and practices that help us to maintain this kind of flexibility.

3. *Deliver working software frequently, from a couple of weeks to a couple of months, with a preference to the shorter time scale.* We deliver *working* software, and we deliver it early and often. We are not content with delivering bundles of documents or plans. We don't count those as true deliveries. Our eye is on the goal of delivering software that satisfies the customer's needs.

4. *Businesspeople and developers must work together daily throughout the project.* In order for a project to be agile, customers, developers, and stakeholders must have significant and frequent interaction. A software project is not like a fire-and-forget weapon. A software project must be continuously guided.

5. *Build projects around motivated individuals. Give them the environment and support they need, and trust them to get the job done.* People are the most important success factor. All other factors—process, environment, management, and so on—are second-order factors and are subject to change if they are having an adverse effect on the people.

6. *The most efficient and effective method of conveying information to and within a development team is face-to-face conversation.* In an agile project, people *talk* to one another. The primary mode of communication is human interaction. Written documents are created and updated incrementally on the same schedule as the software and only as needed.

7. *Working software is the primary measure of progress.* Agile projects measure their progress by measuring the amount of software that is currently meeting the customer's need. They don't measure their progress in terms of the phase they are in or by the volume of documentation that has been produced or by the amount of infrastructure code they have created. They are 30 percent done when 30 percent of the necessary functionality is working.

8. *Agile processes promote sustainable development. The sponsors, developers, and users should be able to maintain a constant pace indefinitely.* An agile project is not run like a 50-yard dash; it is run like a marathon. The team does not take off at full speed and try to maintain that speed for the duration. Rather, it runs at a fast but sustainable pace.

Running too fast leads to burnout, shortcuts, and debacle. Agile teams pace themselves. They don't allow themselves to get too tired. They don't borrow tomorrow's energy to get a bit more done today. They work at a rate that allows them to maintain the highest-quality standards for the duration of the project.

9. *Continuous attention to technical excellence and good design enhances agility.* High quality is the key to high speed. The way to go fast is to keep the software as clean and robust as possible. Thus, all agile team members are committed to producing only the highest quality code they can. They do not make messes and then tell themselves that they'll clean them up when they have more time. They clean any messes as they are made.

10. *Simplicity—the art of maximizing the amount of work not done—is essential.* Agile teams do not try to build the grand system in the sky. Rather, they always take the simplest path that is consistent with their goals. They don't put a lot of importance on anticipating tomorrow's problems; nor do they try to defend against all of them today. Rather, they do the simplest and highest quality work today, confident that it will be easy to change if and when tomorrow's problems arise.

11. *The best architectures, requirements, and designs emerge from self-organizing teams.* An agile team is a self-organizing team. Responsibilities are not handed to individual team members from the outside but rather are communicated to the team as a whole. The team determines the best way to fulfill those responsibilities.

    Agile team members work together on all aspects of the project. Each member is allowed input into the whole. No single team member is solely responsible for the architecture or the requirements or the tests. The team shares those responsibilities, and each team member has influence over them.

12. *At regular intervals, the team reflects on how to become more effective, then tunes and adjusts its behavior accordingly.* An agile team continually adjusts its organization, rules, conventions, relationships, and so on. An agile team knows that its environment is continuously changing and knows that it must change with that environment to remain agile.

Conclusion

The professional goal of every software developer and every development team is to deliver the highest possible value to employers and customers. Yet our projects fail, or fail to deliver value, at a dismaying rate. The upward spiral of process inflation, though well intentioned, is culpable for at least some of this failure. The principles and values of agile software development were formed as a way to help teams break the cycle of process inflation and to focus on simple techniques for reaching their goals.

At the time of this writing, there are many agile processes to choose from: SCRUM,[2] Crystal,[3] feature-driven development (FDD),[4] adaptive software development (ADP),[5] and Extreme Programming (XP).[6] However, the vast majority of successful agile teams have drawn from all these processes to tune their own particular flavor of agility. These adaptations appear to be coalescing around a combination of SCRUM and XP, in which SCRUM practices are used to manage multiple teams that use XP.

Bibliography

[Beck99] Kent Beck, *Extreme Programming Explained: Embrace Change*, Addison-Wesley, 1999.

[Highsmith2000] James A. Highsmith, *Adaptive Software Development: A Collaborative Approach to Managing Complex Systems*, Dorset House, 2000.

[Newkirk2001] James Newkirk and Robert C. Martin, *Extreme Programming in Practice*, Addison-Wesley, 2001.

---

2. www.controlchaos.com

3. crystalmethodologies.org

4. Peter Coad, Eric Lefebvre, and Jeff De Luca, *Java Modeling in Color with UML: Enterprise Components and Process*, Prentice Hall, 1999.

5. [Highsmith2000]

6. [Beck99], [Newkirk2001]

2

Overview of Extreme Programming

© Jennifer M. Kohnke

As developers we need to remember that XP is not the only game in town.

—Pete McBreen

Chapter 1 outlined what agile software development is about. However, the chapter didn't tell us exactly what to do. It gave us some platitudes and goals but little in the way of real direction. This chapter corrects that.

The Practices of Extreme Programming

Whole Team

We want customers, managers, and developers to work closely with one another so that they are all aware of one another's problems and are collaborating to solve those problems. Who is the customer? The customer of an XP team is the person or group that defines and prioritizes features. Sometimes, the customer is a group of business analysts, quality assurance specialists, and/or marketing specialists working in the same company as the developers. Sometimes, the customer is a user representative commissioned by the body of users. Sometimes, the customer is in fact the paying customer. But in an XP project, the customer, however defined, is a member of, and available to, the team.

The best case is for the customer to work in the same room as the developers. Next best is if the customer works within 100' of the developers. The larger the distance, the more difficult it is for the customer to be a true team member. A customer located in another building or in another state it is very difficult to integrate into the team.

What do you do if the customer simply cannot be close by? My advice is to find someone who can be close by and who is willing and able to stand in for the true customer.

User Stories

In order to plan a project, we must know something about the requirements, but we don't need to know very much. For planning purposes, we need to know only enough about a requirement to estimate it. You may think that in order to estimate a requirement, you need to know all its details. But that's not quite true. You have to know that there *are* details, and you have to know roughly the kinds of details there are, but you don't have to know the specifics.

The specific details of a requirement are likely to change with time, especially once the customer begins to see the system come together. Nothing focuses requirements better than seeing the nascent system come to life. Therefore, capturing the specific details about a requirement long before it is implemented is likely to result in wasted effort and premature focusing.

In XP, we get the sense of the details of the requirements by talking them over with the customer. But we do not capture that detail. Rather, the customer writes a few words on an index card that we agree will remind us of the conversation. The developers write an estimate on the card at roughly the same time that the customer writes it. They base that estimate on the sense of detail they got during their conversations with the customer.

A *user story* is a mnemonic token of an ongoing conversation about a requirement. A user story is a planning tool that the customer uses to schedule the implementation of a requirement, based on its priority and estimated cost.

Short Cycles

An XP project delivers working software every two weeks. Each of these two-week iterations produces working software that addresses some of the needs of the stakeholders. At the end of each iteration, the system is demonstrated to the stakeholders in order to get their feedback.

The iteration plan An iteration is usually two weeks in length and represents a minor delivery that may or may not be put into production. The iteration plan is a collection of user stories selected by the customer according to a budget established by the developers.

The developers set the budget for an iteration by measuring how much they got done in the previous iteration. The customer may select any number of stories for the iteration so long as the total of the estimate does not exceed that budget.

Once an iteration has been started, the business agrees not to change the definition or priority of the stories in that iteration. During this time, the developers are free to cut the stories up into *tasks* and to develop the tasks in the order that makes the most technical and business sense.

The release plan XP teams often create a release plan that maps out the next six or so iterations. That plan is known as a release plan. A release is usually three months' worth of work. It represents a major delivery that can usually be put into production. A release plan consists of prioritized collections of user stories that have been selected by the customer according to a budget presented by the developers.

The developers set the budget for the release by measuring how much they got done in the previous release. The customer may select any number of stories for the release, so long as the total of the estimate does not exceed that budget. The business also determines the order in which the stories will be implemented in the release. If the team so desires, it can map out the first few iterations of the release by showing which stories will be completed in which iterations.

Releases are not cast in stone. The business can change the release content at any time. The business can cancel stories, write new stories, or change the priority of a story. However, the business should strive not to change an *iteration*.

Acceptance Tests

The details about the user stories are captured in the form of acceptance tests specified by the customer. The acceptance tests for a story are written immediately preceding, or even concurrently with, the implementation of that story. They are written in a scripting language that allows them to be run automatically and repeatedly.[1] Together, they act to verify that the system is behaving as the customers have specified.

---

1. See www.fitnesse.org

Acceptance tests are written by business analysts, quality assurance specialists, and testers during the iteration. The language they are written in is easy for programmers, customers, and businesspeople to read and understand. It is from these tests that the programmers learn the true detailed operation of the stories they are implementing. These tests become the true requirements document of the project. Every detail about every feature is described in the acceptance tests, and those tests are the final authority as to whether those features are done and correct.

Once an acceptance test passes, it is added to the body of passing acceptance tests and is never allowed to fail again. This growing body of acceptance tests is run several times per day, every time the system is built. If an acceptance tests fails, the build is declared a failure. Thus, once a requirement is implemented, it is never broken. The system is migrated from one working state to another and is never allowed to go unworking for longer than a few hours.

Pair Programming

Code is written by pairs of programmers working together at the same workstation. One member of each pair drives the keyboard and types the code. The other member of the pair watches the code being typed, finding errors and improvements.[2] The two interact intensely. Both are completely engaged in the act of writing software.

The roles change frequently. If the driver gets tired or stuck, the pair partner grabs the keyboard and starts to drive. The keyboard will move back and forth between them several times in an hour. The resultant code is designed and authored by both members. Neither can take more than half the credit.

Pair membership changes frequently. A reasonable goal is to change pair partners at least once per day so that every programmer works in two different pairs each day. Over the course of an iteration, every member of the team should have worked with every other member of the team, and they should have worked on just about everything that was going on in the iteration.

Pair programming dramatically increases the spread of knowledge throughout the team. Although specialties remain, and tasks that require certain specialties will usually belong to the appropriate specialists, those specialists will pair with nearly everyone else on the team. This will spread the specialty throughout the team such that other team members can fill in for the specialists in a pinch. Studies by Williams[3] and Nosek[4] have suggested that pairing does not reduce the efficiency of the programming staff but does significantly reduce the defect rate.

---

2. I have seen pairs in which one member controls the keyboard and the other controls the mouse.
3. [Williams2000], [Cockburn2001]
4. [Nosek98]

Test-Driven Development (TDD)

Chapter 4 discusses this topic in great detail. What follows is a quick overview.

All production code is written in order to make a failing unit test pass. First, we write a unit test that fails because the functionality it is testing for doesn't exist. Then we write the code that makes that test pass.

This iteration between writing test cases and code is very rapid, on the order of a minute or so. The test cases and code evolve together, with the test cases leading the code by a very small fraction. (See Chapter 6 for an example.)

As a result, a very complete body of test cases grows along with the code. These tests allow the programmers to check whether the program works. Programming a pair that makes a small change can run the tests to ensure that nothing has broken. This greatly facilitates *refactoring* (discussed later in this chapter).

When you write code in order to make test cases pass, that code is by definition testable. What's more, there is a strong motivation to decouple modules so that they can be tested independently. Thus, the design of code that is written in this fashion tends to be much less coupled. The principles of object-oriented design (OOD) play a powerful role in helping you with this decoupling (see Section II).

Collective Ownership

A pair has the right to check out *any* module and improve it. No programmers are individually responsible for any one particular module or technology. Everybody works on the graphical user interface (GUI).[5] Everybody works on the middleware. Everybody works on the database. Nobody has more authority than anybody else over a module or a technology.

This doesn't mean that XP denies specialties. If your specialty is the GUI, you are most likely to work on GUI tasks. But you will also be asked to pair on middleware and database tasks. If you decide to learn a second specialty, you can sign up for tasks, and work with specialists, who will teach it to you. You are not confined to your specialty.

Continuous Integration

The programmers check their code in and integrate several times per day. The rule is simple. The first one to check in wins; everybody else merges.

XP teams use nonblocking source control. This means that programmers are allowed to check any module out at any time, regardless of who else may have it checked out. When checking the module back in after modifying it, the programmer must be prepared

---

5. I'm not advocating a three-tiered architecture here. I simply chose three common partitions of software technology.

to merge it with any changes made by anyone who checked the module in earlier. To avoid long merge sessions, the members of the team check their modules very frequently.

A *pair* will work for an hour or two on a task. They create test cases and production code. At some convenient breaking point, probably long before the task is complete, they decide to check the code back in. They first make sure that all the tests run. They integrate their new code into the existing code base. If there is a merge to do, they do it. If necessary, they consult with the programmers who beat them to the check-in. Once their changes are integrated, they build the new system. They run every test in the system, including all currently running acceptance tests. If they broke anything that used to work, they fix it. Once all the tests run, they finish the check-in.

So XP teams will build the system many times each day. They build the *whole* system from end to end.[6] If the final result of a system is a CD-ROM, they cut the CD-ROM. If the final result of the system is an active Web site, they install that Web site, probably on a testing server.

Sustainable Pace

A software project is not a sprint; it is a marathon. A team that leaps off the starting line and starts racing as fast as it can will burn out long before finishing. In order to finish quickly, the team must run at a sustainable pace; it must conserve its energy and alertness. It must intentionally run at a steady, moderate pace.

The XP rule is that a team is not *allowed* to work overtime. The only exception to that rule is that in the last week in a release, a team that is within striking distance of its release goal can sprint to the finish and work overtime.

Open Workspace

The team works together in an open room. Tables are set up with workstations on them. Each table has two or three such workstations. Two chairs are in front of each workstation. The walls are covered with status charts, task breakdowns, Unified Modeling Language (UML) diagrams, and so on.

The sound in this room is a buzz of conversation. Each pair is within earshot of every other pair. Each has the opportunity to hear when another is in trouble. Each knows the state of the other. The programmers are in a position to communicate intensely.

One might think that this would be a distracting environment. It would be easy to fear that you'd never get anything done, because of the constant noise and distraction. In fact, this doesn't turn out to be the case. Moreover, instead of interfering with productivity, a University of Michigan study suggested, working in a "war room" environment may *increase* productivity by a factor of 2.[7]

---

6. Ron Jeffries says, "End to end is farther than you think."

7. www.sciencedaily.com/releases/2000/12/001206144705.htm

The Planning Game

Chapter 3 goes into great detail about the XP planning game. I'll describe it briefly here.

The essence of the planning game is the division of responsibility between business and development. The businesspeople—customers—decide how important a feature is, and the developers decide how much that feature will cost to implement.

At the beginning of each release and each iteration, the developers give the customers a budget. The customers choose stories whose costs total up to that budget and are not allowed to exceed their budget. Developers determine their budget, based on how much they were able to get done in the previous iteration or in the previous release.

With these simple rules in place, and with short iterations and frequent releases, it won't be long before the customers and developers get used to the rhythm of the project. The customers will get a sense for how quickly the developers are going. Based on that sense, the customers will be able to determine how long their project will take and how much it will cost.

Simple Design

An XP team makes its designs as simple and expressive as they can be. Furthermore, the team narrows its focus to consider only the stories that are planned for the current iteration, not worrying about stories to come. Rather, the team migrates the design of the system from iteration to iteration to be the best design for the stories that the system currently implements.

This means that an XP team will probably not start with infrastructure, probably won't select the database first, and probably won't select the middleware first. Rather, the team's first act will be to get the first batch of stories working in the *simplest way possible*. The team will add the infrastructure only when a story comes along that forces it to.

Three XP mantras guide the developer.

1. *Consider the simplest thing that could possibly work.* XP teams always try to find the simplest possible design option for the current batch of stories. If we can make the current stories work with flat files, we might not use a database. If we can make the current stories work with a simple socket connection, we might not use an ORB, or a Web Service. If we can make the current stories work without multithreading, we might not include mutithreading. We try to consider the simplest way to implement the current stories. Then we choose a practical solution that is as close to that simplicity as we can *practically* get.

2. *You aren't going to need it.* Yeah, but we *know* we're going to need that database one day. We *know* we're going to have to have an ORB one day. We *know* we're going to have to support multiple users one day. So we need to put the hooks in for those things *now*, don't we?

    An XP team seriously considers what will happen if it resists the temptation to add infrastructure before it is strictly needed. The team starts from the assumption that it isn't going to need that infrastructure. The team puts the infrastructure in only if it has proof, or at least very compelling evidence, that putting the infrastructure in now will be more cost-effective than waiting.

3. *Once and only once.* XPers don't tolerate duplication of code. Wherever they find it, they eliminate it.

    There are many sources of code duplication. The most obvious are those stretches of code that were captured with a mouse and plopped down in multiple places. When we find those, we eliminate them by creating a function or a base class. Sometimes, two or more algorithms may be remarkably similar and yet differ in subtle ways. We turn those into functions or use the TEMPLATE METHOD pattern (see Chapter 22). Once discovered, we won't tolerate duplication, whatever its source.

    The best way to eliminate redundancy is to create abstractions. After all, if two things are similar, some abstraction must unify them. Thus, the act of eliminating redundancy forces the team to create many abstractions and further reduce coupling.

Refactoring

Chapter 5 covers refactoring in more detail.[8] What follows here is a brief overview.

Code tends to rot. As we add feature after feature and deal with bug after bug, the structure of the code degrades. Left unchecked, this degradation leads to a tangled, unmaintainable mess.

XP teams reverse this degradation through frequent refactoring. Refactoring is the practice of making a series of tiny transformations that improve the structure of the system without affecting its behavior. Each transformation is trivial, hardly worth doing. But together, they combine into significant transformations of the design and architecture of the system.

After each tiny transformation, we run the unit tests to make sure that we haven't broken anything. Then we do the next transformation, and the next, and the next, running the tests after each. In this manner, we keep the system working while transforming its design.

Refactoring is done continuously rather than at the end of the project, the end of the release, or the end of the iteration, or even the end of the day. Refactoring is something we

---

8. [Fowler99]

do every hour or every half hour. Through refactoring, we continuously keep the code as clean, simple, and expressive as it can be.

Metaphor

Metaphor is the only XP practice that is not concrete and direct. Metaphor is the least well understood of all the practices of XP. XPers are pragmatists at heart, and this lack of concrete definition makes us uncomfortable. Indeed, the proponents of XP have often discussed removing metaphor as a practice. Yet in some sense, metaphor is one of the most important practices of all.

Think of a jigsaw puzzle. How do you know how the pieces go together? Clearly, each piece abuts others, and its shape must be perfectly complementary to the pieces it touches. If you were blind and had a very good sense of touch, you could put the puzzle together by diligently sifting through each piece and trying it in position after position.

But something more powerful than the shape of the pieces binds the puzzle together: a picture. The picture is the true guide. The picture is so powerful that if two adjacent pieces of the picture do not have complementary shapes, you *know* that the puzzle maker made a mistake.

That's what the metaphor is. It's the big picture that ties the whole system together. It's the vision of the system that makes the location and shape of all the individual modules obvious. If a module's shape is inconsistent with the metaphor, you know that it is the module that is wrong.

Often, a metaphor boils down to a system of names. The names provide a vocabulary for elements in the system and helps to define their relationships.

For example, I once worked on a system that transmitted text to a screen at 60 characters per second. At that rate, a screen fill could take some time. So we'd allow the program that was generating the text to fill a buffer. When the buffer was full, we'd swap the program out to disk. When the buffer got close to empty, we'd swap the program back in and let it run some more.

We spoke about this system in terms of dump trucks hauling garbage. The buffers were little trucks. The display screen was the dump. The program was the garbage producer. The names all fit together and helped us think about the system as a whole.

As another example, I once worked on a system that analyzed network traffic. Every 30 minutes, it polled dozens of network adapters and pulled down the monitoring data from them. Each network adapter gave us a small block of data composed of several individual variables. We called these blocks "slices." The slices were raw data that needed to be analyzed. The analysis program "cooked" the slices, so it was called "the toaster." We called the individual variables within the slices "crumbs." All in all, it was a useful and entertaining metaphor.

Of course, a metaphor is more than a system of names. A metaphor is a vision for the system. A metaphor guides all the developers to choose appropriate names, select appropriate locations for functions, create appropriate new classes and methods, and so on.

Conclusion

Extreme Programming is a set of simple and concrete practices that combine into an agile development process. XP is a good general-purpose method for developing software. Many project teams will be able to adopt it as is. Many others will be able to adapt it by adding or modifying practices.

Bibliography

[ARC97] Alistair Cockburn, "The Methodology Space," *Humans and Technology*, technical report HaT TR.97.03 (dated 97.10.03), http://members.aol.com/acockburn/papers/methyspace/methyspace.htm.

[Beck99] Kent Beck, *Extreme Programming Explained: Embrace Change*, Addison-Wesley, 1999.

[Beck2003] Kent Beck, *Test-Driven Development by Example*, Addison-Wesley, 2003.

[Cockburn2001] Alistair Cockburn and Laurie Williams, "The Costs and Benefits of Pair Programming," XP2000 Conference in Sardinia, reproduced in Giancarlo Succi and Michele Marchesi, *Extreme Programming Examined*, Addison-Wesley, 2001.

[DRC98] Daryl R. Conner, *Leading at the Edge of Chaos*, Wiley, 1998.

[EWD72] D.J. Dahl, E.W. Dijkstra, and C.A.R. Hoare, *Structured Programming*, Academic Press, 1972.

[Fowler99] Martin Fowler, *Refactoring: Improving the Design of Existing Code*, Addison-Wesley, 1999.

[Newkirk2001] James Newkirk and Robert C. Martin, *Extreme Programming in Practice*, Addison-Wesley, 2001.

[Nosek98] J. T. Nosek, "The Case for Collaborative Programming," *Communications of the ACM*, 1998, pp. 105–108.

[Williams2000] Laurie Williams, Robert R. Kessler, Ward Cunningham, Ron Jeffries, "Strengthening the Case for Pair Programming," *IEEE Software*, July–Aug. 2000.

3

Planning

When you can measure what you are speaking about, and express it in numbers, you know something about it; but when you cannot measure it, when you cannot express it in numbers, your knowledge is of a meager and unsatisfactory kind.

—Lord Kelvin, 1883

What follows is a description of the Planning Game from Extreme Programming.[1] It is similar to the way planning is done in several of the other agile[2] methods: SCRUM,[3]

---

1. [Beck99], [Newkirk2001]

2. www.AgileAlliance.org

3. www.controlchaos.com

Crystal,[4] feature-driven development,[5] and adaptive software development (ADP).[6] However, none of those processes spell it out in as much detail and rigor.

Initial Exploration

At the start of the project, the developers and customers have conversations about the new system in order to identify all the significant features that they can. However, they don't try to identify *all* features. As the project proceeds, the customers will continue to discover more features. The flow of features will not shut off until the project is over.

As a feature is identified, it is broken down into one or more *user stories*, which are written onto index cards or their equivalent. Not much is written on the card except the name of the story (e.g., Login, Add User, Delete User, or Change Password). We aren't trying to capture details at this stage. We simply want something to remind us of the conversations we've been having about the features.

The developers work together to estimate the stories. The estimates are relative, not absolute. We write a number of "points" on a story card to represent the relative cost of the story. We may not be sure just how much time a story point represents, but we do know that a story with 8 points will take twice as long as a story with 4 points.

Spiking, Splitting, and Velocity

Stories that are too large or too small are difficult to estimate. Developers tend to underestimate large stories and overestimate small ones. Any story that is too big should be split into pieces that aren't too big. Any story that is too small should be merged with other small stories.

For example, consider the story "Users can securely transfer money into, out of, and between their accounts." This is a big story. Estimating will be difficult, and probably inaccurate. However, we can split it into many stories that are much easier to estimate:

- Users can log in.
- Users can log out.
- Users can deposit money into their accounts.
- Users can withdraw money from their accounts.
- Users can transfer money from one of their accounts to another account.

When a story is split or merged, it should be reestimated. It is not wise to simply add or subtract the estimate. The whole reason to split or merge a story is to get it to a size at

---

4. [Cockburn2005]

5. Peter Coad, Eric Lefebvre, and Jeff De Luca, *Java Modeling in Color with UML: Enterprise Components and Process*, Prentice Hall, 1999.

6. [Highsmith2000]

which estimation is accurate. It is not surprising to find that a story estimated at 25 points breaks up into stories that add up to 30! Thirty is the more accurate estimate.

Every week, we complete a certain number of stories. The sum of the estimates of the completed stories is a metric known as *velocity*. If we completed 42 points' worth of stories during the previous week, our velocity is 42.

After 3 or 4 weeks, we'll have a good idea of our average velocity. We can use this to predict how much work we'll get done in subsequent weeks. Tracking velocity is one of the most important management tools in an XP project.

At the start of a project, the developers will not have a very good idea of their velocity. They must create an initial guess by whatever means they feel will give the best results. The need for accuracy at this point is not particularly grave, so they don't need to spend an inordinate amount of time on it. Indeed, as good old-fashioned SWAG[7] is usually good enough.

Release Planning

Given a velocity, the customers can get an idea of the cost of each of the stories, as well as its business value and priority. This allows the customers to choose the stories they want done first. This choice is not purely a matter of priority. Something that is important but also expensive may be delayed in favor of something that is less important but much less expensive. Choices like this are *business* decisions. The business folks decide which stories give them the most bang for the buck.

The developers and customers agree on a date for the first release of the project. This is usually a matter of 2–4 months in the future. The customers pick the stories they want implemented within that release and the rough order they want them implemented in. The customers cannot choose more stories than will fit according to the current velocity. Since the velocity is initially inaccurate, this selection is crude. But accuracy is not very important at this point. The release plan can be adjusted as velocity becomes more accurate.

Iteration Planning

Next, the developers and customers choose an iteration size: typically, 1 or 2 weeks. Once again, the customers choose the stories that they want implemented in the first iteration but cannot choose more stories than will fit according to the current velocity.

The order of the stories within the iteration is a technical decision. The developers implement the stories in the order that makes the most technical sense. The developers may work on the stories serially, finishing each one after the next, or may divvy up the stories and work on them all concurrently. It's entirely up to the developers.

---

7. Scientific Wild-Assed Guess

The customers cannot change the stories in the iteration once it has begun. Customers are free to change or reorder any other story in the project but not the ones that the developers are currently working on.

The iteration ends on the specified date, even if all the stories aren't done. The estimates for all the completed stories are totaled, and the velocity for that iteration is calculated. This measure of velocity is then used to plan the next iteration. The rule is very simple: The planned velocity for each iteration is the measured velocity of the previous iteration. If the team got 31 story points done last iteration, it should plan to get 31 story points done in the next. The team's velocity is 31 points per iteration.

This feedback of velocity helps to keep the planning in sync with the team. If the team gains in expertise and skill, the velocity will rise commensurately. If someone is lost from the team, the velocity will fall. If an architecture evolves that facilitates development, the velocity will rise.

Defining "Done"

A story is not done until *all* its acceptance tests pass. Those acceptance tests are automated. They are written by the customer, business analysts, quality assurance specialists, testers, and even programmers, at the very start of each iteration. These tests define the details of the stories and are the final authority on how the stories behave. We'll have more to say about acceptance tests in the next chapter.

Task Planning

At the start of a new iteration, the developers and customers get together to plan. The developers break the stories down into development tasks. A *task* is something that one developer can implement in 4–16 hours. The stories are analyzed, with the customers' help, and the tasks are enumerated as completely as possible.

A list of the tasks is created on a flip chart, whiteboard, or some other convenient medium. Then, one by one, the developers sign up for the tasks they want to implement, estimating each task in arbitrary task points.[8]

Developers may sign up for any kind of task. Database specialists are not constrained to sign up for database tasks. GUI people can sign up for database tasks if they like. Although this may seem inefficient, a mechanism manages that. The benefit is obvious: The more the developers know about the *whole* project, the healthier and more informed the project team is. We want knowledge of the project to spread throughout the team, irrespective of specialty.

---

8. Many developers find it helpful to use "perfect programming hours" as their task points.

Each developer knows how many task points he or she managed to implement in the previous iteration; this number is the developer's *budget*. No one signs up for more points than are in the budget.

Task selection continues until either all tasks are assigned or all developers have used their budgets. If tasks remain, the developers negotiate with each other, trading tasks, based on their various skills. If this doesn't make enough room to get all the tasks assigned, the developers ask the customers to remove tasks or stories from the iteration. If all the tasks are signed up and the developers still have room in their budgets for more work, they ask the customers for more stories.

Half way through the iteration, the team holds a meeting. At this point, half of the *stories* scheduled for the iteration should be complete. If half the *stories* aren't complete, the team tries to reapportion tasks and responsibilities to ensure that all the stories will be complete by the end of the iteration. If the developers cannot find such a reapportionment, the customers need to be told. The customers may decide to pull a task or story from the iteration. At very least, they will name the lowest-priority tasks and stories so that developers avoid working on them.

For example, suppose that the customers selected eight stories totaling 24 story points for the iteration. Suppose also that these were broken down into 42 tasks. At the halfway point of the iteration, we would expect to have 21 tasks and 12 story points complete. Those 12 story points must represent wholly completed stories. Our goal is to complete stories, not simply tasks. The nightmare scenario is to get to the end of the iteration with 90 percent of the tasks complete but no stories complete. At the halfway point, we want to see completed stories that represent half the story points for the iteration.

Iterating

Every 2 weeks, the current iteration ends and the next begins. At the end of each iteration, the current running executable is demonstrated to the customers. The customers are asked to evaluate the look, feel, and performance of the project. They will provide their feedback in terms of new user stories.

The customers see progress frequently. They can measure velocity. They can predict how quickly the team is going and can schedule high-priority stories early. In short, customers have all the data and control they need to manage the project to their liking.

Tracking

Tracking and managing an XP project is a matter of recording the results of each iteration and then using those results to predict what will happen in the next iterations. Consider, for example, Figure 3-1. This graph is called a *velocity chart*. We would normally find it on the wall of the project war room.

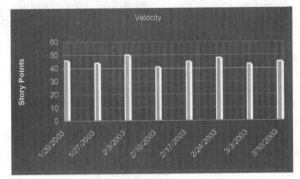

Figure 3-1
Velocity chart

This chart shows how many story points were completed—passed their automated acceptance tests—at the end of each week. Although there is some variation between the weeks, the data clearly shows that this team is completing around 42 story points per week.

Consider also the graph in Figure 3-2. This so-called *burn-down chart* shows, on a week-by-week basis, how many points remain to be completed for the next major milestone or release. The slope of this chart is a reasonable predictor of the end date.

Note that the difference between the bars in the burn-down chart does not equal the height of the bars in the velocity chart. The reason is that new stories are being added to the project. It may also indicate that the developers have re-estimated the stories.

When these two charts are kept on the wall of the project room, anybody can look them over and tell within seconds what the status of the project is. They can tell when the next major milestone will be met and to what degree the scope and estimates are creeping. These two charts are the true bottom line for XP and all the agile methods. In the end, it's all about generating reliable management information.

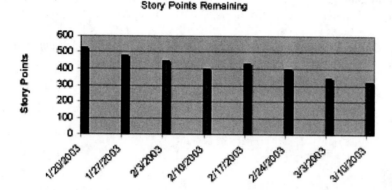

Figure 3-2
Burn-down chart

Conclusion

From iteration to iteration and release to release, the project falls into a predictable and comfortable rhythm. Everyone knows what to expect and when to expect it. Stakeholders see progress frequently and substantially. Rather than being shown notebooks full of diagrams and plans, stakeholders are shown working software that they can touch, feel, and provide feedback on.

Developers see a reasonable plan, based on their own estimates and controlled by their own measured velocity. Developers choose the tasks they feel comfortable working on and keep the quality of their workmanship high.

Managers receive data every iteration. They use this data to control and manage the project. They don't have to resort to pressure, threats, or appeals to loyalty to meet an arbitrary and unrealistic date.

If this sounds like blue sky and apple pie, it's not. The stakeholders won't always be happy with the data that the process produces, especially not at first. Using an agile method does not mean that the stakeholders will get what they want. It simply means that they'll be able to control the team to get the most business value for the least cost.

Bibliography

[Beck99] Kent Beck, *Extreme Programming Explained: Embrace Change*, Addison-Wesley, 1999.

[Cockburn2005] Alistair Cockburn, *Crystal Clear: A Human-Powered Methodolgy for Small Teams*, Addison-Wesley, 2005.

[Highsmith2000] James A. Highsmith, *Adaptive Software Development: A Collaborative Approach to Managing Complex Systems*, Dorset House, 2000.

[Newkirk2001] James Newkirk and Robert C. Martin, *Extreme Programming in Practice*, Addison-Wesley, 2001.

4

Testing

© Jennifer M. Kohnke

Fire is the test of gold; adversity, of strong men.

—Seneca (c. 3 B.C.–A.D. 65)

The act of writing a unit test is more an act of design than of verification. It is also more an act of documentation than of verification. The act of writing a unit test closes a remarkable number of feedback loops, the least of which is the one pertaining to verification of function.

Test-Driven Development

Suppose that we followed three simple rules.

1. Don't write any production code until you have written a failing unit test.

2. Don't write more of a unit test than is sufficient to fail or fail to compile.

3. Don't write any more production code than is sufficient to pass the failing test.

If we worked this way, we'd be working in very short cycles. We'd be writing just enough of a unit test to make it fail and then just enough production code to make it pass. We'd be alternating between these steps every minute or two.

The first and most obvious effect is that every single function of the program has tests that verify its operation. This suite of tests acts as a backstop for further development. It tells us whenever we inadvertently break some existing functionality. We can add functions to the program or change the structure of the program without fear that in the process, we will break something important. The tests tell us that the program is still behaving properly. We are thus much freer to make changes and improvements to our program.

A more important but less obvious effect is that the act of writing the test first forces us into a different point of view. We must view the program we are about to write from the vantage point of a caller of that program. Thus, we are immediately concerned with the interface of the program as well as its function. By writing the test first, we design the software to be *conveniently callable*.

What's more, by writing the test first, we force ourselves to design the program to be *testable*. Designing the program to be callable and testable is remarkably important. In order to be callable and testable, the software has to be decoupled from its surroundings. Thus, the act of writing tests first *forces us to decouple the software*!

Another important effect of writing tests first is that the tests act as an invaluable form of documentation. If you want to know how to call a function or create an object, there is a test that shows you. The tests act as a suite of examples that help other programmers figure out how to work with the code. This documentation is compilable and executable. It will stay current. It cannot lie.

Example of Test-First Design

Just for fun, I recently wrote a version of *Hunt the Wumpus*. This program is a simple adventure game in which the player moves through a cave, trying to kill the Wumpus before being eaten by the Wumpus. The cave is a set of rooms connected by passageways. Each room may have passages to the north, south, east, or west. The player moves about by telling the computer which direction to go.

One of the first tests I wrote for this program was `testMove` (Listing 4-1). This function created a new `WumpusGame`, connected room 4 to room 5 via an east passage, placed the player in room 4, issued the command to move east, and then asserted that the player should be in room 5.

Listing 4-1

```
[Test]

public void TestMove()
{
    WumpusGame g = new WumpusGame();
    g.Connect(4,5,"E");
    g.GetPlayerRoom(4);
    g.East();
    Assert.AreEqual(5, g.GetPlayerRoom());
}
```

All this code was written before any part of WumpusGame was written. I took Ward Cunningham's advice and wrote the test the way I wanted it to read. I trusted that I could make the test pass by writing the code that conformed to the structure implied by the test. This is called *intentional programming*. You state your intent in a test before you implement it, making your intent as simple and readable as possible. You trust that this simplicity and clarity points to a good structure for the program.

Programming by intent immediately led me to an interesting design decision. The test makes no use of a Room class. The action of *connecting* one room to another communicates my intent. I don't seem to need a Room class to facilitate that communication. Instead, I can simply use integers to represent the rooms.

This may seem counterintuitive to you. After all, this program may appear to you to be all about rooms, moving between rooms, finding out what rooms contain, and so on. Is the design implied by my intent flawed because it lacks a Room class?

I could argue that the concept of connections is far more central to the Wumpus game than the concept of room. I could argue that this initial test pointed out a good way to solve the problem. Indeed, I think that is the case, but it is not the point I'm trying to make. The point is that the test illuminated a central design issue at a very early stage. *The act of writing tests first is an act of discerning between design decisions.*

Note that the test tells you how the program works. Most of us could easily write the four named methods of WumpusGame from this simple specification. We could also name and write the three other direction commands without much trouble. If later we wanted to know how to connect two rooms or move in a particular direction, this test will show us how to do it in no uncertain terms. This test acts as a compilable and executable document that describes the program.

Test Isolation

The act of writing tests before production code often exposes areas in the software that ought to be decoupled. For example, Figure 4-1 shows a simple UML diagram of a payroll application. The Payroll class uses the EmployeeDatabase class to fetch an Employee object, asks the `Employee` to calculate its pay, passes that pay to the `CheckWriter` object to produce a check, and, finally, posts the payment to the `Employee` object and writes the object back to the database.

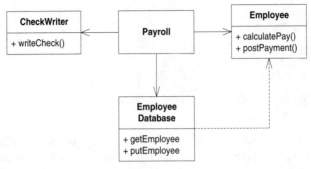

Figure 4-1
Coupled payroll model

Presume that we haven't written any of this code yet. So far, this diagram is simply sitting on a whiteboard after a quick design session.[1] Now we need to write the tests that specify the behavior of the `Payroll` object. A number of problems are associated with writing this test. First, what database do we use? `Payroll` needs to read from some kind of database. Must we write a fully functioning database before we can test the `Payroll` class? What data do we load into it? Second, how do we verify that the appropriate check got printed? We can't write an automated test that looks on the printer for a check and verifies the amount on it!

The solution to these problems is to use the MOCK OBJECT pattern.[2] We can insert interfaces between all the collaborators of `Payroll` and create test stubs that implement these interfaces.

Figure 4-2 shows the structure. The `Payroll` class now uses interfaces to communicate with the `EmployeeDatabase`, `CheckWriter`, and `Employee`. Three MOCK OBJECTS have been created that implement these interfaces. These MOCK OBJECTS are queried by the `PayrollTest` object to see whether the `Payroll` object managed them correctly.

Listing 4-2 shows the intent of the test. It creates the appropriate MOCK OBJECTS, passes them to the `Payroll` object, tells the `Payroll` object to pay all the employees, and then asks the MOCK OBJECTS to verify that all the checks were written correctly and that all the payments were posted correctly.

Of course, this test is simply checking that `Payroll` called all the right functions with all the right data. The test is not checking that checks were written or that a true database

---

1.   [Jeffries2001]

2.   [Mackinnon2000]

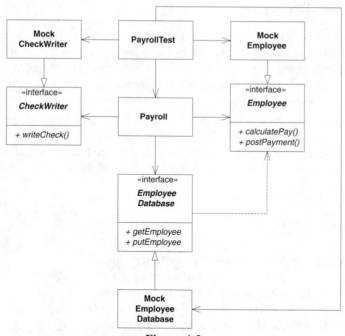

Figure 4-2
Decoupled `Payroll` using MOCK OBJECTS for testing

Listing 4-2
`TestPayroll`

```
[Test]

public void TestPayroll()
{
  MockEmployeeDatabase db = new MockEmployeeDatabase();
  MockCheckWriter w = new MockCheckWriter();
  Payroll p = new Payroll(db, w);
  p.PayEmployees();
  Assert.IsTrue(w.ChecksWereWrittenCorrectly());
  Assert.IsTrue(db.PaymentsWerePostedCorrectly());
}
```

---

was properly updated. Rather, it's checking that the `Payroll` class is behaving as it should in isolation.

You might wonder what the `MockEmployee` is for. It seems feasible that the real `Employee` class could be used instead of a mock. If that were so, I would have no compunction about using it. In this case, I presumed that the `Employee` class was more complex than needed to check the function of `Payroll`.

Serendipitous Decoupling

The decoupling of `Payroll` is a good thing. It allows us to swap in different databases and checkwriters for both testing and extending of the application. I think it is interesting that this decoupling was driven by the need to test. Apparently, the need to isolate the module under test forces us to decouple in ways that are beneficial to the overall structure of the program. *Writing tests before code improves our designs.*

A large part of this book is about design principles for managing dependencies. Those principles give you some guidelines and techniques for decoupling classes and packages. You will find these principles most beneficial if you practice them as part of your unit testing strategy. It is the unit tests that will provide much of the impetus and direction for decoupling.

Acceptance Tests

Unit tests are necessary but insufficient as verification tools. Unit tests verify that the small elements of the system work as they are expected to, but they do not verify that the system works properly as a whole. Unit tests are white box tests[3] that verify the individual mechanisms of the system. Acceptance tests are black box tests[4] that verify that the customer requirements are being met.

Acceptance tests are written by folks who do not know the internal mechanisms of the system. These tests may be written directly by the customer or by business analysts, testers, or quality assurance specialists. Acceptance tests are automated. They are usually composed in a special specification language that is readable and writable by relatively nontechnical people.

Acceptance tests are the ultimate documentation of a feature. Once the customer has written the acceptance tests that verify that a feature is correct, the programmers can read those acceptance tests to truly understand the feature. So, just as unit tests serve as compilable and executable documentation for the internals of the system, acceptance tests serve as compilable and executable documentation of the features of the system. In short, *the acceptance tests become the true requirements document.*

Furthermore, the act of writing acceptance tests first has a profound effect on the architecture of the system. In order to make the system testable, it has to be decoupled at the high architecture level. For example, the user interface has to be decoupled from the

---

3. A test that knows and depends on the internal structure of the module being tested.
4. A test that does not know or depend on the internal structure of the module being tested.

business rules in such a way that the acceptance tests can gain access to those business rules without going through the UI.

In the early iterations of a project, the temptation is to do acceptance tests manually. This is inadvisable because it deprives those early iterations of the decoupling pressure exerted by the need to automate the acceptance tests. When you start the very first iteration knowing full well that you must automate the acceptance tests, you make very different architectural trade-offs. Just as unit tests drive you to make superior design decisions in the small, acceptance tests drive you to make superior architecture decisions in the large.

Consider, again, the payroll application. In our first iteration, we must be able to add and delete employees to and from the database. We must also be able to create paychecks for the employees currently in the database. Fortunately, we have to deal only with salaried employees. The other kinds of employees have been held back until a later iteration.

We haven't written any code yet, and we haven't invested in any design yet. This is the best time to start thinking about acceptance tests. Once again, intentional programming is a useful tool for us to use. We should write the acceptance tests the way we think they should appear, and then we can design the payroll system accordingly.

I want the acceptance tests to be convenient to write and easy to change. I want them to be placed in a collaborative tool and available on the internal network so that I can run them any time I please. Therefore, I'll use the open-source FitNesse tool.[5] FitNesse allows each acceptance test to be written as a simple Web page and accessed and executed from a Web browser.

Figure 4-3 shows an example acceptance test written in FitNesse. The first step of the test is to add two employees to the payroll system. The second step is to pay them. The third step is to make sure that the paychecks were written correctly. In this example, we are assuming that tax is a straight 20 percent deduction.

Clearly, this kind of test is very easy for customers to read and write. But think about what it implies about the structure of the system. The first two tables of the test are functions of the payroll application. If you were writing the payroll system as a reusable framework, they'd correspond to application programming interface (API) functions. Indeed, in order for FitNesse to invoke these functions, the APIs must be written.[6]

Serendipitous Architecture

Note the pressure that the acceptance tests placed on the architecture of the payroll system. The very fact that we considered the tests first led us to the notion of an API for the

---

5. www.fitnesse.org

6. The manner in which FitNesse calls these API functions is beyond the scope of this book. For more information, consult the FitNesse documentation. Also see [Mugridge2005].

First we add two employees.

Add employees.		
id	name	salary
1	Jeff Languid	1000.00
2	Kelp Holland	2000.00

Next we pay them.

Create paychecks.	
pay date	check number
1/31/2001	1000

Make sure 20% straight tax was removed.

Inspect paychecks.		
id	gross pay	net pay
1	1000	800
2	2000	1600

Figure 4-3
Sample acceptance test

functions of the payroll system. Clearly, the UI will use this API to achieve its ends. Note also that the printing of the paychecks must be decoupled from the `Create Paychecks` function. These are good architectural decisions.

Conclusion

The simpler it is to run a suite of tests, the more often those tests will be run. The more the tests are run, the sooner any deviation from those tests will be found. If we can run all the tests several time a day, then the system will never be broken for more than a few minutes. This is a reasonable goal. We simply don't allow the system to backslide. Once it works to a certain level, it never backslides to a lower level.

Yet verification is only one of the benefits of writing tests. Both unit tests and acceptance tests are a form of documentation. That documentation is compilable and executable and therefore accurate and reliable. Moreover, these tests are written in unambiguous languages that are readable by their audience. Programmers can read unit tests because they are written in their programming language. Customers can read acceptance tests because they are written in a simple tabular language.

Possibly the most important benefit of all this testing is the impact it has on architecture and design. To make a module or an application testable, it must also be decoupled. The more testable it is, the more decoupled it is. The act of considering comprehensive acceptance and unit tests has a profoundly positive effect on the structure of the software.

Bibliography

[**Jeffries2001**] Ron Jeffries, *Extreme Programming Installed*, Addison-Wesley, 2001.

[**Mackinnon2000**] Tim Mackinnon, Steve Freeman, and Philip Craig, "Endo-Testing: Unit Testing with Mock Objects," in Giancarlo Succi and Michele Marchesi, *Extreme Programming Examined*, Addison-Wesley, 2001.

[**Mugridge2005**] Rick Mugridge and Ward Cunningham, *Fit for Developing Software: Framework for Integrated Tests*, Addison-Wesley, 2005.

Refactoring

The only factor becoming scarce in a world of abundance is human attention.

—Kevin Kelly, in *Wired*

This chapter is about human attention, about paying attention to what you are doing and making sure that you are doing your best. It is about the difference between getting something to work and getting something right. It is about the value we place in the structure of our code.

In *Refactoring*, his classic book, Martin Fowler defines refactoring as "the process of changing a software system in such a way that it does not alter the external behavior of the code yet improves its internal structure."[1] But why would we want to improve the structure of working code? What about "If it's not broken, don't fix it!"?

Every software module has three functions. First is the function it performs while executing. This function is the reason for the module's existence. The second function of a module is to afford change. Almost all modules will change in the course of their lives, and it is the responsibility of the developers to make sure that such changes are as simple as possible to make. A module that is difficult to change is broken and needs fixing, even though it works. The third function of a module is to communicate to its readers. Developers who are not familiar with the module should be able to read and understand it without undue mental gymnastics. A module that does not communicate is broken and needs to be fixed.

What does it take to make a module easy to read and easy to change? Much of this book is dedicated to principles and patterns whose primary goal is to help you create modules that are flexible and adaptable. But it takes something more than just principles and patterns to make a module that is easy to read and change. It takes attention. It takes discipline. It takes a passion for creating beauty.

A Simple Example of Refactoring: Generating Primes

Consider the code in Listing 5-1. This program generates prime numbers. It is one big function with many single-letter variables and comments to help us read it.

Listing 5-1

`GeneratePrimes.cs, version 1`

```
/// <remark>
/// This class Generates prime numbers up to a user specified
/// maximum. The algorithm used is the Sieve of Eratosthenes.
///
/// Eratosthenes of Cyrene, b. c. 276 BC, Cyrene, Libya --
/// d. c. 194, Alexandria.  The first man to calculate the
/// circumference of the Earth.  Also known for working on
/// calendars with leap years and ran the library at
/// Alexandria.
///
/// The algorithm is quite simple.  Given an array of integers
/// starting at 2.  Cross out all multiples of 2.  Find the
/// next uncrossed integer, and cross out all of its multiples.
/// Repeat until you have passed the square root of the
/// maximum value.
///
/// Written by Robert C. Martin on 9 Dec 1999 in Java
/// Translated to C# by Micah Martin on 12 Jan 2005.
```

---

1. [Fowler99], p. xvi

Listing 5-1 (Continued)

GeneratePrimes.cs, version 1

```
///</remark>

using System;

/// <summary>
/// author: Robert C. Martin
/// </summary>
public class GeneratePrimes
{
  ///<summary>
  /// Generates an array of prime numbers.
  ///</summary>
  ///
  /// <param name="maxValue">The generation limit.</param>
  public static int[] GeneratePrimeNumbers(int maxValue)
  {
    if (maxValue >= 2) // the only valid case
    {
      // declarations
      int s = maxValue + 1; // size of array
      bool[] f = new bool[s];
      int i;

      // initialize array to true.
      for (i = 0; i < s; i++)
        f[i] = true;

      // get rid of known non-primes
      f[0] = f[1] = false;

      // sieve
      int j;
      for (i = 2; i < Math.Sqrt(s) + 1; i++)
      {
        if(f[i]) // if i is uncrossed, cross its multiples.
        {
          for (j = 2 * i; j < s; j += i)
            f[j] = false; // multiple is not prime
        }
      }

      // how many primes are there?
      int count = 0;
      for (i = 0; i < s; i++)
      {
        if (f[i])
          count++; // bump count.
      }

      int[] primes = new int[count];

      // move the primes into the result
      for (i = 0, j = 0; i < s; i++)
```

Listing 5-1 (Continued)

GeneratePrimes.cs, version 1

```
        {
          if (f[i])                 // if prime
             primes[j++] = i;
        }

        return primes;  // return the primes
      }
      else // maxValue < 2
        return new int[0]; // return null array if bad input.
    }
}
```

Unit Testing

The unit test for GeneratePrimes is shown in Listing 5-2. It takes a statistical approach, checking whether the generator can generate primes up to 0, 2, 3, and 100. In the first case, there should be no primes. In the second, there should be one prime, and it should be 2. In the third, there should be two primes, and they should be 2 and 3. In the last case, there should be 25 primes, the last of which is 97. If all these tests pass, I make the assumption that the generator is working. I doubt that this is foolproof, but I can't think of a reasonable scenario in which these tests would pass but the function fail.

Listing 5-2

GeneratePrimesTest.cs

```
using NUnit.Framework;

[TestFixture]
public class GeneratePrimesTest
{
  [Test]
  public void TestPrimes()
  {
    int[] nullArray = GeneratePrimes.GeneratePrimeNumbers(0);
    Assert.AreEqual(nullArray.Length, 0);

    int[] minArray = GeneratePrimes.GeneratePrimeNumbers(2);
    Assert.AreEqual(minArray.Length, 1);
    Assert.AreEqual(minArray[0], 2);

    int[] threeArray = GeneratePrimes.GeneratePrimeNumbers(3);
    Assert.AreEqual(threeArray.Length, 2);
    Assert.AreEqual(threeArray[0], 2);
    Assert.AreEqual(threeArray[1], 3);

    int[] centArray = GeneratePrimes.GeneratePrimeNumbers(100);
    Assert.AreEqual(centArray.Length, 25);
    Assert.AreEqual(centArray[24], 97);
  }
}
```

Refactoring

To help me refactor this program, I am using Visual Studio with the *ReSharper* refactoring add-in from *JetBrains*. This tool makes it trivial to extract methods and rename variables and classes.

It seems pretty clear that the main function wants to be three separate functions. The first initializes all the variables and sets up the sieve. The second executes the sieve, and the third loads the sieved results into an integer array. To expose this structure more clearly, I extracted those functions into three separate methods (Listing 5-3). I also removed a few unnecessary comments and changed the name of the class to `PrimeGenerator`. The tests all still ran.

Extracting the three functions forced me to promote some of the variables of the function to static fields of the class. This makes it much clearer which variables are local and which have wider influence.

Listing 5-3

PrimeGenerator.cs, version 2

```
///<remark>
/// This class Generates prime numbers up to a user specified
/// maximum.  The algorithm used is the Sieve of Eratosthenes.
/// Given an array of integers starting at 2:
/// Find the first uncrossed integer, and cross out all its
/// multiples.  Repeat until there are no more multiples
/// in the array.
///</remark>
using System;

public class PrimeGenerator
{
  private static int s;
  private static bool[] f;
  private static int[] primes;

  public static int[] GeneratePrimeNumbers(int maxValue)
  {
    if (maxValue < 2)
      return new int[0];
    else
    {
      InitializeSieve(maxValue);
      Sieve();
      LoadPrimes();
      return primes;  // return the primes
    }
  }

  private static void LoadPrimes()
  {
    int i;
    int j;
```

Listing 5-3 (Continued)

`PrimeGenerator.cs, version 2`

```
      // how many primes are there?
      int count = 0;
      for (i = 0; i < s; i++)
      {
        if (f[i])
          count++; // bump count.
      }

      primes = new int[count];

      // move the primes into the result
      for (i = 0, j = 0; i < s; i++)
      {
        if (f[i])              // if prime
          primes[j++] = i;
      }
    }

    private static void Sieve()
    {
      int i;
      int j;
      for (i = 2; i < Math.Sqrt(s) + 1; i++)
      {
        if(f[i]) // if i is uncrossed, cross its multiples.
        {
          for (j = 2 * i; j < s; j += i)
            f[j] = false; // multiple is not prime
        }
      }
    }

    private static void InitializeSieve(int maxValue)
    {
      // declarations
      s = maxValue + 1; // size of array
      f = new bool[s];
      int i;

      // initialize array to true.
      for (i = 0; i < s; i++)
        f[i] = true;

      // get rid of known non-primes
      f[0] = f[1] = false;
    }
  }
```

The `InitializeSieve` function is a little messy, so I cleaned it up considerably (Listing 5-4). First, I replaced all usages of the `s` variable with `f.Length`. Then I changed the names of the three functions to something a bit more expressive. Finally, I rearranged the innards of `InitializeArrayOfIntegers` (née `InitializeSieve`) to be a little nicer to read. The tests all still ran.

Listing 5-4

PrimeGenerator.cs, version 3 (partial)

```csharp
public class PrimeGenerator
{
  private static bool[] f;
  private static int[] result;

  public static int[] GeneratePrimeNumbers(int maxValue)
  {
    if (maxValue < 2)
      return new int[0];
    else
    {
      InitializeArrayOfIntegers(maxValue);
      CrossOutMultiples();
      PutUncrossedIntegersIntoResult();
      return result;
    }
  }

  private static void InitializeArrayOfIntegers(int maxValue)
  {
    // declarations
    f = new bool[maxValue + 1];
    f[0] = f[1] = false; //neither primes nor multiples.
    for (int i = 2; i < f.Length; i++)
      f[i] = true;
  }
}
```

Next, I looked at `CrossOutMultiples`. There were a number of statements in this function, and in others, of the form `if (f[ i]  == true)`. The intent was to check whether `i` was uncrossed, so I changed the name of `f` to `unCrossed`. But this led to ugly statements, such as `unCrossed[ i]  = false`. I found the double negative confusing. So I changed the name of the array to `isCrossed` and changed the sense of all the Booleans. The tests all still ran.

I got rid of the initialization that set `isCrossed[ 0]` and `isCrossed[ 1]` to `true` and simply made sure that no part of the function used the `isCrossed` array for indexes less than 2. I extracted the inner loop of the `CrossOutMultiples` function and called it `CrossOutMultiplesOf`. I also thought that `if (isCrossed[ i]  == false)` was confusing, so I created a function called `NotCrossed` and changed the `if` statement to `if (NotCrossed(i))`. The tests all still ran.

I spent a bit of time writing a comment that tried to explain why you have to iterate only up to the square root of the array size. This led me to extract the calculation into a function where I could put the explanatory comment. In writing the comment, I realized that the square root is the maximum prime factor of any of the integers in the array. So I chose that name for the variables and functions that dealt with it. The result of all these refactorings are in Listing 5-5. The tests all still ran.

Listing 5-5
PrimeGenerator.cs, version 4 (partial)

```
public class PrimeGenerator
{
  private static bool[] isCrossed;
  private static int[] result;

  public static int[] GeneratePrimeNumbers(int maxValue)
  {
    if (maxValue < 2)
      return new int[0];
    else
    {
      InitializeArrayOfIntegers(maxValue);
      CrossOutMultiples();
      PutUncrossedIntegersIntoResult();
      return result;
    }
  }

  private static void InitializeArrayOfIntegers(int maxValue)
  {
    isCrossed = new bool[maxValue + 1];
    for (int i = 2; i < isCrossed.Length; i++)
      isCrossed[i] = false;
  }

  private static void CrossOutMultiples()
  {
    int maxPrimeFactor = CalcMaxPrimeFactor();
    for (int i = 2; i < maxPrimeFactor + 1; i++)
    {
      if(NotCrossed(i))
        CrossOutputMultiplesOf(i);
    }
  }

  private static int CalcMaxPrimeFactor()
  {
    // We cross out all multiples of p, where p is prime.
    // Thus, all crossed out multiples have p and q for
    // factors.  If p > sqrt of the size of the array, then
    // q will never be greater than 1.  Thus p is the
    // largest prime factor in the array and is also
    // the iteration limit.

    double maxPrimeFactor = Math.Sqrt(isCrossed.Length) + 1;
    return (int) maxPrimeFactor;
  }

  private static void CrossOutputMultiplesOf(int i)
  {
    for (int multiple = 2*i;
         multiple < isCrossed.Length;
         multiple += i)
      isCrossed[multiple] = true;
  }
```

Listing 5-5 (Continued)

PrimeGenerator.cs, version 4 (partial)

```
private static bool NotCrossed(int i)
{
    return isCrossed[i] == false;
}
}
```

The last function to refactor is PutUncrossedIntegersIntoResult. This method has two parts. The first counts the number of uncrossed integers in the array and creates the result array of that size. The second moves the uncrossed integers into the result array. I extracted the first part into its own function and did some miscellaneous cleanup (Listing 5-6). The tests all still ran.

Listing 5-6

PrimerGenerator.cs, version 5 (partial)

```
private static void PutUncrossedIntegersIntoResult()
{
    result = new int[NumberOfUncrossedIntegers()];
    for (int j = 0, i = 2; i < isCrossed.Length; i++)
    {
        if (NotCrossed(i))
            result[j++] = i;
    }
}

private static int NumberOfUncrossedIntegers()
{
    int count = 0;
    for (int i = 2; i < isCrossed.Length; i++)
    {
        if (NotCrossed(i))
            count++; // bump count.
    }
    return count;
}
```

The Final Reread

Next, I made one final pass over the whole program, reading it from beginning to end, rather like one would read a geometric proof. This is an important step. So far, I've been refactoring fragments. Now I want to see whether the whole program hangs together as a *readable* whole.

First, I realize that I don't like the name InitializeArrayOfIntegers. What's being initialized is not, in fact, an array of integers but an array of Booleans. But `InitializeArrayOfBooleans` is not an improvement. What we are really doing in this method is uncrossing all the relevant integers so that we can then cross out the multiples. So I change the name to `UncrossIntegersUpTo`. I also realize that I don't like the name `isCrossed` for the array of Booleans. So I change it to `crossedOut`. The tests all still run.

One might think that I'm being frivolous with these name changes, but with a refactoring browser, you can afford to do these kinds of tweaks; they cost virtually nothing. Even without a refactoring browser, a simple search and replace is pretty cheap. And the tests strongly mitigate any chance that we might unknowingly break something.

I don't know what I was smoking when I wrote all that `maxPrimeFactor` stuff. Yikes! The square root of the size of the array is not necessarily prime. That method did *not* calculate the maximum prime factor. The explanatory comment was simply *wrong*. So I rewrote the comment to better explain the rationale behind the square root and rename all the variables appropriately.[2] The tests all still run.

What the devil is that +1 doing in there? It must have been paranoia. I was afraid that a fractional square root would convert to an integer that was too small to serve as the iteration limit. But that's silly. The true iteration limit is the largest prime less than or equal to the square root of the size of the array. I'll get rid of the +1.

The tests all run, but that last change makes me pretty nervous. I understand the rationale behind the square root, but I've got a nagging feeling that there may be some corner cases that aren't being covered. So I'll write another test that checks that there are no multiples in any of the prime lists between 2 and 500. (See the `TestExhaustive` function in Listing 5-8.) The new test passes, and my fears are allayed.

The rest of the code reads pretty nicely. So I think we're done. The final version is shown in Listings 5-7 and 5-8.

Listing 5-7

PrimeGenerator.cs (final)

```
///<remark>
/// This class Generates prime numbers up to a user specified
/// maximum.  The algorithm used is the Sieve of Eratosthenes.
/// Given an array of integers starting at 2:
/// Find the first uncrossed integer, and cross out all its
/// multiples.  Repeat until there are no more multiples
/// in the array.
///</remark>
using System;
```

---

2. I once watched Kent Beck refactor this very same program. He did away with the square root altogether. His rationale was that the square root was difficult to understand and that no test that failed if you iterated right up to the size of the array. I can't bring myself to give up the efficiency. I guess that shows my assembly language roots.

Listing 5-7 (Continued)
PrimeGenerator.cs (final)

```csharp
public class PrimeGenerator
{
  private static bool[] crossedOut;
  private static int[] result;

  public static int[] GeneratePrimeNumbers(int maxValue)
  {
    if (maxValue < 2)
      return new int[0];
    else
    {
      UncrossIntegersUpTo(maxValue);
      CrossOutMultiples();
      PutUncrossedIntegersIntoResult();
      return result;
    }
  }

  private static void UncrossIntegersUpTo(int maxValue)
  {
    crossedOut = new bool[maxValue + 1];
    for (int i = 2; i < crossedOut.Length; i++)
      crossedOut[i] = false;
  }

  private static void PutUncrossedIntegersIntoResult()
  {
    result = new int[NumberOfUncrossedIntegers()];
    for (int j = 0, i = 2; i < crossedOut.Length; i++)
    {
      if (NotCrossed(i))
        result[j++] = i;
    }
  }

  private static int NumberOfUncrossedIntegers()
  {
    int count = 0;
    for (int i = 2; i < crossedOut.Length; i++)
    {
      if (NotCrossed(i))
        count++; // bump count.
    }
    return count;
  }

  private static void CrossOutMultiples()
  {
    int limit = DetermineIterationLimit();
    for (int i = 2; i <= limit; i++)
    {
      if(NotCrossed(i))
        CrossOutputMultiplesOf(i);
    }
  }
```

Listing 5-7 (Continued)

PrimeGenerator.cs (final)

```
  private static int DetermineIterationLimit()
  {
    // Every multiple in the array has a prime factor that
    // is less than or equal to the root of the array size,
    // so we don't have to cross off multiples of numbers
    // larger than that root.
    double iterationLimit = Math.Sqrt(crossedOut.Length);
    return (int) iterationLimit;
  }

  private static void CrossOutputMultiplesOf(int i)
  {
    for (int multiple = 2*i;
         multiple < crossedOut.Length;
         multiple += i)
      crossedOut[multiple] = true;
  }

  private static bool NotCrossed(int i)
  {
    return crossedOut[i] == false;
  }
}
```

Listing 5-8

GeneratePrimesTest.cs (final)

```
using NUnit.Framework;

[TestFixture]
public class GeneratePrimesTest
{
  [Test]
  public void TestPrimes()
  {
    int[] nullArray = PrimeGenerator.GeneratePrimeNumbers(0);
    Assert.AreEqual(nullArray.Length, 0);

    int[] minArray = PrimeGenerator.GeneratePrimeNumbers(2);
    Assert.AreEqual(minArray.Length, 1);
    Assert.AreEqual(minArray[0], 2);

    int[] threeArray = PrimeGenerator.GeneratePrimeNumbers(3);
    Assert.AreEqual(threeArray.Length, 2);
    Assert.AreEqual(threeArray[0], 2);
    Assert.AreEqual(threeArray[1], 3);

    int[] centArray = PrimeGenerator.GeneratePrimeNumbers(100);
    Assert.AreEqual(centArray.Length, 25);
    Assert.AreEqual(centArray[24], 97);
  }
```

Listing 5-8 (Continued)

GeneratePrimesTest.cs (final)

```
  [Test]
  public void TestExhaustive()
  {
    for (int i = 2; i<500; i++)
      VerifyPrimeList(PrimeGenerator.GeneratePrimeNumbers(i));
  }

  private void VerifyPrimeList(int[] list)
  {
    for (int i=0; i<list.Length; i++)
      VerifyPrime(list[i]);
  }

  private void VerifyPrime(int n)
  {
    for (int factor=2; factor<n; factor++)
      Assert.IsTrue(n%factor != 0);
  }
}
```

Conclusion

The end result of this program reads much better than it did at the start. It also works a bit better. I'm pretty pleased with the outcome. The program is much easier to understand and is therefore much easier to change. Also, the structure of the program has isolated its parts from one another. This also makes the program much easier to change.

You might be worried that extracting functions that are called only once might adversely affect performance. I think that the increased readability is worth a few extra nanoseconds in most cases. However, there may be deep inner loops where those few nanoseconds will be costly. My advice is to assume that the cost will be negligible and wait to be proved wrong.

Was this worth the time we invested in it? After all, the function worked when we started. I strongly recommend that you *always* practice such refactoring for *every* module you write and for every module you maintain. The time investment is very small compared to the effort you'll be saving yourself and others in the near future.

Refactoring is like cleaning up the kitchen after dinner. The first time you skip cleaning up, you are done with dinner sooner. But the lack of clean dishes and clear working space makes dinner take longer to prepare the next day. This makes you want to skip cleaning again. Indeed, you can always finish dinner faster *today* if you skip cleaning. But the mess builds and builds. Eventually, you are spending an inordinate amount of time hunting for the right cooking utensils, chiseling the encrusted dried food off the dishes, scrubbing them down so they are suitable to cook with, and so on. Dinner takes forever. Skipping the cleanup does not really make dinner go more quickly.

The goal of refactoring, as depicted in this chapter, is to clean your code every day, every hour, and every minute. We don't want the mess to build. We don't want to have to chisel and scrub the encrusted bits that accumulate over time. We want to be able to extend and modify our systems with a minimum of effort. The most important enabler of that ability is the cleanliness of the code.

I can't stress this enough. All the principles and patterns in this book come to naught if the code they are used within is a mess. Before investing in principles and patterns, invest in clean code.

Bibliography

[**Fowler99**] Martin Fowler, *Refactoring: Improving the Design of Existing Code*, Addison-Wesley, 1999.

6

A Programming Episode

Design and programming are human activities; forget that and all is lost.

—Bjarne Stroustrup, 1991

In order to demonstrate agile programming practices, Bob Koss (RSK) and Bob Martin (RCM) will pair program a simple application while you watch like a fly on the wall. We will use test-driven development and a lot of refactoring to create our application. What follows is a pretty faithful reenactment of a programming episode that the two Bobs did in a hotel room in late 2000.

We made lots of mistakes while doing this. Some of the mistakes are in code, some are in logic, some are in design, and some are in requirements. As you read, you will see us flail around in all these areas, identifying and then dealing with our errors and misconceptions.

The process is messy, as all human processes are. The result: Well, the order that came out of such a messy process is amazing.

The program calculates the score of a game of bowling, so it helps if you know the rules. If you don't know the rules of bowling, check out the box on page 99.

The Bowling Game

RCM: Will you help me write a little application that calculates bowling scores?

RSK: (Reflects to himself: The XP practice of pair programming says that I can't say no when asked to help. I suppose that's especially true when it is your boss who is asking.) Sure, Bob, I'd be glad to help.

RCM: OK, great. What I'd like to do is write an application that keeps track of a bowling league. It needs to record all the games, determine the ranks of the teams, determine the winners and losers of each weekly match, and accurately score each game.

RSK: Cool. I used to be a pretty good bowler. This will be fun. You rattled off several user stories; which one would you like to start with?

RCM: Let's begin with scoring a single game.

RSK: OK. What does that mean? What are the inputs and outputs for this story?

RCM: It seems to me that the inputs are simply a sequence of throws. A throw is an integer that tells how many pins were knocked down by the ball. The output is the score for each frame.

RSK: I'm assuming you are acting as the customer in this exercise; so what form do you want the inputs and outputs to be in?

RCM: Yes, I'm the customer. We'll need a function to call to add throws and another function that gets the score. Sort of like:

```
ThrowBall(6);
ThrowBall(3);
Assert.AreEqual(9, GetScore());
```

RSK: OK, we're going to need some test data. Let me sketch out a little picture of a scorecard. [See Figure 6-1.]

1	4	4	5	6		5				0	1	7		6			2	6
5		14		29		49		60		61		77		97		117		133

Figure 6-1
Typical bowling score card

RCM: That guy is pretty erratic.

RSK: Or drunk, but it will serve as a decent acceptance test.

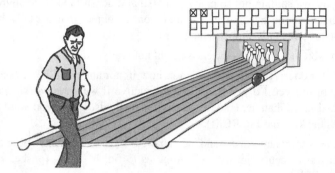

RCM: We'll need others, but let's deal with that later. How should we start? Shall we come up with a design for the system?

RSK: I wouldn't mind a UML diagram showing the problem domain concepts that we might see from the scorecard. That will give us some candidate objects that we can explore further in code.

RCM: (putting on his powerful object designer hat) OK, clearly a game object consists of a sequence of ten frames. Each frame object contains one, two, or three throws.

RSK: Great minds. That was exactly what I was thinking. Let me quickly draw that. [See Figure 6-2.]

Figure 6-2
UML diagram of bowling scorecard

RSK: Well, pick a class, any class. Shall we start at the end of the dependency chain and work backward? That will make testing easier.

RCM: Sure, why not. Let's create a test case for the `Throw` class.

RSK: (starts typing)

```
//ThrowTest.cs--------------------------------
using NUnit.Framework;

[TestFixture]
public class ThrowTest
{
  [Test]
  public void Test???
}
```

RSK: Do you have a clue what the behavior of a `Throw` object should be?

RCM: It holds the number of pins knocked down by the player.

RSK: OK, you just said, in not so many words, that it doesn't really do anything. Maybe we should come back to it and focus on an object that actually has behavior instead of one that's simply a data store.

RCM: Hmm. You mean the `Throw` class might not really exist?

RSK: Well, if it doesn't have any behavior, how important can it be? I don't know if it exists or not yet. I'd just feel more productive if we were working on an object that had more than setters and getters for methods. But if you want to drive . . . (slides the keyboard to RCM).

RCM: Well, let's move up the dependency chain to `Frame` and see whether there are any test cases we can write that will force us to finish `Throw` (pushes the keyboard back to RSK).

RSK: (wondering whether RCM is leading me down a blind alley to educate me or whether he is really agreeing with me) OK, new file, new test case.

```
//FrameTest.cs-------------------------------------
using NUnit.Framework;

[TestFixture]
public class FrameTest
{
  [Test]
  public void Test???
}
```

RCM: OK, that's the second time we've typed that. Now, can you think of any interesting test cases for `Frame`?

RSK: A `Frame` might provide its score, the number of pins on each throw, whether there was a strike or a spare . . .

RCM: OK, show me the code.

RSK: (types)

```
//FrameTest.cs----------------------------
using NUnit.Framework;

[TestFixture]
public class FrameTest
{
    [Test]
    public void TestScoreNoThrows()
    {
      Frame f = new Frame();
      Assert.AreEqual(0, f.Score);
    }
}
//Frame.cs-------------------------------------
public class Frame
```

```
{
    public int Score
    {
      get { return 0; }
    }
}
```

RCM: OK, the test case passes. But `Score` is a really stupid property. It will fail if we add a throw to the `Frame`. So let's write the test case that adds some throws and then checks the score.

```
//FrameTest.cs--------------------------------

[Test]
public void TestAddOneThrow()
{
  Frame f = new Frame();
  f.Add(5);
  Assert.AreEqual(5, f.Score);
}
```

RCM: That doesn't compile. There's no `Add` method in `Frame`.

RSK: I'll bet if you define the method, it will compile ;-)

RCM: (types)

```
//Frame.cs-------------------------------------
public class Frame
{
    public int Score
    {
      get { return 0 };
    }

    public void Add(Throw t)
    {
    }
}
```

RCM: (thinking out loud) This doesn't compile, because we haven't written the `Throw` class.

RSK: Talk to me, Bob. The test is passing an integer, and the method expects a `Throw` object. You can't have it both ways. Before we go down the `Throw` path again, can you describe its behavior?

RCM: Wow! I didn't even notice that I had written `f.Add(5)`. I should have written `f.Add(new Throw(5))`, but that's ugly as hell. What I *really* want to write is `f.Add(5)`.

RSK: Ugly or not, let's leave aesthetics out of it for the time being. Can you describe any behavior of a `Throw` object—binary response, Bob.

RCM: 101101011010100101. I don't know whether there is any behavior in `Throw`; I'm beginning to think that a `Throw` is just an `int`. However, we don't need to consider that yet, since we can write `Frame.Add` to take an `int`.

RSK: Then I think we should do that for no other reason than it's simple. When we feel pain, we can do something more sophisticated.

RCM: Agreed.

```
//Frame.cs-------------------------------------
public class Frame
{
  public int Score
  {
    get { return 0};
  }

  public void Add(int pins)
  {
  }
}
```

RCM: OK, this compiles and fails the test. Now, let's make the test pass.

```
//Frame.cs-------------------------------------
public class Frame
{
    private int score;

  public int Score
  {
    get { return score; }
  }

  public void Add(int pins)
  {
    score += pins;
  }
}
```

RCM: This compiles and passes the tests. But it's clearly simplistic. What's the next test case?

RSK: Can we take a break first?

----------------------------Break----------------------------

RCM: That's better. `Frame.Add` is a fragile function. What if you call it with an 11?

RSK: It can throw an exception if that happens. But who is calling it? Is this going to be an application framework that thousands of people will use and we have to protect against such things, or is this going to be used by you and only you? If the latter, just don't call it with an 11 (chuckle).

RCM: Good point; the tests in the rest of the system will catch an invalid argument. If we run into trouble, we can put the check in later.

So, the `Add` function doesn't currently handle strikes or spares. Let's write a test case that expresses that.

RSK: Hmmmm. If we call `Add(10)` to represent a strike, what should `GetScore()` return? I don't know how to write the assertion, so maybe we're asking the wrong question. Or we're asking the right question of the wrong object.

RCM: When you call `Add(10)`, or `Add(3)` followed by `Add(7)`, calling `Score` on the `Frame` is meaningless. The `Frame` would have to look at later `Frame` instances to calculate its score. If those later `Frame` instances don't exist, it would have to return something ugly, such as `-1`. I don't want to return `-1`.

RSK: Yeah, I hate the `-1` idea too. You've introduced the idea of `Frames` knowing about other `Frames`. Who is holding these different `Frame` objects?

RCM: The `Game` object.

RSK: So `Game` depends on `Frame`, and `Frame` in turn depends back on `Game`. I hate that.

RCM: `Frames` don't have to depend on `Game`; they could be arranged in a linked list. Each `Frame` could hold pointers to its next and previous `Frames`. To get the score from a `Frame`, the `Frame` would look backward to get the score of the previous `Frame` and look forward for any spare or strike balls it needs.

RSK: OK, I'm feeling kind of dumb because I can't visualize this. Show me some code.

RCM: Right. So we need a test case first.

RSK: For `Game` or another test for `Frame`?

RCM: I think we need one for `Game`, since it's `Game` that will build the `Frames` and hook them up to each other.

RSK: Do you want to stop what we're doing on `Frame` and do a mental longjump to `Game`, or do you just want to have a `MockGame` object that does just what we need to get `Frame` working?

RCM: No, let's stop working on `Frame` and start working on `Game`. The test cases in `Game` should prove that we need the linked list of `Frames`.

RSK: I'm not sure how they'll show the need for the list. I need code.

RCM: (types)

```
//GameTest.cs-------------------------------------------
using NUnit.Framework;

[TestFixture]
public class GameTest
{
  [Test]
  public void TestOneThrow()
  {
    Game game = new Game();
```

```
            game.Add(5);
            Assert.AreEqual(5, game.Score);
        }
    }
```

RCM: Does that look reasonable?

RSK: Sure, but I'm still looking for proof for this list of `Frames`.

RCM: Me too. Let's keep following these test cases and see where they lead.

```
        //Game.cs---------------------------------
        public class Game
        {
          public int Score
          {
            get { return 0; }
          }

          public void Add(int pins)
          {
          }
        }
```

RCM: OK; this compiles and fails the test. Now let's make it pass.

```
        //Game.cs---------------------------------
        public class Game
        {
          private int score;

          public int Score
          {
            get { return score; }
          }

          public void Add(int pins)
          {
            score += pins;
          }
        }
```

RCM: This passes. Good.

RSK: I can't disagree with it. But I'm still looking for this great proof of the need for a linked list of `Frame` objects. That's what led us to `Game` in the first place.

RCM: Yeah, that's what I'm looking for, too. I fully expect that once we start injecting spare and strike test cases, we'll have to build `Frames` and tie them together in a linked list. But I don't want to build that until the code forces us to.

RSK: Good point. Let's keep going in small steps on `Game`. What about another test that tests two throws but with no spare?

RCM: OK; that should pass right now. Let's try it.

```
//GameTest.cs--------------------------------

[Test]
public void TestTwoThrowsNoMark()
{
  Game game = new Game();
  game.Add(5);
  game.Add(4);
  Assert.AreEqual(9, game.Score);
}
```

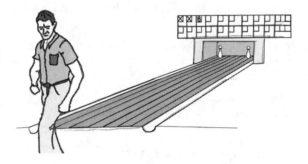

RCM: Yep, that one passes. Now let's try four balls, with no marks.

RSK: Well, that will pass too. I didn't expect this. We can keep adding throws, and we don't ever even need a `Frame`. But we haven't done a spare or a strike yet. Maybe that's when we'll have to make one.

RCM: That's what I'm counting on. However, consider this test case:

```
//TestGame.cs------------------------------------------

[Test]
public void TestFourThrowsNoMark()
{
  Game game = new Game();
  game.Add(5);
  game.Add(4);
  game.Add(7);
  game.Add(2);
  Assert.AreEqual(18, game.Score);
  Assert.AreEqual(9,  game.ScoreForFrame(1));
  Assert.AreEqual(18, game.ScoreForFrame(2));
}
```

RCM: Does this look reasonable?

RSK: It sure does. I forgot that we have to be able to show the score in each frame. Ah, our sketch of the scorecard was serving as a coaster for my Diet Coke. Yeah, that's why I forgot.

RCM: (sigh) OK; first, let's make this test case fail by adding the `ScoreForFrame` method to `Game`.

```
//Game.cs---------------------------------

    public int ScoreForFrame(int frame)
    {
      return 0;
    }
```

RCM: Great; this compiles and fails. Now, how do we make it pass?

RSK: We can start making `Frame` objects. But is that the simplest thing that will get the test to pass?

RCM: No, actually, we could simply create an array of integers in the `Game`. Each call to `Add` would append a new integer onto the array. Each call to `ScoreForFrame` will simply work forward through the array and calculate the score.

```
//Game.cs---------------------------------
public class Game
{
  private int score;
  private int[] throws = new int[21];
  private int currentThrow;

  public int Score
  {
    get { return score; }
  }

  public void Add(int pins)
  {
    throws[currentThrow++] = pins;
    score += pins;
  }

  public int ScoreForFrame(int frame)
  {
    int score = 0;
    for(int ball = 0;
        frame > 0 && ball < currentThrow;
        ball+=2, frame--)
    {
      score += throws[ball] + throws[ball + 1];
    }

    return score;
  }
}
```

RCM: (very satisfied with himself) There, that works.

RSK: Why the magic number 21?

RCM: That's the maximum possible number of throws in a game.

RSK: Yuck. Let me guess; in your youth, you were a UNIX hacker and prided yourself on writing an entire application in one statement that nobody else could decipher.

ScoreForFrame() needs to be refactored to be more communicative. But before we consider refactoring, let me ask another question. Is Game the best place for this method? In my mind, Game is violating the Single-Responsibility Principle. [See Chapter 8.] It is accepting throws, *and* it knows how to score for each frame. What would you think about a Scorer object?

RCM: (makes a rude oscillating gesture with his hand) I don't know where the functions live now; right now, I'm interested in getting the scoring stuff to work. Once we've got that all in place, *then* we can debate the values of the SRP. However, I see your point about the UNIX hacker stuff; let's try to simplify that loop.

```
public int ScoreForFrame(int theFrame)
{
  int ball = 0;
  int score=0;
  for (int currentFrame = 0;
    currentFrame < theFrame;
    currentFrame++)
  {
    score += throws[ball++] + throws[ball++];
  }

  return score;
}
```

RCM: That's a little better, but there are side effects in the score+= expression. They don't matter here, because it doesn't matter which order the two addend expressions are evaluated in. (Or does it? Is it possible that the two increments could be done before either array operations?)

RSK: I suppose we could do an experiment to verify that there aren't any side effects, but that function isn't going to work with spares and strikes. Should we keep trying to make it more readable, or should we push further on its functionality?

RCM: The experiment might have meaning only on certain compilers. Other compilers might use different evaluation orders. I don't know whether this is an issue, but let's get rid of the potential order dependency and then push on with more test cases.

```
public int ScoreForFrame(int theFrame)
{
  int ball = 0;
  int score=0;
  for (int currentFrame = 0;
    currentFrame < theFrame;
    currentFrame++)
  {
```

```
        int firstThrow = throws[ball++];
        int secondThrow = throws[ball++];
        score += firstThrow + secondThrow;
    }

    return score;
}
```

RCM: OK, next test case. Let's try a spare.

```
[Test]
public void TestSimpleSpare()
{
    Game game = new Game();
}
```

RCM: I'm tired of writing this. Let's refactor the test and put the creation of the game in a SetUp function.

```
//GameTest.cs--------------------------------
using NUnit.Framework;

[TestFixture]
public class GameTest
{
    private Game game;

    [SetUp]
    public void SetUp()
    {
        game = new Game();
    }

    [Test]
    public void TestOneThrow()
    {
        game.Add(5);
        Assert.AreEqual(5, game.Score);
    }

    [Test]
    public void TestTwoThrowsNoMark()
    {
        game.Add(5);
        game.Add(4);
        Assert.AreEqual(9, game.Score);
    }

    [Test]
    public void TestFourThrowsNoMark()
    {
        game.Add(5);
        game.Add(4);
```

```
        game.Add(7);
        game.Add(2);
        Assert.AreEqual(18, game.Score);
        Assert.AreEqual(9,  game.ScoreForFrame(1));
        Assert.AreEqual(18, game.ScoreForFrame(2));
      }


      [Test]
      public void TestSimpleSpare()
      {
      }
    }
```

RCM: That's better; now let's write the spare test case.

```
      [Test]
      public void TestSimpleSpare()
      {
        game.Add(3);
        game.Add(7);
        game.Add(3);
        Assert.AreEqual(13, game.ScoreForFrame(1));
      }
```

RCM: OK, that test case fails. Now we need to make it pass.

RSK: I'll drive.

```
      public int ScoreForFrame(int theFrame)
      {
        int ball = 0;
        int score=0;
        for (int currentFrame = 0;
          currentFrame < theFrame;
          currentFrame++)
        {
          int firstThrow = throws[ball++];
          int secondThrow = throws[ball++];

          int frameScore = firstThrow + secondThrow;

          // spare needs next frames first throw
          if ( frameScore == 10 )
            score += frameScore + throws[ball++];
          else
            score += frameScore;
        }

        return score;
      }
```

RSK: Yee-HA! That works!

RCM: (grabbing the keyboard) OK, but I think the increment of `ball` in the `frameScore==10` case shouldn't be there. Here's a test case that proves my point.

```
[Test]
public void TestSimpleFrameAfterSpare()
{
  game.Add(3);
  game.Add(7);
  game.Add(3);
  game.Add(2);
  Assert.AreEqual(13, game.ScoreForFrame(1));
  Assert.AreEqual(18, game.Score);
}
```

RCM: Ha! See, that fails. Now if we just take out that pesky extra increment . . .

```
if ( frameScore == 10 )
    score += frameScore + throws[ball];
```

RCM: Uh, it still fails. Could it be that the `Score` method is wrong? I'll test that by changing the test case to use `ScoreForFrame(2)`.

```
[Test]
public void TestSimpleFrameAfterSpare()
{
  game.Add(3);
  game.Add(7);
  game.Add(3);
  game.Add(2);
  Assert.AreEqual(13, game.ScoreForFrame(1));
  Assert.AreEqual(18, game.ScoreForFrame(2));
}
```

RCM: Hmmmm. That passes. The `Score` property must be messed up. Let's look at it.

```
public int Score
{
  get { return score; }
}

public void Add(int pins)
{
  throws[currentThrow++] = pins;
  score += pins;
}
```

RCM: Yeah, that's wrong. The `Score` property is simply returning the sum of the pins, not the proper score. What we need `Score` to do is call `ScoreForFrame()` with the current frame.

RSK: We don't know what the current frame is. Let's add that message to each of our current tests, one at a time, of course.

RCM: Right.

```
//GameTest.cs-------------------------------

  [Test]
  public void TestOneThrow()
  {
    game.Add(5);
    Assert.AreEqual(5, game.Score);
    Assert.AreEqual(1, game.CurrentFrame);
  }

//Game.cs--------------------------------

  public int CurrentFrame
  {
    get { return 1; }
  }
```

RCM: OK, that works. But it's stupid. Let's do the next test case.

```
  [Test]
  public void TestTwoThrowsNoMark()
  {
    game.Add(5);
    game.Add(4);
    Assert.AreEqual(9, game.Score);
    Assert.AreEqual(1, game.CurrentFrame);
  }
```

RCM: That one's uninteresting; let's try the next.

```
  [Test]
  public void TestFourThrowsNoMark()
  {
    game.Add(5);
    game.Add(4);
    game.Add(7);
    game.Add(2);
    Assert.AreEqual(18, game.Score);
    Assert.AreEqual(9,  game.ScoreForFrame(1));
    Assert.AreEqual(18, game.ScoreForFrame(2));
    Assert.AreEqual(2, game.CurrentFrame);
  }
```

RCM: This one fails. Now let's make it pass.

RSK: I think the algorithm is trivial. Just divide the number of throws by 2, since there are two throws per frame. Unless we have a strike. But we don't have strikes yet, so let's ignore them here too.

RCM: (flails around, adding and suotracting 1 until it works)[1]

```
public int CurrentFrame
{
  get { return 1 + (currentThrow - 1) / 2; }
}
```

RCM: That's isn't very satisfying.

RSK: What if we don't calculate it each time? What if we adjust a `currentFrame` member variable after each throw?

RCM: OK, let's try that.

```
//Game.cs---------------------------------

private int currentFrame;
private bool isFirstThrow = true;


public int CurrentFrame
{
  get { return currentFrame; }
}

public void Add(int pins)
{
  throws[currentThrow++] = pins;
  score += pins;

  if (isFirstThrow)
  {
    isFirstThrow = false;
    currentFrame++;
  }
  else
  {
    isFirstThrow=true;;
  }
}
```

RCM: OK, this works. But it also implies that the current frame is the frame of the last ball thrown, not the frame that the next ball will be thrown into. As long as we remember that, we'll be fine.

RSK: I don't have that good of a memory, so let's make it more readable. But before we go screwing around with it some more, let's pull that code out of `Add()` and put it in a private member function called `AdjustCurrentFrame()` or something.

---

1. Dave Thomas and Andy Hunt call this *programming by coincidence*.

RCM: OK, that sounds good.

```
public void Add(int pins)
{
  throws[currentThrow++] = pins;
  score += pins;

  AdjustCurrentFrame();
}

private void AdjustCurrentFrame()
{
  if (isFirstThrow)
  {
    isFirstThrow = false;
    currentFrame++;
  }
  else
  {
    isFirstThrow=true;;
  }
}
```

RCM: Now let's change the variable and function names to be more clear. What should we call `currentFrame`?

RSK: I kind of like that name. I don't think we're incrementing it in the right place, though. The current frame, to me, is the frame number that I'm throwing in. So it should get incremented right after the last throw in a frame.

RCM: I agree. Let's change the test cases to reflect that; then we'll fix `Adjust-CurrentFrame`.

```
//GameTest.cs--------------------------------
[Test]
public void TestTwoThrowsNoMark()
{
  game.Add(5);
  game.Add(4);
  Assert.AreEqual(9, game.Score);
  Assert.AreEqual(2, game.CurrentFrame);
}

[Test]
public void TestFourThrowsNoMark()
{
  game.Add(5);
  game.Add(4);
  game.Add(7);
  game.Add(2);
  Assert.AreEqual(18, game.Score);
  Assert.AreEqual(9,  game.ScoreForFrame(1));
  Assert.AreEqual(18, game.ScoreForFrame(2));
```

```
  Assert.AreEqual(3, game.CurrentFrame);
}

//Game.cs-------------------------------

private int currentFrame = 1;


private void AdjustCurrentFrame()
{
  if (isFirstThrow)
  {
    isFirstThrow = false;
  }
  else
  {
    isFirstThrow=true;
    currentFrame++;
  }
}
```

RCM: OK, that's working. Now let's test `CurrentFrame` in the two spare cases.

```
[Test]
public void TestSimpleSpare()
{
  game.Add(3);
  game.Add(7);
  game.Add(3);
  Assert.AreEqual(13, game.ScoreForFrame(1));
  Assert.AreEqual(2, game.CurrentFrame);
}

[Test]
public void TestSimpleFrameAfterSpare()
{
  game.Add(3);
  game.Add(7);
  game.Add(3);
  game.Add(2);
  Assert.AreEqual(13, game.ScoreForFrame(1));
  Assert.AreEqual(18, game.ScoreForFrame(2));
  Assert.AreEqual(3, game.CurrentFrame);
}
```

RCM: This works. Now, back to the original problem. We need `Score` to work. We can
       now write `Score` to call `ScoreForFrame(CurrentFrame-1)`.

```
[Test]
public void TestSimpleFrameAfterSpare()
{
  game.Add(3);
  game.Add(7);
```

```
                    game.Add(3);
                    game.Add(2);
                    Assert.AreEqual(13, game.ScoreForFrame(1));
                    Assert.AreEqual(18, game.ScoreForFrame(2));
                    Assert.AreEqual(18, game.Score);
                    Assert.AreEqual(3, game.CurrentFrame);
                  }

          //Game.cs---------------------------------

              public int Score()
              {
                  return ScoreForFrame(CurrentFrame - 1);
              }
```

RCM: This fails the `TestOneThrow` test case. Let's look at it.

```
              [Test]
              public void TestOneThrow()
              {
                  game.Add(5);
                  Assert.AreEqual(5, game.Score);
                  Assert.AreEqual(1, game.CurrentFrame);
              }
```

RCM: With only one throw, the first frame is incomplete. The score method is calling `ScoreForFrame(0)`. This is yucky.

RSK: Maybe, maybe not. Who are we writing this program for, and who is going to be calling `Score`? Is it reasonable to assume that it won't get called on an incomplete frame?

RCM: Yeah. But it bothers me. To get around this, we have to take the `score` out of the `TestOneThrow` test case. Is that what we want to do?

RSK   We could. We could even eliminate the entire `TestOneThrow` test case. It was used to ramp us up to the test cases of interest. Does it really serve a useful purpose now? We still have coverage in all of the other test cases.

RCM: Yeah, I see your point. OK, out it goes. (edits code, runs test, gets green bar) Ahhh, that's better.

Now, we'd better work on the strike test case. After all, we want to see all those
`Frame` objects built into a linked list, don't we? (snicker).

```
[Test]
public void TestSimpleStrike()
{
  game.Add(10);
  game.Add(3);
  game.Add(6);
  Assert.AreEqual(19, game.ScoreForFrame(1));
  Assert.AreEqual(28, game.Score);
  Assert.AreEqual(3, game.CurrentFrame);
}
```

RCM: OK, this compiles and fails as predicted. Now we need to make it pass.

```
//Game.cs---------------------------------
public class Game
{
  private int score;
  private int[] throws = new int[21];
  private int currentThrow;
  private int currentFrame = 1;
  private bool isFirstThrow = true;

  public int Score
  {
    get { return ScoreForFrame(GetCurrentFrame() - 1); }
  }

  public int CurrentFrame
  {
    get { return currentFrame; }
  }

  public void Add(int pins)
  {
    throws[currentThrow++] = pins;
    score += pins;

    AdjustCurrentFrame(pins);
  }

  private void AdjustCurrentFrame(int pins)
  {
    if (isFirstThrow)
    {
      if(pins == 10) //Strike
        currentFrame++;
      else
        isFirstThrow = false;
    }
```

```
      else
      {
        isFirstThrow=true;
        currentFrame++;
      }
    }

    public int ScoreForFrame(int theFrame)
    {
      int ball = 0;
      int score=0;
      for (int currentFrame = 0;
        currentFrame < theFrame;
        currentFrame++)
      {
        int firstThrow = throws[ball++];
        if(firstThrow == 10) //Strike
        {
          score += 10 + throws[ball] + throws[ball+1];
        }
        else
        {
          int secondThrow = throws[ball++];

          int frameScore = firstThrow + secondThrow;

          // spare needs next frames first throw
          if ( frameScore == 10 )
            score += frameScore + throws[ball];
          else
            score += frameScore;
        }
      }

      return score;
    }
  }
```

RCM: OK, that wasn't too hard. Let's see if it can score a perfect game.

```
[Test]
public void TestPerfectGame()
{
  for (int i=0; i<12; i++)
  {
    game.Add(10);
  }
  Assert.AreEqual(300, game.Score);
  Assert.AreEqual(10, game.CurrentFrame);
}
```

RCM: Urg, it's saying that the score is 330. Why would that be?

RSK: Because the current frame is getting incremented all the way to 12.

RCM: Oh! We need to limit it to 10.

```
private void AdjustCurrentFrame(int pins)
{
  if (isFirstThrow)
  {
    if(pins == 10) //Strike
      currentFrame++;
    else
      isFirstThrow = false;
  }
  else
  {
    isFirstThrow=true;
    currentFrame++;
  }

  if(currentFrame > 10)
    currentFrame = 10;
}
```

RCM: Damn, now it's saying that the score is 270. What's going on?

RSK: Bob, the Score property is subtracting 1 from SetCurrentFrame, so it's giving you the score for frame 9, not 10.

RCM: What? You mean I should limit the current frame to 11, not 10? I'll try it.

```
if(currentFrame > 11)
  currentFrame = 11;
```

RCM: OK, so now it gets the score correct but fails because the current frame is 11 and not 10. Ick! this current frame thing is a pain in the butt. We want the current frame to be the frame the player is throwing into, but what does that mean at the end of the game?

RSK: Maybe we should go back to the idea that the current frame is the frame of the last ball thrown.

RCM: Or maybe we need to come up with the concept of the last *completed* frame? After all, the score of the game at any time is the score in the last completed frame.

RSK: A completed frame is a frame that you can write the score into, right?

RCM: Yes, a frame with a spare in it completes after the next ball. A frame with a strike in it completes after the next two balls. A frame with no mark completes after the second ball in the frame.

Wait a minute. We are trying to get the `Score` property to work, right? All we need to do is force `Score` to call `ScoreForFrame(10)` if the game is complete.

RSK: How do we know whether the game is complete?

RCM: If `AdjustCurrentFrame` ever tries to increment `currentFrame` past the tenth frame, the game is complete.

RSK: Wait. All you are saying is that if `CurrentFrame` returns 11, the game is complete; that's the way the code works now!

RCM: Hmm. You mean we should change the test case to match the code?

```
[Test]
public void TestPerfectGame()
{
  for (int i=0; i<12; i++)
  {
    game.Add(10);
  }
  Assert.AreEqual(300, game.Score);
  Assert.AreEqual(11, game.CurrentFrame);
}
```

RCM: Well, that works. But I still feel uneasy about it.

RSK: Maybe something will occur to us later. Right now, I think I see a bug. May I? (grabs keyboard)

```
[Test]
public void TestEndOfArray()
{
  for (int i=0; i<9; i++)
  {
    game.Add(0);
    game.Add(0);
  }
  game.Add(2);
  game.Add(8); // 10th frame spare
  game.Add(10); // Strike in last position of array.
  Assert.AreEqual(20, game.Score);
}
```

RSK: Hmm. That doesn't fail. I thought since the twenty-first position of the array was a strike, the scorer would try to add the twenty-second and twenty-third positions to the score. But I guess not.

RCM: Hmm, you are still thinking about that scorer object, aren't you. Anyway, I see what you were getting at, but since `score` never calls `ScoreForFrame` with a number larger than 10, the last strike is not actually counted as a strike. It's just counted at a 10 to complete the last spare. We never walk beyond the end of the array.

RSK: OK, lets pump our original score card into the program.

```
[Test]
public void TestSampleGame()
{
  game.Add(1);
  game.Add(4);
  game.Add(4);
  game.Add(5);
  game.Add(6);
  game.Add(4);
  game.Add(5);
  game.Add(5);
  game.Add(10);
  game.Add(0);
  game.Add(1);
  game.Add(7);
  game.Add(3);
  game.Add(6);
  game.Add(4);
  game.Add(10);
  game.Add(2);
  game.Add(8);
  game.Add(6);
  Assert.AreEqual(133, game.Score);
}
```

RSK: Well, that works. Are there any other test cases that you can think of?

RCM: Yeah, let's test a few more boundary conditions; how about the poor schmuck who throws 11 strikes and then a final 9?

```
[Test]
public void TestHeartBreak()
{
  for (int i=0; i<11; i++)
    game.Add(10);
  game.Add(9);
  Assert.AreEqual(299, game.Score);
}
```

RCM: That works. OK, how about a tenth frame spare?

```
[Test]
public void TestTenthFrameSpare()
{
  for (int i=0; i<9; i++)
    game.Add(10);
  game.Add(9);
  game.Add(1);
  game.Add(1);
  Assert.AreEqual(270, game.Score);
}
```

RCM: (staring happily at the green bar) "That works, too. I can't think of any more, can you.

RSK: No, I think we've covered them all. Besides, I really want to refactor this mess. I still see the `scorer` object in there somewhere.

RCM: OK, well, the `ScoreForFrame` function is pretty messy. Let's consider it.

```
public int ScoreForFrame(int theFrame)
{
  int ball = 0;
  int score=0;
  for (int currentFrame = 0;
    currentFrame < theFrame;
    currentFrame++)
  {
    int firstThrow = throws[ball++];
    if(firstThrow == 10) //Strike
    {
      score += 10 + throws[ball] + throws[ball+1];
    }
    else
    {
      int secondThrow = throws[ball++];

      int frameScore = firstThrow + secondThrow;

      // spare needs next frames first throw
      if ( frameScore == 10 )
        score += frameScore + throws[ball];
      else
        score += frameScore;
```

```
      }
    }

    return score;
  }
```

RCM: I'd really like to extract the body of that `else` clause into a separate method named `HandleSecondThrow`, but I can't, because it uses `ball`, `firstThrow`, and `secondThrow` local variables.

RSK: We could turn those locals into member variables.

RCM: Yeah, that kind of reinforces your notion that we'll be able to pull the scoring out into its own `scorer` object. OK, let's give that a try.

RSK: (grabs keyboard)

```
private int ball;
private int firstThrow;
private int secondThrow;

public int ScoreForFrame(int theFrame)
{
  ball = 0;
  int score=0;
  for (int currentFrame = 0;
    currentFrame < theFrame;
    currentFrame++)
  {
    firstThrow = throws[ball++];
    if(firstThrow == 10) //Strike
    {
      score += 10 + throws[ball] + throws[ball+1];
    }
    else
    {
      secondThrow = throws[ball++];

      int frameScore = firstThrow + secondThrow;

      // spare needs next frames first throw
      if ( frameScore == 10 )
        score += frameScore + throws[ball];
      else
        score += frameScore;
    }
  }

  return score;
}
```

RSK: This works, so now we can pull the `else` clause out into its own function.

```
public int ScoreForFrame(int theFrame)
{
  ball = 0;
  int score=0;
  for (int currentFrame = 0;
    currentFrame < theFrame;
    currentFrame++)
  {
    firstThrow = throws[ball++];
    if(firstThrow == 10) //Strike
    {
      score += 10 + throws[ball] + throws[ball+1];
    }
    else
    {
      score += HandleSecondThrow();
    }
  }

  return score;
}

private int HandleSecondThrow()
{
  int score = 0;
  secondThrow = throws[ball++];

  int frameScore = firstThrow + secondThrow;

  // spare needs next frames first throw
  if ( frameScore == 10 )
    score += frameScore + throws[ball];
  else
    score += frameScore;
  return score;
}
```

RCM: Look at the structure of `ScoreForFrame`! In pseudocode, it looks something like

```
if strike
  score += 10 + NextTwoBalls;
else
  HandleSecondThrow.
```

RCM: What if we changed it to

```
if strike
  score += 10 + NextTwoBalls;
else if spare
  score += 10 + NextBall;
else
  score += TwoBallsInFrame
```

RSK: Geez! That's pretty much the rules for scoring bowling, isn't it? OK, let's see whether we can get that structure in the real function. First, let's change the way the ball variable is being incremented, so that the three cases manipulate it independently.

```
public int ScoreForFrame(int theFrame)
{
  ball = 0;
  int score=0;
  for (int currentFrame = 0;
    currentFrame < theFrame;
    currentFrame++)
  {
    firstThrow = throws[ball];
    if(firstThrow == 10) //Strike
    {
      ball++;
      score += 10 + throws[ball] + throws[ball+1];
    }
    else
    {
      score += HandleSecondThrow();
    }
  }

  return score;
}

private int HandleSecondThrow()
{
  int score = 0;
  secondThrow = throws[ball + 1];

  int frameScore = firstThrow + secondThrow;

  // spare needs next frames first throw
  if ( frameScore == 10 )
  {
    ball += 2;
    score += frameScore + throws[ball];
  }
  else
  {
    ball += 2;
    score += frameScore;
  }
  return score;
}
```

RCM: (grabs keyboard) OK, now let's get rid of the firstThrow and secondThrow variables and replace them with appropriate functions.

```
public int ScoreForFrame(int theFrame)
{
  ball = 0;
  int score=0;
  for (int currentFrame = 0;
    currentFrame < theFrame;
    currentFrame++)
  {
    firstThrow = throws[ball];
    if(Strike())
    {
      ball++;
      score += 10 + NextTwoBalls;
    }
    else
    {
      score += HandleSecondThrow();
    }
  }

  return score;
}

private bool Strike()
{
  return throws[ball] == 10;
}

private int NextTwoBalls
{
  get { return (throws[ball] + throws[ball+1]); }
}
```

RCM: That step works; let's keep going.

```
private int HandleSecondThrow()
{
  int score = 0;
  secondThrow = throws[ball + 1];

  int frameScore = firstThrow + secondThrow;

  // spare needs next frames first throw
  if (Spare())
  {
    ball += 2;
    score += 10 + NextBall;
  }
  else
  {
    ball += 2;
    score += frameScore;
```

```
      }
      return score;
    }

    private bool Spare()
    {
      return throws[ball] + throws[ball+1] == 10;
    }

    private int NextBall
    {
      get { return throws[ball]; }
    }
```

RCM: OK, that works too. Now let's deal with `frameScore`.

```
    private int HandleSecondThrow()
    {
      int score = 0;
      secondThrow = throws[ball + 1];

      int frameScore = firstThrow + secondThrow;

      // spare needs next frames first throw
      if ( IsSpare() )
      {
        ball += 2;
        score += 10 + NextBall;
      }
      else
      {
        score += TwoBallsInFrame;
        ball += 2;
      }
      return score;
    }

    private int TwoBallsInFrame
    {
      get { return throws[ball] + throws[ball+1]; }
    }
```

RSK: Bob, you aren't incrementing `ball` in a consistent manner. In the spare and strike case, you increment before you calculate the score. In the `TwoBallsInFrame` case, you increment *after* you calculate the score. And the code *depends* on this order! What's up?

RCM: Sorry, I should have explained. I'm planning on moving the increments into `Strike`, `Spare`, and `TwoBallsInFrame`. That way, they'll disappear from the `ScoreForFrame` method, and the method will look just like our pseudocode.

RSK: OK, I'll trust you for a few more steps, but remember, I'm watching.

RCM: OK, now since nobody uses `firstThrow`, `secondThrow`, and `frameScore` any-more, we can get rid of them.

```
public int ScoreForFrame(int theFrame)
{
  ball = 0;
  int score=0;
  for (int currentFrame = 0;
    currentFrame < theFrame;
    currentFrame++)
  {
    if(Strike())
    {
      ball++;
      score += 10 + NextTwoBalls;
    }
    else
    {
      score += HandleSecondThrow();
    }
  }

  return score;
}

private int HandleSecondThrow()
{
  int score = 0;
  // spare needs next frames first throw
  if ( Spare() )
  {
    ball += 2;
    score += 10 + NextBall;
  }
  else
  {
    score += TwoBallsInFrame;
    ball += 2;
  }
  return score;
}
```

RCM: (The sparkle in his eyes is a reflection of the green bar.) Now, since the only vari-able that couples the three cases is `ball`, and since `ball` is dealt with indepen-dently in each case, we can merge the three cases.

```
public int ScoreForFrame(int theFrame)
{
  ball = 0;
  int score=0;
  for (int currentFrame = 0;
    currentFrame < theFrame;
```

```
        currentFrame++)
  {
    if(Strike())
    {
      ball++;
      score += 10 + NextTwoBalls;
    }
    else if ( Spare() )
    {
      ball += 2;
      score += 10 + NextBall;
    }
    else
    {
      score += TwoBallsInFrame;
      ball += 2;
    }
  }

  return score;
}
```

RSK: OK, now we can make the increments consistent and rename the functions to be more explict. (grabs keyboard)

```
public int ScoreForFrame(int theFrame)
{
  ball = 0;
  int score=0;
  for (int currentFrame = 0;
    currentFrame < theFrame;
    currentFrame++)
  {
    if(Strike())
    {
      score += 10 + NextTwoBallsForStrike;
      ball++;
    }
    else if ( Spare() )
    {
      score += 10 + NextBallForSpare;
      ball += 2;
    }
    else
    {
      score += TwoBallsInFrame;
      ball += 2;
    }
  }

  return score;
}
```

```
      private int NextTwoBallsForStrike
      {
        get { return (throws[ball+1] + throws[ball+2]); }
      }

      private int NextBallForSpare
      {
        get { return throws[ball+2]; }
      }
```

RCM: Look at that `ScoreForFrame` method! That's the rules of bowling stated about as succinctly as possible.

RSK: But, Bob, what happened to the linked list of `Frame` objects? (snicker, snicker)

RCM: (sigh) We were bedeviled by the daemons of diagrammatic overdesign. My God, three little boxes drawn on the back of a napkin—`Game`, `Frame`, and `Throw`—and it was still too complicated and just plain wrong.

RSK: We made a mistake starting with the `Throw` class. We should have started with the `Game` class first!

RCM: Indeed! So, next time, let's try starting at the highest level and work down.

RSK: (gasp) Top-down design!??!?!?

RCM: Correction: Top-down *test-first* design. Frankly, I don't know whether this is a good rule. It's just what would have helped us in this case. So next time, I'm going to try it and see what happens.

RSK: Yeah, OK. Anyway, we still have some refactoring to do. The `ball` variable is simply a private iterator for `ScoreForFrame` and its minions. They should all be moved into a different object.

RCM: Oh, yes, your `Scorer` object. You were right, after all. Let's do it.

RSK: (grabs keyboard and takes several small steps punctuated by tests to create)

```
      //Game.cs--------------------------------
      public class Game
      {
        private int score;
        private int currentFrame = 1;
        private bool isFirstThrow = true;
        private Scorer scorer = new Scorer();

        public int Score
        {
          get { return ScoreForFrame(GetCurrentFrame() - 1); }
        }

        public int CurrentFrame
        {
          get { return currentFrame; }
```

```
      }

      public void Add(int pins)
      {
        scorer.AddThrow(pins);
        score += pins;
        AdjustCurrentFrame(pins);
      }

      private void AdjustCurrentFrame(int pins)
      {
        if (isFirstThrow)
        {
          if(pins == 10) //Strike
            currentFrame++;
          else
            isFirstThrow = false;
        }
        else
        {
          isFirstThrow = true;
          currentFrame++;
        }

        if(currentFrame > 11)
          currentFrame = 11;
      }

      public int ScoreForFrame(int theFrame)
      {
        return scorer.ScoreForFrame(theFrame);
      }
    }

    //Scorer.cs---------------------------------
    public class Scorer
    {
      private int ball;
      private int[] throws = new int[21];
      private int currentThrow;

      public void AddThrow(int pins)
      {
        throws[currentThrow++] = pins;
      }

      public int ScoreForFrame(int theFrame)
      {
        ball = 0;
        int score=0;
        for (int currentFrame = 0;
          currentFrame < theFrame;
```

```
      currentFrame++)
  {
    if(Strike())
    {
      score += 10 + NextTwoBallsForStrike;
      ball++;
    }
    else if ( Spare() )
    {
      score += 10 + NextBallForSpare;
      ball += 2;
    }
    else
    {
      score += TwoBallsInFrame;
      ball += 2;
    }
  }

  return score;
}

private int NextTwoBallsForStrike
{
  get { return (throws[ball+1] + throws[ball+2]); }
}

private int NextBallForSpare
{
  get { return throws[ball+2]; }
}

private bool Strike()
{
  return throws[ball] == 10;
}

private int TwoBallsInFrame
{
  get { return throws[ball] + throws[ball+1]; }
}

private bool Spare()
{
  return throws[ball] + throws[ball+1] == 10;
}
}
```

RSK: That's much better. Now the Game simply keeps track of frames, and the Scorer simply calculates the score. The Single-Responsibility Principle rocks!

RCM: Whatever. But it is better. Did you notice that the `score` variable is not being used anymore?

RSK: Ha! You're right. Let's kill it. (gleefully starts erasing things)

```
public void Add(int pins)
{
    scorer.AddThrow(pins);
    AdjustCurrentFrame(pins);
}
```

RSK: Not bad. Now, should we clean up the `AdjustCurrentFrame` stuff?

RCM: OK, let's look at it.

```
private void AdjustCurrentFrame(int pins)
{
    if (isFirstThrow)
    {
        if(pins == 10) //Strike
            currentFrame++;
        else
            isFirstThrow = false;
    }
    else
    {
        isFirstThrow = true;
        currentFrame++;
    }

    if(currentFrame > 11)
        currentFrame = 11;
}
```

RCM: OK, first, let's extract the increments into a single function that also restricts the frame to 11. (Brrrr. I still don't like that 11.)

RSK: Bob, 11 means end of game.

RCM: Yeah. Brrrr. (grabs keyboard, makes a couple of changes punctuated by tests)

```
private void AdjustCurrentFrame(int pins)
{
    if (isFirstThrow)
    {
        if(pins == 10) //Strike
            AdvanceFrame();
        else
            isFirstThrow = false;
    }
    else
    {
        isFirstThrow = true;
        AdvanceFrame();
    }
}
```

```
private void AdvanceFrame()
{
  currentFrame++;
  if(currentFrame > 11)
    currentFrame = 11;
}
```

RCM: OK, that's a little better. Now let's break out the strike case into its own function. (takes a few small steps and runs tests between each)

```
private void AdjustCurrentFrame(int pins)
{
  if (isFirstThrow)
  {
    if(AdjustFrameForStrike(pins) == false)
      isFirstThrow = false;
  }
  else
  {
    isFirstThrow = true;
    AdvanceFrame();
  }
}

private bool AdjustFrameForStrike(int pins)
{
  if(pins == 10)
  {
    AdvanceFrame();
    return true;
  }
  return false;
}
```

RCM: That's pretty good. Now, about that 11.

RSK: You really hate that, don't you?

RCM: Yeah, look at the `Score` property

```
public int Score
{
  get { return ScoreForFrame(GetCurrentFrame() - 1); }
}
```

RCM: That -1 is odd. It's the only place we truly use `CurrentFrame`, and yet we need to adjust what it returns.

RSK: Damn, you're right. How many times have we reversed ourselves on this?

RCM: Too many. But there is it. The code wants `currentFrame` to represent the frame of the last thrown ball, not the frame we are about to throw into.

RSK: Sheesh, that's going to break lots of tests cases.

RCM: Actually, I think we should remove `CurrentFrame` from all the test cases and remove the `CurrentFrame` function itself. Nobody really uses it.

RSK: OK, I get your point. I'll do it. It'll be like putting a lame horse out of its misery. (grabs keyboard)

```
//Game.cs-----------------------------------
public int Score
{
  get { return ScoreForFrame(currentFrame); }
}


private void AdvanceFrame()
{
  currentFrame++;
  if(currentFrame > 10)
    currentFrame = 10;
}
```

RCM: Oh, for crying out loud. You mean to tell me that we were fretting over *that*. All we did was change the limit from 11 to 10 and remove the −1. Cripe.

RSK: Yeah, Uncle Bob, it really wasn't worth all the angst we gave it.

RCM: I hate the side effect in `AdjustFrameForStrike()`. I want to get rid of it. What do you think of this?

```
private void AdjustCurrentFrame(int pins)
{
  if ((isFirstThrow && pins == 10) || (!isFirstThrow))
    AdvanceFrame();
  else
    isFirstThrow = false;
}
```

RSK: I like the idea, and it passes the tests, but I hate the long `if` statement. How about this?

```
private void AdjustCurrentFrame(int pins)
{
  if (Strike(pins) || (!isFirstThrow))
    AdvanceFrame();
  else
    isFirstThrow = false;
}

private bool Strike(int pins)
{
  return (isFirstThrow && pins == 10);
}
```

RCM: Yeah, that's pretty. We could even go one step further:

```
      private void AdjustCurrentFrame(int pins)
      {
        if (LastBallInFrame(pins))
          AdvanceFrame();
        else
          isFirstThrow = false;
      }


      private bool LastBallInFrame(int pins)
      {
        return Strike(pins) || (!isFirstThrow);
      }
```

RSK: Nice!

RCM: OK, looks like we are done. Let's just read through the whole program and see whether it's as simple and communicative as it can be.

```
      //Game.cs--------------------------------
      public class Game
      {
        private int currentFrame = 0;
        private bool isFirstThrow = true;
        private Scorer scorer = new Scorer();

        public int Score
        {
          get { return ScoreForFrame(currentFrame); }
        }

        public void Add(int pins)
        {
          scorer.AddThrow(pins);
          AdjustCurrentFrame(pins);
        }

        private void AdjustCurrentFrame(int pins)
        {
          if (LastBallInFrame(pins))
            AdvanceFrame();
          else
            isFirstThrow = false;
        }

        private bool LastBallInFrame(int pins)
        {
          return Strike(pins) || (!isFirstThrow);
        }

        private bool Strike(int pins)
        {
          return (isFirstThrow && pins == 10);
        }
```

```
      private void AdvanceFrame()
      {
        currentFrame++;
        if(currentFrame > 10)
          currentFrame = 10;
      }

      public int ScoreForFrame(int theFrame)
      {
        return scorer.ScoreForFrame(theFrame);
      }
}

//Scorer.cs--------------------------------
public class Scorer
{
    private int ball;
    private int[] throws = new int[21];
    private int currentThrow;

    public void AddThrow(int pins)
    {
      throws[currentThrow++] = pins;
    }

    public int ScoreForFrame(int theFrame)
    {
      ball = 0;
      int score=0;
      for (int currentFrame = 0;
        currentFrame < theFrame;
        currentFrame++)
      {
        if(Strike())
        {
          score += 10 + NextTwoBallsForStrike;
          ball++;
        }
        else if ( Spare() )
        {
          score += 10 + NextBallForSpare;
          ball += 2;
        }
        else
        {
          score += TwoBallsInFrame;
          ball += 2;
        }
      }

      return score;
```

```
    }

    private int NextTwoBallsForStrike
    {
      get { return (throws[ball+1] + throws[ball+2]); }
    }

    private int NextBallForSpare
    {
      get { return throws[ball+2]; }
    }

    private bool Strike()
    {
      return throws[ball] == 10;
    }

    private int TwoBallsInFrame
    {
      get { return throws[ball] + throws[ball+1]; }
    }

    private bool Spare()
    {
      return throws[ball] + throws[ball+1] == 10;
    }
  }
```

RCM: OK, that looks pretty good. I can't think of anything else to do.

RSK: Yeah, it's pretty. Let's look over the tests for good measure.

```
//GameTest.cs--------------------------------
using NUnit.Framework;

[TestFixture]
public class GameTest
{
  private Game game;

  [SetUp]
  public void SetUp()
  {
    game = new Game();
  }

  [Test]
  public void TestTwoThrowsNoMark()
  {
    game.Add(5);
    game.Add(4);
    Assert.AreEqual(9, game.Score);
  }
```

```
[Test]
public void TestFourThrowsNoMark()
{
  game.Add(5);
  game.Add(4);
  game.Add(7);
  game.Add(2);
  Assert.AreEqual(18, game.Score);
  Assert.AreEqual(9,  game.ScoreForFrame(1));
  Assert.AreEqual(18, game.ScoreForFrame(2));
}

[Test]
public void TestSimpleSpare()
{
  game.Add(3);
  game.Add(7);
  game.Add(3);
  Assert.AreEqual(13, game.ScoreForFrame(1));
}

[Test]
public void TestSimpleFrameAfterSpare()
{
  game.Add(3);
  game.Add(7);
  game.Add(3);
  game.Add(2);
  Assert.AreEqual(13, game.ScoreForFrame(1));
  Assert.AreEqual(18, game.ScoreForFrame(2));
  Assert.AreEqual(18, game.Score);
}

[Test]
public void TestSimpleStrike()
{
  game.Add(10);
  game.Add(3);
  game.Add(6);
  Assert.AreEqual(19, game.ScoreForFrame(1));
  Assert.AreEqual(28, game.Score);
}

[Test]
public void TestPerfectGame()
{
  for (int i=0; i<12; i++)
  {
    game.Add(10);
  }
  Assert.AreEqual(300, game.Score);
```

```
    }

    [Test]
    public void TestEndOfArray()
    {
      for (int i=0; i<9; i++)
      {
        game.Add(0);
        game.Add(0);
      }
      game.Add(2);
      game.Add(8); // 10th frame spare
      game.Add(10); // Strike in last position of array.
      Assert.AreEqual(20, game.Score);
    }

    [Test]
    public void TestSampleGame()
    {
      game.Add(1);
      game.Add(4);
      game.Add(4);
      game.Add(5);
      game.Add(6);
      game.Add(4);
      game.Add(5);
      game.Add(5);
      game.Add(10);
      game.Add(0);
      game.Add(1);
      game.Add(7);
      game.Add(3);
      game.Add(6);
      game.Add(4);
      game.Add(10);
      game.Add(2);
      game.Add(8);
      game.Add(6);
      Assert.AreEqual(133, game.Score);
    }

    [Test]
    public void TestHeartBreak()
    {
      for (int i=0; i<11; i++)
        game.Add(10);
      game.Add(9);
      Assert.AreEqual(299, game.Score);
    }

    [Test]
    public void TestTenthFrameSpare()
```

```
    {
      for (int i=0; i<9; i++)
        game.Add(10);
      game.Add(9);
      game.Add(1);
      game.Add(1);
      Assert.AreEqual(270, game.Score);
    }
  }
```

RSK: That pretty much covers it. Can you think of any more meaningful test cases?

RCM: No, I think that's the set. There aren't any there that I'd be comfortable removing at this point.

RSK: Then we're done.

RCM: I'd say so. Thanks a lot for your help.

RSK: No problem; it was fun.

Conclusion

After writing this chapter, I published it on the Object Mentor Web site.[2] Many people read it and gave their comments. Some folks were disturbed that there was almost no object-oriented design involved. I find this response interesting. Must we have object-oriented design in every application and every program? In this case, the program simply didn't need much of it. The `Scorer` class was really the only concession to OO, and even that was more simple partitioning than true OOD.

Other folks thought that there really should be a `Frame` class. One person went so far as to create a version of the program that contained a `Frame` class. It was much larger and more complex than what you see here.

Some folks felt that we weren't fair to UML. After all, we didn't do a complete design before we began. The funny little UML diagram on the back of the napkin (Figure 6-2) was not a complete design; it did not include sequence diagrams. I find this argument rather odd. It doesn't seem likely to me that adding sequence diagrams to Figure 6-2 would have caused us to abandon the `Throw` and `Frame` classes. Indeed, I think it would have entrenched us in our view that these classes were necessary.

Am I trying to say that diagrams are inappropriate? Of course not. Well, actually, yes, in a way I am. For this program, the diagrams didn't help at all. Indeed, they were a distraction. If we had followed them, we would have wound up with a program that was much more complex than necessary. You might contend that we would also have wound up with a program that was more maintainable, but I disagree. The program you see here

---

2. www.objectmentor.com

is easy to understand and therefore easy to maintain. There are no mismanaged dependencies within it that make it rigid or fragile.

So, yes, diagrams can be inappropriate at times. When are they inappropriate? When you create them without code to validate them *and then intend to follow them*. There is nothing wrong with drawing a diagram to explore an idea. However, having produced a diagram, you should not assume that it is the best design for the task. You may find that the best design will evolve as you take tiny little steps, writing tests first.

In support of this conclusion, let me leave you with the words of General Dwight David Eisenhower: "*In preparing for battle I have always found that plans are useless, but planning is indispensable.*"

Overview of the Rules of Bowling

Bowling is a game that is played by throwing a cantaloupe-sized ball down a narrow alley toward ten wooden pins. The object is to knock down as many pins as possible per throw.

The game is played in ten frames. At the beginning of each frame, all ten pins are set up. The player then gets two tries to knock them all down.

If the player knocks all the pins down on the first try, it is called a "strike," and the frame ends. If the player fails to knock down all the pins with the first ball but succeeds with the second ball, it is called a "spare." After the second ball of the frame, the frame ends even if pins are still standing.

A *strike* frame is scored by adding ten, plus the number of pins knocked down by the next two balls, to the score of the previous frame. A *spare* frame is scored by adding ten, plus the number of pins knocked down by the next ball, to the score of the previous frame. Otherwise, a frame is scored by adding the number of pins knocked down by the two balls in the frame to the score of the previous frame.

If a strike is thrown in the tenth frame, the player may throw two more balls to complete the score of the strike. Likewise, if a spare is thrown in the tenth frame, the player may throw one more ball to complete the score of the spare. Thus, the tenth frame may have three balls instead of two.

1	4	4	5	6	◢	5	◢	◣	0	1	7	◢	6	◢	◣	2	◢	6
5		14		29		49		60		61		77		97		117		133

The preceding scorecard shows a typical, if rather poor, game. In the first frame, the player knocked down one pin with the first ball and four more with the second. Thus, the player's score for the frame is a 5. In the second frame, the player knocked down four pins with the first ball, and five more with the second. That makes nine pins total, added to the previous frame makes 14.

In the third frame, the player knocked down six pins with the first ball and knocked down the rest with the second for a spare. No score can be calculated for this frame until the next ball is rolled.

In the fourth frame, the player knocks down five pins with the first ball. This lets us complete the scoring of the spare in frame 3. The score for frame 3: 10 plus the score in frame 2 (14) plus the first ball of frame 4 (5), or 29. The final ball of frame 4 is a spare.

Frame 5 is a strike. This lets us finish the score of frame 4 which is 29 + 10 + 10 = 49.

Frame 6 is dismal. The first ball went in the gutter and failed to knock down any pins. The second ball knocked down only one pin. The score for the strike in frame 5 is 49 + 10 + 0 + 1 = 60.

The rest you can probably figure out for yourself.

Section II

Agile Design

If *agility* is about building software in tiny increments, how can you ever *design* the software? How can you take the time to ensure that the software has a good structure that is flexible, maintainable, and reusable? If you build in tiny increments, aren't you really setting the stage for lots of scrap and rework in the name of refactoring? Aren't you going to miss the big picture?

In an agile team, the big picture evolves along with the software. With each iteration, the team improves the design of the system so that it is as good as it can be for the system as it is *now*. The team does not spend very much time looking ahead to future requirements and needs. Nor does it try to build in today the infrastructure to support the features that may be needed tomorrow. Rather, the team focuses on the *current* structure of the system, making it as good as it can be.

This is not an abandonment of architecture and design. Rather, it is a way to incrementally evolve the most appropriate architecture and design for the system. It is also a way to keep that design and architecture appropriate as the system grows and evolves over time. Agile development makes the process of design and architecture *continous*.

How do we know how whether the design of a software system is good? Chapter 7 enumerates and describes symptoms of poor design. Such symptoms, or design smells often pervade the overall structure of the software. The chapter demonstrates how those symptoms accumulate in a software project and explains how to avoid them.

The symptoms are:

- *Rigidity.* The design is difficult to change.

- *Fragility.* The design is easy to break.

- *Immobility.* The design is difficult to reuse.

- *Viscosity.* It is difficult to do the right thing.

- *Needless complexity.* Overdesign.

- *Needless repetition.* Mouse abuse.

- *Opacity.* Disorganized expression.

These symptoms are similar in nature to code smells, but are at a higher level. They are smells that pervade the overall structure of the software rather than a small section of code.

As a symptom, a design smell is something that can be measured subjectively if not objectively. Often, the smell is caused by the violation of one of more design principles. Chapters 8–12 describe object-oriented design principles that help developers eliminate the symptoms of poor design—design smells—and build the best designs for the current set of features.

The principles are:

- Chapter 8: The Single-Responsibility Principle (SRP)

- Chapter 9: The Open/Closed Principle (OCP)

- Chapter 10: The Liskov Substitution Principle (LSP)

- Chapter 11: The Dependency-Inversion Principle (DIP)

- Chapter 12: The Interface Segregation Principle (ISP)

These principles are the hard-won product of decades of experience in software engineering. They are not the product of a single mind but represent the integration of the thoughts and writings of a large number of software developers and researchers. Although they are presented here as principles of object-oriented design, they are really special cases of long-standing principles of software engineering.

Agile teams apply principles only to solve smells; they don't apply principles when there are no smells. It would be a mistake to unconditionally conform to a principle just because it is a principle. The principles are there to help us eliminate bad smells. They are not a perfume to be liberally scattered all over the system. Over-conformance to the principles leads to the design smell of needless complexity.

7

What Is Agile Design?

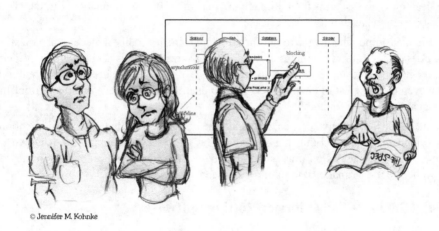

© Jennifer M. Kohnke

After reviewing the software development life cycle as I understood it, I concluded that the only software documentation that actually seems to satisfy the criteria of an engineering design is the source code listings.

—Jack Reeves

In 1992, Jack Reeves wrote a seminal article—"What Is Software Design?"—in the *C++ Journal*.[1] In this article, Reeves argued that the design of a software system is documented primarily by its source code, that diagrams representing the source code are ancillary to

---

1. [Reeves92] This is a great paper. I strongly recommend you read it. It is included in this book in Appendix B on page 687.

the design and are not the design itself. As it turns out, Jack's article was a harbinger of agile development.

In the pages that follow, we often talk about "the design." You should not take that to mean a set of UML diagrams separate from the code. A set of UML diagrams may represent parts of a design, but those diagrams are not *the* design. The design of a software project is an abstract concept. It has to do with the overall shape and structure of the program, as well as the detailed shape and structure of each module, class, and method. The design can be represented by many different media, but its final embodiment is source code. In the end, the source code *is* the design.

Design Smells

If you are lucky, you start a project with a clear picture of what you want the system to be. The design of the system is a vital image in your mind. If you are luckier still, the clarity of that design makes it to the first release.

But then something goes wrong. The software starts to rot like a piece of bad meat. As time goes by, the rotting continues. Ugly, festering sores and boils accumulate in the code, making it more and more difficult to maintain. Eventually, the sheer effort required to make even the simplest of changes becomes so onerous that the developers and front-line managers cry for a redesign.

Such redesigns rarely succeed. Although the designers start out with good intentions, they find that they are shooting at a moving target. The old system continues to evolve and change, and the new design must keep up. The warts and ulcers accumulate in the new design before it ever makes it to its first release.

Design Smells—The Odors of Rotting Software

You know that the software is rotting when it starts to exhibit any of the following odors.

- Rigidity

- Fragility

- Immobility

- Viscosity

- Needless complexity

- Needless repetition

- Opacity

Rigidity

Rigidity is the tendency for software to be difficult to change, even in simple ways. A design is rigid if a single change causes a cascade of subsequent changes in dependent modules. The more modules that must be changed, the more rigid the design.

Most developers have faced this situation in one way or another. They are asked to make what appears to be a simple change. They look the change over and make a reasonable estimate of the work required. But later, as they work through the change, they find that there are unanticipated repercussions to the change. The developers find themselves chasing the change through huge portions of the code, modifying far more modules than they had first estimated, and discovering thread after thread of other changes that they must remember to make. In the end, the changes take far longer than the initial estimate. When asked why their estimate was so poor, they repeat the traditional software developers lament: "It was a lot more complicated than I thought!"

Fragility

Fragility is the tendency of a program to break in many places when a single change is made. Often, the new problems are in areas that have no conceptual relationship with the area that was changed. Fixing those problems leads to even more problems, and the development team begins to resemble a dog chasing its tail.

As the fragility of a module increases, the likelihood that a change will introduce unexpected problems approaches certainty. This seems absurd, but such modules are not at all uncommon. These are the modules that are continually in need of repair, the ones that are never off the bug list. These modules are the ones that the developers know need to be redesigned, but nobody wants to face the spectre of redesigning them. These modules are the ones that get *worse* the more you fix them.

Immobility

A design is immobile when it contains parts that could be useful in other systems, but the effort and risk involved with separating those parts from the original system are too great. This is an unfortunate but very common occurrence.

Viscosity

Viscosity comes in two forms: viscosity of the software and viscosity of the environment. When faced with a change, developers usually find more than one way to make that change. Some of the ways preserve the design; others do not (i.e., they are hacks). When the design-preserving methods are more difficult to use than the hacks, the viscosity of the design is high. It is easy to do the wrong thing but difficult to do the right thing. We want to design our software such that the changes that preserve the design are easy to make.

Viscosity of environment comes about when the development environment is slow and inefficient. For example, if compile times are very long, developers will be tempted to make changes that don't force large recompiles, even though those changes don't preserve the design. If the source code control system requires hours to check in just a few files, developers will be tempted to make changes that require as few check-ins as possible, regardless of whether the design is preserved.

In both cases, a viscous project is one in which the design of the software is difficult to preserve. We want to create systems and project environments that make it easy to preserve and improve the design.

Needless Complexity

A design smells of needless complexity when it contains elements that aren't currently useful. This frequently happens when developers anticipate changes to the requirements and put facilities in the software to deal with those potential changes. At first, this may seem like a good thing to do. After all, preparing for future changes should keep our code flexible and prevent nightmarish changes later.

Unfortunately, the effect is often just the opposite. By preparing for many contingencies, the design becomes littered with constructs that are never used. Some of those preparations may pay off, but many more do not. Meanwhile, the design carries the weight of these unused design elements. This makes the software complex and difficult to understand.

Needless Repetition

Cut and paste may be useful text-editing operations, but they can be disastrous code-editing operations. All too often, software systems are built on dozens or hundreds of repeated code elements. It happens like this: Ralph needs to write some code that *fravles the arvadent*.[2] He looks around in other parts of the code where he suspects other arvadent fravling has occurred and finds a suitable stretch of code. He cuts and pastes that code into his module and makes the suitable modifications.

Unbeknownst to Ralph, the code he scraped up with his mouse was put there by Todd, who scraped it out of a module written by Lilly. Lilly was the first to fravle an arvadent, but she realized that fravling an arvadent was very similar to fravling a garnatosh. She found some code somewhere that fravled a garnatosh, cut and paste it into her module, and modified it as necessary.

When the same code appears over and over again, in slightly different forms, the developers are missing an abstraction. Finding all the repetition and eliminating it with an appropriate abstraction may not be high on their priority list, but it would go a long way toward making the system easier to understand and maintain.

---

2. For those of you who do not have English as your first language, the term *fravle the arvadent* is composed of nonsense words and is meant to imply some nondescript programming activity.

When there is redundant code in the system, the job of changing the system can become arduous. Bugs found in such a repeating unit have to be fixed in every repetition. However, since each repetition is slightly different from every other, the fix is not always the same.

Opacity

Opacity is the tendency of a module to be difficult to understand. Code can be written in a clear and expressive manner, or it can be written in an opaque and convoluted manner. Code that evolves over time tends to become more and more opaque with age. A constant effort to keep the code clear and expressive is required in order to keep opacity to a minimum.

When developers first write a module, the code may seem clear to them. After all, they have immersed themselves in it and understand it at an intimate level. Later, after the intimacy has worn off, they may return to that module and wonder how they could have written anything so awful. To prevent this, developers need to put themselves in their readers' shoes and make a concerted effort to refactor their code so that their readers can understand it. They also need to have their code reviewed by others.

Why Software Rots

In nonagile environments, designs degrade because requirements change in ways that the initial design did not anticipate. Often, these changes need to be made quickly and may be made by developers who are not familiar with the original design philosophy. So, though the change to the design works, it somehow violates the original design. Bit by bit, as the changes continue, these violations accumulate until malignancy sets in.

However, we cannot blame the drifting of the requirements for the degradation of the design. We, as software developers, know full well that requirements change. Indeed, most of us realize that the requirements are the most volatile elements in the project. If our designs are failing owing to the constant rain of changing requirements, it is our designs and practices that are at fault. We must somehow find a way to make our designs resilient to such changes and use practices that protect them from rotting.

An agile team thrives on change. The team invests little up front and so is not vested in an aging initial design. Rather, the team keeps the design of the system as clean and simple as possible and backs it up with lots of unit tests and acceptance tests. This keeps the design flexible and easy to change. The team takes advantage of that flexibility in order to continuously improve the design; thus, each iteration ends with a system whose design is as appropriate as it can be for the requirements in that iteration.

The Copy Program

A Familiar Scenario

Watching a design rot may help illustrate the preceding points. Let's say that your boss comes to you early Monday morning and asks you to write a program that copies characters from the keyboard to the printer. Doing some quick mental exercises in your head, you conclude that this will be less than ten lines of code. Design and coding time should be a lot less than 1 hour. What with cross-functional group meetings, quality education meetings, daily group progress meetings, and the three current crises in the field, this program ought to take you about a week to complete—if you stay after hours. However, you always multiply your estimates by 3.

"Three weeks," you tell your boss. He harumphs and walks away, leaving you to your task.

The initial design You have a bit of time right now before that process review meeting begins, so you decide to map out a design for the program. Using structured design, you come up with the structure chart in Figure 7-1.

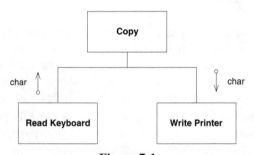

Figure 7-1
Copy program structure chart

There are three modules, or subprograms, in the application. The Copy module calls the other two. The Copy program fetches characters from the Read Keyboard module and routes them to the Write Printer module.

You look at your design and see that it is good. You smile and then leave your office to go to that review. At least you'll be able to get a little sleep there.

On Tuesday, you come in a bit early so that you can finish up the Copy program. Unfortunately, one of the crises in the field has warmed up overnight, and you have to go to the lab and help debug a problem. On your lunch break, which you finally take at 3 PM, you manage to type in the code for the Copy program. The result is Listing 7-1.

You just manage to save the edit when you realize that you are already late for a quality meeting. You know that this is an important one; they are going to be talking about the

---

Listing 7-1

The Copy Program

```
public class Copier
{
  public static void Copy()
  {
    int c;
    while((c=Keyboard.Read()) != -1)
      Printer.Write(c);
  }
}
```

---

magnitude of zero defects. So you wolf down your Twinkies and Coke and head off to the meeting.

On Wednesday, you come in early again, and this time nothing seems to be amiss. So you pull up the source code for the Copy program and begin to compile it. Lo and behold, it compiles first time with no errors! It's a good thing, too, because your boss calls you into an unscheduled meeting about the need to conserve laser printer toner.

On Thursday, after spending 4 hours on the phone walking a service technician in Rocky Mount, North Carolina, through the remote debugging and error-logging commands in one of the more obscure components of the system, you grab a Hoho and then test your Copy program. It works, first time! Good thing, too. Because your new co-op student has just erased the master source code directory from the server, and you have to go find the latest backup tapes and restore it. Of course, the last full backup was taken 3 months ago, and you have 94 incremental backups to restore on top of it.

Friday is completely unbooked. Good thing, too, because it takes all day to get the Copy program successfully loaded into your source code control system.

Of course, the program is a raging success and gets deployed throughout your company. Your reputation as an ace programmer is once again confirmed, and you bask in the glory of your achievements. With luck, you might actually produce 30 lines of code this year!

The requirements they are a'changin' A few months later, your boss comes to you and says that the Copy program should also be able to read from the paper tape reader. You gnash your teeth and roll your eyes. You wonder why people are always changing the requirements. Your program wasn't designed for a paper tape reader! You warn your boss that changes like this are going to destroy the elegance of your design. Nevertheless, your boss is adamant, saying that the users really need to read characters from the paper tape reader from time to time.

So you sigh and plan your modifications. You'd like to add a Boolean argument to the Copy function. If true, you'd read from the paper tape reader; if false, you'd read from the keyboard as before. Unfortunately, so many other programs use the Copy program now that you can't change the interface. Changing the interface would cause weeks and weeks of recompiling and retesting. The system test engineers alone would lynch you, not to mention the seven people in the configuration control group. And the process police would have a field day, forcing all kinds of code reviews for every module that called Copy!

No, changing the interface is out. But then how can you let the Copy program know that it must read from the paper tape reader? Of course! You'll use a global! You'll also use the best and most useful feature of the C family of languages, the ? : operator! Listing 7-2 shows the result.

Listing 7-2

First modification of Copy program

```
public class Copier
{
  //remember to reset this flag
  public static bool ptFlag = false;
  public static void Copy()
  {
    int c;
    while((c=(ptFlag ? PaperTape.Read()
                     : Keyboard.Read())) != -1)
      Printer.Write(c);
  }
}
```

Copy callers who want to read from the paper tape reader must first set the ptFlag to true. Then they can call Copy, and it will happily read from the paper tape reader. Once Copy returns, the caller must reset the ptFlag; otherwise, the next caller may mistakenly read from the paper tape reader rather than from the keyboard. To remind the programmers of their duty to reset this flag, you have added an appropriate comment.

Once again, you release your software to critical acclaim. It is even more successful than before, and hordes of eager programmers are waiting for an opportunity to use it. Life is good.

Give 'em an inch Some weeks later, your boss—who is still your boss despite three corporatewide reorganizations in as many months—tells you that the customers would sometimes like the Copy program to output to the paper tape punch. Customers! They are always ruining your designs. *Writing software would be a lot easier if it weren't for customers.* You tell your boss that these incessant changes are having a profound negative effect on the elegance of your design, warning that if changes continue at this horrid pace, the software will be impossible to maintain before year's end. Your boss nods knowingly and then tells you to make the change anyway.

This design change is similar to the one before it. All we need is another global and another ? : operator! Listing 7-3 shows the result of your endeavors.

You are especially proud of the fact that you remembered to change the comment. Still, you worry that the structure of your program is beginning to topple. Any more changes to the input device will certainly force you to completely restructure the while loop conditional. Perhaps it's time to dust off your resume.

Listing 7-3

Second modification of Copy program

```
public class Copier
{
  //remember to reset these flags
  public static bool ptFlag = false;
  public static bool punchFlag = false;
  public static void Copy()
  {
    int c;
    while((c=(ptFlag ? PaperTape.Read()
                     : Keyboard.Read())) != -1)
      punchFlag ? PaperTape.Punch(c) : Printer.Write(c);
  }
}
```

Expect changes I'll leave it to you to determine just how much of the preceding was satirical exaggeration. The point of the story is to show how the design of a program can rapidly degrade in the presence of change. The original design of the Copy program was simple and elegant. Yet after only two changes, it has begun to show the signs of rigidity, fragility, immobility, complexity, redundancy, and opacity. This trend is certainly going to continue, and the program will become a mess.

We might sit back and blame this on the changes. We might complain that the program was well designed for the original spec and that the subsequent changes to the spec caused the design to degrade. However, this ignores one of the most prominent facts in software development: *Requirements always change!*

Remember, the most volatile things in most software projects are the requirements. The requirements are continuously in a state of flux. This is a fact that we, as developers, must accept! *We live in a world of changing requirements, and our job is to make sure that our software can survive those changes*. If the design of our software degrades because the requirements have changed, we are not being agile.

Agile Design of the Copy Program

An agile development team might begin exactly the same way, with the code in Listing 7-1.[3] When the boss asked to make the program read from the paper tape reader, the developers would have responded by changing the design to be resilient to that kind of change. The result might have been something like Listing 7-4.

---

3. Actually, the practice of test-driven development would very likely force the design to be flexible enough to endure the boss without change. However, in this example, we'll ignore that.

Listing 7-4
Agile version 2 of Copy

```
public interface Reader
{
  int Read();
}

public class KeyboardReader : Reader
{
  public int Read() {return Keyboard.Read();}
}

public class Copier
{
  public static Reader reader = new KeyboardReader();
  public static void Copy()
  {
    int c;
    while((c=(reader.Read())) != -1)
      Printer.Write(c);
  }
}
```

Instead of trying to patch the design to make the new requirement work, the team seizes the opportunity to improve the design so that it will be resilient to that kind of change in the future. From now on, whenever the boss asks for a new kind of input device, the team will be able to respond in a way that does not cause degradation to the Copy program.

The team has followed the *Open/Closed Principle (OCP)*, which we describe in Chapter 9. This principle directs us to design our modules so that they can be extended without modification. That's exactly what the team has done. Every new input device that the boss asks for can be provided without modifying the Copy program.

Note, however, that when it first designed the module, the team did not try to anticipate how the program was going to change. Instead, the team wrote the module in the simplest way possible. It was only when the requirements did eventually change that the team changed the design of the module to be resilient to that kind of change.

One could argue that the team did only half the job. While the developers were protecting themselves from different input devices, they could also have protected themselves from different output devices. However, the team really has no idea whether the output devices will ever change. To add the extra protection now would be work that served no current puprose. It's clear that if such protection is needed it will be easy to add later. So, there's really no reason to add it now.

Following agile practices The agile developers in our example built an abstract class to protect them from changes to the input device. How did they know how to do that? The answer lies with one of the fundamental tenets of object-oriented design.

The initial design of the `Copy` program is inflexible because of the *direction* of its dependencies. Look again at Figure 7-1. Note that the `Copy` module depends directly on the `KeyboardReader` and the `PrinterWriter`. The `Copy` module is a high-level module in this application. It sets the policy of the application. It knows how to copy characters. Unfortunately, it has also been made dependent on the low-level details of the keyboard and the printer. Thus, when the low-level details change, the high-level policy is affected.

Once the inflexibility was exposed, the agile developers knew that the dependency from the `Copy` module to the input device needed to be *inverted*, using the Dependency Inversion Principle (DIP) in Chapter 11, so that `Copy` would no longer depend on the input device. They then used the STRATEGY pattern, discussed in Chapter 22, to create the desired inversion.

So, in short, the agile developers knew what to do because they followed these steps.

1. They detected the problem by following agile practices.

2. They diagnosed the problem by applying design principles.

3. They solved the problem by applying an appropriate design pattern.

The interplay between these three aspects of software development *is* the act of design.

Keeping the design as good as it can be Agile developers are dedicated to keeping the design as appropriate and clean as possible. This is not a haphazard or tentative commitment. Agile developers do not "clean up" the design every few weeks. Rather, they keep the software as clean, simple, and expressive as they possibly can—every day, every hour, and every minute. They never say, "We'll go back and fix that later." They never let the rot begin.

The attitude that agile developers have toward the design of the software is the same attitude that surgeons have toward sterile procedure. Sterile procedure is what makes surgery *possible*. Without it, the risk of infection would be far too high to tolerate. Agile developers feel the same way about their designs. The risk of letting even the tiniest bit of rot begin is too high to tolerate.

The design must remain clean. And since the source code is the most important expression of the design, it too must remain clean. Professionalism dicates that we, as software developers, cannot tolerate code rot.

Conclusion

So, what is agile design? Agile design is a process, not an event. It's the continous application of principles, patterns, and practices to improve the structure and readability of the software. It is the dedication to keep the design of the system as simple, clean, and expressive as possible at all times.

In the chapters that follow, we'll be investigating the principles and patterns of software design. As you read, remember that an agile developer does not apply those principles and patterns to a big, up-front design. Rather, they are applied from iteration to iteration in an attempt to keep the code, and the design it embodies, clean.

Bibliography

[Reeves92] Jack Reeves, "What Is Software Design?," *C++ Journal*, (2), 1992. Also available at www.bleading-edge.com/Publications/C++Journal/Cpjour2.htm.

8

The Single-Responsibility Principle (SRP)

© Jennifer M. Kohnke

None but Buddha himself must take the responsibility of giving out occult secrets . . .

—E. Cobham Brewer 1810–1897, *Dictionary of Phrase and Fable* (1898)

This principle was described in the work of Tom DeMarco[1] and Meilir Page-Jones.[2] They called it *cohesion*, which they defined as the functional relatedness of the elements of a module. In this chapter, we modify that meaning a bit and relate cohesion to the forces that cause a module, or a class, to change.

The Single-Responsibility Principle

A class should have only one reason to change.

Consider the bowling game from Chapter 6. For most of its development, the `Game` class was handling two separate responsibilities: keeping track of the current frame and calculating the score. In the end, RCM and RSK separated these two responsibilities into two classes. The `Game` kept the responsibility to keep track of frames, and the `Scorer` got the responsibility to calculate the score.

Why was it important to separate these two responsibilities into separate classes? The reason is that each responsibility is an axis of change. When the requirements change, that change will be manifest through a change in responsibility among the classes. If a class assumes more than one responsibility, that class will have more than one reason to change.

If a class has more than one responsibility, the responsibilities become coupled. Changes to one responsibility may impair or inhibit the class's ability to meet the others. This kind of coupling leads to fragile designs that break in unexpected ways when changed.

For example, consider the design in Figure 8-1. The `Rectangle` class has two methods shown. One draws the rectangle on the screen, and the other computes the area of the rectangle.

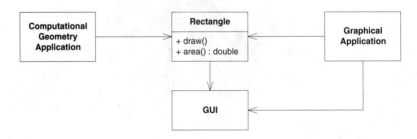

Figure 8-1
More than one responsibility

---

1. [DeMarco79], p. 310

2. [PageJones88], p. 82

Two different applications use the `Rectangle` class. One application does computational geometry. Using `Rectangle` to help it with the mathematics of geometric shapes but never drawing the rectangle on the screen. The other application is graphical in nature and may also do some computational geometry, but it definitely draws the rectangle on the screen.

This design violates SRP. The `Rectangle` class has two responsibilities. The first responsibility is to provide a mathematical model of the geometry of a rectangle. The second responsibility is to render the rectangle on a GUI.

The violation of SRP causes several nasty problems. First, we must include `GUI` in the computational geometry application. In .NET, the GUI assembly would have to be built and deployed with the computational geometry application.

Second, if a change to the `GraphicalApplication` causes the `Rectangle` to change for some reason, that change may force us to rebuild, retest, and redeploy the `ComputationalGeometryApplication`. If we forget to do this, that application may break in unpredictable ways.

A better design is to separate the two responsibilities into two completely different classes, as shown in Figure 8-2. This design moves the computational portions of `Rectangle` into the `GeometricRectangle` class. Now changes made to the way rectangles are rendered cannot affect the `ComputationalGeometryApplication`.

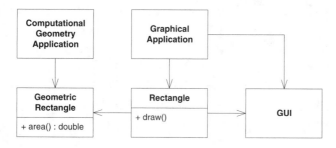

Figure 8-2
Separated responsibilities

Defining a Responsibility

In the context of the SRP, we define a responsibility to be *a reason for change*. If you can think of more than one motive for changing a class, that class has more than one responsibility. This is sometimes difficult to see. We are accustomed to thinking of responsibility in groups. For example, consider the `Modem` interface in Listing 8-1. Most of us will agree that this interface looks perfectly reasonable. The four functions it declares are certainly functions belonging to a modem.

Listing 8-1
Modem.cs -- SRP violation

```
public interface Modem
{
    public void Dial(string pno);
    public void Hangup();
    public void Send(char c);
    public char Recv();
}
```

However, two responsibilities are being shown here. The first responsibility is connection management. The second is data communication. The `dial` and `hangup` functions manage the connection of the modem; the `send` and `recv` functions communicate data.

Should these two responsibilities be separated? That depends on how the application is changing. If the application changes in ways that affect the signature of the connection functions, the design will smell of rigidity, because the classes that call `send` and `read` will have to be recompiled and redeployed more often than we like. In that case, the two responsibilities should be separated, as shown in Figure 8-3. This keeps the client applications from coupling the two responsibilities.

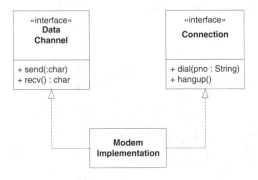

Figure 8-3
Separated modem interface

If, on the other hand, the application is not changing in ways that cause the two responsibilities to change at different times, there is no need to separate them. Indeed, separating them would smell of needless complexity.

There is a corrolary here. *An axis of change is an axis of change only if the changes occur.* It is not wise to apply SRP—or any other principle, for that matter—if there is no symptom.

Separating Coupled Responsibilities

Note that in Figure 8-3, I kept both responsibilities coupled in the `ModemImplem-`
`entation` class. This is not desirable, but it may be necessary. There are often reasons,
having to do with the details of the hardware or operating system, that force us to couple
things that we'd rather not couple. However, by separating their interfaces, we have
decoupled the concepts as far as the rest of the application is concerned.

We may view the `ModemImplementation` class as a kludge or a wart; however, note
that all dependencies flow *away* from it. Nobody needs to depend on this class. Nobody
except `main` needs to know that it exists. Thus, we've put the ugly bit behind a fence. Its
ugliness need not leak out and pollute the rest of the application.

Persistence

Figure 8-4 shows a common violation of SRP. The `Employee` class contains business
rules and persistence control. These two responsibilities should almost never be mixed.
Business rules tend to change frequently, and although persistence may not change as frequently, it changes for completely different reasons. Binding business rules to the persistence subsystem is asking for trouble.

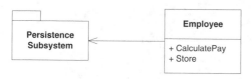

Figure 8-4
Coupled persistence

Fortunately, as we saw in Chapter 4, the practice of test-driven development will usually force these two responsibilities to be separated long before the design begins to smell.
However, if the tests did not force the separation, and if the smells of rigidity and fragility
become strong, the design should be refactored, using the FACADE, DAO (Data Access
Object), or PROXY patterns to separate the two responsibilities.

Conclusion

The Single-Responsibility Principle is one of the simplest of the principles but one of the
most difficult to get right. Conjoining responsibilities is something that we do naturally.
Finding and separating those responsibilities is much of what software design is really
about. Indeed, the rest of the principles we discuss come back to this issue in one way or
another.

Bibliography

[DeMarco79] Tom DeMarco, *Structured Analysis and System Specification,* Yourdon Press Computing Series, 1979.

[PageJones88] Meilir Page-Jones, *The Practical Guide to Structured Systems Design*, 2d. ed., Yourdon Press Computing Series, 1988.

9

The Open/Closed Principle (OCP)

© Jennifer M. Kohnke

Dutch Door*: Noun. A door divided in two horizontally so that either part can be left open or closed.*

—*The American Heritage Dictionary of the English Language, Fourth Edition,* 2000

As Ivar Jacobson has said, "All systems change during their life cycles. This must be borne in mind when developing systems expected to last longer than the first version."[1] How can we create designs that are stable in the face of change and that will last longer than the first version? Bertrand Meyer[2] gave us guidance as long ago as 1988 when he coined the now-famous open/closed principle. To paraphrase him:

> **The Open/Closed Principle (OCP)**
>
> *Software entities (classes, modules, functions, etc.) should be open for exten-sion but closed for modification.*

When a single change to a program results in a cascade of changes to dependent mod-ules, the design smells of rigidity. OCP advises us to refactor the system so that further changes of that kind will not cause more modifications. If OCP is applied well, further changes of that kind are achieved by adding new code, not by changing old code that already works. This may seem like motherhood and apple pie—the golden, unachievable ideal—but in fact, there are some relatively simple and effective strategies for *approach-ing* that ideal.

Description of OCP

Modules that conform to OCP have two primary attributes.

1. They are *open for extension*. This means that the behavior of the module can be extended. As the requirements of the application change, we can extend the module with new behaviors that satisfy those changes. In other words, we are able to change what the module does.

2. They are *closed for modification*. Extending the behavior of a module does not result in changes to the source, or binary, code of the module. The binary executable version of the module—whether in a linkable library, a DLL, or a .EXE file—remains untouched.

It would seem that these two attributes are at odds. The normal way to extend the behavior of a module is to make changes to the source code of that module. A module that cannot be changed is normally thought to have a fixed behavior.

How is it possible that the behaviors of a module can be modified without changing its source code? Without changing the module, how can we change what a module does?

---

1. [Jacobson92], p. 21
2. [Meyer97]

The answer is *abstraction*. In C# or any other object-oriented programming language (OOPL), it is possible to create abstractions that are fixed and yet represent an unbounded group of possible behaviors. The abstractions are abstract base classes, and the unbounded group of possible behaviors are represented by all the possible derivative classes.

It is possible for a module to manipulate an abstraction. Such a module can be closed for modification, since it depends on an abstraction that is fixed. Yet the behavior of that module can be extended by creating new derivatives of the abstraction.

Figure 9-1 shows a simple design that does not conform to OCP. Both the `Client` and `Server` classes are concrete. The `Client` class *uses* the `Server` class. If we want for a `Client` object to use a different server object, the `Client` class must be changed to name the new server class.

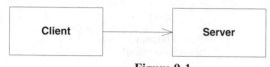

Figure 9-1
`Client` is not open and closed.

Figure 9-2 shows the corresponding design that conforms to the OCP by using the STRATEGY pattern (see Chapter 22). In this case, the `ClientInterface` class is abstract with abstract member functions. The `Client` class uses this abstraction. However, objects of the `Client` class will be using objects of the derivative `Server` class. If we want `Client` objects to use a different server class, a new derivative of the `ClientInterface` class can be created. The `Client` class can remain unchanged.

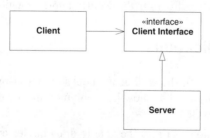

Figure 9-2
STRATEGY pattern: `Client` is both open and closed.

The `Client` has some work that it needs to get done and can describe that work in terms of the abstract interface presented by `ClientInterface`. Subtypes of `Client-Interface` can implement that interface in any manner they choose. Thus, the behavior specified in `Client` can be extended and modified by creating new subtypes of `ClientInterface`.

You may wonder why I named `ClientInterface` the way I did. Why didn't I call it `AbstractServer` instead? The reason, as we will see later, is that *abstract classes are more closely associated to their clients than to the classes that implement them.*

Figure 9-3 shows an alternate structure using the TEMPLATE METHOD pattern (see Chapter 22). The `Policy` class has a set of concrete public functions that implement a policy, similar to the functions of the `Client` in Figure 9-2. As before, those policy functions describe some work that needs to be done in terms of some abstract interfaces. However, in this case, the abstract interfaces are part of the `Policy` class itself. In C#, they would be abstract methods. Those functions are implemented in the subtypes of `Policy`. Thus, the behaviors specified within `Policy` can be extended or modified by creating new derivatives of the `Policy` class.

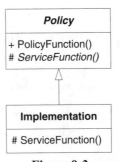

Figure 9-3
TEMPLATE METHOD pattern: Base class is open and closed.

These two patterns are the most common ways of satisfying OCP. They represent a clear separation of generic functionality from the detailed implementation of that functionality.

The `Shape` Application

The `Shape` example has been shown in many books on object-oriented design. This infamous example is normally used to show how polymorphism works. However, this time, we will use it to elucidate OCP.

We have an application that must be able to draw circles and squares on a standard GUI. The circles and squares must be drawn in a particular order. A list of the circles and squares will be created in the appropriate order, and the program must walk the list in that order and draw each circle or square.

Violating OCP

In C, using procedural techniques that do not conform to OCP, we might solve this problem as shown in Listing 9-1. Here, we see a set of data structures that have the same first element but are different beyond that. The first element of each is a type code that identifies the data structure as either a `Circle` or a `Square`. The function `DrawAllShapes` walks an array of pointers to these data structures, examining the type code and then calling the appropriate function, either `DrawCircle` or `DrawSquare`.

Listing 9-1

Procedural solution to the Square/Circle problem

```
--shape.h----------------------------------------
enum ShapeType {circle, square};

struct Shape
{
  ShapeType itsType;
};

--circle.h---------------------------------------
struct Circle
{
  ShapeType itsType;
  double itsRadius;
  Point itsCenter;
};

void DrawCircle(struct Circle*);

--square.h---------------------------------------
struct Square
{
  ShapeType itsType;
  double itsSide;
  Point itsTopLeft;
};

void DrawSquare(struct Square*);

--drawAllShapes.cc-------------------------------
typedef struct Shape *ShapePointer;

void DrawAllShapes(ShapePointer list[], int n)
{
  int i;
  for (i=0; i<n; i++)
  {
    struct Shape* s = list[i];
    switch (s->itsType)
    {
    case square:
      DrawSquare((struct Square*)s);
    break;

    case circle:
      DrawCircle((struct Circle*)s);
    break;
    }
  }
}
```

Because it cannot be closed against new kinds of shapes, the function DrawAllShapes does not conform to OCP. If I wanted to extend this function to be able to draw a list of shapes that included triangles, I would have to modify the function. In fact, I would have to modify the function for any new type of shape that I needed to draw.

Of course, this program is only a simple example. In real life, the switch statement in the DrawAllShapes function would be repeated over and over again in various functions all through the application, each one doing something a little different. There might be one each for dragging shapes, stretching shapes, moving shapes, deleting shapes, and so on. Adding a new shape to such an application means hunting for every place that such switch statements—or if/else chains—exist and adding the new shape to each.

Moreover, it is very unlikely that all the switch statements and if/else chains would be as nicely structured as the one in DrawAllShapes. It is much more likely that the predicates of the if statements would be combined with logical operators or that the case clauses of the switch statements would be combined to "simplify" the local decision making. In some pathological situations, functions may do precisely the same things to Squares that they do to Circles. Such functions would not even have the switch/ case statements or if/else chains. Thus, the problem of finding and understanding all the places where the new shape needs to be added can be nontrivial.

Also, consider the kinds of changes that would have to be made. We'd have to add a new member to the ShapeType enum. Since all the different shapes depend on the declaration of this enum, we'd have to recompile them all.[3] And we'd also have to recompile all the modules that depend on Shape.

So, we not only must change the source code of all switch/case statements or if/ else chains but also alter the binary files, via recompilation, of all the modules that use any of the Shape data structures. Changing the binary files means that any assemblies, DLLs, or other kinds of binary components must be redeployed. The simple act of adding a new shape to the application causes a cascade of subsequent changes to many source modules and even more binary modules and binary components. Clearly, the impact of adding a new shape is very large.

Let's run through this again. The solution in Listing 9-1 is rigid because the addition of Triangle causes Shape, Square, Circle, and DrawAllShapes to be recompiled and redeployed. The solution is fragile because there will be many other switch/case or if/else statements that are both difficult to find and difficult to decipher. The solution is immobile because anyone attempting to reuse DrawAllShapes in another program is required to bring along Square and Circle, even if

---

3. In C/C++, changes to enums can cause a change in the size of the variable used to hold the enum. So, great care must be taken if you decide that you don't need to recompile the other shape declarations.

that new program does not need them. In short, Listing 9-1 exhibits many of the smells of bad design.

Conforming to OCP

Figure 9-2 shows the code for a solution to the square/circle problem that conforms to OCP. In this case, we have written an abstract class named Shape. This abstract class has a single abstract method named Draw. Both Circle and Square are derivatives of the Shape class.

Listing 9-2

OOD solution to Square/Circle problem

```
public interface Shape
{
  void Draw();
}

public class Square : Shape
{
  public void Draw()
  {
    //draw a square
  }
}

public class Circle : Shape
{
  public void Draw()
  {
    //draw a circle
  }
}

  public void DrawAllShapes(IList shapes)
  {
    foreach(Shape shape in shapes)
      shape.Draw();
  }
```

Note that if we want to extend the behavior of the DrawAllShapes function in Listing 9-2 to draw a new kind of shape, all we need do is add a new derivative of the Shape class. The DrawAllShapes function does not need to change. Thus, DrawAllShapes conforms to OCP. Its behavior can be extended without modifying it. Indeed, adding a Triangle class has *absolutely no effect* on any of the modules shown here. Clearly, some part of the system must change in order to deal with the Triangle class, but all the code shown here is immune to the change.

In a real application, the Shape class would have many more methods. Yet adding a new shape to the application is still quite simple, since all that is required is to create the new derivative and implement all its functions. There is no need to hunt through all the application, looking for places that require changes. This solution is not fragile.

Nor is the solution rigid. No existing source modules need to be modified, and no existing binary modules need to be rebuilt—with one exception. The module that creates instances of the new derivative of `Shape` must be modified. Typically, this is done by `main`, in some function called by `main`, or in the method of some object created by `main`.[4]

Finally, the solution is not immobile. `DrawAllShapes` can be reused by any application without the need to bring `Square` or `Circle` along for the ride. Thus, the solution exhibits none of the attributes of bad design mentioned.

This program conforms to OCP. *It is changed by adding new code rather than by changing existing code.* Therefore, the program does not experience the cascade of changes exhibited by nonconforming programs. The only changes required are the addition of the new module and the `main` related change that allows the new objects to be instantiated.

But consider what would happen to the `DrawAllShapes` function from Listing 9-2 if we decided that *all* `Circle`s *should be drawn before any* `Square`s. The `DrawAllShapes` function is not closed against a change, like this. To implement that change, we'll have to go into `DrawAllShapes` and scan the list first for `Circle`s and then again for `Square`s.

Anticipation and "Natural" Structure

Had we anticipated this kind of change, we could have invented an abstraction that protected us from it. The abstractions we chose in Listing 9-2 are more of a hindrance to this kind of change than a help. You may find this surprising; after all, what could be more natural than a `Shape` base class with `Square` and `Circle` derivatives? Why isn't that natural, real-world model the best one to use? Clearly, the answer is that that model is *not* natural in a system in which ordering is coupled to shape type.

This leads us to a disturbing conclusion. In general, no matter how "closed" a module is, there will always be some kind of change against which it is not closed. *There is no model that is natural to all contexts!*

Since closure cannot be complete, it must be strategic. That is, the designer must choose the kinds of changes against which to close the design, must guess at the kinds of changes that are most likely, and then construct abstractions to protect against those changes.

This takes a certain amount of prescience derived from experience. Experienced designers hope that they know the users and the industry well enough to judge the probability of various kinds of changes. These designers then invoke OCP against the most probable changes.

---

4. Such objects are known as *factories*, and we'll have more to say about them in Chapter 29.

This is not easy. It amounts to making educated guesses about the likely kinds of changes that the application will suffer over time. When the designers guess right, they win. When they guess wrong, they lose. And they will certainly guess wrong some of the time.

Also, conforming to OCP is expensive. It takes development time and effort to create the appropriate abstractions. Those abstractions also increase the complexity of the software design. There is a limit to the amount of abstraction that the developers can afford. Clearly, we want to limit the application of OCP to changes that are likely.

How do we know which changes are likely? We do the appropriate research, we ask the appropriate questions, and we use our experience and common sense. And after all that, *we wait until the changes happen!*

Putting the "Hooks" In

How do we protect ourselves from changes? In the previous century, we said that we'd "put the hooks in" for changes that we thought might take place. We felt that this would make our software flexible.

However, the hooks we put in were often incorrect. Worse, they smelled of needless complexity that had to be supported and maintained, even though they weren't used. This is not a good thing. We don't want to load the design with lots of unnecessary abstraction. Rather, we want to wait until we need the abstraction and then put them in.

Fool me once "Fool me once, shame on you. Fool me twice, shame on me." This is a powerful attitude in software design. To keep from loading our software with needless complexity, we may permit ourselves to be fooled *once*. This means that we initially write our code expecting it not to change. When a change occurs, we implement the abstractions that protect us from future changes *of that kind*. In short, we *take the first bullet* and then make sure that we are protected from any more bullets coming from that particular gun.

Stimulating change If we decide to take the first bullet, it is to our advantage to get the bullets flying early and frequently. We want to know what kinds of changes are likely before we are very far down the development path. The longer we wait to find out what kinds of changes are likely, the more difficult it will be to create the appropriate abstractions.

Therefore, we need to stimulate the changes. We do this through several of the means discussed in Chapter 2.

- We write tests first. Testing is one kind of usage of the system. By writing tests first, we force the system to be testable. Therefore, changes in testability will not surprise us later. We will have built the abstractions that make the system testable. We are likely to find that many of these abstractions will protect us from other kinds of changes later.

- We use very short development cycles: days instead of weeks.

- We develop features before infrastructure and frequently show those features to stake-holders.

- We develop the most important features first.

- We release the software early and often. We get it in front of our customers and users as quickly and as often as possible.

Using Abstraction to Gain Explicit Closure

OK, we've taken the first bullet. The user wants us to draw all `Circles` before any `Squares`. Now we want to protect ourselves from any future changes of that kind.

How can we close the `DrawAllShapes` function against changes in the ordering of drawing? Remember that closure is based on abstraction. Thus, in order to close `DrawAllShapes` against ordering, we need some kind of "ordering abstraction." This abstraction would provide an abstract interface through which any possible ordering policy could be expressed.

An ordering policy implies that, given any two objects, it is possible to discover which ought to be drawn first. C# provides such an abstraction. `IComparable` is an interface with one method, `CompareTo`. This method takes an object as a parameter and returns -1 if the receiving object is less than the parameter, 0 if they're equal, and 1 if the receiving object is greater than the parameter.

Figure 9-3 shows what the `Shape` class might look like when it extends the `IComparable` interface.

Listing 9-3
Shape extending IComparable

```
public interface Shape : IComparable
{
  void Draw();
}
```

Now that we have a way to determine the relative ordering of two `Shape` objects, we can sort them and then draw them in order. Listing 9-4 shows the C# code that does this.

Listing 9-4
DrawAllShapes with ordering

```
public void DrawAllShapes(ArrayList shapes)
{
  shapes.Sort();
  foreach(Shape shape in shapes)
    shape.Draw();
}
```

This gives us a means for ordering Shape objects and for drawing them in the appropriate order. But we still do not have a decent ordering abstraction. As it stands, the individual Shape objects will have to override the CompareTo method in order to specify ordering. How would this work? What kind of code would we write in Circle.CompareTo to ensure that Circles were drawn before Squares? Consider Listing 9-5.

Listing 9-5

Ordering a Circle

```
public class Circle : Shape
{
  public int CompareTo(object o)
  {
    if(o is Square)
      return -1;
    else
      return 0;
  }
}
```

It should be very clear that this function, and all its siblings in the other derivatives of Shape, do not conform to OCP. There is no way to close them against new derivatives of Shape. Every time a new derivative of Shape is created, all the CompareTo() functions will need to be changed.[5]

Of course, this doesn't matter if no new derivatives of Shape are ever created. On the other hand, if they are created frequently, this design would cause a significant amount of thrashing. Again, we'd take the first bullet.

Using a Data-Driven Approach to Achieve Closure

If we must close the derivatives of Shape from knowledge of one another, we can use a table-driven approach. Listing 9-6 shows one possibility.

Listing 9-6

Table driven type ordering mechanism

```
/// <summary>
/// This comparer will search the priorities
/// hashtable for a shape's type.  The priorities
/// table defines the odering of shapes.  Shapes
/// that are not found precede shapes that are found.
/// </summary>
public class ShapeComparer : IComparer
{
  private static Hashtable priorities = new Hashtable();
```

---

5. It is possible to solve this problem by using the ACYCLIC VISITOR pattern described in Chapter 35. Showing that solution now would be getting ahead of ourselves a bit. I'll remind you to come back here at the end of that chapter.

Listing 9-6 (Continued)

Table driven type ordering mechanism

```
    static ShapeComparer()
    {
      priorities.Add(typeof(Circle), 1);
      priorities.Add(typeof(Square), 2);
    }

    private int PriorityFor(Type type)
    {
      if(priorities.Contains(type))
        return (int)priorities[type];
      else
        return 0;
    }

    public int Compare(object o1, object o2)
    {
      int priority1 = PriorityFor(o1.GetType());
      int priority2 = PriorityFor(o2.GetType());
      return priority1.CompareTo(priority2);
    }
  }

    public void DrawAllShapes(ArrayList shapes)
    {
      shapes.Sort(new ShapeComparer());
      foreach(Shape shape in shapes)
        shape.Draw();
    }
```

By taking this approach, we have successfully closed the `DrawAllShapes` function against ordering issues in general and each of the `Shape` derivatives against the creation of new `Shape` derivatives or a change in policy that reorders the `Shape` objects by their type (e.g., changing the ordering so that `Squares` are drawn first).

The only item that is not closed against the order of the various `Shapes` is the table itself. And that table can be placed in its own module, separate from all the other modules, so that changes to it do not affect any of the other modules.

Conclusion

In many ways, the Open/Closed Principle is at the heart of object-oriented design. Conformance to this principle is what yields the greatest benefits claimed for object-oriented technology: flexibility, reusability, and maintainability. Yet conformance to this principle is not achieved simply by using an object-oriented programming language. Nor is it a good idea to apply rampant abstraction to every part of the application. Rather, it requires a dedication on the part of the developers to apply abstraction only to those parts of the program that exhibit frequent change. *Resisting premature abstraction is as important as abstraction itself.*

Bibliography

[**Jacobson92**] Ivar Jacobson, Patrick Johnsson, Magnus Christerson, and Gunnar Över-gaard, *Object-Oriented Software Engineering: A Use Case Driven Approach*, Addison-Wesley, 1992.

[**Meyer97**] Bertrand Meyer, *Object Oriented Software Construction*, 2d. ed., Prentice Hall, 1997.

10

The Liskov Substitution Principle (LSP)

© Jennifer M. Kohnke

The primary mechanisms behind the Open/Closed Principle are abstraction and polymorphism. In statically typed languages, such as C#, one of the key mechanisms that supports abstraction and polymorphism is inheritance. It is by using inheritance that we can create derived classes that implement abstract methods in base classes.

What are the design rules that govern this particular use of inheritance? What are the characteristics of the best inheritance hierarchies? What are the traps that will cause us to create hierarchies that do not conform to OCP? These are the questions addressed by the Liskov Substitution Principle (LSP).

> **The Liskov Substitution Principle**
>
> *Subtypes must be substitutable for their base types.*

Barbara Liskov wrote this principle in 1988.[1] She said:

> What is wanted here is something like the following substitution property: If for each
> object o_1 of type S there is an object o_2 of type T such that for all programs P defined in
> terms of T, the behavior of P is unchanged when o_1 is substituted for o_2 then S is a subtype
> of T.

The importance of this principle becomes obvious when you consider the consequences of violating it. Presume that we have a function f that takes as its argument a reference to some base class B. Presume also that when passed to f in the guise of B, some
derivative D of B causes f to misbehave. Then D violates LSP. Clearly, D is fragile in the
presence of f.

The authors of f will be tempted to put in some kind of test for D so that f can behave
properly when a D is passed to it. This test violates *OCP* because now, f is not closed to all
the various derivatives of B. Such tests are a code smell that are the result of inexperienced
developers or, what's worse, developers in a hurry reacting to LSP violations.

Violations of LSP

A Simple Example

Violating LSP often results in the use of runtime type checking in a manner that grossly
violates OCP. Frequently, an explicit `if` statement or `if/else` chain is used to determine
the type of an object so that the behavior appropriate to that type can be selected. Consider
Listing 10-1.

Listing 10-1
A violation of LSP causing a violation of OCP

```
struct Point {double x, y;}

public enum ShapeType {square, circle};

public class Shape
{
    private ShapeType type;
```

---

1. [Liskov88]

Listing 10-1 (Continued)
A violation of LSP causing a violation of OCP

```
public Shape(ShapeType t){type = t;}

public static void DrawShape(Shape s)
{
  if(s.type == ShapeType.square)
    (s as Square).Draw();
  else if(s.type == ShapeType.circle)
    (s as Circle).Draw();
  }
}

public class Circle : Shape
{
  private Point center;
  private double radius;

  public Circle() : base(ShapeType.circle) {}
  public void Draw() {/* draws the circle */}
}

public class Square : Shape
{
  private Point topLeft;
  private double side;

  public Square() : base(ShapeType.square) {}
  public void Draw() {/* draws the square */}
}
```

Clearly, the `DrawShape` function in Listing 10-1 violates OCP. It must know about every possible derivative of the `Shape` class, and it must be changed whenever new derivatives of `Shape` are created. Indeed, many rightly view the structure of this function as anathema to good design. What would drive a programmer to write a function like this?

Consider Joe the Engineer. Joe has studied object-oriented technology and has concluded that the overhead of polymorphism is too high to pay.[2] Therefore, he defined class `Shape` without any abstract functions. The classes `Square` and `Circle` derive from `Shape` and have `Draw()` functions, but they don't override a function in `Shape`. Since `Circle` and `Square` are not substitutable for `Shape`, `DrawShape` must inspect its incoming `Shape`, determine its type, and then call the appropriate `Draw` function.

The fact that `Square` and `Circle` cannot be substituted for `Shape` is a violation of LSP. This violation forced the violation of OCP by `DrawShape`. Thus, *a violation of LSP is a latent violation of OCP.*

---

2. On a reasonably fast machine, that overhead is on the order of 1ns per method invocation, so it's difficult to see Joe's point.

A More Subtle Violation

Of course there are other, far more subtle ways of violating LSP. Consider an application that uses the Rectangle class as described in Listing 10-2.

Listing 10-2
Rectangle class

```
public class Rectangle
{
    private Point topLeft;
    private double width;
    private double height;

    public double Width
    {
        get { return width; }
        set { width = value; }
    }

    public double Height
    {
        get { return height; }
        set { height = value; }
    }
}
```

Imagine that this application works well and is installed in many sites. As is the case with all successful software, its users demand changes from time to time. One day, the users demand the ability to manipulate *squares* in addition to rectangles.

It is often said that inheritance is the *IS-A* relationship. In other words, if a new kind of object can be said to fulfill the IS-A relationship with an old kind of object, the class of the new object should be derived from the class of the old object.

For all normal intents and purposes, a square *is a* rectangle. Thus, it is logical to view the Square class as being derived from the Rectangle class. (See Figure 10-1.)

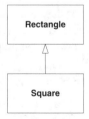

Figure 10-1
Square inherits from Rectangle

This use of the IS-A relationship is sometimes thought to be one of the fundamental techniques of object-oriented analysis, a term frequently used but seldom defined. A square is a rectangle, and so the Square class should be derived from the Rectangle class. However, this kind of thinking can lead to some subtle yet significant problems. Generally, these problem are not foreseen until we see them in code.

Our first clue that something has gone wrong might be the fact that a Square does not need both height and width member variables. Yet it will inherit them from Rectangle. Clearly, this is wasteful. In many cases, such waste is insignificant. But if we must create hundreds of thousands of Square objects—such as a CAD/CAE program in which every pin of every component of a complex circuit is drawn as a square—this waste could be significant.

Let's assume, for the moment, that we are not very concerned with memory efficiency. Other problems ensue from deriving Square from Rectangle. Square will inherit the Width and Height settter properties. These properties are inappropriate for a Square, since the width and height of a square are identical. This is a strong indication that there is a problem. However, there is a way to sidestep the problem. We could override Width and Height as follows:

```
public new double Width
{
  set
  {
    base.Width = value;
    base.Height = value;
  }
}

public new double Height
{
  set
  {
    base.Height = value;
    base.Width = value;
  }
}
```

Now, when someone sets the width of a Square object, its height will change correspondingly. And when someone sets the height, its width will change with it. Thus, the invariants—those properties that must always be true regardless of state—of the Square remain intact. The Square object will remain a mathematically proper square:

```
Square s = new Square();
s.SetWidth(1); // Fortunately sets the height to 1 too.
s.SetHeight(2); // sets width and height to 2. Good thing.
```

But consider the following function:

```
void f(Rectangle r)
{
  r.SetWidth(32); // calls Rectangle.SetWidth
}
```

If we pass a reference to a Square object into this function, the Square object will be corrupted, because the height won't be changed. This is a clear violation of LSP. The f function does not work for derivatives of its arguments. The reason for the failure is that

Width and Height were not declared virtual in Rectangle and are therefore not polymorphic.

We can fix this easily by declaring the setter properties to be virtual. However, when the creation of a derived class causes us to make changes to the base class, it often implies that the design is faulty. Certainly, it violates OCP. We might counter this by saying that forgetting to make Width and Height virtual was the real design flaw and that we are simply fixing it now. However, this is difficult to justify, since setting the height and width of a rectangle are exceedingly primitive operations. By what reasoning would we make them virtual if we did not anticipate the existence of Square?

Still, let's assume that we accept the argument and fix the classes. We wind up with the code in Listing 10-3.

Listing 10-3

Rectangle and Square that are self consistent

```
public class Rectangle
{
  private Point topLeft;
  private double width;
  private double height;

  public virtual double Width
  {
    get { return width; }
    set { width = value; }
  }

  public virtual double Height
  {
    get { return height; }
    set { height = value; }
  }
}

public class Square : Rectangle
{
  public override double Width
  {
    set
    {
      base.Width = value;
      base.Height = value;
    }
  }

  public override double Height
  {
    set
    {
      base.Height = value;
      base.Width = value;
    }
  }
}
```

The real problem Square and Rectangle now appear to work. No matter what you do to a Square object, it will remain consistent with a mathematical square. And regardless of what you do to a Rectangle object, it will remain a mathematical rectangle. Moreover, you can pass a Square into a function that accepts a Rectangle, and the Square will still act like a square and will remain consistent.

Thus, we might conclude that the design is now self-consistent and correct. However, this conclusion would be amiss. A design that is self-consistent is not necessarily consistent with all its users! Consider function g:

```
void g(Rectangle r)
{
  r.Width = 5;
  r.Height = 4;
  if(r.Area() != 20)
    throw new Exception("Bad area!");
}
```

This function invokes the Width and Height members of what it believes to be a Rectangle. The function works just fine for a Rectangle but throws an Exception if passed a Square. So here is the real problem: *The author of* g *assumed that changing the width of a* Rectangle *leaves its height unchanged.*

Clearly, it is reasonable to assume that changing the width of a rectangle does not affect its height! However, not all objects that can be passed as Rectangles satisfy that assumption. If you pass an instance of a Square to a function like g, whose author made that assumption, that function will malfunction. Function g is fragile with respect to the Square/Rectangle hierarchy.

Function g shows that there exist functions that take Rectangle objects but that cannot operate properly on Square objects. Since, for these functions, Square is not substitutable for Rectangle, the relationship between Square and Rectangle violates LSP.

One might contend that the problem lay in function g, that the author had no right to make the assumption that width and height were independent. The author of g would disagree. The function g takes a Rectagle as its argument. There are invariants, statements of truth, that obviously apply to a class named Rectangle, and one of those invariants is that height and width are independent. The author of g had every right to assert this invariant. It is the author of Square who has violated the invariant.

Interestingly enough, the author of Square did not violate an invariant of Square. By deriving Square from Rectangle, the author of Square violated an invariant of Rectangle!

Validity is not intrinsic The Laskov Substitution Principle leads us to a very important conclusion: *A model, viewed in isolation, cannot be meaningfully validated.* The validity of a model can be expressed only in terms of its clients. For example, when we examined the final version of the `Square` and `Rectangle` classes in isolation, we found that they were self-consistent and valid. Yet when we looked at them from the viewpoint of a programmer who made reasonable assumptions about the base class, the model broke down.

When considering whether a particular design is appropriate, one cannot simply view the solution in isolation. One must view it in terms of the reasonable assumptions made by the users of that design.[3]

Who knows what reasonable assumptions the users of a design are going to make? Most such assumptions are not easy to anticipate. Indeed, if we tried to anticipate them all, we'd likely wind up imbuing our system with the smell of needless complexity. Therefore, as with all other principles, it is often best to defer all but the most obvious LSP violations until the related fragility has been smelled.

ISA is about behavior So, what happened? Why did the apparently reasonable model of the `Square` and `Rectangle` go bad? After all, isn't a `Square` a `Rectangle`? Doesn't the IS-A relationship hold?

Not as far as the author of `g` is concerned! A square might be a rectangle, but from `g`'s point of view, a `Square` object is definitely *not* a `Rectangle` object. Why? Because the *behavior* of a `Square` object is not consistent with `g`'s expectation of the behavior of a `Rectangle` object. Behaviorally, a `Square` is not a `Rectangle`, and it is *behavior* that software is really all about. LSP makes it clear that in OOD, the IS-A relationship pertains to *behavior* that can be reasonably assumed and that clients depend on.

Design by contract Many developers may feel uncomfortable with the notion of behavior that is "reasonably assumed." How do you know what your clients will really expect? There is a technique for making those reasonable assumptions explicit and thereby enforcing LSP. The technique is called *design by contract* (DBC) and is expounded by Bertrand Meyer.[4]

Using DBC, the author of a class explicitly states the contract for that class. The contract informs the author of any client code of the behaviors that can be relied on. The contract is specified by declaring preconditions and postconditions for each method. The preconditions

---

3. Often, you will find that those reasonable assumptions are asserted in the unit tests written for the base class. This is yet another good reason to practice test-driven development.

4. [Meyer97], p. 331

must be true in order for the method to execute. On completion, the method guarantees that the postcondition are true.

We can view the postcondition of the `Rectangle.Width` setter as follows:

```
assert((width == w) && (height == old.height));
```

where `old` is the value of the `Rectangle` before `Width` is called. Now the rule for preconditions and postconditions of derivatives, as stated by Meyer, is: "A routine redeclaration [in a derivative] may only replace the original precondition by one equal or weaker, and the original post-condition by one equal or stronger."[5]

In other words, when using an object through its base class interface, the user knows only the preconditions and postconditions of the base class. Thus, derived objects must not expect such users to obey preconditions that are stronger then those required by the base class. That is, users must accept anything that the base class could accept. Also, derived classes must conform to all the postconditions of the base. That is, their behaviors and outputs must not violate any of the constraints established for the base class. Users of the base class must not be confused by the output of the derived class.

Clearly, the postcondition of the `Square.Width setter` is weaker[6] than the postcondition of the `Rectangle.Width setter`, since it does not enforce the constraint `(height == old.height)`. Thus, the `Width property of Square` violates the contract of the base class.

Certain languages, such as Eiffel, have direct support for preconditions and postconditions. You can declare them and have the runtime system verify them for you. C# has no such feature. In C#, we must manually consider the preconditions and postconditions of each method and make sure that Meyer's rule is not violated. Moreover, it can be very helpful to document these preconditions and postconditions in the comments for each method.

Specifying contracts in unit tests Contracts can also be specified by writing unit tests. By thoroughly testing the behavior of a class, the unit tests make the behavior of the class clear. Authors of client code will want to review the unit tests in order to know what to reasonably assume about the classes they are using.

A Real-World Example

Enough of squares and rectangles! Does LSP have a bearing on real software? Let's look at a case study that comes from a project I worked on a few years ago.

---

5. [Meyer97], p. 573
6. The term *weaker* can be confusing. X is weaker than Y if X does not enforce all the constraints of Y. It does not matter how many new constraints X enforces.

Motivation In the early 1990s I purchased a third-party class library that had some container classes.[7] The containers were roughly related to the Bags and Sets of Smalltalk. There were two varieties of Set and two similar varieties of Bag. The first variety was called *bounded* and was based an array. The second was called *unbounded* and was based on a linked list.

The constructor for BoundedSet specified the maximum number of elements the set could hold. The space for these elements was preallocated as an array within the BoundedSet. Thus, if the creation of the BoundedSet succeeded, we could be sure that it had enough memory. Since it was based on an array, it was very fast. There were no memory allocations performed during normal operation. And since the memory was preallocated, we could be sure that operating the BoundedSet would not exhaust the heap. On the other hand, it was wasteful of memory, since it would seldom completely utilize all the space that it had preallocated.

UnboundedSet, on the other hand, had no declared limit on the number of elements it could hold. So long as heap memory was avaliable, the UnboundedSet would continue to accept elements. Therefore, it was very flexible. It was also economical in that it used only the memory necessary to hold the elements that it currently contained. It was also slow, because it had to allocate and deallocate memory as part of its normal operation. Finally, a danger was that its normal operation could exhaust the heap.

I was unhappy with the interfaces of these third-party classes. I did not want my application code to be dependent on them, because I felt that I would want to replace them with better classes later. Thus, I wrapped the third-party containers in my own abstract interface, as shown in Figure 10-2.

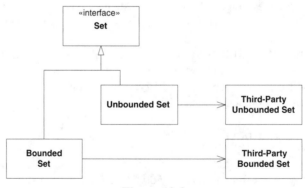

Figure 10-2
Container class adapter layer

---

7. The language was C++, long before the standard container library was available.

I created an interface, called `Set`, that presented abstract `Add`, `Delete`, and `IsMember` functions, as shown in Listing 10-4.[8] This structure unified the unbounded and bounded varieties of the two third-party sets and allowed them to be accessed through a common interface. Thus, some client could accept an argument of type `Set` and would not care whether the actual `Set` it worked on was of the bounded or unbounded variety. (See the `PrintSet` function in Listing 10-5.)

Listing 10-4

Abstract Set class

```
public interface Set
{
  public void Add(object o);
  public void Delete(object o);
  public bool IsMember(object o);
}
```

Listing 10-5

PrintSet

```
void PrintSet(Set s)
{
  foreach(object o in s)
  Console.WriteLine(o.ToString());
}
```

It is a big advantage not to have to know or care what kind of `Set` you are using. It means that the programmer can decide which kind of `Set` is needed in each particular instance, and none of the client functions will be affected by that decision. The programmer may choose an `UnboundedSet` when memory is tight and speed is not critical or may choose a `BoundedSet` when memory is plentiful and speed is critical. The client functions will manipulate these objects through the interface of the base class `Set` and will therefore not know or care which kind of `Set` they are using.

Problem I wanted to add a `PersistentSet` to this hierarchy. A persistent set is can be written out to a stream and then read back in later, possibly by a different application. Unfortunately, the only third-party container that I had access to that also offered persistence was not acceptable. It accepted objects that were derived from the abstract base class `PersistentObject`. I created the hierarchy shown in Figure 10-3.

Note that `PersistentSet` contains an instance of the third-party persistent set, to which it delegates all its methods. Thus, if you call `Add` on the `PersistentSet`, it simply delegates that to the appropriate method of the contained third-party persistent set.

On the surface, this might look all right. However, there is an implication that is rather ugly. Elements that are added to the third-party persistent set must be derived from `PersistentObject`. Since `PersistentSet` simply delegates to the third-party

---

8. The original code has been translated into C# here to make it easier for .NET programmers to understand.

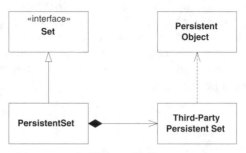

Figure 10-3
PersistentSet hierarchy

persistent set, any element added to `PersistentSet` must therefore derive from `PersistentObject`. Yet the interface of `Set` has no such constraint.

When a client is adding members to the base class `Set`, that client cannot be sure whether the `Set` might be a `PersistentSet`. Thus, the client has no way of knowing whether the elements it adds ought to be derived from `PersistentObject`.

Consider the code for `PersistentSet.Add()` in Listing 10-6. This code makes it clear that if any client tries to add an object that is not derived from the class `PersistentObject` to my `PersistentSet`, a runtime error will ensue. The cast will throw an exception. None of the existing clients of the abstract base class `Set` expect exceptions to be thrown on `Add`. Since these functions will be confused by a derivative of `Set`, this change to the hierarchy violates LSP.

Listing 10-6
Add method in `PersistentSet`
| ```
void Add(object o)
{
   PersistentObject p = (PersistentObject)o;
   thirdPartyPersistentSet.Add(p);
}
``` |

Is this a problem? Certainly. Functions that never before failed when passed a derivative of `Set` may now cause runtime errors when passed a `PersistentSet`. Debugging this kind of problem is relatively difficult, since the runtime error occurs very far away from the logic flaw. The logic flaw is the decision either to pass a `PersistentSet` into a function or to add an object to the `PersistentSet` that is not derived from `PersistentObject`. In either case, the decision might be millions of instructions away from the invocation of the `Add` method. Finding it can be a bear. Fixing it can be worse.

A solution that does *not* conform to the LSP How do we solve this problem? Several years ago, I solved it by convention, which is to say that I did not solve it in source code. Rather, I instated a convention whereby `PersistentSet` and `PersistentObject` were kept hidden from the application. They were known only to one particular module.
```

This module was responsible for reading and writing all the containers to and from the persistent store. When a container needed to be written, its contents were copied into appropriate derivatives of `PersistentObject` and then added to `PersistentSets`, which were then saved on a stream. When a container needed to be read from a stream, the process was inverted. A `PersistentSet` was read from the stream, and then the `PersistentObject`s were removed from the `PersistentSet` and copied into regular, nonpersistent, objects, which were then added to a regular `Set`.

This solution may seem overly restrictive, but it was the only way I could think of to prevent `PersistentSet` objects from appearing at the interface of functions that would want to add nonpersistent objects to them. Moreover, it broke the dependency of the rest of the application on the whole notion of persistence.

Did this solution work? Not really. The convention was violated in several parts of the application by developers who did not understand the necessity for it. That is the problem with conventions: they have to be continually resold to each developer. If the developer has not learned the convention or does not agree with it, the convention will be violated. And one violation can compromise the whole structure.

An LSP-compliant solution How would I solve this now? I would acknowledge that a `PersistentSet` does not have an IS-A relationship with `Set`, that it is not a proper derivative of `Set`. Thus, I would separate the hierarchies but not completely. `Set` and `PersistentSet` have features in common. In fact, it is only the `Add` method that causes the difficulty with LSP. Thus, I would create a hierarchy in which both `Set` and `PersistentSet` were siblings beneath an interface that allowed for membership testing, iteration, and so on (see Figure 10-4). This would allow `PersistentSet` objects to be iterated and tested for membership, and so on, but would not afford the ability to add objects that were not derived from `PersistentObject` to a `PersistentSet`.

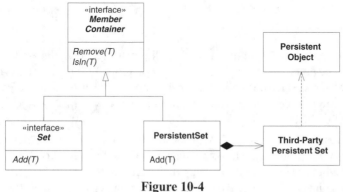

Figure 10-4
An LSP-compliant solution

Factoring Instead of Deriving

Another interesting and puzzling case of inheritance is the case of `Line` and `LineSegment`.[9] Consider Listings 10-7 and 10-8. At first, these two classes appear to be natural candidates for inheritance. `LineSegment` needs every member variable and every member function declared in `Line`. Moreover, `LineSegment` adds a new member function of its own, `Length`, and overrides the meaning of the `IsOn` function. Yet these two classes violate LSP in a subtle way.

Listing 10-7

`Line.cs`

```
public class Line
{
  private Point p1;
  private Point p2;

  public Line(Point p1, Point p2){this.p1=p1; this.p2=p2;}

  public Point P1 { get { return p1; } }
  public Point P2 { get { return p2; } }
  public double Slope { get {/*code*/} }
  public double YIntercept { get {/*code*/} }
  public virtual bool IsOn(Point p) {/*code*/}
}
```

Listing 10-8

`LineSegment.cs`

```
public class LineSegment : Line
{
  public LineSegment(Point p1, Point p2) : base(p1, p2) {}

  public double Length() { get {/*code*/} }
  public override bool IsOn(Point p) {/*code*/}
}
```

A user of `Line` has a right to expect that all points that are colinear with it are on it. For example, the point returned by the `YIntercept` property is the point at which the line intersects the *Y*-axis. Since this point is colinear with the line, users of `Line` have a right to expect that `IsOn(YIntercept) == true`. In many instances of `LineSegment`, however, this statement will fail.

Why is this an important issue? Why not simply derive `LineSegment` from `Line` and live with the subtle problems? This is a judgment call. There are *rare* occasions when it is more expedient to accept a subtle flaw in polymorphic behavior than to attempt to manipulate the design into complete LSP compliance. Accepting compromise instead of pursuing

---

9. Despite the similarity of this example to the `Square/Rectangle` example, it comes from a real application and was subject to the real problems discussed.

perfection is an engineering trade-off. A good engineer learns when compromise is more *profitable* than perfection. However, conformance to LSP *should not be surrendered lightly*. The guarantee that a subclass will always work where its base classes are used is a powerful way to manage complexity. Once it is forsaken, we must consider each subclass individually.

In the case of the `Line` and `LineSegment`, a simple solution illustrates an important tool of OOD. If we have access to both the `Line` and `LineSegment` classes, we can *factor* the common elements of both into an abstract base class. Listings 10-9, 10-10, and 10-11 show the factoring of `Line` and `LineSegment` into the base class `LinearObject`.

Listing 10-9
LinearObject.cs

```
public abstract class LinearObject
{
    private Point p1;
    private Point p2;

    public LinearObject(Point p1, Point p2)
    {this.p1=p1; this.p2=p2;}

    public Point P1 { get { return p1; } }
    public Point P2 { get { return p2; } }

    public double Slope { get {/*code*/} }
    public double YIntercept { get {/*code*/} }

    public virtual bool IsOn(Point p) {/*code*/}
}
```

Listing 10-10
Line.cs

```
public class Line : LinearObject
{
    public Line(Point p1, Point p2) : base(p1, p2) {}
    public override bool IsOn(Point p) {/*code*/}
}
```

Listing 10-11
LineSegment.cs

```
public class LineSegment : LinearObject
{
    public LineSegment(Point p1, Point p2) : base(p1, p2) {}

    public double GetLength() {/*code*/}
    public override bool IsOn(Point p) {/*code*/}
}
```

Representing both `Line` and `LineSegment`, `LinearObject` provides most of the functionality and data members for both subclasses, with the exception of the `IsOn` method, which is abstract. Users of `LinearObject` are not allowed to assume that they understand the extent of the object they are using. Thus, they can accept either a `Line` or a `LineSegment` with no problem. Moreover, users of `Line` will never have to deal with a `LineSegment`.

Factoring is a powerful tool. If qualities can be factored out of two subclasses, there is the distinct possibility that other classes will show up later that need those qualities, too. Of factoring, Rebecca Wirfs-Brock, Brian Wilkerson, and Lauren Wiener say:

> We can state that if a set of classes all support a common responsibility, they should inherit that responsibility from a common superclass.

> If a common superclass does not already exist, create one, and move the common responsibilities to it. After all, such a class is demonstrably useful—you have already shown that the responsibilities will be inherited by some classes. Isn't it conceivable that a later extension of your system might add a new subclass that will support those same responsibilities in a new way? This new superclass will probably be an abstract class.[10]

Listing 10-12 shows how the attributes of `LinearObject` can be used by an unanticipated class: `Ray`. A `Ray` is substitutable for a `LinearObject`, and no user of `LinearObject` would have any trouble dealing with it.

Listing 10-12

`Ray.cs`

```
public class Ray : LinearObject
{
    public Ray(Point p1, Point p2) : base(p1, p2) {/*code*/}
    public override bool IsOn(Point p) {/*code*/}
}
```

Heuristics and Conventions

Some simple heuristics can give you some clues about LSP violations. These heuristics all have to do with derivative classes that somehow *remove* functionality from their base classes. A derivative that does less than its base is usually not substitutable for that base and therefore violates LSP.

Consider Figure 10-13. The f function in `Base` is implemented but in `Derived` is degenerate. Presumably, the author of `Derived` found that function f had no useful purpose in a `Derived`. Unfortunately, the users of `Base` don't know that they shouldn't call f, and so there is a substitution violation.

---

10. [Wirfs-Brock90], p. 113

Listing 10-13

A degenerate function in a derivative

```
public class Base
{
    public virtual void f() {/*some code*/}
}

public class Derived : Base
{
    public override void f() {}
}
```

The presence of degenerate functions in derivatives is not always indicative of an LSP violation, but it's worth looking at them when they occur.

Conclusion

The Open/Closed Principle is at the heart of many of the claims made for object-oriented design. When this principle is in effect, applications are more maintainable, reusable, and robust. The Liskov Substitution Principle is one of the prime enablers of OCP. The substitutability of subtypes allows a module, expressed in terms of a base type, to be extensible without modification. That substitutability must be something that developers can depend on implicitly. Thus, the contract of the base type has to be well and prominently understood, if not explicitly enforced, by the code.

The term *IS-A* is too broad to act as a definition of a subtype. The true definition of a subtype is *substitutable*, where substitutability is defined by either an explicit or implicit contract.

Bibliography

[Liskov88] "Data Abstraction and Hierarchy," Barbara Liskov, *SIGPLAN Notices*, 23(5) (May 1988).

[Meyer97] Bertrand Meyer, *Object-Oriented Software Construction*, 2d. ed., Prentice Hall, 1997.

[Wirfs-Brock90] Rebecca Wirfs-Brock et al., *Designing Object-Oriented Software*, Prentice Hall, 1990.

11

The Dependency-Inversion Principle (DIP)

© Jennifer M. Kohnke

Nevermore
Let the great interests of the State depend
Upon the thousand chances that may sway
A piece of human frailty

—Sir Thomas Noon Talfourd (1795–1854)

> **The Dependency-Inversion Principle**
>
> A. *High-level modules should not depend on low-level modules. Both should depend on abstractions.*
>
> B. *Abstractions should not depend upon details. Details should depend upon abstractions.*

Over the years, many have questioned why I use the word *inversion* in the name of this principle. The reason is that more traditional software development methods, such as structured analysis and design, tend to create software structures in which high-level modules depend on low-level modules and in which policy depends on detail. Indeed, one of the goals of these methods is to define the subprogram hierarchy that describes how the high-level modules make calls to the low-level modules. The initial design of the `Copy` program in Figure 7-1 is a good example of such a hierarchy. The dependency structure of a well-designed object-oriented program is "inverted" with respect to the dependency structure that normally results from traditional procedural methods.

Consider the implications of high-level modules that depend on low-level modules. It is the high-level modules that contain the important policy decisions and business models of an application. These modules contain the identity of the application. Yet when these modules depend on the lower-level modules, changes to the lower-level modules can have direct effects on the higher-level modules and can force them to change in turn.

This predicament is absurd! It is the high-level, policy-setting modules that ought to be influencing the low-level detailed modules. The modules that contain the high-level business rules should take precedence over, and be independent of, the modules that contain the implementation details. High-level modules simply should not depend on low-level modules in any way.

Moreover, it is high-level, policy-setting modules that we want to be able to reuse. We are already quite good at reusing low-level modules in the form of subroutine libraries. When high-level modules depend on low-level modules, it becomes very difficult to reuse those high-level modules in different contexts. However, when the high-level modules are independent of the low-level modules, the high-level modules can be reused quite simply. This principle is at the very heart of framework design.

Layering

According to Booch, "all well structured object-oriented architectures have clearly-defined layers, with each layer providing some coherent set of services through a well-defined and controlled interface."[1] A naive interpretation of this statement might lead a

---

1. [Booch96], p. 54

designer to produce a structure similar to Figure 11-1. In this diagram, the high-level `Policy` layer uses a lower-level `Mechanism` layer, which in turn uses a detailed-level `Utility` layer. Although this may look appropriate, it has the insidious characteristic that the `Policy` layer is sensitive to changes all the way down in the `Utility` layer. *Dependency is transitive*. The `Policy` layer depends on something that depends on the `Utility` layer; thus, the `Policy` layer transitively depends on the `Utility` layer. This is very unfortunate.

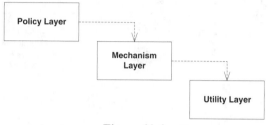

Figure 11-1
Naive layering scheme

Figure 11-2 shows a more appropriate model. Each upper-level layer declares an abstract interface for the services it needs. The lower-level layers are then realized from these abstract interfaces. Each higher-level class uses the next-lowest layer through the abstract interface. Thus, the upper layers do not depend on the lower layers. Instead, the lower layers depend on abstract service interfaces *declared in* the upper layers. Not only is the transitive dependency of `PolicyLayer` on `UtilityLayer` broken; so too is the direct dependency of the `PolicyLayer` on `MechanismLayer`.

Ownership Inversion

Note that the inversion here is one of not only dependencies but also interface ownership. We often think of utility libraries as owning their own interfaces. But when DIP is applied, we find that the clients tend to own the abstract interfaces and that their servers derive from them.

This is sometimes known as the Hollywood principle: "Don't call us; we'll call you."[2] The lower-level modules provide the implementation for interfaces that are declared within, and called by, the upper-level modules.

---

2. [Sweet85]

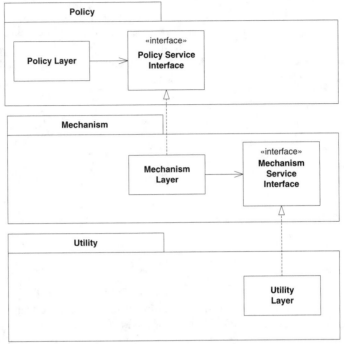

Figure 11-2
Inverted layers

Using this inversion of ownership, PolicyLayer is unaffected by any changes to MechanismLayer or UtilityLayer. Moreover, PolicyLayer can be reused in any context that defines lower-level modules that conform to the PolicyService-Interface. Thus, by inverting the dependencies, we have created a structure that is simultaneously more flexible, durable, and mobile.

In this context, ownership simply means that the owned interfaces are distributed with the owning clients and not with the servers that implement them. The interface is in the same package or library with the client. This forces the server library or package to depend on the client library or package.

Of course, there are times when we don't want the server to depend on the client. This is especially true when there are many clients but only one server. In that case, the clients must agree on the service interface and publish it in a separate package.

Dependence on Abstractions

A somewhat more naive, yet still very powerful, interpretation of DIP is the simple heuristic: "Depend on abstractions." Simply stated, this heuristic recommends that you should not depend on a concrete class and that rather, all relationships in a program should terminate on an abstract class or an interface.

- No variable should hold a reference to a concrete class.

- No class should derive from a concrete class.

- No method should override an implemented method of any of its base classes.

Certainly, this heuristic is usually violated at least once in every program. Somebody has to create the instances of the concrete classes, and whatever module does that will depend on them.[3] Moreover, there seems no reason to follow this heuristic for classes that are concrete but nonvolatile. If a concrete class is not going to change very much, and no other similar derivatives are going to be created, it does very little harm to depend on it.

For example, in most systems, the class that describes a string is concrete. In C#, for example, it is the concrete class `string`. This class is not volatile. That is, it does not change very often. Therefore, it does no harm to depend directly on it.

However, most concrete classes that *we* write as part of an application program *are* volatile. It is *those* concrete classes that we do not want to depend directly on. Their volatility can be isolated by keeping them behind an abstract interface.

This is not a complete solution. There are times when the interface of a volatile class must change, and this change must be propagated to the abstract interface that represents the class. Such changes break through the isolation of the abstract interface.

This is the reason that the heuristic is a bit naive. If, on the other hand, we take the longer view that the client modules or layers declare the service interfaces that they need, the interface will change only when the *client* needs the change. Changes to the classes that implement the abstract interface will not affect the client.

A Simple DIP Example

Dependency inversion can be applied wherever one class sends a message to another. For example, consider the case of the `Button` object and the `Lamp` object.

The `Button` object senses the external environment. On receiving the `Poll` message, the `Button` object determines whether a user has "pressed" it. It doesn't matter what the sensing mechanism is. It could be a button icon on a GUI, a physical button being pressed by a human finger, or even a motion detector in a home security system. The `Button` object detects that a user has either activated or deactivated it.

The `Lamp` object affects the external environment. On receiving a `TurnOn` message, the `Lamp` object illuminates a light of some kind. On receiving a `TurnOff` message, it

---

3. Actually, there are ways around this if you can use strings to create classes. C# allows this. So do several other languages. In such languages, the names of the concrete classes can be passed into the program as configuration data.

extinguishes that light. The physical mechanism is unimportant. It could be an LED on a computer console, a mercury vapor lamp in a parking lot, or even the laser in a laser printer.

How can we design a system such that the `Button` object controls the `Lamp` object? Figure 11-3 shows a naive model. The `Button` object receives `Poll` messages, determines whether the button has been pressed, and then simply sends the `TurnOn` or `TurnOff` message to the `Lamp`.

Figure 11-3
Naive model of a `Button` and a `Lamp`

Why is this naive? Consider the C# code implied by this model (Listing 11-1). Note that the `Button` class depends directly on the `Lamp` class. This dependency implies that `Button` will be affected by changes to `Lamp`. Moreover, it will not be possible to reuse `Button` to control a `Motor` object. In this model, `Button` objects control `Lamp` objects and *only* `Lamp` objects.

Listing 11-1

Button.cs

```
public class Button
{
  private Lamp lamp;
  public void Poll()
  {
    if (/*some condition*/)
      lamp.TurnOn();
  }
}
```

This solution violates DIP. The high-level policy of the application has not been separated from the low-level implementation. The abstractions have not been separated from the details. Without such a separation, the high-level policy automatically depends on the low-level modules, and the abstractions automatically depend on the details.

Finding the Underlying Abstraction

What is the high-level policy? It is the abstraction that underlies the application, the truths that do not vary when the details are changed. It is the system *inside* the system—it is the metaphor. In the `Button/Lamp` example, the underlying abstraction is to detect an on/off gesture from a user and relay that gesture to a target object. What mechanism is used to detect the user gesture? Irrelevant! What is the target object? Irrelevant! These are details that do not impact the abstraction.

The model in Figure 11-3 can be improved by inverting the dependency upon the Lamp object. In Figure 11-4, we see that the Button now holds an association to something called a ButtonServer, which provides the interfaces that Button can use to turn something on or off. Lamp implements the ButtonServer interface. Thus, Lamp is now doing the depending rather than being depended on.

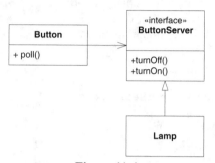

Figure 11-4
Dependency inversion applied to Lamp

The design in Figure 11-4 allows a Button to control any device that is willing to implement the ButtonServer interface. This gives us a great deal of flexibility. It also means that Button objects will be able to control objects that have not yet been invented.

However, this solution also puts a constraint on any object that needs to be controlled by a Button. Such an object *must* implement the ButtonServer interface. This is unfortunate, because these objects may also want to be controlled by a Switch object or some kind of object other than a Button.

By inverting the direction of the dependency and making the Lamp do the depending instead of being depended on, we have made Lamp depend on a different detail: Button. Or have we?

Lamp certainly depends on ButtonServer, but ButtonServer does not depend on Button. Any kind of object that knows how to manipulate the ButtonServer interface will be able to control a Lamp. Thus, the dependency is in name only. And we can fix that by changing the name of ButtonServer to something a bit more generic, such as SwitchableDevice. We can also ensure that Button and SwitchableDevice are kept in separate libraries, so that the use of SwitchableDevice does not imply the use of Button.

In this case, nobody owns the interface. We have the interesting situation whereby the interface can be used by lots of different clients, and implemented by lots of different servers. Thus, the interface needs to stand alone without belonging to either group. In C#, we would put it in a separate namespace and library.[4]

---

4. In dynamic languages such as Smalltalk, Pyrhon, or Ruby, the interface simply wouldn't exist as an explicit source code entity.

The **Furnace Example**

Let's look at a more interesting example. Consider the software that might control the regulator of a furnace. The software can read the current temperature from an I/O channel and instruct the furnace to turn on or off by sending commands to a different I/O channel. The structure of the algorithm might look something like Listing 11-2.

Listing 11-2

Simple algorithm for a thermostat

```
const byte TERMOMETER = 0x86;
const byte FURNACE = 0x87;
const byte ENGAGE = 1;
const byte DISENGAGE = 0;

void Regulate(double minTemp, double maxTemp)
{
  for(;;)
  {
    while (in(THERMOMETER) > minTemp)
      wait(1);
    out(FURNACE,ENGAGE);

    while (in(THERMOMETER) < maxTemp)
      wait(1);
    out(FURNACE,DISENGAGE);
  }
}
```

The high-level intent of the algorithm is clear, but the code is cluttered with lots of low-level details. This code could never be reused with different control hardware.

This may not be much of a loss, since the code is very small. But even so, it is a shame to have the algorithm lost for reuse. We'd rather invert the dependencies and see something like Figure 11-5.

This shows that the `Regulate` function takes two arguments that are both interfaces. The `Thermometer` interface can be read, and the `Heater` interface can be engaged and disengaged. This is all the `Regulate` algorithm needs. Now it can be written as shown in Listing 11-3

This has inverted the dependencies such that the high-level regulation policy does not depend on any of the specific details of the thermometer or the furnace. The algorithm is nicely reusable.

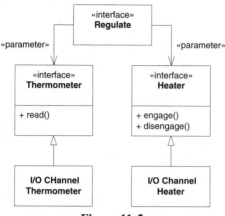

Figure 11-5
Generic regulator

Listing 11-3
Generic regulator

```
void Regulate(Thermometer t, Heater h,
      double minTemp, double maxTemp)
{
  for(;;)
  {
    while (t.Read() > minTemp)
      wait(1);
    h.Engage();

    while (t.Read() < maxTemp)
      wait(1);
    h.Disengage();
  }
}
```

Conclusion

Traditional procedural programming creates a dependency structure in which policy depends on detail. This is unfortunate, since the policies are then vulnerable to changes in the details. Object-oriented programming inverts that dependency structure such that both details and policies depend on abstraction, and service interfaces are often owned by their clients.

Indeed, this inversion of dependencies is the hallmark of good object-oriented design. It doesn't matter what language a program is written in. If its dependencies are inverted, it has an OO design. If its dependencies are not inverted, it has a procedural design.

The principle of dependency inversion is the fundamental low-level mechanism behind many of the benefits claimed for object-oriented technology. Its proper application is necessary for the creation of reusable frameworks. It is also critically important for the construction of code that is resilient to change. Since abstractions and details are isolated from each other, the code is much easier to maintain.

Bibliography

[Booch96] Grady Booch, *Object Solutions: Managing the Object-Oriented Project*, Addison-Wesley, 1996.

[GOF95] Eric Gamma, Richard Helm, Ralph Johnson, and John Vlissides, *Design Patterns: Elements of Reusable Object-Oriented Software*, Addison-Wesley, 1995.

[Sweet85] Richard E. Sweet, "The Mesa Programming Environment," *SIGPLAN Notices*, 20(7) July 1985: 216–229.

12

The Interface Segregation Principle (ISP)

This principle deals with the disadvantages of "fat" interfaces. Classes whose interfaces are not cohesive have "fat" interfaces. In other words, the interfaces of the class can be broken up into groups of methods. Each group serves a different set of clients. Thus, some clients use one group of methods, and other clients use the other groups.

ISP acknowledges that there are objects that require noncohesive interfaces; however, it suggests that clients should not know about them as a single class. Instead, clients should know about abstract base classes that have cohesive interfaces.

Interface Pollution

Consider a security system in which `Door` objects can be locked and unlocked and know whether they are open or closed. (See Listing 12-1.) This `Door` is coded as an interface so that clients can use objects that conform to the `Door` interface without having to depend on particular implementations of `Door`.

Listing 12-1
Security Door
| ```
public interface Door
{
    void Lock();
    void Unlock();
    bool IsDoorOpen();
}
``` |
```

Now consider that one such implementation, `TimedDoor`, needs to sound an alarm when the door has been left open for too long. In order to do this, the `TimedDoor` object communicates with another object called a `Timer`. (See Listing 12-2.)

Listing 12-2

```
public class Timer
{
  public void Register(int timeout, TimerClient client)
  {/*code*/}
}

public interface TimerClient
{
  void TimeOut();
}
```

When an object wishes to be informed about a timeout, it calls the `Register` function of the `Timer`. The arguments of this function are the time of the timeout and a reference to a `TimerClient` object whose `TimeOut` function will be called when the timeout expires.

How can we get the `TimerClient` class to communicate with the `TimedDoor` class so that the code in the `TimedDoor` can be notified of the timeout? There are several alternatives. Figure 12-1 shows a common solution. We force `Door`, and therefore `TimedDoor`, to inherit from `TimerClient`. This ensures that `TimerClient` can register itself with the `Timer` and receive the `TimeOut` message.

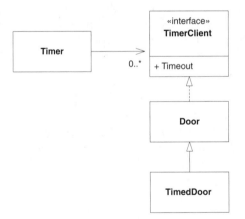

Figure 12-1
`TimerClient` at top of hierarchy

The problem with this solution is that the `Door` class now depends on `TimerClient`. Not all varieties of `Door` need timing. Indeed, the original `Door` abstraction had nothing whatever to do with timing. If timing-free derivatives of `Door` are created, they will have to provide degenerate implementations for the `TimeOut` method a potential violation of

LSP. Moreover, the applications that use those derivatives will have to import the definition of the `TimerClient` class, even though it is not used. That smells of needless complexity and needless redundancy.

This is an example of interface pollution, a syndrome that is common in statically typed languages, such as C#, C++, and Java. The interface of `Door` has been polluted with a method that it does not require. It has been forced to incorporate this method solely for the benefit of one of its subclasses. If this practice is pursued, every time a derivative needs a new method, that method will be added to the base class. This will further pollute the interface of the base class, making it "fat."

Moreover, each time a new method is added to the base class, that method must be implemented or allowed to default in derived classes. Indeed, an associated practice is to add these methods to the base class, giving them degenerate, or default, implementations specifically so that derived classes are not burdened with the need to implement them. As we learned previously, such a practice can violate LSP, leading to maintenance and reusability problems.

Separate Clients Mean Separate Interfaces

`Door` and `TimerClient` represent interfaces that are used by comply different clients. `Timer` uses `TimerClient`, and classes that manipulate doors use `Door`. Since the clients are separate, the interfaces should remain separate, too. Why? Because clients exert forces on their server interfaces.

When we think of forces that cause changes in software, we normally think about how changes to interfaces will affect their users. For example, we would be concerned about the changes to all the users of `TimerClient` if its interface changed. However, there is a force that operates in the other direction. Sometimes, the *user* forces a change to the interface.

For example, some users of `Timer` will register more than one timeout request. Consider the `TimedDoor`. When it detects that the `Door` has been opened, it sends the `Register` message to the `Timer`, requesting a timeout. However, before that timeout expires, the door closes, remains closed for a while, and then opens again. This causes us to register a *new* timeout request before the old one has expired. Finally, the first timeout request expires, and the `TimeOut` function of the `TimedDoor` is invoked. The `Door` alarms falsely.

We can correct this situation by using the convention shown in Listing 12-3. We include a unique `timeOutId` code in each timeout registration and repeat that code in the `TimeOut` call to the `TimerClient`. This allows each derivative of `TimerClient` to know which timeout request is being responded to.

Clearly, this change will affect all the users of `TimerClient`. We accept this, since the lack of the `timeOutId` is an oversight that needs correction. However, the design in Figure 12-1 will also cause `Door`, and all clients of `Door`, to be affected by this fix! This

---

Listing 12-3
Timer with ID

```
public class Timer
{
  public void Register(int timeout,
                       int timeOutId,
                       TimerClient client)
  {/*code*/}
}

public interface TimerClient
{
  void TimeOut(int timeOutID);
}
```

---

smells of rigidity and viscosity. Why should a bug in `TimerClient` have *any* affect on clients of `Door` derivatives that do not require timing? This kind of strange interdependency chills customers and managers to the bone. When a change in one part of the program affects other, completely unrelated parts of the program, the cost and repercussions of changes become unpredictable, and the risk of fallout from the change increases dramatically.

The Interface Segregation Principle

Clients should not be forced to depend on methods they do not use.

When clients are forced to depend on methods they don't use, those clients are subject to changes to those methods. This results in an inadvertent coupling between all the clients. Said another way, when a client depends on a class that contains methods that the client does not use but that other clients *do* use, that client will be affected by the changes that those other clients force on the class. We would like to avoid such couplings where possible, and so we want to separate the interfaces.

Class Interfaces versus Object Interfaces

Consider the `TimedDoor` again. Here is an object that has two separate interfaces used by two separate clients: `Timer` and the users of `Door`. These two interfaces *must* be implemented in the same object, since the implementation of both interfaces manipulates the same data. How can we conform to ISP? How can we separate the interfaces when they must remain together?

The answer lies in the fact that clients of an object do not need to access it through the interface of the object. Rather, they can access it through delegation or through a base class of the object.

Separation Through Delegation

One solution is to create an object that derives from `TimerClient` and delegates to the `TimedDoor`. Figure 12-2 shows this solution. When it wants to register a timeout request with the `Timer`, the `TimedDoor` creates a `DoorTimerAdapter` and registers it with the `Timer`. When the `Timer` sends the `TimeOut` message to the `DoorTimerAdapter`, the `DoorTimerAdapter` delegates the message back to the `TimedDoor`.

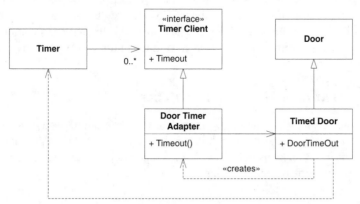

Figure 12-2
Door timer adapter

This solution conforms to ISP and prevents the coupling of `Door` clients to `Timer`. Even if the change to `Timer` shown in Listing 12-3 were to be made, none of the users of `Door` would be affected. Moreover, `TimedDoor` does not have to have the exact same interface as `TimerClient`. The `DoorTimerAdapter` can *translate* the `TimerClient` interface into the `TimedDoor` interface. Thus, this is a very general-purpose solution. (See Listing 12-4.)

Listing 12-4
`TimedDoor.cs`

```
public interface TimedDoor : Door
{
   void DoorTimeOut(int timeOutId);
}

public class DoorTimerAdapter : TimerClient
{
   private TimedDoor timedDoor;

   public DoorTimerAdapter(TimedDoor theDoor)
   {
      timedDoor = theDoor;
   }
```

Listing 12-4 (Continued)

TimedDoor.cs

```
  public virtual void TimeOut(int timeOutId)
  {
    timedDoor.DoorTimeOut(timeOutId);
  }
}
```

However, this solution is also somewhat inelegant. It involves the creation of a new object every time we wish to register a timeout. Moreover, the delegation requires a very small, but still nonzero, amount of runtime and memory. In some application domains, such as embedded real-time control systems, runtime and memory are scarce enough to make this a concern.

Separation Through Multiple Inheritance

Figure 12-3 and Listing 12-5 show how multiple inheritance can be used to achieve ISP. In this model, `TimedDoor` inherits from both `Door` and `TimerClient`. Although clients of both base classes can make use of `TimedDoor`, neither depends on the `TimedDoor` class. Thus, they use the same object through separate interfaces.

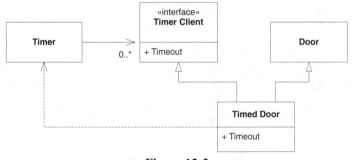

Figure 12-3
Multiply inherited `TimedDoor`

Listing 12-5

TimedDoor.cpp

```
public interface TimedDoor : Door, TimerClient
{
}
```

This solution is my normal preference. The only time I would choose the solution in Figure 12-2 over that in Figure 12-3 is if the translation performed by the `DoorTimerAdapter` object were necessary or if different translations were needed at different times.

The ATM User Interface Example

Now let's consider a slightly more significant example: the traditional automated teller machine (ATM) problem. The user interface of an ATM needs to be very flexible. The output may need to be translated into many different languages and it may need to be presented on a screen, on a braille tablet, or spoken out a speech synthesizer (Figure 12-4). Clearly, this flexibility can be achieved by creating an abstract base class that has abstract methods for all the different messages that need to be presented by the interface.

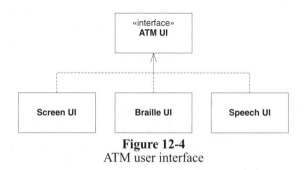

Figure 12-4
ATM user interface

Consider also that each transaction that the ATM can perform is encapsulated as a derivative of the class `Transaction`. Thus, we might have such classes as `DepositTransaction`, `WithdrawalTransaction`, `TransferTransaction`, and so on. Each of these classes invokes `UI` methods. For example, in order to ask the user to enter the amount to be deposited, the `DepositTransaction` object invokes the `RequestDepositAmount` method of the `UI` class. Likewise, in order to ask the user how much money to transfer between accounts, the `TransferTransaction` object calls the `RequestTransferAmount` method of `UI`. This corresponds to the diagram in Figure 12-5.

Note that this is precisely the situation that ISP tells us to avoid. Each of the transactions is using `UI` methods that no other class uses. This creates the possibility that changes to one of the derivatives of `Transaction` will force corresponding change to `UI`, thereby affecting all the other derivatives of `Transaction` and every other class that depends on the `UI` interface. Something smells like rigidity and fragility around here.

For example, if we were to add a `PayGasBillTransaction`, we would have to add new methods to `UI` in order to deal with the unique messages that this transaction would want to display. Unfortunately, since `DepositTransaction`, `WithdrawalTransaction`, and `TransferTransaction` all depend on the `UI` interface, they are all likely to be rebuilt. Worse, if the transactions were all deployed as components in separate assemblies,

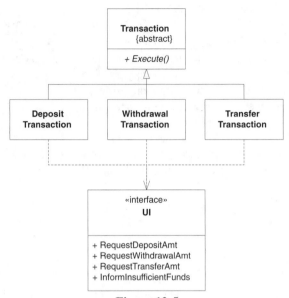

Figure 12-5
ATM transaction hierarchy

those assemblies would very likely have to be redeployed, even though none of their logic was changed. Can you smell the viscosity?

This unfortunate coupling can be avoided by segregating the UI interface into individual interfaces, such as DepositUI, WithdrawUI, and TransferUI. These separate interfaces can then be multiply inherited into the final UI interface. Figure 12-6 and Listing 12-6 show this model.

Whenever a new derivative of the Transaction class is created, a corresponding base class for the abstract UI interface will be needed, and so the UI interface and all its derivatives must change. However, these classes are not widely used. Indeed, they are probably used only by main or whatever process boots the system and creates the concrete UI instance. So the impact of adding new UI base classes is minimized.

A careful examination of Figure 12-6 shows one of the issues with ISP conformance that was not obvious from the TimedDoor example. Note that each transaction must somehow know about its particular version of the UI. DepositTransaction must know about DepositUI, WithdrawTransaction must know about WithdrawalUI, and so on. In Listing 12-6, I have addressed this issue by forcing each transaction to be constructed with a reference to its particular UI. Note that this allows me to use the idiom in Listing 12-7.

This is handy but also forces each transaction to contain a reference member to its UI. In C#, one might be tempted to put all the UI components into a single class. Listing 12-8 shows such an approach. This, however, has an unfortunate effect. The UIGlobals class

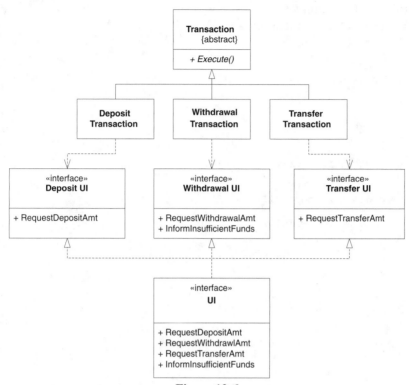

Figure 12-6
Segregated ATM UI interface

Listing 12-6

Segregated ATM UI interface

```
public interface Transaction
{
  void Execute();
}

public interface DepositUI
{
  void RequestDepositAmount();
}

public class DepositTransaction : Transaction
{
  privateDepositUI depositUI;

  public DepositTransaction(DepositUI ui)
  {
    depositUI = ui;
  }
```

Listing 12-6 (Continued)
Segregated ATM UI interface

```
  public virtual void Execute()
  {
    /*code*/
    depositUI.RequestDepositAmount();
    /*code*/
  }
}

public interface WithdrawalUI
{
  void RequestWithdrawalAmount();
}

public class WithdrawalTransaction : Transaction
{
  private WithdrawalUI withdrawalUI;

  public WithdrawalTransaction(WithdrawalUI ui)
  {
    withdrawalUI = ui;
  }

  public virtual void Execute()
  {
    /*code*/
    withdrawalUI.RequestWithdrawalAmount();
    /*code*/
  }
}

public interface TransferUI
{
  void RequestTransferAmount();
}

public class TransferTransaction : Transaction
{
  private TransferUI transferUI;

  public TransferTransaction(TransferUI ui)
  {
    transferUI = ui;
  }

  public virtual void Execute()
  {
    /*code*/
    transferUI.RequestTransferAmount();
    /*code*/
  }
}

public interface UI : DepositUI, WithdrawalUI, TransferUI
{
}
```

Listing 12-7

Interface initialization idiom

```
UI Gui; // global object;

void f()
{
    DepositTransaction dt = new DepositTransaction(Gui);
}
```

---

depends on `DepositUI`, `WithdrawalUI`, and `TransferUI`. This means that a module wishing to use any of the `UI` interfaces transitively depends on all of them, exactly the situation that ISP warns us to avoid. If a change is made to any of the `UI` interfaces, all modules that use `UIGlobals` may be forced to recompile. The `UIGlobals` class has recombined the interfaces that we had worked so hard to segregate!

Listing 12-8

Wrapping the Globals in a class

```
public class UIGlobals
{
    public static WithdrawalUI withdrawal;
    public static DepositUI deposit;
    public static TransferUI transfer;

    static UIGlobals()
    {
        UI Lui = new AtmUI(); // Some UI implementation
        UIGlobals.deposit = Lui;
        UIGlobals.withdrawal = Lui;
        UIGlobals.transfer = Lui;
    }
}
```

Consider now a function `g` that needs access to both the `DepositUI` and the `TransferUI`. Consider also that we wish to pass the user interfaces into this function. Should we write the function declaration like this:

```
void g(DepositUI depositUI, TransferUI transferUI)
```

Or should we write it like this:

```
void g(UI ui)
```

The temptation to write the latter (monadic) form is strong. After all, we know that in the former (polyadic) form, both arguments will refer to the *same object*. Moreover, if we were to use the polyadic form, its invocation might look like this:

```
g(ui, ui);
```

Somehow this seems perverse.

Perverse or not, the polyadic form is often preferable to the monadic form. The monadic form forces `g` to depend on every interface included in `UI`. Thus, when `WithdrawalUI` changes, `g` and all clients of `g` could be affected. This is more perverse than g(ui,ui)! Moreover, we cannot be sure that both arguments of g will *always* refer to the same object! In the future, it may be that the interface objects are separated for some reason. The fact that all interfaces are combined into a single object is information that g does not need to know. Thus, I prefer the polyadic form for such functions.

Clients can often be grouped together by the service methods they call. Such groupings allow segregated interfaces to be created for each group instead of for each client. This greatly reduces the number of interfaces that the service has to realize and prevents the service from depending on each client type.

Sometimes, the methods invoked by different groups of clients will overlap. If the overlap is small, the interfaces for the groups should remain separate. The common functions should be declared in all the overlapping interfaces. The server class will inherit the common functions from each of those interfaces but will implement them only once.

When object-oriented applications are maintained, the interfaces to existing classes and components often change. Sometimes, these changes have a huge impact and force the recompilation and redeployment of a very large part of the system. This impact can be mitigated by adding new interfaces to existing objects rather than changing the existing interface. If clients of the old interface wish to access methods of the new interface, they can query the object for that interface, as shown in Listing 12-9.

Listing 12-9
| ```
void Client(Service s)
{
  if(s is NewService)
  {
    NewService ns = (NewService)s;
    // use the new service interface
  }
}
``` |

As with all principles, care must be taken not to overdo it. The specter of a class with hundreds of different interfaces, some segregated by client and other segregated by version, is frightening indeed.

Conclusion

Fat classes cause bizarre and harmful couplings between their clients. When one client forces a change on the fat class, all the other clients are affected. Thus, clients should have to depend only on methods that they call. This can be achieved by breaking the interface of the fat class into many client-specific interfaces. Each client-specific interface declares only those functions that its particular client or client group invoke. The fat class can then inherit all the client-specific interfaces and implement them. This breaks the dependence of the clients on methods that they don't invoke and allows the clients to be independent of one another.
```

Bibliography

[GOF95] Erich Gamma, Richard Helm, Ralph Johnson, and John Vlissides, *Design Patterns: Elements of Reusable Object-Oriented Software*, Addison-Wesley, 1995.

13

Overview of UML for C# Programmers

Angela Brooks

The Unified Modeling Language (UML) is a graphical notation for drawing diagrams of software concepts. One can use it for drawing diagrams of a problem domain, a proposed software design, or an already completed software implementation. Fowler describes these three levels as *conceptual*, *specification*, and *implementation*.[1] This book deals with the last two.

---

1. [Fowler1999]

Specification- and implementation-level diagrams have a strong connection to source code. Indeed, it is the intent for a specification-level diagram to be turned into source code. Likewise, it is the intent for an implementation-level diagram to describe existing source code. As such, diagrams at these levels must follow certain rules and semantics. Such diagrams have very little ambiguity and a great deal of formality.

On the other hand, diagrams at the conceptual level are not strongly related to source code. Rather, they are related to *human* language. They are a shorthand used to describe concepts and abstractions that exist in the human problem domain. Since they don't follow strong semantic rules, their meaning can be ambiguous and subject to interpretation.

Consider, for example, the following sentence: *A dog is an animal*. We can create a conceptual UML diagram that represents this sentence, as shown in Figure 13-1.

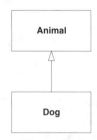

Figure 13-1
Conceptual UML diagram

This diagram depicts two entities—*Animal* and *Dog*—connected by *generalization* relationship. An *Animal* is a generalization of a *Dog*. A *Dog* is a special case of an *Animal*. That's all the diagram means. Nothing more can be inferred from it. We might be asserting that our pet dog, Sparky, is an animal; or, we might be asserting that dogs, as a biological species, belong to the animal kingdom. Thus, the diagram is subject to interpretation.

However, the same diagram at the specification or implementation level has a much more precise meaning:

```
public class Animal {}
public class Dog : Animal {}
```

This source code defines `Animal` and `Dog` as classes connected by an *inheritance* relationship. Whereas the conceptual model says nothing at all about computers, data processing, or programs, the specification model *describes part of a program*.

Unfortunately, the diagrams themselves don't communicate what level they are drawn at. Failure to recognize the level of a diagram is the source of significant miscommunication between programmers and analysts. A conceptual-level diagram *does not* define source code; nor should it. A specification-level diagram that describes the solution to a problem does not have to look anything like the conceptual-level diagram that describes that problem.

All the rest of the diagrams in this book are at the specification/implementation levels and are accompanied by corresponding source code, where feasible. We have seen our last conceptual-level diagram.

Following is a very brief tour of the primary diagrams used in UML. Then, you will be able to read and write most of the UML diagrams you will usually need. What remains, and what subsequent chapters address, are the details and formalisms that you will need to become proficient in UML.

UML has three main kinds of diagrams. *Static diagrams* describe the unchanging logical structure of software elements by depicting classes, objects, and data structures and the relationships that exist among them. *Dynamic diagrams* show how software entities change during execution, depicting the flow of execution, or the way entities change state. *Physical diagrams* show the unchanging physical structure of software entities, depicting physical entities, such as source files, libraries, binary files, data files, and the like, and the relationships that exist among them.

Consider the code in Listing 13-1. This program implements a map based on a simple binary tree algorithm. Familiarize yourself with the code before you consider the diagrams that follow.

Listing 13-1

TreeMap.cs

```
using System;

namespace TreeMap
{
  public class TreeMap
  {
    private TreeMapNode topNode = null;

    public void Add(IComparable key, object value)
    {
      if (topNode == null)
        topNode = new TreeMapNode(key, value);
      else
        topNode.Add(key, value);
    }

    public object Get(IComparable key)
    {
      return topNode == null ? null : topNode.Find(key);
    }
  }

  internal class TreeMapNode
  {
    private static readonly int LESS = 0;
    private static readonly int GREATER = 1;
    private IComparable key;
    private object value;
    private TreeMapNode[] nodes = new TreeMapNode[2];
```

Listing 13-1 (Continued)

TreeMap.cs

```
    public TreeMapNode(IComparable key, object value)
    {
      this.key = key;
      this.value = value;
    }

    public object Find(IComparable key)
    {
      if (key.CompareTo(this.key) == 0) return value;
      return FindSubNodeForKey(SelectSubNode(key), key);
    }

    private int SelectSubNode(IComparable key)
    {
      return (key.CompareTo(this.key) < 0) ? LESS : GREATER;
    }

    private object FindSubNodeForKey(int node, IComparable key)
    {
      return nodes[node] == null ? null : nodes[node].Find(key);
    }

    public void Add(IComparable key, object value)
    {
      if (key.CompareTo(this.key) == 0)
        this.value = value;
      else
        AddSubNode(SelectSubNode(key), key, value);
    }

    private void AddSubNode(int node, IComparable key,
      object value)
    {
      if (nodes[node] == null)
        nodes[node] = new TreeMapNode(key, value);
      else
        nodes[node].Add(key, value);
    }
  }
}
```

Class Diagrams

The *class diagram* in Figure 13-2 shows the major classes and relationships in the program. A TreeMap class has public methods named Add and Get and holds a reference to a TreeMapNode in a variable named topNode. Each TreeMapNode holds a reference to two other TreeMapNode instances in some kind of container named nodes. Each TreeMapNode instance holds references to two other instances in variables named key and value. The key variable holds a reference to some instance that implements the IComparable interface. The value variable simply holds a reference to some object.

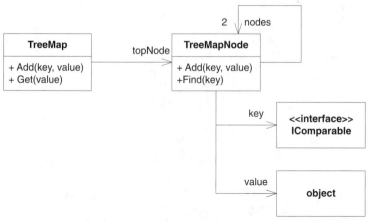

Figure 13-2
Class diagram of `TreeMap`

We'll go over the nuances of class diagrams in Chapter 19. For now, you need to know only a few things.

- Rectangles represent classes, and arrows represent relationships.

- In this diagram, all the relationships are *associations*. Associations are simple data relationships in which one object holds a reference to, and invokes methods on, the other.

- The name on an association maps to the name of the variable that holds the reference.

- A number next to an arrowhead typically shows the number of instances held by the relationship. If that number is greater than 1, some kind of container, usually an array, is implied.

- Class icons can have more than one compartment. The top compartment always holds the name of the class. The other compartments describe functions and variables.

- The «`interface`» notation means that `IComparable` is an interface.

- Most of the notations shown are optional.

Look carefully at this diagram and relate it to the code in Listing 13-1. Note how the association relationships correspond to instance variables. For example, the association from `TreeMap` to `TreeMapNode` is named `topNode` and corresponds to the `topNode` variable within `TreeMap`.

Object Diagrams

Figure 13-3 is an *object diagram*. It shows a set of objects and relationships at a particular moment in the execution of the system. You can view it as a snapshot of memory.

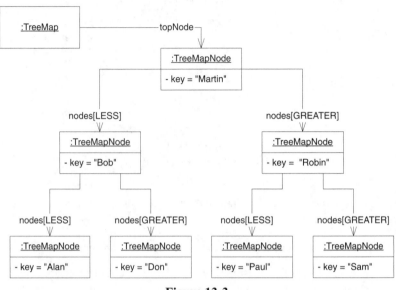

Figure 13-3
`TreeMap` object diagram

In this diagram, the rectangle icons represent objects. You can tell that they are objects because their names are underlined. The name after the colon is the name of the class that the object belongs to. Note that the lower compartment of each object shows the value of that object's `key` variable.

The relationships between the objects are called links and are derived from the associations in Figure 13-2. Note that the links are named for the two array cells in the `nodes` array.

Sequence Diagrams

Figure 13-4 is a *sequence diagram*. It describes how the `TreeMap.Add` method is implemented.

The stick figure represents an unknown caller. This caller invokes the `Add` method on a `TreeMap` object. If the `topNode` variable is `null`, `TreeMap` responds by creating a new `TreeMapNode` and assigning it to `topNode`. Otherwise, the `TreeMap` sends the `Add` message to `topNode`.

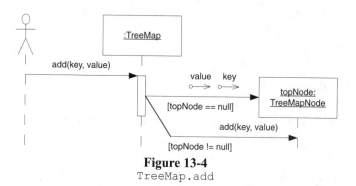

Figure 13-4
`TreeMap.add`

The Boolean expressions inside brackets are called *guards*. They show which path is taken. The message arrow that terminates on the `TreeMapNode` icon represents *construction*. The little arrows with circles are called *data tokens*. In this case, they depict the construction arguments. The skinny rectangle below `TreeMap` is called an *activation*. It depicts how much time the `add` method executes.

Collaboration Diagrams

Figure 13-5 is a *collaboration diagram* depicting the case of `TreeMap.Add` in which `topNode` is not `null`. Collaboration diagrams contain the same information that sequence diagrams contain. However, whereas sequence diagrams make the order of the messages clear, collaboration diagrams make the relationships between the objects clear.

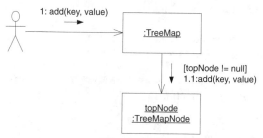

Figure 13-5
Collaboration diagram of one case of `TreeMap.Add`

The objects are connected by relationships called links. A *link* exists wherever one object can send a message to another. Traveling over those links are the messages themselves. They are depicted as the smaller arrows. The messages are labeled with the name of the message, its sequence number, and any guards that apply.

The dot structure of the sequence number shows the calling hierarchy. The `TreeMap.Add` function (message 1) invokes the `TreeMapNode.Add` function (message 1.1). Thus, message 1.1 is the first message sent by the function invoked by message 1.

State Diagrams

UML has a comprehensive notation for finite state machines. Figure 13-6 shows just the barest subset of that notation.

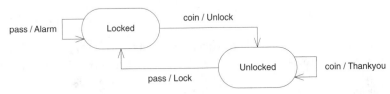

Figure 13-6
State machine of a subway turnstile

Figure 13-6 shows the state machine for a subway turnstile. There are two *states:* `Locked` and `Unlocked`. Two *events* may be sent to the machine. The `coin` event means that the user has dropped a coin into the turnstile. The `pass` event means that the user has passed through the turnstile.

The arrows are called *transitions*. They are labeled with the *event* that triggers the transition and the *action* that the transition performs. When a transition is triggered, it causes the state of the system to change.

We can translate Figure 13-6 to English as follows:

- If we are in the `Locked` state and get a `coin` event, we transition to the `Unlocked` state and invoke the `Unlock` function.

- If we are in the `Unlocked` state and get a `pass` event, we transition to the `Locked` state and invoke the `Lock` function.

- If we are in the `Unlocked` state and get a `coin` event, we stay in the `Unlocked` state and call the `Thankyou` function.

- If we are in the `Locked` state and get a `pass` event, we stay in the `Locked` state and call the `Alarm` function.

State diagrams are extremely useful for figuring out the way a system behaves. They give us the opportunity to explore what the system should do in unexpected cases, such as when a user deposits a coin and then deposits *another* coin for no good reason.

Conclusion

The diagrams shown in this chapter are enough for most purposes. Most programmers could live without any more knowledge of UML than what is shown here.

Bibliography

[Fowler1999] Martin Fowler with Kendall Scott, *UML Distilled: A Brief Guide to the Standard Object Modeling Language*, 2d ed., Addison-Wesley, 1999.

14

Working with Diagrams

Angela Brooks

Before exploring the details of UML, we should talk about when and why we use it. Much harm has been done to software projects through the misuse and overuse of UML.

Why Model?

Why do engineers build models? Why do aerospace engineers build models of aircraft? Why do structural engineers build models of bridges? What purposes do these models serve?

These engineers build models to find out whether their designs will work. Aerospace engineers build models of aircraft and then put them into wind tunnels to see whether they will fly. Structural engineers build models of bridges to see whether they will stand. Architects build models of buildings to see whether their clients will like the way they look. *Models are built to find out whether something will work.*

This implies that models must be testable. It does no good to build a model if you cannot apply criteria to that model in order to test it. If you can't evaluate the model, the model has no value.

Why don't aerospace engineers simply build the plane and try to fly it? Why don't structural engineers simply build the bridge and then see whether it stands? Very simply, airplanes and bridges are a *lot* more expensive than the models. *We investigate designs with models when the models are much cheaper than the real thing we are building.*

Why Build Models of Software?

Can a UML diagram be tested? Is it much cheaper to create and test than the software it represents? In both cases, the answer is nowhere near as clear as it is for aerospace engineers and structural engineers. There are no firm criteria for testing a UML diagram. We can look at it, evaluate it, and apply principles and patterns to it, but in the end, the evaluation is still subjective. UML diagrams are less expensive to draw than software is to write but not by a huge factor. Indeed, there are times when it's easier to change source code than it is to change a diagram. So when does it make sense to use UML?

I wouldn't be writing some of these chapters if UML didn't make sense to use. However, UML is also easy to misuse. *We make use of UML when we have something definitive we need to test and when using UML to test it is cheaper than using code to test it.* For example, let's say that I have an idea for a certain design. I need to test whether the other developers on my team think that it is a good idea. So I write a UML diagram on the whiteboard and ask my teammates for their feedback.

Should We Build Comprehensive Designs Before Coding?

Why do architects, aerospace engineers, and structural engineers all draw blueprints. The reason is that one person can draw the blueprints for a home that will require five or more people to build. A few dozen aerospace engineers can draw blueprints for an airplane that will require thousands of people to build. Blueprints can be drawn without digging foundations, pouring concrete, or hanging windows. In short, it is *much* cheaper to plan a building up front than to try to build it without a plan. It doesn't cost much to throw away a faulty blueprint, but it costs a *lot* to tear down a faulty building.

Once again, things are not so clear-cut in software. It is not at all clear that drawing UML diagrams is much cheaper than writing code. Indeed, many project teams have spent *more* on their diagrams than they have on the code itself. It is also not clear that throwing away a diagram is much cheaper than throwing away code. Therefore, it is not at all clear that creating a comprehensive UML design before writing code is a cost-effective option.

Making Effective Use of UML

Apparently, architecture, aerospace engineering, and structural engineering do not provide a clear metaphor for software development. We cannot blithely use UML the way those other disciplines use blueprints and models (see Appendix B). So, when and why *should* we use UML?

Diagrams are most useful for communicating with others and for helping you work out design problems. It is important that you use only the amount of detail necessary to accomplish your goal. Loading a diagram with lots of adornments is possible but counterproductive. Keep your diagrams simple and clean. UML diagrams are not source code and should not be treated as the place to declare every method, variable, and relationship.

Communicating with Others

UML is enormously convenient for communicating design concepts among software developers. A lot can be done with a small group of developers at a whiteboard. If you have some ideas that you need to communicate to others, UML can be a big benefit.

UML is very good for communicating focused design ideas. For example, the diagram in Figure 14-1 is very clear. We see `LoginPage` deriving from the `Page` class and using the `UserDatabase`. Apparently, the classes `HttpRequest` and `HttpResponse` are needed by `LoginPage`. One could easily imagine a group of developers standing around a whiteboard and debating about a diagram like this. Indeed, the diagram makes it very clear what the code structure would look like.

On the other hand, UML is not particularly good for communicating algorithmic detail. Consider the simple bubble sort code in Listing 14-1. Expressing this simple module in UML is not very satisfying.

Figure 14-2 gives us a rough structure but is cumbersome and reflects none of the interesting details. Figure 14-3 is no easier to read than the code and is substantially more difficult to create. UML for these purposes leaves much to be desired.

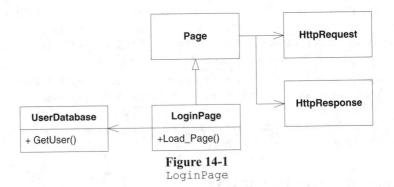

Figure 14-1
LoginPage

Listing 14-1

BubbleSorter.cs

```
public class BubbleSorter
{
  private static int operations;

  public static int Sort(int [] array)
  {
    operations = 0;
    if (array.Length <= 1)
      return operations;

    for (int nextToLast = array.Length-2;
      nextToLast >= 0; nextToLast--)
      for (int index = 0; index <= nextToLast; index++)
        CompareAndSwap(array, index);

    return operations;
  }

  private static void Swap(int[] array, int index)
  {
    int temp = array[index];
    array[index] = array[index+1];
    array[index+1] = temp;
  }

  private static void CompareAndSwap(int[] array, int index)
  {
    if (array[index] > array[index+1])
      Swap(array, index);
    operations++;
  }
}
```

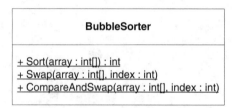

Figure 14-2
`BubbleSorter`

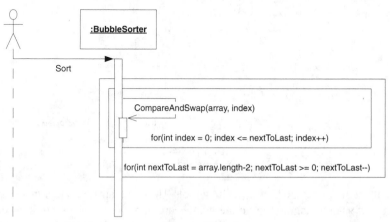

Figure 14-3
`BubbleSorter` sequence diagram

Road Maps

UML can be useful for creating road maps of large software structures. Such road maps give developers a quick way to find out which classes depend on which others and provide a reference to the structure of the whole system.

For example, in Figure 14-4, it is easy to see that `Space` objects have a `PolyLine` constructed of many `Lines` that are derived from `LinearObject`, which contains two `Points`. Finding this structure in code would be tedious. Finding it in a road map diagram is trivial.

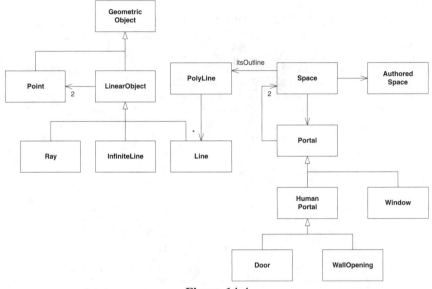

Figure 14-4
Road map diagram

Such road maps can be useful teaching tools. However, any team member ought to be able to throw such a diagram up on the whiteboard at a moment's notice. Indeed, I drew the one in Figure 14-4 from my memory of a system I was working on ten years ago. Such diagrams capture the knowledge that all the developers must keep in their heads in order to work effectively in the system. So, for the most part, there is not much point in going to a lot of trouble to create and archive such documents. Their best use is, once again, at the whiteboard.

Back-End Documentation

The best time to create a design document that you intend to save is at the end of the project, as the last act of the team. Such a document will accurately reflect the state of the design as the team left it and could certainly be useful to an incoming team.

However, there are some pitfalls. UML diagrams need to be carefully considered. We don't want a thousand pages of sequence diagrams! Rather, we want a few salient diagrams that describe the major issues in the system. No UML diagram is worse than one that is cluttered with so many lines and boxes that you get lost in the tangle, as is (Figure 14-5).

What to Keep and What to Throw Away

Get into the habit of throwing UML diagrams away. Better yet, get into the habit of not creating them on a persistent medium. Write them on a whiteboard or on scraps of paper.

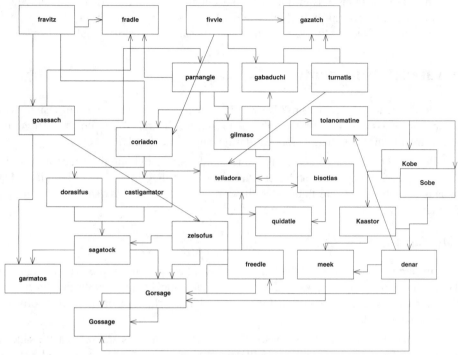

Figure 14-5
A bad but all too common example

Erase the whiteboard frequently, and throw the scraps of paper away. Don't use a CASE tool or a drawing program as a rule. There is a time and place for such tools, but most of your UML should be short-lived.

Some diagrams, however, are useful to save: the ones that express a common design solution in your system. Save the diagrams that record complex protocols that are difficult to see in the code. These are the diagrams that provide road maps for areas of the system that aren't touched very often. These are the diagrams that record designer intent in a way that is better than code can express it.

There is no point in hunting for these diagrams; you'll know them when you see them. There's no point in trying to create these diagrams up front. You'll be guessing, and you'll guess wrong. The useful diagrams will keep showing up over and over again. They'll show up on whiteboards or scraps of paper in design session after design session. Eventually, someone will make a persistent copy of the diagram just so it doesn't have to be drawn again. That is the time to place the diagram in some common area that everyone has access to.

It is important to keep common areas convenient and uncluttered. Putting useful diagrams on a Web server or a networked knowledge base is a good idea. However, don't allow hundreds or thousands of diagrams to accumulate there. Be judicious about which diagrams are truly useful and which could be recreated by anybody on the team at a moment's notice. Keep only those whose long-term survival has lots of value.

Iterative Refinement

How do we create UML diagrams? Do we draw them in one brilliant flash of insight? Do we draw the class diagrams first and then the sequence diagrams? Should we scaffold the whole structure of the system before we flesh in any of the details?

The answer to all these questions is a resounding *no*. Anything that humans do well, they do by taking tiny steps and then evaluating what they have done. The things that humans do not do well are things that they do in great leaps. We want to create useful UML diagrams. Therefore, we will create them in tiny steps.

Behavior First

I like to start with behavior. If I think that UML will help me think a problem through, I'll start by drawing a simple sequence diagram or collaboration diagram of the problem. Consider, for example, the software that controls a cellular phone. How does this software make the phone call?

We might imagine that the software detects each button press and sends a message to some object that controls dialing. So we'll draw a `Button` object and a `Dialer` object and show the `Button` sending many `digit` messages to the `Dialer` (Figure 14-6). (The star means *many*.)

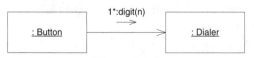

Figure 14-6
A simple sequence diagram

What will the `Dialer` do when it receives a `digit` message? Well, it needs to get the digit displayed on the screen. So perhaps it'll send `displayDigit` to the `Screen` object (Figure 14-7).

Next, the `Dialer` had better cause a tone to be emitted from the speaker. So we'll have it send the `tone` message to the `Speaker` object (Figure 14-8).

At some point, the user will click the Send button, indicating that the call is to go through. At that point, we'll have to tell the cellular radio to connect to the cellular network and pass along the phone number that was dialed (Figure 14-9).

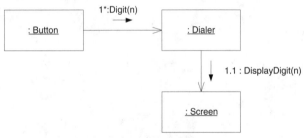

Figure 14-7
Continuation of Figure 14-6

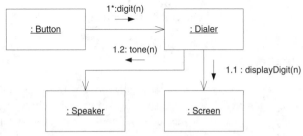

Figure 14-8
Continuation of Figure 14-7

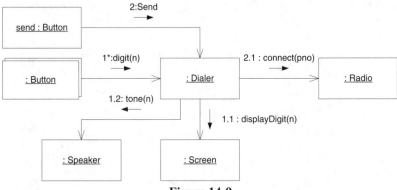

Figure 14-9
Collaboration diagram

Once the connection has been established, the `Radio` can tell the `Screen` to light up the in-use indicator. This message will almost certainly be sent in a different thread of control, which is denoted by the letter in front of the sequence number. The final collaboration diagram is shown in Figure 14-10.

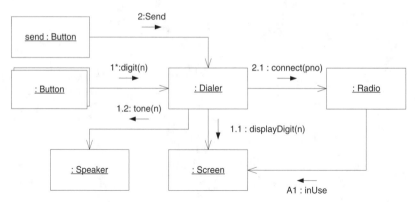

Figure 14-10
Cell phone collaboration diagram

Check the Structure

This little exercise has shown how we build a collaboration from nothing. Note how we invented objects along the way. We didn't know ahead of time that these objects were going to be there; we simply knew that we needed certain things to happen, so we invented objects to do them.

But now, before continuing, we need to examine what this collaboration means to the structure of the code. So we'll create a class diagram (Figure 14-11) that supports the collaboration. This class diagram will have a class for each object in the collaboration and an association for each link in the collaboration.

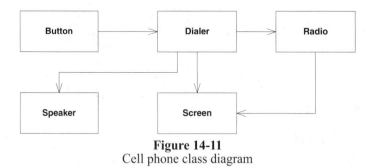

Figure 14-11
Cell phone class diagram

Those of you familiar with UML will note that we have ignored aggregation and composition. That's intentional. There'll be plenty of time to consider whether any of those relationships apply.

What's important to me right now is an analysis of the dependencies. Why should `Button` depend on `Dialer`? If you think about this, it's pretty hideous. Consider the implied code:

```
public class Button
{
  private Dialer itsDialer;
  public Button(Dialer dialer)
  {itsDialer = dialer;}
  ...
}
```

I don't want the source code of `Button` mentioning the source code of `Dialer`. `Button` is a class that I can use in many different contexts. For example, I'd like to use the `Button` class to control the on/off switch or the menu button or the other control buttons on the phone. If I bind the `Button` to the `Dialer`, I won't be able to reuse the `Button` code for other purposes.

I can fix this by inserting an interface between `Button` and `Dialer`, as shown in Figure 14-12. Here, we see that each `Button` is given a token that identifies it. When it detects that the button has been pressed, the `Button` class it invokes the `buttonPressed` method of the `ButtonListener` interface, passing the token. This breaks the dependence of `Button` on `Dialer` and allows `Button` to be used virtually anywhere that needs to receive button presses.

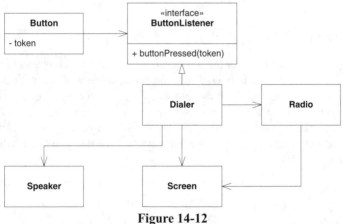

Figure 14-12
Isolating `Button` from `Dialer`

Note that this change has had no effect on the dynamic diagram in Figure 14-10. The objects are all the same; only the classes have changed.

Unfortunately, now we've made `Dialer` know something about `Button`. Why should `Dialer` expect to get its input from `ButtonListener`? Why should it have a method named `buttonPressed` within it? What has the `Dialer` got to do with `Button`?

We can solve this problem, and get rid of all the token nonsense, by using a batch of little adapters (Figure 14-13). The `ButtonDialerAdapter` implements the `ButtonListener` interface, receiving the `buttonPressed` method and sending a `digit(n)` message to the `Dialer`. The `digit` passed to the `Dialer` is held in the adapter.

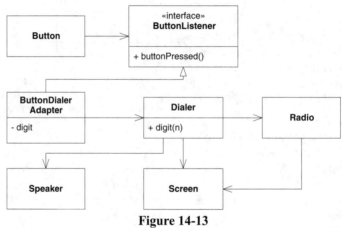

Figure 14-13
Adapting `Button`s to `Dialer`s

Envisioning the Code

We can easily envision the code for the `ButtonDialerAdapter`. It appears in Listing 14-2. Being able to envision the code is *critically* important when working with diagrams. We use the diagrams as a shortcut for code, not a replacement for it. If you are drawing diagrams and cannot envision the code that they represent, you are building castles in the air. *Stop what you are doing and figure out how to translate it to code.* Never let the diagrams become an end unto themselves. You must always be sure that you know what code you are representing.

Listing 14-2
ButtonDialerAdapter.cs

```
public class ButtonDialerAdapter : ButtonListener
{
  private int digit;
  private Dialer dialer;
```

Listing 14-2 (Continued)
ButtonDialerAdapter.cs

```
  public ButtonDialerAdapter(int digit, Dialer dialer)
  {
    this.digit = digit;
    this.dialer = dialer;
  }

  public void ButtonPressed()
  {
    dialer.Digit(digit);
  }
}
```

Evolution of Diagrams

Note that the last change we made in Figure 14-13 has invalidated the dynamic model back in Figure 14-10. The dynamic model knows nothing of the adapters. We'll change that now.

Figure 14-14 shows how the diagrams evolve together in an iterative fashion. You start with a little bit of dynamics. Then you explore what those dynamics imply to the static relationships. You alter the static relationships according to the principles of good design. Then you go back and improve the dynamic diagrams.

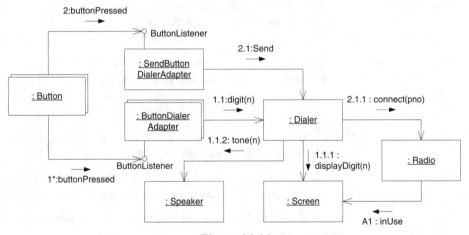

Figure 14-14
Adding adapters to the dynamic model

Each of these steps is *tiny*. We don't want to invest any more than *five minutes* into a dynamic diagram before exploring the static structure implied. We don't want to spend any more than five minutes refining that static structure before we consider the impact on the dynamic behavior. Rather, we want to evolve the two diagrams together using very short cycles.

Remember, we're probably doing this at a whiteboard, and we are probably not recording what we are doing for posterity. We aren't trying to be very formal or very precise. Indeed, the diagrams I have included in the preceding figures are a bit more precise and formal than you would normally have to be. The goal at the whiteboard is not to get all the dots right on your sequence numbers. The goal is to get everybody standing at the board to understand the discussion. The goal is to stop working at the board and start writing code.

When and How to Draw Diagrams

Drawing UML diagrams can be a very useful activity. It can also be a horrible waste of time. A decision to use UML can be either very good or very bad. It depends on how, and how much, you choose to use it.

When to Draw Diagrams and When to Stop

Don't make a rule that everything must be diagrammed. Such rules are worse than useless. Enormous amounts of project time and energy can be wasted in pursuit of diagrams that no one will ever read.

Draw diagrams when:

- Several people need to understand the structure of a particular part of the design because they are all going to be working on it simultaneously. Stop when everyone agrees that they understand.

- You want team consensus, but two or more people disagree on how a particular element should be designed. Put the discussion into a time box, then choose a means for deciding, such as a vote or an impartial judge. Stop at the end of the time box or when the decision can be made. Then erase the diagram.

- You want to play with a design idea, and the diagrams can help you think it through. Stop when you can finish your thinking in code. Discard the diagrams.

- You need to explain the structure of some part of the code to someone else or to yourself. Stop when the explanation would be better done by looking at code.

- It's close to the end of the project, and your customer has requested them as part of a documentation stream for others.

Do not draw diagrams:

- Because the process tells you to.

- Because you feel guilty not drawing them or because you think that's what good designers do. Good designers write code. They draw diagrams only when necessary.

- To create comprehensive documentation of the design phase prior to coding. Such documents are almost never worth anything and consume immense amounts of time.

- For other people to code. True software architects participate in the coding of their designs.

CASE Tools

UML CASE tools can be beneficial but also expensive dust collectors. Be *very* careful about making a decision to purchase and deploy a UML CASE tool.

- *Don't UML CASE tools make it easier to draw diagrams?* No, they make it significantly more difficult. There is a long learning curve to get proficient, and even then the tools are more cumbersome than whiteboards, which are very easy to use. Developers are usually already familiar with them. If not, there is virtually no learning curve.

- *Don't UML CASE tools make it easier for large teams to collaborate on diagrams?* In some cases. However, the vast majority of developers and development projects do not need to be producing diagrams in such quantities and complexities that they require an automated collaborative system to coordinate their diagramming activities. In any case, the best time to purchase a system to coordinate the preparation of UML diagrams is when a manual system has first been put in place, is starting to show the strain, and the only choice is to automate.

- *Don't UML CASE tools make it easier to generate code?* The sum total effort involved in creating the diagrams, generating the code, and then using the generated code is not likely to be less than the cost of simply writing the code in the first place. If there is a gain, it is not an order of magnitude or even a factor of 2. Developers know how to edit text files and use IDEs. Generating code from diagrams may sound like a good idea, but I strongly urge you to measure the productivity increase before you spend a lot of money.

- *What about these CASE tools that are also IDEs and show the code and diagrams together?* These tools are definitely cool. However, the constant presence of UML is not important. The fact that the diagram changes as I modify the code or that the code changes as I modify the diagram does not really help me much. Frankly, I'd rather buy an IDE that has put its effort into figuring out how to help me manipulate my programs rather than my diagrams. Again, measure productivity improvement before making a huge monetary commitment.

In short, look before you leap, and look very hard. There *may* be a benefit to outfitting your team with an expensive CASE tool, but verify that benefit with your own experiments before buying something that could very well turn into shelfware.

But What About Documentation?

Good documentation is essential to any project. Without it, the team will get lost in a sea of code. On the other hand, too much documentation of the wrong kind is worse because you have all this distracting and misleading paper, and you still have the sea of code.

Documentation must be created, but it must be created prudently. The choice of what *not* to document is just as important as the choice of what *to* document. A complex communication protocol needs to be documented. A complex relational schema needs to be documented. A complex reusable framework needs to be documented. However, none of these things need a hundred pages of UML. Software documentation should be *short and to the point*. The value of a software document is inversely proportional to its size.

For a project team of 12 people working on a project of a million lines of code, I would have a total of 25 to 200 pages of persistent documentation, with my preference being for the smaller. These documents would include UML diagrams of the high-level structure of the important modules, ER (Entity-Relationship) diagrams of the relational schema, a page or two about how to build the system, testing instructions, source code control instructions, and so forth. I would put this documentation into a wiki[1] or some collaborative authoring tool so that anyone on the team can access it on the screen and search it and change it as need be.

It takes a lot of work to make a document small, but that work is worth it. People will read small documents. They won't read 1,000-page tomes.

Conclusion

A few folks at a whiteboard can use UML to help them think through a design problem. Such diagrams should be created iteratively, in very short cycles. It is best to explore dynamic scenarios first and then determine their implications on the static structure. It is important to evolve the dynamic and static diagrams together, using very short iterative cycles on the order of five minutes or less.

UML CASE tools can be beneficial in certain cases. But for the normal development team, they are likely to be more of a hindrance than a help. If you think you need a UML CASE tool, even one integrated with an IDE, run some productivity experiments first. Look before you leap.

UML is a tool, not an end in itself. As a tool, it can help you think through your designs and communicate them to others. Use it sparingly, and it will give you great benefit. Overuse it, and it will waste a lot of your time. When using UML, *think small*.

---

1. A Web-based collaborative document authoring tool. See http://c2.com and http://fitnesse.org.

15

State Diagrams

Angela Brooks

UML has a rich set of notations for describing finite state machines (FSMs). In this chapter, we'll look at the most useful bits of that notation. FSMs are an enormously useful tool for writing all kinds of software. I use them for GUIs, communication protocols, and any other type of event-based system. Unfortunately, I find that too many developers are unfamiliar with the concepts of FSMs and are therefore missing many opportunities to simplify. I'll do my small part to correct that in this chapter.

The Basics

Figure 15-1 shows a simple *state transition diagram* (STD) that describes an FSM that controls the way a user logs in to a system. The rounded rectangles represent *states*. The name of each state is in its upper compartment. In the lower compartment are special actions that tell us what to do when the state is entered or exited. For example, as we enter the `Prompting for Login` state, we invoke the `showLoginScreen` action. When we exit that state, we invoke the `hideLoginScreen` action.

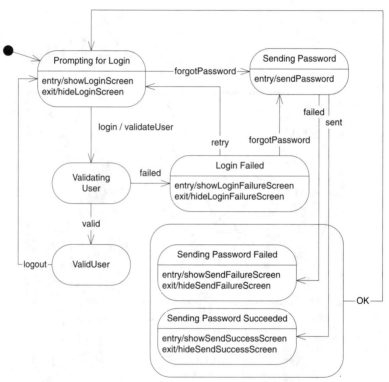

Figure 15-1
Simple login state machine

The arrows between the states are called *transitions*. Each is labeled with the name of the event that triggers the transition. Some are also labeled with an action to be performed when the transition is triggered. For example, if we are in the `Prompting for Login` state and get a `login` event, we transition to the `Validating User` state and invoke the `validateUser` action.

The black circle in the upper left of the diagram is called an *initial pseudostate*. An FSM begins its life following the transition out of this pseudostate. Thus, our state machine starts out transitioning into the `Prompting for Login` state.

I drew a *superstate* around the Sending Password Failed and Sending Password Succeeded states because both states react to the OK event by transitioning to the Prompting for Login state. I didn't want to draw two identical arrows, so I used the convenience of a superstate.

This FSM makes it clear how the login process works and breaks the process down into nice little functions. If we implement all the action functions such as showLoginScreen, validateUser, and sendPassword, and wire them up with the logic shown in the diagram, we can be sure that the login process will work.

Special Events

The lower compartment of a state contains event/action pairs. The entry and exit events are standard, but as you can see from Figure 15-2, you can supply your own events, if you like. If one of these special events occurs while the FSM is in that state, then the corresponding action is invoked.

Figure 15-2
States and special events in UML

Before UML, I used to represent a special event as a transition arrow that looped around back to the same state, as in Figure 15-3. However, this has a slightly different meaning in UML. Any transition that exits a state will invoke the exit action, if any. Likewise, any transition that enters a state will invoke the entry action, if any. Thus, in UML, a reflexive transition, such as that in Figure 15-3, invokes not only myAction but also the exit and entry actions.

Figure 15-3
Reflexive transition

Superstates

As you saw in the login FSM in Figure 15-1, superstates are convenient when you have many states that respond to some of the same events in the same way. You can draw a superstate around those similar states and simply draw the transition arrows leaving the superstate instead of leaving the individual states. Thus, the two diagrams in Figure 15-4 are equivalent.

Superstate transitions can be overridden by drawing explicit transition from the substates. Thus, in Figure 15-5, the `pause` transition for `S3` overrides the default `pause` transition for the `Cancelable` superstate. In this sense, a superstate is rather like a base class. Substates can override their superstate transitions the same way that derived classes can override their base class methods. However, it is inadvisable to push this metaphor too far. The relationship between superstates and substates is not really equivalent to inheritance.

Angela Brooks

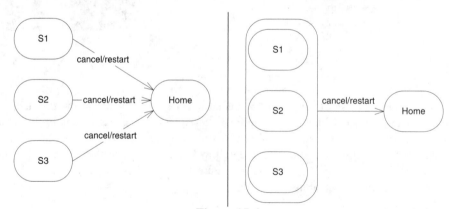

Figure 15-4
Transition: multiple states and superstate

Superstates can have `entry`, `exit`, and special events the same way that normal states can have them. Figure 15-6 shows an FSM in which both superstates and substates have `exit` and `entry` actions. As it transitions from `Some State` into `Sub`, the FSM first invokes the `enterSuper` action, followed by the `enterSub` action. Likewise, if it transitions out of `Sub2` back to `Some State`, the FSM first invokes `exitSub2` and then `exitSuper`. However, since it does not exit the superstate, the `e2` transition from `Sub` to `Sub2` simply invokes `exitSub` and `enterSub2`.

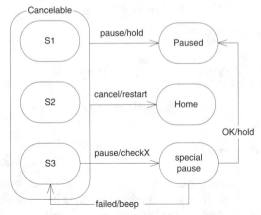

Figure 15-5
Overriding superstate transitions

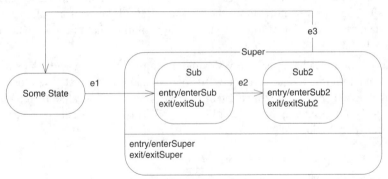

Figure 15-6
Hierarchical invocation of `entry` and `exit` actions

Initial and Final Pseudostates

Figure 15-7 shows two pseudostates that are commonly used in UML. FSMs come into existence *in the process of* transitioning out of the initial pseudostate. The transition leading out of the initial pseudostate cannot have an event, since the event is the creation of the state machine. The transition can, however, have an action. This action will be the first action invoked after the creation of the FSM.

Similarly, an FSM dies in the process of transitioning into the *final pseudostate*. The final pseudostate is never actually reached. Any action on the transition into the final pseudostate will be the last action invoked by the FSM.

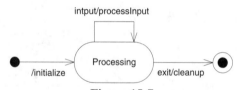

Figure 15-7
Initial and final pseudostates

Using FSM Diagrams

I find diagrams like this to be immensely useful for figuring out state machines for sub-systems whose behavior is well known. On the other hand, most systems that are amena-ble to FSMs do not have behaviors that are well known in advance. Rather, the behaviors of most systems grow and evolve over time. Diagrams aren't a conducive medium for sys-tems that must change frequently. Issues of layout and space intrude on the content of the diagrams. This intrusion can sometimes prevent designers from making needed changes to a design. The specter of reformatting the diagram prevents them from adding a needed class or state and causes them to use a substandard solution that doesn't impact the dia-gram layout.

Text, on the other hand, is a very flexible medium for dealing with change. Layout issues are at a minimum, and there is always room to add lines of text. Therefore, for sys-tems that evolve, I create *state transition tables* (STTs) in text files rather than STDs. Con-sider the STD of the subway turnstile in Figure 15-8. This can be easily represented as an STT, as shown in Table 15-1.

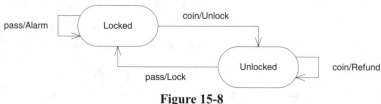

Figure 15-8
Subway turnstile STD

Table 15-1 Subway Turnstile STT

Current State	Event	New State	Action
Locked	coin	Unlocked	Unlock
Locked	pass	Locked	Alarm
Unlocked	coin	Unlocked	Refund
Unlocked	pass	Locked	Lock

The STT is a simple table with four columns. Each row of the table represents a transition. Look at each transition arrow on the diagram. You'll see that the table rows contain the two endpoints of each arrow, as well as the event and action of the arrow. You read the STT by using the following sentence template: "If we are in the Locked state and get a coin event, we go to the Unlocked state and invoke the Unlock function."

This table can be converted into a text file very simply:

```
Locked      coin    Unlocked    Unlock
Locked      pass    Locked      Alarm
Unlocked    coin    Unlocked    Refund
Unlocked    pass    Locked      Lock
```

These 16 words contain all the logic of the FSM.

SMC (state machine compiler) is a simple compiler I wrote in 1989 to read STTs and generate C++ code to implement the logic. Since then, SMC has grown and changed to emit code for various languages. We'll be taking a much closer look at SMC in Chapter 36 when we discuss the STATE pattern. SMC is freely available from the resources section of www.objectmentor.com.

Creating and maintaining FSMs in this form is much easier than trying to maintain diagrams, and generating the code saves lots of time. So, though diagrams can be very useful to help you think through or present an FSM to others, the text form is much more convenient for development.

Conclusion

Finite state machines are a powerful concept for structuring software. UML provides a very powerful notation for visualizing FSMs. However, it is often easier to develop and maintain an FSM by using a textual language rather than diagrams.

The UML state diagram notation is much richer than I have described. There are several other pseudostates, icons, and widgets that you can apply. However, I rarely find them useful. The notation I have described in this chapter is all I ever use.

16

Object Diagrams

Sometimes, it can be useful to show the state of the system at a particular time. Like a snapshot of a running system, a UML object diagram shows the objects, relationships, and attribute values that obtain at a given instant.

A Snapshot in Time

Some time ago, I was involved with an application that allowed users to draw the floor plan of a building on a GUI. The program captured the rooms, doors, windows, and wall openings in the data structure, as shown in Figure 16-1. Although this diagram shows you what kinds of data structures are possible, it does not tell you exactly what objects and relationships are instantiated at any given time.

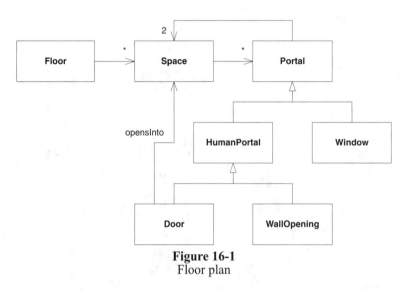

Figure 16-1
Floor plan

Let's assume that a user of our program draws two rooms, a kitchen, and a lunchroom, connected by a wall opening. Both the kitchen and the lunchroom have a window to the outside. The lunchroom also has a door that opens outward to the outside. This scenario is depicted by the object diagram in Figure 16-2. This diagram shows the objects that are in the system and what other objects they are connected to. It shows `kitchen` and the `lunchRoom` as separate instances of `Space`. It shows how these two rooms are connected by a wall opening. It shows that the outside is represented by another instance of space. And it shows all the other objects and relationships that must exist.

Object diagrams like this are useful when you need to show what the internal structure of a system looks like at a particular time, or when the system is in a particular state. An object diagram shows the intent of the designer. It shows the way that certain classes and relationships are going to be used. It can help to show how the system will change as various inputs are given to it.

But be careful; it is easy to get carried away. In the past decade, I have probably drawn fewer than a dozen object diagrams of this kind. The need for them simply has not arisen very frequently. When they are needed, they are indispensable, and that's why I'm including them in this book. However, you aren't going to need them very often, and you should definitely not assume that you need to draw them for every scenario in the system or even for every system.

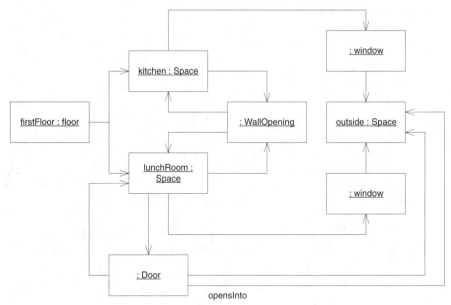

Figure 16-2
Lunchroom and kitchen

Active Objects

Object diagrams are also useful in multi-threaded systems. Consider, for example, the `SocketServer` code in Listing 16-1. This program implements a simple framework that allows you to write socket servers without having to deal with all the nasty threading and synchronization issues that accompany sockets.

Listing 16-1
SocketServer.cs

```
using System.Collections;
using System.Net;
using System.Net.Sockets;
using System.Threading;

namespace SocketServer
{
```

Listing 16-1 (Continued)

SocketServer.cs

```
public interface SocketService
{
  void Serve(Socket s);
}

public class SocketServer
{
  private TcpListener serverSocket = null;
  private Thread serverThread = null;
  private bool running = false;
  private SocketService itsService = null;
  private ArrayList threads = new ArrayList();

  public SocketServer(int port, SocketService service)
  {
    itsService = service;
    IPAddress addr = IPAddress.Parse("127.0.0.1");
    serverSocket = new TcpListener(addr, port);
    serverSocket.Start();
    serverThread = new Thread(new ThreadStart(Server));
    serverThread.Start();
  }

  public void Close()
  {
    running = false;
    serverThread.Interrupt();
    serverSocket.Stop();
    serverThread.Join();
    WaitForServiceThreads();
  }

  private void Server()
  {
    running = true;
    while (running)
    {
      Socket s = serverSocket.AcceptSocket();
      StartServiceThread(s);
    }
  }

  private void StartServiceThread(Socket s)
  {
    Thread serviceThread =
      new Thread(new ServiceRunner(s, this).ThreadStart());
    lock (threads)
    {
      threads.Add(serviceThread);
    }
    serviceThread.Start();
  }
```

```
Listing 16-1  (Continued)
SocketServer.cs
      private void WaitForServiceThreads()
      {
        while (threads.Count > 0)
        {
          Thread t;
          lock (threads)
          {
            t = (Thread) threads[0];
          }

          t.Join();
        }
      }

      internal class ServiceRunner
      {
        private Socket itsSocket;
        private SocketServer itsServer;

        public ServiceRunner(Socket s, SocketServer server)
        {
          itsSocket = s;
          itsServer = server;
        }

        public void Run()
        {
          itsServer.itsService.Serve(itsSocket);
          lock (itsServer.threads)
          {
            itsServer.threads.Remove(Thread.CurrentThread);
          }
          itsSocket.Close();
        }

        public ThreadStart ThreadStart()
        {
          return new ThreadStart(Run);
        }
      }
    }
}
```

The class diagram for this code is shown in Figure 16-3. It's not very inspiring, and it's difficult to see what the intent of this code is from the class diagram. The figure shows all the classes and relationships, but somehow the big picture doesn't come through.

However, look at the object diagram in Figure 16-4. This shows the structure much better than the class diagram does. Figure 16-4 shows that the SocketServer holds onto the serverThread and that the serverThread runs in a delegate named Server(). It shows that the serverThread is responsible for creating all the ServiceRunner instances.

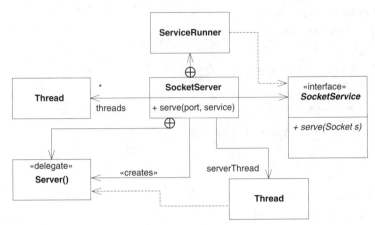

Figure 16-3
SocketServer class diagram

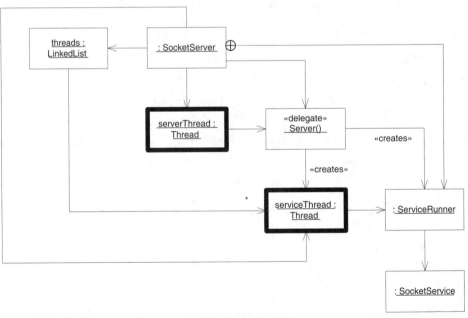

Figure 16-4
SocketServer object diagram

Note the heavy bold lines around the Thread instances. Objects with heavy bold borders represent *active objects*, which act as the head of a thread of control. They contain the methods, such as Start, Abort, Sleep, and so on, that control the thread. In this diagram, all the active objects are instances of `Thread` because all the processing is done in delegates that the `Thread` instances hold references to.

The object diagram is more expressive than the class diagram because the structure of this particular application is built at runtime. In this case, the structure is more about objects than about classes.

Conclusion

Object diagrams provide a snapshot of the state of the system at a particular time. This can be a useful way to depict a system, especially when the system's structure is built dynamically instead of imposed by the static structure of its classes. However, one should be leery of drawing many object diagrams. Most of the time, they can be inferred directly from corresponding class diagrams and therefore serve little purpose.

17

Use Cases

Use cases are a wonderful idea that has been vastly overcomplicated. Over and over again, I have seen teams sitting and spinning in their attempts to write use cases. Typically, such teams thrash on issues of form rather than substance. They argue and debate over preconditions, postconditions, actors, secondary actors, and a bevy of other things that *simply don't matter.*

The real trick to use cases is to *keep them simple.* Don't worry about use case forms; simply write them on *blank* paper or on a *blank* page in a simple word processor or on *blank* index cards. Don't worry about filling in all the details. Details aren't important until much later. Don't worry about capturing *all* the use cases; that's an impossible task.

The one thing to remember about use cases is: *Tomorrow, they are going to change.* No matter how diligently you capture them, no matter how fastidiously you record the details, no matter how thoroughly you think them through, no matter how much effort you apply to exploring and analyzing the requirements: *Tomorrow*, they are going to change.

If something is going to change tomorrow, you don't need to capture its details today. Indeed, you want to postpone the capture of the details until the last possible moment. Think of use cases as *just-in-time requirements*.

Writing Use Cases

Note the title of this section. We *write* use cases; we don't draw them. Use cases are not diagrams. Use cases are textual descriptions of behavioral requirements, written from a certain point of view.

"Wait!" you say. "I know UML has use case diagrams, I've seen them."

Yes, UML does have use case diagrams. However, those diagrams tell you nothing at all about the *content* of the use cases. They are devoid of information about the behavioral requirements that use cases are meant to capture. Use case diagrams in UML capture something else entirely.

A use case is a description of the behavior of a system. That description is written from the point of view of a user who has just told the system to do something in particular. A use case captures the *visible* sequence of events that a system goes through in response to a *single* user stimulus.

A *visible event* is one that the user can see. Use cases do not describe hidden behavior at all. They don't discuss the hidden mechanisms of the system. They describe only those things that a user can see.

Typically, a use case is broken up into two sections. The first is the *primary course*. Here, we describe how the system responds to the stimulus of the user and assume that nothing goes wrong.

For example, here is a typical use case for a point-of-sale system.

Check Out Item:
1. Cashier swipes product over scanner; scanner reads UPC code.
2. Price and description of item, as well as current subtotal, appear on the display facing the customer. The price and description also appear on the cashier's screen.
3. Price and description are printed on receipt.
4. System emits an audible "acknowledgment" tone to tell the cashier that the UPC code was correctly read.

That's the primary course of a use case! Nothing more complex is necessary. Indeed, even that tiny sequence might be too much detail if the use case isn't going to be implemented for a while. We wouldn't want to record this kind of detail until the use case was within a few days or weeks of being implemented.

How can you estimate a use case if you don't record its detail? You talk to the stake-holders about the detail, without necessarily recording it. This will give you the information you need to give a rough estimate. Why not record the detail if you're going to talk to the stakeholders about it? Because tomorrow, the details are going to change. Won't that change affect the estimate? Yes, but over many use cases, those effects integrate out. Recording the detail too early just isn't cost-effective.

If we aren't going to record the details of the use case just yet, what *do* we record? How do we know that the use case even exists if we don't write something down? Write the name of the use case. Keep a list of them in a spreadsheet or a word processor document. Better yet, write the name of the use case on an index card, and maintain a stack of use case cards. Fill in the details as they get closer to implementation.

Alternate Courses

Some of those details will concern things that can go wrong. During the conversations with the stakeholders, you'll want to talk over failure scenarios. Later, as it gets closer and closer to the time when the use case will be implemented, you'll want to think through more and more of those alternative courses. They become addenda to the primary course of the use case. They can be written as follows.

UPC Code Not Read:

If the scanner fails to capture the UPC code, the system should emit the "reswipe" tone, telling the cashier to try again. If after three tries the scanner still does not capture the UPC code, the cashier should enter it manually.

No UPC Code:

If the item does not have a UPC code, the cashier should enter the price manually.

These alternative courses are interesting because they hint at other use cases that the stakeholders might not have identified initially. In this case it, appears necessary to be able to enter the UPC or price manually.

What Else?

What about actors, secondary actors, preconditions, postconditions, and the rest? Don't worry about all that stuff. For the vast majority of the systems you will work on, you won't need to know about all those other things. Should the time come that you need to know more about use cases, you can read Alistair Cockburn's definitive work on the topic.[1] For now, learn to walk before you learn to run. Get used to writing simple use cases. As you master them—defined as having successfully used them in a project—you

---

1. [Cockburn2001]

can ever so carefully and parsimoniously adopt some of the more sophisticated techniques. But remember, don't sit and spin.

Diagramming Use Cases

Of all the diagrams in UML, use case diagrams are the most confusing and the least useful. I recommend that you avoid them entirely, with the exception of the system boundary diagram.

Figure 17-1 shows a system boundary diagram. The large rectangle is the system boundary. Everything inside the rectangle is part of the system under development. Outside the rectangle are the *actors* that *act* on the system. Actors are entities outside the system and provide the stimuli for the system. Typically, actors are human users. They might also be other systems or even devices, such as real-time clocks.

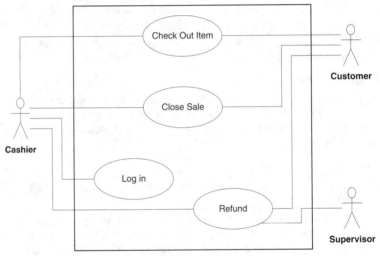

Figure 17-1
System boundary diagram

Inside the boundary rectangle are the use cases: the ovals with names inside. The lines connect the actors to the use cases they stimulate. Avoid using arrows; nobody really knows what the direction of the arrowheads means.

This diagram is almost, but not quite, useless. It contains very little information of use to the programmer, but it makes a good cover page for a presentation to stakeholders.

Use case relationships fall into the category of things that "seemed like a good idea at the time." I suggest that you actively ignore them. They'll add no value to your use cases or to your understanding of the system and will be the source of many never-ending debates about whether to use «extends» or «generalization».

Conclusion

This was a short chapter. That's fitting because the topic is simple. That simplicity must be your attitude toward use cases. If once you proceed down the dark path of use case complexity, forever will it dominate your destiny. Use the force, and keep your use cases simple.

Bibliography

[Cockburn2001] Alistair Cockburn, *Writing Effective Use Cases*, Addison-Wesley, 2001.

18

Sequence Diagrams

Sequence diagrams are the most common of the dynamic models drawn by UML users. As you might expect, UML provides lots and lots of goodies to help you draw truly incomprehensible diagrams. In this chapter, we describe those goodies and try to convince you to use them with great restraint.

I once consulted for a team that had decided to create sequence diagrams for every method of every class. Please don't do this; it's a terrible waste of time. Use sequence diagrams when you have an immediate need to explain to someone how a group of objects collaborate or when you want to visualize that collaboration for yourself. Use them as a tool that you use occasionally to hone your analytical skills rather than as necessary documentation.

The Basics

I first learned to draw sequence diagrams in 1978. James Grenning, a longtime friend and associate, showed them to me while we were working on a project that involved complex communication protocols between computers connected by modems. What I am going to show you here is very close to the simple notation he taught me then, and it should suffice for the vast majority of sequence diagrams that you will need to draw.

Objects, Lifelines, Messages, and Other Odds and Ends

Figure 18-1 shows a typical sequence diagram. The objects and classes involved in the collaboration are shown at the top. Objects have underlined names; classes do not. The stick figure (actor) at left represents an anonymous object. It is the source and sink of all the messages entering and leaving the collaboration. Not all sequence diagrams have such an anonymous actor, but many do.

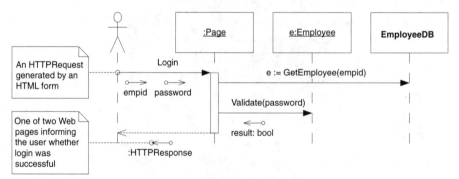

Figure 18-1
Typical sequence diagram

The dashed lines hanging down from the objects and the actor are called *lifelines*. A message being sent from one object to another is shown as an arrow between the two lifelines. Each message is labeled with its name. Arguments appear either in the parentheses that follow the name or next to *data tokens* (the little arrows with the circles on the end). Time is in the vertical dimension, so the lower a message appears, the later it is sent.

The skinny little rectangle on the lifeline of the Page object is called an *activation*. Activations are optional; most diagrams don't need them. Activations represent the time that a function executes. In this case, it shows how long the Login function runs. The two messages leaving the activation to the right were sent by the Login method. The unlabeled dashed arrow shows the `Login` function returning to the actor and passing back a return value.

Note the use of the *e* variable in the `GetEmployee` message. This signifies the value returned by `GetEmployee`. Note also that the `Employee` object is named *e*. You guessed it: They're one and the same. The value that `GetEmployee` returns is a reference to the `Employee` object.

Finally, note that because `EmployeeDB` is a class, its name is not underlined. This can only mean that `GetEmployee` is a static method. Thus, we'd expect `EmployeeDB` to be coded as in Listing 18-1.

Listing 18-1
EmployeeDB.cs

```
public class EmployeeDB
{
    public static Employee GetEmployee(string empid)
    {
        . . .
    }
    . . .
}
```

Creation and Destruction

We can show the creation of an object on a sequence diagram by using the convention shown in Figure 18-2. An unlabeled message terminates on the object to be created, not on its lifeline. We would expect `ShapeFactory` to be implemented as shown in Figure 18-2.

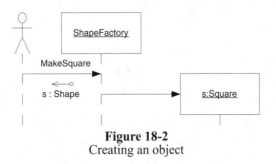

Figure 18-2
Creating an object

Listing 18-2
ShapeFactory.cs

```
public class ShapeFactory
{
    public Shape MakeSquare()
    {
        return new Square();
    }
}
```

In C#, we don't explicitly destroy objects. The garbage collector does all the explicit destruction for us. However, there are times when we want to make it clear that we are done with an object and that, as far as we are concerned, the garbage collector can have it.

Figure 18-3 shows how we denote this in UML. The lifeline of the object to be released comes to a premature end at a large X. The message arrow terminating on the X represents the act of releasing the object to the garbage collector.

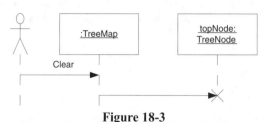

Figure 18-3
Releasing an object to the garbage collector

Listing 18-3 shows the implementation we might expect from this diagram. Note that the `Clear` method sets the `topNode` variable to `null`. Since it is the only object that holds a reference to that `TreeNode` instance, the `TreeMap` will be released to the garbage collector.

Listing 18-3
TreeMap.cs

```
public class TreeMap
{
  private TreeNode topNode;
  public void Clear()
  {
    topNode = null;
  }
}
```

Simple Loops

You can draw a simple loop in a UML diagram by drawing a box around the messages that repeat. The loop condition is enclosed in brackets and is placed somewhere in the box, usually at the lower right. See Figure 18-4.

This is a useful notational convention. However, it is not wise to try to capture algorithms in sequence diagrams. Sequence diagrams should be used to expose the connections between objects, not the nitty-gritty details of an algorithm.

Cases and Scenarios

Don't draw sequence diagrams like Figure 18-5, with lots of objects and scores of messages. Nobody can read them. Nobody *will* read them. They're a huge waste of time. Rather, learn how to draw a few smaller sequence diagrams that capture the *essence* of what you are trying to do. Each sequence diagram should fit on a single page, with plenty of room left for explanatory text. You should not have to shrink the icons down to tiny sizes to get them to fit on the page.

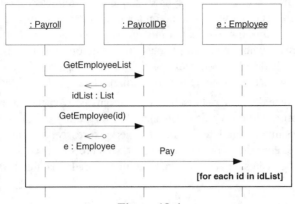

Figure 18-4
A simple loop

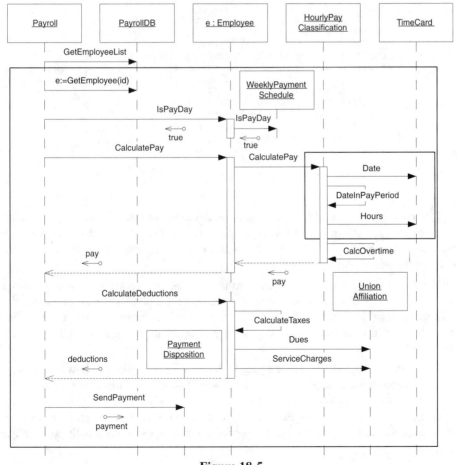

Figure 18-5
An overly complex sequence diagram

Also, don't draw dozens or hundreds of sequence diagrams. If you have too many, they won't be read. Find out what's common about all the scenarios and focus on that. *In the world of UML diagrams, commonalities are much more important than differences.* Use your diagrams to show common themes and common practices. Don't use them to document every little detail. If you really need to draw a sequence diagram to describe the way messages flow, do them succinctly and sparingly. Draw as few of them as possible.

First, ask yourself whether the sequence diagram is even necessary. Code is often more communicative and economical. Listing 18-4, for example, shows what the code for the `Payroll` class might look like. This code is very expressive and stands on its own. We don't need the sequence diagram to understand it, so there's no need to draw the sequence diagram. When code can stand on its own, diagrams are redundant and wasteful.

Listing 18-4

`Payroll.cs`

```
public class Payroll
{
  private PayrollDB itsPayrollDB;
  private PaymentDisposition itsDisposition;
  public void DoPayroll()
  {
    ArrayList employeeList = itsPayrollDB.GetEmployeeList();
    foreach (Employee e in employeeList)
    {
      if (e.IsPayDay())
      {
        double pay = e.CalculatePay();
        double deductions = e.CalculateDeductions();
        itsDisposition.SendPayment(pay - deductions);
      }
    }
  }
}
```

Can code really be used to describe part of a system? In fact, *this should be a goal* of the developers and designers. The team should strive to create code that is expressive and readable. The more the code can describe itself, the fewer diagrams you will need, and the better off the whole project will be.

Second, if you feel that a sequence diagram is necessary, ask yourself whether there is a way to split it up into a small group of scenarios. For example, we could break the large sequence diagram in Figure 18-5 into several much smaller sequence diagrams that would be much easier to read. Consider how much easier the small scenario in Figure 18-6 is to understand.

Third, think about what you are trying to depict. Are you trying to show the details of a low-level operation, as in Figure 18-6, which shows how to calculate hourly pay? Or are you trying to show a high-level view of the overall flow of the system, as in Figure 18-7? In general, high-level diagrams are more useful than low-level ones. High-level diagrams help the reader tie the system together mentally. They expose commonalities more than differences.

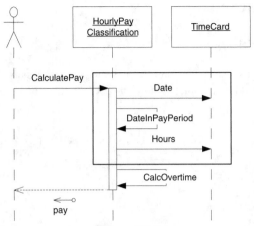

Figure 18-6
One small scenario

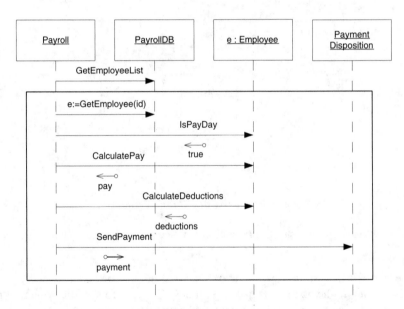

Figure 18-7
A high-level view

Advanced Concepts

Loops and Conditions

It is possible to draw a sequence diagram that completely specifies an algorithm. Figure 18-8 shows the payroll algorithm, complete with well-specified loops and `if` statements.

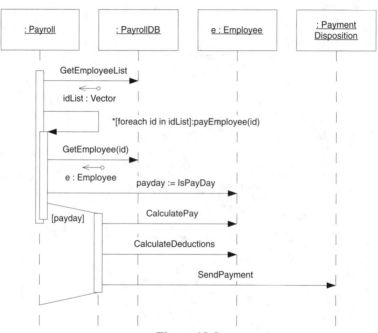

Figure 18-8
Sequence diagram with loops and conditions

The `payEmployee` message is prefixed with a *recurrence* expression that looks like this:

```
*[ foreach id in idList]
```

The star tells us that this is an iteration; the message will be sent repeatedly until the *guard* expression in the brackets is `false`. Although UML has a specific syntax for guard expressions, I find it more useful to use a C#-like pseudocode that suggests the use of an iterator or a `foreach`.

The `payEmployee` message terminates on an activation rectangle that is touching, but offset from, the first. This denotes that there are now two functions executing in the same object. Since the `payEmployee` message is recurrent, the second activation will also be recurrent, and so all the messages depending from it will be part of the loop.

Note the activation that is near the `[ payday]` guard. This denotes an `if` statement. The second activation gets control only if the guard condition is `true`. Thus, if `isPayDay` returns `true`, `calculatePay`, `calculateDeductions`, and `sendPayment` will be executed; otherwise, they won't be.

The fact that it is *possible* to capture all the details of an algorithm in a sequence diagram should not be construed as a license to capture all your algorithms in this manner. The depiction of algorithms in UML is clunky at best. Code such as Listing 18-4 is a *much* better way of expressing an algorithm.

Messages That Take Time

Usually, we don't consider the time it takes to send a message from one object to another. In most OO languages, that time is virtually instantaneous. That's why we draw the message lines horizontally: They don't take any time. In some cases, however, messages *do* take time to send. We could be trying to send a message across a network boundary or in a system where the thread of control can break between the invocation and execution of a method. When this is possible, we can denote it by using *angled* lines, as shown in Figure 18-9.

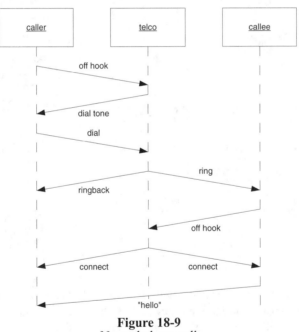

Figure 18-9
Normal phone call

This figure shows a phone call being made. This sequence diagram has three objects. The `caller` is the person making the call. The `callee` is the person being called. The `telco` is the telephone company.

Lifting the phone from the receiver sends the off-hook message to the telco, which responds with a dial tone. Having received the dial tone, the caller dials the phone number of the callee. The telco responds by ringing the callee and playing a ringback tone to the caller. The callee picks up the phone in response to the ring. The telco makes the connection. The callee says "Hello," and the phone call has succeeded.

However, there is another possibility, which demonstrates the usefulness of these kinds of diagrams. Look carefully at Figure 18-10. Note that the diagram starts exactly the same. However, just before the phone rings, the callee picks it up to make a call. The caller is now connected to the callee, but neither party knows it. The caller is waiting for a "Hello," and the callee is waiting for a dial tone. The callee eventually hangs up in frustration, and the caller hears a dial tone.

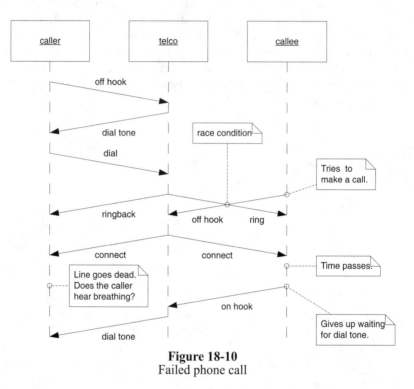

Figure 18-10
Failed phone call

The crossing of the two arrows in Figure 18-10 is called a *race condition*. Race conditions occur when two asynchronous entities can simultaneously invoke incompatible operations. In our case, the telco invoked the *ring* operation, and the callee went off hook. At this point, the parties all had a different notion of the state of the system. The caller was waiting for "Hello," the telco thought its job was done, and the callee was waiting for a dial tone.

Race conditions in software systems can be remarkably difficult to discover and debug. These diagrams can be helpful in finding and diagnosing them. Mostly, they are useful in explaining them to others, once discovered.

Asynchronous Messages

When you send a message to an object, you usually don't expect to get control back until the receiving object has finished executing. Messages that behave this way are called *synchronous messages*. However, in distributed or multithreaded systems, it is possible for the sending object to get control back immediately and for the receiving object to execute in another thread of control. Such messages are called *asynchronous messages*.

Figure 18-11 shows an asynchronous message. Note that the arrowhead is open instead of filled. Look back at all the other sequence diagrams in this chapter. They were all drawn with synchronous (filled arrowhead) messages. It is the elegance—or perversity; take your pick—of UML that such a subtle difference in the arrowhead can have such a profound difference in the represented behavior.

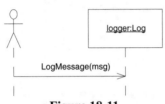

Figure 18-11
Asynchronous message

Previous versions of UML used half-arrowheads to denote asynchronous messages, as shown in Figure 18-12. This is much more visually distinctive. The reader's eye is immediately drawn to the asymmetry of the arrowhead. Therefore, I continue to use this convention, even though it has been superseded in UML 2.0.

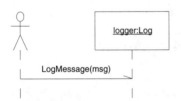

Figure 18-12
Older, better way to depict asynchronous messages

Listing 18-5 and 18-6 show code that could correspond to Figure 18-11. Listing 18-5 shows a unit test for the AsynchronousLogger class in Listing 18-6. Note that the LogMessage function returns immediately after queueing the message. Note also that the message is processed in a completely different thread that is started by the constructor. The TestLog class makes sure that the logMessage method behaves asynchronously by first checking whether the message was queued but not processed, then yielding the processor to other threads, and finally by verifying that the message was processed and removed from the queue.

This is just one possible implementation of an asynchronous message. Other implementations are possible. In general, we denote a message to be asynchronous if the caller can expect it to return before the desired operations are performed.

Listing 18-5

TestLog.cs

```
using System;
using System.Threading;
using NUnit.Framework;

namespace AsynchronousLogger
{
  [TestFixture]
  public class TestLog
  {
    private AsynchronousLogger logger;
    private int messagesLogged;

    [SetUp]
    protected void SetUp()
    {
      messagesLogged = 0;
      logger = new AsynchronousLogger(Console.Out);
      Pause();
    }

    [TearDown]
    protected void TearDown()
    {
      logger.Stop();
    }

    [Test]
    public void OneMessage()
    {
      logger.LogMessage("one message");
      CheckMessagesFlowToLog(1);
    }

    [Test]
    public void TwoConsecutiveMessages()
    {
      logger.LogMessage("another");
      logger.LogMessage("and another");
      CheckMessagesFlowToLog(2);
    }

    [Test]
    public void ManyMessages()
    {
      for (int i = 0; i < 10; i++)
      {
        logger.LogMessage(string.Format("message:{0}", i));
        CheckMessagesFlowToLog(1);
      }
    }
```

Listing 18-5 (Continued)

TestLog.cs

```
    private void CheckMessagesFlowToLog(int queued)
    {
      CheckQueuedAndLogged(queued, messagesLogged);
      Pause();
      messagesLogged += queued;
      CheckQueuedAndLogged(0, messagesLogged);
    }

    private void CheckQueuedAndLogged(int queued, int logged)
    {
      Assert.AreEqual(queued,
                       logger.MessagesInQueue(), "queued");
      Assert.AreEqual(logged,
                       logger.MessagesLogged(), "logged");
    }

    private void Pause()
    {
      Thread.Sleep(50);
    }
  }
}
```

Listing 18-6

AsynchronousLogger.cs

```
using System;
using System.Collections;
using System.IO;
using System.Threading;

namespace AsynchronousLogger
{
  public class AsynchronousLogger
  {
    private ArrayList messages =
      ArrayList.Synchronized(new ArrayList());
    private Thread t;
    private bool running;
    private int logged;
    private TextWriter logStream;

    public AsynchronousLogger(TextWriter stream)
    {
      logStream = stream;
      running = true;
      t = new Thread(new ThreadStart(MainLoggerLoop));
      t.Priority = ThreadPriority.Lowest;
      t.Start();
    }

    private void MainLoggerLoop()
    {
```

Listing 18-6 (Continued)

AsynchronousLogger.cs

```
    while (running)
    {
      LogQueuedMessages();
      SleepTillMoreMessagesQueued();
      Thread.Sleep(10); // Remind me to explain this.
    }
}

private void LogQueuedMessages()
{
  while (MessagesInQueue() > 0)
    LogOneMessage();
}

private void LogOneMessage()
{
  string msg = (string) messages[0];
  messages.RemoveAt(0);
  logStream.WriteLine(msg);
  logged++;
}

private void SleepTillMoreMessagesQueued()
{
  lock (messages)
  {
    Monitor.Wait(messages);
  }
}

public void LogMessage(String msg)
{
  messages.Add(msg);
  WakeLoggerThread();
}

public int MessagesInQueue()
{
  return messages.Count;
}

public int MessagesLogged()
{
  return logged;
}

public void Stop()
{
  running = false;
  WakeLoggerThread();
  t.Join();
}

private void WakeLoggerThread()
{
```

Listing 18-6 (Continued)

`AsynchronousLogger.cs`

```
        lock (messages)
        {
          Monitor.PulseAll(messages);
        }
      }
    }
  }
```

Multiple Threads

Asynchronous messages imply multiple threads of control. We can show several different threads of control in a UML diagram by tagging the message name with a thread identifier, as shown in Figure 18-13.

Note that the name of the message is prefixed with an identifier, such as T1, followed by a colon. This identifier names the thread that the message was sent from. In the diagram, the `AsynchronousLogger` object was created and manipulated by thread T1. The thread that does the message logging, running inside the `Log` object, is named T2.

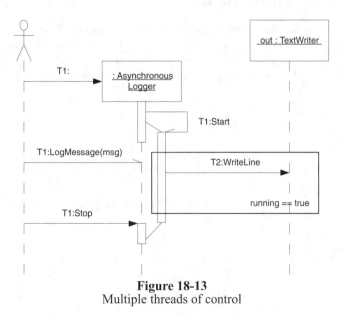

Figure 18-13
Multiple threads of control

As you can see, the thread identifiers don't necessarily correspond to names in the code. Listing 18-6 does not name the logging thread T2. Rather, the thread identifiers are for the benefit of the diagram.

Active Objects

Sometimes, we want to denote that an object has a separate internal thread. Such objects are known as *active objects*. They are shown with a bold outline, as in Figure 18-14.

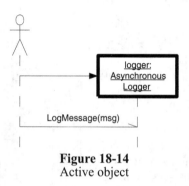

Figure 18-14
Active object

Active objects instantiate and control their own threads. There are no restrictions about their methods. Their methods may run in the object's thread or in the caller's thread.

Sending Messages to Interfaces

Our AsynchronousLogger class is one way to log messages. What if we wanted our application to be able to use many different kinds of loggers? We'd probably create a Logger interface that declared the LogMessage method and derive our AsynchronousLogger class and all the other implementations from that interface. See Figure 18-15.

```
interface Logger {
  void LogMessage(string msg);
}

public class AsynchronousLogger : Logger {
  ...
}
```

Figure 18-15
Simple logger design

The application is going to be sending messages to the `Logger` interface. The application won't know that the object is an `AsychronousLogger`. How can we depict this in a sequence diagram?

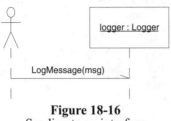

Figure 18-16
Sending to an interface

Figure 18-16 shows the obvious approach. You simply name the object for the interface and be done with it. This may seem to break the rules, since it's impossible to have an instance of an interface. However, all we are saying here is that the `logger` object conforms to the `Logger` type. We aren't saying that we somehow managed to instantiate a naked interface.

Sometimes, however, we know the type of the object and yet want to show the message being sent to an interface. For example, we might know that we have created an `AsynchronousLogger`, but we still want to show the application using only the `Logger` interface. Figure 18-17 shows how this is depicted. We use the interface lollipop on the lifeline of the object.

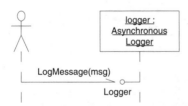

Figure 18-17
Sending to a derived type through an interface

Conclusion

As we have seen, sequence diagrams are a powerful way to communicate the flow of messages in an object-oriented application. We've also hinted that they are easy to abuse and easy to overdo.

An occasional sequence diagram on the whiteboard can be invaluable. A very short paper with five or six sequence diagrams denoting the most common interactions in a subsystem can be worth its weight in gold. On the other hand, a document filled with a thousand sequence diagrams is not likely to be worth the paper it's printed on.

One of the great fallacies of software development in the 1990s was the notion that developers should draw sequence diagrams for all methods *before* writing the code. This always proves to be a very expensive waste of time. Don't do it.

Instead, use sequence diagrams as the tool they were intended to be. Use them at a whiteboard to communicate with others in real time. Use them in a terse document to capture the core salient collaborations of the system.

As far as sequence diagrams are concerned, too few is better than too many. You can always draw one later if you find you need it.

Class Diagrams

UML class diagrams allow us to denote the static contents of—and the relationships between—classes. In a class diagram, we can show the member variables and member functions of a class. We can also show whether one class inherits from another or whether it holds a reference to another. In short, we can depict all the *source code dependencies* between classes.

This can be valuable. It can be much easier to evaluate the dependency structure of a system from a diagram than from source code. Diagrams make certain dependency structures visible. We can *see* dependency cycles and determine how best to break them. We can see when abstract classes depend on concrete classes and can determine a strategy for rerouting such dependencies.

The Basics

Classes

Figure 19-1 shows the simplest form of class diagram. The class named `Dialer` is represented as a simple rectangle. This diagram represents nothing more than the code shown to its right.

<table>
<tr><td>

Dialer

</td><td>

```
public class Dialer
{
}
```

</td></tr>
</table>

Figure 19-1
Class icon

This is the most common way you will represent a class. The classes on most diagrams don't need any more than their name to make clear what is going on.

A class icon can be subdivided into compartments. The top compartment is for the name of the class; the second, for the variables of the class; and the third, is for the methods of the class. Figure 19-2 shows these compartments and how they translate into code.

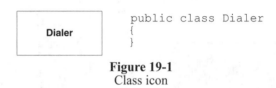

```
public class Dialer
{
    private ArrayList digits;
    private int nDigits;
    public void Digit(int n);
    protected bool RecordDigit(int n);
}
```

Figure 19-2
Class icon compartments with corresponding code

Note the character in front of the variables and functions in the class icon. A dash (-) denotes `private`; a hash (#), `protected`; and a plus (+), `public`.

The type of a variable, or a function argument is shown after the colon following the variable or argument name. Similarly, the return value of a function is shown after the colon following the function.

This kind of detail is sometimes useful but should not be used very often. UML diagrams are not the place to declare variables and functions. Such declarations are better done in source code. Use these adornments only when they are essential to the purpose of the diagram.

Association

Associations between classes most often represent instance variables that hold references to other objects. For example, Figure 19-3 shows an association between `Phone` and `Button`. The direction of the arrow indicates that `Phone` holds a reference to `Button`. The name near the arrowhead is the name of the instance variable. The number near the arrowhead indicates how many references are held.

```
public class Phone
{
    private Button itsButtons[15];
}
```

Figure 19-3
Association

In Figure 19-3, 15 `Button` objects are connected to the `Phone` object. Figure 19-4, shows what happens when there is no limit. A `Phonebook` is connected to *many* `PhoneNumber` objects. (The star means *many*) In C#, this is most commonly implemented with an `ArrayList` or some other collection.

```
public class Phonebook
{
    private ArrayList itsPnos;
}
```

Figure 19-4
One-to-many association

I could have said, "A `Phonebook` *has* many `PhoneNumbers`." Instead, I avoided using the word *has*. This was intentional. The common OO verbs HAS-A and IS-A have led to a number of unfortunate misunderstandings. For now, don't expect me to use the common terms. Rather, I'll use terms that are descriptive of what happens in the software, such as *is connected to*.

Inheritance

You have to be very careful with your arrowheads in UML. Figure 19-5 shows why. The arrowhead pointing at `Employee` denotes *inheritance*.[1] If you draw your arrowheads carelessly, it may be difficult to tell whether you mean inheritance or association. To make it clearer, I often make inheritance relationships vertical and associations horizontal.

In UML, all arrowheads point in the direction of *source code dependency.* Since it is the `SalariedEmployee` class that mentions the name of `Employee`, the arrowhead points at `Employee`. So, in UML, inheritance arrows point at the base class.

```
public class Employee
{
    . . .
}

public class SalariedEmployee : Employee
{
    . . .
}
```

Figure 19-5
Inheritance

UML has a special notation for the kind of inheritance used between a C# class and a C# interface. As shown in Figure 19-6, it is a dashed inheritance arrow.[2] In the diagrams to come, you'll probably catch me forgetting to dash the arrows that point to interfaces. I suggest that you forget to dash the arrows that you draw on whiteboards, too. Life's too short to be dashing arrows.

Figure 19-7 shows another way to convey the same information. Interfaces can be drawn as lollipops on the classes that implement them. We often see this kind of notation in COM designs.

---

1. Actually, it denotes *generalization*, but as far as a C# programmer is concerned, the difference is moot.

2. This is called a *realizes* relationship. There's more to it than simply inheritance of interface, but the difference is beyond the scope of this book and probably beyond the scope of anyone who writes code for a living.

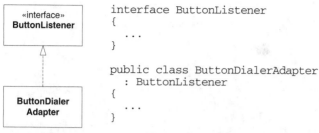

```
interface ButtonListener
{
    ...
}

public class ButtonDialerAdapter
    : ButtonListener
{
    ...
}
```

Figure 19-6
Realizes relationship

ButtonListener

**ButtonDialer
Adapter**

Figure 19-7
Lollipop interface indicator

An Example Class Diagram

Figure 19-8 shows a simple class diagram of part of an ATM system. This diagram is interesting both for what it shows and for what it does not show. Note that I have taken pains to mark all the interfaces. I consider it crucial to make sure that my readers know what classes I intend to be interfaces and which I intend to be implemented. For example, the diagram immediately tells you that `WithdrawalTransaction` talks to a `CashDispenser` interface. Clearly, some class in the system will have to implement the `CashDispenser`, but in this diagram, we don't care which class it is.

Note that I have not been particularly thorough in documenting the methods of the various UI interfaces. Certainly, `WithdrawalUI` will need more than the two methods shown there. What about `PromptForAccount` or `InformCashDispenserEmpty`? Putting those methods in the diagram would clutter it. By providing a representative batch of methods, I've given the reader the idea. That's all that's necessary.

Again note the convention of horizontal association and vertical inheritance. This helps to differentiate these vastly different kinds of relationships. Without a convention like this, it can be difficult to tease the meaning out of the tangle.

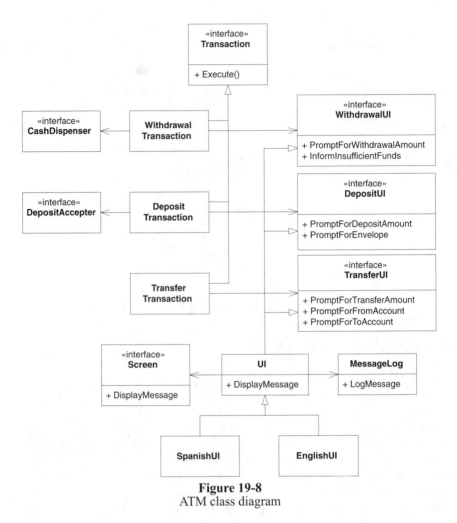

Figure 19-8
ATM class diagram

Note how I've separated the diagram into three distinct zones. The transactions and their actions are on the left, the various UI interfaces are all on the right, and the UI implementation is on the bottom. Note also that the connections between the groupings are minimal and regular. In one case, it is three associations, all pointing the same way. In the other case, it is three inheritance relationships, all merged into a single line. The groupings, and the way they are connected, help the reader to see the diagram in coherent pieces.

You should be able to *see* the code as you look at the diagram. Is Listing 19-1 close to what you expected for the implementation of UI?

Listing 19-1

UI.cs

```
public abstract class UI :
  WithdrawalUI, DepositUI, TransferUI
{
  private Screen itsScreen;
  private MessageLog itsMessageLog;

  public abstract void PromptForDepositAmount();
  public abstract void PromptForWithdrawalAmount();
  public abstract void InformInsufficientFunds();
  public abstract void PromptForEnvelope();
  public abstract void PromptForTransferAmount();
  public abstract void PromptForFromAccount();
  public abstract void PromptForToAccount();

  public void DisplayMessage(string message)
  {
    itsMessageLog.LogMessage(message);
    itsScreen.DisplayMessage(message);
  }
}
```

The Details

A vast number of details and adornments can be added to UML class diagrams. Most of the time, these details and adornments should not be added. But there are times when they can be helpful.

Class Stereotypes

Class stereotypes appear between guillemet[3] characters, usually above the name of the class. We have seen them before. The «interface» denotation in Figure 19-8 is a class stereotype. C# programmers can use two standard stereotypes: «interface» and «utility».

«interface» All the methods of classes marked with this stereotype are abstract. None of the methods can be implemented. Moreover, «interface» classes can have no instance variables. The only variables they can have are static variables. This corresponds exactly to C# interfaces. See Figure 19-9.

I draw interfaces so often that spelling the whole stereotype out at the whiteboard can be pretty inconvenient. So I often use the shorthand in the lower part of Figure 19-9 to make the drawing easier. It's not standard UML, but it's much more convenient.

---

3. The quotation marks that look like double angle brackets « ». These are *not* two less-than and two greater-than signs. If you use doubled inequality operators instead of the appropriate and proper guillemet characters, the UML police *will* find you.

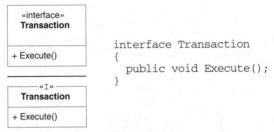

```
interface Transaction
{
    public void Execute();
}
```

Figure 19-9
«interface» class stereotype

«utility» All the methods and variables of a «utility» class are static. Booch used to call these *class utilities*.[4] See Figure 19-10.

```
public class Math
{
    public static readonly double PI =
                                3.14159265358979323;

    public static double Sin(double theta){...}
    public static double Cos(double theta){...}
}
```

Figure 19-10
«utility» class stereotype

You can make your own stereotypes, if you like. I often use the stereotypes «persistent», «C-API», «struct», or «function». Just make sure that the people who are reading your diagrams know what your stereotype means.

Abstract Classes

In UML, there are two ways to denote that a class or a method is abstract. You can write the name in italics, or you can use the `{ abstract}` property. Both options are shown in Figure 19-11.

It's a little difficult to write italics at a whiteboard, and the `{ abstract}` property is wordy. So at the whiteboard, I use the convention shown in Figure 19-12 if I need to denote a class or method as abstract. Again, this isn't standard UML but at the whiteboard is a lot more convenient.[5]

---

4. [Booch94], p. 186

5. Some of you may remember the Booch notation. One of the nice things about that notation was its convenience. It was truly a whiteboard notation.

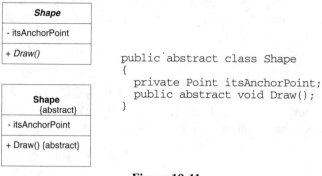

```
public abstract class Shape
{
    private Point itsAnchorPoint;
    public abstract void Draw();
}
```

Figure 19-11
Abstract classes

Figure 19-12
Unofficial denotation of abstract classes

Properties

Properties, such as { abstract} can be added to any class. They represent extra information that's not usually part of a class. You can create your own properties at any time.

Properties are written in a comma-separated list of name/value pairs, like this:

{author=Martin, date=20020429, file=shape.cs, private}

The properties in the preceding example are not part of UML. Also, properties need not be specific to code but can contain any bit of meta data you fancy. The { abstract} property is the only defined property of UML that programmers normally find useful.

A property that does not have a value is assumed to take the Boolean value true. Thus, { abstract} and { abstract = true} are synonyms. Properties are written below and to the right of the name of the class, as shown in Figure 19-13.

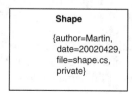

Figure 19-13
Properties

Other than the{ abstract} property, I don't know when you'd find this useful. Personally, in the many years that I've been writing UML diagrams, I've never had occasion to use class properties for anything.

Aggregation

Aggregation is a special form of association that connotes a whole/part relationship. Figure 19-14 shows how it is drawn and implemented. Note that the implementation shown in Figure 19-14 is indistinguishable from association. That's a hint.

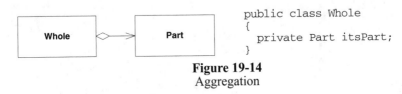

```
public class Whole
{
    private Part itsPart;
}
```

Figure 19-14
Aggregation

Unfortunately, UML does not provide a strong definition for this relationship. This leads to confusion because various programmers and analysts adopt their own pet definitions for the relationship. For that reason, I don't use the relationship at all, and I recommend that you avoid it as well. In fact, this relationship was almost dropped from UML 2.0.

The one hard rule that UML gives us regarding aggregations is simply this: A whole cannot be its own part. Therefore, *instances* cannot form cycles of aggregations. A single object cannot be an aggregate of itself, two objects cannot be aggregates of each other, three objects cannot form a ring of aggregation, and so on. See Figure 19-15.

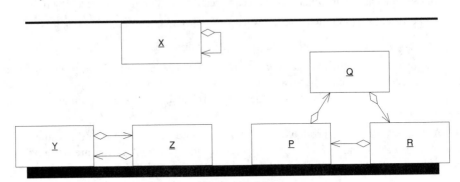

Figure 19-15
Illegal cycles of aggregation between instances

I don't find this to be a particularly useful definition. How often am I concerned about making sure that instances form a directed acyclic graph? Not very often. Therefore, I find this relationship useless in the kinds of diagrams I draw.

Composition

Composition is a special form of aggregation, as shown in Figure 19-16. Again, note that the implementation is indistinguishable from association. This time, however, the reason is that the relationship does not have a lot of use in a C# program. C++ programmers, on the other hand, find a *lot* of use for it.

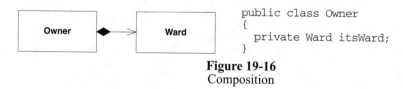

```
public class Owner
{
    private Ward itsWard;
}
```

Figure 19-16
Composition

The same rule applies to composition that applied to aggregation. There can be no cycles of instances. An owner cannot be its own ward. However, UML provides quite a bit more definition for composition.

- An instance of a ward cannot be owned simultaneously by two owners. The object diagram in Figure 19-17 is illegal. Note, however, that the corresponding class diagram is not illegal. An owner can transfer ownership of a ward to another owner.

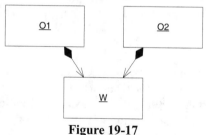

Figure 19-17
Illegal composition

- The owner is responsible for the lifetime of the ward. If the owner is destroyed, the ward must be destroyed with it. If the owner is copied, the ward must be copied with it.

In C#, destruction happens behind the scenes by the garbage collector, so there is seldom a need to manage the lifetime of an object. Deep copies are not unheard of, but the need to show deep-copy semantics on a diagram is rare. So, though I have used composition relationships to describe some C# programs, such use is infrequent.

Figure 19-18 shows how composition is used to denote deep copy. We have a class named Address that holds many strings. Each string holds one line of the address. Clearly, when you make a copy of the Address, you want the copy to change independently of the original. Thus, we need to make a deep copy. The composition relationship between the Address and the Strings indicates that copies need to be deep.[6]

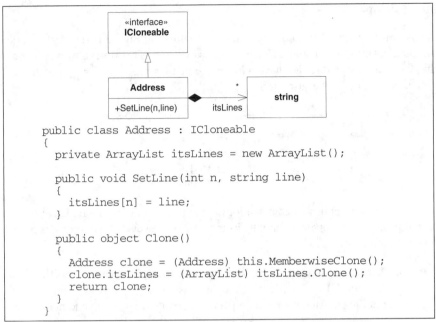

Figure 19-18
Deep copy implied by composition

Multiplicity

Objects can hold arrays or collections of other objects, or they can hold many of the same kind of objects in separate instance variables. In UML, this can be shown by placing a *multiplicity* expression on the far end of the association. Multiplicity expressions can be simple numbers, ranges, or a combination of both. For example, Figure 19-19 shows a BinaryTreeNode, using a multiplicity of 2.

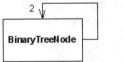

```
public class BinaryTreeNode
{
    private BinaryTreeNode leftNode;
    private BinaryTreeNode rightNode;
}
```

Figure 19-19
Simple multiplicity

---

6. *Exercise:* Why was it enough to clone the itsLines collection? Why didn't I have to clone the actual string instances?

Here are the allowable forms of multiplicity:

- Digit.   The exact number of elements

- * or 0..*   Zero to many

- 0..1   Zero or one, in Java, often implemented with a reference that can
                     be `null`

- 1..*   One to many

- 3..5   Three to five

- 0, 2..5, 9..*   Silly, but legal

Association Stereotypes

Associations can be labeled with stereotypes that change their meaning. Figure 19-20
shows the ones that I use most often.

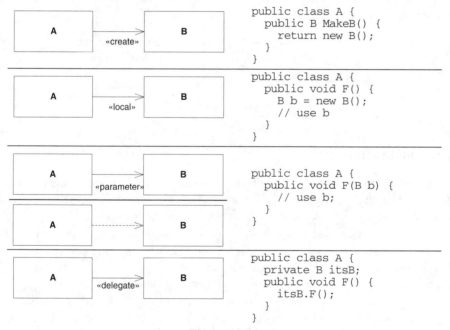

```
public class A {
   public B MakeB() {
      return new B();
   }
}
```

```
public class A {
   public void F() {
      B b = new B();
      // use b
   }
}
```

```
public class A {
   public void F(B b) {
      // use b;
   }
}
```

```
public class A {
   private B itsB;
   public void F() {
      itsB.F();
   }
}
```

Figure 19-20
Association stereotypes

The «create» stereotype indicates that the target of the association is created by the
source. The implication is that the source creates the target and then passes it around to
other parts of the system. In the example, I've shown a typical factory.

The «local» stereotype is used when the source class creates an instance of the target and holds it in a local variable. The implication is that the created instance does not survive the member function that creates it. Thus, it is not held by any instance variable or passed around the system in any way.

The «parameter» stereotype shows that the source class gains access to the target instance though the parameter of one of its member functions. Again, the implication is that the source forgets all about this object once the member function returns. The target is not saved in an instance variable.

Using dashed dependency arrows, as the diagram shows, is a common and convenient idiom for denoting parameters. I usually prefer it to using the «parameter» stereotype.

The «delegate» stereotype is used when the source class forwards a member function invocation to the target. A number of design patterns apply this technique: PROXY, DECO-RATOR, and COMPOSITE.[7] Since I use these patterns a lot, I find the notation helpful.

Nested Classes

Nested classes are represented in UML with an association adorned with a crossed circle, as shown in Figure 19-21.

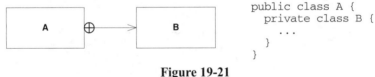

```
public class A {
   private class B {
      ...
   }
}
```

Figure 19-21
Nested class

Association Classes

Associations with multiplicity tell us that the source is connected to many instances of the target, but the diagram doesn't tell us what kind of container class is used. This can be depicted by using an association class, as shown in Figure 19-22.

Association classes show how a particular association is implemented. On the diagram, they appear as a normal class connected to the association with a dashed line. As C# programmers, we interpret this to mean that the source class contains a reference to the association class, which in turn contains references to the target.

Association classes can also be classes that you write in order to hold instances of some other object. Sometimes, these classes enforce business rules. For example, in Figure 19-23, a `Company` class holds many `Employee` instances through `EmployeeContracts`. To be frank, I have never found this notation to be particularly useful.

---

7. [GOF95], pp. 163, 175, 207

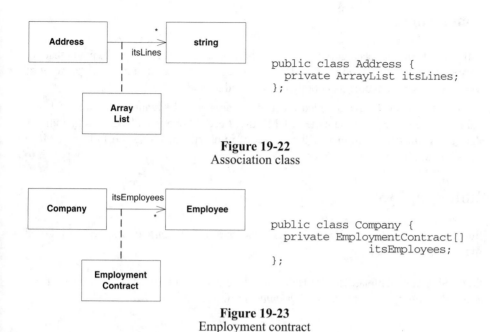

```
public class Address {
    private ArrayList itsLines;
};
```

Figure 19-22
Association class

```
public class Company {
    private EmploymentContract[]
                      itsEmployees;
};
```

Figure 19-23
Employment contract

Association Qualifiers

Association qualifiers are used when the association is implemented through some kind of key or token instead of with a normal C# reference. The example in Figure 19-24 shows a LoginTransaction associated with an Employee. The association is mediated by a member variable named empid, which contains the database key for the Employee.

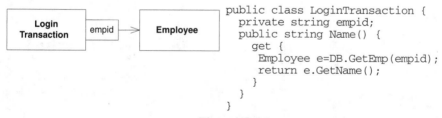

```
public class LoginTransaction {
    private string empid;
    public string Name() {
        get {
            Employee e=DB.GetEmp(empid);
            return e.GetName();
        }
    }
}
```

Figure 19-24
Association qualifier

I find this notation useful in rare situations. Sometimes, it's convenient to show that an object is associated to another through a database or dictionary key. It is important, however, that all the parties reading the diagram know how the qualifier is used to access the object. This is not something that's immediately evident from the notation.

Conclusion

UML has lots of widgets, adornments, and whatchamajiggers. There are so many that you can spend a long time becoming an UML language lawyer, enabling you to do what all lawyers can: write documents nobody else can understand.

In this chapter, I have avoided most of the arcana and byzantine features of UML. Rather, I have shown you the parts of UML that *I* use. I hope that along with that knowledge, I have instilled within you the values of minimalism. Using too little of UML is almost always better than using too much.

Bibliography

[Booch94] Grady Booch, *Object-Oriented Analysis and Design with Applications*, 2d ed. Addison-Wesley, 1994.

[GOF95] Erich Gamma, Richard Helm, Ralph Johnson, and John Vlissides, *Design Patterns: Elements of Reusable Object-Oriented Software*, Addison-Wesley, 1995.

20

Heuristics and Coffee

Angela Brooks

Over the past dozen years, I have taught object-oriented design to professional software developers. My courses are divided into morning lectures and afternoon exercises. For the exercises, I divide the class into teams and have them solve a design problem using UML. The next morning, we choose one or two teams to present their solutions on a whiteboard, and we critique their designs.

I have taught these courses hundreds of times and have noticed a group of design mistakes commonly made by the students. This chapter presents a few of the most common errors, shows why they are errors, and addresses how they can be corrected. Then the chapter goes on to solve the problem in a way that I think resolves all the design forces nicely.

The Mark IV Special Coffee Maker

During the first morning of an OOD class, I present the basic definitions of classes, objects, relationships, methods, polymorphism, and so on. At the same time, I present the basics of UML. Thus, the students learn the fundamental concepts, vocabulary, and tools of object-oriented design.

During the afternoon, I give the class the following exercise to work on: design the software that controls a simple coffee maker. Here is the specification I give them.[1]

Specification

The Mark IV Special makes up to 12 cups of coffee at a time. The user places a filter in the filter holder, fills the filter with coffee grounds, and slides the filter holder into its receptacle. The user then pours up to 12 cups of water into the water strainer and presses the Brew button. The water is heated until boiling. The pressure of the evolving steam forces the water to be sprayed over the coffee grounds, and coffee drips through the filter into the pot. The pot is kept warm for extended periods by a warmer plate, which turns on only if coffee is in the pot. If the pot is removed from the warmer plate while water is being sprayed over the grounds, the flow of water is stopped so that brewed coffee does not spill on the warmer plate. The following hardware needs to be monitored or controlled:

- The heating element for the boiler. It can be turned on or off.

- The heating element for the warmer plate. It can be turned on or off.

- The sensor for the warmer plate. It has three states: `warmerEmpty`, `potEmpty`, `potNotEmpty`.

- A sensor for the boiler, which determines whether water is present. It has two states: `boilerEmpty` or `boilerNotEmpty`.

- The Brew button. This momentary button starts the brewing cycle. It has an indicator that lights up when the brewing cycle is over and the coffee is ready.

- A pressure-relief valve that opens to reduce the pressure in the boiler. The drop in pressure stops the flow of water to the filter. The value can be opened or closed.

---

1. This problem comes from my first book: [Martin1995], p. 60.

The hardware for the Mark IV has been designed and is currently under development. The hardware engineers have even provided a low-level API for us to use, so we don't have to write any bit-twiddling I/O driver code. The code for these interface functions is shown in Listing 20-1. If this code looks strange to you, keep in mind that it was written by hardware engineers.

Listing 20-1
CoffeeMakerAPI.cs

```
namespace CoffeeMaker
{
  public enum WarmerPlateStatus
  {
    WARMER_EMPTY,
    POT_EMPTY,
    POT_NOT_EMPTY
  };

  public enum BoilerStatus
  {
    EMPTY,NOT_EMPTY
  };

  public enum BrewButtonStatus
  {
    PUSHED,NOT_PUSHED
  };

  public enum BoilerState
  {
    ON,OFF
  };

  public enum WarmerState
  {
    ON,OFF
  };

  public enum IndicatorState
  {
    ON,OFF
  };

  public enum ReliefValveState
  {
    OPEN, CLOSED
  };

  public interface CoffeeMakerAPI
  {
    /*
     * This function returns the status of the warmer-plate
     * sensor. This sensor detects the presence of the pot
     * and whether it has coffee in it.
     */
```

Listing 20-1 (Continued)
CoffeeMakerAPI.cs

```
    WarmerPlateStatus GetWarmerPlateStatus();

    /*
     * This function returns the status of the boiler switch.
     * The boiler switch is a float switch that detects if
     * there is more than 1/2 cup of water in the boiler.
     */

    BoilerStatus GetBoilerStatus();

    /*
     * This function returns the status of the brew button.
     * The brew button is a momentary switch that remembers
     * its state. Each call to this function returns the
     * remembered state and then resets that state to
     * NOT_PUSHED.
     *
     * Thus, even if this function is polled at a very slow
     * rate, it will still detect when the brew button is
     * pushed.
     */

    BrewButtonStatus GetBrewButtonStatus();

    /*
     * This function turns the heating element in the boiler
     * on or off.
     */

    void SetBoilerState(BoilerState s);

    /*
     * This function turns the heating element in the warmer
     * plate on or off.
     */

    void SetWarmerState(WarmerState s);

    /*
     * This function turns the indicator light on or off.
     * The indicator light should be turned on at the end
     * of the brewing cycle. It should be turned off when
     * the user presses the brew button.
     */

    void SetIndicatorState(IndicatorState s);

    /*
     * This function opens and closes the pressure-relief
     * valve. When this valve is closed, steam pressure in
     * the boiler will force hot water to spray out over
     * the coffee filter. When the valve is open, the steam
     * in the boiler escapes into the environment, and the
     * water in the boiler will not spray out over the filter.
     */
```

Listing 20-1 (Continued)
CoffeeMakerAPI.cs

```
        void SetReliefValveState(ReliefValveState s);
    }
}
```

If you want a challenge, stop reading here and try to design this software yourself. Remember that you are designing the software for a simple, embedded real-time system. What I expect of my students is a set of class diagrams, sequence diagrams, and state machines.

A Common but Hideous Solution

By far the most common solution that my students present is the one in Figure 20-1. In this diagram, the central `CoffeeMaker` class is surrounded by minions that control the various devices. The `CoffeeMaker` contains a `Boiler`, a `WarmerPlate`, a `Button`, and a `Light`. The `Boiler` contains a `BoilerSensor` and a `BoilerHeater`. The `WarmerPlate` contains a `PlateSensor` and a `PlateHeater`. Finally, two base classes, `Sensor` and `Heater`, act as parents to the `Boiler` and `WarmerPlate` elements, respectively.

It is difficult for beginners to appreciate just how hideous this structure is. Quite a few rather serious errors are lurking in this diagram. Many of them would not be noticed until you tried to code this design and found that the code was absurd.

But before we get to the problems with the design itself, let's look at the problems with the way the UML is created.

Missing methods The biggest problem that Figure 20-1 exhibits is a complete lack of methods. We are writing a *program* here, and programs are about behavior! Where is the behavior in this diagram?

When they create diagrams without methods, designers may be partitioning the software on something other than behavior. Partitionings that are not based on behavior are almost always significant errors. It is the behavior of a system that is the first clue to how the software should be partitioned.

Vapor classes If we consider the methods we might put in the class `Light` we can see how poorly partitioned this particular design is. Clearly, the `Light` object wants to be turned on or turned off. Thus, we might put an `On()` and `Off()` method in class `Light`. What would the implementation of those function look like? See Listing 20-2.

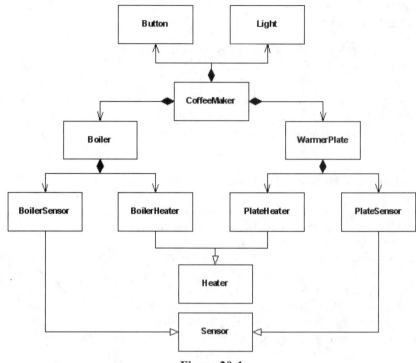

Figure 20-1
Hyperconcrete coffee maker

Listing 20-2

Light.cs

```
public class Light {
  public void On() {
    CoffeeMaker.api.SetIndicatorState(IndicatorState.ON);
  }

  public void Off() {
    CoffeeMaker.api.SetIndicatorState(IndicatorState.OFF);
  }
}
```

Class `Light` has some peculiarities. First, it has no variables. This is odd, since an object usually has some kind of state that it manipulates. What's more, the `On()` and `Off()` methods simply delegate to the `SetIndicatorState` method of the `CoffeeMakerAPI`. Apparently, the `Light` class is nothing more than a call translator and is not doing anything useful.

This same reasoning can be applied to the `Button`, `Boiler`, and `WarmerPlate` classes. They are nothing more than adapters that translate a function call from one form to another. Indeed, they could be removed from the design altogether without changing any of the logic in the `CoffeeMaker` class. That class would simply have to call the `CoffeeMakerAPI` directly instead of through the adapters.

By considering the methods and then the code, we have demoted these classes from the prominent position the hold in Figure 20-1, to mere placeholders without much reason to exist. For this reason, I call them *vapor classes.*

Imaginary Abstraction

Note the `Sensor` and `Heater` base classes in Figure 20-1. The previous section should have convinced you that their derivatives were mere vapor, but what about the base classes themselves? On the surface, they seem to make a lot of sense. But, there doesn't seem to be any place for their derivatives.

Abstractions are tricky things. We humans see them everywhere, but many are not appropriate to be turned into base classes. These, in particular, have no place in this design. We can see this by asking, *Who uses them?*

No class in the system makes use of the `Sensor` or `Heater` class. If nobody uses them, what reason do they have to exist? Sometimes, we might tolerate a base class that nobody uses if it supplied some common code to its derivatives, but these bases have no code in them at all. At best, their methods are abstract. Consider, for example, the `Heater` interface in Listing 20-3. A class with nothing but abstract functions and that no other class uses is officially useless.

Listing 20-3

Heater.cs

```
public interface Heater {
  void TurnOn();
  void TurnOff();
}
```

The `Sensor` class (Listing 20-4) is worse! Like `Heater`, it has abstract methods and no users. What's worse, is that the return value of its sole method is ambiguous. What does the `Sense()` method return? In the `BoilerSensor`, it returns two possible values, but in `WarmerPlateSensor`, it returns three possible values. In short, we cannot specify the contract of the `Sensor` in the interface. The best we can do is say that sensors may return `ints`. This is pretty weak.

Listing 20-4

Sensor.cs

```
public interface Sensor {
  int Sense();
}
```

What happened here is that we read through the specification, found a bunch of likely nouns, made some inferences about their relationships, and then created a UML diagram based on that reasoning. If we accepted these decisions as an architecture and implemented them the way they stand, we'd wind up with an all-powerful `CoffeeMaker` class surrounded by vaporous minions. We might as well program it in C!

God classes Everybody knows that god classes are a bad idea. We don't want to concentrate all the intelligence of a system into a single object or a single function. One of the goals of OOD is the partitioning and distribution of behavior into many classes and many functions. It turns out, however, that many object models that appear to be distributed are the abode of gods in disguise. Figure 20-1 is a prime example. At first glance, it looks like there are lots of classes with interesting behavior. But as we drill down into the code that would implement those classes, we find that only one of those

classes, `CoffeeMaker`, has any interesting behavior; the rest are all imaginary abstractions or vapor classes.

An Improved Solution

Solving the coffee maker problem is an interesting exercise in abstraction. Most developers new to OO find themselves quite surprised by the result.

The trick to solving this (or any) problem is to step back and separate its details from its essential nature. Forget about boilers, valves, heaters, sensors, and all the little details; concentrate on the underlying problem. What is that problem? The problem is: How do you make coffee?

How *do* you make coffee? The simplest, most common solution to this problem is to pour hot water over coffee grounds and to collect the resulting infusion in some kind of vessel. Where do we get the hot water from? Let's call it a `HotWaterSource`. Where do we collect the coffee? Let's call it a `ContainmentVessel`.[2]

Are these two abstractions classes? Does a `HotWaterSource` have behavior that could be captured in software? Does a `ContainmentVessel` do something that software could control? If we think about the Mark IV unit, we could imagine the boiler, valve, and boiler sensor playing the role of the `HotWaterSource`. The `HotWaterSource` would be responsible for heating the water and delivering it over the coffee grounds to drip into the `ContainmentVessel`. We could also imagine the warmer plate and its sensor playing the

---

2. That name is particularly appropriate for the kind of coffee that *I* like to make.

role of the `ContainmentVessel`. It would be responsible for keeping the contained coffee warm and for letting us know whether any coffee was left in the vessel.

How would you capture the previous discussion in a UML diagram? Figure 20-2 shows one possible schema. `HotWaterSource` and `ContainmentVessel` are both represented as classes and are associated by the flow of coffee.

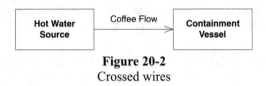

Figure 20-2
Crossed wires

The association shows an error that OO novices commonly make. The association is made with something physical about the problem instead of with the control of software behavior. The fact that coffee flows from the `HotWaterSource` to the `ContainmentVessel` is completely irrelevant to the association between those two classes.

For example, what if the software in the `ContainmentVessel` told the `HotWaterSource` when to start and stop the flow of hot water into the vessel? This might be depicted as shown in Figure 20-3. Note that the `ContainmentVessel` is sending the `Start` message to the `HotWaterSource`. This means that the association in Figure 20-2 is backward. `HotWaterSource` does not depend on the `ContainmentVessel` at all. Rather, the `ContainmentVessel` depends on the `HotWaterSource`.

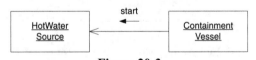

Figure 20-3
Starting the flow of hot water

The lesson here is simply this: Associations are the pathways through which messages are sent between objects. Associations have nothing to do with the flow of physical objects. The fact that hot water flows from the boiler to the pot does not mean that there should be an association from the `HotWaterSource` to the `ContainmentVessel`.

I call this particular mistake *crossed wires* because the wiring between the classes has gotten crossed between the logical and physical domains.

The coffee maker user interface It should be clear that something is missing from our coffee maker model. We have a `HotWaterSource` and a `ContainmentVessel`, but we don't have any way for a human to interact with the system. Somewhere, our system has to listen for commands from a human. Likewise, the system must be able to report its status to its human owners. Certainly, the Mark IV had hardware dedicated to this purpose. The button and the light served as the user interface.

Thus, we'll add a `UserInterface` class to our coffee maker model. This gives us a triad of classes interacting to create coffee under the direction of a user.

Use case 1: User pushes brew button OK, given these three classes, how do their instances communicate? Let's look at several use cases to see whether we can find out what the behavior of these classes is.

Which one of our objects detects the fact that the user has pressed the Brew button? Clearly, it must be the `UserInterface` object. What should this object do when the Brew button is pushed?

Our goal is to start the flow of hot water. However, before we can do that, we'd better make sure that the `ContainmentVessel` is ready to accept coffee. We'd also better make sure that the `HotWaterSource` is ready. If we think about the Mark IV, we're making sure that the boiler is full and that the pot is empty and in place on the warmer.

So, the `UserInterface` object first sends a message to the `HotWaterSource` and the `ContainmentVessel` to see whether they are ready. This is shown in Figure 20-4.

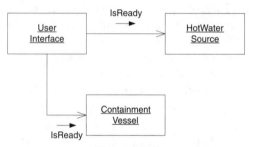

Figure 20-4
Brew button pressed, checking for ready

If either of these queries returns `false`, we refuse to start brewing coffee. The `UserInterface` object can take care of letting the user know that his or her request was denied. In the Mark IV case, we might flash the light a few times.

If both queries return `true`, then we need to start the flow of hot water. The `UserInterface` object should probably send a `Start` message to the `HotWaterSource`. The `HotWaterSource` will then start doing whatever it needs to do to get hot water flowing. In the case of the Mark IV, it will close the valve and turn on the boiler. Figure 20-5 shows the completed scenario.

Use case 2: Containment vessel not ready In the Mark IV, we know that the user can take the pot off the warmer while coffee is brewing. Which one of our objects would detect the fact that the pot had been removed? Certainly, it would be the `ContainmentVessel`. The requirements for the Mark IV tell us that we need to stop the flow of coffee when this happens. Thus, the `ContainmentVessel` must be able to tell

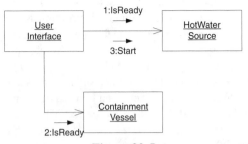

Figure 20-5
Brew button pressed, complete

the `HotWaterSource` to stop sending hot water. Likewise, it needs to be able to tell it to start again when the pot is replaced. Figure 20-6 adds the new methods.

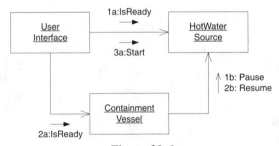

Figure 20-6
Pausing and resuming the flow of hot water

Use case 3: Brewing complete At some point, we will be done brewing coffee and will have to turn off the flow of hot water. Which one of our objects knows when brewing is complete? In the Mark IV's case, the sensor in the boiler tells us that the boiler is empty, so our `HotWaterSource` would detect this. However, it's not difficult to envision a coffee maker in which the `ContainmentVessel` would be the one to detect that brewing was done. For example, what if our coffee maker was plumbed into the water mains and therefore had an infinite supply of water? What if an intense microwave generator heated the water as it flowed through the pipes into a thermally isolated vessel?[3] What if that vessel had a spigot from which users got their coffee? In this case, a sensor in the vessel would know that it was full and that hot water should be shut off.

The point is that in the abstract domain of the `HotWaterSource` and `Containment-Vessel`, neither is an especially compelling candidate for detecting completion of the brew. My solution to that is to ignore the issue. I'll assume that either object can tell the others that brewing is complete.

---

3. OK, I'm having a bit of fun. But what if?

Which objects in our model need to know that brewing is complete? Certainly, the `UserInterface` needs to know, since, in the Mark IV, it must turn the light on. It should also be clear that the `HotWaterSource` needs to know that brewing is over, because it'll need to stop the flow of hot water. In the Mark IV, it'll shut down the boiler and open the valve. Does the `ContainmentVessel` need to know that brewing is complete? Does the `ContainmentVessel` need to do or to keep track of anything special once the brewing is complete? In the Mark IV, it's going to detect an empty pot being put back on the plate, signaling that the user has poured the last of the coffee. This causes the Mark IV to turn the light *off*. So, yes, the `ContainmentVessel` needs to know that brewing is complete. Indeed, the same argument can be used to say that the `UserInterface` should send the `Start` message to the `ContainmentVessel` when brewing starts. Figure 20-7 shows the new messages. Note that I've shown that either `HotWaterSource` or `ContainmentVesslel` can send the `Done` message.

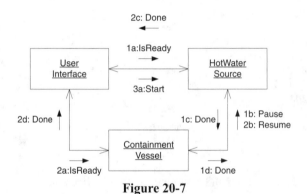

Figure 20-7
Detecting when brewing is complete

Use case 4: Coffee all gone The Mark IV shuts off the light when brewing is complete *and* an empty pot is placed on the plate. Clearly, in our object model, it is the `ContainmentVessel` that should detect this. It will have to send a `Complete` message to the `UserInterface`. Figure 20-8 shows the completed collaboration diagram.

From this diagram, we can draw a class diagram with all the associations intact. This diagram holds no surprises. You can see it in Figure 20-9.

Implementing the Abstract Model

Our object model is reasonably well partitioned. We have three distinct areas of responsibility, and each seems to be sending and receiving messages in a balanced way. There does not appear to be a god object anywhere. Nor does there appear to be any vapor classes.

So far, so good, but how do we implement the Mark IV in this structure? Do we simply implement the methods of these three classes to invoke the `CoffeeMakerAPI`? This

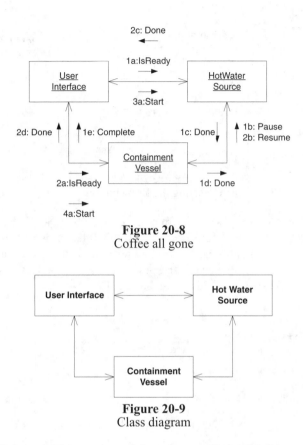

Figure 20-8
Coffee all gone

Figure 20-9
Class diagram

would be a real shame! We've captured the essence of what it takes to make coffee. It would be pitifully poor design if we were to now tie that essence to the Mark IV.

In fact, I'm going to make a rule right now. None of the three classes we have created must ever know *anything* about the Mark IV. This is the Dependency-Inversion Principle (DIP). We are not going to allow the high-level coffee-making policy of this system to depend on the low-level implementation.

OK, then, how will we create the Mark IV implementation? Let's look at all the use cases again. But this time, let's look at them from the Mark IV point of view.

Use case 1: User pushes Brew button How does the UserInterface know that the Brew button has been pushed? Clearly, it must call the CoffeeMakerAPI.GetBrewButtonStatus() function. Where should it call this function? We've already decreed that the UserInterface class itself cannot know about the CoffeeMakerAPI. So where does this call go?

We'll apply DIP and put the call in a derivative of UserInterface. See Figure 20-10 for details.

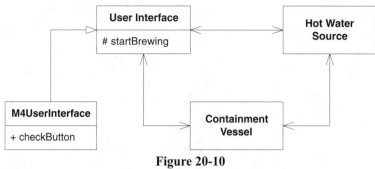

Figure 20-10
Detecting the Brew button

We've derived `M4UserInterface` from `UserInterface`, and we've put a `Check-Button()` method in `M4UserInterface`. When this function is called, it will call the `CoffeeMakerAPI.GetBrewButtonStatus()` function. If the button has been pressed, the fuction will invoke the protected `StartBrewing()` method of `UserInterface`. Listings 20-5 and 20-6 show how this would be coded.

Listing 20-5

M4UserInterface.cs

```
public class M4UserInterface : UserInterface
{
  private void CheckButton()
  {
    BrewButtonStatus status =
      CoffeeMaker.api.GetBrewButtonStatus();
    if (status == BrewButtonStatus.PUSHED)
    {
      StartBrewing();
    }
  }
}
```

Listing 20-6

UserInterface.cs

```
public class UserInterface
{
  private HotWaterSource hws;
  private ContainmentVessel cv;

  public void Done() {}
  public void Complete() {}
  protected void StartBrewing()
  {
    if (hws.IsReady() && cv.IsReady())
    {
      hws.Start();
      cv.Start();
    }
  }
}
```

You might be wondering why I created the protected `StartBrewing()` method at all. Why didn't I simply call the `Start()` functions from `M4UserInterface`? The reason is simple but significant. The `IsReady()` tests and the consequential calls to the `Start()` methods of the `HotWaterSource` and the `ContainmentVessel` are high-level policy that the `UserInterface` class should possess. That code is valid irrespective of whether we are implementing a Mark IV and should therefore not be coupled to the Mark IV derivative. This is yet another example of the Single-Responsibility Principle (SRP). You will see me make this same distinction over and over again in this example. I keep as much code as I can in the high-level classes. The only code I put into the derivatives is code that is directly, inextricably associated with the Mark IV.

Implementing the `IsReady()` functions How are the `IsReady()` methods of `HotWaterSource` and `ContainmentVessel` implemented? It should be clear that these are really only abstract methods and that these classes are therefore abstract classes. The corresponding derivatives `M4HotWaterSource` and `M4ContainmentVessel` will implement them by calling the appropriate `CoffeeMakerAPI` functions. Figure 20-11 shows the new structure, and Listings 20-7 and 20-8 show the implementation of the two derivatives.

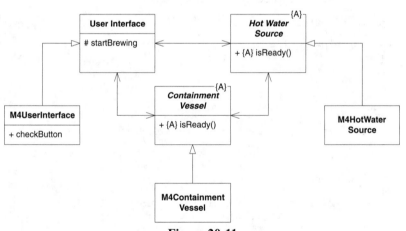

Figure 20-11
Implementing the `isReady` methods

Listing 20-7

M4HotWaterSource.cs

```
public class M4HotWaterSource : HotWaterSource
{
  public override bool IsReady()
  {
    BoilerStatus status =
      CoffeeMaker.api.GetBoilerStatus();
    return status == BoilerStatus.NOT_EMPTY;
  }
}
```

Listing 20-8

M4ContainmentVessel.cs

```
public class M4ContainmentVessel : ContainmentVessel
{
  public override bool IsReady()
  {
    WarmerPlateStatus status =
      CoffeeMaker.api.GetWarmerPlateStatus();
    return status == WarmerPlateStatus.POT_EMPTY;
  }
}
```

Implementing the Start() functions The Start() method of HotWaterSource
is simply an abstract method that is implemented by M4HotWaterSource to invoke the
CoffeeMakerAPI functions that close the valve and turn on the boiler. As I wrote these
functions, I began to get tired of all the CoffeeMaker.api.XXX structures I was writing,
so I did a little refactoring at the same time. The result is in Listing 20-9.

Listing 20-9

M4HotWaterSource.cs

```
public class M4HotWaterSource : HotWaterSource
{
  private CoffeeMakerAPI api;

  public M4HotWaterSource(CoffeeMakerAPI api)
  {
    this.api = api;
  }

  public override bool IsReady()
  {
    BoilerStatus status = api.GetBoilerStatus();
    return status == BoilerStatus.NOT_EMPTY;
  }

  public override void Start()
  {
    api.SetReliefValveState(ReliefValveState.CLOSED);
    api.SetBoilerState(BoilerState.ON);
  }
}
```

The Start() method for the ContainmentVessel is a little more interesting. The
only action that the M4ContainmentVessel needs to take is to remember the brewing
state of the system. As we'll see later, this will allow it to respond correctly when pots are
placed on or removed from the plate. Listing 20-10 shows the code.

Listing 20-10

M4ContainmentVessel1.cs

```
public class M4ContainmentVessel : ContainmentVessel
{
  private CoffeeMakerAPI api;
```

Listing 20-10 (Continued)

M4ContainmentVessell.cs

```
      private bool isBrewing = false;

      public M4ContainmentVessel(CoffeeMakerAPI api)
      {
        this.api = api;
      }

      public override bool IsReady()
      {
        WarmerPlateStatus status = api.GetWarmerPlateStatus();
        return status == WarmerPlateStatus.POT_EMPTY;
      }

      public override void Start()
      {
        isBrewing = true;
      }
    }
```

Calling M4UserInterface.CheckButton How does the flow of control ever get to a place at which the `CoffeeMakerAPI.GetBrewButtonStatus()` function can be called? For that matter, how does the flow of control get to where *any* of the sensors can be detected?

Many of the teams that try to solve this problem get completely hung up on this point. Some don't want to assume that there's a multithreading operating system in the coffee maker, and so they use a polling approach to the sensors. Others want to put multithreading in so that they don't have to worry about polling. I've seen this particular argument go back and forth for an hour or more in some teams.

These teams' mistake—which I eventually point out to them after letting them sweat a bit—is that the choice between threading and polling is completely irrelevant. This decision can be made at the very last minute without harm to the design. Therefore, it is always best to assume that messages can be sent asynchronously, as though there were independent threads, and then put the polling or threading in at the last minute.

The design so far has assumed that somehow, the flow of control will asynchronously get into the `M4UserInterface` object so that it can call `CoffeeMakerAPI.GetBrew-ButtonStatus()`. Now let's assume that we are working in a very minimal platform that does not support threading. This means that we're going to have to poll. How can we make this work?

Consider the `Pollable` interface in Listing 20-11. This interface has nothing but a `Poll()` method. What if `M4UserInterface` implemented this interface? What if the `Main()` program hung in a hard loop, calling this method over and over again? Then the flow of control would continuously be reentering `M4UserInterface`, and we could detect the Brew button.

Listing 20-11

Pollable.cs

```
public interface Pollable
{
   void Poll();
}
```

Indeed, we can repeat this pattern for all three of the M4 derivatives. Each has its own sensors it needs to check. So, as shown in Figure 20-12, we can derive all the M4 derivatives from `Pollable` and call them all from `Main()`.

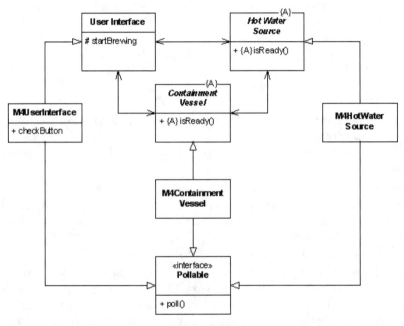

Figure 20-12
Pollable coffee maker

Listing 20-12 shows what the `Main` function might look like. It is placed in a class called `M4CoffeeMaker`. The `Main()` function creates the implemented version of the `api` and then creates the three M4 components. It calls `Init()` functions to wire the components up to each other. Finally, it hangs in an infinite loop, calling `Poll()` on each of the components in turn.

Listing 20-12

M4CoffeeMaker.cs

```
public static void Main(string[] args)
{
   CoffeeMakerAPI api = new M4CoffeeMakerAPI();
```

Listing 20-12 (Continued)

M4CoffeeMaker.cs

```
    M4UserInterface ui = new M4UserInterface(api);
    M4HotWaterSource hws = new M4HotWaterSource(api);
    M4ContainmentVessel cv = new M4ContainmentVessel(api);

    ui.Init(hws,cv);
    hws.Init(ui, cv);
    cv.Init(hws,ui);

    while (true)
    {
      ui.Poll();
      hws.Poll();
      cv.Poll();
    }
  }
}
```

It should now be clear how the M4UserInterface.CheckButton() function gets called. Indeed, it should be clear that this function is really not called CheckButton(). It is called Poll(). Listing 20-13 shows what M4UserInterface looks like now.

Listing 20-13

M4UserInterface.cs

```
  public class M4UserInterface : UserInterface
                               , Pollable
  {
    private CoffeeMakerAPI api;

    public M4UserInterface(CoffeeMakerAPI api)
    {
      this.api = api;
    }

    public void Poll()
    {
      BrewButtonStatus status = api.GetBrewButtonStatus();
      if (status == BrewButtonStatus.PUSHED)
      {
        StartBrewing();
      }
    }
  }
```

Completing the coffee maker The reasoning used in the previous sections can be repeated for each of the other components of the coffee maker. The result is shown in Listings 20-14 through 20-21.

The Benefits of This Design

Despite the trivial nature of the problem, this design shows some very nice characteristics. Figure 20-13 shows the structure. I have drawn a line around the three abstract classes. These classes hold the high-level policy of the coffee maker. Note that all dependencies that cross the line point inward. Nothing inside the line depends on anything outside. Thus, the abstractions are completely separated from the details.

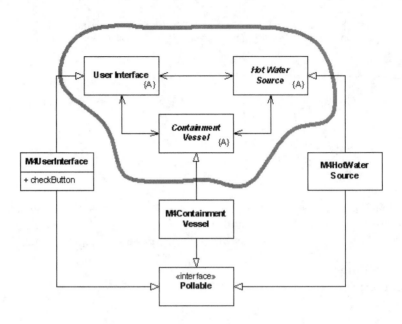

Figure 20-13
Coffee maker components

The abstract classes know nothing of buttons, lights, valves, sensors, or any other of the detailed elements of the coffee maker. By the same token, the derivatives are dominated by those details.

Note that the three abstract classes could be reused to make many different kinds of coffee machines. We could easily use them in a coffee machine that is connected to the water mains and uses a tank and spigot. It seems likely that we could also use them for a coffee vending machine. Indeed, I think we could use it in an automatic tea brewer or even a chicken soup maker. This segregation between high-level policy and detail is the essence of object-oriented design.

The Roots of This Design I did not simply sit down one day and develop this design in a nice straightfoward manner. Indeed, in 1993, my first design for the coffee maker looked much more like Figure 20-1. However, I have written about this problem many times and have used it as an exercise while teaching class after class. So this design has been refined over time.

The code was created, test first, using the unit tests in Listing 20-22. I created the code, based on the structure in Figure 20-13, but put it together incrementally, one failing test case at a time.[4]

I am not convinced that the test cases are complete. If this were more than an example program, I'd do a more exhaustive analysis of the test cases. However, I felt that such an analysis would have been overkill for this book.

OOverkill

This example has certain pedagogical advantages. It is small and easy to understand and shows how the principles of OOD can be used to manage dependencies and separate concerns. On the other hand, its very smallness means that the benefits of that separation probably do not outweigh the costs.

If we were to write the Mark IV coffee maker as an FSM, we'd find that it had 7 states and 18 transitions.[5] We could encode this into 18 lines of SMC code. A simple main loop that polls the sensors would be another ten lines or so, and the action functions that the FSM would invoke would be another couple of dozen. In short, we could write the whole program in less than a page of code.

If we don't count the tests, the OO solution of the coffee maker is *five* pages of code. There is no way that we can justify this disparity. In larger applications, the benefits of dependency management and the separation of concerns clearly outweigh the costs of OOD. In this example, however, the reverse is more likely to be true.

Listing 20-14

UserInterface.cs

```
using System;

namespace CoffeeMaker
{
  public abstract class UserInterface
  {
    private HotWaterSource hws;
    private ContainmentVessel cv;
    protected bool isComplete;

    public UserInterface()
    {
      isComplete = true;
    }
```

---

4. [Beck2002]

5. [Martin1995], p. 65

Listing 20-14 (Continued)

UserInterface.cs

```
    public void Init(HotWaterSource hws, ContainmentVessel cv)
    {
      this.hws = hws;
      this.cv = cv;
    }

    public void Complete()
    {
      isComplete = true;
      CompleteCycle();
    }

    protected void StartBrewing()
    {
      if (hws.IsReady() && cv.IsReady())
      {
        isComplete = false;
        hws.Start();
        cv.Start();
      }
    }

    public abstract void Done();
    public abstract void CompleteCycle();
  }
}
```

Listing 20-15

M4UserInterface.cs

```
using CoffeeMaker;

namespace M4CoffeeMaker
{
  public class M4UserInterface : UserInterface
                              , Pollable
  {
    private CoffeeMakerAPI api;

    public M4UserInterface(CoffeeMakerAPI api)
    {
      this.api = api;
    }

    public void Poll()
    {
      BrewButtonStatus buttonStatus = api.GetBrewButtonStatus();
      if (buttonStatus == BrewButtonStatus.PUSHED)
      {
        StartBrewing();
      }
    }
```

Listing 20-15 (Continued)

M4UserInterface.cs

```
    public override void Done()
    {
      api.SetIndicatorState(IndicatorState.ON);
    }

    public override void CompleteCycle()
    {
      api.SetIndicatorState(IndicatorState.OFF);
    }
  }
}
```

Listing 20-16

HotWaterSource.cs

```
namespace CoffeeMaker
{
  public abstract class HotWaterSource
  {
    private UserInterface ui;
    private ContainmentVessel cv;
    protected bool isBrewing;

    public HotWaterSource()
    {
      isBrewing = false;
    }

    public void Init(UserInterface ui, ContainmentVessel cv)
    {
      this.ui = ui;
      this.cv = cv;
    }

    public void Start()
    {
      isBrewing = true;
      StartBrewing();
    }

    public void Done()
    {
      isBrewing = false;
    }

    protected void DeclareDone()
    {
      ui.Done();
      cv.Done();
      isBrewing = false;
    }

    public abstract bool IsReady();
```

Listing 20-16 (Continued)

HotWaterSource.cs

```
      public abstract void StartBrewing();
      public abstract void Pause();
      public abstract void Resume();
   }
}
```

Listing 20-17

M4HotWaterSource.cs

```csharp
using System;
using CoffeeMaker;

namespace M4CoffeeMaker
{
  public class M4HotWaterSource : HotWaterSource
                                 , Pollable
  {
    private CoffeeMakerAPI api;

    public M4HotWaterSource(CoffeeMakerAPI api)
    {
      this.api = api;
    }

    public override bool IsReady()
    {
      BoilerStatus boilerStatus = api.GetBoilerStatus();
      return boilerStatus == BoilerStatus.NOT_EMPTY;
    }

    public override void StartBrewing()
    {
      api.SetReliefValveState(ReliefValveState.CLOSED);
      api.SetBoilerState(BoilerState.ON);
    }

    public void Poll()
    {
      BoilerStatus boilerStatus = api.GetBoilerStatus();
      if (isBrewing)
      {
        if (boilerStatus == BoilerStatus.EMPTY)
        {
          api.SetBoilerState(BoilerState.OFF);
          api.SetReliefValveState(ReliefValveState.CLOSED);
          DeclareDone();
        }
      }
    }

    public override void Pause()
    {
      api.SetBoilerState(BoilerState.OFF);
```

Listing 20-17 (Continued)

M4HotWaterSource.cs

```csharp
      api.SetReliefValveState(ReliefValveState.OPEN);
    }

    public override void Resume()
    {
      api.SetBoilerState(BoilerState.ON);
      api.SetReliefValveState(ReliefValveState.CLOSED);
    }
  }
}
```

Listing 20-18

ContainmentVessel.cs

```csharp
using System;

namespace CoffeeMaker
{
  public abstract class ContainmentVessel
  {
    private UserInterface ui;
    private HotWaterSource hws;
    protected bool isBrewing;
    protected bool isComplete;

    public ContainmentVessel()
    {
      isBrewing = false;
      isComplete = true;
    }

    public void Init(UserInterface ui, HotWaterSource hws)
    {
      this.ui = ui;
      this.hws = hws;
    }

    public void Start()
    {
      isBrewing = true;
      isComplete = false;
    }

    public void Done()
    {
      isBrewing = false;
    }

    protected void DeclareComplete()
    {
      isComplete = true;
      ui.Complete();
    }
```

Listing 20-18 (Continued)

ContainmentVessel.cs

```
    protected void ContainerAvailable()
    {
      hws.Resume();
    }

    protected void ContainerUnavailable()
    {
      hws.Pause();
    }

    public abstract bool IsReady();
  }
}
```

Listing 20-19

M4ContainmentVessel.cs

```
using CoffeeMaker;

namespace M4CoffeeMaker
{
  public class M4ContainmentVessel : ContainmentVessel
                                   , Pollable
  {
    private CoffeeMakerAPI api;
    private WarmerPlateStatus lastPotStatus;

    public M4ContainmentVessel(CoffeeMakerAPI api)
    {
      this.api = api;
      lastPotStatus = WarmerPlateStatus.POT_EMPTY;
    }

    public override bool IsReady()
    {
      WarmerPlateStatus plateStatus =
                        api.GetWarmerPlateStatus();
      return plateStatus == WarmerPlateStatus.POT_EMPTY;
    }

    public void Poll()
    {
      WarmerPlateStatus potStatus = api.GetWarmerPlateStatus();
      if (potStatus != lastPotStatus)
      {
        if (isBrewing)
        {
          HandleBrewingEvent(potStatus);
        }
        else if (isComplete == false)
        {
          HandleIncompleteEvent(potStatus);
        }
```

Listing 20-19 (Continued)

M4ContainmentVessel.cs

```
          lastPotStatus = potStatus;
      }
    }

    private void
    HandleBrewingEvent(WarmerPlateStatus potStatus)
    {
      if (potStatus == WarmerPlateStatus.POT_NOT_EMPTY)
      {
        ContainerAvailable();
        api.SetWarmerState(WarmerState.ON);
      }
      else if (potStatus == WarmerPlateStatus.WARMER_EMPTY)
      {
        ContainerUnavailable();
        api.SetWarmerState(WarmerState.OFF);
      }
      else
      { // potStatus == POT_EMPTY
        ContainerAvailable();
        api.SetWarmerState(WarmerState.OFF);
      }
    }

    private void
    HandleIncompleteEvent(WarmerPlateStatus potStatus)
    {
      if (potStatus == WarmerPlateStatus.POT_NOT_EMPTY)
      {
        api.SetWarmerState(WarmerState.ON);
      }
      else if (potStatus == WarmerPlateStatus.WARMER_EMPTY)
      {
        api.SetWarmerState(WarmerState.OFF);
      }
      else
      { // potStatus == POT_EMPTY
        api.SetWarmerState(WarmerState.OFF);
        DeclareComplete();
      }
    }
  }
}
```

Listing 20-20

Pollable.cs

```
using System;

namespace M4CoffeeMaker
{
  public interface Pollable
```

Listing 20-20 (Continued)

Pollable.cs

```
    {
      void Poll();
    }
  }
}
```

Listing 20-21

CoffeeMaker.cs

```
using CoffeeMaker;

namespace M4CoffeeMaker
{
  public class M4CoffeeMaker
  {
    public static void Main(string[] args)
    {
      CoffeeMakerAPI api = new M4CoffeeMakerAPI();
      M4UserInterface ui = new M4UserInterface(api);
      M4HotWaterSource hws = new M4HotWaterSource(api);
      M4ContainmentVessel cv = new M4ContainmentVessel(api);

      ui.Init(hws, cv);
      hws.Init(ui, cv);
      cv.Init(ui, hws);

      while (true)
      {
        ui.Poll();
        hws.Poll();
        cv.Poll();
      }
    }
  }
}
```

Listing 20-22

TestCoffeeMaker.cs

```
using M4CoffeeMaker;
using NUnit.Framework;

namespace CoffeeMaker.Test
{
  internal class CoffeeMakerStub : CoffeeMakerAPI
  {
    public bool buttonPressed;
    public bool lightOn;
    public bool boilerOn;
    public bool valveClosed;
    public bool plateOn;
    public bool boilerEmpty;
```

Listing 20-22 (Continued)

`TestCoffeeMaker.cs`

```csharp
    public bool potPresent;
    public bool potNotEmpty;

    public CoffeeMakerStub()
    {
      buttonPressed = false;
      lightOn = false;
      boilerOn = false;
      valveClosed = true;
      plateOn = false;
      boilerEmpty = true;
      potPresent = true;
      potNotEmpty = false;
    }

    public WarmerPlateStatus GetWarmerPlateStatus()
    {
      if (!potPresent)
        return WarmerPlateStatus.WARMER_EMPTY;
      else if (potNotEmpty)
        return WarmerPlateStatus.POT_NOT_EMPTY;
      else
        return WarmerPlateStatus.POT_EMPTY;
    }

    public BoilerStatus GetBoilerStatus()
    {
      return boilerEmpty ?
            BoilerStatus.EMPTY : BoilerStatus.NOT_EMPTY;
    }

    public BrewButtonStatus GetBrewButtonStatus()
    {
      if (buttonPressed)
      {
        buttonPressed = false;
        return BrewButtonStatus.PUSHED;
      }
      else
      {
        return BrewButtonStatus.NOT_PUSHED;
      }
    }

    public void SetBoilerState(BoilerState boilerState)
    {
      boilerOn = boilerState == BoilerState.ON;
    }

    public void SetWarmerState(WarmerState warmerState)
    {
      plateOn = warmerState == WarmerState.ON;
    }
```

Listing 20-22 (Continued)

`TestCoffeeMaker.cs`

```
  public void
  SetIndicatorState(IndicatorState indicatorState)
  {
    lightOn = indicatorState == IndicatorState.ON;
  }

  public void
  SetReliefValveState(ReliefValveState reliefValveState)
  {
    valveClosed = reliefValveState == ReliefValveState.CLOSED;
  }
}

[TestFixture]
public class TestCoffeeMaker
{
  private M4UserInterface ui;
  private M4HotWaterSource hws;
  private M4ContainmentVessel cv;
  private CoffeeMakerStub api;

  [SetUp]
  public void SetUp()
  {
    api = new CoffeeMakerStub();
    ui = new M4UserInterface(api);
    hws = new M4HotWaterSource(api);
    cv = new M4ContainmentVessel(api);
    ui.Init(hws, cv);
    hws.Init(ui, cv);
    cv.Init(ui, hws);
  }

  private void Poll()
  {
    ui.Poll();
    hws.Poll();
    cv.Poll();
  }

  [Test]
  public void InitialConditions()
  {
    Poll();
    Assert.IsFalse(api.boilerOn);
    Assert.IsFalse(api.lightOn);
    Assert.IsFalse(api.plateOn);
    Assert.IsTrue(api.valveClosed);
  }

  [Test]
  public void StartNoPot()
  {
    Poll();
    api.buttonPressed = true;
    api.potPresent = false;
```

Listing 20-22 (Continued)
TestCoffeeMaker.cs

```csharp
      Poll();
      Assert.IsFalse(api.boilerOn);
      Assert.IsFalse(api.lightOn);
      Assert.IsFalse(api.plateOn);
      Assert.IsTrue(api.valveClosed);
    }

    [Test]
    public void StartNoWater()
    {
      Poll();
      api.buttonPressed = true;
      api.boilerEmpty = true;
      Poll();
      Assert.IsFalse(api.boilerOn);
      Assert.IsFalse(api.lightOn);
      Assert.IsFalse(api.plateOn);
      Assert.IsTrue(api.valveClosed);
    }

    [Test]
    public void GoodStart()
    {
      NormalStart();
      Assert.IsTrue(api.boilerOn);
      Assert.IsFalse(api.lightOn);
      Assert.IsFalse(api.plateOn);
      Assert.IsTrue(api.valveClosed);
    }

    private void NormalStart()
    {
      Poll();
      api.boilerEmpty = false;
      api.buttonPressed = true;
      Poll();
    }

    [Test]
    public void StartedPotNotEmpty()
    {
      NormalStart();
      api.potNotEmpty = true;
      Poll();
      Assert.IsTrue(api.boilerOn);
      Assert.IsFalse(api.lightOn);
      Assert.IsTrue(api.plateOn);
      Assert.IsTrue(api.valveClosed);
    }

    [Test]
    public void PotRemovedAndReplacedWhileEmpty()
    {
      NormalStart();
      api.potPresent = false;
```

Listing 20-22 (Continued)

`TestCoffeeMaker.cs`

```csharp
    Poll();
    Assert.IsFalse(api.boilerOn);
    Assert.IsFalse(api.lightOn);
    Assert.IsFalse(api.plateOn);
    Assert.IsFalse(api.valveClosed);

    api.potPresent = true;
    Poll();
    Assert.IsTrue(api.boilerOn);
    Assert.IsFalse(api.lightOn);
    Assert.IsFalse(api.plateOn);
    Assert.IsTrue(api.valveClosed);
  }

  [Test]
  public void PotRemovedWhileNotEmptyAndReplacedEmpty()
  {
    NormalFill();
    api.potPresent = false;
    Poll();
    Assert.IsFalse(api.boilerOn);
    Assert.IsFalse(api.lightOn);
    Assert.IsFalse(api.plateOn);
    Assert.IsFalse(api.valveClosed);

    api.potPresent = true;
    api.potNotEmpty = false;
    Poll();
    Assert.IsTrue(api.boilerOn);
    Assert.IsFalse(api.lightOn);
    Assert.IsFalse(api.plateOn);
    Assert.IsTrue(api.valveClosed);
  }

  private void NormalFill()
  {
    NormalStart();
    api.potNotEmpty = true;
    Poll();
  }

  [Test]
  public void PotRemovedWhileNotEmptyAndReplacedNotEmpty()
  {
    NormalFill();
    api.potPresent = false;
    Poll();
    api.potPresent = true;
    Poll();
    Assert.IsTrue(api.boilerOn);
    Assert.IsFalse(api.lightOn);
    Assert.IsTrue(api.plateOn);
    Assert.IsTrue(api.valveClosed);
  }
```

Listing 20-22 (Continued)

`TestCoffeeMaker.cs`

```
    [Test]
    public void BoilerEmptyPotNotEmpty()
    {
      NormalBrew();
      Assert.IsFalse(api.boilerOn);
      Assert.IsTrue(api.lightOn);
      Assert.IsTrue(api.plateOn);
      Assert.IsTrue(api.valveClosed);
    }

    private void NormalBrew()
    {
      NormalFill();
      api.boilerEmpty = true;
      Poll();
    }


    [Test]
    public void BoilerEmptiesWhilePotRemoved()
    {
      NormalFill();
      api.potPresent = false;
      Poll();
      api.boilerEmpty = true;
      Poll();
      Assert.IsFalse(api.boilerOn);
      Assert.IsTrue(api.lightOn);
      Assert.IsFalse(api.plateOn);
      Assert.IsTrue(api.valveClosed);

      api.potPresent = true;
      Poll();
      Assert.IsFalse(api.boilerOn);
      Assert.IsTrue(api.lightOn);
      Assert.IsTrue(api.plateOn);
      Assert.IsTrue(api.valveClosed);
    }

    [Test]
    public void EmptyPotReturnedAfter()
    {
      NormalBrew  ();
      api   .
      potNotEmpty  = false;
      Poll  ();
      Assert.IsFalse(api.boilerOn);
      Assert.IsFalse(api.lightOn);
      Assert.IsFalse(api.plateOn);
      Assert.IsTrue(api.valveClosed);
    }
  }
}
```

Bibliography

[Beck2002] Kent Beck, *Test-Driven Development*, Addison-Wesley, 2002.

[Martin1995] Robert C. Martin, *Designing Object-Oriented C++ Applications Using the Booch Method*, Prentice Hall, 1995.

Section III

The Payroll Case Study

© Jennifer M. Kohnke

The time has come for our first major case study. We have studied practices and principles. We have discussed the essence of design. We have talked about testing and planning. Now we need to do some real work.

In the next several chapters, we explore the design and implementation of a batch payroll system, a rudimentary specification of which follows. As part of that design and implementation, we will make use of several design patterns: COMMAND, TEMPLATE METHOD, STRATEGY, SINGLETON, NULL OBJECT, FACTORY, and FACADE. These patterns are the topic of the next several chapters. In Chapter 26, we work through the design and implementation of the payroll problem.

There are several ways to read through this case study.

- Read straight through, first learning the design patterns and then seeing how they are applied to the payroll problem.

- If you know the patterns and are not interested in a review, go right to Chapter 26.

- Read Chapter 26 first and then go back and read through the chapters that describe the patterns that were used.

- Read Chapter 26 in bits. When it talks about a pattern you are unfamiliar with, read through the chapter that describes that pattern, and then return to Chapter 26.

Indeed, there are no rules. Pick, or invent, the strategy that works best for you.

Rudimentary Specification of the Payroll System

Following are some of the notes we took while conversing with our customer. (These notes are also given in Chapter 26.)

This system consists of a database of the company's employees, and their associated data, such as time cards. The system must pay all employees the correct amount, on time, by the method that they specify. Also, various deductions must be taken from their pay.

- Some employees work by the hour. They are paid an hourly rate that is one of the fields in their employee record. They submit daily time cards that record the date and the number of hours worked. If they work more than 8 hours per day, they are paid 1.5 times their normal rate for those extra hours. They are paid every Friday.

- Some employees are paid a flat salary. They are paid on the last working day of the month. Their monthly salary is one of the fields in their employee record.

- Some of the salaried employees are also paid a commission based on their sales. They submit sales receipts that record the date and the amount of the sale. Their commission rate is a field in their employee record. They are paid every other Friday.

- Employees can select their method of payment. They may have their paychecks mailed to the postal address of their choice, have their paychecks held by the paymaster for pickup, or request that their paychecks be directly deposited into the bank account of their choice.

- Some employees belong to the union. Their employee record has a field for the weekly dues rate. Their dues must be deducted from their pay. Also, the union may assess service charges against individual union members from time to time. These service charges are submitted by the union on a weekly basis and must be deducted from the appropriate employee's next pay amount.

- The payroll application will run once each working day and pay the appropriate employees on that day. The system will be told what date the employees are to be paid to, so it will generate payments for records from the last time the employee was paid up to the specified date.

Exercise

Before continuing, you might find it instructive to design the payroll system on your own, now. You might want to sketch some initial UML diagrams. Better yet, you might want to write the first few test-first use cases. Apply the principles and practices we've learned so far, and try to create a balanced and healthy design. Remember the coffee maker!

If you are going to do this, take a look at the use cases that follow. Otherwise, skip them; they'll be presented again in Chapter 26.

Use Case 1: Add New Employee

A new employee is added by the receipt of an `AddEmp` transaction. This transaction contains the employee's name, address, and assigned employee number. The transaction has three forms:

1. `AddEmp <EmpID> "<name>" "<address>" H <hrly-rate>`
2. `AddEmp <EmpID> "<name>" "<address>" S <mtly-slry>`
3. `AddEmp <EmpID> "<name>" "<address>" C <mtly-slry> <comm-rate>`

The employee record is created with its fields assigned appropriately.

Alternatives: An error in the transaction structure If the transaction structure is inappropriate, it is printed out in an error message, and no action is taken.

Use Case 2: Deleting an Employee

Employees are deleted when a `DelEmp` transaction is received. The form of this transaction is as follows:

```
DelEmp <EmpID>
```

When this transaction is received, the appropriate employee record is deleted.

Alternative: Invalid or unknown `EmpID` If the `<EmpID>` field is not structured correctly or does not refer to a valid employee record, the transaction is printed with an error message, and no other action is taken.

Use Case 3: Post a `Time Card`

On receipt of a `TimeCard` transaction, the system will create a time card record and associate it with the appropriate employee record:

```
TimeCard <empid> <date> <hours>
```

Alternative 1: The selected employee is not hourly The system will print an appropriate error message and take no further action.

Alternative 2: An error in the transaction structure The system will print an appropriate error message and take no further action.

Use Case 4: Posting a `Sales Receipt`

On receipt of the `SalesReceipt` transaction, the system will create a new sales-receipt record and associate it with the appropriate commissioned employee.

```
SalesReceipt <EmpID> <date> <amount>
```

Alternative 1: The selected employee is not commissioned The system will print an appropriate error message and take no further action.

Alternative 2: An error in the transaction structure The system will print an appropriate error message and take no further action.

Use Case 5: Posting a Union Service Charge

On receipt of this transaction, the system will create a service-charge record and associate it with the appropriate union member:

```
ServiceCharge <memberID> <amount>
```

Alternative: Poorly formed transaction If the transaction is not well formed or if the `<memberID>` does not refer to an existing union member, the transaction is printed with an appropriate error message.

Use Case 6: Changing Employee Details

On receipt of this transaction, the system will alter one of the details of the appropriate employee record. This transaction has several possible variations:

```
ChgEmp <EmpID> Name <name>              Change employee name
ChgEmp <EmpID> Address <address>        Change employee address
ChgEmp <EmpID> Hourly <hourlyRate>      Change to hourly
ChgEmp <EmpID> Salaried <salary>        Change to salaried
```

```
ChgEmp <EmpID> Commissioned <salary> <rate>      Change to commissioned
ChgEmp <EmpID> Hold                               Hold paycheck
ChgEmp <EmpID> Direct <bank> <account>            Direct deposit
ChgEmp <EmpID> Mail <address>                     Mail paycheck
ChgEmp <EmpID> Member <memberID> Dues <rate>      Put employee in union
ChgEmp <EmpID> NoMember                            Cut employee from union
```

Alternative: Transaction Errors If the structure of the transaction is improper, $<EmpID>$ does not refer to a real employee, $<memberID>$ already refers to a member, print a suitable error, and take no further action.

Use Case 7: Run the Payroll for Today

On receipt of the payday transaction, the system finds all those employees who should be paid on the specified date. The system then determines how much they are owed and pays them according to their selected payment method. An audit-trail report is printed showing the action taken for each employee:

```
Payday <date>
```

COMMAND and ACTIVE OBJECT:
Versatility and Multitasking

No man has received from nature the right to command his fellow human beings.

—Denis Diderot (1713–1784)

Of all the design patterns that have been described over the years, COMMAND impresses me as one of the simplest and most elegant. But we shall see, the simplicity is deceptive. The range of uses that COMMAND may be put to is probably without bound.

The simplicity of COMMAND, as shown in Figure 21-1, is almost laughable. Listing 21-1 doesn't do much to dampen the levity. It seems absurd that we can have a pattern that consists of nothing more than an interface with one method.

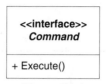

Figure 21-1
COMMAND pattern

Listing 21-1
Command.cs

```
public interface Command
{
   void Execute();
}
```

In fact, this pattern has crossed a very interesting line. And it is in the crossing of this line that all the interesting complexity lies. Most classes associate a suite of methods with a corresponding set of variables. The COMMAND pattern does not do this. Rather, it encapsulates a single function free of any variables.

In strict object-oriented terms, this is anathema, smacking of functional decomposition. It elevates the role of a function to the level of a class. Blasphemy! Yet at this boundary where two paradigms clash, interesting things start to occur.

Simple Commands

Several years ago, I consulted for a large firm that made photocopiers. I was helping one of its development teams with the design and implementation of the embedded real-time software that drove the inner workings of a new copier. We stumbled on the idea of using the COMMAND pattern to control the hardware devices. We created a hierarchy that looked something like Figure 21-2.

The role of these classes should be obvious. Call `Execute()` on a `RelayOnCommand` turns on a relay. Calling `Execute()` on a `MotorOffCommand` turns off a motor. The address of the motor or relay is passed into the object as an argument to its constructor.

With this structure in place, we could now pass `Command` objects around the system and `Execute()` them without knowing precisely what kind of `Command` they represented. This led to some interesting simplifications.

The system was event driven. Relays opened or closed, motors started or stopped, and clutches engaged or disengaged, based on certain events that took place in the system. Many

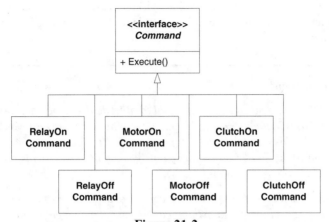

Figure 21-2
Some simple commands for the copier software

of those events were detected by sensors. For example, when an optical sensor determined that a sheet of paper had reached a certain point in the paper path, we'd need to engage a certain clutch. We were able to implement this by simply binding the appropriate ClutchOnCommand to the object that controlled that particular optical sensor. See Figure 21-3.

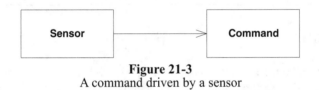

Figure 21-3
A command driven by a sensor

This simple structure has an enormous advantage. The Sensor has no idea what it is doing. Whenever it detects an event, it simply calls Execute() on the Command that it is bound to. This means that the Sensors don't have to know about individual clutches or relays. They don't have to know the mechanical structure of the paper path. Their function becomes remarkably simple.

The complexity of determining which relays to close when certain sensors declare events has moved to an initialization function. At some point during the initialization of the system, each Sensor is bound to an appropriate Command. This puts all the logical interconnections between the sensors and commands—the *wiring*—in one place and gets it out of the main body of the system. Indeed, it would be possible to create a simple text file that described which Sensors were bound to which Commands. The initialization program could read this file and build the system appropriately. Thus, the *wiring* of the system could be determined completely outside the program and could be adjusted without recompilation.

By encapsulating the *notion* of a command, this pattern allowed us to decouple the logical interconnections of the system from the devices that were being connected. This was a huge benefit.

Where'd the *I* go?

In the .NET community, it is conventional to precede the name of an interface with a capital I. *In the preceding example, the interface* Command *would conventionally be named* ICommand. *Although many .NET conventions are good, and in general this book follows them, this particular convention is not favored by your humble authors.*

In general, it is a bad idea to pollute the name of something with an orthogonal concept, especially if that orthogonal concept can change. What if, for example, we decide that ICommand *should be an abstract class instead of an interface? Must we then find all the references to* ICommand *and change them to* Command? *Must we then also recompile and redeploy all the affected assemblies?*

This is the twenty-first century. We have intelligent IDEs that can tell us, with just a mouse-over, whether a class is an interface. It is time for the last vestiges of Hungarian notation to finally be put to rest.

Transactions

The COMMAND pattern has another common use, one we will find useful in the payroll problem: the creation and execution of transactions. Imagine, for example, that we are writing the software that maintains a database of employees (see Figure 21-4). Users can apply a number of operations to that database, such as adding new employees, deleting old employees, or changing the attributes of existing employees.

A user who decides to add a new employee must specify all the information needed to successfully create the employee record. Before acting on that information, the system needs to verify that the information is syntactically and semantically correct. The COMMAND pattern can help with this job. The command object acts as a respository for the unvalidated data, implements the validation methods, and implements the methods that finally execute the transaction.

For example, consider Figure 21-5. The AddEmployeeTransaction contains the same data fields that Employee contains, as well as a pointer to a PayClassification object. These fields and object are created from the data that the user specifies when directing the system to add a new employee.

The Validate method looks over all the data and makes sure that it makes sense. It checks it for syntactic and semantic correctness. It may even check to ensure that the data

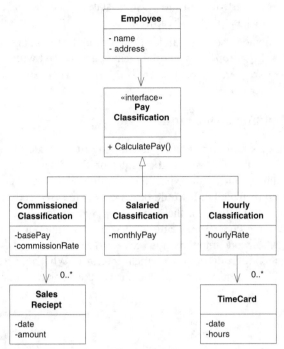

Figure 21-4
Employee database

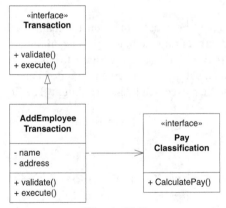

Figure 21-5
AddEmployee transaction

in the transaction is consistent with the existing state of the database. For example, it might ensure that no such employee already exists.

The `Execute` method uses the validated data to update the database. In our simple example, a new `Employee` object would be created and loaded with the fields from the `AddEmployeeTransaction` object. The `PayClassification` object would be moved or copied into the `Employee`.

Physical and Temporal Decoupling

The benefit this give us is in the dramatic decoupling of the code that procures the data from the user, the code that validates and operates on that data, and the business objects themselves. For example, one might expect the data for adding a new employee to be procured from a dialog box in a GUI. It would be a shame if the GUI code contained the validation and execution algorithms for the transaction. Such a coupling would prevent that validation and execution code from being used with other interfaces. By separating the validation and execution code into the `AddEmployeeTransaction` class, we have physically decoupled that code from the procurement interface. What's more, we've separated the code that knows how to manipulate the logistics of the database from the business entities themselves.

Temporal Decoupling

We have also decoupled the validation and execution code in a different way. Once the data has been procured, there is no reason why the validation and execution methods must be called immediately. The transaction objects can be held in a list and validated and executed much later.

Suppose that we have a database that must remain unchanged during the day. Changes may be applied only during the hours between midnight and 1 A.M. It would be a shame to have to wait until midnight and then have to rush to type all the commands in before 1 A.M. It would be much more convenient to type in all the commands, have them validated on the spot, and then executed later, at midnight. The COMMAND pattern gives us this ability.

Undo Method

Figure 21-6 adds the `Undo()` method to the COMMAND pattern. It stands to reason that if the `Execute()` method of a `Command` derivative can be implemented to remember the details of the operation it performs, the `Undo()` method can be implemented to undo that operation and return the system to its original state.

Imagine, for example, an application that allows the user to draw geometric shapes on the screen. A toolbar has buttons that allow the user to draw circles, squares, rectangles, and so on. Let's say that the user clicks the Draw Circle button. The system

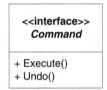

Figure 21-6
Undo variation of the COMMAND pattern

creates a `DrawCircleCommand` and then calls `Execute()` on that command. The `DrawCircleCommand` object tracks the user's mouse, waiting for a click in the drawing window. On receiving that click, it sets the click point as the center of the circle and proceeds to draw an animated circle at that center, with a radius that tracks the current mouse position. When the user clicks again, the `DrawCircleCommand` stops animating the circle and adds the appropriate circle object to the list of shapes currently displayed on the canvas. It also stores the ID of the new circle in a private variable of its own. Then it returns from the `Execute()` method. The system then pushes the expended `DrawCirlceCommand` on the stack of completed commands.

Some time later, the user clicks the Undo button on the toolbar. The system pops the completed commands stack and calls `Undo()` on the resulting `Command` object. On receiving the `Undo()` message, the `DrawCircleCommand` object deletes the circle matching the saved ID from the list of objects currently displayed on the canvas.

With this technique, you can easily implement `Undo` in nearly any application. The code that knows how to undo a command is always right next to the code that knows how to perform the command.

Active Object

One of my favorite uses of the COMMAND pattern is the ACTIVE OBJECT pattern.[1] This old technique for implementing multiple threads of control has been used, in one form or another, to provide a simple multitasking nucleus for thousands of industrial systems.

The idea is very simple. Consider Listings 21-2 and 21-3. An `ActiveObjectEngine` object maintains a linked list of `Command` objects. Users can add new commands to the engine, or they can call `Run()`. The `Run()` function simply goes through the linked list, executing and removing each command.

---

1.   [Lavender96]

Listing 21-2
ActiveObjectEngine.cs

```csharp
using System.Collections;

public class ActiveObjectEngine
{
  ArrayList itsCommands = new ArrayList();

  public void AddCommand(Command c)
  {
    itsCommands.Add(c);
  }

  public void Run()
  {
    while (itsCommands.Count > 0)
    {
      Command c = (Command) itsCommands[0];
      itsCommands.RemoveAt(0);
      c.Execute();
    }
  }
}
```

Listing 21-3
Command.cs

```csharp
public interface Command
{
  void Execute();
}
```

This may not seem very impressive. But imagine what would happen if one of the Command objects in the linked list put itself back on the list. The list would never go empty, and the Run() function would never return.

Consider the test case in Listing 21-4. This test case creates a SleepCommand, which among other things passes a delay of 1,000 ms to the constructor of the SleepCommand. The test case then puts the SleepCommand into the ActiveObjectEngine. After calling Run(), the test case expects that a certain number of milliseconds have elapsed.

Listing 21-4
TestSleepCommand.cs

```csharp
using System;
using NUnit.Framework;

[TestFixture]
public class TestSleepCommand
{
  private class WakeUpCommand : Command
  {
    public bool executed = false;
```

Listing 21-4 (Continued)

TestSleepCommand.cs

```
    public void Execute()
    {
      executed = true;
    }
  }

  [Test]
  public void TestSleep()
  {
    WakeUpCommand wakeup = new WakeUpCommand();
    ActiveObjectEngine e = new ActiveObjectEngine();
    SleepCommand c = new SleepCommand(1000, e, wakeup);
    e.AddCommand(c);
    DateTime start = DateTime.Now;
    e.Run();
    DateTime stop = DateTime.Now;
    double sleepTime = (stop-start).TotalMilliseconds;
    Assert.IsTrue(sleepTime >= 1000,
      "SleepTime " + sleepTime + " expected > 1000");
    Assert.IsTrue(sleepTime <= 1100,
      "SleepTime " + sleepTime + " expected < 1100");
    Assert.IsTrue(wakeup.executed, "Command Executed");
  }
}
```

Let's look at this test case more closely. The constructor of the `SleepCommand` contains three arguments. The first is the delay time, in milliseconds. The second is the `ActiveObjectEngine` that the command will be running in. Finally, there is another command object called `wakeup`. The intent is that the `SleepCommand` will wait for the specified number of milliseconds and will then execute the `wakeup` command.

Listing 21-5 shows the implementation of `SleepCommand`. On execution, `SleepCommand` checks whether it has been executed previously. If not, it records the start time. If the delay time has not passed, it puts itself back in the `ActiveObjectEngine`. If the delay time has passed, it puts the `wakeup` command into the `ActiveObjectEngine`.

Listing 21-5

SleepCommand.cs

```
using System;

public class SleepCommand : Command
{
  private Command wakeupCommand = null;
  private ActiveObjectEngine engine = null;
  private long sleepTime = 0;
  private DateTime startTime;
  private bool started = false;

  public SleepCommand(long milliseconds, ActiveObjectEngine e,
                      Command wakeupCommand)
```

Listing 21-5 (Continued)
SleepCommand.cs

```
  {
    sleepTime = milliseconds;
    engine = e;
    this.wakeupCommand = wakeupCommand;
  }

  public void Execute()
  {
    DateTime currentTime = DateTime.Now;
    if (!started)
    {
      started = true;
      startTime = currentTime;
      engine.AddCommand(this);
    }
    else
    {
      TimeSpan elapsedTime = currentTime - startTime;
      if (elapsedTime.TotalMilliseconds < sleepTime)
      {
        engine.AddCommand(this);
      }
      else
      {
        engine.AddCommand(wakeupCommand);
      }
    }
  }
}
```

We can draw an analogy between this program and a multithreaded program that is waiting for an event. When a thread in a multithreaded program waits for an event, the thread usually invokes an operating system call that blocks the thread until the event has occurred. The program in Listing 21-5 does not block. Instead, if the event it is waiting for (elapsedTime.TotalMilliseconds < sleepTime) has not occurred, the thread simply puts itself back into the ActiveObjectEngine.

Building multithreaded systems using variations of this technique has been, and will continue to be, a very common practice. Threads of this kind have been known as *run-to-completion* tasks (RTC); each Command instance runs to completion before the next Command instance can run. The name RTC implies that the Command instances do not block.

The fact that the Command instances all run to completion gives RTC threads the interesting advantage that they all share the same runtime stack. Unlike the threads in a traditional multithreaded system, it is not necessary to define or allocate a separate runtime stack for each RTC thread. This can be a powerful advantage in memory-constrained systems with many threads.

Continuing our example, Listing 21-6 shows a simple program that makes use of SleepCommand and exhibits multithreaded behavior. This program is called Delayed-Typer.

Listing 21-6
DelayedTyper.cs

```
using System;

public class DelayedTyper : Command
{
  private long itsDelay;
  private char itsChar;
  private static bool stop = false;
  private static ActiveObjectEngine engine =
    new ActiveObjectEngine();

  private class StopCommand : Command
  {
    public void Execute()
    {
      DelayedTyper.stop = true;
    }
  }

  public static void Main(string[] args)
  {
    engine.AddCommand(new DelayedTyper(100, '1'));
    engine.AddCommand(new DelayedTyper(300, '3'));
    engine.AddCommand(new DelayedTyper(500, '5'));
    engine.AddCommand(new DelayedTyper(700, '7'));

    Command stopCommand = new StopCommand();

    engine.AddCommand(
      new SleepCommand(20000, engine, stopCommand));
    engine.Run();
  }

  public DelayedTyper(long delay, char c)
  {
    itsDelay = delay;
    itsChar = c;
  }

  public void Execute()
  {
    Console.Write(itsChar);
    if (!stop)
      DelayAndRepeat();
  }

  private void DelayAndRepeat()
  {
    engine.AddCommand(
      new SleepCommand(itsDelay, engine, this));
  }
}
```

Note that `DelayedTyper` implements `Command`. The `Execute` method simply prints a character that was passed at construction, checks the `stop` flag and, if not set, invokes `DelayAndRepeat`. The `DelayAndRepeat` constructs a `SleepCommand`, using the delay that was passed in at construction, and then inserts the `SleepCommand` into the `ActiveObjectEngine`.

The behavior of this `Command` is easy to predict. In effect, it hangs in a loop, repeatedly typing a specified character and waiting for a specified delay. It exits the loop when the `stop` flag is set.

The Main program of `DelayedTyper` starts several `DelayedTyper` instances going in the `ActiveObjectEngine`, each with its own character and delay, and then invokes a `SleepCommand` that will set the `stop` flag after a while. Running this program produces a simple string of 1s, 3s, 5s, and 7s. Running it again produces a similar but different string. Here are two typical runs:

```
1357113115113711131511317151311131517311113511137115311111357...
1357111315131711131511311713511131151731113151131711351113117...
```

These strings are different because the CPU clock and the real-time clock aren't in perfect sync. This kind of nondeterministic behavior is the hallmark of multithreaded systems.

Nondeterministic behavior is also the source of much woe, anguish, and pain. As anyone who's worked on embedded real-time systems knows, it's tough to debug nondeterministic behavior.

Conclusion

The simplicity of the COMMAND pattern belies its versatility. COMMAND can be used for a wonderful variety of purposes, ranging from database transactions to device control to multithreaded nuclei to GUI do/undo administration.

It has been suggested that the COMMAND pattern breaks the OO paradigm by emphasizing functions over classes. That may be true, but in the real world of the software developer, usefulness trumps theory. The COMMAND pattern can be very useful.

Bibliography

[GOF95] Erich Gamma, Richard Helm, Ralph Johnson, and John Vlissides, *Design Patterns: Elements of Reusable Object-Oriented Software*, Addison-Wesley, 1995

[Lavender96] R. G. Lavender and D. C. Schmidt, "Active Object: An Object Behavioral Pattern for Concurrent Programming," in J. O. Coplien, J. Vlissides, and N. Kerth, eds. *Pattern Languages of Program Design*, Addison-Wesley, 1996.

22

TEMPLATE METHOD and STRATEGY: Inheritance versus Delegation

© Jennifer M. Kohnke

The best strategy in life is diligence.

—Chinese proverb

In the early 1990s—in the early days of OO—we were all quite taken with the notion of inheritance. The implications of the relationship were profound. With inheritance, we could *program by difference!* That is, given a class that did something almost useful to us, we could create a subclass and change only the bits we didn't like. We could reuse code simply by inheriting it! We could establish whole taxonomies of software structures, each level of which reused code from the levels above. It was a brave new world.

Like most brave new worlds, this one turned out to be a bit too starry-eyed. By 1995, it was clear that inheritance was very easy to overuse and that overuse of inheritance was very costly. Gamma, Helm, Johnson, and Vlissides went so far as to stress: *"Favor object composition over class inheritance."*[1] So we cut back on our use of inheritance, often replacing it with composition or delegation.

This chapter is the story of two patterns that epitomize the difference between inheritance and delegation. TEMPLATE METHOD and STRATEGY solve similar problems and can often be used interchangeably. However, TEMPLATE METHOD uses inheritance to solve the problem, whereas STRATEGY uses delegation.

Both TEMPLATE METHOD and STRATEGY solve the problem of separating a generic algorithm from a detailed context. We frequently see the need for this in software design. We have an algorithm that is generically applicable. In order to conform to the Dependency-Inversion Principle (DIP), we want to make sure that the generic algorithm does not depend on the detailed implementation. Rather, we want the generic algorithm and the detailed implementation to depend on abstractions.

TEMPLATE METHOD

Consider all the programs you have written. Many probably have this fundamental `main loop` structure:

```
Initialize();
while (!Done()) // main loop
{
  Idle();        // do something useful.
}
Cleanup();
```

First, we initialize the application. Then we enter the `main loop`, where we do whatever the program needs to do. We might process GUI events or perhaps database records. Finally, once we are done, we exit the `main loop` and clean up before we exit.

This structure is so common that we can capture it in a class named `Application`. Then we can reuse that class for every new program we want to write. Think of it! We never have to write that loop again![2]

---

1. [GOF95], p. 20
2. I've also got this bridge I'd like to sell you.

For example, consider Listing 22-1. Here, we see all the elements of the standard program. The TextReader and TextWriter are initialized. A Main loop reads Fahrenheit
readings from the Console.In and prints out Celsius conversions. At the end, an exit
message is printed.

Listing 22-1

FtoCRaw.cs

```csharp
using System;
using System.IO;

public class FtoCRaw
{
  public static void Main(string[] args)
  {
    bool done = false;
    while (!done)
    {
      string fahrString = Console.In.ReadLine();
      if (fahrString == null || fahrString.Length == 0)
        done = true;
      else
      {
        double fahr = Double.Parse(fahrString);
        double celcius = 5.0/9.0*(fahr - 32);
        Console.Out.WriteLine("F={0}, C={1}",fahr,celcius);
      }
    }
    Console.Out.WriteLine("ftoc exit");
  }
}
```

This program has all the elements of the preceding main loop structure. It does a little
initialization, does its work in a Main loop, and then cleans up and exits.

We can separate this fundamental structure from the ftoc program by using the
TEMPLATE METHOD pattern. This pattern places all the generic code into an implemented
method of an abstract base class. The implemented method captures the generic algorithm
but defers all details to abstract methods of the base class.

So, for example, we can capture the main loop structure in an abstract base class
called Application. See Listing 22-2.

Listing 22-2

Application.cs

```csharp
public abstract class Application
{
  private bool isDone = false;

  protected abstract void Init();
  protected abstract void Idle();
  protected abstract void Cleanup();
```

Listing 22-2 (Continued)
Application.cs

```
  protected void SetDone()
  {
    isDone = true;
  }

  protected bool Done()
  {
    return isDone;
  }

  public void Run()
  {
    Init();
    while (!Done())
      Idle();
    Cleanup();
  }
}
```

This class describes a generic main-loop application. We can see the main loop in the implemented Run function. We can also see that all the work is being deferred to the abstract methods Init, Idle, and Cleanup. The Init method takes care of any initialization we need done. The Idle method does the main work of the program and will be called repeatedly until SetDone is called. The Cleanup method does whatever needs to be done before we exit.

We can rewrite the ftoc class by inheriting from Application and simply filling in the abstract methods. Listing 22-3 show what this looks like.

Listing 22-3
FtoCTemplateMethod.cs

```
using System;
using System.IO;

public class FtoCTemplateMethod : Application
{
  private TextReader input;
  private TextWriter output;

  public static void Main(string[] args)
  {
    new FtoCTemplateMethod().Run();
  }

  protected override void Init()
  {
    input = Console.In;
    output = Console.Out;
  }
```

Listing 22-3 (Continued)
FtoCTemplateMethod.cs

```
protected override void Idle()
{
  string fahrString = input.ReadLine();
  if (fahrString == null || fahrString.Length == 0)
    SetDone();
  else
  {
    double fahr = Double.Parse(fahrString);
    double celcius = 5.0/9.0*(fahr - 32);
    output.WriteLine("F={0}, C={1}", fahr, celcius);
  }
}

protected override void Cleanup()
{
  output.WriteLine("ftoc exit");
}
}
```

It's easy to see how the old `ftoc` application has been fit into the TEMPLATE METHOD pattern.

Pattern Abuse

By this time, you should be thinking *"Is he serious? Does he really expect me to use this `Application` class for all new apps? It hasn't bought me anything, and it's overcomplicated the problem."*

Er..., Yeah.. :^(

I chose the example because it was simple and provided a good platform for showing the mechanics of TEMPLATE METHOD. On the other hand, I don't really recommend building `ftoc` like this.

This is a good example of pattern abuse. Using TEMPLATE METHOD for this particular application is ridiculous. It complicates the program and makes it bigger. Encapsulating the main loop of every application in the universe sounded wonderful when we started, but the practical application is fruitless in this case.

Design patterns are wonderful things. They can help you with many design problems. But the fact that they exist does not mean that they should always be used. In this case, TEMPLATE METHOD was applicable to the problem, but its use was not advisable. The cost of the pattern was higher than the benefit it yielded.

Bubble Sort

So let's look at a slightly more useful example. See Listing 22-4. Note that like Application, Bubble Sort is easy to understand, and so makes a useful teaching tool. However, no one in their right mind would ever use Bubble Sort if they had any significant amount of sorting to do. There are *much* better algorithms.

Listing 22-4

BubbleSorter.cs

```csharp
public class BubbleSorter
{
  static int operations = 0;
  public static int Sort(int [] array)
  {
    operations = 0;
    if (array.Length <= 1)
      return operations;

    for (int nextToLast = array.Length-2;
      nextToLast >= 0; nextToLast--)
      for (int index = 0; index <= nextToLast; index++)
        CompareAndSwap(array, index);

    return operations;
  }

  private static void Swap(int[] array, int index)
  {
    int temp = array[index];
    array[index] = array[index+1];
    array[index+1] = temp;
  }

  private static void CompareAndSwap(int[] array, int index)
  {
    if (array[index] > array[index+1])
      Swap(array, index);
    operations++;
  }
}
```

The BubbleSorter class knows how to sort an array of integers, using the bubble sort algorithm. The Sort method of BubbleSorter contains the algorithm that knows how to do a bubble sort. The two ancillary methods—Swap and CompareAndSwap—deal with the details of integers and arrays and handle the mechanics that the Sort algorithm requires.

Using the TEMPLATE METHOD pattern, we can separate the bubble sort algorithm out into an abstract base class named BubbleSorter. BubbleSorter contains a Sort function implementation that calls an abstract method named OutOfOrder and another called Swap. The OutOfOrder method compares two adjacent elements in the array and returns true if the elements are out of order. The Swap method swaps two adjacent cells in the array.

The Sort method does not know about the array; nor does it care what kinds of objects are stored in the array. It simply calls OutOfOrder for various indices into the array and determines whether those indices should be swapped. See Listing 22-5.

Listing 22-5

BubbleSorter.cs

```
public abstract class BubbleSorter
{
  private int operations = 0;
  protected int length = 0;

  protected int DoSort()
  {
    operations = 0;
    if (length <= 1)
      return operations;

    for (int nextToLast = length-2;
      nextToLast >= 0; nextToLast--)
      for (int index = 0; index <= nextToLast; index++)
      {
        if (OutOfOrder(index))
          Swap(index);
        operations++;
      }

    return operations;
  }

  protected abstract void Swap(int index);
  protected abstract bool OutOfOrder(int index);
}
```

Given BubbleSorter, we can now create simple derivatives that can sort any different kind of object. For example, we could create IntBubbleSorter, which sorts arrays of integers, and DoubleBubbleSorter, which sorts arrays of doubles. See Figure 22-1 and Listings 22-6, and 22-7.

The TEMPLATE METHOD pattern shows one of the classic forms of reuse in object-oriented programming. Generic algorithms are placed in the base class and inherited into different detailed contexts. But this technique is not without its costs. Inheritance is a very strong relationship. Derivatives are inextricably bound to their base classes.

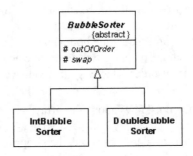

Figure 22-1
Bubble sorter structure

Listing 22-6

IntBubbleSorter.cs

```csharp
public class IntBubbleSorter : BubbleSorter
{
  private int[] array = null;

  public int Sort(int[] theArray)
  {
    array = theArray;
    length = array.Length;
    return DoSort();
  }

  protected override void Swap(int index)
  {
    int temp = array[index];
    array[index] = array[index + 1];
    array[index + 1] = temp;
  }

  protected override bool OutOfOrder(int index)
  {
    return (array[index] > array[index + 1]);
  }
}
```

Listing 22-7

DoubleBubbleSorter.cs

```csharp
public class DoubleBubbleSorter : BubbleSorter
{
  private double[] array = null;

  public int Sort(double[] theArray)
  {
    array = theArray;
    length = array.Length;
    return DoSort();
  }
```

Listing 22-7 (Continued)

`DoubleBubbleSorter.cs`

```
  protected override void Swap(int index)
  {
    double temp = array[index];
    array[index] = array[index + 1];
    array[index + 1] = temp;
  }

  protected override bool OutOfOrder(int index)
  {
    return (array[index] > array[index + 1]);
  }
}
```

For example, the `OutOfOrder` and `Swap` functions of `IntBubbleSorter` are exactly what are needed for other kinds of sort algorithms. But there is no way to reuse `OutOfOrder` and `Swap` in those other sort algorithms. By inheriting `BubbleSorter`, we have doomed `IntBubbleSorter` to be forever bound to `BubbleSorter`. The STRATEGY pattern provides another option.

STRATEGY

The STRATEGY pattern solves the problem of inverting the dependencies of the generic algorithm and the detailed implementation in a very different way. Consider once again the pattern-abusing `Application` problem.

Rather than placing the generic application algorithm into an abstract base class, we place it into a *concrete* class named `ApplicationRunner`. We define the abstract methods that the generic algorithm must call within an interface named `Application`. We derive `FtoCStrategy` from this interface and pass it into the `ApplicationRunner`. `ApplicationRunner` then delegates to this interface. See Figure 22-2 and Listings 22-8 through 22-10.

It should be clear that this structure has both benefits and costs over the TEMPLATE METHOD structure. STRATEGY involves more total classes and more indirection than TEMPLATE METHOD. The delegation pointer within `ApplicationRunner` incurs a slightly higher cost in terms of runtime and data space than inheritance would. On the other hand, if we had many different applications to run, we could reuse the `ApplicationRunner` *instance* and pass in many different implementations of `Application`, thereby reducing the code space overhead.

None of these costs and benefits are overriding. In most cases, none of them matters in the slightest. In the typical case, the most worrisome is the extra class needed by the STRATEGY pattern. However, there is more to consider.

Consider an implementation of the bubble sort that uses the STRATEGY pattern. See Listings 22-11 through 22-13.

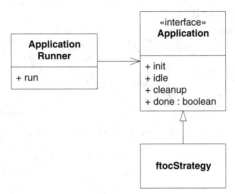

Figure 22-2
STRATEGY structure of the Application algorithm

Listing 22-8

ApplicationRunner.cs

```
public class ApplicationRunner
{
  private Application itsApplication = null;

  public ApplicationRunner(Application app)
  {
    itsApplication = app;
  }
  public void run()
  {
    itsApplication.Init();
    while (!itsApplication.Done())
      itsApplication.Idle();
    itsApplication.Cleanup();
  }
}
```

Listing 22-9

Application.cs

```
public interface Application
{
  void Init();
  void Idle();
  void Cleanup();
  bool Done();
}
```

Listing 22-10

FtoCStrategy.cs

```
using System;
using System.IO;
```

Listing 22-10 (Continued)

FtoCStrategy.cs

```
public class FtoCStrategy : Application
{
  private TextReader input;
  private TextWriter output;
  private bool isDone = false;

  public static void Main(string[] args)
  {
    (new ApplicationRunner(new FtoCStrategy())).run();
  }

  public void Init()
  {
    input = Console.In;
    output = Console.Out;
  }

  public void Idle()
  {
    string fahrString = input.ReadLine();
    if (fahrString == null || fahrString.Length == 0)
      isDone = true;
    else
    {
      double fahr = Double.Parse(fahrString);
      double celcius = 5.0/9.0*(fahr - 32);
      output.WriteLine("F={0}, C={1}", fahr, celcius);
    }
  }

  public void Cleanup()
  {
    output.WriteLine("ftoc exit");
  }

  public bool Done()
  {
    return isDone;
  }
}
```

Listing 22-11

BubbleSorter.cs

```
public class BubbleSorter
{
  private int operations = 0;
  private int length = 0;
  private SortHandler itsSortHandler = null;

  public BubbleSorter(SortHandler handler)
  {
    itsSortHandler = handler;
  }
```

Listing 22-11 (Continued)

BubbleSorter.cs

```csharp
public int Sort(object array)
{
  itsSortHandler.SetArray(array);
  length = itsSortHandler.Length();
  operations = 0;
  if (length <= 1)
    return operations;

  for (int nextToLast = length - 2;
    nextToLast >= 0; nextToLast--)
    for (int index = 0; index <= nextToLast; index++)
    {
      if (itsSortHandler.OutOfOrder(index))
        itsSortHandler.Swap(index);
      operations++;
    }

  return operations;
}
```

Listing 22-12

SortHandler.cs

```csharp
public interface SortHandler
{
  void Swap(int index);
  bool OutOfOrder(int index);
  int Length();
  void SetArray(object array);
}
```

Listing 22-13

IntSortHandler.cs

```csharp
public class IntSortHandler : SortHandler
{
  private int[] array = null;

  public void Swap(int index)
  {
    int temp = array[index];
    array[index] = array[index + 1];
    array[index + 1] = temp;
  }

  public void SetArray(object array)
  {
    this.array = (int[]) array;
  }

  public int Length()
```

Listing 22-13 (Continued)
`IntSortHandler.cs`

```
  {
    return array.Length;
  }

  public bool OutOfOrder(int index)
  {
    return (array[index] > array[index + 1]);
  }
}
```

Note that the `IntSortHandler` class knows nothing whatever of the `BubbleSorter`, having no dependency whatever on the bubble sort implementation. This is not the case with the TEMPLATE METHOD pattern. Look back at Listing 22-6, and you can see that the `IntBubbleSorter` depended directly on `BubbleSorter`, the class that contains the bubble sort algorithm.

The TEMPLATE METHOD approach partially violates DIP. The implementation of the `Swap` and `OutOfOrder` methods depends directly on the bubble sort algorithm. The STRATEGY approach contains no such dependency. Thus, we can use the `IntSortHandler` with `Sorter` implementations other than `BubbleSorter`.

For example, we can create a variation of the bubble sort that terminates early if a pass through the array finds it in order. (See Figure 22-14.) `QuickBubbleSorter` can also use `IntSortHandler` or any other class derived from `SortHandler`.

Listing 22-14
`QuickBubbleSorter.cs`

```
public class QuickBubbleSorter
{
  private int operations = 0;
  private int length = 0;
  private SortHandler itsSortHandler = null;

  public QuickBubbleSorter(SortHandler handler)
  {
    itsSortHandler = handler;
  }

  public int Sort(object array)
  {
    itsSortHandler.SetArray(array);
    length = itsSortHandler.Length();
    operations = 0;
    if (length <= 1)
      return operations;

    bool thisPassInOrder = false;
    for (int nextToLast = length-2;
      nextToLast >= 0 && !thisPassInOrder; nextToLast--)
```

```
┌──────────────────────────────────────────────────────────┐
│ Listing 22-14 (Continued)                                │
│ QuickBubbleSorter.cs                                     │
├──────────────────────────────────────────────────────────┤
      {
        thisPassInOrder = true; //potenially.
        for (int index = 0; index <= nextToLast; index++)
        {
          if (itsSortHandler.OutOfOrder(index))
          {
            itsSortHandler.Swap(index);
            thisPassInOrder = false;
          }
          operations++;
        }
      }

      return operations;
    }
  }
```

Thus, the STRATEGY pattern provides one extra benefit over the TEMPLATE METHOD pattern. Whereas the TEMPLATE METHOD pattern allows a generic algorithm to manipulate many possible detailed implementations, the STRATEGY pattern, by fully conforming to DIP, additionally allows each detailed implementation to be manipulated by many different generic algorithms.

Conclusion

TEMPLATE METHOD is simple to write and simple to use but is also inflexible. STRATEGY is flexible, but you have to create an extra class, instantiate an extra object, and wire the extra object into the system. So the choice between TEMPLATE METHOD and STRATEGY depends on whether you need the flexibility of STRATEGY or can live with the simplicity of TEMPLATE METHOD. Many times, I have opted for TEMPLATE METHOD simply because it is easier to implement and use. For example, I would use the TEMPLATE METHOD solution to the bubble sort problem unless I was very sure that I needed different sort algorithms.

Bibliography

[GOF95] Erich Gamma, Richard Helm, Ralph Johnson, and John Vlissides, *Design Patterns: Elements of Reusable Object-Oriented Software*, Addison-Wesley, 1995.

[PLOPD3] Robert C. Martin, Dirk Riehle, and Frank Buschmann, eds. *Pattern Languages of Program Design 3*, Addison-Wesley, 1998.

23

FACADE and MEDIATOR

© Jennifer M. Kohnke

Symbolism erects a facade of respectability to hide the indecency of dreams.

—Mason Cooley

The two patterns discussed in this chapter have a common purpose: imposing some kind of policy on another group of objects. FACADE imposes policy from above; MEDIATOR, from below. The use of FACADE is visible and constraining; that of MEDIATOR, invisible and enabling.

FACADE

The FACADE pattern is used when you want to provide a simple and specific interface onto a group of objects that have a complex and general interface. Consider, for example, DB.cs in Listing 34-9. This class imposes a very simple interface, specific to

ProductData, on the complex and general interfaces of the classes within the System.Data namespace. Figure 23-1 shows the structure.

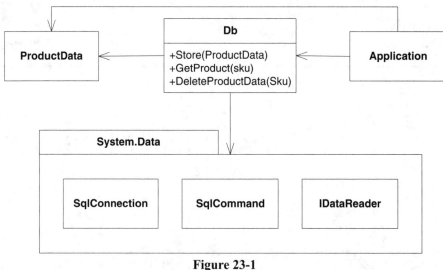

Figure 23-1
The DB FACADE

Notice that the DB class protects the Application from needing to know the intimacies of the System.Data namespace. The class hides all the generality and complexity of System.Data behind a very simple and specific interface.

A FACADE like DB imposes a lot of policy on the usage of System.Data, knowing how to initialize and close the database connection, translate the members of ProductData into database fields and back, and build the appropriate queries and commands to manipulate the database. All that complexity is hidden from users. From the point of view of the Application, System.Data does not exist; it is hidden behind the FACADE.

The use of the FACADE pattern implies that the developers have adopted the convention that all database calls must go through DB. If any part of the Application code goes straight to System.Data rather than through the FACADE, that convention is violated. As such, the FACADE imposes its polices on the application. By convention, DB has become the sole broker of the facilities of System.Data.

FACADE can be used to hide any aspect of a program. However, using FACADE to hide the database has become so common, the pattern is also known as TABLE DATA GATEWAY.

MEDIATOR

The MEDIATOR pattern also imposes policy. However, whereas FACADE imposes its policy in a visible and constraining way, MEDIATOR imposes its policies in a hidden and unconstraining way. For example, the `QuickEntryMediator` class in Listing 23-1 sits quietly behind the scenes and binds a text-entry field to a list. When you type in the text-entry field, the first list element that matches what you have typed is highlighted. This lets you type abbreviations and quickly select a list item.

Listing 23-1

QuickEntryMediator.cs

```
using System;
using System.Windows.Forms;

/// <summary>
/// QuickEntryMediator.  This class takes a TextBox and a
/// ListBox. It assumes that the user will type
/// characters into the TextBox that are prefixes of
/// entries in the ListBox.  It automatically selects the
/// first item in the ListBox that matches the current
/// prefix in the TextBox.
///
/// If the TextField is null, or the prefix does not
/// match any element in the ListBox, then the ListBox
/// selection is cleared.
///
/// There are no methods to call for this object.  You
/// simply create it, and forget it.  (But don't let it
/// be garbage collected...)
///
/// Example:
///
/// TextBox t = new TextBox();
/// ListBox l = new ListBox();
///
/// QuickEntryMediator qem = new QuickEntryMediator(t,l);
///   // that's all folks.
///
/// Originally written in Java
/// by Robert C. Martin, Robert S. Koss
/// on 30 Jun, 1999 2113 (SLAC)
/// Translated to C# by Micah Martin
/// on May 23, 2005 (On the Train)
/// </summary>
public class QuickEntryMediator
{
  private TextBox itsTextBox;
  private ListBox itsList;

  public QuickEntryMediator(TextBox t, ListBox l)
  {
    itsTextBox = t;
    itsList = l;
```

Listing 23-1 (Continued)
QuickEntryMediator.cs

```
        itsTextBox.TextChanged += new EventHandler(TextFieldChanged);
    }

    private void
      TextFieldChanged(object source, EventArgs args)
    {
      string prefix = itsTextBox.Text;

      if (prefix.Length == 0)
      {
        itsList.ClearSelected();
        return;
      }

      ListBox.ObjectCollection listItems = itsList.Items;
      bool found = false;
      for (int i = 0; found == false &&
              i < listItems.Count; i++)
      {
        Object o = listItems[i];
        String s = o.ToString();
        if (s.StartsWith(prefix))
        {
          itsList.SetSelected(i, true);
          found = true;
        }
      }

      if (!found)
      {
        itsList.ClearSelected();
      }
    }
  }
}
```

The structure of the QuickEntryMediator is shown in Figure 23-2. An instance of QuickEntryMediator is constructed with a ListBox and a TextBox. The Quick-EntryMediator registers an EventHandler with the TextBox. This EventHandler invokes the TextFieldChanged method whenever there is a change in the text. This method then finds a ListBox element that is prefixed by the text and selects it.

The users of the ListBox and TextField have no idea that this MEDIATOR exists. It quietly sits there, imposing its policy on those objects without their permission or knowledge.

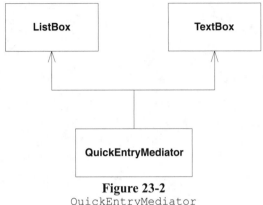

Figure 23-2
QuickEntryMediator

Conclusion

Imposing policy can be done from above, using FACADE, if that policy needs to be big and visible. On the other hand, if subtlety and discretion are needed, MEDIATOR may be the more appropriate choice. FACADES are usually the focal point of a convention. Everyone agrees to use the FACADE instead of the objects beneath it. MEDIATOR, on the other hand, is hidden from the users. Its policy is a fait accompli rather than a matter of convention.

Bibliography

[Fowler03] Martin Fowler, *Patterns of Enterprise Application Architecture*, Addison-Wesley, 2003.

[GOF95] Erich Gamma, Richard Helm, Ralph Johnson, and John Vlissides, *Design Patterns: Elements of Reusable Object-Oriented Software*, Addison-Wesley, 1995.

24

SINGLETON and MONOSTATE

© Jennifer M. Kohnke

Infinite beatitude of existence! It is; and there is none else beside It.

— Edwin A. Abbott, Flatland (1884)

Usually, there is a one-to-many relationship between classes and instances. You can create many instances of most classes. The instances are created when they are needed and are disposed of when their usefulness ends. They come and go in a flow of memory allocations and deallocations.

But some classes should have only one instance. That instance should appear to have come into existence when the program started and should be disposed of only when the program ends. Such objects are sometimes the roots of the application. From the roots, you can find your way to many other objects in the system. Sometimes, these objects are factories, which you can use to create the other objects in the system. Sometimes, these objects are managers, responsible for keeping track of certain other objects and driving them through their paces.

Whatever these objects are, it is a severe logic failure if more than one of them is created. If more than one root is created, access to objects in the application may depend on a chosen root. Programmers, not knowing that more than one root exists, may find themselves looking at a subset of the application objects without knowing it. If more than one factory exists, clerical control over the created objects may be compromised. If more than one manager exists, activities that were intended to be serial may become concurrent.

It may seem that mechanisms to enforce the singularity of these objects is overkill. After all, when you initialize the application, you can simply create one of each and be done with it.[1] In fact, this is usually the best course of action. Such a mechanism should be avoided when there is no immediate and significant need. However, we also want our code to communicate our intent. If the mechanism for enforcing singularity is trivial, the benefit of communication may outweigh the cost of the mechanism.

This chapter is about two patterns that enforce singularity. These patterns have very different cost/benefit trade-offs. In most contexts, their cost is low enough to more than balance the benefit of their expressiveness.

SINGLETON

SINGLETON is a very simple pattern.[2] The test case in Listing 24-1 shows how it should work. The first test function shows that the `Singleton` instance is accessed through the `public static` method `Instance` and that if `Instance` is called multiple times, a reference to the exact same instance is returned each time. The second test case shows that the `Singleton` class has no `public` constructors, so there is no way for anyone to create an instance without using the `Instance` method.

Listing 24-1

Singleton test case

```
using System;
using System.Reflection;
using NUnit.Framework;

[TestFixture]
public class TestSimpleSingleton
```

---

1. I call this the JUST CREATE ONE pattern.

2. [GOF95], p. 127

Listing 24-1 (Continued)
Singleton test case

```
{
  [Test]
  public void TestCreateSingleton()
  {
    Singleton s = Singleton.Instance;
    Singleton s2 = Singleton.Instance;
    Assert.AreSame(s, s2);
  }

  [Test]
  public void TestNoPublicConstructors()
  {
    Type singleton = typeof(Singleton);
    ConstructorInfo[] ctrs = singleton.GetConstructors();
    bool hasPublicConstructor = false;
    foreach(ConstructorInfo c in ctrs)
    {
      if(c.IsPublic)
      {
        hasPublicConstructor = true;
        break;
      }
    }
    Assert.IsFalse(hasPublicConstructor);
  }
}
```

This test case is a specification for the SINGLETON pattern and leads directly to the code shown in Listing 24-2. By inspecting this code, it should be clear that there can never be more than one instance of the Singleton class within the scope of the static variable Singleton.theInstance.

Listing 24-2
Singleton implementation

```
public class Singleton
{
  private static Singleton theInstance = null;
  private Singleton() {}

  public static Singleton Instance
  {
    get
    {
      if (theInstance == null)
        theInstance = new Singleton();
      return theInstance;
    }
  }
}
```

Benefits

- *Cross-platform:* Using appropriate middleware (e.g., Remoting), SINGLETON can be extended to work across many CLRs (Common Language Runtime) and many computers.

- *Applicable to any class:* You can change any class into a SINGLETON simply by making its constructors `private` and adding the appropriate `static` functions and variable.

- *Can be created through derivation:* Given a class, you can create a subclass that is a SINGLETON.

- *Lazy evaluation:* If the SINGLETON is never used, it is never created.

Costs

- *Destruction undefined:* There is no good way to destroy or decommission a SINGLETON. If you add a `decommission` method that nulls out `theInstance`, other modules in the system may still be holding a reference to the SINGLETON. Subsequent calls to `Instance` will cause another instance to be created, causing two concurrent instances to exist. This problem is particularly acute in C++, in which the instance *can be destroyed*, leading to possible dereferencing of a destroyed object.

- *Not inherited:* A class derived from a SINGLETON is not a SINGLETON. If it needs to be a SINGLETON, the `static` function and variable need to be added to it.

- *Efficiency:* Each call to `Instance` invokes the `if` statement. For most of those calls, the `if` statement is useless.

- *Nontransparent:* Users of a SINGLETON know that they are using it, because they must invoke the `Instance` method.

SINGLETON in Action

Assume that we have a Web-based system that allows users to log in to secure areas of a Web server. Such a system will have a database containing user names, passwords, and other user attributes. Assume further that the database is accessed through a third-party API. We could access the database directly in every module that needed to read and write a user. However, this would scatter usage of the third-party API throughout the code and would leave us no place to enforce access or structure conventions.

A better solution is to use the FACADE pattern and create a `UserDatabase` class that provides methods for reading and writing `User` objects.[3] These methods access the

---

3. This special form of the FACADE pattern is known as a GATEWAY. For a detailed discussion of GATEWAYs, see [Fowler03].

third-party API of the database, translating between User objects and the tables and rows of the database. Within the UserDatabase, we can enforce conventions of structure and access. For example, we can guarantee that no User record gets written unless it has a nonblank username. Or, we can serialize access to a User record, making sure that two modules cannot simultaneously read and write it.

The code in Listings 24-3 and 24-4 show a SINGLETON solution. The SINGLETON class is named UserDatabaseSource and implements the UserDatabase interface. Note that the static Instance() method does not have the traditional if statement to protect against multiple creations. Instead, it takes advantage of the .NET initialization facility.

Listing 24-3

UserDatabase interface

```
public interface UserDatabase
{
  User ReadUser(string userName);
  void WriteUser(User user);
}
```

Listing 24-4

UserDatabase Singleton

```
public class UserDatabaseSource : UserDatabase
{
  private static UserDatabase theInstance =
    new UserDatabaseSource();

  public static UserDatabase Instance
  {
    get
    {
      return theInstance;
    }
  }

  private UserDatabaseSource()
  {
  }

  public User ReadUser(string userName)
  {
    // Some Implementation
  }

  public void WriteUser(User user)
  {
    // Some Implementation
  }
}
```

This is an extremely common use of the SINGLETON pattern. It ensures that all database access will be through a single instance of UserDatabaseSource. This makes it easy to put checks, counters, and locks in `UserDatabaseSource` to enforce the access and structure conventions mentioned earlier.

MONOSTATE

The MONOSTATE pattern is another way to achieve singularity. It works through a completely different mechanism. We can see how that mechanism works by studying the `Monostate` test case in Listing 24-5.

The first test function simply describes an object whose x variable can be set and retrieved. But the second test case shows that two instances of the same class behave *as though they were one.* If you set the x variable on one instance to a particular value, you can retrieve that value by getting the x variable of a different instance. It's as though the two instances are simply different names for the same object.

Listing 24-5

Monostate test fixture

```
using NUnit.Framework;

[TestFixture]
public class TestMonostate
{
  [Test]
  public void TestInstance()
  {
    Monostate m = new Monostate();
    for (int x = 0; x < 10; x++)
    {
      m.X = x;
      Assert.AreEqual(x, m.X);
    }
  }

  [Test]
  public void TestInstancesBehaveAsOne()
  {
    Monostate m1 = new Monostate();
    Monostate m2 = new Monostate();

    for (int x = 0; x < 10; x++)
    {
      m1.X = x;
      Assert.AreEqual(x, m2.X);
    }
  }
}
```

If we were to plug the `Singleton` class into this test case and replace all the `new Monostate` statements with calls to `Singleton.Instance`, the test case should still pass. So this test case describes the *behavior* of `Singleton` without imposing the constraint of a single instance!

How can two instances behave as though they were a single object? Quite simply, it means that the two objects must share the same variables. This is easily achieved by making all the variables `static`. Listing 24-6 shows the `Monostate` implementation that passes the preceding test case. Note that the `itsX` variable is `static` but that *none of the methods are*. This is important, as we'll see later.

Listing 24-6

Monostate implementation

```
public class Monostate
{
  private static int itsX;

  public int X
  {
    get { return itsX; }
    set { itsX = value; }
  }
}
```

I find this to be a delightfully twisted pattern. No matter how many instances of `Monostate` you create, they all behave as though they were a *single object*. You can even destroy or decommission all the current instances without losing the data.

Note that the difference between the two patterns is one of behavior versus structure. The SINGLETON pattern enforces the structure of singularity, preventing any more than one instance from being created. MONOSTATE, by contrast, enforces the *behavior* of singularity without imposing structural constraints. To underscore this difference, consider that the MONOSTATE test case is valid for the `Singleton` class but that the SINGLETON test case is not even close to being valid for the `Monostate` class.

Benefits

- *Transparency:* Users do not behave differently from users of a regular object. The users do not need to know that the object is monostate.

- *Derivability:* Derivatives of a monostate are monostates. Indeed, all the derivatives of a monostate are part of the *same* monostate. They all share the same static variables.

- *Polymorphism:* Since the methods of a monostate are not static, they can be overridden in a derivative. Thus, different derivatives can offer different behavior over the same set of static variables.

- *Well-defined creation and destruction:* The variables of a monostate, being static, have well-defined creation and destruction times.

Costs

- *No conversion:* A nonmonostate class cannot be converted into a monostate class through derivation.

- *Efficiency:* Because it is a real object, a monostate may go through many creations and destructions. These operations are often costly.

- *Presence:* The variables of a monostate take up space, even if the monostate is never used.

- *Platform local:* You can't make a monostate work across several CLR instances or across several platforms.

MONOSTATE in Action

Consider implementing the simple finite state machine (FSM) for the subway turnstile shown in Figure 24-1. The turnstile begins its life in the Locked state. If a coin is deposited, the turnstile transitions to the Unlocked state and unlocks the gate, resets any alarm state that might be present, and deposits the coin in its collection bin. If a user passes through the gate at this point, the turnstile transitions back to the Locked state and locks the gate.

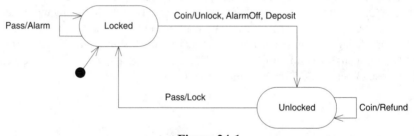

Figure 24-1
Subway turnstile finite state machine

There are two abnormal conditions. If the user deposits two or more coins before passing through the gate, they will be refunded, and the gate will remain unlocked. If the user passes through without paying, an alarm will sound, and the gate will remain locked.

The test program that describes this operation is shown in Listing 24-7. Note that the test methods assume that the Turnstile is a monostate and expects to be able to send events and gather queries from different instances. This makes sense if there will never be more than one instance of the Turnstile.

The implementation of the monostate Turnstile is in Listing 24-8. The base Turnstile class delegates the two event functions, coin and pass, to two derivatives of Turnstile, Locked and Unlocked, that represent the states of the FSM.

Listing 24-7

TurnstileTest

```
using NUnit.Framework;

[TestFixture]
public class TurnstileTest
{
  [SetUp]
  public void SetUp()
  {
    Turnstile t = new Turnstile();
    t.reset();
  }

  [Test]
  public void TestInit()
  {
    Turnstile t = new Turnstile();
    Assert.IsTrue(t.Locked());
    Assert.IsFalse(t.Alarm());
  }

  [Test]
  public void TestCoin()
  {
    Turnstile t = new Turnstile();
    t.Coin();
    Turnstile t1 = new Turnstile();
    Assert.IsFalse(t1.Locked());
    Assert.IsFalse(t1.Alarm());
    Assert.AreEqual(1, t1.Coins);
  }

  [Test]
  public void TestCoinAndPass()
  {
    Turnstile t = new Turnstile();
    t.Coin();
    t.Pass();

    Turnstile t1 = new Turnstile();
    Assert.IsTrue(t1.Locked());
    Assert.IsFalse(t1.Alarm());
    Assert.AreEqual(1, t1.Coins, "coins");
  }

  [Test]
  public void TestTwoCoins()
  {
    Turnstile t = new Turnstile();
    t.Coin();
    t.Coin();

    Turnstile t1 = new Turnstile();
    Assert.IsFalse(t1.Locked(), "unlocked");
    Assert.AreEqual(1, t1.Coins, "coins");
```

Listing 24-7 (Continued)

TurnstileTest

```csharp
      Assert.AreEqual(1, t1.Refunds, "refunds");
      Assert.IsFalse(t1.Alarm());
    }

    [Test]
    public void TestPass()
    {
      Turnstile t = new Turnstile();
      t.Pass();
      Turnstile t1 = new Turnstile();
      Assert.IsTrue(t1.Alarm(), "alarm");
      Assert.IsTrue(t1.Locked(), "locked");
    }

    [Test]
    public void TestCancelAlarm()
    {
      Turnstile t = new Turnstile();
      t.Pass();
      t.Coin();
      Turnstile t1 = new Turnstile();
      Assert.IsFalse(t1.Alarm(), "alarm");
      Assert.IsFalse(t1.Locked(), "locked");
      Assert.AreEqual(1, t1.Coins, "coin");
      Assert.AreEqual(0, t1.Refunds, "refund");
    }

    [Test]
    public void TestTwoOperations()
    {
      Turnstile t = new Turnstile();
      t.Coin();
      t.Pass();
      t.Coin();
      Assert.IsFalse(t.Locked(), "unlocked");
      Assert.AreEqual(2, t.Coins, "coins");
      t.Pass();
      Assert.IsTrue(t.Locked(), "locked");
    }
  }
```

Listing 24-8

Turnstile

```csharp
public class Turnstile
{
  private static bool isLocked = true;
  private static bool isAlarming = false;
  private static int itsCoins = 0;
  private static int itsRefunds = 0;
  protected static readonly
    Turnstile LOCKED = new Locked();
```

Listing 24-8 (Continued)

Turnstile

```
protected static readonly
  Turnstile UNLOCKED = new Unlocked();
protected static Turnstile itsState = LOCKED;

public void reset()
{
  Lock(true);
  Alarm(false);
  itsCoins = 0;
  itsRefunds = 0;
  itsState = LOCKED;
}

public bool Locked()
{
  return isLocked;
}

public bool Alarm()
{
  return isAlarming;
}

public virtual void Coin()
{
  itsState.Coin();
}

public virtual void Pass()
{
  itsState.Pass();
}

protected void Lock(bool shouldLock)
{
  isLocked = shouldLock;
}

protected void Alarm(bool shouldAlarm)
{
  isAlarming = shouldAlarm;
}

public int Coins
{
  get { return itsCoins; }
}

public int Refunds
{
  get { return itsRefunds; }
}
```

Listing 24-8 (Continued)

Turnstile

```
    public void Deposit()
    {
        itsCoins++;
    }

    public void Refund()
    {
        itsRefunds++;
    }
}

internal class Locked : Turnstile
{
    public override void Coin()
    {
        itsState = UNLOCKED;
        Lock(false);
        Alarm(false);
        Deposit();
    }

    public override void Pass()
    {
        Alarm(true);
    }
}

internal class Unlocked : Turnstile
{
    public override void Coin()
    {
        Refund();
    }

    public override void Pass()
    {
        Lock(true);
        itsState = LOCKED;
    }
}
```

This example shows some of the useful features of the MONOSTATE pattern. It takes advantage of the ability for monostate derivatives to be polymorphic and the fact that monostate derivatives are themselves monostates. This example also shows how difficult it can sometimes be to turn a monostate into a nonmonostate. The structure of this solution strongly depends on the monostate nature of Turnstile. If we needed to control more than one turnstile with this FSM, the code would require some significant refactoring.

Perhaps you are concerned about the unconventional use of inheritance in this example. Having Unlocked and Locked derived from Turnstile seems a violation of normal OO principles. However, since Turnstile is a monostate, there are no separate instances of it. Thus, `Unlocked` and `Locked` aren't really separate objects but instead are part of the `Turnstile` abstraction. `Unlocked` and `Locked` have access to the same variables and methods that `Turnstile` does.

Conclusion

It is often necessary to enforce a single instantiation for a particular object. This chapter has shown two very different techniques. SINGLETON makes use of private constructors, a static variable, and a static function to control and limit instantiation. MONOSTATE simply makes all variables of the object static.

SINGLETON is best used when you have an existing class that you want to constrain through derivation and don't mind that everyone will have to call the `Instance()` method to gain access. MONOSTATE is best used when you want the singular nature of the class to be transparent to the users or when you want to use polymorphic derivatives of the single object.

Bibliography

[**Fowler03**] Martin Fowler, *Patterns of Enterprise Application Architecture*, Addison-Wesley, 2003.

[**GOF95**] Erich Gamma, Richard Helm, Ralph Johnson, and John Vlissides, *Design Patterns: Elements of Reusable Object-Oriented Software*, Addison-Wesley, 1995.

[**PLOPD3**] Robert C. Martin, Dirk Riehle, and Frank Buschmann, eds. *Pattern Languages of Program Design 3*, Addison-Wesley, 1998.

NULL OBJECT

Faultily faultless, icily regular, splendidly null, Dead perfection, no more.

—Lord Alfred Tennyson (1809–1892)

Description

Consider the following code:

```
Employee e = DB.GetEmployee("Bob");
if (e != null && e.IsTimeToPay(today))
  e.Pay();
```

We ask the database for an `Employee` object named `"Bob"`. The `DB` object will return `null` if no such object exists. Otherwise, it will return the requested instance of `Employee`. If the employee exists and is owed payment we invoke the `pay` method.

We've all written code like this before. The idiom is common because, in C-based languages, the first expression of the `&&` is evaluated first, and the second is evaluated only if the first is `true`. Most of us have also been burned by forgetting to test for `null`. Common though the idiom may be, it is ugly and error prone.

We can alleviate the tendency toward error by having `DB.GetEmployee` throw an exception instead of returning `null`. However, `try`/`catch` blocks can be even uglier than checking for `null`.

We can address these issues by using the NULL OBJECT pattern.[1] This pattern often eliminates the need to check for `null`, and it can help to simplify the code.

Figure 25-1 shows the structure. `Employee` becomes an interface that has two implementations. `EmployeeImplementation`, the normal implementation, contains all the methods and variables that you would expect an `Employee` object to have. When it finds an employee in the database, `DB.GetEmployee` returns an instance of `Employee-Implementation`. `NullEmployee` is returned only if `DB.GetEmployee` cannot find the employee.

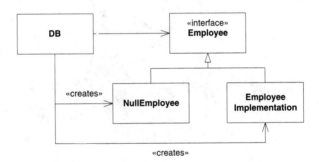

Figure 25-1
NULL OBJECT pattern

`NullEmployee` implements all the methods of `Employee` to do "nothing." What "nothing" is depends on the method. For example, one would expect that `IsTimeToPay` would be implemented to return `false`, since it is never time to pay a `NullEmployee`.

Thus, using this pattern, we can change the original code to look like this:

```
Employee e = DB.GetEmployee("Bob");
if (e.IsTimeToPay(today))
  e.Pay();
```

---

1. [PLOPD3], p. 5. This delightful article is full of wit, irony, and quite practical advice.

This is neither error prone nor ugly. There is a nice consistency to it. DB.Get-Employee *always* returns an instance of Employee. That instance is guaranteed to behave appropriately, regardless of whether the employee was found.

Of course, in many cases, we'll still want to know whether DB.GetEmployee failed to find an employee. This can be accomplished by creating in Employee a static readonly variable that holds the one and only instance of NullEmployee.

Listing 25-1 shows the test case for NullEmployee. In this case, "Bob" does not exist in the database. Note that the test case expects IsTimeToPay to return false. Note also that it expects the employee returned by DB.GetEmployee to be Employee.NULL.

Listing 25-1

EmployeeTest.cs (partial)

```
[Test]
public void TestNull()
{
  Employee e = DB.GetEmployee("Bob");
  if (e.IsTimeToPay(new DateTime()))
    Assert.Fail();
  Assert.AreSame(Employee.NULL, e);
}
```

The DB class is shown in Listing 25-2. Note that, for the purposes of our test, the GetEmployee method simply returns Employee.NULL.

Listing 25-2

DB.cs

```
public class DB
{
  public static Employee GetEmployee(string s)
  {
    return Employee.NULL;
  }
}
```

The Employee class is shown in Listing 25-3. Note that this class has a static variable, NULL, that holds the sole instance of the nested implementation of Employee. NullEmployee implements IsTimeToPay to return false and Pay to do nothing.

Listing 25-3

Employee.cs

```
using System;

public abstract class Employee
{
  public abstract bool IsTimeToPay(DateTime time);
  public abstract void Pay();
```

Listing 25-3 (Continued)
Employee.cs

```
  public static readonly Employee NULL =
    new NullEmployee();

  private class NullEmployee : Employee
  {
    public override bool IsTimeToPay(DateTime time)
    {
      return false;
    }

    public override void Pay()
    {
    }
  }
}
```

Making `NullEmployee` a `private` nested class is a way to make sure that there is only a single instance of it. Nobody else can create other instances of the `NullEmployee`. This is a good thing, because we want to be able to say such things as:

```
  if (e == Employee.NULL)
```

This would be unreliable if it were possible to create many instances of the null employee.

Conclusion

Those of us who have been using C-based languages for a long time have grown accustomed to functions that return `null` or `0` on some kind of failure. We presume that the return value from such functions needs to be tested. The NULL OBJECT pattern changes this. By using this pattern, we can ensure that functions always return valid objects, even when they fail. Those objects that represent failure do "nothing."

Bibliography

[PLOPD3] Robert C. Martin, Dirk Riehle, and Frank Buschmann, eds. *Pattern Languages of Program Design 3*, Addison-Wesley, 1998.

26

The Payroll Case Study:
Iteration 1

© Jennifer M. Kohnke

Everything which is in any way beautiful is beautiful in itself,
and terminates in itself, not having praise as part of itself.

—Marcus Aurelius, circa A.D. 170

The following case study describes the first iteration in the development of a simple batch payroll system. You will find the user stories in this case study to be simplistic. For example, taxes are simply not mentioned. This is typical of an early iteration. It will provide only a very small part of the business value the customers need.

In this chapter, we do the kind of quick analysis and design session that often takes place at the start of a normal iteration. The customer has selected the stories for the iteration, and now we have to figure out how we are going to implement them. Such design sessions are short and cursory, just like this chapter. The UML diagrams you see here are no more than hasty sketches on a whiteboard. The real design work will take place in the next chapter, when we work through the unit tests and implementations.

Rudimentary Specification

Following are some notes we took while conversing with our customer about the stories that were selected for the first iteration.

- Some employees work by the hour. They are paid an hourly rate that is one of the fields in their employee record. They submit daily time cards that record the date and the number of hours worked. If they work more than 8 hours per day, they are paid 1.5 times their normal rate for those extra hours. They are paid every Friday.

- Some employees are paid a flat salary. They are paid on the last working day of the month. Their monthly salary is one of the fields in their employee record.

- Some of the salaried employees are also paid a commission based on their sales. They submit sales receipts that record the date and the amount of the sale. Their commission rate is a field in their employee record. They are paid every other Friday.

- Employees can select their method of payment. They may have their paychecks mailed to the postal address of their choice, have their paychecks held for pickup by the paymaster, or request that their paychecks be directly deposited into the bank account of their choice.

- Some employees belong to the union. Their employee record has a field for the weekly dues rate. Their dues must be deducted from their pay. Also, the union may assess service charges against individual union members from time to time. These service charges are submitted by the union on a weekly basis and must be deducted from the appropriate employee's next pay amount.

- The payroll application will run once each working day and pay the appropriate employees on that day. The system will be told what date the employees are to be paid to, so it will generate payments for records from the last time the employee was paid up to the specified date.

We could begin by generating the database schema. Clearly, this problem calls for some kind of relational database, and the requirements give us a very good idea of what the tables and fields might be. It would be easy to design a workable schema and then start building some queries. However, this approach will generate an application for which the database is the central concern.

Databases are implementation details! Consideration of the database should be deferred as long as possible. Far too many applications were designed with the database in mind from the beginning and so are inextricably tied to those databases. Remember the definition of abstraction: "the amplification of the essential and the elimination of the irrelevant." At this stage of the project, the database is irrelevant; it is merely a technique used for storing and accessing data, nothing more.

Analysis by Use Cases

Instead of starting with the data of the system, let's start by considering the behavior of the system. After all, it is the system's behavior that we are being paid to create.

One way to capture and analyze the behavior of a system is to create *use cases*. As originally described by Jacobson, use cases are very similar to the notion of user stories in XP.[1] A use case is like a user story that has been elaborated with a little more detail. Such elaboration is appropriate once the user story has been selected for implementation in the current iteration.

When we perform use case analysis, we look to the user stories and acceptance tests to find out the kinds of stimuli that the users of this system provide. Then we try to figure out how the system responds to those stimuli. For example, here are the user stories that our customer has chosen for the next iteration:

1. Add a new employee

2. Delete an employee

3. Post a time card

4. Post a sales receipt

5. Post a union service charge

6. Change employee details (e.g., hourly rate, dues rate, etc.)

7. Run the payroll for today

Let's convert each of these user stories into an elaborated use case. We don't need to go into too much detail: just enough to help us think through the design of the code that fulfills each story.

---

1. [Jacobson92]

Adding Employees

Use Case 1: Add New Employee

A new employee is added by the receipt of an `AddEmp` transaction. This transaction contains the employee's name, address, and assigned employee number. The transaction has three forms:

1. `AddEmp <EmpID> "<name>" "<address>" H <hrly-rate>`

2. `AddEmp <EmpID> "<name>" "<address>" S <mtly-slry>`

3. `AddEmp <EmpID> "<name>" "<address>" C <mtly-slry> <com-rate>`

The employee record is created with its fields assigned appropriately.

Alternative 1: An error in the transaction structure

If the transaction structure is inappropriate, it is printed out in an error message, and no action is taken.

Use case 1 hints at an abstraction. The `AddEmp` transaction has three forms, all of which share the `<EmpID>`, `<name>`, and `<address>` fields. We can use the COMMAND pattern to create an `AddEmployeeTransaction` abstract base class with three derivatives: `AddHourlyEmployeeTransaction`, `AddSalariedEmployeeTransaction`, and `AddCommissionedEmployeeTransaction` (see Figure 26-1).

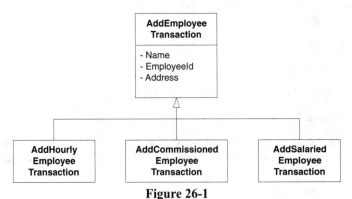

Figure 26-1
`AddEmployeeTransaction` class hierarchy

This structure conforms nicely to the Single-Responsibility Principle (SRP) by splitting each job into its own class. The alternative would be to put all these jobs into a single module. Although doing so might reduce the number of classes in the system and there-fore make the system simpler, it would also concentrate all the transaction-processing code in one place, creating a large and potentially error-prone module.

Use case 1 specifically talks about an employee record, which implies some sort of database. Again. our predisposition to databases may tempt us into thinking about record layouts or the field structure in a relational database table, but we should resist these urges. What the use case is really asking us to do is create an employee. What is the object model of an employee? A better question might be: What do the three transactions create? In my view, they create three kinds of employee objects, mimicking the three kinds of AddEmp transactions. Figure 26-2 shows a possible structure.

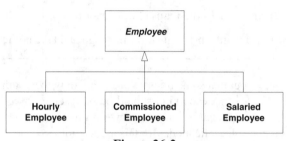

Figure 26-2
Possible Employee class hierarchy

Deleting Employees

Use Case 2: Deleting an Employee

Employees are deleted when a DelEmp transaction is received. The form of this transaction is as follows:

    DelEmp <EmpID>

When this transaction is received, the appropriate employee record is deleted.

Alternative 1: Invalid or unknown EmpID

If the <EmpID> field is not structured correctly or does not refer to a valid employee record, the transaction is printed with an error message, and no other action is taken.

Other than the obvious DeleteEmployeeTransaction class, I'm not getting any partic-ular insight from use case 2. Let's move on.

Posting Time Cards

Use Case 3: Post a `Time Card`

On receipt of a `TimeCard` transaction, the system will create a time card record and associate it with the appropriate employee record.

    `TimeCard <empid> <date> <hours>`

Alternative 1: The selected employee is not hourly

The system will print an appropriate error message and take no further action.

Alternative 2: An error in the transaction structure

The system will print an appropriate error message and take no further action.

This use case points out that some transactions apply only to certain kinds of employees, strengthening the idea that each kind should be represented by different classes. In this case, there is also an association implied between time cards and hourly employees. Figure 26-3 shows a possible static model for this association.

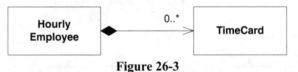

Figure 26-3
Association between `HourlyEmployee` and `TimeCard`

Posting Sales Receipts

Use Case 4: Post a `Sales Receipt`

On receipt of the `SalesReceipt` transaction, the system will create a new sales-receipt record and associate it with the appropriate commissioned employee.

    `SalesReceipt <EmpID> <date> <amount>`

Alternative 1: The selected employee not commissioned

The system will print an appropriate error message and take no further action.

Alternative 2: An error in the transaction structure

The system will print an appropriate error message and take no further action.

This use case is very similar to use case 3 and implies the structure shown in Figure 26-4.

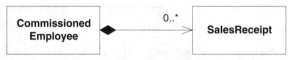

Figure 26-4
Commissioned employees and sales receipts

Posting a Union Service Charge

Use Case 5: Post a Union Service Charge

On receipt of this transaction, the system will create a service-charge record and associate it with the appropriate union member.

    `ServiceCharge <memberID> <amount>`

Alternative 1: Poorly formed transaction

If the transaction is not well formed or if the `<memberID>` does not refer to an existing union member, the transaction is printed with an appropriate error message.

This use case shows that union members are not accessed through employee IDs. The union maintains its own identification numbering scheme for union members. Thus, the system must be able to associate union members and employees. There are many ways to provide this kind of association, so to avoid being arbitrary, let's defer this decision until later. Perhaps constraints from other parts of the system will force our hand one way or another.

One thing is certain. There is a direct association between union members and their service charges. Figure 26-5 shows a possible static model for this association.

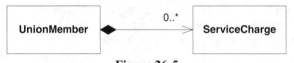

Figure 26-5
Union members and service charges

Changing Employee Details

Use Case 6: Changing Employee Details

Upon receipt of this transaction, the system will alter one of the details of the appropriate employee record. There are several possible variations to this transaction.

ChgEmp <EmpID> Name <name>	Change employee name
ChgEmp <EmpID> Address <address>	Change employee address
ChgEmp <EmpID> Hourly <hourlyRate>	Change to hourly
ChgEmp <EmpID> Salaried <salary>	Change to salaried
ChgEmp <EmpID> Commissioned <salary> <rate>	Change to commissioned
ChgEmp <EmpID> Hold	Hold paycheck
ChgEmp <EmpID> Direct <bank> <account>	Direct deposit
ChgEmp <EmpID> Mail <address>	Mail paycheck
ChgEmp <EmpID> Member <memberID> Dues <rate>	Put employee in union
ChgEmp <EmpID> NoMember	Cut employee from union

Alternative 1: Transaction errors

If the structure of the transaction is improper, <EmpID> does not refer to a real employee, or <memberID> already refers to a member, the system will print a suitable error and take no further action.

This use case is very revealing. It has told us all the employee aspects that must be changeable. The fact that we can change an employee from hourly to salaried means that the diagram in Figure 26-2 is certainly invalid. Instead, it would probably be more appropriate to use the STRATEGY pattern for calculating pay. The Employee class could hold a strategy class named PaymentClassification, as in Figure 26-6. This is an advantage because we can change the PaymentClassification object without changing any other part of the Employee object. When an hourly employee is changed to a salaried employee, the HourlyClassification of the corresponding Employee object is replaced with a SalariedClassification object.

PaymentClassification objects come in three varieties. The HourlyClassification objects maintain the hourly rate and a list of TimeCard objects. The Salaried-Classification objects maintain the monthly salary figure. The Commissioned-Classification objects maintain a monthly salary, a commission rate, and a list of SalesReceipt objects.

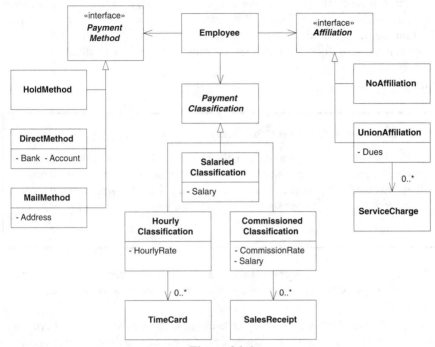

Figure 26-6
Revised class diagram for `Payroll`: the core model

The method of payment must also be changeable. Figure 26-6 implements this idea by using the STRATEGY pattern and deriving three kinds of `PaymentMethod` classes. If the `Employee` object contains a `MailMethod` object, the corresponding employee will have paychecks mailed to the address recorded in the `MailMethod` object. If the `Employee` object contains a `DirectMethod` object, the corresponding employee's pay will be directly deposited into the bank account recorded in the `DirectMethod` object. If the `Employee` contains a `HoldMethod` object, the corresponding employee's paychecks will be sent to the paymaster to be held for pickup.

Finally, Figure 26-6 applies the NULL OBJECT pattern to union membership. Each `Employee` object contains an `Affiliation` object, which has two forms. If the `Employee` contains a `NoAffiliation` object, the corresponding employee's pay is not adjusted by any organization other than the employer. However, if the `Employee` object contains a `UnionAffiliation` object, that employee must pay the dues and service charges that are recorded in that `UnionAffiliation` object.

This use of these patterns makes this system conform well to the Open/Closed Principle (OCP). The `Employee` class is closed against changes in payment method, payment classification, and union affiliation. New methods, classifications, and affiliations can be added to the system without affecting `Employee`.

Figure 26-6 is becoming our *core model*, or architecture. It's at the heart of everything that the payroll system does. There will be many other classes and designs in the payroll application, but they will all be secondary to this fundamental structure. Of course, this structure is not cast in stone. We will be modifying it along with everything else.

Payday

Use Case 7: Run the Payroll for Today

On receipt of the payday transaction, the system finds all those employees that should be paid on the specified date. The system then determines how much they are owed and pays them according to their selected payment method. An audit-trail report is printed showing the action taken for each employee.

```
Payday <date>
```

Although it is easy to understand the intent of this use case, it is not so simple to determine what impact it has on the static structure of Figure 26-6. We need to answer several questions.

First, how does the `Employee` object know how to calculate its pay? Certainly, the system must tally up an hourly employee's time cards and multiply by the hourly rate. Similarly, the system must tally up a commissioned employee's sales receipts, multiply by the commission rate, and add the base salary. But where does this get done? The ideal place seems to be in the `PaymentClassification` derivatives. These objects maintain the records needed to calculate pay, so they should probably have the methods for determining pay. Figure 26-7 shows a collaboration diagram that describes how this might work.

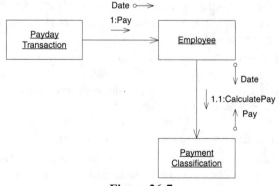

Figure 26-7
Calculating an employee's pay

When asked to calculate pay, the `Employee` object refers this request to its `PaymentClassification` object. The algorithm used depends on the type of `PaymentClassification` that the `Employee` object contains. Figures 26-8 through 26-10 show the three possible scenarios.

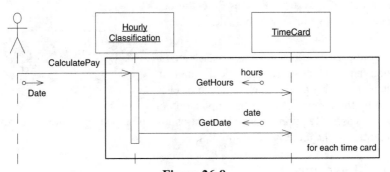

Figure 26-8
Calculating an hourly employee's pay

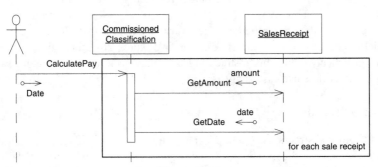

Figure 26-9
Calculating a commissioned employee's pay

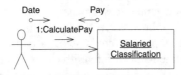

Figure 26-10
Calculating a salaried employee's pay

Reflection: Finding the Underlying Abstractions

So far, we have learned that a simple use case analysis can provide a wealth of information and insights into the design of a system. Figures 26-6 through 26-10 resulted from thinking about the use cases, that is, thinking about behavior.

To use the OCP effectively, we must hunt for abstractions and find those that underlie the application. Often, these abstractions are not stated or even alluded to by the requirements of the application or even the use cases. Requirements and use cases may be too steeped in details to express the generalities of the underlying abstractions.

Employee Payment

Let's look again at the requirements. We see statements like this: "Some employees work by the hour" and "Some employees are paid a flat salary" and "Some . . . employees are paid a commission." This hints at the following generalization: All employees are paid, but they are paid by different schemes. The abstraction here is that *all employees are paid*. Our model of the `PaymentClassification` in Figures 26-7 through 26-10 expresses this abstraction nicely. Thus, this abstraction has already been found among our user stories by doing a very simple use case analysis.

Payment Schedule

Looking for other abstractions, we find "They are paid every Friday," "They are paid on the last working day of the month," and "They are paid every other Friday." This leads us to another generality: *All employees are paid according to a schedule*. The abstraction here is the notion of the *schedule*. It should be possible to ask an `Employee` object whether a certain date is its payday. The use cases barely mention this. The requirements associate an employee's schedule and payment classification. Specifically, hourly employees are paid weekly, salaried employees are paid monthly, and employees receiving commissions are paid biweekly; however, is this association essential? Might not the policy change one day, so that employees could select a particular schedule or employees belonging to different departments or different divisions could have different schedules? Might not schedule policy change independent of payment policy? Certainly, this seems likely.

If, as the requirements imply, we delegated the issue of schedule to the `Payment-Classification` class, our class could not be closed against issues of change in schedule. When we changed payment policy, we would also have to test schedule; when we changed schedules, we would also have to test payment policy. Both OCP and SRP would be violated.

An association between schedule and payment policy could lead to bugs in which a change to a particular payment policy caused incorrect scheduling of certain employees. Bugs like this may make sense to programmers, but they strike fear in the hearts of managers and users. They fear, and rightly so, that if schedules can be broken by a change to payment policy, *any* change made *anywhere* might cause problems in *any* other unrelated part of the system. They fear that they cannot predict the effects of a change. When effects cannot be predicted, confidence is lost, and the program assumes the status of "dangerous and unstable" in the minds of its managers and users.

Despite the essential nature of the schedule abstraction, our use case analysis failed to give us any direct clues about its existence. To spot it required careful consideration of the requirements and an insight into the wiles of the user community. Overreliance on tools and procedures and underreliance on intelligence and experience are recipes for disaster.

Figures 26-11 and 26-12 show the static and dynamic models for the schedule abstraction. As you can see, we've used the STRATEGY pattern yet again. The `Employee` class contains the abstract `PaymentSchedule` class. The three varieties of `PaymentSchedule` correspond to the three known schedules by which employees are paid.

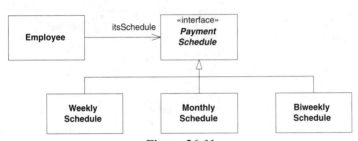

Figure 26-11
Static model of a `Schedule` abstraction

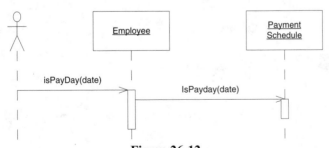

Figure 26-12
Dynamic model of a `Schedule` abstraction

Payment Methods

Another generalization we can make from the requirements is that *all employees receive their pay by some method*. The abstraction is the `PaymentMethod` class. Interestingly enough, this abstraction is already expressed in Figure 26-6.

Affiliations

The requirements imply that employees may have affiliations with a union; however, the union may not be the only organization that has a claim to some of an employee's pay. Employees might want to make automatic contributions to certain charities or have their dues to professional associations paid automatically. The generalization therefore becomes that *the employee may be affiliated with many organizations that should be automatically paid from the employee's paycheck*.

The corresponding abstraction is the `Affiliation` class that is shown in Figure 26-6. That figure, however, does not show the `Employee` containing more than one `Affiliation`, and it shows the presence of a `NoAffiliation` class. This design does not quite fit the abstraction we now think we need. Figures 26-13 and 26-14 show the static and dynamic models that represent the `Affiliation` abstraction.

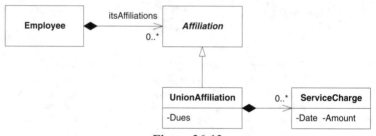

Figure 26-13
Static structure of `Affiliation` abstraction

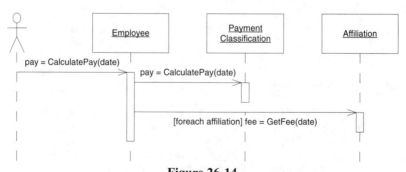

Figure 26-14
Dynamic structure of `Affiliation` abstraction

The list of `Affiliation` objects has obviated the need to use the NULL OBJECT pattern for unaffiliated employees. Now, the list of affiliations for an employee who has no affiliation will simply be empty.

Conclusion

This is a good start on a design. By elaborating the user stories into use cases and hunting through those use cases for abstractions, we've created a *shape* for the system. An architecture is burgeoning. Note, however, that this architecture has been created by looking at only the first few user stories. We did not do a comprehensive review of every requirement in the system. Nor did we demand that every user story and use case be perfect. We also did not do an exhaustive design of the system, complete with class and sequence diagrams for every jot and title that we could think of.

Thinking about design is important. Thinking about design in small, incremental steps is *critical*. Doing too much is worse than doing too little. In this chapter, the amount we did was just about right. It feels unfinished, but it's enough for us to understand and make progress with.

Bibliography

[**Jacobson92**] Ivar Jacobson, *Object-Oriented Software Engineering: A Use Case Driven Approach*, Addison-Wesley, 1992.

27

The Payroll Case Study: Implementation

© Jennifer M. Kohnke

It's long past time we started writing the code that supports and verifies the designs we've been spinning. I'll be creating that code in very small, incremental steps, but I'll show it to you only at convenient points in the text. Don't let the fact that you see only fully formed snapshots of code mislead you into thinking that I wrote it in that form. In fact, between each batch of code you see, there will have been dozens of edits, compiles, and test cases, each one making a tiny, evolutionary change in the code.

You'll also see quite a bit of UML. Think of this UML as a quick diagram that I sketch on a whiteboard to show you, my pair partner, what I have in mind. UML makes a convenient medium for us to communicate by.

Transactions

We begin by thinking about the transactions that represent the use cases. Figure 27-1 shows that we represent transactions as an interface named `Transaction`, which has a method named `Execute()`. This is, of course, the COMMAND pattern. The implementation of the `Transaction` class is shown in Listing 27-1.

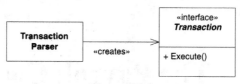

Figure 27-1
Transaction interface

Listing 27-1
Transaction.cs

```
namespace Payroll
{
  public interface Transaction
  {
    void Execute();
  }
}
```

Adding Employees

Figure 27-2 shows a potential structure for the transactions that add employees. Note that it is within these transactions that the employees' payment schedule is associated with their payment classification. This is appropriate, since the transactions are contrivances instead of part of the core model. Thus, for example, the core model is unaware that hourly employeess are paid weekly. The association between payment classificaton and payment schedule is merely part of one of the peripheral contrivances and can be changed at any time. For example, we could easily add a transaction that allows us to change employee schedules.

This decision conforms nicely to OCP and SRP. It is the responsibility of the transactions, not the core model, to specify the association between payment type and payment schedule. What's more, that association can be changed without changing the core model.

Note, too, that the default payment method is to hold the paycheck with the paymaster. If an employee wants a different payment method, it must be changed with the appropriate `ChgEmp` transaction.

As usual, we begin writing code by writing tests first. The test case in Listing 27-2 shows that the `AddSalariedTransaction` is working correctly. The code to follow will make that test case pass.

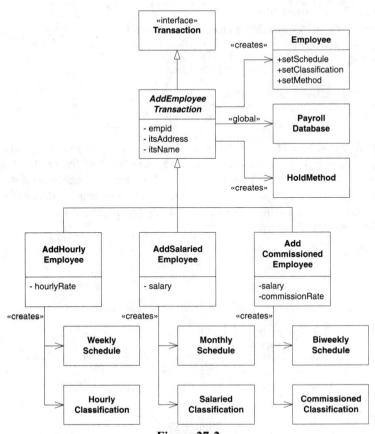

Figure 27-2
Static model of AddEmployeeTransaction

Listing 27-2

PayrollTest.TestAddSalariedEmployee

```
[Test]
public void TestAddSalariedEmployee()
{
  int empId = 1;
  AddSalariedEmployee t =
    new AddSalariedEmployee(empId, "Bob", "Home", 1000.00);
  t.Execute();

  Employee e = PayrollDatabase.GetEmployee(empId);
  Assert.AreEqual("Bob", e.Name);

  PaymentClassification pc = e.Classification;
  Assert.IsTrue(pc is SalariedClassification);
  SalariedClassification sc = pc as SalariedClassification;
```

Listing 27-2 (Continued)
PayrollTest.TestAddSalariedEmployee

```
    Assert.AreEqual(1000.00, sc.Salary, .001);
    PaymentSchedule ps = e.Schedule;
    Assert.IsTrue(ps is MonthlySchedule);

    PaymentMethod pm = e.Method;
    Assert.IsTrue(pm is HoldMethod);
}
```

The payroll database The `AddEmployeeTransaction` class uses a class called `PayrollDatabase`. For the moment, this class maintains all the existing `Employee` objects in a `Hashtable` that is keyed by `empID`. The class also maintains a `Hashtable` that maps union `memberID`s to `empID`s. We'll figure out how to make the contents persistent later. The structure for this class appears in Figure 27-3. `PayrollDatabase` is an example of the FACADE pattern.

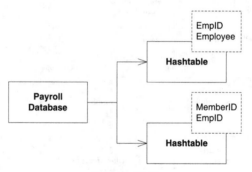

Figure 27-3
Static structure of `PayrollDatabase`

Listing 27-3 shows a rudimentary implementation of the `PayrollDatabase`. This implementation is meant to help us with our initial test cases. It does not yet contain the hash table that maps member IDs to `Employee` instances.

Listing 27-3
PayrollDatabase.cs

```
using System.Collections;

namespace Payroll
{
  public class PayrollDatabase
  {
    private static Hashtable employees = new Hashtable();

    public static void AddEmployee(int id, Employee employee)
    {
      employees[id] = employee;
    }
```

Listing 27-3 (Continued)
PayrollDatabase.cs

```
        public static Employee GetEmployee(int id)
        {
            return employees[id] as Employee;
        }
    }
}
```

In general, I consider database implementations to be details. Decisions about those details should be deferred as long as possible. Whether this particular database will be implemented with a relational database management system (RDBMS), or flat files, or an object-oriented database management system (OODBMS), is irrelevant at this point. Right now, I'm simply interested in creating the API that will provide database services to the rest of the application. I'll find appropriate implementations for the database later.

Deferring details about the database is an uncommon but very rewarding practice. Database decisions can usually wait until we have much more knowledge about the software and its needs. By waiting, we avoid the problem of putting too much infrastructure into the database. Rather, we implement only enough database facility for the current needs of the application.

Using TEMPLATE METHOD to add employees Figure 27-4 shows the dynamic model for adding an employee. Note that the `AddEmployeeTransaction` object sends messages to *itself* in order to get the appropriate `PaymentClassification` and `PaymentSchedule` objects. These messages are implemented in the derivatives of the `AddEmployeeTransaction` class. This is an application of the TEMPLATE METHOD pattern.

Listing 27-4 shows the implementation of the TEMPLATE METHOD pattern in the `AddEmployeeTransaction` class. This class implements the `Execute()` method to call two pure virtual functions that will be implemented by derivatives. These functions, `MakeSchedule()` and `MakeClassification()`, return the `PaymentSchedule` and `PaymentClassification` objects that the newly created `Employee` needs. The `Execute()` method then binds these objects to the `Employee` and saves the `Employee` in the `PayrollDatabase`.

Two things are of particular interest here. First, when the TEMPLATE METHOD pattern is applied, as it is here, for the sole purpose of creating objects, it goes by the name FACTORY METHOD. Second, it is conventional for the creation methods in the FACTORY METHOD pattern to be named `MakeXXX()`. I realized both of these issues while I was writing the code, and that is why the method names differ between the code and the diagram.

Should I have gone back and changed the diagram? I didn't see the need in this case. I don't intend for that diagram to be used as a reference by anyone else. Indeed, if this were a real project, that diagram would have been drawn on a whiteboard and would probably now be on the verge of being erased.

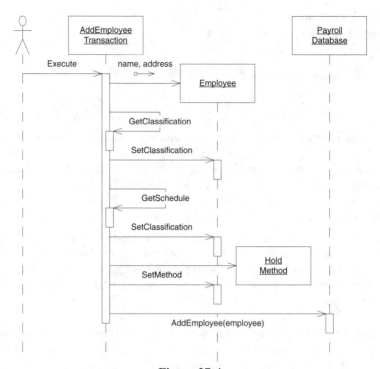

Figure 27-4
Dynamic model for adding an employee

Listing 27-4

AddEmployeeTransaction.cs

```
namespace Payroll
{
  public abstract class AddEmployeeTransaction : Transaction
  {
    private readonly int empid;
    private readonly string name;
    private readonly string address;

    public AddEmployeeTransaction(int empid,
      string name, string address)
    {
      this.empid = empid;
      this.name = name;
      this.address = address;
    }

    protected abstract
      PaymentClassification MakeClassification();
    protected abstract
      PaymentSchedule MakeSchedule();
```

Listing 27-4 (Continued)

AddEmployeeTransaction.cs

```
    public void Execute()
    {
        PaymentClassification pc = MakeClassification();
        PaymentSchedule ps = MakeSchedule();
        PaymentMethod pm = new HoldMethod();

        Employee e = new Employee(empid, name, address);
        e.Classification = pc;
        e.Schedule = ps;
        e.Method = pm;
        PayrollDatabase.AddEmployee(empid, e);
    }
  }
}
```

Listing 27-5 shows the implementation of the AddSalariedEmployee class. This class derives from AddEmployeeTransaction and implements the MakeSchedule() and MakeClassification() methods to pass back the appropriate objects to AddEmployeeTransaction.Execute().

Listing 27-5

AddSalariedEmployee.cs

```
namespace Payroll
{
  public class AddSalariedEmployee : AddEmployeeTransaction
  {
    private readonly double salary;

    public AddSalariedEmployee(int id, string name,
      string address, double salary)
      : base(id, name, address)
    {
      this.salary = salary;
    }

    protected override
      PaymentClassification MakeClassification()
    {
      return new SalariedClassification(salary);
    }

    protected override PaymentSchedule MakeSchedule()
    {
      return new MonthlySchedule();
    }
  }
}
```

The AddHourlyEmployee and AddCommissionedEmployee are left as exercises for you. Remember to write your test cases first.

Deleting Employees

Figures 27-5 and 27-6 present the static and dynamic models for the transactions that delete employees. Listing 27-6 shows the test case for deleting an employee. Listing 27-7 shows the implementation of `DeleteEmployeeTransaction`. This is a very typical implementation of the COMMAND pattern. The constructor stores the data that the `Execute()` method eventually operates on.

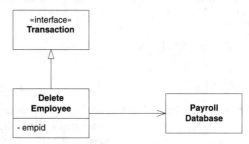

Figure 27-5
Static model for `DeleteEmployee` transaction

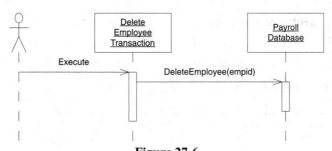

Figure 27-6
Dynamic model for `DeleteEmployee` transaction

Listing 27-6
`PayrollTest.DeleteEmployee`

```
[Test]
public void DeleteEmployee()
{
  int empId = 4;
  AddCommissionedEmployee t =
    new AddCommissionedEmployee(
    empId, "Bill", "Home", 2500, 3.2);
  t.Execute();

  Employee e = PayrollDatabase.GetEmployee(empId);
  Assert.IsNotNull(e);
```

Listing 27-6 (Continued)

`PayrollTest.DeleteEmployee`

```
        DeleteEmployeeTransaction dt =
            new DeleteEmployeeTransaction(empId);
        dt.Execute();

        e = PayrollDatabase.GetEmployee(empId);
        Assert.IsNull(e);
    }
```

Listing 27-7

`DeleteEmployeeTransaction.cs`

```
namespace Payroll
{
    public class DeleteEmployeeTransaction : Transaction
    {
        private readonly int id;

        public DeleteEmployeeTransaction(int id)
        {
            this.id = id;
        }

        public void Execute()
        {
            PayrollDatabase.DeleteEmployee(id);
        }
    }
}
```

By now, you have noticed that the `PayrollDatabase` provides static access to its fields. In effect, `PayrollDatabase.employees` is a global variable. For decades, textbooks and teachers have been discouraging the use of global variables, with good reason. Still, global variables are not intrinsically evil or harmful. This particular situation is an ideal choice for a global variable. There will ever be only one instance of the `PayrollDatabase` methods and variables, and it needs to be known by a wide audience.

You might think that this could be better accomplished by using the SINGLETON or MONOSTATE patterns. It is true that these would serve the purpose. However, they do so by using global variables themselves. A SINGLETON or a MONOSTATE is, by definition, a global entity. In this case, I felt that a SINGLETON or a MONOSTATE would smell of needless complexity. It's easier to simply keep the database global.

Time Cards, Sales Receipts, and Service Charges

Figure 27-7 shows the static structure for the transaction that posts time cards to employees. Figure 27-8 shows the dynamic model. The basic idea is that the transaction gets the `Employee` object from the `PayrollDatabase`, asks the `Employee` for its `PaymentClassification` object, and then creates and adds a `TimeCard` object to that `PaymentClassification`.

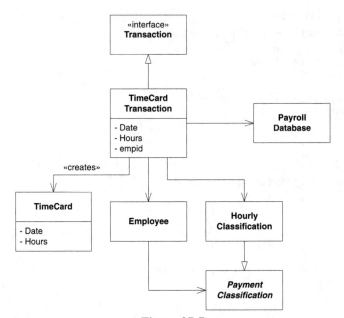

Figure 27-7
Static structure of `TimeCardTransaction`

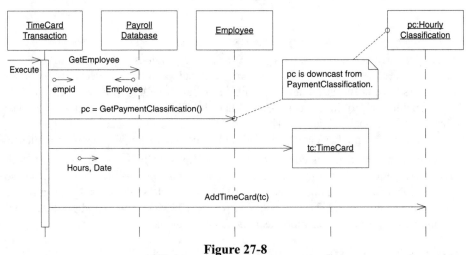

Figure 27-8
Dynamic model for posting a `TimeCard`

Note that we cannot add `TimeCard` objects to general `PaymentClassification` objects; we can add them only to `HourlyClassification` objects. This implies that we must downcast the `PaymentClassification` object received from the `Employee` object to an `HourlyClassification` object. This is a good use for the `as` operator in C# (see Listing 27-10).

Listing 27-8 shows one of the test cases that verifies that time cards can be added to hourly employees. This test code simply creates an hourly employee and adds it to the database. Then it creates a `TimeCardTransaction`, invokes `Execute()`, and checks whether the employee's `HourlyClassification` contains the appropriate `TimeCard`.

Listing 27-8

`PayrollTest.TestTimeCardTransaction`

```
[Test]
public void TestTimeCardTransaction()
{
  int empId = 5;
  AddHourlyEmployee t =
    new AddHourlyEmployee(empId, "Bill", "Home", 15.25);
  t.Execute();
  TimeCardTransaction tct =
    new TimeCardTransaction(
      new DateTime(2005, 7, 31), 8.0, empId);
  tct.Execute();

  Employee e = PayrollDatabase.GetEmployee(empId);
  Assert.IsNotNull(e);

  PaymentClassification pc = e.Classification;
  Assert.IsTrue(pc is HourlyClassification);
  HourlyClassification hc = pc as HourlyClassification;

  TimeCard tc = hc.GetTimeCard(new DateTime(2005, 7, 31));
  Assert.IsNotNull(tc);
  Assert.AreEqual(8.0, tc.Hours);
}
```

Listing 27-9 shows the implementation of the `TimeCard` class. There's not much to this class right now. It's simply a data class.

Listing 27-9

`TimeCard.cs`

```
using System;

namespace Payroll
{
  public class TimeCard
  {
    private readonly DateTime date;
    private readonly double hours;

    public TimeCard(DateTime date, double hours)
    {
      this.date = date;
      this.hours = hours;
    }
```

Listing 27-9 (Continued)
`TimeCard.cs`

```
      public double Hours
      {
        get { return hours; }
      }

      public DateTime Date
      {
        get { return date; }
      }
    }
  }
```

Listing 27-10 shows the implementation of the `TimeCardTransaction` class. Note the use of `InvalidOperationExceptions`. This is not particularly good long-term practice but suffices this early in development. After we get some idea of what the exceptions ought to be, we can come back and create meaningful exception classes.

Listing 27-10
`TimeCardTransaction.cs`

```
using System;

namespace Payroll
{
  public class TimeCardTransaction : Transaction
  {
    private readonly DateTime date;
    private readonly double hours;
    private readonly int empId;

    public TimeCardTransaction(
      DateTime date, double hours, int empId)
    {
      this.date = date;
      this.hours = hours;
      this.empId = empId;
    }

    public void Execute()
    {
      Employee e = PayrollDatabase.GetEmployee(empId);

      if (e != null)
      {
        HourlyClassification hc =
          e.Classification as HourlyClassification;

        if (hc != null)
          hc.AddTimeCard(new TimeCard(date, hours));
        else
          throw new InvalidOperationException(
            "Tried to add timecard to" +
              "non-hourly employee");
      }
```

Listing 27-10 (Continued)
TimeCardTransaction.cs

```
      else
        throw new InvalidOperationException(
          "No such employee.");
    }
  }
}
```

Figures 27-9 and 27-10 show a similar design for the transaction that posts sales receipts to a commissioned employee. I've left the implementation of these classes as an exercise.

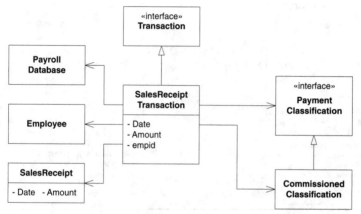

Figure 27-9
Static model for `SalesReceiptTransaction`

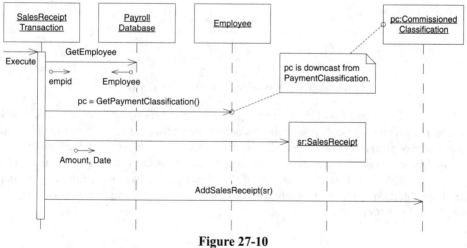

Figure 27-10
Dynamic model for `SalesReceiptTransaction`

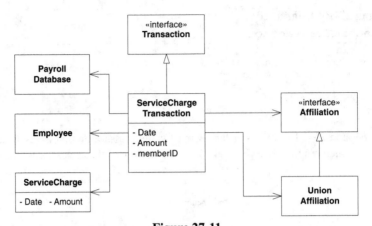

Figure 27-11
Static model for ServiceChargeTransaction

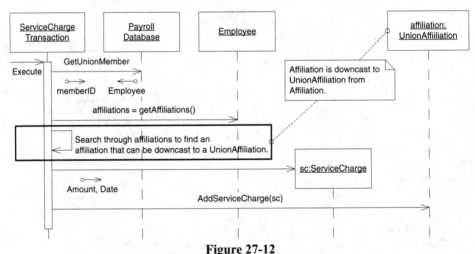

Figure 27-12
Dynamic model for ServiceChargeTransaction

Figures 27-11 and 27-12 show the design for the transaction that posts service charges to union members. These designs point out a mismatch between the transaction model and the core model that we have created. Our core Employee object can be affiliated with many different organizations, but the transaction model assumes that any affiliation must be a union affiliation. Thus, the transaction model provides no way to identify a particular kind of affiliation. Instead, it simply assumes that if we are posting a service charge, the employee has a union affiliation.

The dynamic model addresses this dilemma by searching the set of `Affiliation` objects contained by the `Employee` object for a `UnionAffiliation` object. The model then adds the `ServiceCharge` object to that `UnionAffiliation`.

Listing 27-11 shows the test case for the `ServiceChargeTransaction`. It simply creates an hourly employee, adds a `UnionAffiliation` to it, makes sure that the appropriate member ID is registered with the `PayrollDatabase`, creates and executes a `ServiceChargeTransaction`, and, finally, makes sure that the appropriate `ServiceCharge` was indeed added to `Employee`'s `UnionAffiliation`.

Listing 27-11
`PayrollTest.AddServiceCharge`

```
[Test]
public void AddServiceCharge()
{
  int empId = 2;
  AddHourlyEmployee t = new AddHourlyEmployee(
    empId, "Bill", "Home", 15.25);
  t.Execute();
  Employee e = PayrollDatabase.GetEmployee(empId);
  Assert.IsNotNull(e);
  UnionAffiliation af = new UnionAffiliation();
  e.Affiliation = af;
  int memberId = 86; // Maxwell Smart
  PayrollDatabase.AddUnionMember(memberId, e);
  ServiceChargeTransaction sct =
    new ServiceChargeTransaction(
    memberId, new DateTime(2005, 8, 8), 12.95);
  sct.Execute();
  ServiceCharge sc =
    af.GetServiceCharge(new DateTime(2005, 8, 8));
  Assert.IsNotNull(sc);
  Assert.AreEqual(12.95, sc.Amount, .001);
}
```

When I drew the UML in Figure 27-12, I thought that replacing `NoAffiliation` with a list of affiliations was a better design. I thought it was more flexible and less complex. After all, I could add new affiliations any time I wanted, and I didn't have to create the `NoAffiliation` class. However, when writing the test case in Listing 27-11, I realized that setting the `Affiliation` property on `Employee` was better than calling `AddAffiliation`. After all, the requirements do not ask that an employee have more than one `Affiliation`, so there is no need to use a cast to select from potentially many kinds. Doing so would be more complex than necessary.

This is an example of why doing too much UML without verifying it in code can be dangerous. The code can tell you things about your design that the UML cannot. Here, I was putting structures into the UML that weren't needed. Maybe one day they'd come in handy, but they have to be maintained between now and then. The cost of that maintenance may not be worth the benefit.

In this case, even though the cost of maintaining the downcast is relatively slight, I'm not going to use it; it's much simpler to implement without a list of `Affiliation` objects. So I'll keep the NULL OBJECT pattern in place with the `NoAffiliation` class.

Listing 27-12 shows the implementation of the `ServiceChargeTransaction`. It is indeed much simpler without the loop looking for `UnionAffiliation` objects. It simply gets the `Employee` from the database, downcasts its `Affillation` to a `UnionAffilliation`, and adds the `ServiceCharge` to it.

Listing 27-12
ServiceChargeTransaction.cs

```csharp
using System;

namespace Payroll
{
  public class ServiceChargeTransaction : Transaction
  {
    private readonly int memberId;
    private readonly DateTime time;
    private readonly double charge;

    public ServiceChargeTransaction(
      int id, DateTime time, double charge)
    {
      this.memberId = id;
      this.time = time;
      this.charge = charge;
    }

    public void Execute()
    {
      Employee e = PayrollDatabase.GetUnionMember(memberId);

      if (e != null)
      {
        UnionAffiliation ua = null;
        if(e.Affiliation is UnionAffiliation)
          ua = e.Affiliation as UnionAffiliation;

        if (ua != null)
          ua.AddServiceCharge(
            new ServiceCharge(time, charge));
        else
          throw new InvalidOperationException(
            "Tries to add service charge to union"
            + "member without a union affiliation");
      }
      else
        throw new InvalidOperationException(
          "No such union member.");
    }
  }
}
```

Changing Employees

Figure 27-13 show the static structure for the transactions that change the attributes of an employee. This
structure is easily derived from use case 6. All the
transactions take an `EmpID` argument, so we can
create a top-level base class called `Change-`
`EmployeeTransaction`. Below this base class are
the classes that change single attributes, such as
`ChangeNameTransaction` and `ChangeAddressTransaction`. The transactions that
change classifications have a commonality of purpose in that they all modify the same
field of the `Employee` object. Thus, they can be grouped together under an abstract base,
`ChangeClassificationTransaction`. The same is true of the transactions that change
the payment and the affiliations. This can be seen by the structure of `Change-`
`MethodTransaction` and `ChangeAffiliationTransaction`.

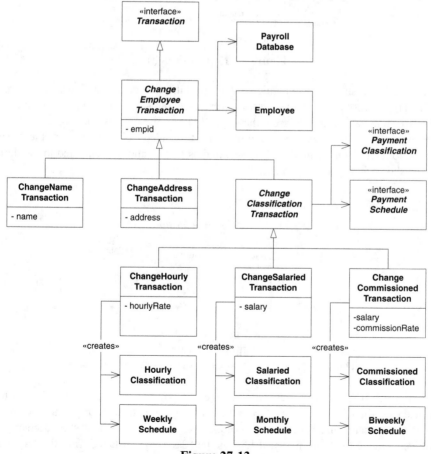

Figure 27-13
Static model for `ChangeEmployeeTransaction`

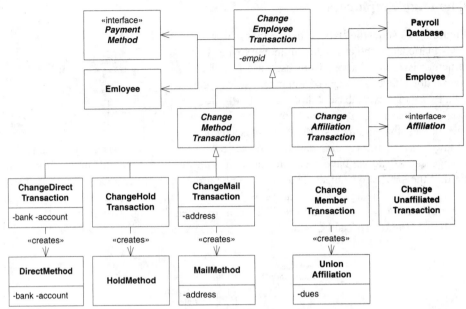

Figure 27-13 (Continued)

Figure 27-14 shows the dynamic model for all the change transactions. Again, we see the TEMPLATE METHOD pattern in use. In every case, the Employee object corresponding to the EmpID must be retrieved from the PayrollDatabase. Thus, the Execute function of ChangeEmployeeTransaction implements this behavior and then sends the Change message to itself. This method will be declared as virtual and implemented in the derivatives, as shown in Figures 27-15 and 27-16.

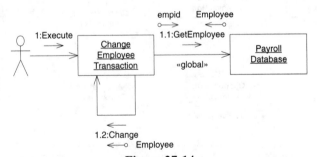

Figure 27-14
Dynamic model for ChangeEmployeeTransaction

Listing 27-13 shows the test case for the ChangeNameTransaction. This simple test case uses the AddHourlyEmployee transaction to create an hourly employee named Bill. It then creates and executes a ChangeNameTransaction that should change the employee's name to Bob. Finally, it fetches the Employee instance from the Payroll-Database and verifies that the name has been changed.

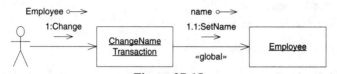

Figure 27-15
Dynamic model for `ChangeNameTransaction`

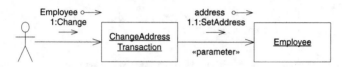

Figure 27-16
Dynamic model for `ChangeAddressTransaction`

Listing 27-13

`PayrollTest.TestChangeNameTransaction()`

```
[Test]
public void TestChangeNameTransaction()
{
  int empId = 2;
  AddHourlyEmployee t =
    new AddHourlyEmployee(empId, "Bill", "Home", 15.25);
  t.Execute();
  ChangeNameTransaction cnt =
    new ChangeNameTransaction(empId, "Bob");
  cnt.Execute();
  Employee e = PayrollDatabase.GetEmployee(empId);
  Assert.IsNotNull(e);
  Assert.AreEqual("Bob", e.Name);
}
```

Listing 27-14 shows the implementation of the abstract base class
`ChangeEmployeeTransaction`. The structure of the TEMPLATE METHOD pattern is
clearly in evidence. The `Execute()` method simply reads the appropriate `Employee`
instance from the `PayrollDatabase` and, if successful, invokes the abstract `Change()`
method.

Listing 27-14

`ChangeEmployeeTransaction.cs`

```
using System;

namespace Payroll
{
  public abstract class ChangeEmployeeTransaction : Transaction
  {
    private readonly int empId;

    public ChangeEmployeeTransaction(int empId)
    {
      this.empId = empId;
    }
```

Listing 27-14 (Continued)
ChangeEmployeeTransaction.cs

```
    public void Execute()
    {
      Employee e = PayrollDatabase.GetEmployee(empId);

      if(e != null)
        Change(e);
      else
        throw new InvalidOperationException(
          "No such employee.");
    }

    protected abstract void Change(Employee e);
  }
}
```

Listing 27-15 shows the implementation of the `ChangeNameTransaction`. The second half of the TEMPLATE METHOD can easily be seen. The `Change()` method is implemented to change the name of the `Employee` argument. The structure of the `ChangeAddressTransaction` is very similar and is left as an exercise.

Listing 27-15
ChangeNameTransaction.cs

```
namespace Payroll
{
  public class ChangeNameTransaction :
    ChangeEmployeeTransaction
  {
    private readonly string newName;

    public ChangeNameTransaction(int id, string newName)
    : base(id)
    {
      this.newName = newName;
    }

    protected override void Change(Employee e)
    {
      e.Name = newName;
    }
  }
}
```

Changing Classification. Figure 27-17 shows how the hierarchy beneath `Change-ClassificationTransaction` is envisioned. The TEMPLATE METHOD pattern is used yet again. All these transactions must create a new `PaymentClassification` object and then hand it to the `Employee` object. This is accomplished by sending the `GetClassification` message to itself. This abstract method is implemented in each of the classes derived from `ChangeClassificationTransaction`, as shown in Figures 27-18 through Figure 27-20.

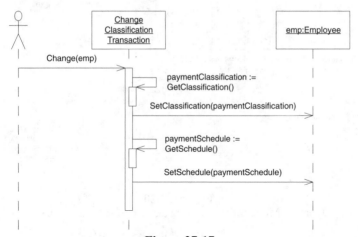

Figure 27-17
Dynamic model of ChangeClassificationTransaction

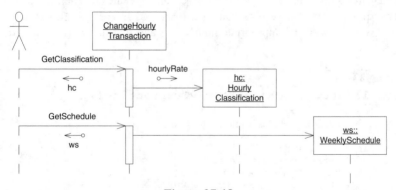

Figure 27-18
Dynamic model of ChangeHourlyTransaction

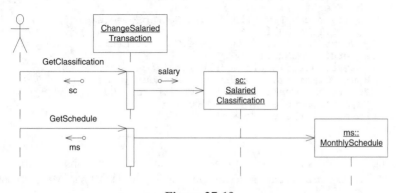

Figure 27-19
Dynamic model of ChangeSalariedTransaction

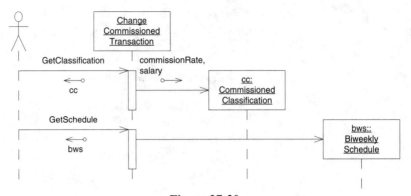

Figure 27-20
Dynamic Model of `ChangeCommissionedTransaction`

Listing 27-16 shows the test case for the `ChangeHourlyTransaction`. The test case uses an `AddCommissionedEmployee` transaction to create a commissioned employee and then creates a `ChangeHourlyTransaction` and executes it. The transaction fetches the changed employee and verifies that its `PaymentClassification` is an `Hourly-Classification` with the appropriate hourly rate and that its `PaymentSchedule` is a `WeeklySchedule`.

Listing 27-16
`PayrollTest.TestChangeHourlyTransaction()`

```
[Test]
public void TestChangeHourlyTransaction()
{
    int empId = 3;
    AddCommissionedEmployee t =
      new AddCommissionedEmployee(
      empId, "Lance", "Home", 2500, 3.2);
    t.Execute();
    ChangeHourlyTransaction cht =
      new ChangeHourlyTransaction(empId, 27.52);
    cht.Execute();
    Employee e = PayrollDatabase.GetEmployee(empId);
    Assert.IsNotNull(e);
    PaymentClassification pc = e.Classification;
    Assert.IsNotNull(pc);
    Assert.IsTrue(pc is HourlyClassification);
    HourlyClassification hc = pc as HourlyClassification;
    Assert.AreEqual(27.52, hc.HourlyRate, .001);
    PaymentSchedule ps = e.Schedule;
    Assert.IsTrue(ps is WeeklySchedule);
}
```

Listing 27-17 shows the implementation of the abstract base class `ChangeClassificationTransaction`. Once again, the TEMPLATE METHOD pattern is easy to pick out. The `Change()` method invokes the two abstract getters for the, `Classification` and `Schedule` properties and uses the values from these properties to set the classification and schedule of the `Employee`.

Listing 27-17
ChangeClassificationTransaction.cs

```
namespace Payroll
{
  public abstract class ChangeClassificationTransaction
    : ChangeEmployeeTransaction
  {
    public ChangeClassificationTransaction(int id)
      : base (id)
    {}

    protected override void Change(Employee e)
    {
      e.Classification = Classification;
      e.Schedule = Schedule;
    }

    protected abstract
      PaymentClassification Classification { get; }
    protected abstract PaymentSchedule Schedule { get; }
  }
}
```

The decision to use properties instead of `get` functions was made as the code was being written. Again, we see the tension between the diagrams and the code.

Listing 27-18 shows the implementation of the `ChangeHourlyTransaction` class. This class completes the TEMPLATE METHOD pattern by implementing the getters for the `Classification` and `Schedule` properties that it inherited from `Change-ClassificationTransaction`. The class implements the `Classification` getter to return a newly created `HourlyClassification` and implements the `Schedule` getter to return a newly created `WeeklySchedule`.

Listing 27-18
ChangeHourlyTransaction.cs

```
namespace Payroll
{
  public class ChangeHourlyTransaction
    : ChangeClassificationTransaction
  {
    private readonly double hourlyRate;

    public ChangeHourlyTransaction(int id, double hourlyRate)
      : base(id)
    {
      this.hourlyRate = hourlyRate;
    }
```

Listing 27-18 (Continued)

ChangeHourlyTransaction.cs

```
    protected override PaymentClassification Classification
    {
      get { return new HourlyClassification(hourlyRate); }
    }

    protected override PaymentSchedule Schedule
    {
      get { return new WeeklySchedule(); }
    }
  }
}
```

As always, the `ChangeSalariedTransaction` and `ChangeCommissionedTransaction` are left as an exercise.

A similar mechanism is used for the implementation of `ChangeMethodTransaction`. The abstract `Method` property is used to select the proper derivative of `PaymentMethod`, which is then handed to the `Employee` object (see Figures 27-21 through 27-24).

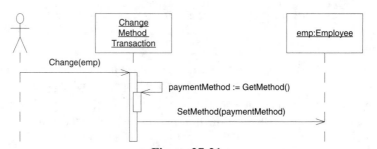

Figure 27-21
Dynamic model of `ChangeMethodTransaction`

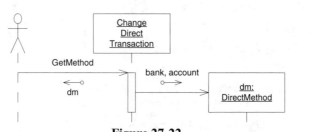

Figure 27-22
Dynamic model of `ChangeDirectTransaction`

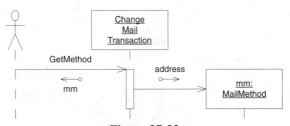

Figure 27-23
Dynamic model of `ChangeMailTransaction`

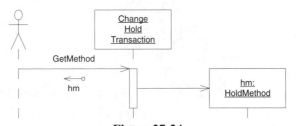

Figure 27-24
Dynamic model of `ChangeHoldTransaction`

The implementation of these classes turned out to be straightforward and unsurprising. They too are left as an exercise.

Figure 27-25 shows the implementation of the `ChangeAffiliationTransaction`. Once again, we use the TEMPLATE METHOD pattern to select the `Affiliation` derivative that should be handed to the `Employee` object. (See Figures 27-26 through 27-28).

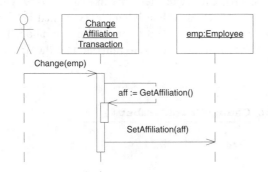

Figure 27-25
Dynamic model of `ChangeAffiliationTransaction`

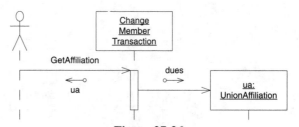

Figure 27-26
Dynamic model of `ChangeMemberTransaction`

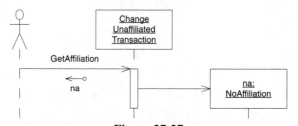

Figure 27-27
Dynamic model of `ChangeUnaffiliatedTransaction`

What Was I Smoking?

I got quite a surprise when I went to implement this design. Look closely at the dynamic diagrams for the affiliation transactions. Can you spot the problem?

As always, I began the implementation by writing the test case for `Change-MemberTransaction`. You can see this test case in Listing 27-19. The test case starts out straightforward enough. It creates an hourly employee named Bill and then creates and executes a `ChangeMemberTransaction` to put Bill in the union. Then it checks to see that Bill has a `UnionAffiliation` bound to him and that the `UnionAffiliation` has the right dues rate.

Listing 27-19
`PayrollTest.ChangeUnionMember()`

```
[Test]
public void ChangeUnionMember()
{
  int empId = 8;
  AddHourlyEmployee t =
    new AddHourlyEmployee(empId, "Bill", "Home", 15.25);
  t.Execute();
  int memberId = 7743;
  ChangeMemberTransaction cmt =
    new ChangeMemberTransaction(empId, memberId, 99.42);
  cmt.Execute();
  Employee e = PayrollDatabase.GetEmployee(empId);
  Assert.IsNotNull(e);
```

Listing 27-19 (Continued)
`PayrollTest.ChangeUnionMember()`

```
      Affiliation affiliation = e.Affiliation;
      Assert.IsNotNull(affiliation);
      Assert.IsTrue(affiliation is UnionAffiliation);
      UnionAffiliation uf = affiliation as UnionAffiliation;
      Assert.AreEqual(99.42, uf.Dues, .001);
      Employee member =PayrollDatabase.GetUnionMember(memberId);
      Assert.IsNotNull(member);
      Assert.AreEqual(e, member);
    }
```

The surprise is hidden in the last few lines of the test case. Those lines make sure that the `PayrollDatabase` has recorded Bill's membership in the union. Nothing in the existing UML diagrams makes sure that this happens. The UML is concerned only with the appropriate `Affiliation` derivative being bound to the `Employee`. I didn't notice the deficit at all. Did you?

I merrily coded the transactions as per the diagrams and then watched the unit test fail. Once the failure occurred, it was obvious what I had neglected. What was not obvious was the solution to the problem. How do I get the membership to be recorded by `ChangeMemberTransaction` but erased by `ChangeUnaffiliatedTransaction`?

The answer was to add to `ChangeAffiliationTransaction` another abstract method, named `RecordMembership(Employee)`. This function is implemented in `ChangeMemberTransaction` to bind the `memberId` to the `Employee` instance. In the `ChangeUnaffiliatedTransaction`, it is implemented to erase the membership record.

Listing 27-20 shows the resulting implementation of the abstract base class `ChangeAffiliationTransaction`. Again, the use of the TEMPLATE METHOD pattern is obvious.

Listing 27-20
`ChangeAffiliationTransaction.cs`

```
namespace Payroll
{
  public abstract class ChangeAffiliationTransaction :
      ChangeEmployeeTransaction
  {
    public ChangeAffiliationTransaction(int empId)
      : base(empId)
    {}

    protected override void Change(Employee e)
    {
      RecordMembership(e);
      Affiliation affiliation = Affiliation;
      e.Affiliation = affiliation;
    }

    protected abstract Affiliation Affiliation { get; }
    protected abstract void RecordMembership(Employee e);
  }
}
```

Listing 27-21 shows the implementation of `ChangeMemberTransaction`. This is not particularly complicated or interesting. On the other hand, the implementation of `ChangeUnaffiliatedTransaction` in Listing 27-22 is a bit more substantial. The `RecordMembership` function has to decide whether the current employee is a union member. If so, it gets the `memberId` from the `UnionAffiliation` and erases the membership record.

Listing 27-21
ChangeMemberTransaction.cs

```
namespace Payroll
{
  public class ChangeMemberTransaction :
ChangeAffiliationTransaction
  {
    private readonly int memberId;
    private readonly double dues;

    public ChangeMemberTransaction(
      int empId, int memberId, double dues)
      : base(empId)
    {
      this.memberId = memberId;
      this.dues = dues;
    }

    protected override Affiliation Affiliation
    {
      get { return new UnionAffiliation(memberId, dues); }
    }

    protected override void RecordMembership(Employee e)
    {
      PayrollDatabase.AddUnionMember(memberId, e);
    }
  }
}
```

Listing 27-22
ChangeUnaffiliatedTransaction.cs

```
namespace Payroll
{
  public class ChangeUnaffiliatedTransaction
   : ChangeAffiliationTransaction
  {}
    public ChangeUnaffiliatedTransaction(int empId)
      : base(empId)
    {}

    protected override Affiliation Affiliation
    {
      get { return new NoAffiliation(); }
    }

    protected override void RecordMembership(Employee e)
```

Listing 27-22 (Continued)

ChangeUnaffiliatedTransaction.cs

```
      {
        Affiliation affiliation = e.Affiliation;
        if(affiliation is UnionAffiliation)
        {
          UnionAffiliation unionAffiliation =
            affiliation as UnionAffiliation;
          int memberId = unionAffiliation.MemberId;
          PayrollDatabase.RemoveUnionMember(memberId);
        }
      }
    }
}
```

I can't say that I'm very pleased with this design. It bothers me that the Change-UnaffiliatedTransaction must know about UnionAffiliation. I could solve this by putting RecordMembership and EraseMembership abstract methods in the Affiliation class. However, this would force UnionAffiliation and NoAffiliation to know about the PayrollDatabase. And I'm not very happy about that, either.[1]

Still, the implementation as it stands is pretty simple and violates OCP only slightly. The nice thing is that very few modules in the system know about Change-UnaffiliatedTransaction, so its extra dependencies aren't doing very much harm.

Paying Employees

Finally, it is time to consider the transaction that is at the root of this application: the transaction that instructs the system to pay the appropriate employees. Figure 27-28 shows the static structure of the PaydayTransaction class. Figure 27-29 and Figure 27-30 describe the dynamic behavior.

The dynamic models express a great deal of polymorphic behavior. The algorithm used by the CalculatePay message depends on the kind of PaymentClassification that the Employee object contains. The algorithm used to determine whether a date is a payday depends on the kind of PaymentSchedule that the Employee contains. The algorithm used to send the payment to the Employee depends on the type of the PaymentMethod object. This high degree of abstraction allows the algorithms to be closed against the addition of new kinds of payment classifications, schedules, affiliations, or payment methods.

---

1. I could use the VISITOR pattern to solve this problem, but that would probably be way overengineered.

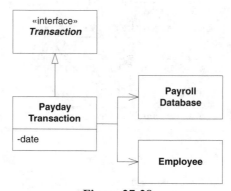

Figure 27-28
Static model of `PaydayTransaction`

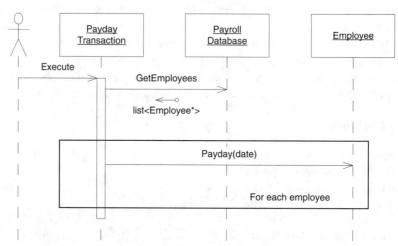

Figure 27-29
Dynamic model for `PaydayTransaction`

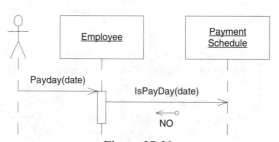

Figure 27-30
Dynamic model scenario: "Payday is not today."

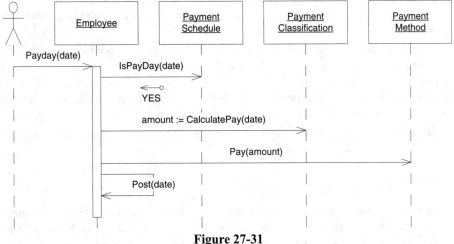

Figure 27-31
Dynamic model scenario: "Payday is today."

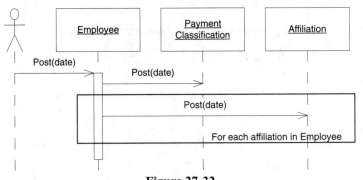

Figure 27-32
Dynamic model scenario: Posting payment

The algorithms depicted in Figure 27-31 and Figure 27-32 introduce the concept of *posting*. After the correct pay amount has been calculated and sent to the Employee, the payment is posted; that is, the records involved in the payment are updated. Thus, we can define the CalculatePay method as calculating the pay from the last posting until the specified date.

Developers and business decisions Where did this notion of posting come from? It certainly wasn't mentioned in the user stories or the use cases. As it happens, I cooked it up as a way to solve a problem that I perceived. I was concerned that the Payday method might be called multiple times with the same date or with a date in the same pay period, so I wanted to make sure that the employee was not paid more than once. I did this on my own initiative, without asking my customer. It just seemed the right thing to do.

In effect, I made a business decision, deciding that multiple runs of the payroll program should produce different results. I should have asked my customer or project manager about this, since they might have very different ideas.

In checking with the customer,[2] I find that the idea of posting goes against his intent. The customer wants to be able to run the payroll system and then review the paychecks. If any of them are wrong, the customer wants to correct the payroll information and run the payroll program again. The customer tells me that I should never consider time cards or sales receipts for dates outside the current pay period.

So, we have to ditch the posting scheme. It seemed like a good idea at the time, but it was not what the customer wanted.

Paying Salaried Employees

The two test cases in Listing 27-23 test whether a salaried employee is being paid appropriately. The first test case makes sure that the employee is paid on the last day of the month. The second test case makes sure that the employee is not paid if it is not the last day of the month.

Listing 27-23
`PayrollTest.PaySingleSalariedEmployee et al.`

```
[Test]
public void PaySingleSalariedEmployee()
{
  int empId = 1;
  AddSalariedEmployee t = new AddSalariedEmployee(
    empId, "Bob", "Home", 1000.00);
  t.Execute();
  DateTime payDate = new DateTime(2001, 11, 30);
  PaydayTransaction pt = new PaydayTransaction(payDate);
  pt.Execute();
  Paycheck pc = pt.GetPaycheck(empId);
  Assert.IsNotNull(pc);
  Assert.AreEqual(payDate, pc.PayDate);
  Assert.AreEqual(1000.00, pc.GrossPay, .001);
  Assert.AreEqual("Hold", pc.GetField("Disposition"));
  Assert.AreEqual(0.0, pc.Deductions, .001);
  Assert.AreEqual(1000.00, pc.NetPay, .001);
}

[Test]
public void PaySingleSalariedEmployeeOnWrongDate()
{
  int empId = 1;
  AddSalariedEmployee t = new AddSalariedEmployee(
    empId, "Bob", "Home", 1000.00);
  t.Execute();
  DateTime payDate = new DateTime(2001, 11, 29);
```

---

2.   OK, the customer is me.

> **Listing 27-23 (Continued)**
> **PayrollTest.PaySingleSalariedEmployee et al.**
>
> ```
>   PaydayTransaction pt = new PaydayTransaction(payDate);
>   pt.Execute();
>   Paycheck pc = pt.GetPaycheck(empId);
>   Assert.IsNull(pc);
> }
> ```

Listing 27-24 shows the `Execute()` function of `PaydayTransaction`. It iterates through all the `Employee` objects in the database, asking each employee if the date on this transaction is its pay date. If so, it creates a new paycheck for the employee and tells the employee to fill in its fields.

> **Listing 27-24**
> **PaydayTransaction.Execute()**
>
> ```
> public void Execute()
> {
>   ArrayList empIds = PayrollDatabase.GetAllEmployeeIds();
>
>   foreach(int empId in empIds)
>   {
>     Employee employee = PayrollDatabase.GetEmployee(empId);
>     if (employee.IsPayDate(payDate)) {
>       Paycheck pc = new Paycheck(payDate);
>       paychecks[empId] = pc;
>       employee.Payday(pc);
>     }
>   }
> }
> ```

Listing 27-25 shows `MonthlySchedule.cs`. Note that it implements `IsPayDate` to return `true` only if the argument date is the last day of the month.

> **Listing 27-25**
> **MonthlySchedule.cs**
>
> ```
> using System;
>
> namespace Payroll
> {
>   public class MonthlySchedule : PaymentSchedule
>   {
>     private bool IsLastDayOfMonth(DateTime date)
>     {
>       int m1 = date.Month;
>       int m2 = date.AddDays(1).Month;
>       return (m1 != m2);
>     }
>
>     public bool IsPayDate(DateTime payDate)
>     {
>       return IsLastDayOfMonth(payDate);
>     }
>   }
> }
> ```

Listing 27-26 shows the implementation of `Employee.PayDay()`. This function is the generic algorithm for calculating and dispatching payment for all employees. Notice the rampant use of the STRATEGY pattern. All detailed calculations are deferred to the contained strategy classes: `classification`, `affiliation`, and `method`.

Listing 27-26

Employee.Paysay()

```
public void Payday(Paycheck paycheck)
{
  double grossPay = classification.CalculatePay(paycheck);
  double deductions =
    affiliation.CalculateDeductions(paycheck);
  double netPay = grossPay - deductions;
  paycheck.GrossPay = grossPay;
  paycheck.Deductions = deductions;
  paycheck.NetPay = netPay;
  method.Pay(paycheck);
}
```

Paying Hourly Employees

Getting the hourly employees paid is a good example of the incrementalism of test-first design. I started with very trivial test cases and worked my way up to increasingly complex ones. I'll show the test cases first, and then show the production code that resulted from them.

Listing 27-27 shows the simplest case. We add an hourly employee to the database and then pay that employee. Since there aren't any time cards, we expect the paycheck to have a zero value. The utility function `ValidateHourlyPaycheck` represents a refactoring that happened later. At first, that code was simply buried inside the test function. This test case passed after returning `true` from `WeeklySchedule.IsPayDate()`.

Listing 27-27

PayrollTest.TestPaySingleHourlyEmployeeNoTimeCards()

```
[Test]
public void PayingSingleHourlyEmployeeNoTimeCards()
{
  int empId = 2;
  AddHourlyEmployee t = new AddHourlyEmployee(
    empId, "Bill", "Home", 15.25);
  t.Execute();
  DateTime payDate = new DateTime(2001, 11, 9);
  PaydayTransaction pt = new PaydayTransaction(payDate);
  pt.Execute();
  ValidateHourlyPaycheck(pt, empId, payDate, 0.0);
}

private void ValidateHourlyPaycheck(PaydayTransaction pt,
  int empid, DateTime payDate, double pay)
{
  Paycheck pc = pt.GetPaycheck(empid);
  Assert.IsNotNull(pc);
```

Listing 27-27 (Continued)

PayrollTest.TestPaySingleHourlyEmployeeNoTimeCards()

```
    Assert.AreEqual(payDate, pc.PayDate);
    Assert.AreEqual(pay, pc.GrossPay, .001);
    Assert.AreEqual("Hold", pc.GetField("Disposition"));
    Assert.AreEqual(0.0, pc.Deductions, .001);
    Assert.AreEqual(pay, pc.NetPay, .001);
  }
```

Listing 27-28 shows two test cases. The first tests whether we can pay an employee after adding a single time card. The second tests whether we can pay overtime for a card that has more than 8 hours on it. Of course, I didn't write these two test cases at the same time. Instead, I wrote the first one and got it working, and then I wrote the second one.

Listing 27-28

PayrollTest.PaySingleHourlyEmployee...()

```
[Test]
public void PaySingleHourlyEmployeeOneTimeCard()
{
  int empId = 2;
  AddHourlyEmployee t = new AddHourlyEmployee(
    empId, "Bill", "Home", 15.25);
  t.Execute();
  DateTime payDate = new DateTime(2001, 11, 9); // Friday

  TimeCardTransaction tc =
    new TimeCardTransaction(payDate, 2.0, empId);
  tc.Execute();
  PaydayTransaction pt = new PaydayTransaction(payDate);
  pt.Execute();
  ValidateHourlyPaycheck(pt, empId, payDate, 30.5);
}

[Test]
public void PaySingleHourlyEmployeeOvertimeOneTimeCard()
{
  int empId = 2;
  AddHourlyEmployee t = new AddHourlyEmployee(
    empId, "Bill", "Home", 15.25);
  t.Execute();
  DateTime payDate = new DateTime(2001, 11, 9); // Friday

  TimeCardTransaction tc =
    new TimeCardTransaction(payDate, 9.0, empId);
  tc.Execute();
  PaydayTransaction pt = new PaydayTransaction(payDate);
  pt.Execute();
  ValidateHourlyPaycheck(pt, empId, payDate,
    (8 + 1.5)*15.25);
}
```

Getting the first test case working was a matter of changing `HourlyClass-ification.CalculatePay` to loop through the time cards for the employee, add up the

hours, and multiply by the pay rate. Getting the second test working forced me to change
the function to calculate straight and overtime hours.

The test case in Listing 27-29 makes sure that we don't pay hourly employees unless
the `PaydayTransaction` is constructed with a Friday.

Listing 27-29
PayrollTest.PaySingleHourlyEmployeeOnWrongDate()

```
[Test]
public void PaySingleHourlyEmployeeOnWrongDate()
{
  int empId = 2;
  AddHourlyEmployee t = new AddHourlyEmployee(
    empId, "Bill", "Home", 15.25);
  t.Execute();
  DateTime payDate = new DateTime(2001, 11, 8); // Thursday

  TimeCardTransaction tc =
    new TimeCardTransaction(payDate, 9.0, empId);
  tc.Execute();
  PaydayTransaction pt = new PaydayTransaction(payDate);
  pt.Execute();

  Paycheck pc = pt.GetPaycheck(empId);
  Assert.IsNull(pc);
}
```

Listing 27-30 is a test case that makes sure that we can calculate the pay for an
employee who has more than one time card.

Listing 27-30
PayrollTest.PaySingleHourlyEmployeeTwoTimeCards()

```
[Test]
public void PaySingleHourlyEmployeeTwoTimeCards()
{
  int empId = 2;
  AddHourlyEmployee t = new AddHourlyEmployee(
    empId, "Bill", "Home", 15.25);
  t.Execute();
  DateTime payDate = new DateTime(2001, 11, 9); // Friday

  TimeCardTransaction tc =
    new TimeCardTransaction(payDate, 2.0, empId);
  tc.Execute();
  TimeCardTransaction tc2 =
    new TimeCardTransaction(payDate.AddDays(-1), 5.0, empId);
  tc2.Execute();
  PaydayTransaction pt = new PaydayTransaction(payDate);
  pt.Execute();
  ValidateHourlyPaycheck(pt, empId, payDate, 7*15.25);
}
```

Finally, the test case in Listing 27-31 proves that we will pay an employee only for
time cards in the current pay period. Time cards from other pay periods are ignored.

Listing 27-31

PayrollTest.Test...WithTimeCardsSpanningTwoPayPeriods()

```
[Test]
public void
TestPaySingleHourlyEmployeeWithTimeCardsSpanningTwoPayPeriods()
{
  int empId = 2;
  AddHourlyEmployee t = new AddHourlyEmployee(
    empId, "Bill", "Home", 15.25);
  t.Execute();
  DateTime payDate = new DateTime(2001, 11, 9); // Friday
  DateTime dateInPreviousPayPeriod =
    new DateTime(2001, 11, 2);

  TimeCardTransaction tc =
    new TimeCardTransaction(payDate, 2.0, empId);
  tc.Execute();
  TimeCardTransaction tc2 = new TimeCardTransaction(
    dateInPreviousPayPeriod, 5.0, empId);
  tc2.Execute();
  PaydayTransaction pt = new PaydayTransaction(payDate);
  pt.Execute();
  ValidateHourlyPaycheck(pt, empId, payDate, 2*15.25);
}
```

The code that makes all this work was grown incrementally, one test case at a time. The structure you see in the code that follows evolved from test case to test case. Listing 27-32 shows the appropriate fragments of HourlyClassification.cs. We simply loop through the time cards. For each time card, we check whether if it is in the pay period. If so, we calculate the pay it represents.

Listing 27-32

HourlyClassification.cs (fragment)

```
public double CalculatePay(Paycheck paycheck)
{
  double totalPay = 0.0;
  foreach(TimeCard timeCard in timeCards.Values)
  {
    if(IsInPayPeriod(timeCard, paycheck.PayDate))
      totalPay += CalculatePayForTimeCard(timeCard);
  }
  return totalPay;
}

private bool IsInPayPeriod(TimeCard card,
                           DateTime payPeriod)
{
  DateTime payPeriodEndDate = payPeriod;
  DateTime payPeriodStartDate = payPeriod.AddDays(-5);

  return card.Date <= payPeriodEndDate &&
    card.Date >= payPeriodStartDate;
}
```

Listing 27-32 (Continued)

HourlyClassification.cs (fragment)

```
private double CalculatePayForTimeCard(TimeCard card)
{
  double overtimeHours = Math.Max(0.0, card.Hours - 8);
  double normalHours = card.Hours - overtimeHours;
  return hourlyRate * normalHours +
    hourlyRate * 1.5 * overtimeHours;
}
```

Listing 27-33 shows that the WeeklySchedule pays only on Fridays.

Listing 27-33

WeeklySchedule.IsPayDate()

```
public bool IsPayDate(DateTime payDate)
{
  return payDate.DayOfWeek == DayOfWeek.Friday;
}
```

Calculating the pay for commissioned employees is left as an exercise. There shouldn't be any big surprises.

Pay periods: A design problem Now it's time to implement the union dues and service charges. I'm contemplating a test case that will add a salaried employee, convert it into a union member, and then pay the employee and ensure that the dues were subtracted from the pay. The coding is shown in Listing 27-34.

Listing 27-34

PayrollTest.SalariedUnionMemberDues()

```
[Test]
public void SalariedUnionMemberDues()
{
  int empId = 1;
  AddSalariedEmployee t = new AddSalariedEmployee(
    empId, "Bob", "Home", 1000.00);
  t.Execute();
  int memberId = 7734;
  ChangeMemberTransaction cmt =
    new ChangeMemberTransaction(empId, memberId, 9.42);
  cmt.Execute();
  DateTime payDate = new DateTime(2001, 11, 30);
  PaydayTransaction pt = new PaydayTransaction(payDate);
  pt.Execute();
  Paycheck pc = pt.GetPaycheck(empId);
  Assert.IsNotNull(pc);
  Assert.AreEqual(payDate, pc.PayDate);
  Assert.AreEqual(1000.0, pc.GrossPay, .001);
  Assert.AreEqual("Hold", pc.GetField("Disposition"));
  Assert.AreEqual(???, pc.Deductions, .001);
  Assert.AreEqual(1000.0 - ???, pc.NetPay, .001);
}
```

Note the **???** in the last two lines of the test case. What should I put there? The user stories tell me that union dues are weekly, but salaried employees are paid monthly. How many weeks are in each month? Should I simply multiply the dues by 4? That's not very accurate. I'll ask the customer what he wants.[3]

The customer tells me that union dues are accrued every Friday. So what I need to do is count the number of Fridays in the pay period and multiply by the weekly dues. There are five Fridays in November 2001, the month the test case is written for. So I can modify the test case appropriately.

Counting the Fridays in a pay period implies that I need to know what the starting and ending dates of the pay period are. I have done this calculation before in the function `IsInPayPeriod` in Listing 27-32. (You probably wrote a similar one for the `CommissionedClassification`.) This function is used by the `CalculatePay` function of the `HourlyClassification` object to ensure that time cards only from the pay period are tallied. Now it seems that the `UnionAffiliation` object must call this function, too.

But wait! What is this function doing in the `HourlyClassification` class? We've already determined that the association between the payment schedule and the payment classification is accidental. The function that determines the pay period ought to be in the `PaymentSchedule` class, not in the `PaymentClassification` class!

It is interesting that our UML diagrams didn't help us catch this problem. The problem surfaced only when I started thinking about the test cases for `UnionAffiliation`. This is yet another example of how necessary coding feedback is to any design. Diagrams can be useful, but reliance on them without feedback from the code is risky business.

So, how do we get the pay period out of the `PaymentSchedule` hierarchy and into the `PaymentClassification` and `Affiliation` hierarchies? These hierarchies do not know anything about each other. I have an idea about this. We could put the pay period dates into the `Paycheck` object. Right now, the `Paycheck` simply has the end date of the pay period. We ought to be able to get the start date in there too.

Listing 27-35 shows the change made to `PaydayTransaction.Execute()`. Note that when the `Paycheck` is created, it is passed both the start and end dates of the pay period. Note also that it is the `PaymentSchedule` that calculates both. The changes to `Paycheck` should be obvious.

Listing 27-35
PaydayTransaction.Execute()

```
public void Execute()
{
  ArrayList empIds = PayrollDatabase.GetAllEmployeeIds();

  foreach(int empId in empIds)
  {
    Employee employee = PayrollDatabase.GetEmployee(empId);
```

---

3. And so Bob talks to himself yet again. Go to www.google.com/groups and look up "Schizophrenic Robert Martin."

Listing 27-35 (Continued)

`PaydayTransaction.Execute()`

```
    if (employee.IsPayDate(payDate))
    {
      DateTime startDate =
        employee.GetPayPeriodStartDate(payDate);
      Paycheck pc = new Paycheck(startDate, payDate);
      paychecks[empId] = pc;
      employee.Payday(pc);
    }
  }
}
```

The two functions in `HourlyClassification` and `CommissionedClassification` that determined whether `TimeCards` and `SalesReceipts` were within the pay period have been merged and moved into the base class `PaymentClassification`. See Listing 27-36.

Listing 27-36

`PaymentClassification.IsInPayPeriod(...)`

```
public bool IsInPayPeriod(DateTime theDate, Paycheck paycheck)
{
  DateTime payPeriodEndDate = paycheck.PayPeriodEndDate;
  DateTime payPeriodStartDate = paycheck.PayPeriodStartDate;
  return (theDate >= payPeriodStartDate)
    && (theDate <= payPeriodEndDate);
}
```

Now we are ready to calculate the employee's union dues in `UnionAffilliation.CalculateDeductions`. The code in Listing 27-37 shows how this is done. The two dates that define the pay period are extracted from the paycheck and are passed to a utility function that counts the number of Fridays between them. This number is then multiplied by the weekly dues rate to calculate the dues for the pay period.

Listing 27-37

`UnionAffiliation.CalculateDeductions(...)`

```
public double CalculateDeductions(Paycheck paycheck)
{
  double totalDues = 0;

  int fridays = NumberOfFridaysInPayPeriod(
    paycheck.PayPeriodStartDate, paycheck.PayPeriodEndDate);
  totalDues = dues * fridays;
  return totalDues;
}

private int NumberOfFridaysInPayPeriod(
  DateTime payPeriodStart, DateTime payPeriodEnd)
{
  int fridays = 0;
  for (DateTime day = payPeriodStart;
    day <= payPeriodEnd; day.AddDays(1))
```

Listing 27-37 (Continued)

`UnionAffiliation.CalculateDeductions(...)`

```
  {
    if (day.DayOfWeek == DayOfWeek.Friday)
      fridays++;
  }
  return fridays;
}
```

The last two test cases have to do with union service charges. The first test case, shown in Listing 27-38, makes sure that we deduct service charges appropriately.

Listing 27-38

`PayrollTest.HourlyUnionMemberServiceCharge()`

```
[Test]
public void HourlyUnionMemberServiceCharge()
{
  int empId = 1;
  AddHourlyEmployee t = new AddHourlyEmployee(
    empId, "Bill", "Home", 15.24);
  t.Execute();
  int memberId = 7734;
  ChangeMemberTransaction cmt =
    new ChangeMemberTransaction(empId, memberId, 9.42);
  cmt.Execute();
  DateTime payDate = new DateTime(2001, 11, 9);
  ServiceChargeTransaction sct =
    new ServiceChargeTransaction(memberId, payDate, 19.42);
  sct.Execute();
  TimeCardTransaction tct =
    new TimeCardTransaction(payDate, 8.0, empId);
  tct.Execute();
  PaydayTransaction pt = new PaydayTransaction(payDate);
  pt.Execute();
  Paycheck pc = pt.GetPaycheck(empId);
  Assert.IsNotNull(pc);
  Assert.AreEqual(payDate, pc.PayPeriodEndDate);
  Assert.AreEqual(8*15.24, pc.GrossPay, .001);
  Assert.AreEqual("Hold", pc.GetField("Disposition"));
  Assert.AreEqual(9.42 + 19.42, pc.Deductions, .001);
  Assert.AreEqual((8*15.24)-(9.42 + 19.42),pc.NetPay, .001);
}
```

The second test case, which posed something of a problem for me, is shown it in Listing 27-39. This test case makes sure that service charges dated outside the current pay period are not deducted.

Listing 27-39

`PayrollTest.ServiceChargesSpanningMultiplePayPeriods()`

```
[Test]
public void ServiceChargesSpanningMultiplePayPeriods()
{
  int empId = 1;
```

Listing 27-39 (Continued)

`PayrollTest.ServiceChargesSpanningMultiplePayPeriods()`

```
    AddHourlyEmployee t = new AddHourlyEmployee(
      empId, "Bill", "Home", 15.24);
    t.Execute();
    int memberId = 7734;
    ChangeMemberTransaction cmt =
      new ChangeMemberTransaction(empId, memberId, 9.42);
    cmt.Execute();
    DateTime payDate = new DateTime(2001, 11, 9);
    DateTime earlyDate =
      new DateTime(2001, 11, 2); // previous Friday
    DateTime lateDate =
      new DateTime(2001, 11, 16); // next Friday
    ServiceChargeTransaction sct =
      new ServiceChargeTransaction(memberId, payDate, 19.42);
    sct.Execute();
    ServiceChargeTransaction sctEarly =
      new ServiceChargeTransaction(memberId,earlyDate,100.00);
    sctEarly.Execute();
    ServiceChargeTransaction sctLate =
      new ServiceChargeTransaction(memberId,lateDate,200.00);
    sctLate.Execute();
    TimeCardTransaction tct =
      new TimeCardTransaction(payDate, 8.0, empId);
    tct.Execute();
    PaydayTransaction pt = new PaydayTransaction(payDate);
    pt.Execute();
    Paycheck pc = pt.GetPaycheck(empId);
    Assert.IsNotNull(pc);
    Assert.AreEqual(payDate, pc.PayPeriodEndDate);
    Assert.AreEqual(8*15.24, pc.GrossPay, .001);
    Assert.AreEqual("Hold", pc.GetField("Disposition"));
    Assert.AreEqual(9.42 + 19.42, pc.Deductions, .001);
    Assert.AreEqual((8*15.24) - (9.42 + 19.42),
      pc.NetPay, .001);
  }
```

To implement this, I wanted `UnionAffiliation::CalculateDeductions` to call `IsInPayPeriod`. Unfortunately, we just put `IsInPayPeriod` in the `PaymentClass-ification` class. (See Listing 27-36.) It was convenient to put it there while it was the derivatives of `PaymentClassification` that needed to call it. But now other classes need it as well. So I moved the function into a `DateUtil` class. After all, the function is simply determining whether a given date is between two other given dates. (See Listing 27-40.)

Listing 27-40

`DateUtil.cs`

```
using System;

namespace Payroll
{
  public class DateUtil
```

Listing 27-40 (Continued)

DateUtil.cs

```
    {
      public static bool IsInPayPeriod(
        DateTime theDate, DateTime startDate, DateTime endDate)
      {
        return (theDate >= startDate) && (theDate <= endDate);
      }
    }
  }
```

So now, finally, we can finish the `UnionAffiliation::CalculateDeductions` function. I leave that as an exercise for you.

Listing 27-41 shows the implementation of the `Employee` class.

Listing 27-41

Employee.cs

```
using System;

namespace Payroll
{
  public class Employee
  {
    private readonly int empid;
    private string name;
    private readonly string address;
    private PaymentClassification classification;
    private PaymentSchedule schedule;
    private PaymentMethod method;
    private Affiliation affiliation = new NoAffiliation();

    public Employee(int empid, string name, string address)
    {
      this.empid = empid;
      this.name = name;
      this.address = address;
    }

    public string Name
    {
      get { return name; }
      set { name = value; }
    }

    public string Address
    {
      get { return address; }
    }

    public PaymentClassification Classification
    {
      get { return classification; }
      set { classification = value; }
    }
```

Listing 27-41 (Continued)
Employee.cs

```csharp
    public PaymentSchedule Schedule
    {
      get { return schedule; }
      set { schedule = value; }
    }

    public PaymentMethod Method
    {
      get { return method; }
      set { method = value; }
    }

    public Affiliation Affiliation
    {
      get { return affiliation; }
      set { affiliation = value; }
    }

    public bool IsPayDate(DateTime date)
    {
      return schedule.IsPayDate(date);
    }

    public void Payday(Paycheck paycheck)
    {
      double grossPay = classification.CalculatePay(paycheck);
      double deductions =
        affiliation.CalculateDeductions(paycheck);
      double netPay = grossPay - deductions;
      paycheck.GrossPay = grossPay;
      paycheck.Deductions = deductions;
      paycheck.NetPay = netPay;
      method.Pay(paycheck);
    }

    public DateTime GetPayPeriodStartDate(DateTime date)
    {
      return schedule.GetPayPeriodStartDate(date);
    }
  }
}
```

Main Program

The main payroll program can now be expressed as a loop that parses transactions from an input source and then executes them. Figures 27-33 and 27-34 describe the statics and dynamics of the main program. The concept is simple: The `PayrollApplication` sits in a loop, alternately requesting transactions from the `TransactionSource` and then telling those `Transaction` objects to `Execute`. Note that this is different from the diagram in Figure 27-1 and represents a shift in our thinking to a more abstract mechanism.

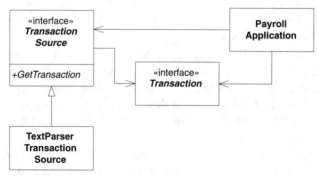

Figure 27-33
Static model for the main program

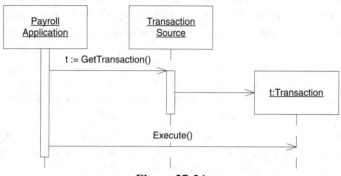

Figure 27-34
Dynamic model for the main program

`TransactionSource` is an interface that we can implement in several ways. The static diagram shows the derivative named `TextParserTransactionSource`, which reads an incoming text stream and parses out the transactions as described in the use cases. This object then creates the appropriate `Transaction` objects and sends them along to the `PayrollApplication`.

The separation of interface from implementation in the `TransactionSource` allows the source of the transactions to vary. For example, we could easily interface the `PayrollApplication` to a `GUITransactionSource` or a `RemoteTransaction-Source`.

The Database

Now that most of the application has been analyzed, designed, and implemented, we can consider the role of the database. The class `PayrollDatabase` clearly encapsulates something involving persistence. The objects contained within the `PayrollDatabase` must live longer than any particular run of the application. How should this be implemented? Clearly, the transient mechanism used by the test cases is not sufficient for the real system. We have several options.

We could implement `PayrollDatabase` by using an object-oriented database management system (OODBMS). This would allow the objects to reside within the permanent storage of the database. As designers, we would have little more work to do, since the OODBMS would not add much new to our design. One of the great benefits of OODBMS products is that they have little or no impact on the object model of the applications. As far as the design is concerned, the database barely exists.[4]

Another option would be to use simple flat text files to record the data. On initialization, the `PayrollDatabase` object could read that file and build the necessary objects in memory. At the end of the program, the `PayrollDatabase` object could write a new version of the text file. Certainly, this option would not suffice for a company with hundreds of thousands of employees or one that wanted real-time concurrent access to its payroll database. However, it might suffice for a smaller company, and it could certainly be used as a mechanism for testing the rest of the application classes without investing in a big database system.

Still another option would be to incorporate a relational database management system (RDBMS) into the `PayrollDatabase` object. The implementation of the `Payroll-Database` object would then make the appropriate queries to the RDMBS to temporarily create the necessary objects in memory.

The point is that any of these mechanisms would work. Our application has been designed in such a way that it does not know or care what the underlying implementation of the database is. As far as the application is concerned, the database is simply mechanisms for managing storage.

Databases should usually not be considered as a major factor of the design and implementation. As we have shown here, they can be left for last and handled as a detail.[5] By doing so, we leave open a number of interesting options for implementing the needed persistence and creating mechanisms to test the rest of the application. We also do not tie ourselves to any particular database technology or product. We have the freedom to choose the database we need, based on the rest of the design, and we maintain the freedom to change or replace that database product in the future as needed.

---

4. This is optimistic. In a simple application, such as payroll, the use of an OODBMS would have very little impact on the design of the program. As applications become more and more complicated, the amount of impact that the OODBMS has on the application increases. Still, the impact is far less than what an RDBMS would have.

5. Sometimes, the nature of the database is one of the requirements of the application. RDBMSs provide powerful query and reporting systems that may be listed as application requirements. However, even when such requirements are explicit, the designers should still decouple the application design from the database design. The application design should not have to depend on any particular kind of database.

Conclusion

In roughly 32 diagrams in Chapters 26 and 27, we have documented the design and implementation of the payroll application. The design uses a large amount of abstraction and polymorphism. The result is that large portions of the design are closed against changes of payroll policy. For example, the application could be changed to deal with employees who were paid quarterly, based on a normal salary and a bonus schedule. This change would require *addition* to the design, but little of the existing design and code would change.

During this design process, we rarely considered whether we were performing analysis, design, or implementation. Instead, we concentrated on issues of clarity and dependency management. We tried to find the underlying abstractions wherever possible. The result is that we have a good design for a payroll application, and we have a core of classes that are germane to the problem domain as a whole.

About This Chapter

The diagrams in this chapter are derived from the Booch diagrams in the corresponding chapter of my 1995 book.[6] Those diagrams were created in 1994. As I created them, I also wrote some of the code that implemented them, to make sure that the diagrams made sense. However, I did not write anywhere near the amount of code presented here. Therefore, the diagrams did not benefit from significant feedback from the code and tests. This lack of feedback shows.

This chapter appears in my 2002 book.[7] I wrote the code for that chapter in C++ in the order presented here. In every case, test cases were written before production code. In many cases, those tests were created incrementally, evolving as the production code also evolved. The production code was written to comply with the diagrams, so long as that made sense. In several cases, it did not make sense, and so I changed the design of the code.

One of the first places that this happened was when I decided against multiple `Affiliation` instances in the `Employee` object. Another was when I found that I had not considered recording the employee's membership in the union in the `ChangeMember-Transaction`.

This is normal. When you design without feedback, you will necessarily make errors. It was the feedback imposed by the tests cases and running code that found these errors for us.

This chapter was translated from C++ into C# by my coauthor, Micah Martin. Special attention was paid to C# conventions and styles, so that the code would not look too much like C#++. (You can find the final version of this code on the Prentice Hall Web site or on www.objectmentor.com/PPP/payroll.net.zip.) The diagrams were left unchanged, except that we replaced composition relationships with associations.

---

6. [Martin1995]

7. [Martin2002]

Bibliography

[Jacobson92] Ivar Jacobson, *Object-Oriented Software Engineering: A Use Case Driven Approach*, Addison-Wesley, 1992.

[Martin1995] *Designing Object-Oriented C++ Aplications Using the Booch Method*, Prentice Hall, 1995.

[Martin2002] *Agile Software Development: Principles, Patterns, and Practices*, Prentice Hall, 2002.

Section IV

Packaging the Payroll System

THIS SIDE UP

© Jennifer M. Kohnke

In this section, we explore the principles of design that help us split a large software system into packages. Chapter 28 discusses those principles. Chapter 29 describes a pattern that we'll use to help improve the packaging structure. Chapter 30 shows how the principles and pattern can be applied to the payroll system.

28

Principles of Package and Component Design

© Jennifer M. Kohnke

Nice package.

—Anthony

As software applications grow in size and complexity, they require some kind of high-level organization. Classes are convenient unit for organizing small applications but are too finely grained to be used as the sole organizational unit for large applications. Something "larger" than a class is needed to help organize large applications. That something is called a *package*, or a *component*.

Packages and Components

The term *package* has been overloaded with many meanings in software. For our purposes, we focus on one particular kind of package, often called a *component*. A component is an independently deployable *binary* unit. In .NET, components are often called *assemblies* and are carried within DLLs.

As vitally important elements of large software systems, components allow such systems to be decomposed into smaller binary deliverables. If the dependencies between the components are well managed, it is possible to fix bugs and add features by redeploying only those components that have changed. More important, *the design of large systems depends critically on good component design*, so that individual teams can focus on isolated components instead of worrying about the whole system.

In UML, packages can be used as containers for groups of classes. These packages can represent subsystems, libraries, or components. By grouping classes into packages, we can reason about the design at a higher level of abstraction. If those packages are components, we can use them to manage the development and distribution of the software. Our goal in this chapter is to learn how to partition the classes in an application according to some criteria and then allocate the classes in those partitions to independently deployable components.

But classes often have dependencies on other classes, and these dependencies often cross component boundaries. Thus, the components will have dependency relationships with each other. The relationships between components express the high-level organization of the application and need to be managed.

This begs a large number of questions.

1. What are the principles for allocating classes to components?

2. What design principles govern the relationships between components?

3. Should components be designed before classes (top down)? Or should classes be designed before components (bottom up)?

4. How are components physically represented? In C#? In the development environment?

5. Once created, to what purpose will we put these components?

This chapter outlines six principles for managing the contents and relationships between components. The first three, principles of package cohesion, help us allocate classes to packages. The last three principles govern package coupling and help us determine how packages should be interrelated. The last two principles also describe a set of *dependency management metrics* that allow developers to measure and characterize the dependency structure of their designs.

Principles of Component Cohesion: Granularity

The principles of component cohesion help developers decide how to partition classes into components. These principles depend on the fact that at least some of the classes and their interrelationships have been discovered. Thus, these principles take a bottom-up view of partitioning.

The Reuse/Release Equivalence Principle (REP)

> **The granule of reuse is the granule of release.**

What do you expect from the author of a class library that you are planning to reuse? Certainly, you want good documentation, working code, well-specified interfaces, and so on. But there are other things you want, too.

First, to make it worth your while to reuse this person's code, you want the author to guarantee to maintain it for you. After all, if you have to maintain it, you are going to have to invest a tremendous amount of time into it, time that might be better spent designing a smaller and better component for yourself.

Second, you are going to want the author to notify you of any changes planned to the interface and functionality of the code. But notification is not enough. The author must give you the choice to refuse to use any new versions. After all, the author might introduce a new version just as you are entering a severe schedule crunch or might make changes to the code that are simply incompatible with your system.

In either case, should you decide to reject that version, the author must guarantee to support your use of the old version for a time. Perhaps that time is as short as 3 months or as long as a year; that is something for the two of you to negotiate. But the author can't simply cut you loose and refuse to support you. If the author won't agree to support your use of older versions, you may have to seriously consider whether you want to use that code and be subject to the author's capricious changes.

This issue is primarily political. It has to do with the clerical and support effort that must be provided if other people are going to reuse code. But those political and clerical issues have a profound effect on the packaging structure of software. In order to provide the guarantees that reusers need, authors organize their software into reusable components and then track those components with release numbers.

Thus, REP states that the granule of reuse, a component, can be no smaller than the granule of release. Anything that we reuse must also be released and tracked. It is not realistic for a developer to simply write a class and then claim that it is reusable. Reusability comes only after a tracking system is in place and offers the guarantees of notification, safety, and support that the potential reusers will need.

REP gives us our first hint at how to partition our design into components. Since reusability must be based on components, reusable components must contain reusable classes. So, at least some components should comprise reusable sets of classes.

It may seem disquieting that a political force would affect the partitioning of our software, but software is not a mathematically pure entity that can be structured according to mathematically pure rules. Software is a human product that supports human endeavors. Software is created by humans and is used by humans. And if software is going to be reused, it must be partitioned in a manner that humans find convenient for that purpose.

What does this tell us about the internal structure of a component? One must consider the internal contents from the point of view of potential reusers. If a component contains software that should be reused, it should not also contain software that is not designed for reuse. *Either all the classes in a component are reusable, or none of them are.*

Further, it's not simply reusability that is the criterion; we must also consider who the reuser is. Certainly, a container class library is reusable, and so is a financial framework. But we would not want them to be part of the same component, for many people who would like to reuse a container class library would have no interest in a financial framework. Thus, we want all the classes in a component to be reusable by the same audience. We do not want an audience to find that a component consists of some classes that are needed, and others that are wholly inappropriate.

The Common Reuse Principle (CRP)

> **The classes in a component are reused together. If you reuse one of the classes in a component, you reuse them all.**

This principle helps us to decide which classes should be placed into a component. CRP states that classes that tend to be reused together belong in the same component.

Classes are seldom reused in isolation. Generally, reusable classes collaborate with other classes that are part of the reusable abstraction. CRP states that these classes belong together in the same component. In such a component, we would expect to see classes that have lots of dependencies on each other. A simple example might be a container class and its associated iterators. These classes are reused together because they are tightly coupled. Thus, they ought to be in the same component.

But CRP tells us more than simply what classes to put together into a component. It also tells us what classes *not* to put in the component. When one component uses another, a dependency is created between the components. It may be that the using component uses only one class within the used component. However, that doesn't weaken the dependency. The using component still depends on the used component. Every time the used component is released, the using component must be revalidated and rereleased. This is true even if the used component is being released because of changes to a class that the using component doesn't care about.

Moreover, it is common for components to live in DLLs. If the used component is released as a DLL, the using code depends on the entire DLL. Any modification to that DLL, even if that modification is to a class that the using code does not care about, will still cause a new version of the DLL to be released. The new DLL will still have to be redeployed, and the using code will still have to be revalidated.

Thus, I want to make sure that when I depend on a component, I depend on every class in that component. To say this another way, I want to make sure that the classes that I put into a component are inseparable, that it is impossible to depend on some and not the others. Otherwise, I will be revalidating and redeploying more than is necessary and will be wasting significant effort.

Therefore, CRP tells us more about what classes shouldn't be together than what classes should be together. CRP says that classes that are not tightly bound to each other with class relationships should not be in the same component.

The Common Closure Principle (CCP)

> **The classes in a component should be closed together against the same kinds of changes. A change that affects a component affects all the classes in that component and no other components.**

This is the Single-Responsibility Principle (SRP) restated for components. Just as SRP says that a class should not contain multiple reasons to change, CCP says that a component should not have multiple reasons to change.

In most applications, maintainability is more important that reusability. If the code in an application must change, you would prefer the changes to occur all in one component rather than being distributed through many components. If changes are focused into a single component, we need redeploy only the one changed component. Other components that don't depend on the changed component do not need to be revalidated or redeployed.

CCP prompts us to gather together in one place all the classes that are likely to change for the same reasons. If two classes are so tightly bound, either physically or conceptually, that they always change together, they belong in the same component. This minimizes the workload related to releasing, revalidating, and redistributing the software.

This principle is closely associated with the Open/Closed Principle (OCP). For it is "closure" in the OCP sense of the word that this principle is dealing with. OCP states that classes should be closed for modification but open for extension. But as we learned, 100 percent closure is not attainable. Closure must be strategic. We design our systems such that they are closed to the most common kinds of changes that we have experienced.

CCP amplifies this by grouping together classes that are open to certain types of changes into the same components. Thus, when a change in requirements comes along, that change has a good chance of being restricted to a minimal number of components.

Summary of Component Cohesion

In the past, our view of cohesion was much simpler. We used to think that cohesion was simply the attribute of a module to perform one, and only one, function. However, the three principles of component cohesion describe a much more complex kind of cohesion. In choosing the classes to group together into a component, we must consider the opposing forces involved in reusability and developability.

Balancing these forces with the needs of the application is nontrivial. Moreover, the balance is almost always dynamic. That is, the partitioning that is appropriate today might not be appropriate next year. Thus, the composition of the component will likely jitter and evolve with time as the focus of the project changes from developability to reusability.

Principles of Component Coupling: Stability

The next three principles deal with the relationships between components. Here again, we will run into the tension between developability and logical design. The forces that impinge on the architecture of a component structure are technical, political, and volatile.

The Acyclic Dependencies Principle (ADP)

> **Allow no cycles in the component dependency graph.**

Have you ever worked all day, gotten some stuff working, and then gone home, only to arrive the next morning to find that your stuff no longer works? Why doesn't it work? Because somebody stayed later than you and changed something you depend on! I call this "the morning-after syndrome."

The "morning-after syndrome" occurs in development environments in which many developers are modifying the same source files. In relatively small projects with only a few developers, it isn't too big a problem. But as the size of the project and the development team grows, the mornings after can get pretty nightmarish. It is not uncommon for weeks to go by without being able to build a stable version of the project. Instead, everyone keeps on changing and changing their code, trying to make it work with the last changes that someone else made.

Over the past several decades, two solutions to this problem have evolved: the weekly build and ADP. Both solutions have come from the telecommunications industry.

The weekly build The weekly build is common in medium-sized projects. It works like this: For the first 4 days of the week, all the developers ignore one another. They all work on private copies of the code and don't worry about integrating with one another. Then, on Friday, they integrate all their changes and build the system. This has the wonderful advantage of allowing the developers to live in an isolated world for four days out of five. The disadvantage, of course, is the large integration penalty that is paid on Friday.

Unfortunately, as the project grows, it becomes less feasible to finish integrating on Friday. The integration burden grows until it starts to overflow into Saturday. A few such Saturdays are enough to convince the developers that integration should begin on Thursday. And so the start of integration slowly creeps toward the middle of the week.

As the duty cycle of development versus integration decreases, the efficiency of the team decreases, too. Eventually, this becomes so frustrating that the developers or the project managers declare that the schedule should be changed to a biweekly build. This suffices for a time, but the integration time continues to grow with project size.

This eventually leads to a crisis. To maintain efficiency, the build schedule has to be continually lengthened. Yet lengthening the build schedule increases project risks. Integration and testing become more and more difficult, and the team loses the benefit of rapid feedback.

Eliminating dependency cycles The solution to this problem is to partition the development environment into releasable components. The components become units of work that can be the responsibility of a developer or a team of developers. When developers get a component working, they release it for use by the other developers. They give it a release number, and move it into a directory for other teams to use, and continue to modify their component in their own private areas. Everyone else uses the released version.

As new releases of a component are made, other teams can decide whether to immediately adopt the new release. If they decide not to, they simply continue using the old release. Once they decide that they are ready, they begin to use the new release.

Thus, none of the teams are at the mercy of the others. Changes made to one component do not need to have an immediate effect on other teams. Each team can decide for itself when to adapt its component to new releases of the components they use. Moreover, integration happens in small increments. There is no single point at which all developers must come together and integrate everything they are doing.

This is a very simple and rational process and is widely used. However, to make it work, you must *manage* the dependency structure of the components. *There can be no cycles*. If there are cycles in the dependency structure, the morning-after syndrome cannot be avoided.

Consider the component diagram in Figure 28-1. Here, we see a rather typical structure of components assembled into an application. The function of this application is unimportant for the purpose of this example. What *is* important is the dependency structure of the components. Note that this structure is a *directed graph*. The components are the *nodes*, and the dependency relationships are the *directed edges*.

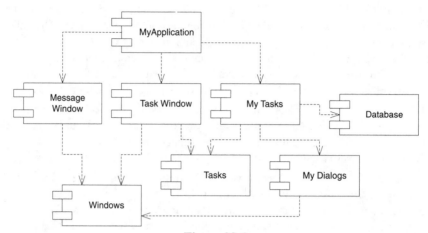

Figure 28-1
Component structures are a directed acyclic graph.

Now note one more thing. Regardless of which component you begin at, it is impossible to follow the dependency relationships and wind up back at that component. This structure has no cycles. It is a *directed acyclic graph* (DAG).

Now, note what happens when the team responsible for MyDialogs makes a new release of its component. It is easy to find out who is affected by this release; you simply follow the dependency arrows backward. Thus, MyTasks and MyApplication are both going to be affected. The developers currently working on those components will have to decide when they should integrate with the new release of MyDialogs.

When MyDialogs is released, it has no effect on many of the other components in the system. They don't know about MyDialogs and don't care when it changes. This is nice. It means that the impact of releasing MyDialogs is relatively small.

When the developers working on the MyDialogs component would like to run a test of that component, all they need do is build their version of MyDialogs with the version of the Windows component they are currently using. None of the other components in the system need be involved. This is nice; it means that the developers working on MyDialogs have relatively little work to do to set up a test and have relatively few variables to consider.

When it is time to release the whole system, it is done from the bottom up. First, the Windows component is compiled, tested, and released, followed by MessageWindow and MyDialogs, then Task, and then TaskWindow and Database. MyTasks is next and, finally, MyApplication. This process is very clear and easy to deal with. We know how to build the system because we understand the dependencies between its parts.

The effect of a cycle in the component dependency graph Let us say that a new requirement forces us to change one of the classes in MyDialogs such that it makes use of a class in `MyApplication`. This creates a dependency cycle, as shown in the component diagram of Figure 28-2.

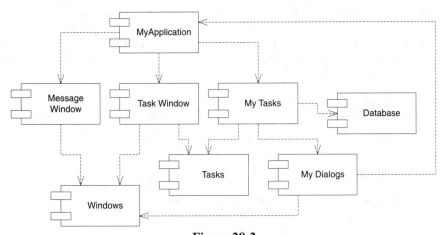

Figure 28-2
A component diagram with a cycle

This cycle creates some immediate problems. For example, the developers working on the `MyTasks` component know that in order to release, they must be compatible with `Tasks`, `MyDialogs`, `Database`, and `Windows`. However, with the cycle in place, they must now also be compatible with `MyApplication`, `TaskWindow`, and `MessageWindow`. That is, `MyTasks` now depends on *every other component in the system*. This makes `MyTasks` very difficult to release. `MyDialogs` suffers the same fate. In fact, the cycle forces `MyApplication`, `MyTasks`, and `MyDialogs` to always be released at the same time. They have, in effect, become one large component. All the developers who are working in any of those components will experience the morning-after syndrome once again. They will be stepping all over one another, since they must all be using exactly the same release of one another's components.

But this is only part of the trouble. Consider what happens when we want to test the `Mydialogs` component. We find that we must reference every other component in the system, including the `Database` component. This means that we have to do a *complete build* just to test `MyDialogs`. This is intolerable.

Have you ever wondered why you have to reference so many different libraries and so much of everybody else's stuff just to run a simple unit test of one of your classes? It is probably because there are cycles in the dependency graph. Such cycles make it very difficult to isolate modules. Unit testing and releasing become very difficult and error prone. Further, compile times grow geometrically with the number of modules. Moreover, when there are cycles in the dependency graph, it can be very difficult to work out what order to build the components in. Indeed, there may be no correct order, which can lead to some nasty problems.

Breaking the cycle It is always possible to break a cycle of components and reinstate the dependency graph as a DAG. There are two primary mechanisms.

1. Apply the Dependency-Inversion Principle (DIP). In the case of Figure 28-2, we could create an abstract base class that has the interface that `MyDialogs` needs. We could then put that abstract base into `MyDialogs` and inherit it into `MyApplication`. This inverts the dependency between `MyDialogs` and `MyApplication`, thus breaking the cycle. See Figure 28-3.

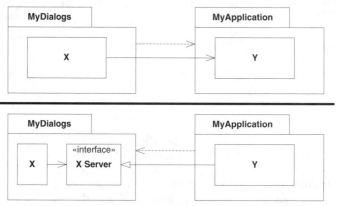

Figure 28-3
Breaking the cycle with dependency inversion

Note that once again, that we named the interface after the client rather than the server. This is yet another application of the rule that interfaces belong to clients.

2. Create a new component that both `MyDialogs` and `MyApplication` depend on. Move the class(es) that they both depend on into that new component. See Figure 28-4.

The second solution implies that the component structure is volatile in the presence of changing requirements. Indeed, as the application grows, the component-dependency structure jitters and grows. Thus, the dependency structure must always be monitored for cycles. When cycles occur, they must be broken somehow. Sometimes, this will mean creating a new component, making the dependency structure grow.

Top-down versus bottom-up design The issues we have discussed so far lead to an inescapable conclusion. The component structure cannot be designed from the top down in the absence of code. Rather, that structure evolves as the system grows and changes.

Some of you may find this to be counterintuitive. We have come to expect that large-grained decompositions, such as components, are also high-level *functional* decompositions. When we see a large-grained grouping, such as a component dependency structure, we feel that the components ought to somehow represent the functions of the system.

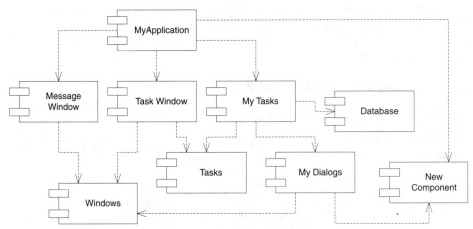

Figure 28-4
Breaking the cycle with a new component

Although it is true that components offer services and functions to one another, there is more to it than that.

The component-dependency structure is a map of the *buildability* of the application. This is why component structures can't be completely designed at the start of the project. This is also why they are not strictly based on functional decomposition. As more and more classes accumulate in the early stages of implementation and design, there is a growing need to manage the dependencies so that the project can be developed without the morning-after syndrome. Moreover, we want to keep changes as localized as possible, so we start paying attention to SRP and CCP and collocate classes that are likely to change together.

As the application continues to grow, we become concerned about creating reusable elements. Thus, CRP begins to dictate the composition of the components. Finally, as cycles appear, ADP is applied, and the component-dependency graph jitters and grows for reasons that have more to do with dependency structure than with function.

If we tried to design the component-dependency structure before we had designed any classes, we would likely fail rather badly. We would not know much about common closure, we would be unaware of any reusable elements, and we would almost certainly create components that produced dependency cycles. Thus, the component-dependency structure grows and evolves with the logical design of the system.

It does not take long, however, for the component structure to settle down into something that is stable enough to support multiple-team development. Once this happens, the teams can focus on their own components. Communication between teams can be restricted to the component boundaries. This enables many teams to work concurrently on the same project with a minimum of overhead.

Keep in mind, however, that the structure of the components will continue to jitter and change as development proceeds. This prevents perfect isolation between the component teams. Those teams will have to work together as the shapes of the components push and pull against each other.

The Stable-Dependencies Principle (SDP)

> **Depend in the direction of stability.**

Designs cannot be completely static. Some volatility is necessary if the design is to be maintained. We accomplish this by conforming to CCP. Using this principle, we create components that are sensitive to certain kinds of changes. These components are *designed* to be volatile; we *expect* them to change.

Any component that we expect to be volatile should not be depended on by a component that is difficult to change! Otherwise, the volatile component will also be difficult to change.

It is the perversity of software that a module that you have designed to be easy to change can be made difficult to change by someone else simply hanging a dependency upon it. Not a line of source code in your module need change, and yet your module will suddenly be difficult to change. By conforming to SDP, we ensure that modules that are intended to be easy to change are not depended on by modules that are more difficult to change than they are.

Stability What is meant by stability? Stand a penny on its side. Is it stable in that position? You'd likely say that it was not. However, unless disturbed, it will remain in that position for a very long time. Thus, stability has nothing directly to do with frequency of change. The penny is not changing, but it is difficult to think of it as stable.

Webster says that something is stable if it is "not easily moved."[1] Stability is related to the amount of work required to make a change. The penny is not stable, because it requires very little work to topple it. On the other hand, a table is very stable, because it takes a considerable amount of effort to turn it over.

How does this relate to software? Many factors make a software component difficult to change: its size, complexity, clarity, and so on. But we are going to ignore all those factors and focus on something different. One sure way to make a software component difficult to change is to make lots of other software components depend on it. A component with lots of incoming dependencies is very stable, because it requires a great deal of work to reconcile any changes with all the dependent components.

---

1. Webster's *Third New International Dictionary*

Figure 28-5 shows X, a stable component. This component has three components depending on it and therefore has three good reasons not to change. We say that it is *responsible* to those three components. On the other hand, X depends on nothing, so it has no external influence to make it change. We say that it is *independent*.

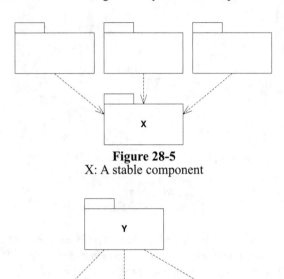

Figure 28-5
X: A stable component

Figure 28-6
Y: An instable component

Figure 28-6, on the other hand, shows a very instable component. Y has no other components depending on it; we say that it is irresponsible. Y also has three components that it depends on, so changes may come from three external sources. We say that Y is dependent.

Stability metrics How can we measure the stability of a component? One way is to count the number of dependencies that enter and leave that component. These counts will allow us to calculate the *positional* stability of the component:

- *Ca* (afferent couplings): The number of classes outside this component that depend on classes within this component

- *Ce* (efferent couplings): The number of classes inside this component that depend on classes outside this component

- *I* (Instability): $I = \dfrac{Ce}{Ca + Ce}$

This metric has the range [0,1]. I = 0 indicates a maximally stable component. I = 1 indicates a maximally instable component.

The *Ca* and *Ce* metrics are calculated by counting the number of *classes* outside the component in question that have dependencies on the classes inside the component in question. Consider the example in Figure 28-7:

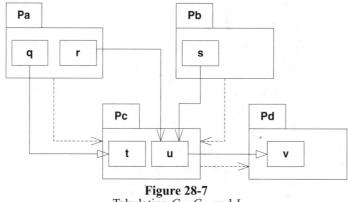

Figure 28-7
Tabulating *Ca*, *Ce*, and *I*

The dashed arrows between the components represent component's dependencies. The relationships between the classes of those components show how those dependencies are implemented. There are inheritance and association relationships.

Now, let's say that we want to calculate the stability of the component Pc. We find that three classes outside Pc depend on classes in Pc. Thus, $Ca = 3$. Moreover, there is one class outside Pc that classes in Pc depend on. Thus, $Ce = 1$, and $I = 1/4$.

In C#, these dependencies are typically represented by `using` statements. Indeed, the *I* metric is easiest to calculate when you have organized your source code such that there is one class in each source file. In C#, the *I* metric can be calculated by counting `using` statements and fully qualified names.

When the *I* metric is 1, it means that no other component depends on this component ($Ca = 0$), and this component does depend on other components ($Ce > 0$). This is as instable as a component can get; it is *irresponsible* and *dependent*. Its lack of dependents gives it no reason *not* to change, and the components that it depends on may give it ample reason *to* change.

On the other hand, when the *I* metric is 0, the component is depended on by other components ($Ca > 0$) but does not itself depend on any other components ($Ce = 0$). It is *responsible* and *independent*. Such a component is as stable as it can get. Its dependents make it difficult to change, and it has no dependencies that might force it to change.

According to SDP, the *I* metric of a component should be larger than the *I* metrics of the components that it depends on. That is, *I* metrics should decrease in the direction of dependency.

Variable component stablility If all the components in a system were maximally stable, the system would be unchangeable. This is not a desirable situation. Indeed, we want to design our component structure so that some components are instable and some are stable. Figure 28-8 shows an ideal configuration for a system with three components.

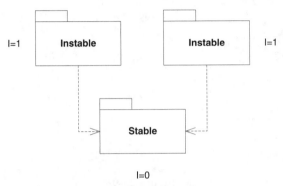

Figure 28-8
Ideal component configuration

The changeable components are on top and depend on the stable component at the bottom. Putting the instable components at the top of the diagram is a useful convention, since any arrow that points *up* is violating SDP.

Figure 28-9 shows how SDP can be violated. Flexible is a component that we intend to be easy to change. We want Flexible to be instable, with an *I* metric close to 0. However, some developer, working in the component named Stable, has hung a dependency on Flexible. This violates SDP, since the *I* metric for Stable is much lower than the *I* metric for Flexible. As a result, Flexible will no longer be easy to change. A change to Flexible will force us to deal with Stable and all its dependents.

To fix this, we somehow have to break the dependence of Stable on Flexible. Why does this dependency exist? Let's assume that within Flexible is a class C that another class U within Stable needs to use. See Figure 28-10.

We can fix this by using DIP. We create an interface called IU and put it in a component named UInterface. We make sure that this interface declares all the methods that U needs to use. We then make C inherit from this interface. See Figure 28-11. This breaks the dependency of Stable on Flexible and forces both components to be dependent on UInterface. UInterface is very stable ($I = 0$), and Flexible retains its necessary instability ($I = 1$). All the dependencies now flow in the direction of *decreasing I*.

High-level design placement Some software in the system should not change very often. This software represents the high-level architecture and design decisions. We don't want these architectural decisions to be volatile. Thus, the software that encapsulates the high-level design of the system should be put into stable components ($I = 0$). The instable components ($I = 1$) should contain only the software that is likely to change.

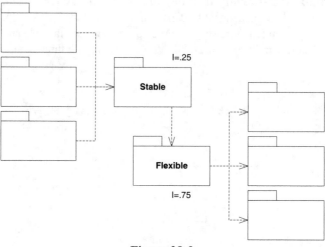

Figure 28-9
Violation of SDP

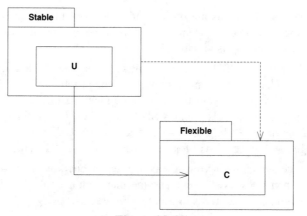

Figure 28-10
The cause of the bad dependency

However, if the high-level design is put into stable components, the source code that represents that design will be difficult to change, which could make the design inflexible. How can a component that is maximally stable ($I = 0$) be flexible enough to withstand change? The answer is to be found in OCP. This principle tells us that it is possible and desirable to create classes that are flexible enough to be extended without requiring modification. What kinds of classes conform to this principle? The answer is *Abstract* classes.

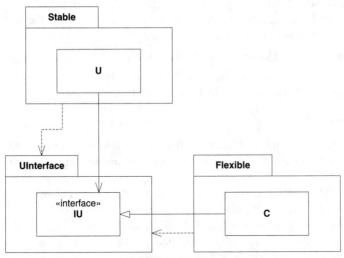

Figure 28-11
Fixing the stability violation, using DIP

The Stable-Abstractions Principle (SAP)

> **A component should be as abstract as it is stable.**

This principle sets up a relationship between stability and abstractness. It says that a stable component should also be abstract so that its stability does not prevent it from being extended. On the other hand, it says that an instable component should be concrete, since its instability allows the concrete code within it to be easily changed.

Thus, if a component is to be stable, it should also consist of abstract classes so that it can be extended. Stable components that are extensible are flexible and do not overly constrain the design.

Combined, SAP and SDP amount to DIP for components. This is true because the SDP says that dependencies should run in the direction of stability, and SAP says that stability implies abstraction. Thus, dependencies run in the direction of abstraction.

However, DIP deals with classes. With classes, there are no shades of gray. A class either is abstract or is not. The combination of SDP and SAP deals with components and allows that a component can be partially abstract and partially stable.

Measuring abstraction The A metric is a measure of the abstractness of a component. Its value is simply the ratio of abstract classes in a component to the total number of classes in the component, where

Nc is the number of classes in the component.

Na is the number of abstract classes in the component. Remember, an abstract class is a class with at least one abstract method and cannot be instantiated:

A (Abstractness). $A = \dfrac{Na}{Nc}$

The A metric ranges from 0 to 1. Zero implies that the component has no abstract classes at all. A value of 1 implies that the component contains nothing but abstract classes.

The main sequence We are now in a position to define the relationship between stability (I) and abstractness (A). We can create a graph with A on the vertical axis and I on the horizontal axis. If we plot the two "good" kinds of components on this graph, we will find the components that are maximally stable and abstract at the upper left at (0,1). The components that are maximally instable and concrete are at the lower right at (1,0). See Figure 28-12.

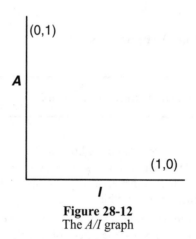

Figure 28-12
The A/I graph

Not all components can fall into one of these two positions. Components have degrees of abstraction and stability. For example, it is very common for one abstract class to derive from another abstract class. The derivative is an abstraction that has a dependency. Thus, though it is maximally abstract, it will not be maximally stable. Its dependency will decrease its stability.

Since we cannot enforce that all components sit at either (0,1) or (1,0), we must assume that a locus of points on the A/I graph defines reasonable positions for components. We can infer what that locus is by finding the areas where components should *not* be, that is, zones of *exclusion*. See Figure 28-13.

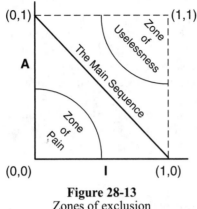

Figure 28-13
Zones of exclusion

Consider a component in the area near (0,0). This component is highly stable and concrete. Such a component is not desirable, because it is rigid. It cannot be extended, because it is not abstract. And it is very difficult to change, because of its stability. Thus, we do not normally expect to see well-designed components sitting near (0,0). The area around (0,0) is a zone of exclusion, the *zone of pain*.

It should be noted that in some cases, components do indeed fall within the zone of pain. An example would be a component representing a database schema. Database schemas are notoriously volatile, extremely concrete, and are highly depended upon. This is one of the reasons that the interface between OO applications and databases is so difficult and that schema updates are generally painful.

Another example of a component that sits near (0,0) is a component that holds a concrete utility library. Although such a component has an I metric of 1, it may in fact be nonvolatile. Consider a "string" component, for example. Even though all the classes within it are concrete, it is nonvolatile. Such components are harmless in the (0,0) zone, since they are not likely to be changed. Indeed, we can consider a third axis of the graph being that of volatility. If so, the graph in Figure 28-13 shows the plane at volatility = 1.

Consider a component near (1,1). This location is undesirable, because it is maximally abstract and yet has no dependents. Such components are useless. Thus, this is called the *zone of uselessness*.

It seems clear that we'd like our volatile components to be as far from both zones of exclusion as possible. The locus of points that is maximally distant from each zone is the line that connects (1,0) and (0,1). This line is known as the *main sequence*.[2]

A component that sits on the main sequence is not "too abstract" for its stability; nor is it "too instable" for its abstractness. It is neither useless nor particularly painful. It is

---

2. The name *main sequence* was adopted because of my interest in astronomy and HR (Hertzsprung-Russell) diagrams.

depended on to the extent that it is abstract, and it depends upon others to the extent that it is concrete.

Clearly, the most desirable positions for a component to hold are at one of the two endpoints of the main sequence. However, in my experience, less than half the components in a project can have such ideal characteristics. Those other components have the best characteristics if they are on or close to the main sequence.

Distance from the main sequence This leads us to our last metric. If it is desirable for components to be on or close to the main sequence, we can create a metric that measures how far away a component is from this ideal.

D (Distance). $D = \dfrac{|A + I - 1|}{\sqrt{2}}$. This ranges from $[0,{\sim}0.707]$.

D' (Normalized distance). $D' = |A + I - 1|$. This metric is much more convenient than D, since it ranges from $[0,1]$. Zero indicates that the component is directly on the main sequence. One indicates that the component is as far away as possible from the main sequence.

Given this metric, a design can be analyzed for its overall conformance to the main sequence. The D metric for each component can be calculated. Any component that has a D value that is not near 0 can be reexamined and restructured. In fact, this kind of analysis has been a great aid to me in helping to define components that are more maintainable and less sensitive to change.

Statistical analysis of a design is also possible. One can calculate the mean and variance of all the D metrics for the components within a design. One would expect a conformant design to have a mean and variance close to 0. The variance can be used to establish "control limits" that can identify components that are "exceptional" in comparison to all the others. See Figure 28-14.

In this scatter plot—not based on real data—we see that the bulk of the components lie along the main sequence but that some of them are more than one standard deviation ($Z = 1$) away from the mean. These aberrant components are worth looking at. For some reason, they are either very abstract with few dependents or very concrete with many dependents.

Another way to use the metrics is to plot the D' metric of each component over time. Figure 28-15 shows a mock-up of such a plot. You can see that some strange dependencies have been creeping into the `Payroll` component over the last few releases. The plot shows a control threshold at $D' = 0.1$. The R2.1 point has exceeded this control limit, so it would be worth our while to find out why this component is so far from the main sequence.

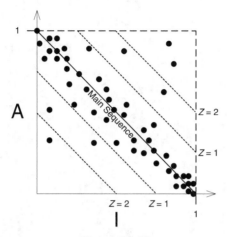

Figure 28-14
Scatter plot of component D scores

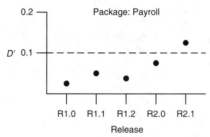

Figure 28-15
Time plot of a single component's D' scores

Conclusion

The *dependency management metrics* described in this chapter measure the conformance of a design to a pattern of dependency and abstraction that I think is a "good" pattern. Experience has shown that certain dependencies are good and others are bad. This pattern reflects that experience. However, a metric is not a god; it is merely a measurement against an arbitrary standard. It is certainly possible that the standard chosen in this chapter is appropriate only for certain applications and not for others. It may also be that far better metrics can be used to measure the quality of a design.

29

FACTORY

© Jennifer M. Kohnke

The man who builds a factory builds a temple.

—Calvin Coolidge (1872–1933)

The Dependency-Inversion Principle (DIP) (Chapter 11) tells us that we should prefer dependencies on abstract classes and avoid dependencies on concrete classes, especially when those classes are volatile. Therefore, the following snippet of code violates this principle:

```
Circle c = new Circle(origin, 1);
```

`Circle` is a concrete class. Therefore, those modules that create instances of `Circle` must violate DIP. Indeed, any line of code that uses the `new` keyword violates DIP.

There are times when violating DIP is mostly harmless, which is pretty good coverage. The more likely a concrete class is to change, the more likely that depending on it will lead to trouble. But if the concrete class is not volatile, depending on it is not worrisome. For example, creating instances of `string` does not bother me. Depending on `string` is very safe because `string` is not likely to change any time soon.

On the other hand, when we are actively developing an application, many concrete classes are very volatile, so depending on them is problematic. We'd rather depend on an abstract interface to shield us from the majority of the changes.

The FACTORY pattern allows us to create instances of concrete objects while depending only on abstract interfaces. Therefore, it can be of great assistance during active development when those concrete classes are highly volatile.

Figure 29-1 shows the problematic scenario. We have a class named `SomeApp` that depends on the interface `Shape`. `SomeApp` uses instances of `Shape` solely through the `Shape` interface and does not use any of the specific methods of `Square` or `Circle`. Unfortunately, `SomeApp` also creates instances of `Square` and `Circle` and thus has to depend on the concrete classes.

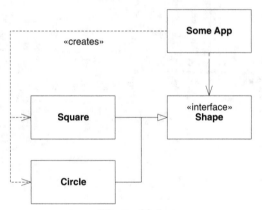

Figure 29-1
An app that violates DIP to create concrete classes

We can fix this by applying the FACTORY pattern to `SomeApp`, as in Figure 29-2. Here, we see the `ShapeFactory` interface, which has two methods: `MakeSquare` and `MakeCircle`. The `MakeSquare` method returns an instance of a `Square`, and the `MakeCircle` method returns an instance of a `Circle`. However, the return type of both functions is `Shape`.

Listing 29-1 shows what the `ShapeFactory` code looks like. Listing 29-2 shows `ShapeFactoryImplementation`.

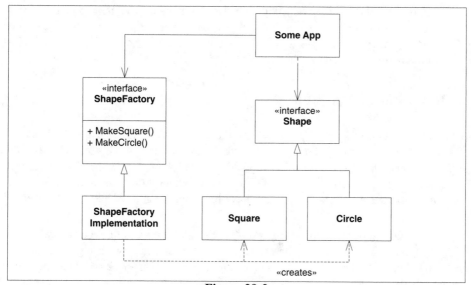

Figure 29-2
Application of FACTORY to SomeApp

Listing 29-1

ShapeFactory.cs

```
public interface ShapeFactory
{
   Shape MakeCircle();
   Shape MakeSquare();
}
```

Listing 29-2

ShapeFactoryImplementation.cs

```
public class ShapeFactoryImplementation : ShapeFactory
{
   public Shape MakeCircle()
   {
     return new Circle();
   }

   public Shape MakeSquare()
   {
     return new Square();
   }
}
```

Note that this completely solves the problem of depending on concrete classes. The application code no longer depends on `Circle` or `Square`, yet it still manages to create instances of them. It manipulates those instances through the `Shape` interface and never invokes methods that are specific to `Square` or `Circle`.

The problem of depending on a concrete class has been moved. Someone must create `ShapeFactoryImplementation`, but nobody else ever needs to create `Square` or `Circle`. `ShapeFactoryImplementation` will most likely be created by `Main` or an initialization function attached to `Main`.

A Dependency Problem

Astute readers will recognize a problem with this form of the FACTORY pattern. The class `ShapeFactory` has a method for each of the derivatives of `Shape`. This results in a *name-only dependency* that makes it difficult to add new derivatives to `Shape`. Every time we add a new `Shape` derivative, we have to add a new method to the `ShapeFactory` interface. In most cases, this means that we'll have to recompile and redeploy all the users of `ShapeFactory`.[1]

We can get rid of this dependency problem by sacrificing a little type safety. Instead of giving `ShapeFactory` one method for every `Shape` derivative, we can give it only one `make` function that takes a `string`. For example, look at Listing 29-3. This technique requires that `ShapeFactoryImplementation` use an `if/else` chain on the incoming argument to select which derivative of `Shape` to instantiate. This is shown in Listings 29-4 and 29-5.

Listing 29-3

A snippet that creates a circle

```
[Test]
public void TestCreateCircle()
{
    Shape s = factory.Make("Circle");
    Assert.IsTrue(s is Circle);
}
```

Listing 29-4

ShapeFactory.cs

```
public interface ShapeFactory
{
    Shape Make(string name);
}
```

Listing 29-5

ShapeFactoryImplementation.cs

```
public class ShapeFactoryImplementation : ShapeFactory
{
    public Shape Make(string name)
```

---

1. Again, this isn't exactly necessary in C#. You might get away without recompiling and redeploying clients of a changed interface. But it's a risky business.

Listing 29-5

ShapeFactoryImplementation.cs

```
    {
      if(name.Equals("Circle"))
        return new Circle();
      else if(name.Equals("Square"))
        return new Square();
      else
        throw new Exception(
          "ShapeFactory cannot create: {0}", name);
    }
  }
```

One might argue that this is dangerous, because callers who misspell the name of a shape will get a runtime error instead of a compile-time error. This is true. However, if you are writing the appropriate unit tests and are applying test-driven development, you'll catch these runtime errors long before they become problems.

Static versus Dynamic Typing

The trade-off that we've just witnessed between type safety and flexibility typifies the ongoing debate over language styles. On the one side are statically typed languages, such as C#, C++, and Java, which check types at compile time and emit compilation errors if the declared types aren't consistent. On the other hand, dynamically typed languages, such as Python, Ruby, Groovy, and Smalltalk, do their type checking at runtime. The compiler does not insist on type consistence; nor, indeed, does the syntax of these languages permit such checking.

As we saw in the FACTORY example, static typing can lead to dependency knots that force modifications to source files for the sole purpose of maintaining type consistency. In our case, we have to change the ShapeFactory interface whenever a new derivative of Shape is added. These changes can force rebuilds and redeployments that would otherwise be unecessary. We solved that problem when we relaxed type safety and depended on our unit tests to catch type errors; we gained the flexibility to add new derivatives of Shape without changing ShapeFactory.

Proponents of statically typed languages contend that the compile-time safety is worth the minor dependency issues, the increased rate of source code modification, and the increased rate of rebuild and redeployment. The other side argues that unit tests will find most of the problems that static typing would find and that the burden of source code modification, rebuild, and redeployment is therefore unecessary.

I find it interesting that the rise in popularity of dynamically typed languages is, so far tracking the rise in adoption of test-driven development (TTD). Perhaps programmers who adopt TDD are finding that it changes the safety versus flexibility equation. Perhaps those programmers are gradually becoming convinced that the flexibility of dynamically typed languages outweighs the benefits of static type checking.

Perhaps we are at the crest of popularity of the statically typed languages. If the current trend continues, we may find that the next major industrial language is more related to Smalltalk than to C++.

Substitutable Factories

One of the great benefits of using factories is the ability to substitute one implementation of a factory for another. In this way, you can substitute families of objects within an application.

For example, imagine an application that had to adapt to many different database implementations. In our example, let's assume that the users can either use flat files or purchase an Oracle adapter. We might use the PROXY pattern to isolate the application from the database implementation.[2] We might also use factories to instantiate the proxies. Figure 29-3 shows the structure.

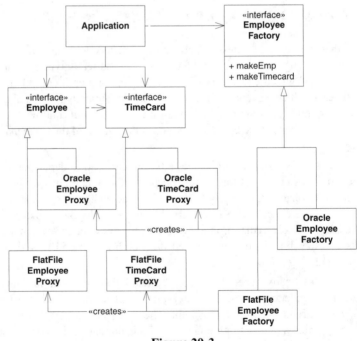

Figure 29-3
Substitutable factory

---

2. We'll study PROXY in Chapter 34. Right now, all you need to know is that a `Proxy` is a class that knows how to read particular objects out of particular kinds of databases.

Note the two implementations of `EmployeeFactory`. One creates proxies that work with flat files, and the other creates proxies that work with Oracle. Note also that the application does not know or care which implementation is being used.

Using Factories for Test Fixtures

When writing unit tests, we often want to test the behavior of a module in isolation from the modules it uses. For example, we might have a `Payroll` application that uses a database (see Figure 29-4). We may wish to test the function of the `Payroll` module without using the database at all.

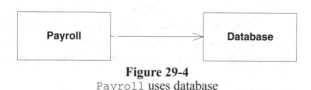

Figure 29-4
`Payroll` uses database

We can accomplish this by using an abstract interface for the database. One implementation of this abstract interface uses the real database. Another implementation is test code written to simulate the behavior of the database and to check that the database calls are being made correctly. Figure 29-5 shows the structure. The `PayrollTest` module tests the `PayrollModule` by making calls to it and also implements the `Database` interface so that it can trap the calls that `Payroll` makes to the database. This allows `PayrollTest` to ensure that `Payroll` is behaving properly. It also allows `PayrollTest` to simulate many kinds of database failures and problems that are otherwise difficult to create. This is a testing pattern known as SELF-SHUNT, also sometimes known as *mocking* or *spoofing*.

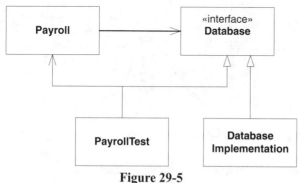

Figure 29-5
`PayrollTest` SELF-SHUNTs database

How does `Payroll` get the instance of `PayrollTest` it uses as the `Database`? Certainly, `Payroll` isn't going to do the creation of `PayrollTest`. Just as clearly, `Payroll` must somehow get a reference to the `Database` implementation it's going to use.

In some cases, it is perfectly natural for `PayrollTest` to pass the `Database` reference to `Payroll`. In other cases, it may be that `PayrollTest` must set a global variable to refer to the `Database`. In still others, `Payroll` may be fully expecting to create the `Database` instance. In that last case, we can use a `Factory` to fool `Payroll` into creating the test version of the `Database` by passing an alternative factory to `Payroll`.

Figure 29-6 shows a possible structure. The `Payroll` module acquires the factory through a global variable—or a static variable in a global class—named `Gdatabase-Factory`. The `PayrollTest` module implements `DatabaseFactory` and sets a reference to itself into that `GdatabaseFactory`. When `Payroll` uses the factory to create a `Database`, the `PayrollTest` module traps the call and passes back a reference to itself. Thus, `Payroll` is convinced that it has created the `PayrollDatabase`, and yet the `PayrollTest` module can fully spoof the `Payroll` module and trap all database calls.

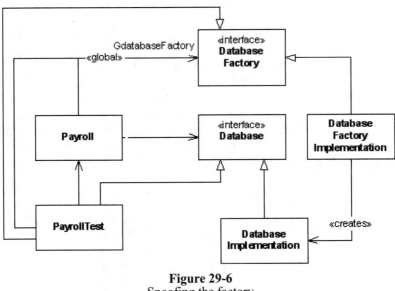

Figure 29-6
Spoofing the factory

Importance of Factories

A strict interpretation of DIP would insist on using factories for every volatile class in the system. What's more, the power of the FACTORY pattern is seductive. These two factors can sometimes lure developers into using factories by default. This is an extreme that I don't recommend.

I don't start out using factories. I put them into the system only when the need for them becomes great enough. For example, if it becomes necessary to use the PROXY pattern, it will probably become necessary to use a factory to create the persistent objects. Or, if through unit testing, I come across situations in which I must spoof the creator of an object, I will likely use a factory. But I don't start out assuming that factories will be necessary.

Factories are a complexity that can often be avoided, especially in the early phases of an evolving design. When they are used by default, factories dramatically increase the difficulty of extending the design. In order to create a new class, one may have to create as many as four new classes: the two interface classes that represent the new class and its factory and the two concrete classes that implement those interfaces.

Conclusion

Factories are powerful tools. They can be of great benefit in conforming to DIP. They allow high-level policy modules to create instances of objects without depending on the concrete implementations of those objects. Factories also make it possible to swap in completely different families of implementations for a group of classes. However, factories are a complexity that can often be avoided. Using them by default is seldom the best course of action.

Bibliography

[GOF95] Erich Gamma, Richard Helm, Ralph Johnson, and John Vlissides, *Design Patterns: Elements of Reusable Object-Oriented Software*, Addison-Wesley, 1995.

The Payroll Case Study: Package Analysis

© Jennifer M. Kohnke

Rule of thumb: if you think something is clever and sophisticated, beware—
it is probably self-indulgence.

—Donald A. Norman, *The Design of Everyday Things*, 1990

We have done a great deal of analysis, design, and implementation of the payroll problem. However, we still have many decisions to make. For one thing, only two programmers—Bob and Micah—have been working on the problem. The current structure of the development environment is consistent with this. All the program files are located in a single directory. There is no higher-order structure. There are no packages, no subsystems, no releasable components other than the entire application. This will not do going forward.

We must assume that as this program grows, the number of people working on it will grow, too. In order to make it convenient for multiple developers, we are going to have to partition the source code into components—assemblies, DLLs—that can be conveniently checked out, modified, and tested.

The payroll application currently consists of 4,382 lines of code divided into about 63 classes and 80 source files. Although this is not a huge number, it does represent an organizational burden. How should we manage these source files and divide them into independently deployable components?

Similarly, how should we divide the work of implementation so that the development can proceed smoothly without the programmers' getting in one another's way? We would like to divide the classes into groups that are convenient for individuals or teams to checkout and support.

Component Structure and Notation

Figure 30-1 shows a possible component structure for the payroll application. We will address the appropriateness of this structure later. For now, we will confine ourselves to how such a structure is documented and used.

By convention, component diagrams are drawn with the dependencies pointing downward. Components at the top are dependent. Components at the bottom are depended on.

Figure 30-1 has divided the payroll application into eight components. The `PayrollApplication` component contains the `PayrollApplication` class and the `TransactionSource` and `TextParserTransactionSource` classes. The `Transactions` component contains the complete `Transaction`-class hierarchy. The constituents of the other components should be clear by carefully examining the diagram.

The dependencies should also be clear. The `PayrollApplication` component depends on the `Transactions` component because the `PayrollApplication` class calls the `Transaction::Execute` method. The `Transactions` component depends on the `PayrollDatabase` component because each of the many derivatives of `Transaction` communicates directly with the `PayrollDatabase` class. The other dependencies are likewise justifiable.

What criteria did we use to group these classes into components? We simply stuck the classes that look like they belonged together into the same components. As we learned in Chapter 28, this is probably not a good idea, however.

Consider what happens if we make a change to the `Classifications` component. This change will force a recompilation and retest of the `EmployeeDatabase` component, and well it should. But it will also force a recompilation and retest of the `Transactions`

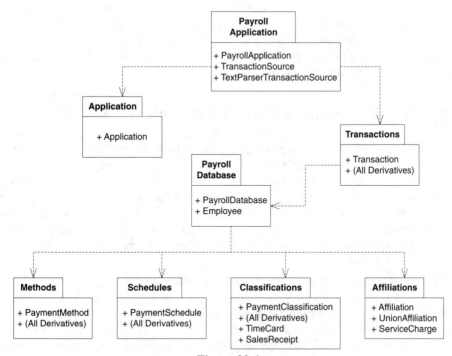

Figure 30-1
Possible payroll component diagram

component. Certainly, the ChangeClassificationTransaction and its three derivatives from Figure 27-13 *should* be recompiled and retested, but why should the others be
recompiled and retested?

Technically, those other transactions don't need recompilation and retest. However, if
they are part of the Transactions component, and if that component is going to be
rereleased to deal with the changes to the Classifications component, it could be
viewed as irresponsible not to recompile and retest the component as a whole. Even if all
the transactions aren't recompiled and retested, the package itself must be rereleased and
redeployed, and then all its clients will require revalidation at the very least and probably
recompilation as well.

The classes in the Transactions component do not share the same closure. Each
one is sensitive to its own particular changes. The ServiceChargeTransaction is open
to changes to the ServiceCharge class, whereas the TimeCardTransaction is open to
changes to the TimeCard class. In fact, as Figure 30-1 implies, some portion of the
Transactions component is dependent on nearly every other part of the software. Thus,
this component suffers a high rate of release. Every time something is changed anywhere
below, the Transactions component will have to be revalidated and rereleased.

The `PayrollApplication` package is even more sensitive: Any change to any part of the system will affect this package, so its release rate must be enormous. You might think that this is inevitable—that as one climbs higher up the package-dependency hierarchy, the release rate must increase. Fortunately, however, this is not true, and avoiding this symptom is one of the major goals of OOD.

Applying the Common Closure Principle (CCP)

Consider Figure 30-2, which groups the classes of the payroll application together according to their closure. For example, the `PayrollApplication` component contains the `PayrollApplication` and `TransactionSource` classes. Both of these two classes depend on the abstract `Transaction` class, which is in the `PayrollDomain` component. Note that the `TextParserTransactionSource` class is in another component that depends on the abstract `PayrollApplication` class. This creates an upside-down structure in which the details depend on the generalities, and the generalities are independent. This conforms to DIP.

The most striking case of generality and independence is the `PayrollDomain` component. This component contains the *essence* of the whole system, yet it depends upon nothing! Examine this component carefully. It contains `Employee`, `PaymentClassification`, `PaymentMethod`, `PaymentSchedule`, `Affiliation`, and `Transaction`. This component contains all the major abstractions in our model, yet it has no dependencies. Why? Because all the classes it contains are abstract.

Consider the `Classifications` component, which contains the three derivatives of `PaymentClassification`, along with the `ChangeClassificationTransaction` class and its three derivatives, as well as `TimeCard` and `SalesReceipt`. Note that any change made to these nine classes is isolated; other than `TextParser`, no other component is affected! Such isolation also holds for the `Methods` component, the `Schedules` component and the `Affiliations` component. This is quite a bit of isolation.

Note that the bulk of the detailed code that will eventually be written is in components that have few or no dependents. Since almost nothing depends on them, we call them *irresponsible*. The code within those components is tremendously flexible; it can be changed without affecting many other parts of the project. Note also that the most general packages of the system contain the least amount of code. These components are heavily depended on but depend on nothing. Since many components depend on them, we call them *responsible*, and since they don't depend upon anything, we call them *independent*. Thus, the amount of responsible code (i.e., code in which changes would affect lots of other code) is very small. Moreover, that small amount of responsible code is also independent, which means that no other modules will induce it to change. This upside-down structure, with highly independent and responsible generalities at the bottom and highly irresponsible and dependent details at the top, is the hallmark of object-oriented design.

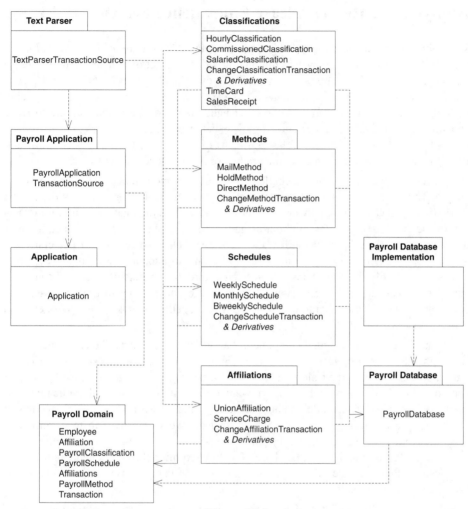

Figure 30-2
A closed-component hierarchy for the payroll application

Compare Figure 30-1 with Figure 30-2. Note that the details at the bottom of Figure 30-1 are independent and highly responsible. This is the wrong place for details! Details should depend on the major architectural decisions of the system and should not be depended on. Note also that the generalities—the components that define the architecture of the system—are irresponsible and highly dependent. Thus, the components that define the architectural decisions depend on, and are thus constrained by, the components that contain the implementation details. This is a violation of SAP. It would be better if the architecture constrained the details!

Applying the Reuse/Release Equivalence Principle (REP)

What portions of the payroll application can we reuse? Another division of our company wanting to reuse our payroll system but having a different set of policies could not reuse `Classifications`, `Methods`, `Schedules`, or `Affiliations` but could reuse `PayrollDomain`, `PayrollApplication`, `Application`, `PayrollDatabase`, and, possibly, `PDImplementation`. On the other hand, another department wanting to write software that analyzed the current employee database could reuse `PayrollDomain`, `Classifications`, `Methods`, `Schedules`, `Affiliations`, `PayrollDatabase`, and `PDImplementation`. In each case, the granule of reuse is a component.

Seldom, if ever, would only a single class from a component be reused. The reason is simple: The classes within a component should be cohesive. That is, that they depend on one another and cannot be easily or sensibly separated. It would make no sense, for example, to use the `Employee` class without using the `PaymentMethod` class. In fact, in order to do so, you would have to modify the `Employee` class so that it did not contain a `PaymentMethod` instance. Certainly, we don't want to support the kind of reuse that forces us to modify the reused components. Therefore, the granule of reuse is the component. This gives us another cohesion criterion to use when trying to group classes into components: The classes should not only be closed together but also reusable together in conformance with REP.

Consider again our original component diagram in Figure 30-1. The components that we might like to reuse, such as `Transactions` or `PayrollDatabase`, are not easily reusable, because they drag along a lot of extra baggage. The `PayrollApplication` component depends on everything. If we wanted to create a new payroll application that used a different set of schedule, method, affiliation, and classification policies, we would not be able to use this package as a whole. Instead, we would have to take individual classes from `PayrollApplication`, `Transactions`, `Methods`, `Schedules`, `Classifications`, and `Affiliations`. By disassembling the components in this way, we destroy their release structure. We cannot say that release 3.2 of `Payroll-Application` is reusable.

Since Figure 30-1 violates CRP, the reuser, having accepted the reusable fragments of our various components, will not be able to depend on our release structure. By reusing the `PaymentMethod` class, the reuser is affected by a new release of `Methods`. Most of the time, the changes will be to classes not being reused, yet the reuser must still track our new release number and probably recompile and retest the code.

This will be so difficult to manage that the reuser's most likely strategy will be to make a copy of the reusable components and evolve that copy separately from ours. This is not reuse. The two pieces of code will become different and will require independent support, effectively doubling the support burden.

These problems are not exhibited by the structure in Figure 30-2. The components in that structure are easier to reuse. `PayrollDomain` does not drag along much baggage. It is reusable independently of any of the derivatives of `PaymentMethod`, `PaymentClass-ification`, `PaymentSchedule`, and so on.

The astute reader will notice that the component diagram in Figure 30-2 does not completely conform to CRP. Specifically, the classes within `PayrollDomain` do not form the smallest reusable unit. The `Transaction` class does not need to be reused with the rest of the component. We could design many applications that access the `Employee` and its fields but never use a `Transaction`.

This suggests a change to the component diagram, as shown in Figure 30-3. This separates the transactions from the elements they manipulate. For example, the classes in the `MethodTransactions` component manipulate the classes in the `Methods` component.

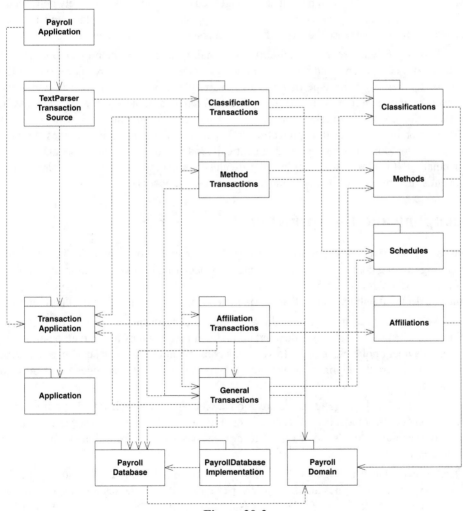

Figure 30-3
Updated payroll component diagram

We have moved the `Transaction` class into a new component, named `Transaction-Application`, which also contains `TransactionSource` and a class named `Transaction-Application`. These three form a reusable unit. The `PayrollApplication` class has now become the grand unifier. It contains the main program and also a derivative of `TransactionApplication`, called `PayrollApplication`, which ties the `TextParser-TransactionSource` to the `TransactionApplication`.

These manipulations have added yet another layer of abstraction to the design. The `TransactionApplication` component can now be reused by any application that obtains `Transactions` from a `TransactionSource` and then `Executes` them. The `PayrollApplication` component is no longer reusable, since it is extremely dependent. However, the `TransactionApplication` component has taken its place and is more general. Now, we can reuse the `PayrollDomain` component without any `Transactions`.

This certainly improves the reusability and maintainability of the project, but the cost is five extra components and a more complex dependency architecture. The value of the trade-off depends on the type of reuse that we might expect and the rate at which we expect the application to evolve. If the application remains stable and few clients reuse it, perhaps this change is overkill. On the other hand, if many applications will reuse this structure or if we expect the application to experience many changes, perhaps the new structure would be superior; it's a judgment call, and it should be driven by data rather a speculation. It is best to start simple and grow the component structure as necessary. Component structures can always be made more elaborate, if necessary.

Coupling and Encapsulation

Just as the coupling among classes is managed by encapsulation boundaries in C#, so the couplings among components can be managed by declaring the classes within them public or private. If a class within one component is to be used by another component, that class must be declared public. A class that is private to a component should be declared internal.

We may want to hide certain classes within a component to prevent afferent couplings. `Classifications` is a detailed component that contains the implementations of several payment policies. In order to keep this component on the main sequence, we want to limit its afferent couplings, so we hide the classes that other packages don't need to know about.

`TimeCard` and `SalesReceipt` are good choices for internal classes. They are implementation details of the mechanisms for calculating an employee's pay. We want to remain free to alter these details, so we need to prevent anyone else from depending on their structure.

A quick glance at Figures 27-7 through 27-10 and Listing 27-10 shows that the `TimeCardTransaction` and `SalesReceiptTransaction` classes already depend on `TimeCard` and `SalesReceipt`. We can easily resolve this problem, however, as shown in Figures 30-4 and 30-5.

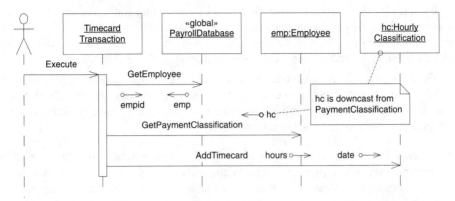

Figure 30-4
Revision to `TimeCardTransaction` to protect `TimeCard` privacy

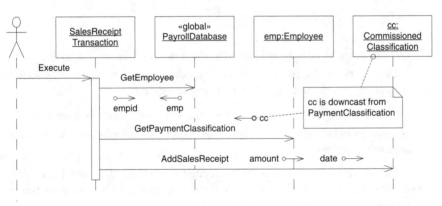

Figure 30-5
Revision to `SalesReceiptTransaction` to protect `SalesReceipt` privacy

Metrics

As we showed in Chapter 28, we can quantify the attributes of cohesion, coupling, stability, generality, and conformance to the main sequence with a few simple metrics. But why should we want to? To paraphrase Tom DeMarco: You can't manage what you can't control, and you can't control what you don't measure.[1] To be effective software engineers or software managers, we must be able to control software development practice. If we don't measure it, however, we will never have that control.

By applying the heuristics that follow, and by calculating some fundamental metrics about our OODs, we can begin to correlate those metrics with measured performance of the software and of the teams that develop it. The more metrics we gather, the more information we will have, and the more control we will eventually be able to exert.

The metrics we describe have been successfully applied to a number of projects since 1994. Several automatic tools will calculate them for you, and they are not difficult to calculate by hand. It is also not difficult to write a simple shell, Python, or Ruby script to walk through your source files and calculate them.[2]

- H (*relational cohesion*) can be represented as the average number of internal relationships per class in a component. Let R be the number of class relationships that are internal to the component (i.e., that do not connect to classes outside the component). Let N be the number of classes within the component). The extra 1 in the formula prevents $H = 0$ when $N = 1$ and represents the relationship that the package has to all its classes:

$$H = \frac{R+1}{N}$$

- C_a (*afferent coupling*) can be calculated as the number of classes from other components that depend on the classes within the subject component. These dependencies are class relationships, such as inheritance and association.

- C_e (*efferent coupling*) can be calculated as the number of classes in other components that the classes in the subject component depend on. As before, these dependencies are class relationships.

- A (*abstractness*, or *generality*) can be calculated as the ratio of the number of abstract classes or interfaces in the component to the total number of classes and interfaces in the component.[3] This metric ranges from 0 to 1.

$$A = \frac{\text{AbstractClasses}}{\text{TotalClasses}}$$

- I (*instability*) can be calculated as the ratio of efferent coupling to total coupling. This metric also ranges from 0 to 1.

$$I = \frac{C_e}{C_e + C_a}$$

---

2. For an example of a shell script, you can download depend.sh from the freeware section of www.objectmentor.com.

3. One might think that a better formula for A is the ratio of abstract methods to total methods within the package. However, I have found that this formula weakens the abstraction metric too much. Even one abstract method makes a class abstract, and the power of that abstraction is more significant than the fact that the class may have dozens of concrete methods, especially when DIP is being followed.

- D (distance from the main sequence) = $|(A + I - 1) \div D2|$. The main sequence is idealized by the line $A + I = 1$. The formula calculates the distance of any particular component from the main sequence. It ranges from ~.7 to 0; the closer to 0, the better.[4]

$$D = \frac{|A + I - 1|}{\sqrt{2}}$$

- D' (normalized distance from the main sequence) represents the D metric normalized to the range [0,1]. It is perhaps a little more convenient to calculate and to interpret. The value 0 represents a component that is coincident with the main sequence. The value 1 represents a component that is as far from the main sequence as is possible.

$$D' = |A + I - 1|$$

Applying the Metrics to the Payroll Application

Table 30-1 shows how the classes in the payroll model have been allocated to components. Figure 30-6 shows the component diagram for the payroll application with all the metrics calculated. And Table 30-2 shows all of the metrics calculated for each component.

Each dependency in Figure 30-6 is adorned with two numbers. The number closest to the depender represents the number of that component's classes that depend on the dependee. The number closest to the dependee represents the number of that component's classes that the depender component depends on.

Each component in Figure 30-6 is adorned with the metrics that apply to it. Many of these metrics are encouraging. `PayrollApplication`, `PayrollDomain`, and `Payroll-Database`, for example, have high relational cohesion and are either on or close to the main sequence. However, the `Classifications`, `Methods`, and `Schedules` components show generally poor relational cohesion and are almost as far from the main sequence as is possible!

These numbers tell us that the partitioning of the classes into components is weak. If we don't find a way to improve the numbers, the development environment will be sensitive to change, which may cause unnecessary rerelease and retesting. Specifically, we have low-abstraction components, such as `ClassificationTransaction`, depending heavily on other low-abstraction components, such as `Classifications`. Classes with

---

4. It is impossible to plot any package outside the unit square on the A versus I graph, because neither A nor I can exceed 1. The main sequence bisects this square from (0,1) to (1,0). Within the square the points that are farthest from the main sequence are the two corners (0,0) and (1,1). Their distance from the main sequence is

$$\frac{\sqrt{2}}{2} = 0.70710678\ldots$$

Table 30-1 Class Allocation to Component

Component	Classes in Component		
Affiliations	ServiceCharge	UnionAffiliation	
AffiliationTransactions	ChangeAffiliationTransaction ServiceChargeTransaction	ChangeUnaffiliatedTransaction	ChangeMemberTransaction
Application	Application		
Classifications	CommissionedClassification SalesReceipt	HourlyClassification Timecard	SalariedClassification
ClassificationTransaction	ChangeClassificationTransaction ChangeSalariedTransaction	ChangeCommissionedTransaction SalesReceiptTransaction	ChangeHourlyTransaction TimecardTransaction
GeneralTransactions	AddCommissionedEmployee AddSalariedEmployee ChangeNameTransaction	AddEmployeeTransaction ChangeAddressTransaction DeleteEmployeeTransaction	AddHourlyEmployee ChangeEmployeeTransaction PaydayTransaction
Methods	DirectMethod	HoldMethod	MailMethod
MethodTransactions	ChangeDirectTransaction ChangeMethodTransaction	ChangeHoldTransaction	ChangeMailTransaction
PayrollApplication	PayrollApplication		
PayrollDatabase	PayrollDatabase		
PayrollDatabaseImplementation	PayrollDatabaseImplementation		
PayrollDomain	Affiliation PaymentMethod	Employee PaymentSchedule	PaymentClassification
Schedules	BiweeklySchedule	MonthlySchedule	WeeklySchedule
TextParserTransactionSource	TextParserTransactionSource		
TransactionApplication	TransactionApplication	Transaction	TransactionSource

Table 30-2 Metrics for Each Component Q

Component Name	N	A	Ca	Ce	R	H	I	A	D	D'
Affiliations	2	0	2	1	1	1	0.33	0	0.47	0.67
AffilliationTransactions	4	1	1	7	2	0.75	0.88	0.25	0.09	0.12
Application	1	1	1	0	0	1	0	1	0	0
Classifications	5	0	8	3	2	0.06	0.27	0	0.51	0.73
ClassificationTransaction	6	1	1	14	5	1	0.93	0.17	0.07	0.10
GeneralTransactions	9	2	4	12	5	0.67	0.75	0.22	0.02	0.03
Methods	3	0	4	1	0	0.33	0.20	0	0.57	0.80
MethodTransactions	4	1	1	6	3	1	0.86	0.25	0.08	0.11
PayrollApplication	1	0	0	2	0	1	1	0	0	0
PayrollDatabase	1	1	11	1	0	1	0.08	1	0.06	0.08
PayrollDatabaseImpl...	1	0	0	1	0	1	1	0	0	0
PayrollDomain	5	4	26	0	4	1	0	0.80	0.14	0.20
Schedules	3	0	6	1	0	0.33	0.14	0	0.61	0.86
TextParserTransactionSource	1	0	1	20	0	1	0.95	0	0.03	0.05
TransactionApplication	3	3	9	1	2	1	0.1	1	0.07	0.10

low abstraction contain most of the detailed code and are therefore likely to change, which will force rerelease of the components that depend on them. Thus, the `Classification-Transaction` component will have a very high release rate since it is subject to both its own high change rate and that of `Classifications`. As much as possible, we would like to limit the sensitivity of our development environment to change.

Clearly, if we have only two or three developers, they will be able to manage the development environment in their heads, and the need to maintain components on the main sequence, for this purpose, will not be great. The more developers there are, however, the more difficult it is to keep the development environment sane. Moreover, the work required to obtain these metrics is minimal compared to the work required to do even a single retest and rerelease.[5] Therefore, it is a judgment call as to whether the work of computing these metrics will be a short-term loss or gain.

---

5. I spent about 2 hours compiling by hand the statistics and computing the metrics for the payroll example. Had I used one of the commercially available tools, it would have taken virtually no time at all.

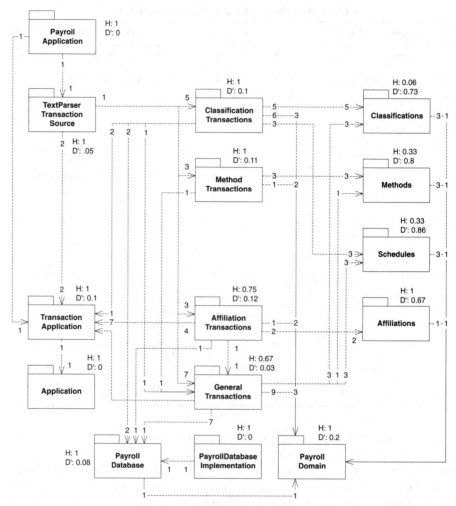

Figure 30-6
Component diagram with metrics

Object Factories

`Classifications` and `ClassificationTransaction` are so heavily depended on because the classes within them must be instantiated. For example, the `TextParser-TransactionSource` class must be able to create `AddHourlyEmployeeTransaction` objects; thus, there is an afferent coupling from the `TextParserTransactionSource` package to the `ClassificationTransactions` package. Also, the `ChangeHourly-Transaction` class must be able to create `HourlyClassification` objects, so there is an afferent coupling from `ClassificationTransaction` to `Classifications`.

Almost every other use of the objects within these components is through their abstract interface. Were it not for the need to create each concrete object, the afferent couplings on these components would not exist. For example, if `TextParser-TransactionSource` did not need to create the different transactions, it would not depend on the four packages containing the transaction implementations.

This problem can be significantly mitigated by using the FACTORY pattern. Each component provides an object factory that is responsible for creating all the public objects within that package.

The object factory for `TransactionImplementation` Figure 30-7 shows how to build an object factory for the `TransactionImplementation` component. The `TransactionFactory` component contains the abstract base class, which defines the abstract methods that represent the constructors for the concrete transaction objects. The `TransactionImplementation` component contains the concrete derivative of the `TransactionFactory` class and uses all the concrete transactions in order to create them.

The `TransactionFactory` class has a static member declared as a `TransactionFactory` pointer. This member must be initialized by the main program to point to an instance of the concrete `TransactionFactoryImplementation` object.

Initializing the factories If other factories are to create objects using the object factories, the static members of the abstract object factories must be initialized to point to the appropriate concrete factory. This must be done before any user attempts to use the factory. The best place to do this is usually the main program, which means that the main program depends on all the factories *and* on all the concrete packages. Thus, each concrete package will have at least one afferent coupling from the main program. This will force the concrete package off the main sequence a bit, but it cannot be helped.[6] It means that we must rerelease the main program every time we change any of the concrete components. Of course, we should probably rerelease the main program for each change anyway, since it will need to be tested regardless. Figures 30-8 and 30-9 show the static and dynamic structure of the main program in relation to the object factories.

Rethinking the Cohesion Boundaries

We initially separated `Classifications`, `Methods`, `Schedules`, and `Affiliations` in Figure 30-1. At the time, it seemed like a reasonable partitioning. After all, other users may want to reuse our schedule classes without reusing our affiliation classes. This partitioning was maintained after we split out the transactions into their own components, creating a dual hierarchy. Perhaps this was too much. The diagram in Figure 30-6 is very tangled.

---

6. As a practical solution, I usually ignore couplings from the main program.

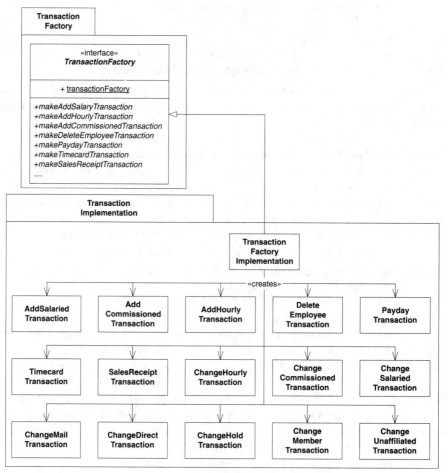

Figure 30-7
Object factory for transactions

A tangled package diagram makes the management of releases difficult if it is done by hand. Although component diagrams would work well with an automated project-planning tool, most of us don't have that luxury. Thus, we need to keep our component diagrams as simple as is practical.

In my view, the transaction partitioning is more important than the functional partitioning. Thus, we will merge the transactions into a single Transaction-Implementation component. We will also merge the Classifications, Schedules, Methods, and Affiliations components into a single PayrollImplementation package.

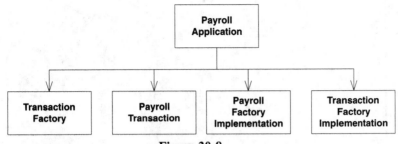

Figure 30-8
Static structure of main program and object factories

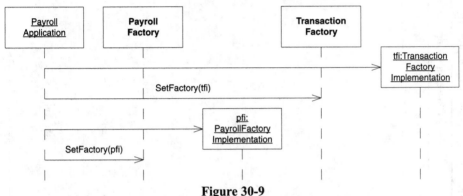

Figure 30-9
Dynamic structure of main program and object factories

The Final Packaging Structure

Table 30-3 shows the final allocation of classes to components. Table 30-4 contains the metrics spreadsheet. Figure 30-10 shows the final component structure, which uses object factories to bring the concrete components near the main sequence

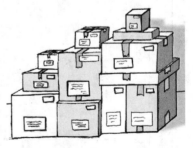

The metrics on this diagram are heartening. The relational cohesions are all very high, thanks in part to the relationships of the concrete factories to the objects they create, and there are no significant deviations from the main sequence. Thus, the couplings between our components are appropriate to a sane development environment. Our abstract components are closed, reusable, and heavily depended on but have few dependencies of their own. Our concrete components are segregated on the basis of reuse, are heavily dependent on the abstract components, and are not heavily depended on themselves.

Table 30-3 Final Allocation of Classes to Components

Components	Classes in Components		
AbstractTransactions	AddEmployeeTransaction	ChangeAffiliationTransaction	ChangeEmployeeTransaction
	ChangeClassificationTransaction	ChangeMethodTransaction	
Application	Application		
PayrollApplication	PayrollApplication		
PayrollDatabase	PayrollDatabase		
PayrollDatabaseImplementation	PayrollDatabaseImplementation		
PayrollDomain	Affiliation	Employee	PaymentClassification
	PaymentMethod	PaymentSchedule	
PayrollFactory	PayrollFactory		
PayrollImplementation	BiweeklySchedule	CommissionedClassification	DirectMethod
	HoldMethod	HourlyClassification	MailMethod
	MonthlySchedule	PayrollFactoryImplementation	SalariedClassification
	SalesReceipt	ServiceCharge	Timecard
	UnionAffiliation	WeeklySchedule	
TextParserTransactionSource	TextParserTransactionSource		
TransactionApplication	Transaction	TransactionApplication	TransactionSource
TransactionFactory	TransactionFactory		
TransactionImplementation	AddCommissionedEmployee	AddHourlyEmployee	AddSalariedEmployee
	ChangeAddressTransaction	ChangeCommissionedTransaction	ChangeDirectTransaction
	ChangeHoldTransaction	ChangeHourlyTransaction	ChangeMailTransaction
	ChangeMemberTransaction	ChangeNameTransaction	ChangeSalariedTransaction
	ChangeUnaffiliatedTransaction	DeleteEmployee	PaydayTransaction
	SalesReceiptTransaction	ServiceChargeTransaction	TimecardTransaction
	TransactionFactoryImplementation		

Table 30-4 Metrics Spreadsheet

Component Name	N	A	Ca	Ce	R	H	I	A	D	D'
AbstractTransactions	5	5	13	1	0	0.20	0.07	1	0.05	0.07
Application	1	1	1	0	0	1	0	1	0	0
PayrollApplication	1	0	0	5	0	1	1	0	0	0
PayrollDatabase	1	1	19	5	0	1	0.21	1	0.15	0.21
PayrollDatabase-Implementation	1	0	0	1	0	1	1	0	0	0
PayrollDomain	5	4	30	0	4	1	0	0.80	0.14	0.20
PayrollFactory	1	1	12	4	0	1	0.25	1	0.18	0.25
PayrollImplementation	14	0	1	5	3	0.29	0.83	0	0.12	0.17
TextParserTransactionSource	1	0	1	3	0	1	0.75	0	0.18	0.25
TransactionApplication	3	3	14	1	3	1.33	0.07	1	0.05	0.07
TransactionFactory	1	1	3	1	0	1	0.25	1	0.18	0.25
TransactionImplementation	19	0	1	14	0	0.05	0.93	0	0.05	0.07

Conclusion

The need to manage component structures is a function of the size of the program and the size of the development team. Even small teams need to partition the source code so that team members can stay out of one another's way. Large programs can become opaque masses of source files without some kind of partitioning structure. The principles and metrics described in this chapter have helped me, and many other development teams, manage their component dependency structures.

Bibliography

[Booch94] Grady Booch, *Object-Oriented Analysis and Design with Applications*, 2d ed., Addison-Wesley, 1994.

[DeMarco82] Tom DeMarco, *Controlling Software Projects*, Yourdon Press, 1982.

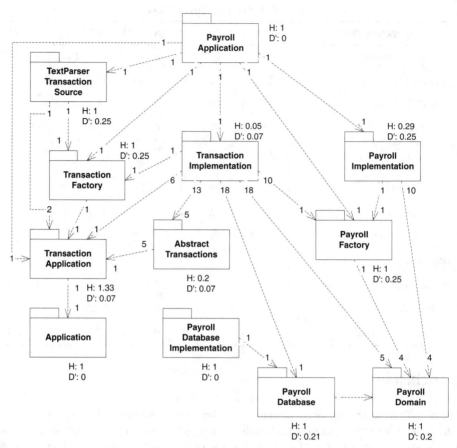

Figure 30-10
Final payroll component structure

31

COMPOSITE

A composite is a euphemism for a lie. It's disorderly. It's dishonest and it's not journalism.

—Fred W. Friendly, 1984

The COMPOSITE pattern is a very simple pattern that has significant implications. The fundamental structure of the COMPOSITE pattern is shown in Figure 31-1. Here, we see a hierarchy based on shapes. The `Shape` base class has two derivative shapes: `Circle` and `Square`. The third derivative is the composite. `CompositeShape` keeps a list of many `Shape` instances. When called on `CompositeShape`, `Draw()` delegates that method to all the `Shape` instances in the list.

Thus, an instance of `CompositeShape` appears to the system to be a single `Shape`. It can be passed to any function or object that takes a `Shape`, and it will behave like a

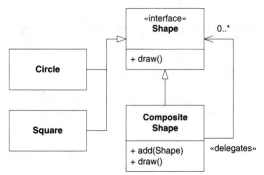

Figure 31-1
COMPOSITE pattern

Shape. However, it is really a proxy[1] for a group of Shape instances. Listings 31-1 and 31-2 show one possible implementation of CompositeShape.

Listing 31-1

Shape.cs

```
public interface Shape
{
   void Draw();
}
```

Listing 31-2

CompositeShape.cs

```
using System.Collections;

public class CompositeShape : Shape
{
   private ArrayList itsShapes = new ArrayList();
   public void Add(Shape s)
   {
     itsShapes.Add(s);
   }

   public void Draw()
   {
     foreach (Shape shape in itsShapes)
       shape.Draw();
   }
}
```

---

1. Note the similarity in structure to the PROXY pattern.

COMPOSITE **Commands**

Consider our discussion of Sensors and Command objects in Chapter 21. Figure 21-3 showed a Sensor class using a Command class. On detecting its stimulus, the Sensor called Do() on the Command.

What I failed to mention then was that often, a Sensor had to execute more than one Command. For example, when it reached a certain point in the paper path, the paper would trip an optical sensor. That sensor then stopped a motor, started another, and engaged a particular clutch.

At first, we took this to mean that every Sensor class would have to maintain a list of Command objects (see Figure 31-2). However, we soon recognized that whenever it needed to execute more than one Command, a Sensor always treated those Command objects identically. That is, it simply iterated over the list and called Do() on each Command. This was ideal for the COMPOSITE pattern.

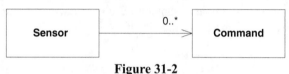

Figure 31-2
Sensor containing many Commands

So we left the Sensor class alone and created a CompositeCommand, as shown in Figure 31-3. This meant that we didn't have to change the Sensor or the Command. We were able to add the plurality of Commands to a Sensor without changing either. This is an application of OCP.

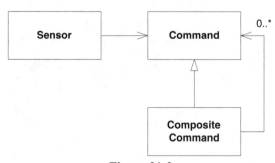

Figure 31-3
CompositeCommand

Multiplicity or No Multiplicity

This leads to an interesting issue. We were able to make our `Sensors` behave as though they contained many `Commands`, without having to modify the `Sensors`. There must be many other situations like this in normal software design. There must be times when you could use COMPOSITE rather than building a list or vector of objects.

In other words, the association between `Sensor` and `Command` is 1:1. We were tempted to change that association to 1:many. But instead, we found a way to get 1:many behavior without a 1:many relationship. A 1:1 relationship is much easier to understand, code, and maintain than a 1:many relationship is, so this was clearly the right design trade-off. How many of the 1:many relationships in your current project could be 1:1 if you used COMPOSITE?

Of course, not all 1:many relationship can be reverted to 1:1 by using COMPOSITE. Only those in which every object in the list is treated identically are candidates. For example, if you maintained a list of employees and searched through that list for employees whose paydate is today, you probably shouldn't use the COMPOSITE pattern, because you wouldn't be treating all the employees identically.

Conclusion

Quite a few 1:many relationships qualify for conversion to COMPOSITE. The advantages are significant. Instead of duplicating the list management and iteration code in each of the clients, that code appears only once in the composite class.

32

Observer: Evolving into a Pattern

© Jennifer M. Kohnke

I prefer to describe my profession as that of a "Contemporary Anthropological Interactive
OBSERVER" because it has just the right amount of flair. Besides,
"stalker" is such an ugly word.

—Anonymous

This chapter serves a special purpose. In it, I describe the OBSERVER[1] pattern, but that is a
minor objective. The primary objective of this chapter is to demonstrate how your design
and code can evolve to use a pattern.

---

1. [GOF95], p. 293

The preceding chapters made use of many patterns. Often, they were presented without showing how the code evolved to use the pattern. This might give you the idea that patterns are simply something you insert into your code and designs in completed form. This is not what I advise. Rather, I prefer to evolve the code I am working on in the direction of a pattern. I may get to the pattern, or I may not. It depends on whether the issues get resolved. It is not uncommon for me to start with a pattern in mind and wind up at a very different place.

This chapter sets up a simple problem and then shows how the design and code evolve to solve that problem. The goal of the evolution is the OBSERVER pattern. At each stage of the evolution, I describe the issues I'm trying to resolve and then show the steps that resolve them. With luck, we'll wind up with an OBSERVER.

The Digital Clock

We have a clock object that catches millisecond interrupts, known as tics, from the operating system and turns them into the time of day. This object knows how to calculate seconds from milliseconds, minutes from seconds, hours from minutes, days from hours, and so on. It knows how many days are in a month and how many months are in a year. It knows all about leap years, when to have them, and when not. It knows about time. See Figure 32-1.

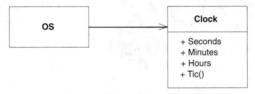

Figure 32-1
`Clock` object

We'd like to create a digital clock that sits on our desktop and continuously displays the time of day. What is the simplest way to accomplish this? We could write this:

```
public void DisplayTime()
{
  while (true)
  {
    int sec = clock.Seconds;
    int min = clock.Minutes;
    int hour = clock.Hours;
    ShowTime(hour, min, sec);
  }
}
```

Clearly, this is suboptimal. It consumes all available CPU cycles to repeatedly display the time. Most of those displays will be wasted because the time will not have changed. It may be that this solution would be adequate in a digital watch or a digital wall clock, since in those systems, conserving CPU cycles is not very important. However, we don't want this CPU hog running on our desktop.

Thus, the way in which the time moves from the clock to the display is going to be nontrivial. What mechanism should I use? Before first, I need to ask another question. How do I test that the mechanism is doing what I want?

The fundamental problem I am exploring is how to get data from the Clock to the DigitalClock. I'm going to assume that the Clock object and the DigitalClock object both exist. My interest is in how to connect them. I can test that connection simply by making sure that the data I get from the Clock is the same data I send to the DigitalClock.

A simple way to do that is to create one interface that pretends to be the Clock and another interface that pretends to be the DigitalClock. Then I can write special test objects that implement those interfaces and verify that the connection between them works as expected. See Figure 32-2.

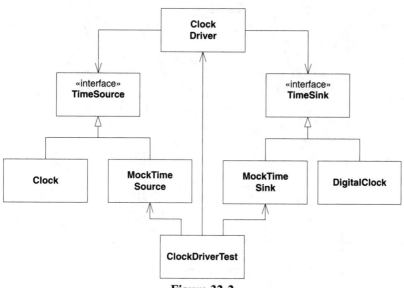

Figure 32-2
Testing the DigitalClock

The ClockDriverTest object will connect the ClockDriver to the two mock objects through the TimeSource and TimeSink interfaces and will then check each of the mock objects to ensure that the ClockDriver managed to move the time from the source to the sink. If necessary, the ClockDriverTest will also ensure that efficiency is being conserved.

I think it's interesting that we have added interfaces to the design simply as a result of considering how to test it. In order to test a module, you have to be able to isolate it from the other modules in the system, just as we have isolated the ClockDriver from the Clock and DigitalClock. Considering tests first helps us to minimize the coupling in our designs.

OK, how does the ClockDriver work? Clearly, in order to be efficient, the Clock-Driver must detect when the time in the TimeSource object has changed. Then, and only then, should it move the time to the TimeSink object. How can the ClockDriver know when the time has changed? It could poll the TimeSource, but that simply recreates the CPU hog problem.

The simplest way for the ClockDriver to know when the time has changed is for the Clock object to tell it. We could pass the ClockDriver to the Clock through the TimeSource interface, and then, when the time changes, the Clock can update the ClockDriver. The ClockDriver will, in turn, set the time on the ClockSink. See Figure 32-3.

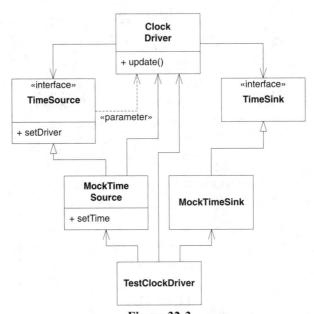

Figure 32-3
Getting the TimeSource to update the ClockDriver

Note the dependency from the TimeSource to the ClockDriver. It is there because the argument to the SetDriver method is a ClockDriver. I'm not very happy with this, since it implies that TimeSource objects must use ClockDriver objects in every case. However, I'll defer doing anything about this until I get this working.

Listing 32-1 shows the test case for the ClockDriver. Note that the test case creates a ClockDriver, binds a MockTimeSource and a MockTimeSink to it, and then sets the time in the source and expects the time to magically arrive at the sink. The rest of the code is shown in Listings 32-2 through 32-6 .

Listing 32-1

ClockDriverTest.cs

```
using NUnit.Framework;

[TestFixture]
public class ClockDriverTest
{
  [Test]
  public void TestTimeChange()
  {
    MockTimeSource source = new MockTimeSource();
    MockTimeSink sink = new MockTimeSink();
    ClockDriver driver = new ClockDriver(source,sink);
    source.SetTime(3,4,5);
    Assert.AreEqual(3, sink.GetHours());
    Assert.AreEqual(4, sink.GetMinutes());
    Assert.AreEqual(5, sink.GetSeconds());

    source.SetTime(7,8,9);
    Assert.AreEqual(7, sink.GetHours());
    Assert.AreEqual(8, sink.GetMinutes());
    Assert.AreEqual(9, sink.GetSeconds());
  }
}
```

Listing 32-2

TimeSource.cs

```
public interface TimeSource
{
  void SetDriver(ClockDriver driver);
}
```

Listing 32-3

TimeSink.cs

```
public interface TimeSink
{
  void SetTime(int hours, int minutes, int seconds);
}
```

Listing 32-4

ClockDriver.cs

```
public class ClockDriver
{
  private readonly TimeSink sink;

  public ClockDriver(TimeSource source, TimeSink sink)
```

Listing 32-4 (Continued)
`ClockDriver.cs`

```
  {
    source.SetDriver(this);
    this.sink = sink;
  }

  public void Update(int hours, int minutes, int seconds)
  {
    sink.SetTime(hours, minutes, seconds);
  }
}
```

Listing 32-5
`MockTimeSource.cs`

```
public class MockTimeSource : TimeSource
{
  private ClockDriver itsDriver;

  public void SetTime(int hours, int minutes, int seconds)
  {
    itsDriver.Update(hours, minutes, seconds);
  }

  public void SetDriver(ClockDriver driver)
  {
    itsDriver = driver;
  }
}
```

Listing 32-6
`MockTimeSink.cs`

```
public class MockTimeSink : TimeSink
{
  private int itsHours;
  private int itsMinutes;
  private int itsSeconds;

  public int GetHours()
  {
    return itsHours;
  }

  public int GetMinutes()
  {
    return itsMinutes;
  }

  public int GetSeconds()
  {
    return itsSeconds;
  }
```

Listing 32-6 (Continued)

MockTimeSink.cs

```
  public void SetTime(int hours, int minutes, int seconds)
  {
    itsHours = hours;
    itsMinutes = minutes;
    itsSeconds = seconds;
  }
}
```

Now that it works, I can think about cleaning it up. I don't like the dependency from TimeSource to ClockDriver. I don't like it because I want the TimeSource interface to be usable by anybody, not just ClockDriver objects. As it stands, only ClockDriver instances can use a TimeSource. We can fix this by creating an interface that TimeSource can use and that ClockDriver can implement (see Figure 32-4). We'll call this interface ClockObserver. See Listings 32-7 through 32-10. The code in **boldface** has changed.

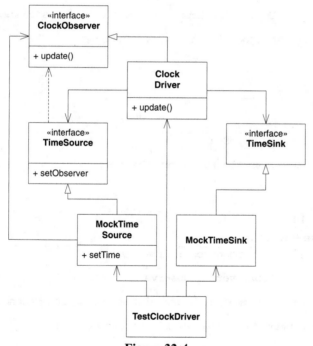

Figure 32-4
Breaking the dependency of TimeSource on ClockDriver

Listing 32-7

ClockObserver.cs

```
public interface ClockObserver
{
  void Update(int hours, int minutes, int secs);
}
```

Listing 32-8

ClockDriver.cs

```
public class ClockDriver : ClockObserver
{
  private readonly TimeSink sink;

  public ClockDriver(TimeSource source, TimeSink sink)
  {
    source.SetObserver(this);
    this.sink = sink;
  }

  public void Update(int hours, int minutes, int seconds)
  {
    sink.SetTime(hours, minutes, seconds);
  }
}
```

Listing 32-9

TimeSource.cs

```
public interface TimeSource
{
  void SetObserver(ClockObserver observer);
}
```

Listing 32-10

MockTimeSource.cs

```
public class MockTimeSource : TimeSource
{
  private ClockObserver itsObserver;

  public void SetTime(int hours, int minutes, int seconds)
  {
    itsObserver.Update(hours, minutes, seconds);
  }

  public void SetObserver(ClockObserver observer)
  {
    itsObserver = observer;
  }
}
```

This is better. Now anybody can make use of `TimeSource` by implementing `ClockObserver` and calling `SetObserver`, passing themselves in as the argument.

I'd like to be able to have more than one `TimeSink` getting the time. One might implement a digital clock. Another might be used to supply the time to a reminder service. Still another might start my nightly backup. In short, I'd like a single `TimeSource` to be able to supply the time to multiple `TimeSink` objects.

How do I do this? Right now, I create a `ClockDriver` with a single `TimeSource` and a single `TimeSink`. How should I specify multiple `TimeSink` instances? I could change the constructor of the `ClockDriver` to take only `TimeSource` and then add a method named `addTimeSink` that allows you to add `TimeSink` instances whenever you want.

The thing I don't like about this is that I now have two indirections. I have to tell the `TimeSource` who the `ClockObserver` is by calling `SetObserver`. Then I also have to tell the `ClockDriver` who the `TimeSink` instances are. Is this double indirection really necessary?

Looking at `ClockObserver` and `TimeSink`, I see that they both have the `SetTime` method. It looks as though `TimeSink` could implement `ClockObserver`. If I did this, my test program could create a `MockTimeSink` and call `SetObserver` on the `TimeSource`. I could get rid of the `ClockDriver` and `TimeSink` altogether! Listing 32-11 shows the changes to `ClockDriverTest`.

Listing 32-11
ClockDriverTest.cs

```
using NUnit.Framework;

[TestFixture]
public class ClockDirverTest
{
  [Test]
  public void TestTimeChange()
  {
    MockTimeSource source = new MockTimeSource();
    MockTimeSink sink = new MockTimeSink();
    source.SetObserver(sink);

    source.SetTime(3,4,5);
    Assert.AreEqual(3, sink.GetHours());
    Assert.AreEqual(4, sink.GetMinutes());
    Assert.AreEqual(5, sink.GetSeconds());

    source.SetTime(7,8,9);
    Assert.AreEqual(7, sink.GetHours());
    Assert.AreEqual(8, sink.GetMinutes());
    Assert.AreEqual(9, sink.GetSeconds());
  }
}
```

This means that `MockTimeSink` should implement `ClockObserver` rather than `TimeSink`. See Listing 32-12. These changes work fine. Why did we think we needed a `ClockDriver` in the first place? Figure 32-5 shows the UML. Clearly, this is much simpler.

Listing 32-12
MockTimeSink.cs

```
public class MockTimeSink : ClockObserver
{
  private int itsHours;
  private int itsMinutes;
  private int itsSeconds;

  public int GetHours()
  {
    return itsHours;
  }

  public int GetMinutes()
  {
    return itsMinutes;
  }

  public int GetSeconds()
  {
    return itsSeconds;
  }

  public void Update(int hours, int minutes, int secs)
  {
    itsHours = hours;
    itsMinutes = minutes;
    itsSeconds = secs;
  }
}
```

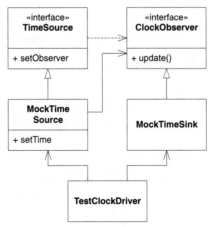

Figure 32-5
Removing `ClockDriver` and `TimeSink`

OK, now we can handle multiple `TimeSink` objects by changing the `setObserver` function to `registerObserver` and making sure that all the registered `ClockObserver` instances are held in a list and updated appropriately. This requires another change to the test program. Listing 32-13 shows the changes. I also did a little refactoring of the test program to make it smaller and easier to read.

Listing 32-13
ClockDriverTest.cs

```
using NUnit.Framework;

[TestFixture]
public class ClockDriverTest
{
    private MockTimeSource source;
    private MockTimeSink sink;

    [SetUp]
    public void SetUp()
    {
        source = new MockTimeSource();
        sink = new  MockTimeSink();
        source.RegisterObserver(sink);
    }

    private void AssertSinkEquals(
        MockTimeSink sink, int hours, int mins, int secs)
    {
        Assert.AreEqual(hours, sink.GetHours());
        Assert.AreEqual(mins, sink.GetMinutes());
        Assert.AreEqual(secs, sink.GetSeconds());
    }

    [Test]
    public void TestTimeChange()
    {
        source.SetTime(3,4,5);
        AssertSinkEquals(sink, 3,4,5);

        source.SetTime(7,8,9);
        AssertSinkEquals(sink, 7,8,9);
    }

    [Test]
    public void TestMultipleSinks()
    {
        MockTimeSink sink2 = new MockTimeSink();
        source.RegisterObserver(sink2);

        source.SetTime(12,13,14);
        AssertSinkEquals(sink, 12,13,14);
        AssertSinkEquals(sink2, 12,13,14);
    }
}
```

The change needed to make this work is pretty simple. We change `MockTimeSource` to hold all registered observers in an `ArrayList`. Then, when the time changes, we iterate through that list and call `Update` on all the registered `ClockObservers`. Listings 32-14 and 32-15 show the changes. Figure 32-6 shows the corresponding UML.

Listing 32-14

TimeSource.cs

```
public interface TimeSource
{
   void RegisterObserver(ClockObserver observer);
}
```

Listing 32-15

MockTimeSource.cs

```
using System.Collections;

public class MockTimeSource : TimeSource
{
   private ArrayList itsObservers = new ArrayList();

   public void SetTime(int hours, int mins, int secs)
   {
      foreach(ClockObserver observer in itsObservers)
        observer.Update(hours, mins, secs);
   }

   public void RegisterObserver(ClockObserver observer)
   {
      itsObservers.Add(observer);
   }
}
```

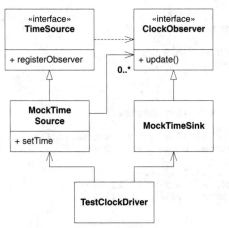

Figure 32-6
Handling multiple `TimeSink` objects

This is pretty nice, but I don't like the fact that the `MockTimeSource` has to deal with the registration and update. It implies that the `Clock`, and every other derivative of `Time-Source`, will have to duplicate that registration and update code. I don't think `Clock` should have to deal with registration and update. I also don't like the idea of duplicate code. So I'd like to move all that stuff into the `TimeSource`. Of course, this will mean that `TimeSource` will have to change from an interface to a class. It also means that `MockTimeSource` will shrink to near nothing. Listings 32-16 and 32-17, and Figure 32-7 show the changes.

Listing 32-16

TimeSource.cs

```
using System.Collections;

public abstract class TimeSource
{
  private ArrayList itsObservers = new ArrayList();

  protected void Notify(int hours, int mins, int secs)
  {
    foreach(ClockObserver observer in itsObservers)
      observer.Update(hours, mins, secs);
  }

  public void RegisterObserver(ClockObserver observer)
  {
    itsObservers.Add(observer);
  }
}
```

Listing 32-17

MockTimeSource.cs

```
public class MockTimeSource : TimeSource
{
  public void SetTime(int hours, int mins, int secs)
  {
    Notify(hours, mins, secs);
  }
}
```

This is pretty cool. Now, anybody can derive from `TimeSource`. All they have to do to get the observers updated is to call `Notify`. But there is still something I don't like about it. `MockTimeSource` inherits directly from `TimeSource`. This means that `Clock` must also derive from `TimeSource`. Why should `Clock` have to depend upon registration and update? `Clock` is simply a class that knows about time. Making it depend upon `TimeSource` seems necessary and undesirable.

I know how I'd solve this in C++. I'd create a subclass, called `ObservableClock`, of both `TimeSource` and `Clock`. I'd override `Tic` and `SetTime` in `ObservableClock` to call `Tic` or `SetTime` in `Clock` and then call `Notify` in `TimeSource`. See Listings 32-8 and 32-18.

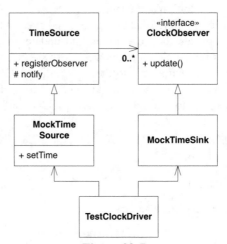

Figure 32-7
Moving registration and update into `TimeSource`

Listing 32-18

ObservableClock.cc (C++)

```
class ObservableClock : public Clock, public TimeSource
{
  public:
    virtual void tic()
    {
      Clock::tic();
      TimeSource::notify(getHours(),
                         getMinutes(),
                         getSeconds());
    }

    virtual void aetTime(int hours, int minutes, int seconds)
    {
      Clock::setTime(hours, minutes, seconds);
      TimeSource::notify(hours, minutes, seconds);
    }
};
```

Unfortunately, we don't have this option in C#, because the language can't deal with multiple inheritance of classes. So, in C#, we either have to leave things as they are or use a delegation hack. The delegation hack is shown in Listings 32-19 through 32-21 and Figure 32-9.

Note that the `MockTimeSource` class implements `TimeSource` and contains a reference to an instance of `TimeSourceImplementation`. Note also that all calls to the `RegisterObserver` method of `MockTimeSource` are delegated to that `TimeSource-Implementation` object. So, too, `MockTimeSource.SetTime` invokes `Notify` on the `TimeSourceImplementation` instance.

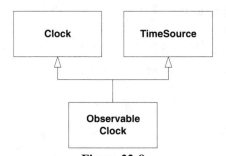

Figure 32-8
Using multiple inheritance in C++ to separate `Clock` from `TimeSource`

Listing 32-19

TomeSource.cs

```
public interface TimeSource
{
   void RegisterObserver(ClockObserver observer);
}
```

Listing 32-20

TimeSourceImplementation.cs

```
using System.Collections;

public class TimeSourceImplementation : TimeSource
{
   private ArrayList itsObservers = new ArrayList();

   public void Notify(int hours, int mins, int secs)
   {
     foreach(ClockObserver observer in itsObservers)
       observer.Update(hours, mins, secs);
   }

   public void RegisterObserver(ClockObserver observer)
   {
     itsObservers.Add(observer);
   }
}
```

Listing 32-21

MockTimeSource.cs

```
public class MockTimeSource : TimeSource
{
   TimeSourceImplementation timeSourceImpl =
     new TimeSourceImplementation();

   public void SetTime(int hours, int mins, int secs)
   {
     timeSourceImpl.Notify(hours, mins, secs);
   }
```

Listing 32-21 (Continued)

MockTimeSource.cs

```
public void RegisterObserver(ClockObserver observer)
{
    timeSourceImpl.RegisterObserver(observer);
}
}
```

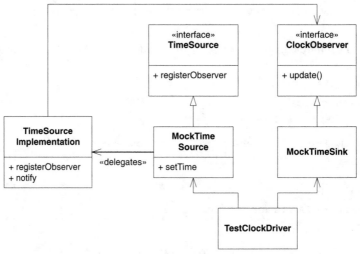

Figure 32-9
`Observer` delegation hack in C#

This is ugly but has the advantage that `MockTimeSource` does not extend a class. This means that if we were to create `ObservableClock`, it could extend `Clock`, implement `TimeSource`, and delegate to `TimeSourceImplementation` (see Figure 32-10). This solves the problem of `Clock` depending on the registration and update stuff but does so at a nontrivial price.

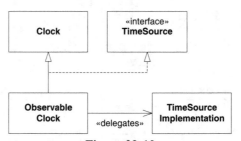

Figure 32-10
The delegation hack for `ObservableClock`

So, let's go back to the way things were in Figure 32-7, before we went down this rat-hole. We'll simply live with the fact that Clock has to depend upon all the registration and update stuff.

TimeSource is a stupid name for what the class does. It started out good, back when we had a ClockDriver. But things have changed an awful lot since then. We should change the name to something that suggests registration and update. The OBSERVER pattern calls this class Subject. Ours seems to be specific to time, so we could call it TimeSubject, but that's not a very intuitive name. We could use the old moniker Observable, but that doesn't ring my chimes, either: TimeObservable? No.

Perhaps it is the specificity of the "push model"[2] observer that is the problem. If we change to a "pull model," we could make the class generic. Then we could change the name of TimeSource to Subject, and everybody familiar with the OBSERVER pattern would know what it meant.

This is not a bad option. Rather than pass the time in the Notify and Update methods, we can have the TimeSink ask the MockTimeSource for the time. We don't want the MockTimeSink to know about the MockTimeSource, so we'll create an interface that the MockTimeSink can use to get the time. The MockTimeSource and the Clock will implement this interface. We'll call this interface TimeSource. The final state of the code and UML are in Figure 32-11 and Listings 32-22 through 32-27.

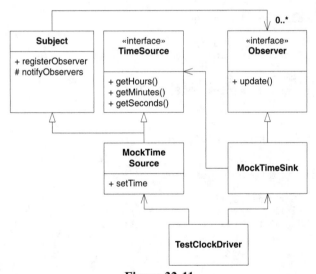

Figure 32-11
Final version of the Observer applied to MockTimeSource and MockTimeSink

---

2. "Push model" observers push data from the subject to the observer by passing it in the Notify and Update methods. "Pull model" observers pass nothing in the Notify and Update methods and depend on the observing object to query the observed object on receiving an update. See [GOF95].

Listing 32-22

ObserverTest.cs

```csharp
using NUnit.Framework;

[TestFixture]
public class ObserverTest
{
  private MockTimeSource source;
  private MockTimeSink sink;

  [SetUp]
  public void SetUp()
  {
    source = new MockTimeSource();
    sink = new  MockTimeSink();
    source.RegisterObserver(sink);
  }

  private void AssertSinkEquals(
    MockTimeSink sink, int hours, int mins, int secs)
  {
    Assert.AreEqual(hours, sink.GetHours());
    Assert.AreEqual(mins, sink.GetMinutes());
    Assert.AreEqual(secs, sink.GetSeconds());
  }

  [Test]
  public void TestTimeChange()
  {
    source.SetTime(3,4,5);
    AssertSinkEquals(sink, 3,4,5);

    source.SetTime(7,8,9);
    AssertSinkEquals(sink, 7,8,9);
  }

  [Test]
  public void TestMultipleSinks()
  {
    MockTimeSink sink2 = new MockTimeSink();
    source.RegisterObserver(sink2);

    source.SetTime(12,13,14);
    AssertSinkEquals(sink, 12,13,14);
    AssertSinkEquals(sink2, 12,13,14);
  }
}
```

Listing 32-23

Observer.cs

```csharp
public interface Observer
{
  void Update();
}
```

Listing 32-24

Subject.cs

```
using System.Collections;

public class Subject
{
  private ArrayList itsObservers = new ArrayList();

  public void NotifyObservers()
  {
    foreach(Observer observer in itsObservers)
      observer.Update();
  }

  public void RegisterObserver(Observer observer)
  {
    itsObservers.Add(observer);
  }
}
```

Listing 32-25

TimeSource.cs

```
public interface TimeSource
{
  int GetHours();
  int GetMinutes();
  int GetSeconds();
}
```

Listing 32-26

MockTimeSource.cs

```
public class MockTimeSource : Subject, TimeSource
{
  private int itsHours;
  private int itsMinutes;
  private int itsSeconds;

  public void SetTime(int hours, int mins, int secs)
  {
    itsHours = hours;
    itsMinutes = mins;
    itsSeconds = secs;
    NotifyObservers();
  }

  public int GetHours()
  {
    return itsHours;
  }

  public int GetMinutes()
```

Listing 32-26 (Continued)
MockTimeSource.cs

```
  {
    return itsMinutes;
  }

  public int GetSeconds()
  {
    return itsSeconds;
  }
}
```

Listing 32-27
MockTimeSink.cs

```
public class MockTimeSink : Observer
{
  private int itsHours;
  private int itsMinutes;
  private int itsSeconds;
  private TimeSource itsSource;

  public MockTimeSink(TimeSource source)
  {
    itsSource = source;
  }

  public int GetHours()
  {
    return itsHours;
  }

  public int GetMinutes()
  {
    return itsMinutes;
  }

  public int GetSeconds()
  {
    return itsSeconds;
  }

  public void Update()
  {
    itsHours = itsSource.GetHours();
    itsMinutes = itsSource.GetMinutes();
    itsSeconds = itsSource.GetSeconds();
  }
}
```

The OBSERVER Pattern

OK, so now that we've been through the example and evolved our code to the OBSERVER pattern, it might be interesting to study what it is. The canonical form of OBSERVER is shown in Figure 32-12. In this example, Clock is being observed by DigitalClock, which registers with the Subject interface of Clock. Whenever the time changes for any reason, Clock calls the Notify method of Subject. The Notify method of Subject invokes the Update method of each registered Observer. Thus, DigitalClock will receive an Update message whenever the time changes, using that opportunity to ask Clock for the time and then display it.

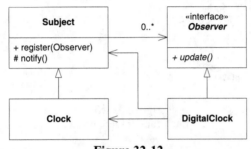

Figure 32-12
Canonical pull-model Observer

OBSERVER is one of those patterns that, once you understand it, you see uses for it everywhere. The indirection is very cool. You can register observers with all kinds of objects rather than writing those objects to explicitly call you. Although this indirection is a useful way to manage dependencies, it can easily be taken to extremes. Overuse of OBSERVER tends to make systems difficult to understand and trace.

Models

The OBSERVER pattern has two primary models. Figure 32-12 shows the *pull-model* OBSERVER. This model gets its name from the fact that the DigitalClock must pull the time information from the Clock object after receiving the Update message.

The advantage of the pull model is its simplicity of implementation and the fact that the Subject and Observer classes can be standard reusable elements in a library. However, imagine that you are observing an employee record with a thousand fields and that you have just received an Update message. Which of the thousand fields changed?

When Update is called on the ClockObserver, the response is obvious. The ClockObserver needs to pull the time from the Clock and display it. But when Update is called on the EmployeeObserver, the response is not so obvious. We don't know what happened. We don't know what to do. Perhaps the employee's name changed, or maybe the employee's salary changed. Maybe the employee got a new boss. Or maybe the employee's bank account changed. We need help.

This help can be given in the push-model form of the OBSERVER pattern. The structure of the push model is shown in Figure 32-13. Note that the `Notify` and `Update` methods both take an argument. The argument is a hint, passed from `Employee` to `SalaryObserver` through the `Notify` and `Update` methods. That hint tells `SalaryObserver` what kind of change the `Employee` record experienced.

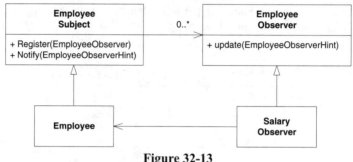

Figure 32-13
Push-model OBSERVER

The `EmployeeObserverHint` argument of `Notify` and `Update` might be an enumeration of some kind, a string, or a more complex data structure containing the old and new values of some field. Whatever it is, its value is being pushed toward the observer.

Choosing between the two OBSERVER models is simply a matter of the complexity of the observed object. If the observed object is complex and the observer needs a hint, the push model is appropriate. If the observed object is simple, a pull model will do fine.

Management of OOD Principles

The principle that most drives the OBSERVER pattern is the Open/Closed Principle (OCP). The motivation for using the pattern is so that you can add new observing objects without changing the observed object. Thus, the observed object stays closed.

From Figure 32-12, it should be clear that `Clock` is substitutable for `Subject` and that `DigitalClock` is substitutable for `Observer`. Thus, the Liskov Substitution Principle (LSP) is applied.

`Observer` is an abstract class, and the concrete `DigitialClock` depends on it. The concrete methods of `Subject` also depend on it. Thus, the Dependency-Inversion Principle (DIP) is applied in this case. You might think that since `Subject` has no abstract methods, the dependency between `Clock` and `Subject` violates DIP. However, `Subject` is a class that ought never to be instantiated. It makes sense only in the context of a derived class. Thus, `Subject` is logically abstract, even though it has no abstract methods. We can enforce the abstractness of `Subject` by giving it a pure virtual destructor in C++ or by making its constructors protected.

There are hints of the Interface Segregation Principle (ISP) in Figure 32-11. The `Subject` and `TimeSource` classes segregate the clients of the `MockTimeSource`, providing specialized interfaces for each of those clients.

Conclusion

So, we made it. We started with a design problem and, through reasonable evolution, brought it pretty close to the canonical OBSERVER pattern. You might complain that since I knew that I wanted to arrive at the OBSERVER, I simply arranged it so that I would. I won't deny it. But that's not really the issue.

If you are familiar with design patterns, an appropriate pattern will very likely pop into your mind when you're faced with a design problem. The question, then, is whether to implement that pattern directly or instead to evolve it into place through a series of small steps. This chapter showed what the second option is like. Rather than simply leaping to the conclusion that the OBSERVER pattern was the best choice for the problem at hand, I slowly maneuvered the code in that direction.

At any point during that evolution, I could have found that my problem was solved and stopped evolving. Or, I might have found that I could solve the problem by changing course and going in a different direction.

I drew in this chapter some of the diagrams for your benefit. I thought it would be easier for you to follow what I was doing by showing you an overview in a diagram. Had I not been trying to expose and expound, I would not have created them. However, *a few* of the diagrams were created for *my* benefit. There were times when I simply needed to stare at the structure that I had created so I could see where to go next.

Had I not been writing a book, I would have drawn these diagrams by hand on a scrap of paper or a whiteboard. I would not have taken the time to use a drawing tool. There are no circumstances that I know of in which using a drawing tool is faster than using a napkin.

Having used the diagrams to help me evolve the code, I would not have kept the diagrams. In every case, the ones I drew for myself were intermediate steps.

Is there value in keeping diagrams at this level of detail? Clearly, if you are trying to expose your reasoning, as I am doing in this book, they come in pretty handy. But usually, we are not trying to document the evolutionary path of a few hours of coding. Usually, these diagrams are transient and are better thrown away. At *this* level of detail, the code is generally good enough to act as its own documentation. At higher levels, this is not always true.

Bibliography

[GOF95] Erich Gamma, Richard Helm, Ralph Johnson, and John Vlissides, *Design Patterns: Elements of Reusable Object-Oriented Software*, Addison-Wesley, 1995.

[PLOPD3] Robert C. Martin, Dirk Riehle, and Frank Buschmann, eds. *Pattern Languages of Program Design 3*, Addison-Wesley, 1998.

33

ABSTRACT SERVER, ADAPTER, and BRIDGE

Politicians are the same all over.
They promise to build a bridge even where there is no river.

—Nikita Khrushchev

In the mid-1990s I was deeply involved with the discussions that coursed through the comp.object newsgroup. Those of us who posted messages on that newsgroup argued furiously about various strategies of analysis and design. At one point, we decided that a concrete example would help us evaluate one another's positions. So we chose a very simple design problem and proceeded to present our favorite solutions.

The design problem was extraordinarily simple. We determined to show how we would design the software inside a simple table lamp. The table lamp has a switch and a light. You could ask the switch whether it was on or off, and you could tell the light to turn on or off: nice, simple problem.

The debate raged for months. Some people used a simple approach of only a switch and a light object. Others thought there ought to be a lamp object that contained the switch and the light. Still others thought that electricity should be an object. One person suggested a power cord object.

Despite the absurdity of most of those arguments, the design model is interesting to explore. Consider Figure 33-1. We can certainly make this design work. The `Switch` object can poll the state of the actual switch and can send appropriate `turnOn` and `turnOff` messages to the `Light` object.

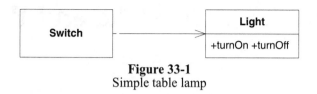

Figure 33-1
Simple table lamp

What don't we like about this design? Two of our design principles are being violated by this design: the Dependency-Inversion Principle (DIP) and the Open/Closed Principle. (OCP) The violation of DIP is easy to see; the dependency from `Switch` to `Light` is a dependency on a concrete class. DIP tells us to prefer dependencies on abstract classes. The violation of OCP is a little less direct but is more to the point. We don't like this design, because it forces us to drag a `Light` along everywhere we need a `Switch`. `Switch` cannot be easily extended to control objects other than `Light`.

ABSTRACT SERVER

You might be thinking that you could inherit a `Switch` subclass that would control something other than a light, as in Figure 33-2. But this doesn't solve the problem, because `FanSwitch` still inherits the dependency on `Light`. Wherever you take a `FanSwitch`, you'll have to bring `Light` along. In any case, that particular inheritance relationship also violates DIP.

To solve the problem, we invoke one of the simplest of all design patterns: ABSTRACT SERVER (see Figure 33-3). By introducing an interface between the `Switch` and the `Light`, we have made it possible for `Switch` to control anything that implements that interface. This immediately satisfies both DIP and OCP.

As an interesting aside, note that the interface is named for its client. It is called `Switchable` rather than `Light`. We've talked about this before, and we'll probably do so

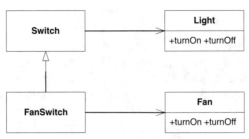

Figure 33-2
A bad way to extend `Switch`

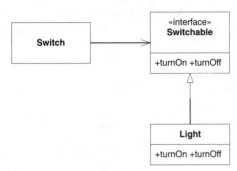

Figure 33-3
ABSTRACT SERVER solution to the table lamp problem

again. Interfaces belong to the client, not to the derivative. The logical binding between the client and the interface is stronger than that between the interface and its derivatives. The logical binding is so strong that it makes no sense to deploy `Switch` without `Switchable`, and yet it makes perfect sense to deploy `Switchable` without `Light`. The strength of the logical bonds is at odds with the strength of the physical bonds. Inheritance is a much stronger physical bond than association is.

In the early 1990s, we used to think that the physical bond ruled. Reputable books recommended that inheritance hierarchies be placed together in the same physical package. This seemed to make sense, since inheritance is such a strong physical bond. But over the past decade, we have learned that the physical strength of inheritance is misleading and that inheritance hierarchies should usually not be packaged together. Rather, clients tend to be packaged with the interfaces they control.

This misalignment of the strength of logical and physical bonds is an artifact of statically typed languages, such as C#. Dynamically typed languages, such as Smalltalk, Python, and Ruby, don't have the misalignment, because they don't use inheritance to achieve polymorphic behavior.

ADAPTER

A problem with the design in Figure 33-3 is the potential violation of the Single-Responsibility Principle (SRP). We have bound together two things, `Light` and `Switchable`, that may not change for the same reasons. What if we can't add the inheritance relationship to `Light`? What if we purchased `Light` from a third party and don't have the source code? What if we want a `Switch` to control a class that we can't derive from `Switchable`? Enter the ADAPTER.[1]

Figure 33-4 shows how an `Adapter` can be used to solve the problem. The adapter derives from `Switchable` and delegates to `Light`. This solves the problem neatly. Now we can have any object that can be turned on or off controlled by a `Switch`. All we need to do is create the appropriate adapter. Indeed, the object need not even have the same `turnOn` and `turnOff` methods that `Switchable` has. The adapter can be *adapted* to the interface of the object.

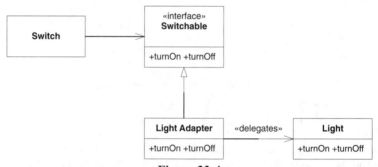

Figure 33-4
Solving the table lamp problem with ADAPTER

Adapters don't come cheap. You need to write the new class, and you need to instantiate the adapter and bind the adapted object to it. Then, every time you invoke the adapter, you have to pay for the time and space required for the delegation. So clearly, you don't want to use adapters all the time. The ABSTRACT SERVER solution is quite appropriate for most situations. In fact, even the initial solution in Figure 33-1 is pretty good unless you happen to *know* that there are other objects for `Switch` to control.

The Class Form of ADAPTER

The `LightAdapter` class in Figure 33-4 is known as an *object-form adapter*. Another approach, known as the *class-form adapter*, is shown in Figure 33-5. In this form, the

---

1. We've seen the ADAPTER before, in Figures 10-2 and 10-3.

adapter object inherits from both the Switchable interface and the Light class. This form is a tiny bit more efficient than the object form and is a bit easier to use but at the expense of using the high coupling of inheritance.

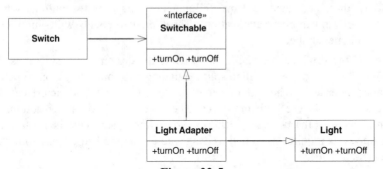

Figure 33-5
Solving the table lamp problem with ADAPTER

The Modem Problem, ADAPTERs, and LSP

Consider the situation in Figure 33-6. We have a large number of modem clients all making use of the Modem interface. The Modem interface is implemented by several derivatives, including HayesModem, USRoboticsModem, and ErniesModem. This is a pretty common situation. It conforms nicely to OCP, LSP, and DIP. Clients are unaffected when there are new kinds of modems to deal with. Suppose that this situation were to continue for several years. Suppose that there were hundreds of modem clients all making happy use of the Modem interface.

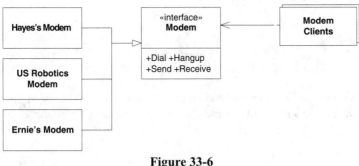

Figure 33-6
Modem problem

Now suppose that our customers have given us a new requirement. Certain kinds of modems, called dedicated modems,[2] don't dial. but sit at both ends of a dedicated connection. Several new applications use these dedicated modems and don't bother to dial. We'll call these the DedUsers. However, our customers want all the current modem clients to be able to use these dedicated modems, Telling us that they don't want to have to modify the hundreds of modem client applications. Those modem clients will simply be told to dial dummy phone numbers.

If we had our druthers, we might want to alter the design of our system as shown in Figure 33-7. We'd make use of ISP to split the dialing and communications functions into two separate interfaces. The old modems would implement both interfaces, and the modem clients would use both interfaces. The DedUsers would use nothing but the Modem interface, and the DedicatedModem would implement only the Modem interface. Unfortunately, this requires us to make changes to all the modem clients, something that our customers forbade.

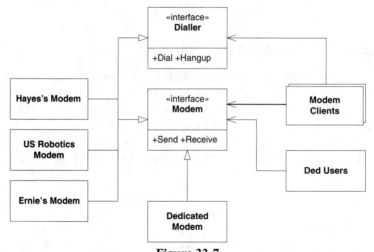

Figure 33-7
Ideal solution to the modem problem

So what do we do? We can't separate the interfaces as we'd like, yet we must provide a way for all the modem clients to use DedicatedModem. One possible solution is to

---

2. All modems used to be dedicated; it is only in recent geological epochs that modems took on the ability to dial. In the early Jurassic period, you rented a breadbox-sized modem from the phone company and connected it to another modem through dedicated lines that you also rented from the phone company. (Life was good for the phone company in the Jurassic.) If you wanted to dial, you rented another breadbox-sized unit called an autodialer.

derive `DedicatedModem` from `Modem` and to implement the `Dial` and `Hangup` functions to do nothing, as follows:

```
class DedicatedModem : Modem
{
    public virtual void Dial(char phoneNumber[10]) {}
    public virtual void Hangup() {}
    public virtual void Send(char c)
    {...}
    public virtual char Receive()
    {...}
}
```

Degenerate functions are a sign that we may be violating LSP. The users of the base class may be expecting `Dial` and `Hangup` to significantly change the state of the modem. The degenerate implementations in `DedicatedModem` may violate those expectations.

Let's presume that the modem clients were written to expect their modems to be dormant until `Dial` is called and to return to dormancy when `Hangup` is called. In other words, they don't expect any characters to be coming out of modems that aren't dialed. `DedicatedModem` violates this expectation. It will return characters before `Dial` has been called and will continue to return them after `Hangup` has been called. Thus, `Dedicated-Modem` may crash some of the modem clients.

You might suggest that the problem is with the modem clients. They aren't written very well if they crash on unexpected input. I'd agree with that. But it's going to be difficult to convince the folks who have to maintain the modem clients to make changes to their software because we are adding a new kind of mode. Not only does this violate OCP, but also it's just plain frustrating. Besides, our customer has explicitly forbidden us to change the modem clients.

A kludge solution We can simulate a connection status in `Dial` and `Hangup` of `DedicatedModem`. We can refuse to return characters if `Dial` has not been called or after `Hangup` has been called. If we make this change, all the modem clients will be happy and won't have to change. *All we have to do is convince the DedUsers to call dial and hangup.* See Figure 33-8.

You might imagine that the folks who are building the `DedUsers` find this pretty frustrating. They are explicitly using `DedicatedModem`. *Why should they have to call Dial and Hangup?* However, they haven't written their software yet, so it's easier to get them to do what we want.

A tangled web of dependencies. Months later, when there are hundreds of `Ded-Users`, our customers present us with a new change. It seems that all these years, our programs have not had to dial international phone numbers. That's why they got away with the char[10] in dial. Now, however, our customers want us to be able to dial phone numbers of arbitrary length. They have a need to make international calls, credit card calls, PIN-identified calls, and so on.

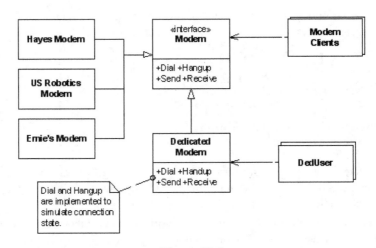

Figure 33-8
Kludging `DedicatedModem` to simulate connection state

Clearly, all the modem clients must be changed. They were written to expect `char[ 10]` for the phone number. Our customers authorize this change because they have no choice, and hordes of programmers are put to the task. Just as clearly, the classes in the `modem` hierarchy must change to accommodate the new phone number size. Our little team can deal with that. *Unfortunately, we now have to go to the authors of the DedUsers and tell them that they have to change their code!* You might imagine how happy they'll be about that. They aren't calling `dial` because they need to. They are calling `Dial` because we told them they have to. And now they are going through an expensive maintenance job because they did what we told them to do.

This is the kind of nasty dependency tangle that many projects find themselves in. A kludge in one part of the system creates a nasty thread of dependency that eventually causes problems in what ought to be a completely unrelated part of the system.

ADAPTER to the rescue We could have prevented this fiasco by using ADAPTER to solve the initial problem, as shown in Figure 33-9. In this case, `DedicatedModem` does not inherit from `Modem`. The modem clients use `DedicatedModem` indirectly through the `DedicatedModemAdapter`. This adapter implements `Dial` and `Hangup` to simulate the connection state. The adapter delegates `send` and `recieve` calls to the `DedicatedModem`.

Note that this eliminates all the difficulties we had before. Modem clients are seeing the connection behavior that they expect, and `DedUsers` don't have to fiddle with `dial` or `hangup`. When the phone number requirement changes, the `DedUsers` will be unaffected. Thus, by putting the adapter in place, we have fixed both LSP and OCP violations.

Note that the kludge still exists. The adapter is still simulating connection state. You may think that this is ugly, and I'd certainly agree with you. However, note that all the dependencies point *away* from the adapter. The kludge is isolated from the system, tucked

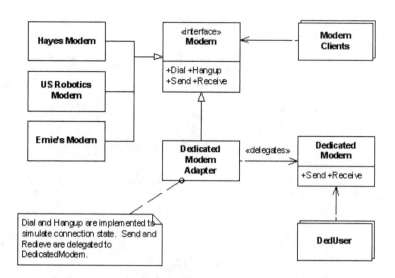

Figure 33-9
Solving the modem problem with ADAPTER

away in an adapter that barely anybody knows about. The only hard dependency on that adapter will likely be in the implementation of some factory[3] somewhere.

Bridge

There is another way to look at this problem. The need for a dedicated modem has added a new degree of freedom to the Modem type hierarchy. When the Modem type was conceived, it was simply an interface for a set of different hardware devices. Thus, we had HayesModem, USRModem, and ErniesModem deriving from the base Modem class. Now, however, it appears that there is another way to cut at the modem hierarchy. We could have DialModem and DedicatedModem deriving from Modem.

Merging these two independent hierarchies can be done as shown in Figure 33-10. Each of the leaves of the type hierarchy puts either a dialup or dedicated behavior onto the hardware it controls. A DedicatedHayesModem object controls a Hayes modem in a dedicated context.

This is not an ideal structure. Every time we add a new piece of hardware, we must create *two* new classes: one for the dedicated case and one for the dialup case. Every time we add a new connection type, we have to create *three* new classes, one for each of the different pieces of hardware. If these two degrees of freedom are at all volatile, we could soon wind up with a large number of derived classes.

---

3. See Chapter 29.

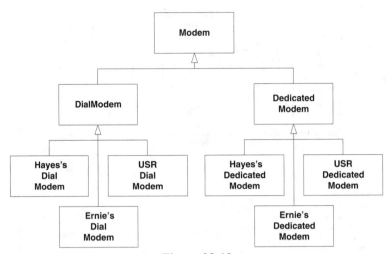

Figure 33-10
Solving the modem problem by merging type hierarchies

We can solve this problem by applying the BRIDGE pattern. This pattern often helps when a type hierarchy has more than one degree of freedom. Rather than merge the hierarchies, we can separate them and tie them together with a bridge.

Figure 33-11 shows the structure. We split the modem hierarchy into two hierarchies. One represents the connection method, and the other represents the hardware.

Modem users continue to use the Modem interface. ModemConnectionController implements the Modem interface. The derivatives of ModemConnectionController control the connection mechanism. DialModemController simply passes the dial and hangup method to dialImp and hangImp in the ModemConnectionController base class. Those methods then delegate to the ModemImplementation class, where they are deployed to the appropriate hardware controller. DedModemController implements dial and hangup to simulate the connection state. It passes send and receive to sendImp and receiveImp, which are then delegated to the ModemImplementation hierarchy as before.

Note that the four imp functions in the ModemConnectionController base class are protected; they are to be used strictly by derivatives of ModemConnection-Controller. No one else should be calling them.

This structure is complex but interesting. We are able to create it without affecting the modem users, yet it allows us to completely separate the connection policies from the hardware implementation. Each derivative of ModemConnectionController represents a new connection policy. That policy can use sendImp, receiveImp, dialImp, and hangImp to implement that policy. New imp functions could be created without affecting the users. ISP could be used to add new interfaces to the connection controller classes.

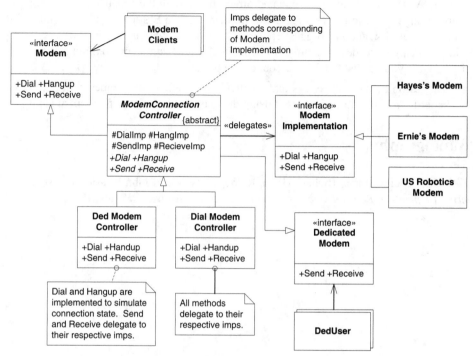

Figure 33-11
BRIDGE solution to the modem problem

This could create a migration path that the modem clients could slowly follow toward an API that is higher level than `dial` and `hangup`.

Conclusion

One might be tempted to suggest that the real problem with the `Modem` scenario is that the original designers got the design wrong. They should have known that connection and communication were separate concepts. Had they done a little more analysis, they would have found this and corrected it. So, it is tempting to blame the problem on insufficient analysis.

Poppycock! There is no such thing as *enough* analysis. No matter how much time you spend trying to figure out the perfect software structure, you will always find that the customer introduces a change that violates that structure.

There is no escape from this. There are no perfect structures. There are only structures that try to balance the current costs and benefits. Over time, those structures must change as the requirements of the system change. The trick to managing that change is to keep the system as simple and as flexible as possible.

The ADAPTER solution is simple and direct. It keeps all the dependencies pointing in the right direction, and it's very simple to implement. The BRIDGE solution is quite a bit more complex. I would not suggest embarking down that road until you had very strong evidence that you needed to completely separate the connection and communication policies and that you needed to add new connection policies.

The lesson here, as always, is that a pattern is something that comes with both costs and benefits. You should find yourself using the ones that best fit the problem at hand.

Bibliography

[GOF95] Erich Gamma, Richard Helm, Ralph Johnson, and John Vlissides, *Design Patterns: Elements of Reusable Object-Oriented Software*, Addison-Wesley, 1995.

34

PROXY AND GATEWAY:
Managing Third-Party APIs

*I am endeavoring, ma'am, to construct a mnemonic circuit
using stone knives and bearskins.*

—Spock

There are many barriers in software systems. When we move data from our program into the database, we are crossing the database barrier. When we send a message from one computer to another, we are crossing the network barrier.

Crossing these barriers can be complicated. If we aren't careful, our software will be more about the barriers than about the problem to be solved. The PROXY pattern helps us cross such barriers while keeping the program centered on the problem to be solved.

Proxy

Imagine that we are writing a shopping cart system for a Web site. Such a system might have objects for the customer, the order (the cart), and the products in the order. Figure 34-1 shows a possible structure. This structure is simplistic but will serve for our purposes.

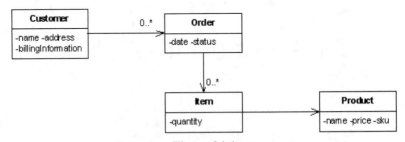

Figure 34-1
Simple shopping cart object model

If we consider the problem of adding a new item to an order, we might come up with the code in Listing 34-1. The AddItem method of class Order simply creates a new Item holding the appropriate Product and quantity and then adds that Item to its internal ArrayList of Items.

Listing 34-1
Adding an item to the Object model

```
public class Order
{
  private ArrayList items = new ArrayList();

  public void AddItem(Product p, int qty)
  {
    Item item = new Item(p, qty);
    items.Add(item);
  }
}
```

Now imagine that these objects represent data kept in a relational database. Figure 34-2 shows the tables and keys that might represent the objects. To find the orders for a given customer, you find all orders that have the customer's cusid. To find all the items in a given order, you find the items that have the order's orderId. To find the products referenced by the items, you use the product's sku.

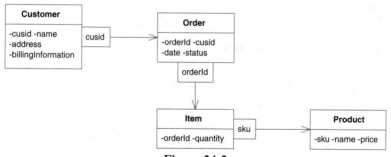

Figure 34-2
Shopping cart relational data model

If we want to add an item row for a particular order, we'd use something like Listing 34-2. This code makes ADO.NET calls to directly manipulate the relational data model.

Listing 34-2

Adding an item to the relational model

```
public class AddItemTransaction : Transaction
{
  public void AddItem(int orderId, string sku, int qty)
  {
    string sql = "insert into items values(" +
      orderId + "," + sku + "," + qty + ")";
    SqlCommand command = new SqlCommand(sql, connection);
    command.ExecuteNonQuery();
  }
}
```

These two code snippets are very different, but they perform the same logical function. They both connect an item to an order. The first ignores the existence of a database, and the second glories in it.

Clearly, the shopping cart program is all about orders, items, and products. Unfortunately, if we use the code in Listing 34-2, we make it about SQL statements, database connections, and piecing together query strings. This is a significant violation of SRP and possibly CCP. Listing 34-2 mixes two concepts that change for different reasons. It mixes the concept of the items and orders with the concept of relational schemas and SQL. If either concept must change for any reason, the other concept will be affected. Listing 34-2 also violates DIP, since the policy of the program depends on the details of the storage mechanism.

The PROXY pattern is a way to cure these ills. To explore this, let's set up a test program that demonstrates the behavior of creating an order and calculating the total price. The salient part of this program is shown in Listing 34-3.

The simple code that passes this test is shown in Listings 34-4 through 34-6. The code makes use of the simple object model in Figure 34-1. It does not assume that there is a database anywhere.

Listing 34-3

```
Test program creates order and verifies calculation of price.
  [Test]
  public void TestOrderPrice()
  {
    Order o = new Order("Bob");
    Product toothpaste = new Product("Toothpaste", 129);
    o.AddItem(toothpaste, 1);
    Assert.AreEqual(129, o.Total);
    Product mouthwash = new Product("Mouthwash", 342);
    o.AddItem(mouthwash, 2);
    Assert.AreEqual(813, o.Total);
  }
```

Listing 34-4

Order.cs

```
public class Order
{
  private ArrayList items = new ArrayList();

  public Order(string cusid)
  {
  }

  public void AddItem(Product p, int qty)
  {
    Item item = new Item(p,qty);
    items.Add(item);
  }

  public int Total
  {
    get
    {
      int total = 0;
      foreach(Item item in items)
      {
        Product p = item.Product;
        int qty = item.Quantity;
        total += p.Price * qty;
      }
      return total;
    }
  }
}
```

Listing 34-5

Product.cs

```
public class Product
{
  private int price;
```

Listing 34-5 (Continued)

Product.cs

```
    public Product(string name, int price)
    {
      this.price = price;
    }

    public int Price
    {
      get { return price; }
    }
  }
```

Listing 34-6

Item.cs

```
public class Item
{
  private Product product;
  private int quantity;

  public Item(Product p, int qty)
  {
    product = p;
    quantity = qty;
  }

  public Product Product
  {
    get { return product; }
  }

  public int Quantity
  {
    get { return quantity; }
  }
}
```

Figures 34-3 and 34-4 show how the PROXY pattern works. Each object to be proxied is split into three parts. The first is an interface that declares all the methods that clients will want to invoke. The second is an implementation that implements those methods without knowledge of the database. The third is the proxy that knows about the database.

Consider the Product class. We have proxied it by replacing it with an interface. This interface has all the same methods that Product has. The ProductImplementation class implements the interface almost exactly as before. The ProductDBProxy implements all the methods of Product to fetch the product from the database, create an instance of ProductImplementation, and then delegate the message to it.

The sequence diagram in Figure 34-4 shows how this works. The client sends the Price message to what it thinks is a Product but what is in fact a ProductDBProxy. The ProductDBProxy fetches the ProductImplementation from the database and then delegates the Price property to it.

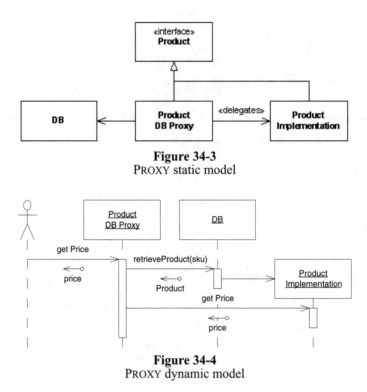

Figure 34-3
PROXY static model

Figure 34-4
PROXY dynamic model

Neither the client nor the `ProductImplementation` knows that this has happened. The database has been inserted into the application without either party knowing about it. That's the beauty of the PROXY pattern. In theory, it can be inserted in between two collaborating objects without their having to know about it. Thus, it can be used to cross a barrier, such as a database or a network, without either participant knowing about it.

In reality, using proxies is nontrivial. To get an idea what some of the problems are, let's try to add the PROXY pattern to the simple shopping cart application.

Implementing PROXY

The simplest `Proxy` to create is for the `Product` class. For our purposes, the product table represents a simple dictionary. It will be loaded in one place with all the products. There is no other manipulation of this table, and that makes the proxy relatively trivial.

To get started, we need a simple database utility that stores and retrieves product data. The proxy will use this interface to manipulate the database. Listing 34-7 shows the test program for what I have in mind. Listings 34-8 and 34-9 make that test pass.

Listing 34-7

`DbTest.cs`

```
[TestFixture]
public class DBTest
{

  [SetUp]
  public void SetUp()
  {
    DB.Init();
  }

  [TearDown]
  public void TearDown()
  {
    DB.Close();
  }

  [Test]
  public void StoreProduct()
  {
    ProductData storedProduct = new ProductData();
    storedProduct.name = "MyProduct";
    storedProduct.price = 1234;
    storedProduct.sku = "999";
    DB.Store(storedProduct);
    ProductData retrievedProduct =
      DB.GetProductData("999");
    DB.DeleteProductData("999");
    Assert.AreEqual(storedProduct, retrievedProduct);
  }
}
```

Listing 34-8

`ProductData.cs`

```
public class ProductData
{
  private string name;
  private int price;
  private string sku;

  public ProductData(string name,
    int price, string sku)
  {
    this.name = name;
    this.price = price;
    this.sku = sku;
  }

  public ProductData() {}
```

Listing 34-8 (Continued)

ProductData.cs

```
  public override bool Equals(object o)
  {
    ProductData pd = (ProductData)o;
    return name.Equals(pd.name) &&
      sku.Equals(pd.sku) &&
      price==pd.price;
  }

  public override int GetHashCode()
  {
    return name.GetHashCode() ^
      sku.GetHashCode() ^
      price.GetHashCode();
  }
}
```

Listing 34-9

```
public class Db
{
  private static SqlConnection connection;

  public static void Init()
  {
    string connectionString =
      "Initial Catalog=QuickyMart;" +
      "Data Source=marvin;" +
      "user id=sa;password=abc;";
    connection = new SqlConnection(connectionString);
    connection.Open();
  }

  public static void Store(ProductData pd)
  {
    SqlCommand command = BuildInsertionCommand(pd);
    command.ExecuteNonQuery();
  }

  private static SqlCommand
    BuildInsertionCommand(ProductData pd)
  {
    string sql =
      "INSERT INTO Products VALUES (@sku, @name, @price)";
    SqlCommand command = new SqlCommand(sql, connection);
    command.Parameters.Add("@sku", pd.sku);
    command.Parameters.Add("@name", pd.name);
    command.Parameters.Add("@price", pd.price);

    return command;
  }

  public static ProductData GetProductData(string sku)
```

Listing 34-9 (Continued)

```
  {
    SqlCommand command = BuildProductQueryCommand(sku);
    IDataReader reader = ExecuteQueryStatement(command);
    ProductData pd = ExtractProductDataFromReader(reader);
    reader.Close();
    return pd;
  }

  private static
  SqlCommand BuildProductQueryCommand(string sku)
  {
    string sql = "SELECT * FROM Products WHERE sku = @sku";
    SqlCommand command = new SqlCommand(sql, connection);
    command.Parameters.Add("@sku", sku);
    return command;
  }

  private static ProductData
    ExtractProductDataFromReader(IDataReader reader)
  {
    ProductData pd = new ProductData();
    pd.Sku = reader["sku"].ToString();
    pd.Name = reader["name"].ToString();
    pd.Price = Convert.ToInt32(reader["price"]);
    return pd;
  }

  public static void DeleteProductData(string sku)
  {
    BuildProductDeleteStatement(sku).ExecuteNonQuery();
  }

  private static SqlCommand
    BuildProductDeleteStatement(string sku)
  {
    string sql = "DELETE from Products WHERE sku = @sku";
    SqlCommand command = new SqlCommand(sql, connection);
    command.Parameters.Add("@sku", sku);
    return command;
  }

  private static IDataReader
    ExecuteQueryStatement(SqlCommand command)
  {
    IDataReader reader = command.ExecuteReader();
    reader.Read();
    return reader;
  }

  public static void Close()
  {
    connection.Close();
  }
}
```

The next step in implementing the proxy is to write a test that shows how it works. This test adds a product to the database, creates a `ProductProxy` with the `sku` of the stored product, and attempts to use the accessors of `Product` to acquire the data from the proxy. See Listing 34-10.

Listing 34-10

ProxyTest.cs

```
[TestFixture]
public class ProxyTest
{
  [SetUp]
  public void SetUp()
  {
    Db.Init();
    ProductData pd = new ProductData();
    pd.sku = "ProxyTest1";
    pd.name = "ProxyTestName1";
    pd.price = 456;
    Db.Store(pd);
  }

  [TearDown]
  public void TearDown()
  {
    Db.DeleteProductData("ProxyTest1");
    Db.Close();
  }

  [Test]
  public void ProductProxy()
  {
    Product p = new ProductProxy("ProxyTest1");
    Assert.AreEqual(456, p.Price);
    Assert.AreEqual("ProxyTestName1", p.Name);
    Assert.AreEqual("ProxyTest1", p.Sku);
  }
}
```

In order to make this work, we have to separate the interface of `Product` from its implementation. So I changed `Product` to an interface and created `ProductImp` to implement it (see Listings 34-11 and 34-12). This forced me to make changes to `TestShoppingCart` (not shown) to use `ProductImp` instead of `Product`.

Listing 34-11

Product.cs

```
public interface Product
{
  int Price {get;}
  string Name {get;}
  string Sku {get;}
}
```

Listing 34-12
ProductImpl.cs

```
public class ProductImpl : Product
{
  private int price;
  private string name;
  private string sku;

  public ProductImpl(string sku, string name, int price)
  {
    this.price = price;
    this.name = name;
    this.sku = sku;
  }

  public int Price
  {
    get { return price; }
  }

  public string Name
  {
    get { return name; }
  }

  public string Sku
  {
    get { return sku; }
  }
}
```

Listing 34-13

```
public class ProductProxy : Product
{
  private string sku;

  public ProductProxy(string sku)
  {
    this.sku = sku;
  }

  public int Price
  {
    get
    {
      ProductData pd = Db.GetProductData(sku);
      return pd.price;
    }
  }

  public string Name
  {
    get
```

Listing 34-13 (Continued)

```
    {
        ProductData pd = Db.GetProductData(sku);
        return pd.name;
    }
  }

  public string Sku
  {
    get { return sku; }
  }
}
```

The implementation of this proxy is trivial. In fact, it doesn't quite match the canonical form of the pattern shown in Figures 34-3 and 34-4. This was an unexpected surprise. My intent was to implement the PROXY pattern. But when the implementation finally materialized, the canonical pattern made no sense.

The canonical pattern would have had `ProductProxy` create a `ProductImp` in every method. It would then have delegated that method or property to the `ProductImp`, as follows:

```
public int Price
{
  get
  {
    ProductData pd = Db.GetProductData(sku);
    ProductImpl p =
      new ProductImpl(pd.Name, pd.Sku, pd.Price);
    return pd.Price;
  }
}
```

The creation of the `ProductImp` is a complete waste of programmer and computer resources. The `ProductProxy` already has the data that the `ProductImp` accessors would return. So there is no need to create, and then delegate to, the `ProductImp`. This is yet another example of how the code may lead you away from the patterns and models you expected.

Note that the `Sku` property of `ProductProxy` in Listing 34-13 takes this theme one step further. It doesn't even bother to hit the database for the `sku`. Why should it? It already has the `sku`.

You might be thinking that the implementation of `ProductProxy` is very inefficient. It hits the database for each accessor. Wouldn't it be better if it cached the `ProductData` item in order to avoid hitting the database?

This change is trivial, but the only thing driving us to do it is our fear. At this point, we have no data to suggest that this program has a performance problem. Besides, we know that the database engine too is doing some caching. So it's not clear what building our own cache would buy us. We should wait until we see indications of a performance problem before we invent trouble for ourselves.

Our next step is to create the proxy for `Order`. Each `Order` instance contains many `Item` instances. In the relational schema (Figure 34-2), this relationship is captured within the `Item` table. Each row of the `Item` table contains the key of the `Order` that contains it. In the object model, however, the relationship is implemented by an `ArrayList` within `Order` (see Listing 34-4). Somehow, the proxy is going to have to translate between the two forms.

We begin by posing a test case that the proxy must pass. This test adds a few dummy products to the database, obtains proxies to those products, and uses them to invoke `AddItem` on an `OrderProxy`. Finally, the test asks the `OrderProxy` for the total price (see Listing 34-14). The intent of this test case is to show that an `OrderProxy` behaves just like an `Order` but obtains its data from the database instead of from in-memory objects.

Listing 34-14

`ProxyTest.cs`

```
[Test]
public void OrderProxyTotal()
{
  Db.Store(new ProductData("Wheaties", 349, "wheaties"));
  Db.Store(new ProductData("Crest", 258, "crest"));
  ProductProxy wheaties = new ProductProxy("wheaties");
  ProductProxy crest = new ProductProxy("crest");
  OrderData od = Db.NewOrder("testOrderProxy");
  OrderProxy order = new OrderProxy(od.orderId);
  order.AddItem(crest, 1);
  order.AddItem(wheaties, 2);
  Assert.AreEqual(956, order.Total);
}
```

In order to make this test case work, we have to implement a few new classes and methods. The first we'll tackle is the `NewOrder` method of `Db`. This method appears to return an instance of something called an `OrderData`. `OrderData` is just like `Product-Data`: a simple data structure that represents a row of the `Order` database table. The method is shown in Listing 34-15.

Listing 34-15

`OrderData.cs`

```
public class OrderData
{
  public string customerId;
  public int orderId;

  public OrderData() {}

  public OrderData(int orderId, string customerId)
  {
    this.orderId = orderId;
    this.customerId = customerId;
  }
}
```

Don't be offended by the use of public data members. This is not an object in the true sense. It is simply a container for data. It has no interesting behavior that needs to be encapsulated. Making the data variables private, and providing getters and setters would be a waste of time. I could have used a `struct` instead of a class, but I want the `OrderData` to be passed by reference rather than by value.

Now we need to write the `NewOrder` function of `Db`. Note that when we call it in Listing 34-14, we provide the ID of the owning customer but do not provide the `orderId`. Each `Order` needs an `orderId` to act as its key. What's more, in the relational schema, each `Item` refers to this `orderId` as a way to show its connection to the `Order`. Clearly, the `orderId` must be unique. How does it get created? Let's write a test to show our intent. See Listing 34-16.

Listing 34-16

DbTest.cs

```
[Test]
public void OrderKeyGeneration()
{
  OrderData o1 = Db.NewOrder("Bob");
  OrderData o2 = Db.NewOrder("Bill");
  int firstOrderId = o1.orderId;
  int secondOrderId = o2.orderId;
  Assert.AreEqual(firstOrderId + 1, secondOrderId);
}
```

This test shows that we expect the `orderId` to somehow automatically increment every time a new `Order` is created. This is easily implemented by allowing `SqlServer` to generate the next `orderId`; we can get the value by calling the database method `scope_identity()`. See Listing 34-17.

Listing 34-17

```
public static OrderData NewOrder(string customerId)
{
  string sql = "INSERT INTO Orders(cusId) VALUES(@cusId); " +
    "SELECT scope_identity()";
  SqlCommand command = new SqlCommand(sql, connection);
  command.Parameters.Add("@cusId", customerId);
  int newOrderId = Convert.ToInt32(command.ExecuteScalar());
  return new OrderData(newOrderId, customerId);
}
```

Now we can start to write `OrderProxy`. As with `Product`, we need to split `Order` into an interface and an implementation. So `Order` becomes the interface, and `OrderImp` becomes the implementation. See Listings 34-18 and 34-19.

Listing 34-18

Order.cs

```
public interface Order
{
  string CustomerId { get; }
  void AddItem(Product p, int quantity);
  int Total { get; }
}
```

Listing 34-19

`OrderImpl.cs`

```
public class OrderImp : Order
{
  private ArrayList items = new ArrayList();
  private string customerId;

  public OrderImp(string cusid)
  {
    customerId = cusid;
  }

  public string CustomerId
  {
    get { return customerId; }
  }

  public void AddItem(Product p, int qty)
  {
    Item item = new Item(p, qty);
    items.Add(item);
  }

  public int Total
  {
    get
    {
      int total = 0;
      foreach(Item item in items)
      {
        Product p = item.Product;
        int qty = item.Quantity;
        total += p.Price * qty;
      }
      return total;
    }
  }
}
```

How do I implement `AddItem` in the proxy? Clearly, the proxy cannot delegate to `OrderImp.AddItem`! Rather, the proxy is going to have to insert an `Item` row in the database. On the other hand, I *really want* to delegate `OrderProxy.Total` to `Order-Imp.Total`, because I want the business rules—the policy for creating totals—to be encapsulated in `OrderImp`. The whole point of building proxies is to separate database implementation from business rules.

In order to delegate the `Total` property, the proxy is going to have to build the complete `Order` object along with all its contained `Items`. Thus, in `OrderProxy.Total`, we are going to have to read in all the items from the database, call `AddItem` on an empty `OrderImp` for each item we find, and then call `Total` on that `OrderImp`. Thus, the `OrderProxy` implementation ought to look something like Listing 34-20.

This implies the existence of an `ItemData` class and a few `Db` functions for manipulating `ItemData` rows. These are shown in Listings 34-21 through 34-23.

Listing 34-20

```
public class OrderProxy : Order
{
  private int orderId;

  public OrderProxy(int orderId)
  {
    this.orderId = orderId;
  }

  public int Total
  {
    get
    {
      OrderImp imp = new OrderImp(CustomerId);
      ItemData[] itemDataArray = Db.GetItemsForOrder(orderId);
      foreach(ItemData item in itemDataArray)
        imp.AddItem(new ProductProxy(item.sku), item.qty);
      return imp.Total;
    }
  }

  public string CustomerId
  {
    get
    {
      OrderData od = Db.GetOrderData(orderId);
      return od.customerId;
    }
  }

  public void AddItem(Product p, int quantity)
  {
    ItemData id =
      new ItemData(orderId, quantity, p.Sku);
    Db.Store(id);
  }

  public int OrderId
  {
    get { return orderId; }
  }
}
```

Listing 34-21

ItemData.cs

```
public class ItemData
{
  public int orderId;
  public int qty;
  public string sku = "junk";

  public ItemData() {}
```

Listing 34-21 (Continued)
ItemData.cs

```
public ItemData(int orderId, int qty, string sku)
{
  this.orderId = orderId;
  this.qty = qty;
  this.sku = sku;
}

public override bool Equals(Object o)
{
  if(o is ItemData)
  {
    ItemData id = o as ItemData;
    return orderId == id.orderId &&
      qty == id.qty &&
      sku.Equals(id.sku);
  }
  return false;
}
}
```

Listing 34-22

```
[Test]
public void StoreItem()
{
  ItemData storedItem = new ItemData(1, 3, "sku");
  Db.Store(storedItem);
  ItemData[] retrievedItems = Db.GetItemsForOrder(1);
  Assert.AreEqual(1, retrievedItems.Length);
  Assert.AreEqual(storedItem, retrievedItems[0]);
}

[Test]
public void NoItems()
{
  ItemData[] id = Db.GetItemsForOrder(42);
  Assert.AreEqual(0, id.Length);
}
```

Listing 34-23

```
public static void Store(ItemData id)
{
  SqlCommand command = BuildItemInsersionStatement(id);
  command.ExecuteNonQuery();
}

private static SqlCommand
  BuildItemInsersionStatement(ItemData id)
{
  string sql = "INSERT INTO Items(orderId,quantity,sku) " +
    "VALUES (@orderID, @quantity, @sku)";
  SqlCommand command = new SqlCommand(sql, connection);
```

Listing 34-23 (Continued)

```
    command.Parameters.Add("@orderId", id.orderId);
    command.Parameters.Add("@quantity", id.qty);
    command.Parameters.Add("@sku", id.sku);
    return command;
}

public static ItemData[] GetItemsForOrder(int orderId)
{
  SqlCommand command =
    BuildItemsForOrderQueryStatement(orderId);
  IDataReader reader = command.ExecuteReader();
  ItemData[] id = ExtractItemDataFromResultSet(reader);
  reader.Close();
  return id;
}

private static SqlCommand
  BuildItemsForOrderQueryStatement(int orderId)
{
  string sql = "SELECT * FROM Items " +
    "WHERE orderid = @orderId";
  SqlCommand command = new SqlCommand(sql, connection);
  command.Parameters.Add("@orderId", orderId);
  return command;
}

private static ItemData[]
  ExtractItemDataFromResultSet(IDataReader reader)
{
  ArrayList items = new ArrayList();
  while (reader.Read())
  {
    int orderId = Convert.ToInt32(reader["orderId"]);
    int quantity = Convert.ToInt32(reader["quantity"]);
    string sku = reader["sku"].ToString();
    ItemData id = new ItemData(orderId, quantity, sku);
    items.Add(id);
  }
  return (ItemData[]) items.ToArray(typeof (ItemData));
}

public static OrderData GetOrderData(int orderId)
{
  string sql = "SELECT cusid FROM orders " +
    "WHERE orderid = @orderId";
  SqlCommand command = new SqlCommand(sql, connection);
  command.Parameters.Add("@orderId", orderId);
  IDataReader reader = command.ExecuteReader();

  OrderData od = null;
  if (reader.Read())
    od = new OrderData(orderId, reader["cusid"].ToString());
  reader.Close();
  return od;
}
```

Listing 34-23 (Continued)

```
public static void Clear()
{
  ExecuteSql("DELETE FROM Items");
  ExecuteSql("DELETE FROM Orders");
  ExecuteSql("DELETE FROM Products");
}

private static void ExecuteSql(string sql)
{
  SqlCommand command = new SqlCommand(sql, connection);
  command.ExecuteNonQuery();
}
```

Summary

This example should have dispelled any false illusions about the elegance and simplicity of using proxies. Proxies are not trivial to use. The simple delegation model implied by the canonical pattern seldom materializes so neatly. Rather, we find ourselves short circuiting the delegation for trivial getters and setters. For methods that manage 1:N relationships, we find ourselves *delaying* the delegation and moving it into other methods, just as the delegation for AddItem was moved into Total. Finally, we face the specter of caching.

We didn't do any caching in this example. The tests all run in less than a second, so there was no need to worry overmuch about performance. But in a real application, the issue of performance, and the need for intelligent caching, is likely to arise. I do not suggest that you automatically implement a caching strategy because you fear that performance will otherwise be too slow. Indeed, I have found that adding caching too early is a good way to *decrease* performance. Rather, if you fear that performance may be a problem, I recommend that you conduct some experiments to *prove* that it will be a problem. Once proven, and *only once proven*, you should start considering how to speed things up.

For all the troublesome nature of proxies, they have one powerful benefit: *the separation of concerns.* In our example, the business rules and the database have been completely separated. OrderImp has no dependence on the database. If we want to change the database schema or the database engine, we can do so without affecting Order, OrderImp, or any of the other business domain classes.

If separation of business rules from database implementation is critically important, PROXY can be a good pattern to use. For that matter, PROXY can be used to separate business rules from *any* kind of implementation issue. It can be used to keep the business rules from being polluted by such things as COM, CORBA, EJB, and so on. It is a way to keep the business rule assets of your project separate from the implementation mechanisms that are currently in vogue.

Databases, Middleware, and Other Third-Party Interfaces

Third-party APIs are a fact of life for software engineers. We buy database engines, middleware engines, class libraries, threading libraries, and so on. Initially, we use these APIs by making direct calls to them from our application code (see Figure 34-5).

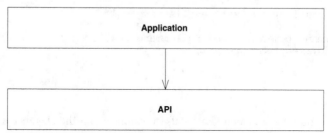

Figure 34-5
Initial relationship between an application and a third-party API

Over time, however, we find that our application code becomes more and more polluted with such API calls. In a database application, for example, we may find more and more SQL strings littering the code that also contains the business rules.

This becomes a problem when the third-party API changes. For databases, it also becomes a problem when the schema changes. As new versions of the API or schema are released, more and more of the application code has to be reworked to align with those changes.

Eventually, the developers decide that they must insulate themselves from these changes. So they invent a layer that separates the application business rules from the third-party API (see Figure 34-6). They concentrate into this layer all the code that uses the third-party API and all the concepts that related to the API rather than to the business rules of the application.

Such layers, such as ADO.NET can sometimes be purchased. They separate the application code from the database engine. Of course, they are also third-party APIs in and of themselves, and therefore the application may need to be insulated even from them.

Note that there is a transitive dependency from the `Application` to the `API`. In some applications, that indirect dependence is still enough to cause problems. ADO.NET, for example, does not insulate the application from the details of the schema.

In order to attain even better insulation, we need to invert the dependency between the application and the layer (see Figure 34-7). This keeps the application from knowing anything about the third-party API, either directly or indirectly. In the case of a database, it keeps the application from direct knowledge of the schema. In the case of a middleware engine, it keeps the application from knowing anything about the data types used by that middleware processor.

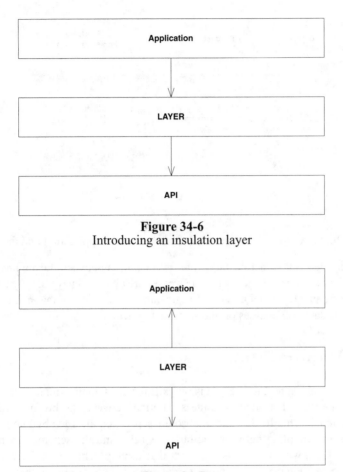

Figure 34-6
Introducing an insulation layer

Figure 34-7
Inverting the dependency between the application and the layer

This arrangement of dependencies is precisely what the PROXY pattern achieves. The application does not depend on the proxies at all. Rather the proxies depend on the application, and on the API. This concentrates all knowledge of the mapping between the application and the API into the proxies.

This concentration of knowledge means that the proxies are nightmares. Whenever the API changes, the proxies change. Whenever the application changes, the proxies change. The proxies can become very difficult to deal with.

It's good to know where your nightmares live. Without the proxies, the nightmares would be spread throughout the application code.

Most applications don't need proxies. Proxies are a heavyweight solution. When I see proxy solutions in use, my recommendation in most cases is to take them out and use

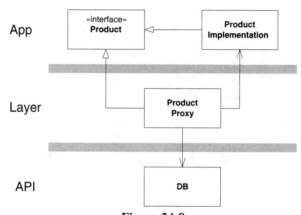

Figure 34-8
How the Proxy inverts the dependency between the application and the layer

something simpler. But sometimes, the intense separation between the application and the API afforded by proxies is beneficial. Those cases are almost always in very large systems that undergo frequent schema and/or API thrashing, or in systems that can ride on top of many different database engines or middleware engines.

TABLE DATA GATEWAY

PROXY is a difficult pattern to use and is overkill for most applications. I would not use it unless convinced that I needed absolute separation between the business rules and the database schema. Normally, the kind of absolute separation afforded by PROXY is not necessary, and some coupling between the business rules and the schema can be tolerated. TABLE DATA GATEWAY (TDG) is a pattern that usually achieves sufficient separation, without the cost of PROXY. Also known as data access object (DAO), this pattern uses a specialized FACADE for each type of object we wish to store in the database (see Figure 34-9).

OrderGateway (Listing 34-24) is an interface that the application uses to access the persistence layer for Order objects. This interface has the method Insert for persisting new Orders and a method Find for retrieving already persisted Orders.

DbOrderGateway (Listing 34-25) implements the OrderGateway and moves Order instances between the object model and the relational database. It has a connection to an SqlServer instance and uses the same schema used previously in the PROXY example.[1]

---

1. I have to say that I hate the database access systems in today's major platforms. The idea of building up SQL strings and executing them is messy at best and certainly baroque. It's a shame that we have to write programs to generate SQL which was meant to be read and written by humans but that instead is parsed and interpreted by the database engine. A more direct mechanism could (and should) be found. Many teams use persistence frameworks, such as NHibernate, to hide the worst of the arcane SQL manipulations, and this is a good thing. However, these frameworks merely hide what ought to be eliminated.

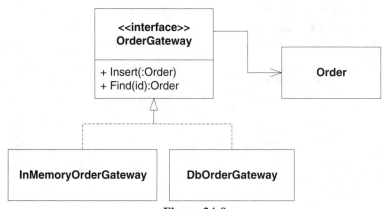

Figure 34-9
TABLE DATA GATEWAY pattern

Listing 34-24

`OrderGateway.cs`

```
public interface OrderGateway
{
  void Insert(Order order);
  Order Find(int id);
}
```

Listing 34-25

`DbOrderGateway.cs`

```
public class DbOrderGateway : OrderGateway
{
  private readonly ProductGateway productGateway;
  private readonly SqlConnection connection;

  public DbOrderGateway(SqlConnection connection,
                        ProductGateway productGateway)
  {
    this.connection = connection;
    this.productGateway = productGateway;
  }

  public void Insert(Order order)
  {
    string sql = "insert into Orders (cusId) values (@cusId)" +
      "; select scope_identity()";
    SqlCommand command = new SqlCommand(sql, connection);
    command.Parameters.Add("@cusId", order.CustomerId);
    int id = Convert.ToInt32(command.ExecuteScalar());
    order.Id = id;

    InsertItems(order);
  }
```

Listing 34-25 (Continued)

`DbOrderGateway.cs`

```csharp
public Order Find(int id)
{
  string sql = "select * from Orders where orderId = @id";
  SqlCommand command = new SqlCommand(sql, connection);
  command.Parameters.Add("@id", id);
  IDataReader reader = command.ExecuteReader();

  Order order = null;
  if(reader.Read())
  {
    string customerId = reader["cusId"].ToString();
    order = new Order(customerId);
    order.Id = id;
  }
  reader.Close();

  if(order != null)
    LoadItems(order);

  return order;
}

private void LoadItems(Order order)
{
  string sql =
    "select * from Items where orderId = @orderId";
  SqlCommand command = new SqlCommand(sql, connection);
  command.Parameters.Add("@orderId", order.Id);
  IDataReader reader = command.ExecuteReader();

  while(reader.Read())
  {
    string sku = reader["sku"].ToString();
    int quantity = Convert.ToInt32(reader["quantity"]);
    Product product = productGateway.Find(sku);
    order.AddItem(product, quantity);
  }
}

private void InsertItems(Order order)
{
  string sql = "insert into Items (orderId, quantity, sku)" +
    "values (@orderId, @quantity, @sku)";

  foreach(Item item in order.Items)
  {
    SqlCommand command = new SqlCommand(sql, connection);
    command.Parameters.Add("@orderId", order.Id);
    command.Parameters.Add("@quantity", item.Quantity);
    command.Parameters.Add("@sku", item.Product.Sku);
    command.ExecuteNonQuery();
  }
}
}
```

The other implementation of OrderGateway is InMemoryOrderGateway (Listing 34-26). InMemoryOrderGateway will save and retrieve Orders just like the DbOrderGateway, but stores the data in memory, using a Hashtable. Persisting data in memory seems rather silly, since all will be lost when the application exits. However, as we'll see later, doing so is invaluable when it comes to testing.

Listing 34-26

InMemoryOrderGateway.cs

```
public class InMemoryOrderGateway : OrderGateway
{
  private static int nextId = 1;
  private Hashtable orders = new Hashtable();

  public void Insert(Order order)
  {
    orders[nextId++] = order;
  }

  public Order Find(int id)
  {
    return orders[id] as Order;
  }
}
```

We also have a ProductGateway interface (Listing 34-27) along with its DB implementation (Listing 34-28) and its in-memory implementation (Listing 34-29). Although we could also have a ItemGateway to acess data in our Items table, it's not neccessary. The application is not interested in Items outside the context of an Order, so the DbOrderGateway deals with both the Orders table and Items table of our schema.

Listing 34-27

ProductGateway.cs

```
public interface ProductGateway
{
  void Insert(Product product);
  Product Find(string sku);
}
```

Listing 34-28

DbProductGateway.cs

```
public class DbProductGateway : ProductGateway
{
  private readonly SqlConnection connection;

  public DbProductGateway(SqlConnection connection)
  {
    this.connection = connection;
  }
```

Listing 34-28 (Continued)

`DbProductGateway.cs`

```
public void Insert(Product product)
{
    string sql = "insert into Products (sku, name, price)" +
      " values (@sku, @name, @price)";
    SqlCommand command = new SqlCommand(sql, connection);
    command.Parameters.Add("@sku", product.Sku);
    command.Parameters.Add("@name", product.Name);
    command.Parameters.Add("@price", product.Price);
    command.ExecuteNonQuery();
}

public Product Find(string sku)
{
    string sql = "select * from Products where sku = @sku";
    SqlCommand command = new SqlCommand(sql, connection);
    command.Parameters.Add("@sku", sku);
    IDataReader reader = command.ExecuteReader();

    Product product = null;
    if(reader.Read())
    {
      string name = reader["name"].ToString();
      int price = Convert.ToInt32(reader["price"]);
      product = new Product(name, sku, price);
    }
    reader.Close();

    return product;
  }
}
```

Listing 34-29

`InMemoryProductGateway.cs`

```
public class InMemoryProductGateway : ProductGateway
{
  private Hashtable products = new Hashtable();

  public void Insert(Product product)
  {
    products[product.Sku] = product;
  }

  public Product Find(string sku)
  {
    return products[sku] as Product;
  }
}
```

The `Product` (Listing 34-30), `Order` (Listing 34-31), and `Item` (Listing 34-32) classes are simple data transfer objects (DTO) that conform to the original object model.

Listing 34-30

Product.cs

```csharp
public class Product
{
  private readonly string name;
  private readonly string sku;
  private int price;

  public Product(string name, string sku, int price)
  {
    this.name = name;
    this.sku = sku;
    this.price = price;
  }

  public int Price
  {
    get { return price; }
  }

  public string Name
  {
    get { return name; }
  }

  public string Sku
  {
    get { return sku; }
  }
}
```

Listing 34-31

Order.cs

```csharp
public class Order
{
  private readonly string cusid;
  private ArrayList items = new ArrayList();
  private int id;

  public Order(string cusid)
  {
    this.cusid = cusid;
  }

  public string CustomerId
  {
    get { return cusid; }
  }

  public int Id
  {
    get { return id; }
    set { id = value; }
  }

  public int ItemCount
```

Listing 34-31 (Continued)

`Order.cs`

```
    {
      get { return items.Count; }
    }

    public int QuantityOf(Product product)
    {
      foreach(Item item in items)
      {
        if(item.Product.Sku.Equals(product.Sku))
          return item.Quantity;
      }
      return 0;
    }

    public void AddItem(Product p, int qty)
    {
      Item item = new Item(p,qty);
      items.Add(item);
    }

    public ArrayList Items
    {
      get { return items; }
    }

    public int Total
    {
      get
      {
        int total = 0;
        foreach(Item item in items)
        {
          Product p = item.Product;
          int qty = item.Quantity;
          total += p.Price * qty;
        }
        return total;
      }
    }
}
```

Listing 34-32

`Item.cs`

```
public class Item
{
  private Product product;
  private int quantity;

  public Item(Product p, int qty)
  {
    product = p;
    quantity = qty;
  }
```

Listing 34-32 (Continued)
Item.cs

```
  public Product Product
  {
    get { return product; }
  }

  public int Quantity
  {
    get { return quantity; }
  }
}
```

Testing and In-Memory TDGs

Anyone who has practiced test-driven development will attest to the fact that tests add up quickly. Before you know it, you'll have hundreds of tests. The time it takes to execute all the tests grows every day. Many of these tests will involve the persistence layer; if the real database is being used for each, you might as well take a coffee break every time you run the test suite. Hitting the database hundreds of times can be time consuming. This is where the InMemoryOrderGateway comes in handy. Since it stores data in memory, the overhead of external persistence is sidestepped.

Using the InMemoryGateway objects when testing saves a significant amout of time when executing tests. It also allows you to forget about configuration and database details, simplifying the test code. Furthermore, you don't have to cleanup or restore an in-memory database at the end of a test; you can simply release it to the garbage collector.

InMemoryGateway objects also come in handy for acceptance testing. Once you've got the InMemoryGateway classes, it's possible to run the whole application without the persistent database. I've found this to be handy on more than one occasion. You'll see that the InMemoryOrderGateway has very little code and that what code it does have is trivial.

Of course, some of your unit tests and acceptance tests should use the persistent versions of the gateways. You *do* have to make sure that your system works with the real database. However, most of your tests can be redirected to the in-memory gateways.

With all the benefits of in-memory gateways, it makes a lot of sense to write and use them where appropriate. Indeed, when I use the TABLE DATA GATEWAY pattern, I start by writing the InMemoryGateway implementation and hold off on writing the DbGateway classes. It's quite possible to build a great deal of the application by using only the InMemoryGateway classes. The application code doesn't know that it's not really using the database. This means that it's not important to worry about which database tools you're going to use or what the schema will look like until much later. In fact, the DbGateways can be one of the last components to be implemented.

Testing the DB Gateways

Listings 34-34 and 34-35 show the unit tests for the DBProductGateway and the DBOrderGateway. The structure of these tests is interesting because they share a common abstract base class: AbstractDBGatewayTest.

Note that the constructor for DbOrderGateway requires an instance of Product-Gateway. Note also that the InMemoryProductGateway rather than the DbProductGateway is being used in the tests. The code works fine despite this trick, and we save a few round-trips to the database when we run the tests.

Listing 34-33
AbstractDbGatewayTest.cs

```csharp
public class AbstractDbGatewayTest
{
  protected SqlConnection connection;
  protected DbProductGateway gateway;
  protected IDataReader reader;

  protected void ExecuteSql(string sql)
  {
    SqlCommand command =
      new SqlCommand(sql, connection);
    command.ExecuteNonQuery();
  }

  protected void OpenConnection()
  {
    string connectionString =
      "Initial Catalog=QuickyMart;" +
        "Data Source=marvin;" +
          "user id=sa;password=abc;";
    connection = new SqlConnection(connectionString);
    this.connection.Open();
  }

  protected void Close()
  {
    if(reader != null)
      reader.Close();
    if(connection != null)
      connection.Close();
  }
}
```

Listing 34-34
DbProductGatewayTest.cs

```csharp
[TestFixture]
public class DbProductGatewayTest : AbstractDbGatewayTest
{
  private DbProductGateway gateway;
```

Listing 34-34 (Continued)

DbProductGatewayTest.cs

```
[SetUp]
public void SetUp()
{
  OpenConnection();
  gateway = new DbProductGateway(connection);
  ExecuteSql("delete from Products");
}

[TearDown]
public void TearDown()
{
  Close();
}

[Test]
public void Insert()
{
  Product product = new Product("Peanut Butter", "pb", 3);
  gateway.Insert(product);

  SqlCommand command =
    new SqlCommand("select * from Products", connection);
  reader = command.ExecuteReader();

  Assert.IsTrue(reader.Read());
  Assert.AreEqual("pb", reader["sku"]);
  Assert.AreEqual("Peanut Butter", reader["name"]);
  Assert.AreEqual(3, reader["price"]);

  Assert.IsFalse(reader.Read());
}

[Test]
public void Find()
{
  Product pb = new Product("Peanut Butter", "pb", 3);
  Product jam = new Product("Strawberry Jam", "jam", 2);

  gateway.Insert(pb);
  gateway.Insert(jam);

  Assert.IsNull(gateway.Find("bad sku"));

  Product foundPb = gateway.Find(pb.Sku);
  CheckThatProductsMatch(pb, foundPb);

  Product foundJam = gateway.Find(jam.Sku);
  CheckThatProductsMatch(jam, foundJam);
}

  private static void CheckThatProductsMatch(Product pb, Product
pb2)
```

Listing 34-34 (Continued)

`DbProductGatewayTest.cs`

```
  {
    Assert.AreEqual(pb.Name,   pb2.Name);
    Assert.AreEqual(pb.Sku,   pb2.Sku);
    Assert.AreEqual(pb.Price, pb2.Price);
  }
}
```

Listing 34-35

`DbOrderGatewayTest.cs`

```
[TestFixture]
public class DbOrderGatewayTest : AbstractDbGatewayTest
{
  private DbOrderGateway gateway;
  private Product pizza;
  private Product beer;

  [SetUp]
  public void SetUp()
  {
    OpenConnection();

    pizza = new Product("Pizza", "pizza", 15);
    beer = new Product("Beer", "beer", 2);
    ProductGateway productGateway =
      new InMemoryProductGateway();
    productGateway.Insert(pizza);
    productGateway.Insert(beer);

    gateway = new DbOrderGateway(connection, productGateway);
    ExecuteSql("delete from Orders");
    ExecuteSql("delete from Items");
  }

  [TearDown]
  public void TearDown()
  {
    Close();
  }

  [Test]
  public void Find()
  {
    string sql = "insert into Orders (cusId) " +
      "values ('Snoopy'); select scope_identity()";
    SqlCommand command = new SqlCommand(sql, connection);
    int orderId = Convert.ToInt32(command.ExecuteScalar());
    ExecuteSql(String.Format("insert into Items (orderId, " +
      "quantity, sku) values ({0}, 1, 'pizza')", orderId));
    ExecuteSql(String.Format("insert into Items (orderId, " +
      "quantity, sku) values ({0}, 6, 'beer')", orderId));
```

Listing 34-35 (Continued)

DbOrderGatewayTest.cs

```
      Order order = gateway.Find(orderId);

      Assert.AreEqual("Snoopy", order.CustomerId);
      Assert.AreEqual(2, order.ItemCount);
      Assert.AreEqual(1, order.QuantityOf(pizza));
      Assert.AreEqual(6, order.QuantityOf(beer));
    }

    [Test]
    public void Insert()
    {
      Order order = new Order("Snoopy");
      order.AddItem(pizza, 1);
      order.AddItem(beer, 6);

      gateway.Insert(order);

      Assert.IsTrue(order.Id != -1);

      Order foundOrder = gateway.Find(order.Id);
      Assert.AreEqual("Snoopy", foundOrder.CustomerId);
      Assert.AreEqual(2, foundOrder.ItemCount);
      Assert.AreEqual(1, foundOrder.QuantityOf(pizza));
      Assert.AreEqual(6, foundOrder.QuantityOf(beer));

    }
  }
```

Using Other Patterns with Databases

Four other patterns that can be used with databases are EXTENSION OBJECT, VISITOR, DECORATOR, and FACADE.[2]

1. **Extension Object:** Imagine an extension object that knows how to write the extended object on a database. In order to write such an object, you would ask it for an extension object that matched the `Database` key, cast it to a `DatabaseWriter-Extension`, and then invoke the `write` function:

```
Product p = /* some function that returns a Product */
ExtensionObject e = p.GetExtension("Database");
if (e != null)
{
  DatabaseWriterExtension dwe = (DatabaseWriterExtension) e;
  e.Write();
}
```

---

2. The first three patterns are discussed in Chapter 35. Facade is discussed in Chapter 23.

2. **Visitor:** Imagine a visitor hierarchy that knows how to write the visited object on a database. You would write an object on the database by creating the appropriate type of visitor and then calling `Accept` on the object to be written:

```
Product p = /* some function that returns a Product */
DatabaseWriterVisitor dwv = new DatabaseWritierVisitor();
p.Accept(dwv);
```

3. **Decorator:** There are two ways to use a decorator to implement databases. You can decorate a business object and give it read and write methods, or you can decorate a data object that knows how to read and write itself and give it business rules. The latter approach is not uncommon when using object-oriented databases. The business rules are kept out of the OODB schema and added in with decorators.

4. **Facade:** This is my favorite starting point; indeed, TABLE DATA GATEWAY is simply a special case of FACADE. On the down side, FACADE does not completely decouple the business rule objects from the database. Figure 34-10 shows the structure. The `DatabaseFacade` class simply provides methods for reading and writing all the necessary objects. This couples the objects to the `DatabaseFacade` and vice versa. The objects know about the facade because they are often the ones that call the read and write functions. The facade knows about the objects because it must use their accessors and mutators to implement the read and write functions.

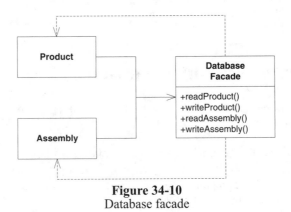

Figure 34-10
Database facade

    This coupling can cause problems in larger applications, but in smaller apps or in apps that are just starting to grow, it's a pretty effective technique. If you start using a facade and then later decide to change to one of the other patterns to reduce coupling, the facade is pretty easy to refactor.

Conclusion

It is very tempting to anticipate the need for PROXY long before the need exists. This is almost never a good idea. I recommend that you start with TABLE DATA GATEWAY or some other kind of FACADE and then refactor as necessary. You'll save yourself time and trouble if you do.

Bibliography

[**Fowler03**] Martin Fowler, *Patterns of Enterprise Application Architecture*, Addison-Wesley, 2003.

[**GOF95**] Erich Gamma, Richard Helm, Ralph Johnson, and John Vlissides, *Design Patterns: Elements of Reusable Object-Oriented Software*, Addison-Wesley, 1995.

[**Martin97**] Robert C. Martin, "Design Patterns for Dealing with Dual Inheritance Hierarchies," *C++ Report*, April 1997.

Visitor

© Jennifer M. Kohnke

"'Tis some visitor," I muttered, "tapping at my chamber door;
Only this and nothing more."

—Edgar Allen Poe, *The Raven*

You need to add a new method to a hierarchy of classes, but the act of adding it will be painful or damaging to the design. This is a common problem. For example, suppose that you have a hierarchy of Modem objects. The base class has the generic methods common to all modems. The derivatives represent the drivers for many different modem manufacturers and types. Suppose also that you have a requirement to add a new method, named `configureForUnix`, to the hierarchy. This method will configure the modem to work with the UNIX operating system. The method will do something different in each modem derivative, because each modem has its own particular idiosyncrasies for setting its configuration, and dealing with UNIX.

Unfortunately, adding `configureForUnix` begs a terrible set of questions. What about Windows, what about OSX, what about Linux? Must we really add a new method to the `Modem` hierarchy for every new operating system that we use? Clearly, this is ugly. We'll never be able to close the `Modem` interface. Every time a new operating system comes along, we'll have to change that interface and redeploy all the modem software.

The VISITOR family allows new methods to be added to existing hierarchies without modifying the hierarchies. The patterns[1] in this family are

- VISITOR
- ACYCLIC VISITOR
- DECORATOR
- EXTENSION OBJECT

VISITOR

Consider the `Modem` hierarchy in Figure 35-1. The `Modem` interface contains the generic methods that all modems can implement. Three derivatives are shown: one that drives a Hayes modem, one that drives a Zoom modem, and one that drives the modem card produced by Ernie, one of our hardware engineers. How can we configure these modems for UNIX without putting the `ConfigureForUnix` method in the `Modem` interface? We can use a technique called *dual dispatch*, the mechanism at the heart of the VISITOR pattern.

Figure 35-2 shows the VISITOR structure, and Listings 35-1 through 35-5 show the corresponding C# code. Listing 35-6 shows the test code that both verifies that VISITOR works and demonstrates how another programmer should use it.

Note that the visitor hierarchy has a method in for every derivative of the visited (`Modem`) hierarchy. This is a kind of 90° rotation: from derivatives to methods.

The test code shows that to configure a modem for UNIX, a programmer creates an instance of the `UnixModemConfigurator` class and passes it to the `Accept` function of the `Modem`. The appropriate `Modem` derivative will then call `Visit(this)` on Modem-`Visitor`, the base class of `UnixModemConfigurator`. If that derivative is a `Hayes`, `Visit(this)` will call `public void Visit(Hayes)`, which will deploy to the `public void Visit(Hayes)` function in `UnixModemConfigurator`, which then configures the `Hayes` modem for `Unix`.

---

1. [GOF95]. For Acyclic Visitor and Extension Object, see [PLOPD3].

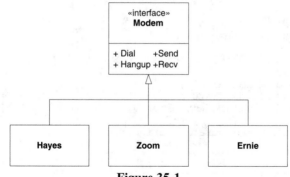

Figure 35-1
Modem hierarchy

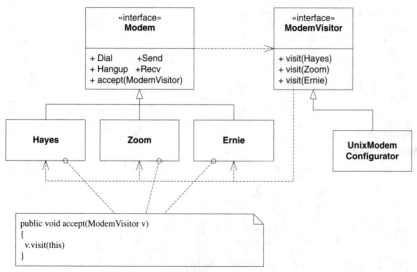

Figure 35-2
VISITOR

Listing 35-1

Modem.cs

```
public interface Modem
{
  void Dial(string pno);
  void Hangup();
  void Send(char c);
  char Recv();
  void Accept(ModemVisitor v);
}
```

Listing 35-2

HayesModem.cs

```
public class HayesModem : Modem
{
  public void Dial(string pno){}
  public void Hangup(){}
  public void Send(char c){}
  public char Recv() {return (char)0;}
  public void Accept(ModemVisitor v) {v.Visit(this);}

  public string configurationString = null;
}
```

Listing 35-3

ZoomModem.cs

```
public class ZoomModem
{
  public void Dial(string pno){}
  public void Hangup(){}
  public void Send(char c){}
  public char Recv() {return (char)0;}
  public void Accept(ModemVisitor v) {v.Visit(this);}

  public int configurationValue = 0;
}
```

Listing 35-4

ErnieModem.cs

```
public class ErnieModem
{
  public void Dial(string pno){}
  public void Hangup(){}
  public void Send(char c){}
  public char Recv() {return (char)0;}
  public void Accept(ModemVisitor v) {v.Visit(this);}

  public string internalPattern = null;
}
```

Listing 35-5

UnixModemConfigurator.cs

```
public class UnixModemConfigurator : ModemVisitor
{
  public void Visit(HayesModem m)
  {
    m.configurationString = "&s1=4&D=3";
  }

  public void Visit(ZoomModem m)
  {
    m.configurationValue = 42;
  }
```

Listing 35-5 (Continued)

`UnixModemConfigurator.cs`

```
    public void Visit(ErnieModem m)
    {
      m.internalPattern = "C is too slow";
    }
  }
```

Listing 35-6

`ModemVisitorTest.cs`

```
[TestFixture]
public class ModemVisitorTest
{
  private UnixModemConfigurator v;
  private HayesModem h;
  private ZoomModem z;
  private ErnieModem e;

  [SetUp]
  public void SetUp()
  {
    v = new UnixModemConfigurator();
    h = new HayesModem();
    z = new ZoomModem();
    e = new ErnieModem();
  }

  [Test]
  public void HayesForUnix()
  {
    h.Accept(v);
    Assert.AreEqual("&s1=4&D=3", h.configurationString);
  }

  [Test]
  public void ZoomForUnix()
  {
    z.Accept(v);
    Assert.AreEqual(42, z.configurationValue);
  }

  [Test]
  public void ErnieForUnix()
  {
    e.Accept(v);
    Assert.AreEqual("C is too slow", e.internalPattern);
  }
}
```

Having built this structure, new operating system configuration functions can be added by adding new derivatives of `ModemVisitor` without altering the `Modem` hierarchy in any way. So the VISITOR pattern substitutes derivatives of `ModemVisitor` for methods in the `Modem` hierarchy.

This *dual dispatch* involves two polymorphic dispatches. The first is the `Accept` function, which resolves the type of the object that `Accept` is called on. The second dispatch—the `Visit` method called from the resolved `Accept` method—resolves to the particular function to be executed.

The two dispatches of VISITOR form a matrix of functions. In our modem example, one axis of the matrix is the various types of modems; the other axis, the various types of operating systems. Every cell in this matrix is filled in with a function that describes how to initialize the particular modem for the particular operating system.

VISITOR is fast. It requires only two polymorphic dispatches, regardless of the breadth or depth of the visited hierarchy.

ACYCLIC VISITOR

Note that the base class of the visited (`Modem`) hierarchy depends on the base class of the visitor hierarchy (`ModemVisitor`). Note also that the base class of the visitor hierarchy has a function for each derivative of the visited hierarchy. This cycle of dependencies ties all the visited derivatives—all the modems—together, making difficult to compile the visitor structure incrementally or to add new derivatives to the visited hierarchy.

The VISITOR pattern works well in programs in which the hierarchy to be modified does not need new derivatives very often. If `Hayes`, `Zoom`, and `Ernie` were the only `Modem` derivatives that were likely to be needed or if the incidence of new `Modem` derivatives was expected to be infrequent, VISITOR would be appropriate.

On the other hand, if the visited hierarchy is highly volatile, such that many new derivatives will need to be created, the visitor base class (e.g., `ModemVisitor`) will have to be modified and recompiled along with all its derivatives every time a new derivative is added to the visited hierarchy.

ACYCLIC VISITOR can be used to solve these problems.[2] (See Figure 35-3.) This variation breaks the dependency cycle by making the `Visitor` base class (`ModemVisitor`) *degenerate*, that is, without methods. Therefore, this class does not depend on the derivatives of the visited hierarchy.

The visitor derivatives also derive from visitor interfaces. There is one visitor interface for each derivative of the visited hierarchy. This is a 180° rotation from derivatives to interfaces. The `Accept` functions in the visited derivatives cast the visitor base class to the appropriate visitor interface. If the cast succeeds, the method invokes the appropriate visit function. Listings 35-7 through 35-16 show the code.

---

2. [PLOPD3], p. 93

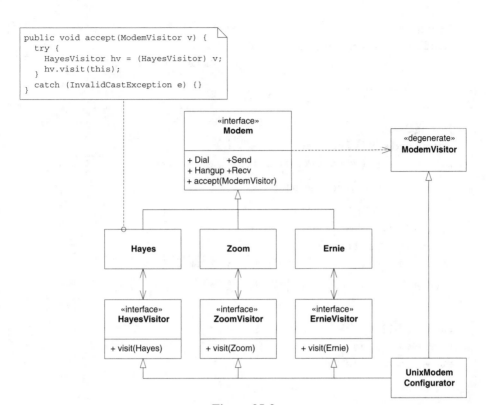

Figure 35-3
ACYCLIC VISITOR

Listing 35-7

Modem.cs

```
public interface Modem
{
   void Dial(string pno);
   void Hangup();
   void Send(char c);
   char Recv();
   void Accept(ModemVisitor v);
}
```

Listing 35-8

ModemVisitor.cs

```
public interface ModemVisitor
{
}
```

Listing 35-9

ErnieModemVisitor.cs

```
public interface ErnieModemVisitor : ModemVisitor
{
  void Visit(ErnieModem m);
}
```

Listing 35-10

HayesModemVisitor.cs

```
public interface HayesModemVisitor : ModemVisitor
{
  void Visit(HayesModem m);
}
```

Listing 35-11

ZoomModemVisitor.cs

```
public interface ZoomModemVisitor : ModemVisitor
{
  void Visit(ZoomModem m);
}
```

Listing 35-12

ErnieModem.cs

```
public class ErnieModem
{
  public void Dial(string pno){}
  public void Hangup(){}
  public void Send(char c){}
  public char Recv() {return (char)0;}
  public void Accept(ModemVisitor v)
  {
    if(v is ErnieModemVisitor)
      (v as ErnieModemVisitor).Visit(this);
  }

  public string internalPattern = null;
}
```

Listing 35-13

HayesModem.cs

```
public class HayesModem : Modem
{
  public void Dial(string pno){}
  public void Hangup(){}
  public void Send(char c){}
  public char Recv() {return (char)0;}
  public void Accept(ModemVisitor v)
  {
    if(v is HayesModemVisitor)
      (v as HayesModemVisitor).Visit(this);
  }

  public string configurationString = null;
}
```

Listing 35-14

ZoomModem.cs

```
public class ZoomModem
{
  public void Dial(string pno){}
  public void Hangup(){}
  public void Send(char c){}
  public char Recv() {return (char)0;}
  public void Accept(ModemVisitor v)
  {
    if(v is ZoomModemVisitor)
      (v as ZoomModemVisitor).Visit(this);
  }

  public int configurationValue = 0;
}
```

Listing 35-15

UnixModemConfigurator.cs

```
public class UnixModemConfigurator
  : HayesModemVisitor, ZoomModemVisitor, ErnieModemVisitor
{
  public void Visit(HayesModem m)
  {
    m.configurationString = "&s1=4&D=3";
  }

  public void Visit(ZoomModem m)
  {
    m.configurationValue = 42;
  }

  public void Visit(ErnieModem m)
  {
    m.internalPattern = "C is too slow";
  }
}
```

Listing 35-16

ModemVisitorTest.cs

```
[TestFixture]
public class ModemVisitorTest
{
  private UnixModemConfigurator v;
  private HayesModem h;
  private ZoomModem z;
  private ErnieModem e;

  [SetUp]
  public void SetUp()
  {
    v = new UnixModemConfigurator();
    h = new HayesModem();
    z = new ZoomModem();
    e = new ErnieModem();
  }
```

Listing 35-16 (Continued)
`ModemVisitorTest.cs`

```
[Test]
public void HayesForUnix()
{
  h.Accept(v);
  Assert.AreEqual("&s1=4&D=3", h.configurationString);
}

[Test]
public void ZoomForUnix()
{
  z.Accept(v);
  Assert.AreEqual(42, z.configurationValue);
}

[Test]
public void ErnieForUnix()
{
  e.Accept(v);
  Assert.AreEqual("C is too slow", e.internalPattern);
}
}
```

This breaks the dependency cycle and makes it easier to add visited derivatives and to do incremental compilations. Unfortunately, it also makes the solution much more complex. Worse still, the timing of the cast can depend on the width and breadth of the visited hierarchy and is therefore difficult to characterize.

For hard real-time systems, the large and unpredictable execution time of the cast may make the ACYCLIC VISITOR inappropriate. For other systems, the complexity of the pattern may disqualify it. But for those systems in which the visited hierarchy is volatile and incremental compilation important, this pattern can be a good option.

Earlier, I explained how the VISITOR pattern created a matrix of functions, with the visited type on one axis and the function to be performed on the other. ACYCLIC VISITOR creates a *sparse* matrix. The visitor classes do not have to implement `Visit` functions for each visited derivative. For example, if `Ernie` modems cannot be configured for UNIX, the `UnixModemConfigurator` will not implement the `ErnieVisitor` interface.

Uses of VISITOR

Report generation The VISITOR pattern is commonly used to walk large data structures and to generate reports. The value of the VISITOR in this case is that the data structure objects do not have to have any report-generation code. New reports can be added by adding new VISITORs rather than by changing the code in the data structures. This means that reports can be placed in separate components and individually deployed only to those customers needing them.

Consider a simple data structure that represents a bill of materials (BOM) (see Figure 35-4). We could generate an unlimited number of reports from this data structure. We could generate a report of the total cost of an assembly or a report that listed all the piece-parts in an assembly.

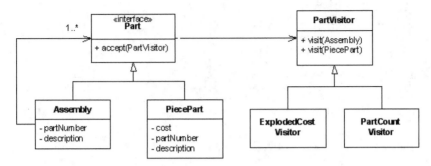

Figure 35-4
Structure of bill of materials report generator

Each of these reports could be generated by methods in the `Part` class. For example, `ExplodedCost` and `PieceCount` could be added to the `Part` class. These properties would be implemented in each derivative of `Part` such that the appropriate reporting was accomplished. Unfortunately, every new report that the customers wanted would force us to change the `Part` hierarchy.

The Single-Responsibility Principle (SRP) told us that we want to separate code that changes for different reasons. The `Part` hierarchy may change as new kinds of parts are needed. However, it should not change because new kinds of reports are needed. Thus, we'd like to separate the reports from the `Part` hierarchy. The VISITOR structure shown in Figure 35-4 shows how this can be accomplished.

Each new report can be written as a new visitor. We write the `Accept` function of `Assembly` to visit the visitor and also call `Accept` on all the contained `Part` instances. Thus, the entire tree is traversed. For each node in the tree, the appropriate `Visit` function is called on the report. The report accumulates the necessary statistics. The report can then be queried for the interesting data and presented to the user.

This structure allows us to create an unlimited number of reports without affecting the part hierarchy. Moreover, each report can be compiled and distributed independently of all the others. This is nice. Listings 35-17 through 35-23 show how this looks in C#.

Listing 35-17

Part.cs

```
public interface Part
{
   string PartNumber { get; }
   string Description { get; }
   void Accept(PartVisitor v);
}
```

Listing 35-18

Assembly.cs

```csharp
public class Assembly : Part
{
  private IList parts = new ArrayList();
  private string partNumber;
  private string description;

  public Assembly(string partNumber, string description)
  {
    this.partNumber = partNumber;
    this.description = description;
  }

  public void Accept(PartVisitor v)
  {
    v.Visit(this);
    foreach(Part part in Parts)
      part.Accept(v);
  }
  public void Add(Part part)
  {
    parts.Add(part);
  }

  public IList Parts
  {
    get { return parts; }
  }

  public string PartNumber
  {
    get { return partNumber; }
  }

  public string Description
  {
    get { return description; }
  }
}
```

Listing 35-19

PiecePart.cs

```csharp
public class PiecePart : Part
{
  private string partNumber;
  private string description;
  private double cost;

  public PiecePart(string partNumber,
    string description,
    double cost)
  {
    this.partNumber = partNumber;
    this.description = description;
    this.cost = cost;
  }
```

Listing 35-19 (Continued)
PiecePart.cs

```
  public void Accept(PartVisitor v)
  {
    v.Visit(this);
  }

  public string PartNumber
  {
    get { return partNumber; }
  }

  public string Description
  {
    get { return description; }
  }

  public double Cost
  {
    get { return cost; }
  }
}
```

Listing 35-20
PartVisitor.cs

```
public interface PartVisitor
{
  void Visit(PiecePart pp);
  void Visit(Assembly a);
}
```

Listing 35-21
ExplosiveCostExplorer.cs

```
public class ExplodedCostVisitor : PartVisitor
{
  private double cost = 0;

  public double Cost
  {
    get { return cost; }
  }

  public void Visit(PiecePart p)
  {
    cost += p.Cost;
  }

  public void Visit(Assembly a)
  {}
}
```

Listing 35-22

`PartCountVisitor.cs`

```csharp
public class PartCountVisitor : PartVisitor
{
  private int pieceCount = 0;
  private Hashtable pieceMap = new Hashtable();

  public void Visit(PiecePart p)
  {
    pieceCount++;
    string partNumber = p.PartNumber;
    int partNumberCount = 0;
    if (pieceMap.ContainsKey(partNumber))
      partNumberCount = (int)pieceMap[partNumber];

    partNumberCount++;
    pieceMap[partNumber] = partNumberCount;
  }

  public void Visit(Assembly a)
  {
  }

  public int PieceCount
  {
    get { return pieceCount; }
  }

  public int PartNumberCount
  {
    get { return pieceMap.Count; }
  }

  public int GetCountForPart(string partNumber)
  {
    int partNumberCount = 0;
    if (pieceMap.ContainsKey(partNumber))
      partNumberCount = (int)pieceMap[partNumber];
    return partNumberCount;
  }
}
```

Listing 35-23

`BOMReportTest.cs`

```csharp
[TestFixture]
public class BOMReportTest
{
  private PiecePart p1;
  private PiecePart p2;
  private Assembly a;

  [SetUp]
  public void SetUp()
  {
    p1 = new PiecePart("997624", "MyPart", 3.20);
    p2 = new PiecePart("7734", "Hell", 666);
```

Listing 35-23 (Continued)
BOMReportTest.cs

```
    a = new Assembly("5879", "MyAssembly");
  }

  [Test]
  public void CreatePart()
  {
    Assert.AreEqual("997624", p1.PartNumber);
    Assert.AreEqual("MyPart", p1.Description);
    Assert.AreEqual(3.20, p1.Cost, .01);
  }

  [Test]
  public void CreateAssembly()
  {
    Assert.AreEqual("5879", a.PartNumber);
    Assert.AreEqual("MyAssembly", a.Description);
  }

  [Test]
  public void Assembly()
  {
    a.Add(p1);
    a.Add(p2);
    Assert.AreEqual(2, a.Parts.Count);
    PiecePart p = a.Parts[0] as PiecePart;
    Assert.AreEqual(p, p1);
    p = a.Parts[1] as PiecePart;
    Assert.AreEqual(p, p2);
  }

  [Test]
  public void AssemblyOfAssemblies()
  {
    Assembly subAssembly = new Assembly("1324", "SubAssembly");
    subAssembly.Add(p1);
    a.Add(subAssembly);

    Assert.AreEqual(subAssembly, a.Parts[0]);
  }

  private class TestingVisitor : PartVisitor
  {
    public IList visitedParts = new ArrayList();

    public void Visit(PiecePart p)
    {
      visitedParts.Add(p);
    }

    public void Visit(Assembly assy)
    {
      visitedParts.Add(assy);
    }
  }
```

Listing 35-23 (Continued)
BOMReportTest.cs

```
[Test]
public void VisitorCoverage()
{
  a.Add(p1);
  a.Add(p2);

  TestingVisitor visitor = new TestingVisitor();
  a.Accept(visitor);

  Assert.IsTrue(visitor.visitedParts.Contains(p1));
  Assert.IsTrue(visitor.visitedParts.Contains(p2));
  Assert.IsTrue(visitor.visitedParts.Contains(a));
}

private Assembly cellphone;

private void SetUpReportDatabase()
{
  cellphone = new Assembly("CP-7734", "Cell Phone");
  PiecePart display = new PiecePart("DS-1428",
                                    "LCD Display",
                                    14.37);
  PiecePart speaker = new PiecePart("SP-92",
                                    "Speaker",
                                    3.50);
  PiecePart microphone = new PiecePart("MC-28",
                                       "Microphone",
                                       5.30);
  PiecePart cellRadio = new PiecePart("CR-56",
                                      "Cell Radio",
                                      30);
  PiecePart frontCover = new PiecePart("FC-77",
                                       "Front Cover",
                                       1.4);
  PiecePart backCover = new PiecePart("RC-77",
                                      "RearCover",
                                      1.2);
  Assembly keypad = new Assembly("KP-62", "Keypad");
  Assembly button = new Assembly("B52", "Button");
  PiecePart buttonCover = new PiecePart("CV-15",
                                        "Cover",
                                        .5);
  PiecePart buttonContact = new PiecePart("CN-2",
                                          "Contact",
                                          1.2);
  button.Add(buttonCover);
  button.Add(buttonContact);
  for (int i = 0; i < 15; i++)
    keypad.Add(button);
  cellphone.Add(display);
  cellphone.Add(speaker);
  cellphone.Add(microphone);
  cellphone.Add(cellRadio);
  cellphone.Add(frontCover);
```

Listing 35-23 (Continued)

BOMReportTest.cs

```
    cellphone.Add(backCover);
    cellphone.Add(keypad);
  }

  [Test]
  public void ExplodedCost()
  {
    SetUpReportDatabase();
    ExplodedCostVisitor v = new ExplodedCostVisitor();
    cellphone.Accept(v);
    Assert.AreEqual(81.27, v.Cost, .001);
  }

  [Test]
  public void PartCount()
  {
    SetUpReportDatabase();
    PartCountVisitor v = new PartCountVisitor();
    cellphone.Accept(v);
    Assert.AreEqual(36, v.PieceCount);
    Assert.AreEqual(8, v.PartNumberCount);
    Assert.AreEqual(1, v.GetCountForPart("DS-1428"), "DS-
      1428");
    Assert.AreEqual(1, v.GetCountForPart("SP-92"), "SP-92");
    Assert.AreEqual(1, v.GetCountForPart("MC-28"), "MC-28");
    Assert.AreEqual(1, v.GetCountForPart("CR-56"), "CR-56");
    Assert.AreEqual(1, v.GetCountForPart("RC-77"), "RC-77");
    Assert.AreEqual(15, v.GetCountForPart("CV-15"), "CV-15");
    Assert.AreEqual(15, v.GetCountForPart("CN-2"), "CN-2");
    Assert.AreEqual(0, v.GetCountForPart("Bob"), "Bob");
  }
}
```

Other uses In general, the VISITOR pattern can be used in any application having a data structure that needs to be interpreted in various ways. Compilers often create intermediate data structures that represent syntactically correct source code. These data structures are then used to generate compiled code. One could imagine visitors for each processor and/or optimization scheme. One could also imagine a visitor that converted the intermediate data structure into a cross-reference listing or even a UML diagram.

Many applications make use of configuration data structures. One could imagine the various subsystems of the application initializing themselves from the configuration data by walking it with their own particular visitors.

Whatever visitors are used, the data structure being used is independent of the uses to which it is being put. New visitors can be created, existing visitors can be changed, and all can be redeployed to installed sites without the recompilation or redeployment of the existing data structures. This is the power of the VISITOR.

DECORATOR

The VISITOR pattern gave us a way to add methods to existing hierarchies without changing those hierarchies. Another pattern that accomplishes this is DECORATOR.

Consider once again the `Modem` hierarchy in Figure 35-1. Imagine that we have an application that has many users. Sitting at a computer, each user can ask the system to call out to another computer, using the computer's modem. Some of the users like to hear their modem's dial. Others like their modems to be silent.

We could implement this by querying the user preferences at every location in the code where the modem is dialed. If the user wants to hear the modem, we set the speaker volume high; otherwise, we turn it off:

```
. . .
Modem m = user.Modem;
if (user.WantsLoudDial())
  m.Volume = 11; // it's one more than 10, isn't it?
m.Dial(...);
. . .
```

The specter of seeing this stretch of code duplicated hundreds of times throughout the application conjures images of 80-hour weeks and heinous debugging sessions. It is something to be avoided.

Another option would be to set a flag in the modem object itself and have the `Dial` method inspect it and set the volume accordingly:

```
. . .
public class HayesModem : Modem
{
  private bool wantsLoudDial = false;

  public void Dial(...)
  {
    if (wantsLoudDial)
    {
      Volume = 11;
    }
    . . .
  }
  . . .
}
```

This is better but must still be duplicated for every derivative of `Modem`. Authors of new derivatives of `Modem` must remember to replicate this code. Depending on programmers' memories is pretty risky business.

We could resolve this with the TEMPLATE METHOD[3] pattern by changing `Modem` from an interface to a class, having it hold the `wantsLoudDial` variable, and having it test that variable in the dial function before it calls the `DialForReal` function:

```
...
public abstract class Modem
{
  private bool wantsLoudDial = false;

  public void Dial(...)
  {
    if (wantsLoudDial)
    {
      Volume = 11;
    }
    DialForReal(...)
  }

  public abstract void DialForReal(...);
}
```

This is better still, but why should `Modem` be affected by the whims of the user in this way? Why should `Modem` know about loud dialing? Must it then be modified every time the user has some other odd request, such as logging out before hangup?

Once again, the Common Closure Principle (CCP) comes into play. We want to separate those things that change for different reasons. We can also invoke the Single-Responsibility Principle (SRP), since the need to dial loudly has nothing to do with the intrinsic functions of `Modem` and should therefore not be part of `Modem`.

DECORATOR solves the issue by creating a completely new class: `LoudDialModem`. `LoudDialModem` derives from `Modem` and delegates to a contained instance of `Modem`, catching the `Dial` function and setting the volume high before delegating. Figure 35-5 shows the structure.

Now the decision to dial loudly can be made in one place. At the place in the code where the user sets preferences, a `LoudDialModem` can be created if loud dialing is requested, and the user's modem can be passed into it. `LoudDialModem` will delegate all calls made to it to the user's modem, so the user won't notice any difference. The `Dial` method, however, will first set the volume high before delegating to the user's modem. The `LoudDialModem` can then become the user's modem without anybody else in the system being affected. Listings 35-24 through 35-27 show the code.

---

3. See Chapter 22.

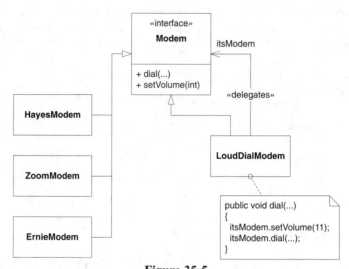

Figure 35-5
DECORATOR: LoudDialModem

Listing 35-24

Modem.cs

```
public interface Modem
{
  void Dial(string pno);
  int SpeakerVolume { get; set; }
  string PhoneNumber { get; }
}
```

Listing 35-25

HayesModem.cs

```
public class HayesModem : Modem
{
  private string phoneNumber;
  private int speakerVolume;

  public void Dial(string pno)
  {
    phoneNumber = pno;
  }

  public int  SpeakerVolume
  {
    get { return speakerVolume; }
    set { speakerVolume = value; }
  }
}
```

Listing 35-25 (Continued)

HayesModem.cs

```csharp
  public string PhoneNumber
  {
    get { return phoneNumber; }
  }
}
```

Listing 35-26

LoudDialModem.cs

```csharp
public class LoudDialModem : Modem
{
  private Modem itsModem;

  public LoudDialModem(Modem m)
  {
    itsModem = m;
  }

  public void Dial(string pno)
  {
    itsModem.SpeakerVolume = 10;
    itsModem.Dial(pno);
  }

  public int SpeakerVolume
  {
    get { return itsModem.SpeakerVolume; }
    set { itsModem.SpeakerVolume = value; }
  }

  public string PhoneNumber
  {
    get { return itsModem.PhoneNumber; }
  }
```

Listing 35-27

ModemDecoratorTest.cs

```csharp
[TestFixture]
public class ModemDecoratorTest
{
  [Test]
  public void CreateHayes()
  {
    Modem m = new HayesModem();
    Assert.AreEqual(null, m.PhoneNumber);
    m.Dial("5551212");
    Assert.AreEqual("5551212", m.PhoneNumber);
    Assert.AreEqual(0, m.SpeakerVolume);
    m.SpeakerVolume = 10;
    Assert.AreEqual(10, m.SpeakerVolume);
  }
```

Listing 35-27 (Continued)

ModemDecoratorTest.cs

```
[Test]
public void LoudDialModem()
{
  Modem m = new HayesModem();
  Modem d = new LoudDialModem(m);
  Assert.AreEqual(null, d.PhoneNumber);
  Assert.AreEqual(0, d.SpeakerVolume);
  d.Dial("5551212");
  Assert.AreEqual("5551212", d.PhoneNumber);
  Assert.AreEqual(10, d.SpeakerVolume);

  }
}
```

Sometimes, two or more decorators may exist for the same hierarchy. For example, we may wish to decorate the Modem hierarchy with LogoutExitModem, which sends the string 'exit' whenever the Hangup method is called. This second decorator will have to duplicate all the delegation code that we have already written in LoudDialModem. We can eliminate this duplicate code by creating a new class, ModemDecorator, that supplies all the delegation code. Then the actual decorators can simply derive from ModemDecorator and override only those methods that they need to. Figure 35-6 and Listings 35-28 and 35-29 show the structure.

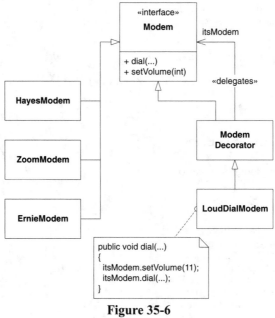

Figure 35-6
ModemDecorator

Listing 35-28
ModemDecorator.cs

```
public class ModemDecorator
{
  private Modem modem;

  public ModemDecorator(Modem m)
  {
    modem = m;
  }

  public void Dial(string pno)
  {
    modem.Dial(pno);
  }

  public int SpeakerVolume
  {
    get { return modem.SpeakerVolume; }
    set { modem.SpeakerVolume = value; }
  }

  public string PhoneNumber
  {
    get { return modem.PhoneNumber; }
  }

  protected Modem Modem
  {
    get { return modem; }
  }
}
```

Listing 35-29
LoudDialModem.cs

```
public class LoudDialModem : ModemDecorator
{
  public LoudDialModem(Modem m) : base(m)
  {}

  public void Dial(string pno)
  {
    Modem.SpeakerVolume = 10;
    Modem.Dial(pno);
  }
}
```

EXTENSION OBJECT

Still another way to add functionality to a hierarchy without changing it is to use the EXTENSION OBJECT pattern. This pattern is more complex than the others but is also much more powerful and flexible. Each object in the hierarchy maintains a list of special extension objects. Each object also provides a method that allows the extension object to be looked up by name. The extension object provides methods that manipulate the original hierarchy object.

For example, let's assume that we have a BOM system again. We need to develop the ability for each object in this hierarchy to create an XML representation of itself. We could put `toXML` methods in the hierarchy, but this would violate CCP. It may be that we don't want BOM stuff and XML stuff in the same class. We could create XML by using a VISITOR, but that doesn't allow us to separate the XML-generating code for each type of BOM object. In a VISITOR, all the XML-generating code for each BOM class would be in the same VISITOR object. What if we want to separate the XML generation for each different BOM object into its own class?

EXTENSION OBJECT provides a nice way to accomplish this goal. The code that follows shows the BOM hierarchy with two kinds of extension object: one kind converts BOM objects into XML; the other kind converts BOM objects into CSV (comma-separated-value) strings. The first kind is accessed by `GetExtension("XML")`; the second, by `GetExtension("CSV")`. The structure is shown in Figure 35-7 and was taken from the completed code. The «marker» stereotype denotes a marker interface; that is, an interface with no methods.

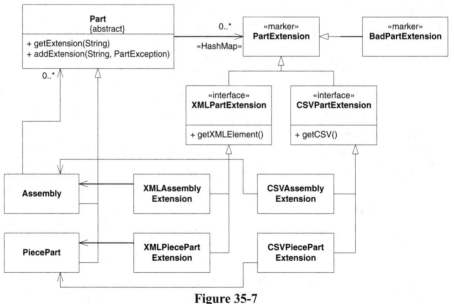

Figure 35-7
Extension Object

The code is in Listings 35-30 through 35-41. It is important to understand that I did not simply write this code from scratch. Rather, I evolved the code from test case to test case. The first source file (Listing 35-30) shows all the test cases. They were written in the order shown. Each test case was written before there was any code that could make it pass. Once each test case was written and failing, the code that made it pass was written. The code was never more complicated than necessary to make the *existing* test cases pass. Thus, the code evolved in tiny increments from working base to working base. I knew that I was trying to build the EXTENSION OBJECT pattern and used that to guide the evolution.

Listing 35-30
BomXmlTest.CS

```
[TestFixture]
public class BomXmlTest
{
  private PiecePart p1;
  private PiecePart p2;
  private Assembly a;

  [SetUp]
  public void SetUp()
  {
    p1 = new PiecePart("997624", "MyPart", 3.20);
    p2 = new PiecePart("7734", "Hell", 666);
    a = new Assembly("5879", "MyAssembly");
  }

  [Test]
  public void CreatePart()
  {
    Assert.AreEqual("997624", p1.PartNumber);
    Assert.AreEqual("MyPart", p1.Description);
    Assert.AreEqual(3.20, p1.Cost, .01);
  }

  [Test]
  public void CreateAssembly()
  {
    Assert.AreEqual("5879", a.PartNumber);
    Assert.AreEqual("MyAssembly", a.Description);
  }

  [Test]
  public void Assembly()
  {
    a.Add(p1);
    a.Add(p2);
    Assert.AreEqual(2, a.Parts.Count);
    Assert.AreEqual(a.Parts[0], p1);
    Assert.AreEqual(a.Parts[1], p2);
  }

  [Test]
  public void AssemblyOfAssemblies()
  {
    Assembly subAssembly = new Assembly("1324", "SubAssembly");
    subAssembly.Add(p1);
    a.Add(subAssembly);

    Assert.AreEqual(subAssembly, a.Parts[0]);
```

Listing 35-30 (Continued)
BomXmlTest.CS

```
  }

  private string ChildText(
    XmlElement element, string childName)
  {
    return Child(element, childName).InnerText;
  }

  private XmlElement Child(XmlElement element, string childName)
  {
    XmlNodeList children =
      element.GetElementsByTagName(childName);
    return children.Item(0) as XmlElement;
  }

  [Test]
  public void PiecePart1XML()
  {
    PartExtension e = p1.GetExtension("XML");
    XmlPartExtension xe = e as XmlPartExtension;
    XmlElement xml = xe.XmlElement;
    Assert.AreEqual("PiecePart", xml.Name);
    Assert.AreEqual("997624",
      ChildText(xml, "PartNumber"));
    Assert.AreEqual("MyPart",
      ChildText(xml, "Description"));
    Assert.AreEqual(3.2,
      Double.Parse(ChildText(xml, "Cost")), .01);
  }

  [Test]
  public void PiecePart2XML()
  {
    PartExtension e = p2.GetExtension("XML");
    XmlPartExtension xe = e as XmlPartExtension;
    XmlElement xml = xe.XmlElement;
    Assert.AreEqual("PiecePart", xml.Name);
    Assert.AreEqual("7734",
      ChildText(xml, "PartNumber"));
    Assert.AreEqual("Hell",
      ChildText(xml, "Description"));
    Assert.AreEqual(666,
      Double.Parse(ChildText(xml, "Cost")), .01);
  }

  [Test]
  public void SimpleAssemblyXML()
  {
    PartExtension e = a.GetExtension("XML");
    XmlPartExtension xe = e as XmlPartExtension;
    XmlElement xml = xe.XmlElement;
    Assert.AreEqual("Assembly", xml.Name);
    Assert.AreEqual("5879",
      ChildText(xml, "PartNumber"));
```

Listing 35-30 (Continued)

BomXmlTest.CS

```
        Assert.AreEqual("MyAssembly",
          ChildText(xml, "Description"));
        XmlElement parts = Child(xml, "Parts");
        XmlNodeList partList = parts.ChildNodes;
        Assert.AreEqual(0, partList.Count);
    }

    [Test]
    public void AssemblyWithPartsXML()
    {
        a.Add(p1);
        a.Add(p2);
        PartExtension e = a.GetExtension("XML");
        XmlPartExtension xe = e as XmlPartExtension;
        XmlElement xml = xe.XmlElement;
        Assert.AreEqual("Assembly", xml.Name);
        Assert.AreEqual("5879",
          ChildText(xml, "PartNumber"));
        Assert.AreEqual("MyAssembly",
          ChildText(xml, "Description"));

        XmlElement parts = Child(xml, "Parts");
        XmlNodeList partList = parts.ChildNodes;
        Assert.AreEqual(2, partList.Count);

        XmlElement partElement =
          partList.Item(0) as XmlElement;
        Assert.AreEqual("PiecePart", partElement.Name);
        Assert.AreEqual("997624",
          ChildText(partElement, "PartNumber"));

        partElement = partList.Item(1) as XmlElement;
        Assert.AreEqual("PiecePart", partElement.Name);
        Assert.AreEqual("7734",
          ChildText(partElement, "PartNumber"));
    }

    [Test]
    public void PiecePart1toCSV()
    {
        PartExtension e = p1.GetExtension("CSV");
        CsvPartExtension ce = e as CsvPartExtension;
        String csv = ce.CsvText;
        Assert.AreEqual("PiecePart,997624,MyPart,3.2", csv);
    }

    [Test]
    public void PiecePart2toCSV()
    {
        PartExtension e = p2.GetExtension("CSV");
        CsvPartExtension ce = e as CsvPartExtension;
        String csv = ce.CsvText;
        Assert.AreEqual("PiecePart,7734,Hell,666", csv);
    }
```

Listing 35-30 (Continued)

BomXmlTest.CS

```
[Test]
public void SimpleAssemblyCSV()
{
  PartExtension e = a.GetExtension("CSV");
  CsvPartExtension ce = e as CsvPartExtension;
  String csv = ce.CsvText;
  Assert.AreEqual("Assembly,5879,MyAssembly", csv);
}

[Test]
public void AssemblyWithPartsCSV()
{
  a.Add(p1);
  a.Add(p2);
  PartExtension e = a.GetExtension("CSV");
  CsvPartExtension ce = e as CsvPartExtension;
  String csv = ce.CsvText;

  Assert.AreEqual("Assembly,5879,MyAssembly," +
    "{PiecePart,997624,MyPart,3.2}," +
    "{PiecePart,7734,Hell,666}"
    , csv);
}

[Test]
public void BadExtension()
{
  PartExtension pe = p1.GetExtension(
    "ThisStringDoesn'tMatchAnyException");
  Assert.IsTrue(pe is BadPartExtension);
}
}
```

Listing 35-31

Part.cs

```
public abstract class Part
{
  Hashtable extensions = new Hashtable();

  public abstract string PartNumber { get; }
  public abstract string Description { get; }

  public void AddExtension(string extensionType,
    PartExtension extension)
  {
    extensions[extensionType] = extension;
  }

  public PartExtension GetExtension(string extensionType)
  {
    PartExtension pe =
      extensions[extensionType] as PartExtension;
    if (pe == null)
      pe = new BadPartExtension();
    return pe;
  }
}
```

Listing 35-32

PartExtension.cs

```
public interface PartExtension
{
}
```

Listing 35-33

PiecePart.cs

```
public class PiecePart : Part
{
  private string partNumber;
  private string description;
  private double cost;

  public PiecePart(string partNumber,
    string description,
    double cost)
  {
    this.partNumber = partNumber;
    this.description = description;
    this.cost = cost;
    AddExtension("CSV", new CsvPiecePartExtension(this));
    AddExtension("XML", new XmlPiecePartExtension(this));
  }

  public override string PartNumber
  {
    get { return partNumber; }
  }

  public override string Description
  {
    get { return description; }
  }

  public double Cost
  {
    get { return cost; }
  }
}
```

Listing 35-34

Assembly.cs

```
public class Assembly : Part
{
  private IList parts = new ArrayList();
  private string partNumber;
  private string description;

  public Assembly(string partNumber, string description)
  {
    this.partNumber = partNumber;
```

Listing 35-34 (Continued)

Assembly.cs

```
        this.description = description;
        AddExtension("CSV", new CsvAssemblyExtension(this));
        AddExtension("XML", new XmlAssemblyExtension(this));
    }

    public void Add(Part part)
    {
        parts.Add(part);
    }

    public IList Parts
    {
        get { return parts; }
    }

    public override string PartNumber
    {
        get { return partNumber; }
    }

    public override string Description
    {
        get { return description; }
    }
}
```

Listing 35-35

XmlPartExtension.cs

```
public abstract class XmlPartExtension : PartExtension
{
    private static XmlDocument document = new XmlDocument();

    public abstract XmlElement XmlElement { get; }

    protected XmlElement NewElement(string name)
    {
        return document.CreateElement(name);
    }

    protected XmlElement NewTextElement(
        string name, string text)
    {
        XmlElement element = document.CreateElement(name);
        XmlText xmlText = document.CreateTextNode(text);
        element.AppendChild(xmlText);
        return element;
    }
}
```

Listing 35-36
XmlPiecePartExtension.cs

```
public class XmlPiecePartExtension : XmlPartExtension
{
  private PiecePart piecePart;

  public XmlPiecePartExtension(PiecePart part)
  {
    piecePart = part;
  }

  public override XmlElement XmlElement
  {
    get
    {
      XmlElement e = NewElement("PiecePart");
      e.AppendChild(NewTextElement(
        "PartNumber", piecePart.PartNumber));
      e.AppendChild(NewTextElement(
        "Description", piecePart.Description));
      e.AppendChild(NewTextElement(
        "Cost", piecePart.Cost.ToString()));

      return e;
    }
  }
}
```

Listing 35-37
XmlAssemblyExtension.cs

```
public class XmlAssemblyExtension : XmlPartExtension
{
  private Assembly assembly;

  public XmlAssemblyExtension(Assembly assembly)
  {
    this.assembly = assembly;
  }

  public override XmlElement XmlElement
  {
    get
    {
      XmlElement e = NewElement("Assembly");
      e.AppendChild(NewTextElement(
        "PartNumber", assembly.PartNumber));
      e.AppendChild(NewTextElement(
        "Description", assembly.Description));

      XmlElement parts = NewElement("Parts");
      foreach(Part part in assembly.Parts)
```

Listing 35-37 (Continued)

XmlAssemblyExtension.cs

```
        {
          XmlPartExtension xpe =
            part.GetExtension("XML")
            as XmlPartExtension;
          parts.AppendChild(xpe.XmlElement);
        }
        e.AppendChild(parts);

        return e;
      }
    }
}
```

Listing 35-38

CsvPartExtension.cs

```
public interface CsvPartExtension : PartExtension
{
  string CsvText { get; }
}
```

Listing 35-39

CsvPiecePartExtension.cs

```
public class CsvPiecePartExtension : CsvPartExtension
{
  private PiecePart piecePart;

  public CsvPiecePartExtension(PiecePart part)
  {
    piecePart = part;
  }

  public string CsvText
  {
    get
    {
      StringBuilder b =
        new StringBuilder("PiecePart,");
      b.Append(piecePart.PartNumber);
      b.Append(",");
      b.Append(piecePart.Description);
      b.Append(",");
      b.Append(piecePart.Cost);
      return b.ToString();
    }
  }
}
```

Listing 35-40
CsvAssemblyExtension.cs

```
public class CsvAssemblyExtension : CsvPartExtension
{
  private Assembly assembly;

  public CsvAssemblyExtension(Assembly assy)
  {
    assembly = assy;
  }

  public string CsvText
  {
    get
    {
      StringBuilder b =
        new StringBuilder("Assembly,");
      b.Append(assembly.PartNumber);
      b.Append(",");
      b.Append(assembly.Description);

      foreach(Part part in assembly.Parts)
      {
        CsvPartExtension cpe =
          part.GetExtension("CSV")
          as CsvPartExtension;
        b.Append(",{");
        b.Append(cpe.CsvText);
        b.Append("}");
      }
      return b.ToString();
    }
  }
}
```

Listing 35-41
BadPartExtension.cs

```
public class BadPartExtension : PartExtension
{
}
```

Note that the extension objects are loaded into each BOM object by that object's constructor. This means that, to some extent, the BOM objects still depend on the XML and CSV classes. If even this tenuous dependency needs to be broken, we could create a FACTORY[4] object that creates the BOM objects and loads their extensions.

---

4. See Chapter 29.

The fact that the extension objects can be loaded into the object creates a great deal of flexibility. Certain extension objects can be inserted or deleted from objects depending upon the state of the system. It would be easy to get carried away with this flexibility. For the most part, you probably won't find it necessary. Indeed, the original implementation of `PiecePart.GetExtention(String extensionType)` looked like this.

```
public PartExtension GetExtension(String extensionType)
{
  if (extensionType.Equals("XML"))
    return new XmlPiecePartExtension(this);

  else if (extensionType.Equals("CSV"))
    return new XmlAssemblyExtension(this);

  return new BadPartExtension();
}
```

I wasn't particularly thrilled with this, because it was virtually identical to the code in `Assembly.GetExtension`. The `Hashtable` solution in `Part` avoids this duplication and is simpler. Anyone reading it will know exactly how extension objects are accessed.

Conclusion

The VISITOR family of patterns provides us with a number of ways to modify the behavior of a hierarchy of classes without having to change them. Thus, they help us maintain the Open/Closed Principle. They also provide mechanisms for segregating various kinds of functionality, keeping classes from getting cluttered with many different functions. As such, they help us maintain the Common Closure Principle. It should be clear that LSP and DIP are also applied to the structure of the VISITOR family.

The VISITOR patterns are seductive. It is easy to get carried away with them. Use them when they help, but maintain a healthy skepticism about their necessity. Often, something that can be solved with a VISITOR can also be solved by something simpler.[5]

---

5. Now that you've read this chapter, you may wish to go back to Chapter 9 and solve the problem of ordering the shapes.

Bibliography

[GOF95] Erich Gamma, Richard Helm, Ralph Johnson, and John Vlissides, *Design Patterns: Elements of Reusable Object-Oriented Software*, Addison-Wesley, 1995.

[PLOPD3] Robert C. Martin, Dirk Riehle, and Frank Buschmann, eds. *Pattern Languages of Program Design 3*, Addison-Wesley, 1998.

36

State

A state without the means of some change is without the means of its conservation.

—Edmund Burke (1729–1797)

Finite state automata are among the most useful abstractions in the software arsenal and are almost universally applicable. They provide a simple and elegant way to explore and define the behavior of a complex system. They also provide a powerful implementation strategy that is easy to understand and easy to modify. I use them in all levels of a system, from controlling the high-level GUI to the lowest-level communication protocols.

We studied the notation and basic operation of FSMs in Chapter 15. Now let's look at the patterns for implementing them. Consider the subway turnstile in Figure 36-1 once again.

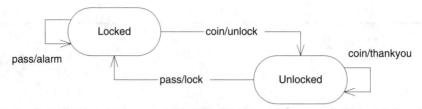

Figure 36-1
Turnstile FSM that covers abnormal events

Nested `Switch/Case` Statements

There are many different strategies for implementing an FSM. The first, and most direct,
is through nested `switch/case` statements. Listing 36-1 shows one such implementation.

Listing 36-1

Turnstile.cs (nested switch/case implementation)

```
public enum State {LOCKED, UNLOCKED};
public enum Event {COIN, PASS};

public class Turnstile
{
  // Private
  internal State state = State.LOCKED;

  private TurnstileController turnstileController;

  public Turnstile(TurnstileController action)
  {
    turnstileController = action;
  }

  public void HandleEvent(Event e)
  {
    switch (state)
    {
      case State.LOCKED:
        switch (e)
        {
          case Event.COIN:
            state = State.UNLOCKED;
            turnstileController.Unlock();
            break;
          case Event.PASS:
            turnstileController.Alarm();
            break;
        }
        break;
      case State.UNLOCKED:
```

Listing 36-1 (Continued)

Turnstile.cs (nested switch/case implementation)

```
            switch (e)
            {
              case Event.COIN:
                turnstileController.Thankyou();
                break;
              case Event.PASS:
                state = State.LOCKED;
                turnstileController.Lock();
                break;
            }
            break;
        }
    }
}
```

The nested switch/case statement divides the code into four mutually exclusive zones, each corresponding to one of the transitions in the STD. Each zone changes the state as needed and then invokes the appropriate action. Thus, the zone for Locked and Coin changes the state to Unlocked and calls Unlock.

Some interesting aspects to this code have nothing to do with the nested switch/case statement. In order for them to make sense, you need to see the unit test that I used to check this code. See Listings 36-2 and 36-3.

Listing 36-2

TurnstileController.cs

```
public interface TurnstileController
{
  void Lock();
  void Unlock();
  void Thankyou();
  void Alarm();
}
```

Listing 36-3

TurnstileTest.cs

```
[TestFixture]
public class TurnstileTest
{
  private Turnstile turnstile;
  private TurnstileControllerSpoof controllerSpoof;

  private class TurnstileControllerSpoof : TurnstileController
  {
    public bool lockCalled = false;
    public bool unlockCalled = false;
    public bool thankyouCalled = false;
    public bool alarmCalled = false;
```

Listing 36-3 (Continued)
TurnstileTest.cs

```
        public void Lock(){lockCalled = true;}
        public void Unlock(){unlockCalled = true;}
        public void Thankyou(){thankyouCalled = true;}
        public void Alarm(){alarmCalled = true;}
    }

    [SetUp]
    public void SetUp()
    {
        controllerSpoof = new TurnstileControllerSpoof();
        turnstile = new Turnstile(controllerSpoof);
    }

    [Test]
    public void InitialConditions()
    {
        Assert.AreEqual(State.LOCKED, turnstile.state);
    }

    [Test]
    public void CoinInLockedState()
    {
        turnstile.state = State.LOCKED;
        turnstile.HandleEvent(Event.COIN);
        Assert.AreEqual(State.UNLOCKED, turnstile.state);
        Assert.IsTrue(controllerSpoof.unlockCalled);
    }

    [Test]
    public void CoinInUnlockedState()
    {
        turnstile.state = State.UNLOCKED;
        turnstile.HandleEvent(Event.COIN);
        Assert.AreEqual(State.UNLOCKED, turnstile.state);
        Assert.IsTrue(controllerSpoof.thankyouCalled);
    }

    [Test]
    public void PassInLockedState()
    {
        turnstile.state = State.LOCKED;
        turnstile.HandleEvent(Event.PASS);
        Assert.AreEqual(State.LOCKED, turnstile.state);
        Assert.IsTrue(controllerSpoof.alarmCalled);
    }

    [Test]
    public void PassInUnlockedState()
    {
        turnstile.state = State.UNLOCKED;
        turnstile.HandleEvent(Event.PASS);
        Assert.AreEqual(State.LOCKED, turnstile.state);
        Assert.IsTrue(controllerSpoof.lockCalled);
    }
}
```

The Internal Scope State Variable

Note the four test functions `CoinInLockedState`, `CoinInUnlockedState`, `PassInLockedState`, and `PassInUnlockedState`. These functions test the four transitions of the FSM separately by forcing the `state` variable of the `Turnstile` to the state they want to check and then invoking the event they want to verify. In order for the test to access the `state` variable `c`, it cannot be `private`. So I gave it internal access and wrote a comment indicating my intent to make it `private`.

Object-oriented dogma insists that all instance variables of a class ought to be private. I have blatantly ignored this rule, and by doing so, I have broken the encapsulation of `Turnstile`.

Or have I? Make no mistake about it: I would rather have kept the `state` variable `private`. However, to do so would have denied my test code the ability to force its value. I could have created the appropriate `CurrentState` `get` and `set` property with internal scope, but that seems ridiculous. I was not trying to expose the `state` variable to any class other than `TestTurnstile`, so why should I create a `get` and `set` property that implies that anyone in the assembly can get and set that variable?

Testing the Actions

Note the `TurnstileController` interface in Listing 36-2. This was put in place specifically so that the `TestTurnstile` class could ensure that the `Turnstile` class was invoking the right action methods in the right order. Without this interface, it would have been much more difficult to ensure that the state machine was working properly.

This is an example of the impact that testing has on design. Had I simply written the state machine without giving thought to testing, it is unlikely that I would have created the `TurnstileController` interface. That would have been unfortunate. The `Turnstile-Controller` interface nicely decouples the logic of the FSM from the actions it needs to perform. Another FSM, using very different logic, can use the `TurnstileController` without any impact at all.

The need to create test code that verifies each unit in isolation forces us to decouple the code in ways we might not otherwise think of. Thus, testability is a force that drives the design to a less coupled state.

Costs and Benefits

For simple state machines, the nested `switch/case` implementation is both elegant and efficient. All the states and events are visible on one or two pages of code. However, for larger FSMs, the situation changes. In a state machine with dozens of states and events, the code devolves into page after page of `case` statements. There are no convenient locators to help you see where, in the state machine, you are reading. Maintaining long, nested `switch/case` statements can be a very difficult and error-prone job.

Another cost of the nested `switch/case` is that there is no good separation between the logic of the FSM and the code that implements the actions. That separation is strongly present in Listing 36-1 because the actions are implemented in a derivative of the `TurnstileController`. However, in most nested `switch/case` FSMs that I have seen, the implementation of the actions is buried in the `case` statements. Indeed, this is still possible in Listing 36-1.

Transition Tables

A common technique for implementing FSMs is to create a data table that describes the transitions. This table is interpreted by an engine that handles the events. The engine looks up the transition that matches the event, invokes the appropriate action, and changes the state. Listing 36-4 shows the code that creates the transition table, and Listing 36-5 shows the transition engine. Both of these listings are snippets from the full implementation (Listing 36-6).

Listing 36-4

Building the turnstile transition table

```
public Turnstile(TurnstileController controller)
{
  Action unlock = new Action(controller.Unlock);
  Action alarm = new Action(controller.Alarm);
  Action thankYou = new Action(controller.Thankyou);
  Action lockAction = new Action(controller.Lock);

  AddTransition(
    State.LOCKED,    Event.COIN, State.UNLOCKED, unlock);
  AddTransition(
    State.LOCKED,    Event.PASS, State.LOCKED,    alarm);
  AddTransition(
    State.UNLOCKED, Event.COIN, State.UNLOCKED, thankYou);
  AddTransition(
    State.UNLOCKED, Event.PASS, State.LOCKED,    lockAction);
}
```

Listing 36-5

The transition engine

```
public void HandleEvent(Event e)
{
  foreach(Transition transition in transitions)
  {
    if(state == transition.startState &&
       e == transition.trigger)
    {
      state = transition.endState;
      transition.action();
    }
  }
}
```

Using Table Interpretation

Listing 36-6 is the full implementation showing how a finite state machine can be implemented by interpreting a list of transition data structures. This code is completely compatible with `TurnstileController` (Listing 36-2) and the `TurnstileTest` (Listing 36-3).

Listing 36-6

Turnstile.cs full implementation

```
Turnstile.cs using table interpretation.
public enum State {LOCKED, UNLOCKED};
public enum Event {COIN, PASS};

public class Turnstile
{
  // Private
  internal State state = State.LOCKED;

  private IList transitions = new ArrayList();

  private delegate void Action();

  public Turnstile(TurnstileController controller)
  {
    Action unlock = new Action(controller.Unlock);
    Action alarm = new Action(controller.Alarm);
    Action thankYou = new Action(controller.ThankYou);
    Action lockAction = new Action(controller.Lock);

    AddTransition(
      State.LOCKED,    Event.COIN, State.UNLOCKED, unlock);
    AddTransition(
      State.LOCKED,    Event.PASS, State.LOCKED,    alarm);
    AddTransition(
      State.UNLOCKED, Event.COIN, State.UNLOCKED, thankYou);
    AddTransition(
      State.UNLOCKED, Event.PASS, State.LOCKED,    lockAction);
  }

  public void HandleEvent(Event e)
  {
    foreach(Transition transition in transitions)
    {
      if(state == transition.startState &&
        e == transition.trigger)
      {
        state = transition.endState;
        transition.action();
      }
    }
  }

  private void AddTransition(State start, Event e, State end, Action
  action)
  {
    transitions.Add(new Transition(start, e, end, action));
  }
```

Listing 36-6 (Continued)

Turnstile.cs full implementation

```
  private class Transition
  {
    public State startState;
    public Event trigger;
    public State endState;
    public Action action;

    public Transition(State start, Event e, State end,Action a)
    {
      this.startState = start;
      this.trigger = e;
      this.endState = end;
      this.action = a;
    }
  }
}
```

Costs and Benefits

One powerful benefit is that the code that builds the transition table reads like a canonical state transition table. The four `AddTransition` lines can be very easily understood. The logic of the state machine is all in one place and is not contaminated with the implementation of the actions.

Maintaining an FSM like this is very easy compared to the nested `switch/case` implementation. To add a new transition, one simply adds a new `AddTransition` line to the `Turnstile` constructor.

Another benefit of this approach is that the table can easily be changed at runtime. This allows for dynamic alteration of the logic of the state machine. I have used mechanisms like that to allow hot patching of FSMs.

Still another benefit is that multiple tables can be created, each representing a different FSM logic. These tables can be selected at runtime, based on starting conditions.

The cost of the approach is primarily speed. It takes time to search through the transition table. For large state machines, that time may become significant.

The STATE Pattern

Another technique for implementing FSMs is the STATE pattern.[1] This pattern combines much of the efficiency of the nested `switch/case` statement with much of the flexibility of interpreting a transition table.

---

1. [GOF95], p. 305

Figure 36-2 shows the structure of the solution. The `Turnstile` class has `public` methods for the events and `protected` methods for the actions. It holds a reference to an interface called `TurnstileState`. The two derivatives of `TurnstileState` represent the two states of the FSM.

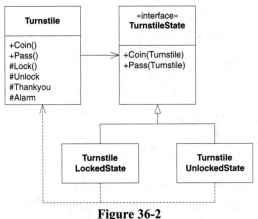

Figure 36-2
The STATE pattern for the `Turnstile` class

When one of the two event methods of `Turnstile` is invoked, it delegates that event to the `TurnstileState` object. The methods of `TurnstileLockedState` implement the appropriate actions for the `Locked` state. The methods of `TurnstileUnlocked-State` implement the appropriate actions for the `Unlocked` state. To change the state of the FSM, the reference in the `Turnstile` object is assigned to an instance of one of these derivatives.

Listing 36-7 shows the `TurnstileState` interface and its two derivatives. The state machine is easily visible in the four methods of those derivatives. For example, the `Coin` method of `LockedTurnstileState` tells the `Turnstile` object to change state to the unlocked state and then invokes the `Unlock` action function of `Turnstile`.

Listing 36-7
Turnstile.cs

```
public interface TurnstileState
{
  void Coin(Turnstile t);
  void Pass(Turnstile t);
}

internal class LockedTurnstileState : TurnstileState
{
  public void Coin(Turnstile t)
  {
    t.SetUnlocked();
    t.Unlock();
  }
```

Listing 36-7 (Continued)
Turnstile.cs

```
  public void Pass(Turnstile t)
  {
    t.Alarm();
  }
}

internal class UnlockedTurnstileState : TurnstileState
{
  public void Coin(Turnstile t)
  {
    t.Thankyou();
  }

  public void Pass(Turnstile t)
  {
    t.SetLocked();
    t.Lock() ;
  }
}
```

The `Turnstile` class is shown in Listing 36-8. Note the `static` variables that hold
the derivatives of `TurnstileState`. These classes have no variables and therefore never
need to have more than one instance. Holding the instances of the `TurnstileState`
derivatives in variables obviates the need to create a new instance every time the state
changes. Making those variables `static` obviates the need to create new instances of the
derivatives in the event that we need more than one instance of `Turnstile`.

Listing 36-8
Turnstile.cs

```
public class Turnstile
{
    internal static TurnstileState lockedState =
      new LockedTurnstileState();

    internal static TurnstileState unlockedState =
      new UnlockedTurnstileState();

    private TurnstileController turnstileController;
    internal TurnstileState state = unlockedState;

    public Turnstile(TurnstileController action)
    {
      turnstileController = action;
    }

    public void Coin()
    {
      state.Coin(this);
    }

    public void Pass()
```

Listing 36-8 (Continued)
`Turnstile.cs`

```
  {
    state.Pass(this);
  }

  public void SetLocked()
  {
    state = lockedState;
  }

  public void SetUnlocked()
  {
    state = unlockedState;
  }

  public bool IsLocked()
  {
    return state == lockedState;
  }

  public bool IsUnlocked()
  {
    return state == unlockedState;
  }

  internal void Thankyou()
  {
    turnstileController.Thankyou();
  }

  internal void Alarm()
  {
    turnstileController.Alarm();
  }

  internal void Lock()
  {
    turnstileController.Lock();
  }

  internal void Unlock()
  {
    turnstileController.Unlock();
  }
}
```

STATE versus STRATEGY

Figure 36-2 is strongly reminiscent of the STRATEGY pattern.[2] Both have a context class, and both delegate to a polymorphic base class that has several derivatives. The difference

---

2. See Chapter 22.

(see Figure 36-3) is that in STATE, the derivatives hold a reference back to the context class. The primary function of the derivatives is to select and invoke methods of the context class through that reference. In the STRATEGY pattern, no such constraint or intent exists. The STRATEGY derivatives are not required to hold a reference to the context and are not required to call methods on the context. Thus, all instances of the STATE pattern are also instances of the STRATEGY pattern, but not all instances of STRATEGY are STATE.

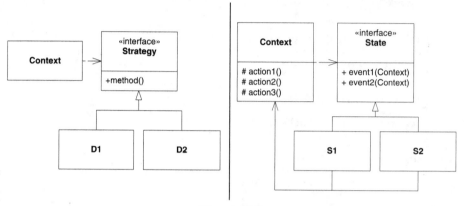

Figure 36-3
STATE versus STRATEGY

Costs and Benefits

The STATE pattern provides a strong separation between the actions and the logic of the state machine. The actions are implemented in the `Context` class, and the logic is distributed through the derivatives of the `State` class. This makes it very simple to change one without affecting the other. For example, it would be very easy to reuse the actions of the `Context` class with a different state logic by simply using a different set of derivatives of the `State` class. Alternatively, we could create `Context` subclasses that modify or replace the actions without affecting the logic of the `State` derivatives.

Another benefit of this technique is that it is very efficient. It is probably just as efficient as the nested `switch/case` implementation. Thus, we have the flexibility of the table-driven approach with the efficiency of the nested `switch/case` approach.

The cost of this technique is twofold. First, the writing of the `State` derivatives is tedious at best. Writing a state machine with 20 states can be mind numbing. Second, the logic is distributed. There is no single place to go to see it all. This makes the code difficult to maintain. This is reminiscent of the obscurity of the nested `switch/case` approach.

The State Machine Compiler (SMC)

The tedium of writing the derivatives of `State`, and the need to have a single place to express the logic of the state machine led me to write the SMC compiler that I described in Chapter 15. The input to the compiler is shown in Listing 36-9. The syntax is

```
currentState
{
  event newState action
  ...
}
```

The four lines at the top of Listing 36-9 identify the name of the state machine, the name of the context class, the initial state, and the name of the exception that will be thrown in the event of an illegal event.

Listing 36-9

Turnstile.sm

```
FSMName Turnstile
Context TurnstileActions
Initial Locked
Exception FSMError
{
    Locked
    {
        Coin    Unlocked    Unlock
        Pass    Locked      Alarm
    }
    Unlocked
    {
        Coin    Unlocked    Thankyou
        Pass    Locked      Lock
    }
}
```

In order to use this compiler, you must write a class that declares the action functions. The name of this class is specified in the `Context` line. I called it `TurnstileActions`. See Listing 36-10.

Listing 36-10

TurnstileActions.cs

```
public abstract class TurnstileActions
{
  public virtual void Lock() {}
  public virtual void Unlock() {}
  public virtual void Thankyou() {}
  public virtual void Alarm() {}
}
```

The compiler generates a class that derives from the context. The name of the generated class is specified in the `FSMName` line. I called it `Turnstile`.

I could have implemented the action functions in `TurnstileActions`. However, I am more inclined to write another class that derives from the generated class and implements the action functions there. This is shown in Listing 36-11.

Listing 36-11

TurnstileFSM.cs

```csharp
public class TurnstileFSM : Turnstile
{
  private readonly TurnstileController controller;

  public TurnstileFSM(TurnstileController controller)
  {
    this.controller = controller;
  }

  public override void Lock()
  {
    controller.Lock();
  }

  public override void Unlock()
  {
    controller.Unlock();
  }

  public override void Thankyou()
  {
    controller.Thankyou();
  }

  public override void Alarm()
  {
    controller.Alarm();
  }
}
```

That's all we have to write. SMC generates the rest. The resulting structure is shown in Figure 36-4. We call this a three-level FSM.[3]

The three levels provide the maximum in flexibility at a very low cost. We can create many different FSMs simply by deriving them from `TurnstileActions`. We can also implement the actions in many different ways simply by deriving from `Turnstile`.

Note that the generated code is completely isolated from the code that you have to write. You never have to modify the generated code. You don't even have to look at it. You can pay it the same level of attention that you pay to binary code.

---

3. [PLOPD1], p. 383

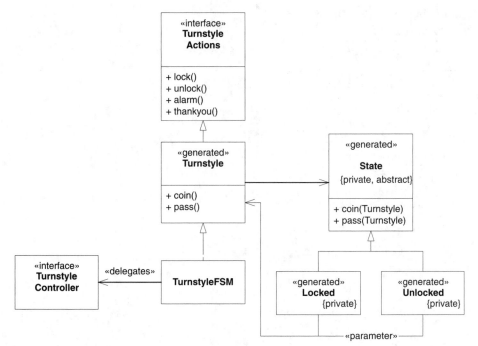

Figure 36-4
Three-level FSM

`Turnstile.cs` Generated by SMC, and Other Support Files

Listings 36-12 through 36-14 complete the code for the SMC example of the turnstile.
`Turnstile.cs` was generated by SMC. The generator creates a bit of cruft, but the code
is not bad.

Listing 36-12
`Turnstile.cs`

```
//--------------------------------------------
//
// FSM:       Turnstile
// Context:   TurnstileActions
// Exception: FSMError
// Version:
// Generated: Monday 07/18/2005 at 20:57:53 CDT
//
//--------------------------------------------

//--------------------------------------------
//
// class Turnstile
//     This is the Finite State Machine class
//
```

Listing 36-12 (Continued)

Turnstile.cs

```
public class Turnstile : TurnstileActions
{
  private State itsState;
  private static string itsVersion = "";

  // instance variables for each state
  private Unlocked itsUnlockedState;
  private Locked itsLockedState;

  // constructor
  public Turnstile()
  {
    itsUnlockedState = new Unlocked();
    itsLockedState = new Locked();

    itsState = itsLockedState;

    // Entry functions for: Locked
  }

  // accessor functions

  public string GetVersion()
  {
    return itsVersion;
  }
  public string GetCurrentStateName()
  {
    return itsState.StateName();
  }
  public State GetCurrentState()
  {
    return itsState;
  }
  public State GetItsUnlockedState()
  {
    return itsUnlockedState;
  }
  public State GetItsLockedState()
  {
    return itsLockedState;
  }

  // Mutator functions

  public void SetState(State value)
  {
    itsState = value;
  }
  // event functions - forward to the current State

  public void Pass()
  {
    itsState.Pass(this);
  }
```

Listing 36-12 (Continued)
Turnstile.cs

```csharp
    public void Coin()
    {
      itsState.Coin(this);
    }

}
//--------------------------------------------
//
// public class State
//     This is the base State class
//
public abstract class State
{
  public abstract string StateName();

  // default event functions

  public virtual void Pass(Turnstile name)
  {
      throw new FSMError( "Pass", name.GetCurrentState());
  }
  public virtual void Coin(Turnstile name)
  {
      throw new FSMError( "Coin", name.GetCurrentState());
  }
}
//--------------------------------------------
//
// class Unlocked
//     handles the Unlocked State and its events
//
public class Unlocked : State
{
  public override string StateName()
    { return "Unlocked"; }

  //
  // responds to Coin event
  //
  public override void Coin(Turnstile name)
  {
    name.Thankyou();

    // change the state
    name.SetState(name.GetItsUnlockedState());
  }

  //
  // responds to Pass event
  //
  public override void Pass(Turnstile name)
  {
    name.Lock();
```

Listing 36-12 (Continued)

Turnstile.cs

```
      // change the state
      name.SetState(name.GetItsLockedState());
    }
}

//-------------------------------------------
//
// class Locked
//    handles the Locked State and its events
//
public class Locked : State
{
  public override string StateName()
    { return "Locked"; }

  //
  // responds to Coin event
  //
  public override void Coin(Turnstile name)
  {
    name.Unlock();

    // change the state
    name.SetState(name.GetItsUnlockedState());
  }

  //
  // responds to Pass event
  //
  public override void Pass(Turnstile name)
  {
    name.Alarm();

    // change the state
    name.SetState(name.GetItsLockedState());
  }
}
```

FSMError is the exception that we told SMC to throw in case of an illegal event. The turnstile example is so simple that there can't be an illegal event, so the exception is useless. However, larger state machines have events that should not occur in certain states. Those transitions are never mentioned in the input to SMC. Thus, if such an event were ever to occur, the generated code would throw the exception.

Listing 36-13

FSMError.cs

```
public class FSMError : ApplicationException
{
  private static string message =
    "Undefined transition from state: {0} with event: {1}.";
```

Listing 36-13 (Continued)

FSMError.cs

```
    public FSMError(string theEvent, State state)
      : base(string.Format(message, state.StateName(), theEvent))
    {
    }
  }
}
```

The test code for the SMC-generated state machine is very similar to all the other test programs we've written in this chapter. The differences are minor.

Listing 36-14

```
[TestFixture]
public class SMCTurnstileTest
{
  private Turnstile turnstile;
  private TurnstileControllerSpoof controllerSpoof;

  private class TurnstileControllerSpoof : TurnstileController
  {
    public bool lockCalled = false;
    public bool unlockCalled = false;
    public bool thankyouCalled = false;
    public bool alarmCalled = false;

    public void Lock(){lockCalled = true;}
    public void Unlock(){unlockCalled = true;}
    public void Thankyou(){thankyouCalled = true;}
    public void Alarm(){alarmCalled = true;}
  }

  [SetUp]
  public void SetUp()
  {
    controllerSpoof = new TurnstileControllerSpoof();
    turnstile = new TurnstileFSM(controllerSpoof);
  }

  [Test]
  public void InitialConditions()
  {
    Assert.IsTrue(turnstile.GetCurrentState() is Locked);
  }

  [Test]
  public void CoinInLockedState()
  {
    turnstile.SetState(new Locked());
    turnstile.Coin();
    Assert.IsTrue(turnstile.GetCurrentState() is Unlocked);
    Assert.IsTrue(controllerSpoof.unlockCalled);
  }

  [Test]
  public void CoinInUnlockedState()
```

Listing 36-14 (Continued)

```
    {
        turnstile.SetState(new Unlocked());
        turnstile.Coin();
        Assert.IsTrue(turnstile.GetCurrentState() is Unlocked);
        Assert.IsTrue(controllerSpoof.thankyouCalled);
    }

    [Test]
    public void PassInLockedState()
    {
        turnstile.SetState(new Locked());
        turnstile.Pass();
        Assert.IsTrue(turnstile.GetCurrentState() is Locked);
        Assert.IsTrue(controllerSpoof.alarmCalled);
    }

    [Test]
    public void PassInUnlockedState()
    {
        turnstile.SetState(new Unlocked());
        turnstile.Pass();
        Assert.IsTrue(turnstile.GetCurrentState() is Locked);
        Assert.IsTrue(controllerSpoof.lockCalled);
    }
}
```

The `TurnstileController` class is identical to all the others that appeared in this chapter. You can see it in Listing 36-2.

Following is the DOS command used to invoke SMC. You'll note that SMC is a Java program. Although it's written in Java, it is capable of generating C# code in addition to Java and C++ code.

```
java -classpath .\smc.jar smc.Smc -g
smc.generator.csharp.SMCSharpGenerator turnstileFSM.sm
```

Costs and Benefits

Clearly, we've managed to maximize the benefits of the various approaches. The description of the FSM is contained in once place and is very easy to maintain. The logic of the FSM is strongly isolated from the implementation of the actions, enabling each to be changed without impact on the other. The solution is efficient and elegant and requires a minimum of coding.

The cost is in the use of SMC. You have to procure, and learn how to use, another tool. In this case, however, the tool is remarkably simple to install and use, and it's free.

Classes of State Machine Application

I use state machines and SMC for several classes of application.

High-Level Application Policies for GUIs

One of the goals of the graphical revolution in the 1980s, was to create *stateless* interfaces for humans to use. At that time, computer interfaces were dominated by textual approaches using hierarchical menus. It was easy to get lost in the menu structure, losing track of what *state* the screen was in. GUIs helped mitigate that problem by minimizing the number of state changes that the screen went through. In modern GUIs, a great deal of work is put into keeping common features on the screen at all times and making sure that the user does not get confused by hidden states.

It is ironic, then, that the code that implements these "stateless" GUIs is strongly state driven. In such GUIs, the code must figure out which menu items and buttons to gray out, which subwindows should appear, which tab should be activated, where the focus ought to be put, and so on. All these decisions are decisions about the state of the interface.

I learned a long time ago that controlling these factors is a nightmare unless you organize them into a single control structure. That control structure is best characterized as an FSM. Since those days, I have been writing almost all my GUIs using FSMs generated by SMC or its predecessors.

Consider the state machine in Listing 36-15. This machine controls the GUI for the login portion of an application. On getting a start event, the machine puts up a login screen. Once the user presses the Enter key, the machine checks the password. If the password is good, the machine goes to the `loggedIn` state and starts the user process (not shown). If the password is bad, the machine displays a screen so informing the user. The user can try again by clicking the OK button but otherwise clicks the Cancel button. If a bad password is entered three times in a row (`thirdBadPassword` event), the machine locks the screen until the administrator password is entered.

Listing 36-15
login.sm

```
Initial init
{
  init
  {
    start logginIn displayLoginScreen
  }

  logginIn
  {
    enter checkingPassword checkPassword
    cancel init clearScreen
  }

  checkingPassword
  {
    passwordGood loggedIn startUserProcess
    passwordBad notifyingPasswordBad displayBadPasswordScreen
    thirdBadPassword screenLocked displayLockScreen
  }
```

Listing 36-15 (Continued)
`login.sm`

```
   notifyingPasswordBad
   {
     OK checkingPassword displayLoginScreen
     cancel init clearScreen
   }

   screenLocked
   {
     enter checkingAdminPassword checkAdminPassword
   }

   checkingAdminPassword
   {
     passwordGood init clearScreen
     passwordBad screenLocked displayLockScreen
   }
 }
```

What we've done here is to capture the high-level policy of the application in a state machine. This high-level policy lives in one place and is easy to maintain. It vastly simplifies the rest of the code in the system, because that code is not mixed with the policy code.

Clearly, this approach can be used for interfaces other than GUIs. Indeed, I have used similar approaches for textual and machine/machine interfaces as well. But GUIs tend to be more complex than those others, so the need for them, and the volume of them, is greater.

GUI Interaction Controllers

Imagine that you want to allow your users to draw rectangles on the screen. The gestures they use are as follows. A user clicks the rectangle icon in the pallet window, positions the mouse in the canvas window at one corner of the rectangle, presses the mouse button, and drags the mouse toward the desired second corner. As the user drags, an animated image of the potential rectangle appears on the screen. The user manipulates the rectangle to the desired shape by continuing to hold the mouse button down while dragging the mouse. When the rectangle is right, the user releases the mouse button. The program then stops the animation and draws a fixed rectangle on the screen.

Of course, the user can abort this at any time by clicking a different pallet icon. If the user drags the mouse out of the canvas window, the animation disappears. If the mouse returns to the canvas window, the animation reappears.

Finally, having finished drawing a rectangle, the user can draw another one simply by clicking and dragging again in the canvas window. There is no need to click the rectangle icon in the pallet.

What I have described here is a FSM. The state transition diagram appears in Figure 36-5. The solid circle with the arrow denotes the starting state of the state machine.[4] The solid circle with the open circle around it is the final state of the machine.

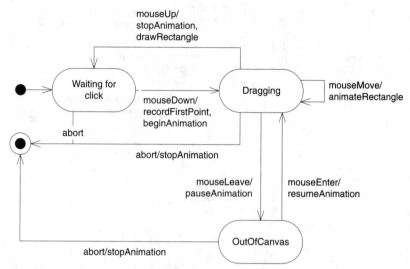

Figure 36-5
Rectangle interaction state machine

GUI interactions are rife with FSMs. They are driven by the incoming events from the user. Those events cause changes in the state of the interaction.

Distributed Processing

Distributed processing is yet another situation in which the state of the system changes based on incoming events. For example, suppose that you had to transfer a large block of information from one node on a network to another. Suppose also that because network response time is precious, you need to chop up the block and send it as a group of small packets.

The state machine depicting this scenario is shown in Figure 36-6. It starts by requesting a transmission session, proceeds by sending each packet and waiting for an acknowledgment, and finishes by terminating the session.

---

4.   See Chapter 13, "State Diagrams."

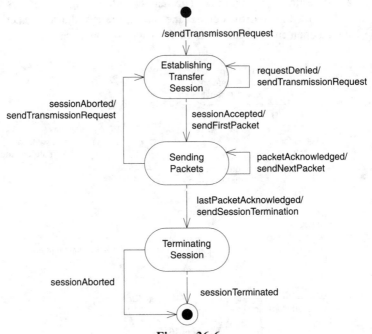

Figure 36-6
Sending large block, using many packets

Conclusion

Finite state machines are underutilized. In many scenarios their use would help to create clearer, simpler, more flexible, and more accurate code. Making use of the STATE pattern and simple tools for generating the code from state transition tables can be of great assistance.

Bibliography

[GOF95] Erich Gamma, Richard Helm, Ralph Johnson, and John Vlissides, *Design Patterns: Elements of Reusable Object-Oriented Software*, Addison-Wesley, 1995.

[PLOPD1] James O. Coplien and Douglas C. Schmidt, *Pattern Languages of Program Design*, Addison-Wesley, 1995.

37

The Payroll Case Study:
The Database

"Experts often possess more data than judgement."

—Colin Powell

In previous chapters, we implemented all the business logic for the payroll application. That implementation had a class, `PayrollDatabase`, that stored all the payroll data in RAM. This worked fine for our purpose at the time. However, it seems obvious that this

603

system will need a more persistent form of data storage. This chapter explains how to provide that persistence by storing the data in a relational database.

Building the Database

The choice of database technology is usually made more for political reasons than for technical reasons. Database and platform companies have done a good job of convincing the market that these choices are of critical importance. Loyalties and allegiances form around database and platform providers for reasons that are more human than technical. So you should not read too much into our choice of Microsoft SQL Server to persist the data for our application.

The schema that we'll be using is shown in Figure 37-1. The Employee table is central. It stores the immediate data for an employee, along with string constants that determine

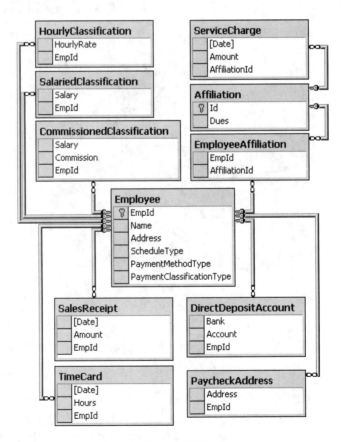

Figure 37-1
Payroll schema

the `PaymentSchedule`, `PaymentMethod`, and `PaymentClassification`. `PaymentClassifications` have data of their own that will be persisted in the corresponding `HourlyClassification`, `SalariedClassification`, and `CommissionedClassification` tables. Each references the `Employee` it belongs to, via the `EmpId` column. This column has a constraint to make sure that an `Employee` record with the given `EmpId` exists in the `Employee` table. `DirectDepositAccount` and `PaycheckAddress` hold the data appropriate to their `PaymentMethod` and are likewise constrained by the `EmpId` column. `SalesReceipt` and `TimeCard` are straightforward. The `Affiliation` table holds such data as the union members and is linked to the `Employee` table via `EmpoyeeAffiliation`.

A Flaw in the Code Design

You may recall that the `PayrollDatabase` was filled with nothing but `public static` methods. This decision is no longer appropriate. How do we start using a real database in the code without breaking all the tests that use the `static` methods? We don't want to overwrite the `PayrollDatabase` class to use a real database. That would force all our existing unit tests to use the real database. It would be nice if `PayrollDatabase` were an interface so we could easily swap out different implementations. One implementation would store data in memory like it does now, so that our tests can continue to run quickly. Another implementation would store data in a real database.

To achieve this new design, we'll have to perform a few refactorings, running the unit tests after each step to make sure we're not breaking the code. First, we'll create an instance of the `PayrollDatabase` and store it in a `static` variable: `instance`. Then we'll go through each `static` method in `PayrollDatabase` and rename it to include the word `static`. Then we'll extract the method body into a new non-`static` method of the same name. (See Listing 37-1.)

Listing 37-1
Example refactoring

```
public class PayrollDatabase
{
  private static PayrollDatabase instance;

  public static void AddEmployee_Static(Employee employee)
  {
    instance.AddEmployee(employee);
  }

  public void AddEmployee(Employee employee)
  {
    employees[employee.EmpId] = employee;
  }
```

Now we need to find every call to `PayrollDatabase.AddEmployee_Static()` and replace it with `PayrollDatabase.instance.AddEmployee()`. Once they have all been changed, we can delete the `static` version of the method. The same has to be done with each `static` method, of course.

That leaves every database invocation going through the `PayrollData-base.instance` variable. We would like `PayrollDatabase` to be an interface. So we need to find another home for that `instance` variable. Certainly, `PayrollTest` should hold such a variable, since it can then be used by all the tests. For the application, a good place is in each `Transaction` derivative. The `PayrollDatabase` instance will have to be passed into the constructor and stored as an instance variable of each `Transaction`. Rather than duplicate this code, let's simply put the `PayrollDatabase` instance in the `Transaction` base class. `Transaction` is an interface, so we'll have to convert it into an abstract class, as in Listing 37-2.

Listing 37-2

`Transaction.cs`

```
public abstract class Transaction
{
    protected readonly PayrollDatabase database;

    public Transaction(PayrollDatabase database)
    {
        this.database = database;
    }

    public abstract void Execute();
}
```

Now that nobody is using the `PayrollDatabase.instance`, we can delete it. Before we convert `PayrollDatabase` into an interface, we need a new implementation that extends `PayrollDatabase`. Since the current implementation stores everything in memory, we'll call the new class `InMemoryPayrollDatabase` (Listing 37-3) and use it wherever `PayrollDatabase` is instantiated. Finally, `PayrollDatabase` can be reduced to an interface (Listing 37-4) and we can begin work on the real database implementation.

Listing 37-3

`InMemoryPayrollDatabase.cs`

```
public class InMemoryPayrollDatabase : PayrollDatabase
{
    private static Hashtable employees = new Hashtable();
    private static Hashtable unionMembers = new Hashtable();

    public void AddEmployee(Employee employee)
    {
        employees[employee.EmpId] = employee;
    }

    // etc...
}
```

Listing 37-4

PayrollDatabase.cs

```
public interface PayrollDatabase
{
  void AddEmployee(Employee employee);
  Employee GetEmployee(int id);
  void DeleteEmployee(int id);
  void AddUnionMember(int id, Employee e);
  Employee GetUnionMember(int id);
  void RemoveUnionMember(int memberId);
  ArrayList GetAllEmployeeIds();
}
```

Adding an Employee

With our design refactored, we can now create SqlPayrollDatabase. This class implements the PayrollDatabase interface to persist data in an SQL Server database with the schema in Figure 37-1. Along with SqlPayrollDatabase, we'll create SqlPayroll-DatabaseTest for unit tests. Listing 37-5 shows the first test.

Listing 37-5

SqlPayrollDatabaseTest.cs

```
[TestFixture]
public class Blah
{
  private SqlPayrollDatabase database;

  [SetUp]
  public void SetUp()
  {
    database = new SqlPayrollDatabase();
  }

  [Test]
  public void AddEmployee()
  {
    Employee employee = new Employee(123,
      "George", "123 Baker St.");
    employee.Schedule = new MonthlySchedule();
    employee.Method =
      new DirectDepositMethod("Bank 1", "123890");
    employee.Classification =
      new SalariedClassification(1000.00);
    database.AddEmployee(123, employee);

    SqlConnection connection = new SqlConnection(
      "Initial Catalog=Payroll;Data Source=localhost;" +
      "user id=sa;password=abc");
    SqlCommand command = new SqlCommand(
      "select * from Employee", connection);
    SqlDataAdapter adapter = new SqlDataAdapter(command);
    DataSet dataset = new DataSet();
    adapter.Fill(dataset);
```

Listing 37-5 (Continued)

`SqlPayrollDatabaseTest.cs`

```
        DataTable table = dataset.Tables["table"];

        Assert.AreEqual(1, table.Rows.Count);
        DataRow row = table.Rows[0];
        Assert.AreEqual(123, row["EmpId"]);
        Assert.AreEqual("George", row["Name"]);
        Assert.AreEqual("123 Baker St.", row["Address"]);
    }
}
```

This test makes a call to `AddEmployee()`, then queries the database to make sure that the data was saved. Listing 37-6 shows the brute-force code to make it pass.

Listing 37-6

`SqlPayrollDatabase.cs`

```
public class SqlPayrollDatabase : PayrollDatabase
{
    private readonly SqlConnection connection;

    public SqlPayrollDatabase()
    {
        connection = new SqlConnection(
            "Initial Catalog=Payroll;Data Source=localhost;" +
            "user id=sa;password=abc");
        connection.Open();
    }

    public void AddEmployee(Employee employee)
    {
        string sql = "insert into Employee values (" +
            "@EmpId, @Name, @Address, @ScheduleType, " +
            "@PaymentMethodType, @PaymentClassificationType)";
        SqlCommand command = new SqlCommand(sql, connection);

        command.Parameters.Add("@EmpId", employee.EmpId);
        command.Parameters.Add("@Name", employee.Name);
        command.Parameters.Add("@Address", employee.Address);
        command.Parameters.Add("@ScheduleType",
            employee.Schedule.GetType().ToString());
        command.Parameters.Add("@PaymentMethodType",
            employee.Method.GetType().ToString());
        command.Parameters.Add("@PaymentClassificationType",
            employee.Classification.GetType().ToString());

        command.ExecuteNonQuery();
    }
}
```

This test passes once but fails every other time it is run. We get an exception from SQL Server, saying that we can't insert duplicate keys. So we'll have to clear the `Employee` table before each test. Listing 37-7 shows how this can be added to the `SetUp` method.

Listing 37-7

SqlPayrollDatabaseTest.SetUp()

```
[SetUp]
public void SetUp()
{
  database = new SqlPayrollDatabase();

  SqlConnection connection = new SqlConnection(
    "Initial Catalog=Payroll;Data Source=localhost;" +
    "user id=sa;password=abc");connection.Open();
  SqlCommand command = new SqlCommand(
    "delete from Employee", connection);
  command.ExecuteNonQuery();
  connection.Close();
}
```

This code does the trick, but it's sloppy. A connection is created in SetUp and in the
AddEmployee test. One connection created in SetUp and closed in TearDown should be
enough. Listing 37-8 shows a refactored version.

Listing 37-8

SqlPayrollDatabaseTest.cs

```
[TestFixture]
public class Blah
{
  private SqlPayrollDatabase database;
  private SqlConnection connection;

  [SetUp]
  public void SetUp()
  {
    database = new SqlPayrollDatabase();

    connection = new SqlConnection(
      "Initial Catalog=Payroll;Data Source=localhost;" +
      "user id=sa;password=abc");
    connection.Open();
    new SqlCommand("delete from Employee",
      this.connection).ExecuteNonQuery();
  }

  [TearDown]
  public void TearDown()
  {
    connection.Close();
  }

  [Test]
  public void AddEmployee()
  {
    Employee employee = new Employee(123,
      "George", "123 Baker St.");
    employee.Schedule = new MonthlySchedule();
    employee.Method =
```

Listing 37-8 (Continued)

SqlPayrollDatabaseTest.cs

```
        new DirectDepositMethod("Bank 1", "123890");
    employee.Classification =
        new SalariedClassification(1000.00);
    database.AddEmployee(employee);

    SqlCommand command = new SqlCommand(
        "select * from Employee", connection);
    SqlDataAdapter adapter = new SqlDataAdapter(command);
    DataSet dataset = new DataSet();
    adapter.Fill(dataset);
    DataTable table = dataset.Tables["table"];

    Assert.AreEqual(1, table.Rows.Count);
    DataRow row = table.Rows[0];
    Assert.AreEqual(123, row["EmpId"]);
    Assert.AreEqual("George", row["Name"]);
    Assert.AreEqual("123 Baker St.", row["Address"]);
  }
}
```

In Listing 37-6, you can see that the `Employee` table columns `ScheduleType`, `PaymentMethodType`, and `PaymentClassificationType` were populated with class names. Althoug this works, it's a bit lengthy. Instead, we'll use more concise keywords. Starting with the schedule type, Listing 37-9 shows how `MonthlySchedules` are saved. Listing 37-10 shows the part of `SqlPayrollDatabase` that satisfies this test.

Listing 37-9

SqlPayrollDatabaseTest.ScheduleGetsSaved()

```
[Test]
public void ScheduleGetsSaved()
{
  Employee employee = new Employee(123,
    "George", "123 Baker St.");
  employee.Schedule = new MonthlySchedule();
  employee.Method = new DirectDepositMethod();
  employee.Classification = new SalariedClassification(1000.00);
  database.AddEmployee(123, employee);

  SqlCommand command = new SqlCommand(
    "select * from Employee", connection);
  SqlDataAdapter adapter = new SqlDataAdapter(command);
  DataSet dataset = new DataSet();
  adapter.Fill(dataset);
  DataTable table = dataset.Tables["table"];

  Assert.AreEqual(1, table.Rows.Count);
  DataRow row = table.Rows[0];
  Assert.AreEqual("monthly", row["ScheduleType"]);
  }
```

Listing 37-10

SqlPayrollDatabase.cs (partial)

```
public void AddEmployee(int id, Employee employee)
{
  ...
  command.Parameters.Add("@ScheduleType",
    ScheduleCode(employee.Schedule));
  ...
}

private static string ScheduleCode(PaymentSchedule schedule)
{
  if(schedule is MonthlySchedule)
    return "monthly";
  else
    return "unknown";
}
```

The observant reader will notice the beginning of an OCP violation in Listing 37-10. The ScheduleCode() method contains an if/else statement to determine whether the schedule is a MonthlySchedule. Soon we'll add another if/else clause for WeeklySchedule and then another for BiweeklySchedule. Every time a new type of payment schedule is added to the system, this if/else chain will have to be modified again.

One alternative is to get the schedule code from the PaymentSchedule hierarchy. We could add a polymorphic property, such as string DatabaseCode, that returns the appropriate value. But that would introduce an SRP violation to the PaymentSchedule hierarchy.

The SRP violation is ugly. It creates an unnecessary coupling between the database and the application and invites other modules to extend this coupling by making use of the ScheduleCode. On the other hand, the OCP violation is encapsulated within the Sql-PayrollDatabase class and is not likely to leak out. So for the time being, we'll live with the OCP violation.

In writing the next test case, we find plenty of opportunity to remove duplicate code. Listing 37-11 shows the SqlPayrollDatabaseTest after some refactoring and with some new test cases. Listing 37-12 shows the SqlPayrollDatabase changes that make the test pass.

Listing 37-11

SqlPayrollDatabaseTest.cs (partial)

```
[SetUp]
public void SetUp()
{
  ...
  CleanEmployeeTable();

  employee = new Employee(123, "George", "123 Baker St.");
  employee.Schedule = new MonthlySchedule();
```

Listing 37-11 (Continued)

SqlPayrollDatabaseTest.cs (partial)

```
    employee.Method = new DirectDepositMethod();
    employee.Classification= new SalariedClassification(1000.00);
}
private void ClearEmployeeTable()
{
  new SqlCommand("delete from Employee",
                 this.connection).ExecuteNonQuery();
}

private DataTable LoadEmployeeTable()
{
  SqlCommand command = new SqlCommand(
    "select * from Employee", connection);
  SqlDataAdapter adapter = new SqlDataAdapter(command);
  DataSet dataset = new DataSet();
  adapter.Fill(dataset);
  return dataset.Tables["table"];
}

[Test]
public void ScheduleGetsSaved()
{
  CheckSavedScheduleCode(new MonthlySchedule(), "monthly");
  ClearEmployeeTable();
  CheckSavedScheduleCode(new WeeklySchedule(), "weekly");
  ClearEmployeeTable();
  CheckSavedScheduleCode(new BiWeeklySchedule(), "biweekly");
}

private void CheckSavedScheduleCode(
  PaymentSchedule schedule, string expectedCode)
{
  employee.Schedule = schedule;
  database.AddEmployee(123, employee);

  DataTable table = LoadEmployeeTable();
  DataRow row = table.Rows[0];

  Assert.AreEqual(expectedCode, row["ScheduleType"]);
}
```

Listing 37-12

SqlPayrollDatabase.cs (partial)

```
private static string ScheduleCode(PaymentSchedule schedule)
{
  if(schedule is MonthlySchedule)
    return "monthly";
  if(schedule is WeeklySchedule)
    return "weekly";
  if(schedule is BiWeeklySchedule)
    return "biweekly";
  else
    return "unknown";
}
```

Listing 37-13 shows a new test for saving the `PaymentMethods`. This code follows the pattern used of saving the schedules. Listing 37-14 shows the new database code.

Listing 37-13

SqlPayrollDatabaseTest.cs (partial)

```
[Test]
public void PaymentMethodGetsSaved()
{
  CheckSavedPaymentMethodCode(new HoldMethod(), "hold");
  ClearEmployeeTable();
  CheckSavedPaymentMethodCode(
    new DirectDepositMethod("Bank -1", "0987654321"),
    "directdeposit");
  ClearEmployeeTable();
  CheckSavedPaymentMethodCode(
    new MailMethod("111 Maple Ct."), "mail");
}
private void CheckSavedPaymentMethodCode(
  PaymentMethod method, string expectedCode)
{
  employee.Method = method;
  database.AddEmployee(employee);

  DataTable table = LoadTable("Employee");
  DataRow row = table.Rows[0];

  Assert.AreEqual(expectedCode, row["PaymentMethodType"]);
}
```

Listing 37-14

SqlPayrollDatabase.cs (partial)

```
public void AddEmployee(int id, Employee employee)
{
  ...
  command.Parameters.Add("@PaymentMethodType",
    PaymentMethodCode(employee.Method));
  ...
}

private static string PaymentMethodCode(PaymentMethod method)
{
  if(method is HoldMethod)
    return "hold";
  if(method is DirectDepositMethod)
    return "directdeposit";
  if(method is MailMethod)
    return "mail";
  else
    return "unknown";
}
```

All the tests pass. But hold on a minute: `DirectDepositMethod` and `MailMethod` have data of their own that needs to be saved. The `DirectDepositAccount` and `PaycheckAddress` tables need to be populated when saving an `Employee` with either payment method. Listing 37-15 shows the test for saving `DirectDepositMethod`.

Listing 37-15

SqlPayrollDatabaseTest.cs (partial)

```
[Test]
public void DirectDepositMethodGetsSaved()
{
  CheckSavedPaymentMethodCode(
    new DirectDepositMethod("Bank -1", "0987654321"),
    "directdeposit");

  SqlCommand command = new SqlCommand(
    "select * from DirectDepositAccount", connection);
  SqlDataAdapter adapter = new SqlDataAdapter(command);
  DataSet dataset = new DataSet();
  adapter.Fill(dataset);
  DataTable table = dataset.Tables["table"];

  Assert.AreEqual(1, table.Rows.Count);
  DataRow row = table.Rows[0];
  Assert.AreEqual("Bank -1", row["Bank"]);
  Assert.AreEqual("0987654321", row["Account"]);
  Assert.AreEqual(123, row["EmpId"]);
}
```

While looking at the code to figure out how to make this test pass, we realized that
we'll need another if/else statement. The first, we added to figure out what value to
stick in the PaymentMethodType column, which is bad enough. The second one is to figure out which table needs to be populated. These if/else OCP violations are starting to
accumulate. We need a solution that uses only one if/else statement. It's shown in Listing 37-16, where we introduce some member variables to help out.

Listing 37-16

SqlPayrollDatabase.cs (partial)

```
public void AddEmployee(int id, Employee employee)
{
  string sql = "insert into Employee values (" +
    "@EmpId, @Name, @Address, @ScheduleType, " +
    "@PaymentMethodType, @PaymentClassificationType)";
  SqlCommand command = new SqlCommand(sql, connection);

  command.Parameters.Add("@EmpId", id);
  command.Parameters.Add("@Name", employee.Name);
  command.Parameters.Add("@Address", employee.Address);
  command.Parameters.Add("@ScheduleType",
    ScheduleCode(employee.Schedule));
  SavePaymentMethod(employee);
  command.Parameters.Add("@PaymentMethodType", methodCode);
  command.Parameters.Add("@PaymentClassificationType",
    employee.Classification.GetType().ToString());

  command.ExecuteNonQuery();
}
```

Listing 37-16 (Continued)

`SqlPayrollDatabase.cs (partial)`

```
private void SavePaymentMethod(Employee employee)
{
  PaymentMethod method = employee.Method;
  if(method is HoldMethod)
    methodCode = "hold";
  if(method is DirectDepositMethod)
  {
    methodCode = "directdeposit";
    DirectDepositMethod ddMethod =
      method as DirectDepositMethod;
    string sql = "insert into DirectDepositAccount" +
      "values (@Bank, @Account, @EmpId)";
    SqlCommand command = new SqlCommand(sql, connection);
    command.Parameters.Add("@Bank", ddMethod.Bank);
    command.Parameters.Add("@Account", ddMethod.AccountNumber);
    command.Parameters.Add("@EmpId", employee.EmpId);
    command.ExecuteNonQuery();
  }
  if(method is MailMethod)
    methodCode = "mail";
  else
    methodCode = "unknown";
}
```

The tests *fail!* Oops. There's an error coming from SQL Server, saying that we can't add an entry to `DirectDepositAccount`, because the related `Employee` record doesn't exist. So the `DirectDepositAcount` table has to be populated *after* the `Employee` table is populated. But this brings up an interesting dilemma. What if the command to insert the employee succeeds but the command to insert the payment method fails? The data becomes corrupt. We end up with an employee with no payment method, and we can't have that.

A common solution is to use *transactions.* With transactions, if any part of the transaction fails, the whole transaction is canceled, and nothing is saved. It's still unfortunate when a save fails, but saving nothing is better than corrupting the database. Before we tackle this problem, let's get our current tests passing. Listing 37-17 continues the code evolution.

Listing 37-17

`SqlPayrollDatabase.cs (partial)`

```
public void AddEmployee(int id, Employee employee)
{
  PrepareToSavePaymentMethod(employee);

  string sql = "insert into Employee values (" +
    "@EmpId, @Name, @Address, @ScheduleType, " +
    "@PaymentMethodType, @PaymentClassificationType)";
  SqlCommand command = new SqlCommand(sql, connection);

  command.Parameters.Add("@EmpId", id);
  command.Parameters.Add("@Name", employee.Name);
```

Listing 37-17 (Continued)

`SqlPayrollDatabase.cs (partial)`

```
    command.Parameters.Add("@Address", employee.Address);
    command.Parameters.Add("@ScheduleType",
      ScheduleCode(employee.Schedule));
    SavePaymentMethod(employee);
    command.Parameters.Add("@PaymentMethodType", methodCode);
    command.Parameters.Add("@PaymentClassificationType",
      employee.Classification.GetType().ToString());

    command.ExecuteNonQuery();

    if(insertPaymentMethodCommand != null)
      insertPaymentMethodCommand.ExecuteNonQuery();
  }

  private void PrepareToSavePaymentMethod(Employee employee)
  {
    PaymentMethod method = employee.Method;
    if(method is HoldMethod)
      methodCode = "hold";
    else if(method is DirectDepositMethod)
    {
      methodCode = "directdeposit";
      DirectDepositMethod ddMethod =
        method as DirectDepositMethod;
      string sql = "insert into DirectDepositAccount" +
        "values (@Bank, @Account, @EmpId)";
      insertPaymentMethodCommand =
        new SqlCommand(sql, connection);
      insertPaymentMethodCommand.Parameters.Add(
        "@Bank", ddMethod.Bank);
      insertPaymentMethodCommand.Parameters.Add(
        "@Account", ddMethod.AccountNumber);
      insertPaymentMethodCommand.Parameters.Add(
        "@EmpId", employee.EmpId);
    }
    else if(method is MailMethod)
      methodCode = "mail";
    else
      methodCode = "unknown";
  }
```

Frustratingly, this still does not pass the tests. This time, the database is complaining when we clear the `Employee` table, because that would leave the `DirectDeposit-Account` table with a missing reference. So we'll have to clear both tables in the `SetUp` method. After being careful to clear the `DirectDepositAccount` table first, I'm rewarded with a green bar. That's nice.

The `MailMethod` still needs to be saved. Let's take care of this before venturing on to transactions. To test that the `PaycheckAddress` table is populated, we'll have to load it. This will be the third time duplicating the code to load a table, so it's past time to refactor. Renaming `LoadEmployeeTable` to `LoadTable` and adding the table name as a parameter makes the code sparkle. Listing 37-18 shows this change, along with the new test.

Listing 37-19 contains the code that makes it pass—after adding a statement to clear the PaycheckAddress table in the SetUp method, that is.

Listing 37-18

SqlPayrollDatabaseTest.cs (partial)

```
private DataTable LoadTable(string tableName)
{
  SqlCommand command = new SqlCommand(
    "select * from " + tableName, connection);
  SqlDataAdapter adapter = new SqlDataAdapter(command);
  DataSet dataset = new DataSet();
  adapter.Fill(dataset);
  return dataset.Tables["table"];
}

[Test]
public void MailMethodGetsSaved()
{
  CheckSavedPaymentMethodCode(
    new MailMethod("111 Maple Ct."), "mail");

  DataTable table = LoadTable("PaycheckAddress");

  Assert.AreEqual(1, table.Rows.Count);
  DataRow row = table.Rows[0];
  Assert.AreEqual("111 Maple Ct.", row["Address"]);
  Assert.AreEqual(123, row["EmpId"]);
}
```

Listing 37-19

SqlPayrollDatabase.cs (partial)

```
private void PrepareToSavePaymentMethod(Employee employee)
{
  ...
  else if(method is MailMethod)
  {
    methodCode = "mail";
    MailMethod mailMethod = method as MailMethod;
    string sql = "insert into PaycheckAddress " +
      "values (@Address, @EmpId)";
    insertPaymentMethodCommand =
      new SqlCommand(sql, connection);
    insertPaymentMethodCommand.Parameters.Add(
      "@Address", mailMethod.Address);
    insertPaymentMethodCommand.Parameters.Add(
      "@EmpId", employee.EmpId);
  }
  ...
}
```

Transactions

Now it's time to make this database operation transactional. Performing SQL Server transaction with .NET is a breeze. The `System.Data.SqlClient.SqlTransaction` class is all you need. However, we can't use it without first having a failing test. How do you test that a database operation is transactional?

If we can start the database operation by allowing the first command to execute successfully and then force a failure in a subsequent command, we can check the database to make sure that no data was saved. So how do you get an operation to succeed and another to fail? Well, let's take as an example our `Employee` with a `DirectDepositMethod`. We know that the employee data gets saved first, followed by the direct-deposit account data. If we can force the insert into the `DirectDepositAccount` table to fail, that'll do the trick. Passing a null value into the `DirectDepositMethod` object should cause a failure, especially considering that the `DirectDepositAccount` table doesn't allow any null values. With Listing 37-20, we're off.

Listing 37-20

SqlPayrollDatabaseTest.cs (partial)

```
[Test]
public void SaveIsTransactional()
{
  // Null values won't go in the database.
  DirectDepositMethod method =
    new DirectDepositMethod(null, null);
  employee.Method = method;
  try
  {
    database.AddEmployee(123, employee);
    Assert.Fail("An exception needs to occur" +
        "for this test to work.");
  }
  catch(SqlException)
  {}

  DataTable table = LoadTable("Employee");
  Assert.AreEqual(0, table.Rows.Count);
}
```

This does indeed cause a failure. The `Employee` record was added to the database, and the `DirectDepositAccount` record was not added. This is the situation that must be avoided. Listing 37-21 demonstrates the use of the `SqlTransaction` class to make our database operation transactional.

Listing 37-21

SqlPayrollDatabase.cs (partial)

```
public void AddEmployee(int id, Employee employee)
{
  SqlTransaction transaction =
    connection.BeginTransaction("Save Employee");
```

Listing 37-21 (Continued)

SqlPayrollDatabase.cs (partial)

```
try
{
  PrepareToSavePaymentMethod(employee);

  string sql = "insert into Employee values (" +
    "@EmpId, @Name, @Address, @ScheduleType, " +
    "@PaymentMethodType, @PaymentClassificationType)";
  SqlCommand command = new SqlCommand(sql, connection);

  command.Parameters.Add("@EmpId", id);
  command.Parameters.Add("@Name", employee.Name);
  command.Parameters.Add("@Address", employee.Address);
  command.Parameters.Add("@ScheduleType",
    ScheduleCode(employee.Schedule));
  command.Parameters.Add("@PaymentMethodType", methodCode);
  command.Parameters.Add("@PaymentClassificationType",
    employee.Classification.GetType().ToString());

  command.Transaction = transaction;
  command.ExecuteNonQuery();

  if(insertPaymentMethodCommand != null)
  {
    insertPaymentMethodCommand.Transaction = transaction;
    insertPaymentMethodCommand.ExecuteNonQuery();
  }

  transaction.Commit();
}
catch(Exception e)
{
  transaction.Rollback();
  throw e;
}
}
```

The tests pass! That was easy. Now to clean up the code. See Listing 37-22.

Listing 37-22

SqlPayrollDatabase.cs (partial)

```
public void AddEmployee(int id, Employee employee)
{
  PrepareToSavePaymentMethod(employee);
  PrepareToSaveEmployee(employee);

  SqlTransaction transaction =
    connection.BeginTransaction("Save Employee");
  try
  {
    ExecuteCommand(insertEmployeeCommand, transaction);
    ExecuteCommand(insertPaymentMethodCommand, transaction);
    transaction.Commit();
  }
```

Listing 37-22 (Continued)

SqlPayrollDatabase.cs (partial)

```
  catch(Exception e)
  {
    transaction.Rollback();
    throw e;
  }
}

private void ExecuteCommand(SqlCommand command,
  SqlTransaction transaction)
{
  if(command != null)
  {
    command.Connection = connection;
    command.Transaction = transaction;
    command.ExecuteNonQuery();
  }
}

private void PrepareToSaveEmployee(Employee employee)
{
  string sql = "insert into Employee values (" +
    "@EmpId, @Name, @Address, @ScheduleType, " +
    "@PaymentMethodType, @PaymentClassificationType)";
  insertEmployeeCommand = new SqlCommand(sql);

  insertEmployeeCommand.Parameters.Add(
    "@EmpId", employee.EmpId);
  insertEmployeeCommand.Parameters.Add(
    "@Name", employee.Name);
  insertEmployeeCommand.Parameters.Add(
    "@Address", employee.Address);
  insertEmployeeCommand.Parameters.Add(
    "@ScheduleType",ScheduleCode(employee.Schedule));
  insertEmployeeCommand.Parameters.Add(
    "@PaymentMethodType", methodCode);
  insertEmployeeCommand.Parameters.Add(
    "@PaymentClassificationType",
    employee.Classification.GetType().ToString());
}

private void PrepareToSavePaymentMethod(Employee employee)
{
  PaymentMethod method = employee.Method;
  if(method is HoldMethod)
    methodCode = "hold";
  else if(method is DirectDepositMethod)
  {
    methodCode = "directdeposit";
    DirectDepositMethod ddMethod =
      method as DirectDepositMethod;
    insertPaymentMethodCommand =
      CreateInsertDirectDepositCommand(ddMethod, employee);
  }
```

Listing 37-22 (Continued)

`SqlPayrollDatabase.cs (partial)`

```
    else if(method is MailMethod)
    {
      methodCode = "mail";
      MailMethod mailMethod = method as MailMethod;
      insertPaymentMethodCommand =
        CreateInsertMailMethodCommand(mailMethod, employee);
    }
    else
      methodCode = "unknown";
}

private SqlCommand CreateInsertDirectDepositCommand(
  DirectDepositMethod ddMethod, Employee employee)
{
  string sql = "insert into DirectDepositAccount " +
    "values (@Bank, @Account, @EmpId)";
  SqlCommand command = new SqlCommand(sql);
  command.Parameters.Add("@Bank", ddMethod.Bank);
  command.Parameters.Add("@Account", ddMethod.AccountNumber);
  command.Parameters.Add("@EmpId", employee.EmpId);
  return command;
}

private SqlCommand CreateInsertMailMethodCommand(
  MailMethod mailMethod, Employee employee)
{
  string sql = "insert into PaycheckAddress " +
    "values (@Address, @EmpId)";
  SqlCommand command = new SqlCommand(sql);
  command.Parameters.Add("@Address", mailMethod.Address);
  command.Parameters.Add("@EmpId", employee.EmpId);
  return command;
}
```

At this point, the `PaymentClassification` still remains unsaved. Implementing this portion of code involves no new tricks and is left up to the reader.

As your humble narrator completed this last task, a flaw in the code became apparent. `SqlPayrollDatabase` will likely be instantiated very early on in the application life cycle and used extensively. With this in mind, take a look at the `insertPaymentMethodCommand` member variable. This variable is given a value when saving an employee with either a direct-deposit or mail-payment method but not when saving an employee with a hold-payment method. Yet the variable is never cleared. What would happen if we save a employee with a mail-payment method and then another with a hold-payment method? Listing 37-23 puts the scenario in a test case.

Listing 37-23

`SqlPayrollDatabaseTest.cs (partial)`

```
[Test]
public void SaveMailMethodThenHoldMethod()
{
  employee.Method = new MailMethod("123 Baker St.");
```

Listing 37-23 (Continued)
`SqlPayrollDatabaseTest.cs (partial)`

```
    database.AddEmployee(employee);

    Employee employee2 = new Employee(321, "Ed", "456 Elm St.");
    employee2.Method = new HoldMethod();
    database.AddEmployee(employee2);

    DataTable table = LoadTable("PaycheckAddress");
    Assert.AreEqual(1, table.Rows.Count);
  }
```

The test fails because the two records were added to the `PaycheckAddress` table. The `insertPaymentMethodCommand` is loaded with a command to add the `MailMethod` for the first employee. When the second employe was saved, the residual command was left behind because the `HoldMethod` doesn't require any extra command, and it was executed a second time.

There are several ways to fix this, but something else bugs me. We originally set off to implement the `SqlPayrollDatabase.AddEmployee` method, and in doing so, we created a plethora of private helper methods. This has really cluttered the poor `SqlPayrollDatabase` class. It's time to create a class that will handle the saving of an employee: a `SaveEmployeeOperation` class. `AddEmployee()` will create a new instance of `SaveEmployeeOperation` every time it's called. This way, we won't have to null the commands, and the `SqlPayrollDatabase` becomes much cleaner. We're not changing any functionality with this change. It's simply a refactoring, so there's no need for new tests.

First, I create the `SaveEmployeeOperation` class and copy over the code to save the employee. I have to add a constructor and a new method, `Execute()`, to initiate the save. Listing 37-24 shows the budding class.

Listing 37-24
`SaveEmployeeOperation.cs (partial)`

```
public class SaveEmployeeOperation
{
  private readonly Employee employee;
  private readonly SqlConnection connection;

  private string methodCode;
  private string classificationCode;
  private SqlCommand insertPaymentMethodCommand;
  private SqlCommand insertEmployeeCommand;
  private SqlCommand insertClassificationCommand;

  public SaveEmployeeOperation(
    Employee employee, SqlConnection connection)
  {
    this.employee = employee;
    this.connection = connection;
  }
```

Listing 37-24 (Continued)
SaveEmployeeOperation.cs (partial)

```
public void Execute()
{
/*
All the code to save an Employee
*/
}
```

Then I change the `SqlPayrollDatabase.AddEmplyee()` method to create a new instance of `SaveEmployeeOperation` and execute it (shown in Listing 37-25). All the tests pass, including `SaveMailMethodThenHoldMethod`. Once all the copied code is deleted, `SqlPayrollDatabase` becomes much cleaner.

Listing 37-25
SqlPayrollDatabase.AddEmployee()

```
public void AddEmployee(Employee employee)
{
  SaveEmployeeOperation operation =
    new SaveEmployeeOperation(employee, connection);
  operation.Execute();
}
```

Loading an Employee

Now it's time to see whether we can load `Employee` objects from the database. Listing 37-26 shows the first test. As you can see, I didn't cut any corners in writing it. It first saves an employee object, using the `SqlPayrollDatabase.AddEmployee()` method, which we've already written and tested. Then the test attempts to load the employee, using `SqlPayrollDatabase.GetEmployee()`. Each aspect of the loaded `Employee` object is checked, including the payment schedule, payment method, and payment classification. The test obviously fails at first, and much work is needed before it will pass.

Listing 37-26
SqlPayrollDatabaseTest.cs (partial)

```
public void LoadEmployee()
{
  employee.Schedule = new BiWeeklySchedule();
  employee.Method =
    new DirectDepositMethod("1st Bank", "0123456");
  employee.Classification =
    new SalariedClassification(5432.10);
  database.AddEmployee(employee);

  Employee loadedEmployee = database.GetEmployee(123);
  Assert.AreEqual(123, loadedEmployee.EmpId);
  Assert.AreEqual(employee.Name,  loadedEmployee.Name);
  Assert.AreEqual(employee.Address, loadedEmployee.Address);
```

Listing 37-26 (Continued)

SqlPayrollDatabaseTest.cs (partial)

```
    PaymentSchedule schedule = loadedEmployee.Schedule;
    Assert.IsTrue(schedule is BiWeeklySchedule);

    PaymentMethod method = loadedEmployee.Method;
    Assert.IsTrue(method is DirectDepositMethod);
    DirectDepositMethod ddMethod = method as DirectDepositMethod;
    Assert.AreEqual("1st Bank", ddMethod.Bank);
    Assert.AreEqual("0123456", ddMethod.AccountNumber);

    PaymentClassification classification =
      loadedEmployee.Classification;
    Assert.IsTrue(classification is SalariedClassification);
    SalariedClassification salariedClassification =
      classification as SalariedClassification;
    Assert.AreEqual(5432.10, salariedClassification.Salary);
  }
```

The last refactoring we did when we implemented the AddEmployee() method was to extract a class, SaveEmployeeOperation, that contained all the code to fulfill its one purpose: to save an employee. We'll use this same pattern right off the bat when implementing the code to load an employee. Of course, we'll be doing this test first as well. However, there is going to be one fundamental difference. In testing the ability to load an employee, we will not touch the database, save the preceding test. We will thoroughly test the ability to load an employee, but we'll do it all without connecting to the database.

Listing 37-27 is the beginning of the LoadEmployeeOperationTest case. The first test, LoadEmployeeDataCommand, creates a new LoadEmployeeOperation object, using an employee ID and null for the database connection. The test then gets the SqlCommand for loading the data from the Employee table and tests its structure. We could execute this command against the database, but what does that buy us? First, it complicates the test, since we'd have to load data before we could execute the query. Second, we're already testing the ability to connect to the database in SqlPayrollDatabaseTest.LoadEmployee(). There's no need to test it over and over again. Listing 37-28 shows the start of LoadEmployeeOperation, along with the code that satisfies this first test.

Listing 37-27

LoadEmployeeOperationTest.cs

```
using System.Data;
using System.Data.SqlClient;
using NUnit.Framework;
using Payroll;

namespace PayrollDB
{
  [TestFixture]
  public class LoadEmployeeOperationTest
  {
    private LoadEmployeeOperation operation;
    private Employee employee;
```

```
Listing 37-27 (Continued)
LoadEmployeeOperationTest.cs

    [SetUp]
    public void SetUp()
    {
      employee = new Employee(123, "Jean", "10 Rue de Roi");
      operation = new LoadEmployeeOperation(123, null);

      operation.Employee = employee;
    }

    [Test]
    public void LoadingEmployeeDataCommand()
    {
      operation = new LoadEmployeeOperation(123, null);
      SqlCommand command = operation.LoadEmployeeCommand;
      Assert.AreEqual("select * from Employee " +
        "where EmpId=@EmpId", command.CommandText);
      Assert.AreEqual(123, command.Parameters["@EmpId"].Value);
    }
  }
}
```

```
Listing 37-28
LoadEmployeeOperation.cs

using System.Data.SqlClient;
using Payroll;

namespace PayrollDB
{
  public class LoadEmployeeOperation
  {
    private readonly int empId;
    private readonly SqlConnection connection;
    private Employee employee;

    public LoadEmployeeOperation(
      int empId, SqlConnection connection)
    {
      this.empId = empId;
      this.connection = connection;
    }

    public SqlCommand LoadEmployeeCommand
    {
      get
      {
        string sql = "select * from Employee " +
          "where EmpId=@EmpId";
        SqlCommand command = new SqlCommand(sql, connection);
        command.Parameters.Add("@EmpId", empId);
        return command;
      }
    }
  }
}
```

The tests pass at this point, so we've got a good start. But the command alone doesn't get us very far; we'll have to create an `Employee` object from the data that's retrieved from the database. One way to load data from the database is to dump it into a `DataSet` object, as we did in earlier tests. This technique is quite convenient because our tests can create a `DataSet` that would look exactly like what would be created were we really querying the database. The test in Listing 37-29 shows how this is done, and Listing 37-30 has the corresponding production code.

Listing 37-29

LoadEmployeeOperationTest.LoadEmployeeData()

```
[Test]
public void LoadEmployeeData()
{
  DataTable table = new DataTable();
  table.Columns.Add("Name");
  table.Columns.Add("Address");
  DataRow row = table.Rows.Add(
    new object[]{"Jean", "10 Rue de Roi"});

  operation.CreateEmplyee(row);

  Assert.IsNotNull(operation.Employee);
  Assert.AreEqual("Jean", operation.Employee.Name);
  Assert.AreEqual("10 Rue de Roi",
    operation.Employee.Address);
}
```

Listing 37-30

LoadEmployeeOperation.cs (partial)

```
public void CreateEmplyee(DataRow row)
{
  string name = row["Name"].ToString();
  string address = row["Address"].ToString();
  employee = new Employee(empId, name, address);
}
```

With this test passing, we can move on to loading payment schedules. Listings 37-31 and 37-32 show the test and production code that loads the first of the `PaymentSchedule` classes: `WeeklySchedule`.

Listing 37-31

LoadEmployeeOperationTest.LoadingSchedules()

```
[Test]
public void LoadingSchedules()
{
  DataTable table = new DataTable();
  table.Columns.Add("ScheduleType");
  DataRow row = table.NewRow();
  row.ItemArray = new object[] {"weekly"};

  operation.AddSchedule(row);
```

Listing 37-31 (Continued)

LoadEmployeeOperationTest.LoadingSchedules()

```
    Assert.IsNotNull(employee.Schedule);
    Assert.IsTrue(employee.Schedule is WeeklySchedule);
  }
```

Listing 37-32

LoadEmployeeOperation.cs (partial)

```
public void AddSchedule(DataRow row)
{
    string scheduleType = row["ScheduleType"].ToString();
    if(scheduleType.Equals("weekly"))
        employee.Schedule = new WeeklySchedule();
}
```

With a little refactoring, we can easily test the loading of all the PaymentSchedule types. Since we've been creating a few DataTable objects so far in the tests and will be creating many more, extracting this dry task out into a new method will turn out to be handy. See Listings 37-33 and 37-34 for the changes.

Listing 37-33

LoadEmployeeOperationTest.LoadingSchedules() (refactored)

```
[Test]
public void LoadingSchedules()
{
    DataRow row = ShuntRow("ScheduleType", "weekly");
    operation.AddSchedule(row);
    Assert.IsTrue(employee.Schedule is WeeklySchedule);

    row = ShuntRow("ScheduleType", "biweekly");
    operation.AddSchedule(row);
    Assert.IsTrue(employee.Schedule is BiWeeklySchedule);

    row = ShuntRow("ScheduleType", "monthly");
    operation.AddSchedule(row);
    Assert.IsTrue(employee.Schedule is MonthlySchedule);
}

private static DataRow ShuntRow(
    string columns, params object[] values)
{
    DataTable table = new DataTable();
    foreach(string columnName in columns.Split(','))
        table.Columns.Add(columnName);
    return table.Rows.Add(values);
}
```

Listing 37-34

LoadEmployeeOperation.cs (partial)

```
public void AddSchedule(DataRow row)
{
    string scheduleType = row["ScheduleType"].ToString();
```

Listing 37-34 (Continued)

`LoadEmployeeOperation.cs (partial)`

```
  if(scheduleType.Equals("weekly"))
    employee.Schedule = new WeeklySchedule();
  else if(scheduleType.Equals("biweekly"))
    employee.Schedule = new BiWeeklySchedule();
  else if(scheduleType.Equals("monthly"))
    employee.Schedule = new MonthlySchedule();
}
```

Next, we can work on loading the payment methods. See Listings 37-35 and 37-36.

Listing 37-35

`LoadEmployeeOperationTest.LoadingHoldMethod()`

```
[Test]
public void LoadingHoldMethod()
{
  DataRow row = ShuntRow("PaymentMethodType", "hold");
  operation.AddPaymentMethod(row);
  Assert.IsTrue(employee.Method is HoldMethod);
}
```

Listing 37-36

`LoadEmployeeOperation.cs (partial)`

```
public void AddPaymentMethod(DataRow row)
{
  string methodCode = row["PaymentMethodType"].ToString();
  if(methodCode.Equals("hold"))
    employee.Method = new HoldMethod();
}
```

That was easy. However, loading the rest of the payment methods is not easy. Consider loading an `Employee` with a `DirectDepositMethod`. First, we'll read the `Employee` table. In the `PaymentMethodType` column the value "`directdeposit`" tells us that we need to create a `DirectDepositMethod` object for this employee. To create a `DirectDepositMethod`, we'll need the bank account data stored in the `DirectDeposit-Account` table. Therefore, the `LoadEmployeeOperation.AddPaymentMethod()` method will have to create a new `sql` command to retrieve that data. To test this, we'll have to put data into the `DirectDepositAccount` table first.

In order to properly test the ability to load payment methods without touching the database, we'll have to create a new class: `LoadPaymentMethodOperation`. This class will be responsible for determining which `PaymentMethod` to create and for loading the data to create it. Listing 37-37 shows the new test fixture: `LoadPaymentMethod-OperationTest` with the test to load `HoldMethod` objects. Listing 37-38 shows the `LoadPaymentMethod` class with the first bit of code, and Listing 37-39 shows how `LoadEmployeeOperation` uses this new class.

Listing 37-37

LoadPaymentMethodOperationTest.cs

```csharp
using NUnit.Framework;
using Payroll;

namespace PayrollDB
{
  [TestFixture]
  public class LoadPaymentMethodOperationTest
  {
    private Employee employee;
    private LoadPaymentMethodOperation operation;

    [SetUp]
    public void SetUp()
    {
      employee = new Employee(567, "Bill", "23 Pine Ct");
    }

    [Test]
    public void LoadHoldMethod()
    {
      operation = new LoadPaymentMethodOperation(
          employee, "hold", null);
      operation.Execute();
      PaymentMethod method = this.operation.Method;
      Assert.IsTrue(method is HoldMethod);
    }
  }
}
```

Listing 37-38

LoadPaymentMethodOperation.cs

```csharp
using System;
using System.Data;
using System.Data.SqlClient;
using Payroll;

namespace PayrollDB
{
  public class LoadPaymentMethodOperation
  {
    private readonly Employee employee;
    private readonly string methodCode;
    private PaymentMethod method;

    public LoadPaymentMethodOperation(
      Employee employee, string methodCode)
    {
      this.employee = employee;
      this.methodCode = methodCode;
    }
```

Listing 37-38 (Continued)

LoadPaymentMethodOperation.cs

```
    public void Execute()
    {
      if(methodCode.Equals("hold"))
        method = new HoldMethod();
    }

    public PaymentMethod Method
    {
      get { return method; }
    }
  }
}
```

Listing 37-39

LoadEmployeeOperation.cs (partial)

```
public void AddPaymentMethod(DataRow row)
{
  string methodCode = row["PaymentMethodType"].ToString();
  LoadPaymentMethodOperation operation =
    new LoadPaymentMethodOperation(employee, methodCode);
  operation.Execute();
  employee.Method = operation.Method;
}
```

Again, loading the `HoldMethod` proves easy. For loading the `DirectDeposit-Method`, we'll have to create an `SqlCommand` that will be used to retrieve the data, and then we'll have to create an instance of `DirectDepositMethod` from the loaded data. Listings 37-40 and 37-41 show tests and production code to do this. Note that the test `CreateDirectDepositMethodFromRow` borrows the `ShuntRow` method, from `LoadEmployeeOperationTest`. It's a handy method so we'll let it slide for now. But at some point, we'll have to find a better place for `ShuntRow` to be shared.

Listing 37-40

LoadPaymentMethodOperationTest.cs (partial)

```
[Test]
public void LoadDirectDepositMethodCommand()
{
  operation = new LoadPaymentMethodOperation(
    employee, "directdeposit") ;
  SqlCommand command = operation.Command;
  Assert.AreEqual("select * from DirectDepositAccount " +
    "where EmpId=@EmpId", command.CommandText);
  Assert.AreEqual(employee.EmpId,
    command.Parameters["@EmpId"].Value);
}

[Test]
public void CreateDirectDepositMethodFromRow()
{
  operation = new LoadPaymentMethodOperation(
    employee, "directdeposit");
```

Listing 37-40 (Continued)

LoadPaymentMethodOperationTest.cs (partial)

```
    DataRow row = LoadEmployeeOperationTest.ShuntRow(
      "Bank,Account", "1st Bank", "0123456");
    operation.CreatePaymentMethod(row);

    PaymentMethod method = this.operation.Method;
    Assert.IsTrue(method is DirectDepositMethod);
    DirectDepositMethod ddMethod =
      method as DirectDepositMethod;
    Assert.AreEqual("1st Bank", ddMethod.Bank);
    Assert.AreEqual("0123456", ddMethod.AccountNumber);
  }
```

Listing 37-41

LoadPaymentMethodOperation.cs (partial)

```
public SqlCommand Command
{
  get
  {
    string sql = "select * from DirectDepositAccount" +
      "where EmpId=@EmpId";
    SqlCommand command = new SqlCommand(sql);
    command.Parameters.Add("@EmpId", employee.EmpId);
    return command;
  }
}

public void CreatePaymentMethod(DataRow row)
{
  string bank = row["Bank"].ToString();
  string account = row["Account"].ToString();
  method = new DirectDepositMethod(bank, account);
}
```

That leaves the loading of `MailMethod` objects. Listing 37-42 shows a test for creating the SQL. In attempting to implement the production code, things get interesting. In the `Command` property, we need an `if/else` statement to determine which table name will be used in the query. In the `Execute()` method, we'll need another `if/else` statement to determine which type of `PaymentMethod` to instantiate. This seems familiar. As before, duplicate `if/else` statements are a smell to be avoided.

The `LoadPaymentMethodOperation` class has to be restructured so that only one `if/else` is needed. With a little creativity and the use of delegates, the problem is solved. Listing 37-43 shows a restructured `LoadPaymentMethodOperation`.

Listing 37-42

LoadPaymentMethodOperationTest.LoadMailMethodCommand()

```
[Test]
public void LoadMailMethodCommand()
{
  operation = new LoadPaymentMethodOperation(employee, "mail");
```

Listing 37-42 (Continued)
LoadPaymentMethodOperationTest.LoadMailMethodCommand()

```
    SqlCommand command = operation.Command;
    Assert.AreEqual("select * from PaycheckAddress " +
      "where EmpId=@EmpId", command.CommandText);
    Assert.AreEqual(employee.EmpId,
      command.Parameters["@EmpId"].Value);
  }
```

Listing 37-43
LoadPaymentMethodOperation.cs (refactored)

```
public class LoadPaymentMethodOperation
{
  private readonly Employee employee;
  private readonly string methodCode;
  private PaymentMethod method;
  private delegate void PaymentMethodCreator(DataRow row);
  private PaymentMethodCreator paymentMethodCreator;
  private string tableName;

  public LoadPaymentMethodOperation(
    Employee employee, string methodCode)
  {
    this.employee = employee;
    this.methodCode = methodCode;
  }

  public void Execute()
  {
    Prepare();
    DataRow row = LoadData();
    CreatePaymentMethod(row);
  }

  public void CreatePaymentMethod(DataRow row)
  {
    paymentMethodCreator(row);
  }

  public void Prepare()
  {
    if(methodCode.Equals("hold"))
      paymentMethodCreator =
    new PaymentMethodCreator(CreateHoldMethod);
    else if(methodCode.Equals("directdeposit"))
    {
      tableName = "DirectDepositAccount";
      paymentMethodCreator = new PaymentMethodCreator(
    CreateDirectDepositMethod);
    }
    else if(methodCode.Equals("mail"))
    {
      tableName = "PaycheckAddress";
    }
  }
```

Listing 37-43 (Continued)
LoadPaymentMethodOperation.cs (refactored)

```
  private DataRow LoadData()
  {
    if(tableName != null)
      return LoadEmployeeOperation.LoadDataFromCommand(Command);
    else
      return null;
  }

  public PaymentMethod Method
  {
    get { return method; }
  }

  public SqlCommand Command
  {
    get
    {
      string sql = String.Format(
        "select * from {0} where EmpId=@EmpId", tableName);
      SqlCommand command = new SqlCommand(sql);
      command.Parameters.Add("@EmpId", employee.EmpId);
      return command;
    }
  }

  public void CreateDirectDepositMethod(DataRow row)
  {
    string bank = row["Bank"].ToString();
    string account = row["Account"].ToString();
    method = new DirectDepositMethod(bank, account);
  }

  private void CreateHoldMethod(DataRow row)
  {
    method = new HoldMethod();
  }
}
```

This refactoring was a little more involved than most. It required a change to the tests. The tests need to call `Prepare()` before they get the command to load the Payment-Method. Listing 37-44 shows this change and the final test for creating the `MailMethod`. Listing 37-45 contains the final bit of code in the `LoadPaymentMethodOperation` class.

Listing 37-44
LoadPaymentMethodOperationTest.cs (partial)

```
[Test]
public void LoadMailMethodCommand()
{
  operation = new LoadPaymentMethodOperation(employee, "mail");
  operation.Prepare();
  SqlCommand command = operation.Command;
```

Listing 37-44 (Continued)
`LoadPaymentMethodOperationTest.cs (partial)`

```
    Assert.AreEqual("select * from PaycheckAddress " +
      "where EmpId=@EmpId", command.CommandText);
    Assert.AreEqual(employee.EmpId,
      command.Parameters["@EmpId"].Value);
  }

  [Test]
  public void CreateMailMethodFromRow()
  {
    operation = new LoadPaymentMethodOperation(employee, "mail");
    operation.Prepare();
    DataRow row = LoadEmployeeOperationTest.ShuntRow(
      "Address", "23 Pine Ct");
    operation.CreatePaymentMethod(row);

    PaymentMethod method = this.operation.Method;
    Assert.IsTrue(method is MailMethod);
    MailMethod mailMethod = method as MailMethod;
    Assert.AreEqual("23 Pine Ct", mailMethod.Address);
  }
```

Listing 37-45
`LoadPaymentMethodOperation.cs (partial)`

```
public void Prepare()
{
  if(methodCode.Equals("hold"))
    paymentMethodCreator =
      new PaymentMethodCreator(CreateHoldMethod);
  else if(methodCode.Equals("directdeposit"))
  {
    tableName = "DirectDepositAccount";
    paymentMethodCreator =
      new PaymentMethodCreator(CreateDirectDepositMethod);
  }
  else if(methodCode.Equals("mail"))
  {
    tableName = "PaycheckAddress";
    paymentMethodCreator =
      new PaymentMethodCreator(CreateMailMethod);
  }
}

private void CreateMailMethod(DataRow row)
{
  string address = row["Address"].ToString();
  method = new MailMethod(address);
}
```

With all the `PaymentMethods` loaded, we are left with the `PaymentClass-ifications` to do. To load the classifications, we'll create a new class, `LoadPayment-ClassificationOperation`, and the corresponding test fixture. This is very similar to what we've done so far and is left up to you to complete.

After that's complete, we can go back to the `SqlPayrollDatabaseTest.Load-Employee` test. Hmm. It still fails. It seems that we've forgotten a bit of wiring. Listing 37-46 shows the changes that have to be made to make the test pass.

Listing 37-46

LoadEmployeeOperation.cs (partial)

```
public void Execute()
{
    string sql = "select *  from Employee where EmpId = @EmpId";
    SqlCommand command = new SqlCommand(sql, connection);
    command.Parameters.Add("@EmpId", empId);

    DataRow row = LoadDataFromCommand(command);

    CreateEmplyee(row);
    AddSchedule(row);
    AddPaymentMethod(row);
    AddClassification(row);
}

public void AddSchedule(DataRow row)
{
    string scheduleType = row["ScheduleType"].ToString();
    if(scheduleType.Equals("weekly"))
      employee.Schedule = new WeeklySchedule();
    else if(scheduleType.Equals("biweekly"))
      employee.Schedule = new BiWeeklySchedule();
    else if(scheduleType.Equals("monthly"))
      employee.Schedule = new MonthlySchedule();
}

private void AddPaymentMethod(DataRow row)
{
    string methodCode = row["PaymentMethodType"].ToString();
    LoadPaymentMethodOperation operation =
      new LoadPaymentMethodOperation(employee, methodCode);
    operation.Execute();
    employee.Method = operation.Method;
}

private void AddClassification(DataRow row)
{
    string classificationCode =
row["PaymentClassificationType"].ToString();
    LoadPaymentClassificationOperation operation =
      new LoadPaymentClassificationOperation(employee,
classificationCode);
    operation.Execute();
    employee.Classification = operation.Classification;
}
```

You may notice that there is plenty of duplication in the `LoadOperation` classes. Also, the tendency to refer to this group of classes as `LoadOperations` suggests that they should derive from a common base class. Such a base class would provide a home for all the duplicate code shared among its would-be derivatives. This refactoring is left to you.

What Remains?

The `SqlPayrollDatabase` class can save new `Employee` objects and load `Employee` objects. But it's not complete. What would happen if we save an `Employee` object that was already saved in the database? This still needs to be handled. Also, we haven't done anything about time cards, sales receipts, or union affiliations. Based on the work that we've accomplished so far, adding this functionality should be fairly straightforward and is, again, left to you.

38

The Payroll User Interface:
MODEL VIEW PRESENTER

As far as the customer is concerned, the Interface is the product.

—Jef Raskin

Our payroll application is coming together nicely at this point. It supports adding hourly, salary, and commissioned employees. Each employee's payments may be delivered by mail, direct deposit, or held in the office. The system can calculate the pay for each employee and have it delivered on a variety of schedules. Furthermore, all the data created and used by the system is persisted in a relational database.

In its current state, the system supports all the needs of our customer. In fact, it was put into production last week. It was installed on a computer in the Human Resources department, and Joe was trained to use it. Joe receives companywide requests to add new employees or change existing employees. He enters each request by adding the appropriate transaction text to a text file that is processed every night. Joe has been very grumpy recently, but he became very happy when he heard that we're going to build a user interface for the payroll system. This UI should make the payroll system easier to use. Joe is happy about this because everyone will be able to enter his or her own transactions instead of sending them to Joe to type into the transaction file.

Deciding what type of interface to build required a long discussion with the customer. One option proposed was a text-based interface whereby users would traverse menus, using keystrokes and entering data via the keyboard. Although text interfaces are easy to build, they can be less than easy to use. Besides, most users today consider them to be "clunky."

A Web interface was also considered. Web applications are great because they don't usually require any installation on the user's machines and can be used from any computer connected to the office intranet. But building Web interfaces is complicated because they appear to tie the application to a large and complex infrastructure of Web servers, application servers, and tiered architectures.[1] This infrastructure needs to be purchased, installed, configured, and administered. Web systems also tie us to such technologies as HTML, CSS, and JavaScript and force us into a somewhat stilted user model reminiscent of the 3270 green-screen applications of the 1970s.

Our users, and our company, wanted something simple to use, build, install, and administer. So in the end, we opted for a GUI desktop application. GUI desktop applications provide a more powerful set of UI functionality and can be less complicated to build than a Web interface. Our initial implementation won't be deployed over a network, so we won't need any of the complex infrastructure that Web systems seem to require.

Of course, desktop GUI applications have some disadvantages. They are not portable and are not easily distributed. However, since all the users of the payroll system work in the same office and use company computers, it was agreed that these disadvantages don't cost us as much as the Web architecture would. So we decided to use Windows Forms to build our UI.

Since UIs can be tricky, we'll limit our first release to adding employees. This first small release will give us some valuable feedback. First, we'll find out how complicated the UI is to build. Second, Joe will use the new UI and will tell us how much easier life is—we hope. Armed with this information, we will know better how to proceed to build

---

1. Or so it seems to the unwary software architect. In many unfortunate cases, this extra infrastructure provides much more benefit to the vendors than to the users.

the rest of the UI. It is also possible that the feedback from this first small release might suggest that a text-based or Web interface would be better. If that happens, it would be better to know before we invested effort in the whole application.

The form of the UI is less important than the internal architecture. Whether desktop or Web, UIs are usually volatile and tend to change more often than the business rules beneath them. Thus, it will behoove us to carefully separate the business logic from the user interface. Toward that end, we'll write as little code in the Windows Forms as possible. Instead, we'll put the code in plain C# classes that will work together with the Windows Forms. This separation strategy protects the business rules from the volatility of the UI. Changes to the UI code won't affect the business rules. Moreover, if one day we decide to switch to a Web interface, the business rule code will already have been separated.

The Interface

Figure 38-1 shows the general idea for the UI that we'll build. The menu named Action contains a list of all the supported actions. Selecting an action opens an appropriate form for creating the selected action. For example, Figure 38-2 shows the form that appears when Add Employee is selected. For the time being, Add Employee is the only action we're interested in.

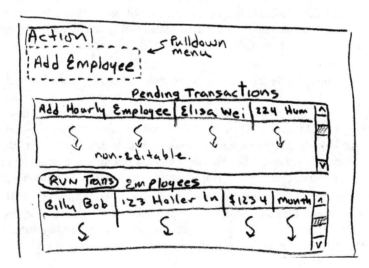

Figure 38-1
Initial payroll user interface

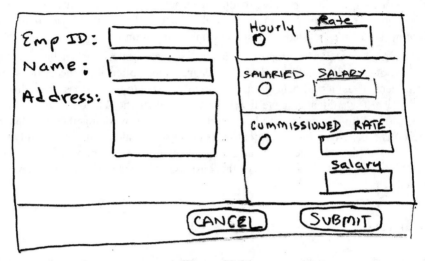

Figure 38-2
Add Employee transaction form

Near the top of the Payroll window is a text box labeled Pending Transactions. Payroll is a batch system. Transactions are entered throughout the day but are not executed until night, when they are all executed together as a batch. This top text box is a list of all the pending transaction that have been collected but not yet executed. In Figure 38-1 we can see that there is one pending transaction to add an hourly employee. The format of this list is readable, but we'll probably want to make it look prettier down the road. For now, this should do.

The bottom text box is labeled Employees and contains a list of employees who already exist in the system. Executing `AddEmployeeTransactions` will add more employees to this list. Again, we can imagine a much better way to display the employees. A tabular format would be nice. There could be a column for each bit a data, along with a column for the date of the last paycheck, amount paid to date, and so on. Records for hourly and commissioned employees would include a link to a new window that would list their time cards and sales receipts, respectively. That will have to wait, though.

In the middle is a button labeled Run Transactions, which does just as it suggests. Clicking it will invoke the batch, executing all the pending transactions and updating the employee list. Unfortunately, someone will have to click this button to initiate the batch. This is a temporary solution until we create an automatic schedule to do it.

Implementation

We can't get very far with the payroll window without being able to add transactions, so we'll start with the form to add an employee transaction, shown in Figure 38-2. Let's think about the business rules that have to be achieved through this window. We need to collect all the information to create a transaction. This can be achieved as the user fills out the form. Based on the information, we need to figure out what type of `AddEmployeeTransaction` to create and then put that transaction in the list to be processed later. This will all be triggered by a click of the Submit button.

That about covers it for the business rules, but we need other behaviors to make the UI more usable. The Submit button, for example, should remain disabled until all the required information is supplied. Also, the text box for hourly rate should be disabled unless the Hourly radio button is on. Likewise, the Salary, Base Salary, and Commission text boxes should remain disabled until the appropriate radio button is clicked.

We must be careful to separate the business behavior from the UI behavior. To do so, we'll use the MODEL VIEW PRESENTER design pattern. Figure 38-3 shows a UML design for how we'll use MODEL VIEW PRESENTER for our current task. You can see that the design has three components: the model, the view, and the presenter. The model in this case represents the `AddEmployeeTransaction` class and its derivatives. The view is a Windows Form called `AddEmployeeWindow`, shown in Figure 38-2. The presenter, a class called `AddEmployeePresenter`, glues the UI to the model. `AddEmployee-Presenter` contains all the business logic for this particular part of the application, whereas `AddEmployeeWindow` contains none. Instead, `AddEmployeeWindow` confines itself to the UI behavior, delegating all the business decisions to the presenter.

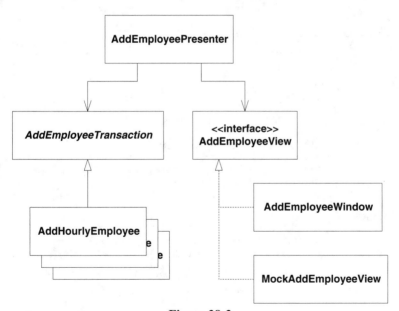

Figure 38-3
MODEL VIEW PRESENTER pattern for adding an employee transaction

An alternative to using MODEL VIEW PRESENTER is to push all the business logic into the Windows Form. In fact, this approach is very common but quite problematic. When the business rules are embedded in the UI code, not only do you have an SRP violation, but also the business rules are much more difficult to automatically test. Such tests would have to involve clicking buttons, reading labels, selecting items in a combo box, and fidgeting with other types of controls. In other words, in order to test the business rules, we'd have to actually *use* the UI. Tests that use the UI are fragile because minor changes to the UI controls have a large impact on the tests. They're also tricky because getting UIs in a test harness is a challenge in and of itself. Also, later down the road, we may decide that a Web interface is needed, and business logic embedded in the Windows form code would have to be duplicated in the ASP.NET code.

The observant reader will have noticed that the AddEmployeePresenter does not directly depend on the AddEmployeeWindow. The AddEmployeeView interface inverts the dependency. Why? Most simply, to make testing easier. Getting user interfaces under test is challenging. If AddEmployeePresenter was directly dependent upon AddEmployeeWindow, AddEmployeePresenterTest would also have to depend on AddEmployeeWindow, and that would be unfortunate. Using the interface and MockAddEmployeeView greatly simplifies testing.

Listing 38-1 and Listing 38-2 show the AddEmployeePresenterTest and Add-EmployeePresenter, respectively. This is where the story begins.

Listing 38-1

AddEmployeePresenterTest.cs

```
using NUnit.Framework;
using Payroll;

namespace PayrollUI
{
  [TestFixture]
  public class AddEmployeePresenterTest
  {
    private AddEmployeePresenter presenter;
    private TransactionContainer container;
    private InMemoryPayrollDatabase database;
    private MockAddEmployeeView view;

    [SetUp]
    public void SetUp()
    {
      view = new MockAddEmployeeView();
      container = new TransactionContainer(null);
      database = new InMemoryPayrollDatabase();
      presenter = new AddEmployeePresenter(
        view, container, database);
    }

    [Test]
    public void Creation()
```

Listing 38-1 (Continued)
`AddEmployeePresenterTest.cs`

```csharp
  {
    Assert.AreSame(container,
      presenter.TransactionContainer);
  }

  [Test]
  public void AllInfoIsCollected()
  {
    Assert.IsFalse(presenter.AllInformationIsCollected());
    presenter.EmpId = 1;
    Assert.IsFalse(presenter.AllInformationIsCollected());
    presenter.Name = "Bill";
    Assert.IsFalse(presenter.AllInformationIsCollected());
    presenter.Address = "123 abc";
    Assert.IsFalse(presenter.AllInformationIsCollected());
    presenter.IsHourly = true;
    Assert.IsFalse(presenter.AllInformationIsCollected());
    presenter.HourlyRate = 1.23;
    Assert.IsTrue(presenter.AllInformationIsCollected());

    presenter.IsHourly = false;
    Assert.IsFalse(presenter.AllInformationIsCollected());
    presenter.IsSalary = true;
    Assert.IsFalse(presenter.AllInformationIsCollected());
    presenter.Salary = 1234;
    Assert.IsTrue(presenter.AllInformationIsCollected());

    presenter.IsSalary = false;
    Assert.IsFalse(presenter.AllInformationIsCollected());
    presenter.IsCommission = true;
    Assert.IsFalse(presenter.AllInformationIsCollected());
    presenter.CommissionSalary = 123;
    Assert.IsFalse(presenter.AllInformationIsCollected());
    presenter.Commission = 12;
    Assert.IsTrue(presenter.AllInformationIsCollected());
  }

  [Test]
  public void ViewGetsUpdated()
  {
    presenter.EmpId = 1;
    CheckSubmitEnabled(false, 1);

    presenter.Name = "Bill";
    CheckSubmitEnabled(false, 2);

    presenter.Address = "123 abc";
    CheckSubmitEnabled(false, 3);

    presenter.IsHourly = true;
    CheckSubmitEnabled(false, 4);

    presenter.HourlyRate = 1.23;
    CheckSubmitEnabled(true, 5);
  }
```

Listing 38-1 (Continued)
AddEmployeePresenterTest.cs

```
    private void CheckSubmitEnabled(bool expected, int count)
    {
      Assert.AreEqual(expected, view.submitEnabled);
      Assert.AreEqual(count, view.submitEnabledCount);
      view.submitEnabled = false;
    }

    [Test]
    public void CreatingTransaction()
    {
      presenter.EmpId = 123;
      presenter.Name = "Joe";
      presenter.Address = "314 Elm";

      presenter.IsHourly = true;
      presenter.HourlyRate = 10;
      Assert.IsTrue(presenter.CreateTransaction()
        is AddHourlyEmployee);

      presenter.IsHourly = false;
      presenter.IsSalary = true;
      presenter.Salary = 3000;
      Assert.IsTrue(presenter.CreateTransaction()
        is AddSalariedEmployee);

      presenter.IsSalary = false;
      presenter.IsCommission = true;
      presenter.CommissionSalary = 1000;
      presenter.Commission = 25;
      Assert.IsTrue(presenter.CreateTransaction()
        is AddCommissionedEmployee);
    }

    [Test]
    public void AddEmployee()
    {
      presenter.EmpId = 123;
      presenter.Name = "Joe";
      presenter.Address = "314 Elm";
      presenter.IsHourly = true;
      presenter.HourlyRate = 25;

      presenter.AddEmployee();

      Assert.AreEqual(1, container.Transactions.Count);
      Assert.IsTrue(container.Transactions[0]
        is AddHourlyEmployee);
    }
  }
}
```

Listing 38-2
AddEmployeePresenter.cs

```csharp
using Payroll;

namespace PayrollUI
{
  public class AddEmployeePresenter
  {
    private TransactionContainer transactionContainer;
    private AddEmployeeView view;
    private PayrollDatabase database;

    private int empId;
    private string name;
    private string address;
    private bool isHourly;
    private double hourlyRate;
    private bool isSalary;
    private double salary;
    private bool isCommission;
    private double commissionSalary;
    private double commission;

    public AddEmployeePresenter(AddEmployeeView view,
      TransactionContainer container,
      PayrollDatabase database)
    {
      this.view = view;
      this.transactionContainer = container;
      this.database = database;
    }

    public int EmpId
    {
      get { return empId; }
      set
      {
        empId = value;
        UpdateView();
      }
    }

    public string Name
    {
      get { return name; }
      set
      {
        name = value;
        UpdateView();
      }
    }

    public string Address
    {
      get { return address; }
```

Listing 38-2 (Continued)

`AddEmployeePresenter.cs`

```csharp
      set
      {
        address = value;
        UpdateView();
      }
    }

    public bool IsHourly
    {
      get { return isHourly; }
      set
      {
        isHourly = value;
        UpdateView();
      }
    }

    public double HourlyRate
    {
      get { return hourlyRate; }
      set
      {
        hourlyRate = value;
        UpdateView();
      }
    }

    public bool IsSalary
    {
      get { return isSalary; }
      set
      {
        isSalary = value;
        UpdateView();
      }
    }

    public double Salary
    {
      get { return salary; }
      set
      {
        salary = value;
        UpdateView();
      }
    }

    public bool IsCommission
    {
      get { return isCommission; }
      set
      {
        isCommission = value;
        UpdateView();
      }
```

Listing 38-2 (Continued)
AddEmployeePresenter.cs

```csharp
  }

  public double CommissionSalary
  {
    get { return commissionSalary; }
    set
    {
      commissionSalary = value;
      UpdateView();
    }
  }

  public double Commission
  {
    get { return commission; }
    set
    {
      commission = value;
      UpdateView();
    }
  }

  private void UpdateView()
  {
    if(AllInformationIsCollected())
      view.SubmitEnabled = true;
    else
      view.SubmitEnabled = false;
  }

  public bool AllInformationIsCollected()
  {
    bool result = true;
    result &= empId > 0;
    result &= name != null && name.Length > 0;
    result &= address != null && address.Length > 0;
    result &= isHourly || isSalary || isCommission;
    if(isHourly)
      result &= hourlyRate > 0;
    else if(isSalary)
      result &= salary > 0;
    else if(isCommission)
    {
      result &= commission > 0;
      result &= commissionSalary > 0;
    }
    return result;
  }

  public TransactionContainer TransactionContainer
  {
    get { return transactionContainer; }
  }
```

```
Listing 38-2 (Continued)
AddEmployeePresenter.cs
      public virtual void AddEmployee()
      {
        transactionContainer.Add(CreateTransaction());
      }

      public Transaction CreateTransaction()
      {
        if(isHourly)
          return new AddHourlyEmployee(
            empId, name, address, hourlyRate, database);
        else if(isSalary)
          return new AddSalariedEmployee(
            empId, name, address, salary, database);
        else
          return new AddCommissionedEmployee(
            empId, name, address, commissionSalary,
            commission, database);
      }
    }
  }
```

Starting with the SetUp method of the test, we see what's involved in instantiating the AddEmployeePresenter. It takes three parameters. The first is an AddEmployee-View, for which we use a MockAddEmployeeView in the test. The second is a TransactionContainer so that it has a place to put the AddEmployeeTransaction that it will create. The last parameter is a PayrollDatabase instance that won't be used directly but is needed as a parameter to the AddEmployeeTransaction constructors.

The first test, Creation, is almost embarrassingly silly. When first sitting down to write code, it can be difficult to figure out what to test first. It often helps to test the simplest thing you can think of. Doing so gets the ball rolling, and subsequent tests come much more naturally. The Creation test is an artifact of this practice. It makes sure that the container parameter was saved, and it could probably be deleted at this point.

The next test, AllInfoIsCollected, is much more interesting. One of the responsibilities of the AddEmployeePresenter is to collect all the information required to create a transaction. Partial data won't do, so the presenter has to know when *all* the necessary data has been collected. This test says that the presenter needs a methods called AllInformationIsCollected, that returns a boolean value. The test also demonstrates how the presenter's data is entered through properties. Each piece of data is entered here one by one. At each step, the presenter is asked whether it has all the data it needs and asserts the expected response. In AddEmployeePresenter, we can see that each property simply stores the value in a field. AllInformationIsCollected does a bit of Boolean algebra as it checks that each field has been provided.

When the presenter has all the information it needs, the user may submit the data adding the transaction. But not until the presenter is content with the data provided should the user be able to submit the form. So it is the presenter's responsibility to inform the user when the form can be submitted. This is tested by the method `ViewGetsUpdated`. This test provides data, one piece at a time to the presenter. Each time, the test checks to make sure that the presenter properly informs the view whether submission should be enabled.

Looking in the presenter, we can see that each property makes a call to `UpdateView`, which in turn calls the `SaveEnabled` property on the view. Listing 38-3 shows the `AddEmployeeView` interface with `SubmitEnabled` declared. `AddEmployeePresenter` informs that submitting should be enabled by calling the `SubmitEnabled` property. Now we don't particularly care what `SubmitEnabled` does at this point. We simply want to make sure that it is called with the right value. This is where the `AddEmployeeView` interface comes in handy. It allows us to create a mock view to make testing easier. In `MockAddEmployeeView`, shown in Listing 38-4, there are two fields: `submitEnabled`, which records the last values passed in, and `submitEnabledCount`, which keeps track of how many times `SubmitEnabled` is invoked. These trivial fields make the test a breeze to write. All the test has to do is check the `submitEnabled` field to make sure that the presenter called the `SubmitEnabled` property with the right value and check `submitEnabledCount` to make sure that it was invoked the correct number of times. Imagine how awkward the test would have been if we had to dig into forms and window controls.

Listing 38-3
AddEmployeeView.cs

```
namespace PayrollUI
{
  public interface AddEmployeeView
  {
    bool SubmitEnabled { set; }
  }
}
```

Listing 38-4
MockAddEmployeeView.xs

```
namespace PayrollUI
{
  public class MockAddEmployeeView : AddEmployeeView
  {
    public bool submitEnabled;
    public int submitEnabledCount;

    public bool SubmitEnabled
    {
      set
      {
        submitEnabled = value;
        submitEnabledCount++;
      }
    }
  }
}
```

Something interesting happened in this test. We were careful to test how `AddEmployeePresenter` behaves when data is entered into the view rather than testing what happens when data is entered. In production, when all the data is entered, the Submit button will become enabled. We could have tested that; instead, we tested how the presenter behaves. We tested that when all the data is entered, the presenter will send a message to the view, telling it to enable submission.

This style of testing is called behavior-driven development. The idea is that you should not think of tests as tests, where you make assertions about state and results. Instead, you should think of tests as *specifications of behavior*, in which you describe how the code is supposed to behave.

The next test, `CreatingTransaction`, demonstrates that `AddEmployeePresenter` creates the proper transaction, based on the data provided. `AddEmployeePresenter` uses an `if/else` statement, based on the payment type, to figure out which type of transaction to create.

That leaves one more test, `AddEmployee`. When the all the data is collected and the transaction is created, the presenter must save the transaction in the `TransactionContainer` so that it can be used later. This test makes sure that this happens.

With `AddEmployeePresenter` implemented, we have all the business rules in place to create `AddEmployeeTransactions`. Now all we need is user interface.

Building a Window

Designing the Add Employee window GUI code was a breeze. With Visual Studio's designer, it's simply a matter of dragging some controls around to the right place. This code is generated for us and is not included in the following listings. Once the window is designed, we have more work to do. We need to implement some behavior in the UI and wire it to the presenter. We also need a test for it all. Listing 38-5 shows `AddEmployeeWindowTest`, and Listing 38-6 shows `AddEmployeeWindow`.

Listing 38-5
AddEmployeeWindowTest.cs

```
using NUnit.Framework;

namespace PayrollUI
{
  [TestFixture]
  public class AddEmployeeWindowTest
  {
    private AddEmployeeWindow window;
    private AddEmployeePresenter presenter;
    private TransactionContainer transactionContainer;

    [SetUp]
    public void SetUp()
    {
      window = new AddEmployeeWindow();
```

Listing 38-5 (Continued)
AddEmployeeWindowTest.cs

```
    transactionContainer = new TransactionContainer(null);
    presenter = new AddEmployeePresenter(
      window, transactionContainer, null);

    window.Presenter = presenter;
    window.Show();
  }

  [Test]
  public void StartingState()
  {
    Assert.AreSame(presenter, window.Presenter);
    Assert.IsFalse(window.submitButton.Enabled);
    Assert.IsFalse(window.hourlyRateTextBox.Enabled);
    Assert.IsFalse(window.salaryTextBox.Enabled);
    Assert.IsFalse(window.commissionSalaryTextBox.Enabled);
    Assert.IsFalse(window.commissionTextBox.Enabled);
  }

  [Test]
  public void PresenterValuesAreSet()
  {
    window.empIdTextBox.Text = "123";
    Assert.AreEqual(123, presenter.EmpId);

    window.nameTextBox.Text = "John";
    Assert.AreEqual("John", presenter.Name);

    window.addressTextBox.Text = "321 Somewhere";
    Assert.AreEqual("321 Somewhere", presenter.Address);

    window.hourlyRateTextBox.Text = "123.45";
    Assert.AreEqual(123.45, presenter.HourlyRate, 0.01);

    window.salaryTextBox.Text = "1234";
    Assert.AreEqual(1234, presenter.Salary, 0.01);

    window.commissionSalaryTextBox.Text = "123";
    Assert.AreEqual(123, presenter.CommissionSalary, 0.01);

    window.commissionTextBox.Text = "12.3";
    Assert.AreEqual(12.3, presenter.Commission, 0.01);

    window.hourlyRadioButton.PerformClick();
    Assert.IsTrue(presenter.IsHourly);

    window.salaryRadioButton.PerformClick();
    Assert.IsTrue(presenter.IsSalary);
    Assert.IsFalse(presenter.IsHourly);

    window.commissionRadioButton.PerformClick();
    Assert.IsTrue(presenter.IsCommission);
    Assert.IsFalse(presenter.IsSalary);
  }
```

Listing 38-5 (Continued)
AddEmployeeWindowTest.cs

```
   [Test]
   public void EnablingHourlyFields()
   {
     window.hourlyRadioButton.Checked = true;
     Assert.IsTrue(window.hourlyRateTextBox.Enabled);

     window.hourlyRadioButton.Checked = false;
     Assert.IsFalse(window.hourlyRateTextBox.Enabled);
   }

   [Test]
   public void EnablingSalaryFields()
   {
     window.salaryRadioButton.Checked = true;
     Assert.IsTrue(window.salaryTextBox.Enabled);

     window.salaryRadioButton.Checked = false;
     Assert.IsFalse(window.salaryTextBox.Enabled);
   }

   [Test]
   public void EnablingCommissionFields()
   {
     window.commissionRadioButton.Checked = true;
     Assert.IsTrue(window.commissionTextBox.Enabled);
     Assert.IsTrue(window.commissionSalaryTextBox.Enabled);

     window.commissionRadioButton.Checked = false;
     Assert.IsFalse(window.commissionTextBox.Enabled);
     Assert.IsFalse(window.commissionSalaryTextBox.Enabled);
   }

   [Test]
   public void EnablingAddEmployeeButton()
   {
     Assert.IsFalse(window.submitButton.Enabled);

     window.SubmitEnabled = true;
     Assert.IsTrue(window.submitButton.Enabled);

     window.SubmitEnabled = false;
     Assert.IsFalse(window.submitButton.Enabled);
   }

   [Test]
   public void AddEmployee()
   {
     window.empIdTextBox.Text = "123";
     window.nameTextBox.Text = "John";
     window.addressTextBox.Text = "321 Somewhere";
     window.hourlyRadioButton.Checked = true;
     window.hourlyRateTextBox.Text = "123.45";

     window.submitButton.PerformClick();
```

Listing 38-5 (Continued)

`AddEmployeeWindowTest.cs`

```
      Assert.IsFalse(window.Visible);
      Assert.AreEqual(1,
        transactionContainer.Transactions.Count);
    }
  }
}
```

Listing 38-6

`AddEmployeeWindow.cs`

```csharp
using System;
using System.Windows.Forms;

namespace PayrollUI
{
  public class AddEmployeeWindow : Form, AddEmployeeView
  {
    public System.Windows.Forms.TextBox empIdTextBox;
    private System.Windows.Forms.Label empIdLabel;
    private System.Windows.Forms.Label nameLabel;
    public System.Windows.Forms.TextBox nameTextBox;
    private System.Windows.Forms.Label addressLabel;
    public System.Windows.Forms.TextBox addressTextBox;
    public System.Windows.Forms.RadioButton hourlyRadioButton;
    public System.Windows.Forms.RadioButton salaryRadioButton;
    public System.Windows.Forms.RadioButton commissionRadioButton;
    private System.Windows.Forms.Label hourlyRateLabel;
    public System.Windows.Forms.TextBox hourlyRateTextBox;
    private System.Windows.Forms.Label salaryLabel;
    public System.Windows.Forms.TextBox salaryTextBox;
    private System.Windows.Forms.Label commissionSalaryLabel;
    public System.Windows.Forms.TextBox commissionSalaryTextBox;
    private System.Windows.Forms.Label commissionLabel;
    public System.Windows.Forms.TextBox commissionTextBox;
    private System.Windows.Forms.TextBox textBox2;
    private System.Windows.Forms.Label label1;
    private System.ComponentModel.Container components = null;
    public System.Windows.Forms.Button submitButton;
    private AddEmployeePresenter presenter;

    public AddEmployeeWindow()
    {
      InitializeComponent();
    }

    protected override void Dispose( bool disposing )
    {
      if( disposing )
      {
        if(components != null)
        {
          components.Dispose();
        }
      }
      base.Dispose( disposing );
```

Listing 38-6 (Continued)
AddEmployeeWindow.cs

```csharp
        }

    #region Windows Form Designer generated code
    // snip
    #endregion

    public AddEmployeePresenter Presenter
    {
      get { return presenter; }
      set { presenter = value; }
    }

    private void hourlyRadioButton_CheckedChanged(
      object sender, System.EventArgs e)
    {
      hourlyRateTextBox.Enabled = hourlyRadioButton.Checked;
      presenter.IsHourly = hourlyRadioButton.Checked;
    }

    private void salaryRadioButton_CheckedChanged(
      object sender, System.EventArgs e)
    {
      salaryTextBox.Enabled = salaryRadioButton.Checked;
      presenter.IsSalary = salaryRadioButton.Checked;
    }

    private void commissionRadioButton_CheckedChanged(
      object sender, System.EventArgs e)
    {
      commissionSalaryTextBox.Enabled =
        commissionRadioButton.Checked;
      commissionTextBox.Enabled =
        commissionRadioButton.Checked;
      presenter.IsCommission =
        commissionRadioButton.Checked;
    }

    private void empIdTextBox_TextChanged(
      object sender, System.EventArgs e)
    {
      presenter.EmpId = AsInt(empIdTextBox.Text);
    }

    private void nameTextBox_TextChanged(
      object sender, System.EventArgs e)
    {
      presenter.Name = nameTextBox.Text;
    }

    private void addressTextBox_TextChanged(
      object sender, System.EventArgs e)
    {
      presenter.Address = addressTextBox.Text;
    }
```

Listing 38-6 (Continued)

AddEmployeeWindow.cs

```csharp
    private void hourlyRateTextBox_TextChanged(
      object sender, System.EventArgs e)
    {
      presenter.HourlyRate = AsDouble(hourlyRateTextBox.Text);
    }

    private void salaryTextBox_TextChanged(
      object sender, System.EventArgs e)
    {
      presenter.Salary = AsDouble(salaryTextBox.Text);
    }

    private void commissionSalaryTextBox_TextChanged(
      object sender, System.EventArgs e)
    {
      presenter.CommissionSalary =
        AsDouble(commissionSalaryTextBox.Text);
    }

    private void commissionTextBox_TextChanged(
      object sender, System.EventArgs e)
    {
      presenter.Commission = AsDouble(commissionTextBox.Text);
    }

    private void addEmployeeButton_Click(
      object sender, System.EventArgs e)
    {
      presenter.AddEmployee();
      this.Close();
    }

    private double AsDouble(string text)
    {
      try
      {
        return Double.Parse(text);
      }
      catch (Exception)
      {
        return 0.0;
      }
    }

    private int AsInt(string text)
    {
      try
      {
        return Int32.Parse(text);
      }
      catch (Exception)
      {
        return 0;
      }
    }
```

Listing 38-6 (Continued)

AddEmployeeWindow.cs

```
    public bool SubmitEnabled
    {
      set { submitButton.Enabled = value; }
    }
  }
}
```

Despite all my griping about how painful it is to test GUI code, testing Windows Form code is relatively easy. There are some pitfalls, however. For some silly reason, known only to programmers at Microsoft, half of the functionality of the controls does not work unless they are *displayed* on the screen. It is for this reason that you'll find the call window.Show() in the SetUp of the test fixture. When the tests are executed, you can see the window appearing and quickly disappearing for each test. This is annoying but bearable. Anything that slows down the tests or otherwise makes them clumsy makes it more likely that the tests will not be run.

Another limitation is that you cannot easily invoke all the events on a control. With buttons and buttonlike controls, you can call PerformClick, but events such as MouseOver, Leave, Validate, and others are not so easy. An extension for NUnit, called NUnitForms, can help with these problems and more. Our tests are simple enough to get by without extra help.

In the SetUp of our test, we create an instance of AddEmployeeWindow and give it an instance of AddEmployeePresenter. Then in the first test, StartingState, we make sure that several controls are disabled: hourlyRateTextBox, salaryTextBox, commissionSalaryTextBox, and commissionTextBox. Only one or two of these fields are needed, and we don't know which ones until the user chooses the payment type. To avoid confusing the user by leaving all the fields enabled, they'll remain disabled until needed. The rules for enabling these controls are specified in three tests: EnablingHourlyFields, EnablingSalaryField, and EnablingCommission-Fields. EnablingHourlyFields, for example, demonstrates how the hourly-RateTextBox is enabled when the hourlyRadioButton is turned on and disabled when the radio button is turned off. This is achieved by registering an EventHandler with each RadioButton. Each EventHandler enables and disables the appropriate text boxes.

The test, PresenterValuesAreSet, is an important one. The presenter know what to do with the data, but it's the view's responsibility to populate the data. Therefore, whenever a field in the view is changed, it calls the corresponding property on the presenter. For each TextBox in the form, we use the Text property to change the value and then check to make sure that the presenter is properly updated. In AddEmployeeWindow, each TextBox has an EventHandler registered on the TextChanged event. For the RadioButton controls, we call the PerformClick method in the test and again make sure that the presenter is informed. The RadioButton's EventHandlers take care of this.

`EnablingAddEmployeeButton` specifies how the `submitButton` is enabled when the `SubmitEnabled` property is set to `true`, and reverse. Remember that in `AddEmployeePresenterTest`, we didn't care what this property did. Now we do care. The view must respond properly when the `SubmitEnabled` property is changed; however, `AddEmployeePresenterTest` was not the right place to test it. `AddEmployee-WindowTest` focuses on the behavior of the `AddEmployeeWindow`, and it *is* the right place to test this unit of code.

The final test here is `AddEmployee`, which fills in a valid set of fields, clicks the Submit button, asserts that the window is no longer visible, and makes sure that a transaction was added to the `transactionContainer`. To make this pass, we register an `EventHandler`, on the `submitButton`, that calls `AddEmployee` on the presenter and then closes the window. If you think about it, the test is doing a lot of work just to make sure that the `AddEmployee` method was called. It has to populate all the fields and then check the `transactionContainer`. Some might argue that instead, we should use a mock presenter so we can easily check that the method was called. To be honest, I wouldn't put up a fight if my pair partner were to bring it up. But the current implementation doesn't bother me too much. It's healthy to include a few high-level tests like this. They help to make sure that the pieces can be integrated properly and that the system works the way it should when put together. Normally, we'd have a suite of acceptance tests that do this at an even higher level, but it doesn't hurt to do it a bit in the unit tests—just a bit, though.

With this code in place, we now have a working form for creating `AddEmployee-Transactions`. But it won't get used until we have the main Payroll window working and wired up to load our `AddEmployeeWindow`.

The Payroll Window

In building the Payroll view, shown in Figure 38-4, we'll use the same MODEL VIEW PRESENTER pattern used in the Add Employee view.

Listings 38-7 and 38-8 show all the code in this part of the design. Altogether, the development of this view is very similar to that of the Add Employee view. For that reason, we will not pay it much attention. Of particular note, however, is the `ViewLoader` hierarchy.

Sooner or later in developing this window, we'll get around to implementing an `EventHandler` for the Add Employee `MenuItem`. This `EventHandler` will call the `AddEmployeeActionInvoked` method on `PayrollPresenter`. At this point, the `AddEmployeeWindow` needs to pop up. Is `PayrollPresenter` supposed to instantiate `AddEmployeeWindow`? So far, we have done well to decouple the UI from the application. Were it to instantiate the `AddEmployeeWindow`, `PayrollPresenter` would be violating DIP. Yet someone must create `AddEmployeeWindow`.

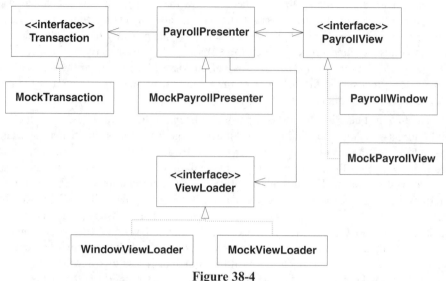

Figure 38-4
Design of the Payroll view

FACTORY pattern to the rescue! This is the exact problem that FACTORY was designed to solve. ViewLoader, and its derivatives, are in fact an implementation of the FACTORY pattern. It declares two methods: LoadPayrollView and LoadAddEmployeeView. WindowsViewLoader implements these methods to create Windows Forms and display them. The MockViewLoader, which can easily replace the WindowsViewLoader, makes testing much easier.

With the ViewLoader in place, PayrollPresenter need not depend on any Windows form classes. It simply makes a call to the LoadAddEmployeeView on its reference to ViewLoader. If the need ever arises, we can change the whole user interface for Payroll by swapping the ViewLoader implementation. No code needs to change. That's power! That's OCP!

Listing 38-7
PayrollPresenterTest.cs

```
using System;
using NUnit.Framework;
using Payroll;

namespace PayrollUI
{
  [TestFixture]
  public class PayrollPresenterTest
  {
    private MockPayrollView view;
    private PayrollPresenter presenter;
    private PayrollDatabase database;
```

Listing 38-7 (Continued)

`PayrollPresenterTest.cs`

```csharp
    private MockViewLoader viewLoader;

    [SetUp]
    public void SetUp()
    {
      view = new MockPayrollView();
      database = new InMemoryPayrollDatabase();
      viewLoader = new MockViewLoader();
      presenter = new PayrollPresenter(database, viewLoader);
      presenter.View = view;
    }

    [Test]
    public void Creation()
    {
      Assert.AreSame(view, presenter.View);
      Assert.AreSame(database, presenter.Database);
      Assert.IsNotNull(presenter.TransactionContainer);
    }

    [Test]
    public void AddAction()
    {
      TransactionContainer container =
        presenter.TransactionContainer;
      Transaction transaction = new MockTransaction();

      container.Add(transaction);

      string expected = transaction.ToString()
        + Environment.NewLine;
      Assert.AreEqual(expected, view.transactionsText);
    }

    [Test]
    public void AddEmployeeAction()
    {
      presenter.AddEmployeeActionInvoked();

      Assert.IsTrue(viewLoader.addEmployeeViewWasLoaded);
    }

    [Test]
    public void RunTransactions()
    {
      MockTransaction transaction = new MockTransaction();
      presenter.TransactionContainer.Add(transaction);
      Employee employee =
        new Employee(123, "John", "123 Baker St.");
      database.AddEmployee(employee);

      presenter.RunTransactions();

      Assert.IsTrue(transaction.wasExecuted);
```

Listing 38-7 (Continued)

PayrollPresenterTest.cs

```
        Assert.AreEqual("", view.transactionsText);
        string expectedEmployeeTest = employee.ToString()
          + Environment.NewLine;
        Assert.AreEqual(expectedEmployeeTest, view.employeesText);
    }
  }
}
```

Listing 38-8

PayrollPresenter.cs

```
using System;
using System.Text;
using Payroll;

namespace PayrollUI
{
  public class PayrollPresenter
  {
    private PayrollView view;
    private readonly PayrollDatabase database;
    private readonly ViewLoader viewLoader;
    private TransactionContainer transactionContainer;

    public PayrollPresenter(PayrollDatabase database,
      ViewLoader viewLoader)
    {
      this.view = view;
      this.database = database;
      this.viewLoader = viewLoader;
      TransactionContainer.AddAction addAction =
        new TransactionContainer.AddAction(TransactionAdded);
      transactionContainer = new TransactionContainer(addAction);
    }

    public PayrollView View
    {
      get { return view; }
      set { view = value; }
    }

    public TransactionContainer TransactionContainer
    {
      get { return transactionContainer; }
    }

    public void TransactionAdded()
    {
      UpdateTransactionsTextBox();
    }

    private void UpdateTransactionsTextBox()
    {
      StringBuilder builder = new StringBuilder();
```

Listing 38-8 (Continued)
PayrollPresenter.cs

```csharp
      foreach(Transaction transaction in
        transactionContainer.Transactions)
      {
        builder.Append(transaction.ToString());
        builder.Append(Environment.NewLine);
      }
      view.TransactionsText = builder.ToString();
    }

    public PayrollDatabase Database
    {
      get { return database; }
    }

    public virtual void AddEmployeeActionInvoked()
    {
      viewLoader.LoadAddEmployeeView(transactionContainer);
    }

    public virtual void RunTransactions()
    {
      foreach(Transaction transaction in
        transactionContainer.Transactions)
        transaction.Execute();

      transactionContainer.Clear();
      UpdateTransactionsTextBox();
      UpdateEmployeesTextBox();
    }

    private void UpdateEmployeesTextBox()
    {
      StringBuilder builder = new StringBuilder();
      foreach(Employee employee in database.GetAllEmployees())
      {
        builder.Append(employee.ToString());
        builder.Append(Environment.NewLine);
      }
      view.EmployeesText = builder.ToString();
    }
  }
}
```

Listing 38-9
PayrollView.cs

```csharp
namespace PayrollUI
{
  public interface PayrollView
  {
    string TransactionsText { set; }

    string EmployeesText { set; }
```

Listing 38-9 (Continued)

PayrollView.cs

```
    PayrollPresenter Presenter { set; }
  }
}
```

Listing 38-10

MockPayrollView.cs

```
namespace PayrollUI
{
  public class MockPayrollView : PayrollView
  {
    public string transactionsText;
    public string employeesText;
    public PayrollPresenter presenter;

    public string TransactionsText
    {
      set { transactionsText = value; }
    }

    public string EmployeesText
    {
      set { employeesText = value; }
    }

    public PayrollPresenter Presenter
    {
      set { presenter = value; }
    }

  }
}
```

Listing 38-11

ViewLoader.cs

```
namespace PayrollUI
{
  public interface ViewLoader
  {
    void LoadPayrollView();
    void LoadAddEmployeeView(
      TransactionContainer transactionContainer);
  }
}
```

Listing 38-12

MockViewLoader.cs

```
namespace PayrollUI
{
  public class MockViewLoader : ViewLoader
```

Listing 38-12 (Continued)
MockViewLoader.cs

```
  {
    public bool addEmployeeViewWasLoaded;
    private bool payrollViewWasLoaded;

    public void LoadPayrollView()
    {
      payrollViewWasLoaded = true;
    }

    public void LoadAddEmployeeView(
      TransactionContainer transactionContainer)
    {
      addEmployeeViewWasLoaded = true;
    }
  }
}
```

Listing 38-13
WindowViewLoaderTest.cs

```
using System.Windows.Forms;
using NUnit.Framework;
using Payroll;

namespace PayrollUI
{
  [TestFixture]
  public class WindowViewLoaderTest
  {
    private PayrollDatabase database;
    private WindowViewLoader viewLoader;

    [SetUp]
    public void SetUp()
    {
      database = new InMemoryPayrollDatabase();
      viewLoader = new WindowViewLoader(database);
    }

    [Test]
    public void LoadPayrollView()
    {
      viewLoader.LoadPayrollView();

      Form form = viewLoader.LastLoadedView;
      Assert.IsTrue(form is PayrollWindow);
      Assert.IsTrue(form.Visible);

      PayrollWindow payrollWindow = form as PayrollWindow;
      PayrollPresenter presenter = payrollWindow.Presenter;
      Assert.IsNotNull(presenter);
      Assert.AreSame(form, presenter.View);
    }
```

Listing 38-13 (Continued)

WindowViewLoaderTest.cs

```
    [Test]
    public void LoadAddEmployeeView()
    {
      viewLoader.LoadAddEmployeeView(
        new TransactionContainer(null));

      Form form = viewLoader.LastLoadedView;
      Assert.IsTrue(form is AddEmployeeWindow);
      Assert.IsTrue(form.Visible);

      AddEmployeeWindow addEmployeeWindow =
        form as AddEmployeeWindow;
      Assert.IsNotNull(addEmployeeWindow.Presenter);
    }
  }
}
```

Listing 38-14

WindowViewLoader.cs

```
using System.Windows.Forms;
using Payroll;

namespace PayrollUI
{
  public class WindowViewLoader : ViewLoader
  {
    private readonly PayrollDatabase database;
    private Form lastLoadedView;

    public WindowViewLoader(PayrollDatabase database)
    {
      this.database = database;
    }

    public void LoadPayrollView()
    {
      PayrollWindow view = new PayrollWindow();
      PayrollPresenter presenter =
        new PayrollPresenter(database, this);

      view.Presenter = presenter;
      presenter.View = view;

      LoadView(view);
    }

    public void LoadAddEmployeeView(
      TransactionContainer transactionContainer)
    {
      AddEmployeeWindow view = new AddEmployeeWindow();
      AddEmployeePresenter presenter =
        new AddEmployeePresenter(view,
          transactionContainer, database);
```

Listing 38-14 (Continued)
WindowViewLoader.cs

```
        view.Presenter = presenter;

        LoadView(view);
    }

    private void LoadView(Form view)
    {
        view.Show();
        lastLoadedView = view;
    }

    public Form LastLoadedView
    {
        get { return lastLoadedView; }
    }
    }
}
```

Listing 38-15
PayrollWindowTest.cs

```
using NUnit.Framework;

namespace PayrollUI
{
    [TestFixture]
    public class PayrollWindowTest
    {
        private PayrollWindow window;
        private MockPayrollPresenter presenter;

        [SetUp]
        public void SetUp()
        {
            window = new PayrollWindow();
            presenter = new MockPayrollPresenter();
            window.Presenter = this.presenter;
            window.Show();
        }

        [TearDown]
        public void TearDown()
        {
            window.Dispose();
        }

        [Test]
        public void TransactionsText()
        {
            window.TransactionsText = "abc 123";
            Assert.AreEqual("abc 123",
                window.transactionsTextBox.Text);
        }
```

Listing 38-15 (Continued)
`PayrollWindowTest.cs`

```
    [Test]
    public void EmployeesText()
    {
      window.EmployeesText = "some employee";
      Assert.AreEqual("some employee",
        window.employeesTextBox.Text);
    }

    [Test]
    public void AddEmployeeAction()
    {
      window.addEmployeeMenuItem.PerformClick();
      Assert.IsTrue(presenter.addEmployeeActionInvoked);
    }

    [Test]
    public void RunTransactions()
    {
      window.runButton.PerformClick();
      Assert.IsTrue(presenter.runTransactionCalled);
    }
  }
}
```

Listing 38-16
`PayrollWinow.cs`

```
namespace PayrollUI
{
  public class PayrollWindow : System.Windows.Forms.Form,
                               PayrollView
  {
    private System.Windows.Forms.MainMenu mainMenu1;
    private System.Windows.Forms.Label label1;
    private System.Windows.Forms.Label employeeLabel;
    public System.Windows.Forms.TextBox employeesTextBox;
    public System.Windows.Forms.TextBox transactionsTextBox;
    public System.Windows.Forms.Button runButton;
    private System.ComponentModel.Container components = null;
    private System.Windows.Forms.MenuItem actionMenuItem;
    public System.Windows.Forms.MenuItem addEmployeeMenuItem;
    private PayrollPresenter presenter;

    public PayrollWindow()
    {
      InitializeComponent();
    }

    protected override void Dispose( bool disposing )
    {
      if( disposing )
      {
        if(components != null)
        {
```

Listing 38-16 (Continued)

PayrollWinow.cs

```
            components.Dispose();
          }
        }
        base.Dispose( disposing );
      }

      #region Windows Form Designer generated code
      //snip
      #endregion

      private void addEmployeeMenuItem_Click(
        object sender, System.EventArgs e)
      {
        presenter.AddEmployeeActionInvoked();
      }

      private void runButton_Click(
        object sender, System.EventArgs e)
      {
        presenter.RunTransactions();
      }

      public string TransactionsText
      {
        set { transactionsTextBox.Text = value; }
      }

      public string EmployeesText
      {
        set { employeesTextBox.Text = value; }
      }

      public PayrollPresenter Presenter
      {
        get { return presenter; }
        set { presenter = value; }
      }

    }
  }
```

Listing 38-17

TransactionContainerTest.cs

```
using System.Collections;
using NUnit.Framework;
using Payroll;

namespace PayrollUI
{
  [TestFixture]
  public class TransactionContainerTest
  {
    private TransactionContainer container;
```

Listing 38-17 (Continued)

`TransactionContainerTest.cs`

```csharp
      private bool addActionCalled;
      private Transaction transaction;

      [SetUp]
      public void SetUp()
      {
        TransactionContainer.AddAction action =
          new TransactionContainer.AddAction(SillyAddAction);
        container = new TransactionContainer(action);
        transaction = new MockTransaction();
      }

      [Test]
      public void Construction()
      {
        Assert.AreEqual(0, container.Transactions.Count);
      }

      [Test]
      public void AddingTransaction()
      {
        container.Add(transaction);

        IList transactions = container.Transactions;
        Assert.AreEqual(1, transactions.Count);
        Assert.AreSame(transaction, transactions[0]);
      }

      [Test]
      public void AddingTransactionTriggersDelegate()
      {
        container.Add(transaction);

        Assert.IsTrue(addActionCalled);
      }

      private void SillyAddAction()
      {
        addActionCalled = true;
      }
    }
  }
```

Listing 38-18

`TransactionContainer.cs`

```csharp
using Payroll;

namespace PayrollUI
{
  public class TransactionContainer
  {
    public delegate void AddAction();
```

Listing 38-18 (Continued)
TransactionContainer.cs

```
    private IList transactions = new ArrayList();
    private AddAction addAction;

    public TransactionContainer(AddAction action)
    {
      addAction = action;
    }

    public IList Transactions
    {
      get { return transactions; }
    }

    public void Add(Transaction transaction)
    {
      transactions.Add(transaction);
      if(addAction != null)
        addAction();
    }

    public void Clear()
    {
      transactions.Clear();
    }
  }
}
```

The Unveiling

A lot of work has gone into this payroll application, and at last we'll see it come alive with its new graphical user interface. Listing 38-19 contains the PayrollMain class, the entry point for the application. Before we can load the Payroll view, we need an instance of the database. In this code listing, an InMemoryPayrollDatabase is being created. This is for demonstration purposes. In production, we'd create an SqlPayrollDatabase that would link up to our SQL Server database. But the application will happily run with the InMemoryPayrollDatabase while all the data is saved in memory and loaded in memory.

Next, an instance of WindowViewLoader is created. LoadPayrollView is called, and the application is started. We can now compile, run it, and add as many employees to the system as we like.

Listing 38-19
PayrollMain.cs

```
using System.Windows.Forms;
using Payroll;

namespace PayrollUI
```

Listing 38-19 (Continued)
`PayrollMain.cs`

```
{
  public class PayrollMain
  {
    public static void Main(string[] args)
    {
      PayrollDatabase database =
        new InMemoryPayrollDatabase();
      WindowViewLoader viewLoader =
        new WindowViewLoader(database);

      viewLoader.LoadPayrollView();
      Application.Run(viewLoader.LastLoadedView);
    }
  }
}
```

Conclusion

Joe will be happy to see what we've done for him. We'll build a production release and let him try it out. Surely he'll have comments about how the user interface is crude and unpolished. There will be quirks that slow him down or aspects that he finds confusing. User interfaces are difficult to get right. So we'll pay close attention to his feedback and go back for another round. Next, we'll add actions to change employee details. Then we'll add actions to submit time cards and sales receipts. Finally we'll handle payday. This is all left to you, of course.

Bibliography

http://daveastels.com/index.php?p=5

www.martinfowler.com/eaaDev/ModelViewPresenter.html

http://nunitforms.sourceforge.net/

www.objectmentor.com/resources/articles/TheHumbleDialogBox.pdf

Appendix A

A Satire of Two Companies

I've got a good mind to join a club and beat you over the head with it!

—Rufus T. Firefly

Rufus Inc.: Project Kickoff

Your name is Bob. The date is January 3, 2001, and your head still aches from the recent millennial revelry. You are sitting in a conference room with several managers and a group of your peers. You are a project team leader. Your boss is there, and he has brought along all of his team leaders. His boss called the meeting.

"We have a new project to develop," says your boss's boss. Call him BB. The points in his hair are so long that they scrape the ceiling. Your boss's points are just starting to grow, but he eagerly awaits the day when he can leave Brylcream stains on the acoustic tiles. BB describes

Rupert Industries: Project Alpha

Your name is Robert. The date is January 3, 2001. The quiet hours spent with your family this holiday have left you refreshed and ready for work. You are sitting in a conference room with your team of professionals. The manager of the division called the meeting.

"We have some ideas for a new project," says the division manager. Call him Russ. He is a high-strung British chap with more energy than a fusion reactor. He is ambitious and driven but understands the value of a team.

Russ describes the essence of the new market opportunity the company has

the essence of the new market they have identified and the product they want to develop to exploit this market.

"We must have this new project up and working by fourth quarter—October 1," BB demands. "Nothing is of higher priority, so we are canceling your current project."

The reaction in the room is stunned silence. Months of work are simply going to be thrown away. Slowly, a murmur of objection begins to circulate around the conference table.

His points give off an evil green glow as BB meets the eyes of everyone in the room. One by one, that insidious stare reduces each attendee to quivering lumps of protoplasm. It is clear that he will brook no discussion on this matter.

Once silence has been restored, BB says, "We need to begin immediately. How long will it take you to do the analysis?"

You raise your hand. Your boss tries to stop you, but his spitwad misses you and you are unaware of his efforts.

"Sir, we can't tell you how long the analysis will take until we have some requirements."

"The requirements document won't be ready for 3 or 4 weeks," BB says, his points vibrating with frustration. "So, *pretend* that you have the requirements in front of you now. How long will you require for analysis?"

No one breathes. Everyone looks around to see whether anyone has some idea.

"If analysis goes beyond April 1, we have a problem. Can you finish the analysis by then?"

identified and introduces you to Jane, the marketing manager, who is responsible for defining the products that will address it.

Addressing you, Jane says, "We'd like to start defining our first product offering as soon as possible. When can you and your team meet with me?"

You reply, "We'll be done with the current iteration of our project this Friday. We can spare a few hours for you between now and then. After that, we'll take a few people from the team and dedicate them to you. We'll begin hiring their replacements and the new people for your team immediately."

"Great," says Russ, "but I want you to understand that it is critical that we have something to exhibit at the trade show coming up this July. If we can't be there with something significant, we'll lose the opportunity."

"I understand," you reply. "I don't yet know what it is that you have in mind, but I'm sure we can have something by July. I just can't tell you what that something will be right now. In any case, you and Jane are going to have complete control over what we developers do, so you can rest assured that by July, you'll have the most important things that can be accomplished in that time ready to exhibit."

Russ nods in satisfaction. He knows how this works. Your team has always kept him advised and allowed him to steer their development. He has the utmost confidence that your team will work on the most important things first and will produce a high-quality product.

* * *

"So, Robert," says Jane at their first meeting, "How does your team feel about being split up?"

Your boss visibly gathers his courage: "We'll find a way, sir!" His points grow 3 mm, and your headache increases by two Tylenol.

"Good." BB smiles. "Now, how long will it take to do the design?"

"Sir," you say. Your boss visibly pales. He is clearly worried that his 3 mms are at risk. "Without an analysis, it will not be possible to tell you how long design will take."

BB's expression shifts beyond austere. "*PRETEND* you have the analysis already!" he says, while fixing you with his vacant, beady little eyes. "How long will it take you to do the design?"

Two Tylenol are not going to cut it. Your boss, in a desperate attempt to save his new growth, babbles: "Well, sir, with only six months left to complete the project, design had better take no longer than 3 months."

"I'm glad you agree, Smithers!" BB says, beaming. Your boss relaxes. He knows his points are secure. After a while, he starts lightly humming the Brylcream jingle.

BB continues, "So, analysis will be complete by April 1, design will be complete by July 1, and that gives you 3 months to implement the project. This meeting is an example of how well our new consensus and empowerment policies are working. Now, get out there and start working. I'll expect to see TQM plans and QIT assignments on my desk by next week. Oh, and don't forget that your cross-functional team meetings and reports will be needed for next month's quality audit."

"We'll miss working with each other," you answer, *"but some of us were getting pretty tired of that last project and are looking forward to a change. So, what are you people cooking up?"*

Jane beams. "You know how much trouble our customers currently have . . ." And she spends a half hour or so describing the problem and possible solution.

"OK, wait a second" you respond. "I need to be clear about this." And so you and Jane talk about how this system might work. Some of her ideas aren't fully formed. You suggest possible solutions. She likes some of them. You continue discussing.

During the discussion, as each new topic is addressed, Jane writes user story cards. Each card represents something that the new system has to do. The cards accumulate on the table and are spread out in front of you. Both you and Jane point at them, pick them up, and make notes on them as you discuss the stories. The cards are powerful mnemonic devices that you can use to represent complex ideas that are barely formed.

At the end of the meeting, you say, "OK, I've got a general idea of what you want. I'm going to talk to the team about it. I imagine they'll want to run some experiments with various database structures and presentation formats. Next time we meet, it'll be as a group, and we'll start identifying the most important features of the system."

A week later, your nascent team meets with Jane. They spread the existing user story cards out on the table and begin to get into some of the details of the system.

"Forget the Tylenol," you think to yourself as you return to your cubicle. "I need bourbon."

Visibly excited, your boss comes over to you and says, "Gosh, what a great meeting. I think we're really going to do some world shaking with this project." You nod in agreement, too disgusted to do anything else.

"Oh," your boss continues, "I almost forgot." He hands you a 30-page document. "Remember that the SEI is coming to do an evaluation next week. This is the evaluation guide. You need to read through it, memorize it, and then shred it. It tells you how to answer any questions that the SEI auditors ask you. It also tells you what parts of the building you are allowed to take them to and what parts to avoid. We are determined to be a CMM level 3 organization by June!"

* * *

You and your peers start working on the analysis of the new project. This is difficult because you have no requirements. But from the 10-minute introduction given by BB on that fateful morning, you have some idea of what the product is supposed to do.

Corporate process demands that you begin by creating a use case document. You and your team begin enumerating use cases and drawing oval and stick diagrams.

Philosophical debates break out among the team members. There is disagreement as to whether certain use cases should be connected with <<extends>> or <<includes>> relationships. Competing models are created, but nobody knows how to evaluate them. The debate continues, effectively paralyzing progress.

The meeting is very dynamic. Jane presents the stories in the order of their importance. There is much discussion about each one. The developers are concerned about keeping the stories small enough to estimate and test. So they continually ask Jane to split one story into several smaller stories. Jane is concerned that each story have a clear business value and priority, so as she splits them, she makes sure that this stays true.

The stories accumulate on the table. Jane writes them, but the developers make notes on them as needed. Nobody tries to capture everything that is said; the cards are not meant to capture everything but are simply reminders of the conversation.

As the developers become more comfortable with the stories, they begin writing estimates on them. These estimates are crude and budgetary, but they give Jane an idea of what the story will cost.

At the end of the meeting, it is clear that many more stories could be discussed. It is also clear that the most important stories have been addressed and that they represent several months worth of work. Jane closes the meeting by taking the cards with her and promising to have a proposal for the first release in the morning.

* * *

The next morning, you reconvene the meeting. Jane chooses five cards and places them on the table.

"According to your estimates, these cards represent about one perfect team-week's worth of work. The last iteration of the previous project managed to get one perfect team-week done in 3 real weeks. If we can get these five stories done in 3

After a week, somebody finds the iceberg.com Web site, which recommends disposing entirely of <<extends>> and <<includes>> and replacing them with <<precedes>> and <<uses>>. The documents on this Web site, authored by Don Sengroiux, describes a method known as stalwart-analysis, which claims to be a step-by-step method for translating use cases into design diagrams.

More competing use case models are created using this new scheme, but again, people can't agree on how to evaluate them. The thrashing continues.

More and more, the use case meetings are driven by emotion rather than by reason. If it weren't for the fact that you don't have requirements, you'd be pretty upset by the lack of progress you are making.

The requirements document arrives on February 15. And then again on February 20, 25, and every week thereafter. Each new version contradicts the previous one. Clearly, the marketing folks who are writing the requirements, empowered though they might be, are not finding consensus.

At the same time, several new competing use case templates have been proposed by the various team members. Each template presents its own particularly creative way of delaying progress. The debates rage on.

On March 1, Prudence Putrigence, the process proctor, succeeds in integrating all the competing use case forms and templates into a single, all-encompassing form. Just the blank form is 15 pages long. She has managed to include every field that appeared on all the competing templates. She also presents a 159-page document describing how to fill out the use

weeks, we'll be able to demonstrate them to Russ. That will make him feel very comfortable about our progress."

Jane is pushing it. The sheepish look on her face lets you know that she knows it too. You reply, "Jane, this is a new team, working on a new project. It's a bit presumptuous to expect that our velocity will be the same as the previous team's. However, I met with the team yesterday afternoon, and we all agreed that our initial velocity should, in fact, be set to one perfect-week for every 3 real-weeks. So you've lucked out on this one."

"Just remember," you continue, "that the story estimates and the story velocity are very tentative at this point. We'll learn more when we plan the iteration and even more when we implement it."

Jane looks over her glasses at you as if to say "Who's the boss around here, anyway?" and then smiles and says, "Yeah, don't worry. I know the drill by now."

Jane then puts 15 more cards on the table. She says, "If we can get all these cards done by the end of March, we can turn the system over to our beta test customers. And we'll get good feedback from them."

You reply, "OK, so we've got our first iteration defined, and we have the stories for the next three iterations after that. These four iterations will make our first release."

"So," says Jane, can you really do these five stories in the next 3 weeks?"

"I don't know for sure, Jane," you reply. "Let's break them down into tasks and see what we get."

So Jane, you, and your team spend the next several hours taking each of the five case form. All current use cases must be rewritten according to the new standard.

You marvel to yourself that it now requires 15 pages of fill-in-the-blank and essay questions to answer the question: What should the system do when the user presses Return?

The corporate process (authored by L. E. Ott, famed author of "Holistic Analysis: A Progressive Dialectic for Software Engineers") insists that you discover all primary use cases, 87 percent of all secondary use cases, and 36.274 percent of all tertiary use cases before you can complete analysis and enter the design phase. You have no idea what a tertiary use case is. So in an attempt to meet this requirement, you try to get your use case document reviewed by the marketing department, which you hope will know what a tertiary use case is.

Unfortunately, the marketing folks are too busy with sales support to talk to you. Indeed, since the project started, you have not been able to get a single meeting with marketing, which has provided a never-ending stream of changing and contradictory requirements documents.

While one team has been spinning endlessly on the use case document, another team has been working out the domain model. Endless variations of UML documents are pouring out of this team. Every week, the model is reworked. The team members can't decide whether to use <<interfaces>> or <<types>> in the model. A huge disagreement has been raging on the proper syntax and application of OCL. Others on the team just got back from a 5-day class on catabolism, and have been producing incredibly detailed and arcane diagrams that nobody else can fathom.

stories that Jane chose for the first iteration and breaking them down into small tasks. The developers quickly realize that some of the tasks can be shared between stories and that other tasks have commonalities that can probably be taken advantage of. It is clear that potential designs are popping into the developers' heads. From time to time, they form little discussion knots and scribble UML diagrams on some cards.

Soon, the whiteboard is filled with the tasks that, once completed, will implement the five stories for this iteration. You start the sign-up process by saying, "OK, let's sign up for these tasks."

"I'll take the initial database generation." says Pete. "That's what I did on the last project, and this doesn't look very different. I estimate it at two of my perfect workdays."

"OK, well, then, I'll take the login screen," says Joe.

"Aw, darn," says Elaine, the junior member of the team, "I've never done a GUI, and I kinda wanted to try that one."

"Ah, the impatience of youth," Joe says sagely, with a wink in your direction. "You can assist me with it, young Jedi." To Jane: "I think it'll take me about three of my perfect workdays."

One by one, the developers sign up for tasks and estimate them in terms of their own perfect workdays. Both you and Jane know that it is best to let the developers volunteer for tasks than to assign the tasks to them. You also know full well that you daren't challenge any of the developers' estimates. You know these people, and you trust them. You know that they are going to do the very best they can.

On March 27, with one week to go before analysis is to be complete, you have produced a sea of documents and diagrams but are no closer to a cogent analysis of the problem than you were on January 3.

* * *

And then, a miracle happens.

* * *

On Saturday, April 1, you check your e-mail from home. You see a memo from your boss to BB. It states unequivocally that you are done with the analysis!

You phone your boss and complain. "How could you have told BB that we were done with the analysis?"

"Have you looked at a calendar lately?" he responds. "It's April 1!"

The irony of that date does not escape you. "But we have so much more to think about. So much more to analyze! We haven't even decided whether to use <<extends>> or <<precedes>>!"

"Where is your evidence that you are not done?" inquires your boss, impatiently.

"Whaaa . . . ."

But he cuts you off. "Analysis can go on forever; it has to be stopped at some point. And since this is the date it was scheduled to stop, it has been stopped. Now, on Monday, I want you to gather up all existing analysis materials and put them into a public folder. Release that folder to Prudence so that she can log it in the CM system by Monday afternoon. Then get busy and start designing."

As you hang up the phone, you begin to consider the benefits of keeping a bottle of bourbon in your bottom desk drawer.

* * *

The developers know that they can't sign up for more perfect workdays than they finished in the last iteration they worked on. Once each developer has filled his or her schedule for the iteration, they stop signing up for tasks.

Eventually, all the developers have stopped signing up for tasks. But, of course, tasks are still left on the board.

"I was worried that that might happen," you say, "OK, there's only one thing to do, Jane. We've got too much to do in this iteration. What stories or tasks can we remove?"

Jane sighs. She knows that this is the only option. Working overtime at the beginning of a project is insane, and projects where she's tried it have not fared well.

So Jane starts to remove the least-important functionality. "Well, we really don't need the login screen just yet. We can simply start the system in the logged-in state."

"Rats!" cries Elaine. "I really wanted to do that."

"Patience, grasshopper." says Joe. "Those who wait for the bees to leave the hive will not have lips too swollen to relish the honey."

Elaine looks confused.

Everyone looks confused.

"So . . . ," Jane continues, "I think we can also do away with . . ."

And so, bit by bit, the list of tasks shrinks. Developers who lose a task sign up for one of the remaining ones.

The negotiation is not painless. Several times, Jane exhibits obvious frustration and impatience. Once, when tensions

They threw a party to celebra,e the on-time completion of the analysis phase. BB gave a colon-stirring speech on empowerment. And your boss, another 3 mm taller, congratulated his team on the incredible show of unity and teamwork. Finally, the CIO takes the stage to tell everyone that the SEI audit went very well and to thank everyone for studying and shredding the evaluation guides that were passed out. Level 3 now seems assured and will be awarded by June. (Scuttlebutt has it that managers at the level of BB and above are to receive significant bonuses once the SEI awards level 3.)

As the weeks flow by, you and your team work on the design of the system. Of course, you find that the analysis that the design is supposedly based on is flawed—no, useless; no, worse than useless. But when you tell your boss that you need to go back and work some more on the analysis to shore up its weaker sections, he simply states, "The analysis phase is over. The only allowable activity is design. Now get back to it."

So, you and your team hack the design as best you can, unsure of whether the requirements have been properly analyzed. Of course, it really doesn't matter much, since the requirements document is still thrashing with weekly revisions, and the marketing department still refuses to meet with you.

The design is a nightmare. Your boss recently misread a book named *The Finish Line* in which the author, Mark DeThomaso, blithely suggested that design documents should be taken down to code-level detail.

are especially high, Elaine volunteers, "I'll work extra hard to make up some of the missing time." You are about to correct her when, fortunately, Joe looks her in the eye and says, "When once you proceed down the dark path, forever will it dominate your destiny."

In the end, an iteration acceptable to Jane is reached. It's not what Jane wanted. Indeed, it is significantly less. But it's something the team feels that can be achieved in the next 3 weeks. And, after all, it still addresses the most important things that Jane wanted in the iteration.

"So, Jane," you say when things had quieted down a bit, "when can we expect acceptance tests from you?"

Jane sighs. This is the other side of the coin. For every story the development team implements, Jane must supply a suite of acceptance tests that prove that it works. And the team needs these long before the end of the iteration, since they will certainly point out differences in the way Jane and the developers imagine the system's behavior.

"I'll get you some example test scripts today," Jane promises. "I'll add to them every day after that. You'll have the entire suite by the middle of the iteration."

* * *

The iteration begins on Monday morning with a flurry of Class, Responsibilities, Collaborators sessions. By mid-morning, all the developers have assembled into pairs and are rapidly coding away.

"And now, my young apprentice," Joe says to Elaine, "you shall learn the mysteries of test-first design!"

"If we are going to be working at that level of detail," you ask, "why don't we simply write the code instead?"

"Because then you wouldn't be designing, of course. And the only allowable activity in the design phase is design!"

"Besides," he continues, "we have just purchased a companywide license for Dandelion! This tool enables 'Round the Horn Engineering!' You are to transfer all design diagrams into this tool. It will automatically generate our code for us! It will also keep the design diagrams in sync with the code!"

Your boss hands you a brightly colored shrink-wrapped box containing the Dandelion distribution. You accept it numbly and shuffle off to your cubicle. Twelve hours, eight crashes, one disk reformatting, and eight shots of 151 later, you finally have the tool installed on your server. You consider the week your team will lose while attending Dandelion training. Then you smile and think, "Any week I'm not here is a good week."

Design diagram after design diagram is created by your team. Dandelion makes it very difficult to draw these diagrams. There are dozens and dozens of deeply nested dialog boxes with funny text fields and check boxes that must all be filled in correctly. And then there's the problem of moving classes between packages.

At first, these diagram are driven from the use cases. But the requirements are changing so often that the use cases rapidly become meaningless.

Debates rage about whether VISITOR or DECORATOR design patterns should be used. One developer refuses to use VISITOR in any form, claiming that it's not a

"Wow, that sounds pretty rad," Elaine replies. "How do you do it?"

Joe beams. It's clear that he has been anticipating this moment. "OK, what does the code do right now?"

"Huh?" replied Elaine, "It doesn't do anything at all; there is no code."

"So, consider our task; can you think of something the code should do?"

"Sure," Elaine said with youthful assurance, "First, it should connect to the database."

"And thereupon, what must needs be required to connecteth the database?"

"You sure talk weird," laughed Elaine. "I think we'd have to get the database object from some registry and call the Connect() *method.*

"Ah, astute young wizard. Thou perceivest correctly that we requireth an object within which we can cacheth the database object."

"Is 'cacheth' really a word?"

"It is when I say it! So, what test can we write that we know the database registry should pass?"

Elaine sighs. She knows she'll just have to play along. "We should be able to create a database object and pass it to the registry in a Store() *method. And then we should be able to pull it out of the registry with a* Get() *method and make sure it's the same object."*

"Oh, well said, my prepubescent sprite!"

"Hay!"

"So, now, let's write a test function that proves your case."

properly object-oriented construct. Some-one refuses to use multiple inheritance, since it is the spawn of the devil.

Review meetings rapidly degenerate into debates about the meaning of object orientation, the definition of analysis versus design, or when to use aggregation versus association.

Midway through the design cycle, the marketing folks announce that they have rethought the focus of the system. Their new requirements document is completely restructured. They have eliminated several major feature areas and replaced them with feature areas that they anticipate customer surveys will show to be more appropriate.

You tell your boss that these changes mean that you need to reanalyze and redesign much of the system. But he says, "The analysis phase is over. The only allowable activity is design. Now get back to it."

You suggest that it might be better to create a simple prototype to show to the marketing folks and even some potential customers. But your boss says, "The analysis phase is over. The only allowable activity is design. Now get back to it."

Hack, hack, hack, hack. You try to create some kind of a design document that might reflect the new requirements documents. However, the revolution of the requirements has not caused them to stop thrashing. Indeed, if anything, the wild oscillations of the requirements document have only increased in frequency and amplitude. You slog your way through them.

On June 15, the Dandelion database gets corrupted. Apparently, the corruption has been progressive. Small errors in the

"But shouldn't we write the database object and registry object first?"

"Ah, you've much to learn, my young impatient one. Just write the test first."

"But it won't even compile!"

"Are you sure? What if it did?"

"Uh . . ."

"Just write the test, Elaine. Trust me." And so Joe, Elaine, and all the other developers began to code their tasks, one test case at a time. The room in which they worked was abuzz with the conversations between the pairs. The murmur was punctuated by an occasional high five when a pair managed to finish a task or a difficult test case.

As development proceeded, the developers changed partners once or twice a day. Each developer got to see what all the others were doing, and so knowledge of the code spread generally throughout the team.

Whenever a pair finished something significant—whether a whole task or simply an important part of a task—they integrated what they had with the rest of the system. Thus, the code base grew daily, and integration difficulties were minimized.

The developers communicated with Jane on a daily basis. They'd go to her whenever they had a question about the functionality of the system or the interpretation of an acceptance test case.

Jane, good as her word, supplied the team with a steady stream of acceptance test scripts. The team read these carefully and thereby gained a much better understanding of what Jane expected the system to do.

By the beginning of the second week, there was enough functionality to demon-

DB accumulated over the months into bigger and bigger errors. Eventually, the CASE tool just stopped working. Of course, the slowly encroaching corruption is present on all the backups.

Calls to the Dandelion technical support line go unanswered for several days. Finally, you receive a brief e-mail from Dandelion, informing you that this is a known problem and that the solution is to purchase the new version, which they promise will be ready some time next quarter, and then reenter all the diagrams by hand.

* * *

Then, on July 1 another miracle happens! You are done with the design!

Rather than go to your boss and complain, you stock your middle desk drawer with some vodka.

* * *

They threw a party to celebrate the on-time completion of the design phase and their graduation to CMM level 3. This time, you find BB's speech so stirring that you have to use the restroom before it begins.

New banners and plaques are all over your workplace. They show pictures of eagles and mountain climbers, and they talk about teamwork and empowerment. They read better after a few scotches. That reminds you that you need to clear out your file cabinet to make room for the brandy.

You and your team begin to code. But you rapidly discover that the design is lacking in some significant areas. Actually, it's lacking any significance at all. You convene a design session in one of the conference rooms to try to work through some of the nastier problems. But your

strate to Jane. She watched eagerly as the demonstration passed test case after test case.

"This is really cool," Jane said as the demonstration finally ended. "But this doesn't seem like one-third of the tasks. Is your velocity slower than anticipated?"

You grimace. You'd been waiting for a good time to mention this to Jane but now she was forcing the issue.

"Yes, unfortunately, we are going more slowly than we had expected. The new application server we are using is turning out to be a pain to configure. Also, it takes forever to reboot, and we have to reboot it whenever we make even the slightest change to its configuration."

Jane eyes you with suspicion. The stress of last Monday's negotiations had still not entirely dissipated. She says, "And what does this mean to our schedule? We can't slip it again, we just can't. Russ will have a fit! He'll haul us all into the woodshed and ream us some new ones."

You look Jane right in the eyes. There's no pleasant way to give someone news like this. So you just blurt out, "Look, if things keep going like they're going, we're not going to be done with everything by next Friday. Now it's possible that we'll figure out a way to go faster. But, frankly, I wouldn't depend on that. You should start thinking about one or two tasks that could be removed from the iteration without ruining the demonstration for Russ. Come hell or high water, we are going to give that demonstration on Friday, and I don't think you want us to choose which tasks to omit."

"Aw for—chrisakes!" Jane barely manages to stifle yelling that last word as she stalks away, shaking her head.

boss catches you at it and disbands the meeting, saying, "The design phase is over. The only allowable activity is coding. Now get back to it."

The code generated by Dandelion is really hideous. It turns out that you and your team were using association and aggregation the wrong way, after all. All the generated code has to be edited to correct these flaws. Editing this code is extremely difficult because it has been instrumented with ugly comment blocks that have special syntax that Dandelion needs in order to keep the diagrams in sync with the code. If you accidentally alter one of these comments, the diagrams will be regenerated incorrectly. It turns out that "Round the Horn Engineering" requires an awful lot of effort.

The more you try to keep the code compatible with Dandelion, the more errors Dandelion generates. In the end, you give up and decide to keep the diagrams up to date manually. A second later, you decide that there's no point in keeping the diagrams up to date at all. Besides, who has time?

Your boss hires a consultant to build tools to count the number of lines of code that are being produced. He puts a big thermometer graph on the wall with the number 1,000,000 on the top. Every day, he extends the red line to show how many lines have been added.

Three days after the thermometer appears on the wall, your boss stops you in the hall. "That graph isn't growing quickly enough. We need to have a million lines done by October 1."

"We aren't even sh-sh-sure that the proshect will require a m-million linezh," you blather.

Not for the first time, you say to yourself, "Nobody ever promised me project management would be easy." You are pretty sure it won't be the last time, either.

* * *

Actually, things went a bit better than you had hoped. The team did, in fact, have to drop one task from the iteration, but Jane had chosen wisely, and the demonstration for Russ went without a hitch.

Russ was not impressed with the progress, but neither was he dismayed. He simply said, "This is pretty good. But remember, we have to be able to demonstrate this system at the trade show in July, and at this rate, it doesn't look like you'll have all that much to show."

Jane, whose attitude had improved dramatically with the completion of the iteration, responded to Russ by saying, "Russ, this team is working hard, and well. When July comes around, I am confident that we'll have something significant to demonstrate. It won't be everything, and some of it may be smoke and mirrors, but we'll have something."

Painful though the last iteration was, it had calibrated your velocity numbers. The next iteration went much better. Not because your team got more done than in the last iteration but simply because the team didn't have to remove any tasks or stories in the middle of the iteration.

By the start of the fourth iteration, a natural rhythm has been established. Jane, you, and the team know exactly what to expect from one another. The team is running hard, but the pace is sustainable. You are confident that the team can keep up this pace for a year or more.

"We have to have a million lines done by October 1," your boss reiterates. His points have grown again, and the Grecian formula he uses on them creates an aura of authority and competence. "Are you sure your comment blocks are big enough?"

Then, in a flash of managerial insight, he says, "I have it! I want you to institute a new policy among the engineers. No line of code is to be longer than 20 characters. Any such line must be split into two or more—preferably more. All existing code needs to be reworked to this standard. That'll get our line count up!"

You decide not to tell him that this will require two unscheduled work months. You decide not to tell him anything at all. You decide that intravenous injections of pure ethanol are the only solution. You make the appropriate arrangements.

Hack, hack, hack, and hack. You and your team madly code away. By August 1, your boss, frowning at the thermometer on the wall, institutes a mandatory 50-hour workweek.

Hack, hack, hack, and hack. By September 1st, the thermometer is at 1.2 million lines and your boss asks you to write a report describing why you exceeded the coding budget by 20 percent. He institutes mandatory Saturdays and demands that the project be brought back down to a million lines. You start a campaign of re-merging lines.

Hack, hack, hack, and hack. Tempers are flaring; people are quitting; QA is raining trouble reports down on you. Customers are demanding installation and user manuals; salespeople are demanding advance demonstrations for special customers; the requirements document is still

The number of surprises in the schedule diminishes to near zero; however, the number of surprises in the requirements does not. Jane and Russ frequently look over the growing system and make recommendations or changes to the existing functionality. But all parties realize that these changes take time and must be scheduled. So the changes do not cause anyone's expectations to be violated.

In March, there is a major demonstration of the system to the board of directors. The system is very limited and is not yet in a form good enough to take to the trade show, but progress is steady, and the board is reasonably impressed.

The second release goes even more smoothly than the first. By now, the team has figured out a way to automate Jane's acceptance test scripts. The team has also refactored the design of the system to the point that it is really easy to add new features and change old ones.

The second release was done by the end of June and was taken to the trade show. It had less in it than Jane and Russ would have liked, but it did demonstrate the most important features of the system. Although customers at the trade show noticed that certain features were missing, they were very impressed overall. You, Russ, and Jane all returned from the trade show with smiles on your faces. You all felt as though this project was a winner.

Indeed, many months later, you are contacted by Rufus Inc. That company had been working on a system like this for its internal operations. Rufus has canceled the development of that system after a death-march project and is negotiating to license your technology for its environment.

Indeed, things are looking up!

thrashing, the marketing folks are complaining that the product isn't anything like they specified, and the liquor store won't accept your credit card anymore. Something has to give. On September 15, BB calls a meeting.

As he enters the room, his points are emitting clouds of steam. When he speaks, the bass overtones of his carefully manicured voice cause the pit of your stomach to roll over. "The QA manager has told me that this project has less than 50 percent of the required features implemented. He has also informed me that the system crashes all the time, yields wrong results, and is hideously slow. He has also complained that he cannot keep up with the continuous train of daily releases, each more buggy than the last!"

He stops for a few seconds, visibly trying to compose himself. "The QA manager estimates that, at this rate of development, we won't be able to ship the product until December!"

Actually, you think it's more like March, but you don't say anything.

"December!" BB roars with such derision that people duck their heads as though he were pointing an assault rifle at them. "December is absolutely out of the question. Team leaders, I want new estimates on my desk in the morning. I am hereby mandating 65-hour work weeks until this project is complete. And it better be complete by November 1."

As he leaves the conference room, he is heard to mutter: "Empowerment—bah!"

* * *

Your boss is bald; his points are mounted on BB's wall. The fluorescent lights reflecting off his pate momentarily dazzle you.

"Do you have anything to drink?" he asks. Having just finished your last bottle of Boone's Farm, you pull a bottle of Thunderbird from your bookshelf and pour it into his coffee mug. "What's it going to take to get this project done?" he asks.

"We need to freeze the requirements, analyze them, design them, and then implement them," you say callously.

"By November 1?" your boss exclaims incredulously. "No way! Just get back to coding the damned thing." He storms out, scratching his vacant head.

A few days later, you find that your boss has been transferred to the corporate research division. Turnover has skyrocketed. Customers, informed at the last minute that their orders cannot be fulfilled on time, have begun to cancel their orders. Marketing is reevaluating whether this product aligns with the overall goals of the company. Memos fly, heads roll, policies change, and things are, overall, pretty grim.

Finally, by March, after far too many sixty-five-hour weeks, a very shaky version of the software is ready. In the field, bug-discovery rates are high, and the technical support staff are at their wits' end, trying to cope with the complaints and demands of the irate customers. Nobody is happy.

In April, BB decides to buy his way out of the problem by licensing a product produced by Rupert Industries and redistributing it. The customers are mollified, the marketing folks are smug, and you are laid off.

Appendix B

What Is Software?

I can still remember where I was when I had the insight that eventually led to the following article. In the summer of 1986 I was working a temporary consulting assignment at the China Lake Naval Weapons Center in California. While there, I took the opportunity to attend a panel discussion on Ada. At one point, someone in the audience asked the typical question "Are software developers engineers?" I don't remember the actual answer, but I do recall that it didn't really seem to address the question. So I sat back and started thinking about how I would answer such a question. I am not sure how, but something in the ensuing discussion caused me to recall an article I had read in *Datamation* magazine almost 10 years before that. That article had been a rationale for why engineers needed to be good writers (I think that is what it was about—it has been a long time), but the key point I got from the article was the author's contention that the end result of an engineering process was a document. In other words, engineers produced documents, not things. Other people took those documents and produced things. So, my wandering mind asked the question, "Out of all the documentation that software projects normally generate, was there anything that could truly be considered an engineering document?" The answer that came to me was yes there was such a document, and only one—the source code.[1]

Looking at the source code as an engineering document—a design—turned my view of my chosen profession upside down. It changed the way I looked at everything. Also, the more I thought about it, the more I felt that it explained an awful lot of the problems that software projects typically encountered. Or rather, I felt that the fact that most people did not understand this distinction, or actively rejected it, explained a lot of things. Several more years went by before the opportunity presented itself for me to make my argument

---

1. Jack Reeves, "What Is Software Design?" *C++ Journal*, 2(2), 1992: Reprinted with permission. ©Jack W. Reeves 1992.

publicly. An article about software design in *The C++ Journal* prompted me to write a letter to the editor about the topic. After an exchange of letters, Livleen Singh, the editor, agreed to publish my thoughts on the topic as an article. What follows is the result.

***

—Jack Reeves, December 22, 2001

Object oriented techniques, and C++ in particular, seem to be taking the software world by storm. Numerous articles and books have appeared describing how to apply the new techniques. In general, the questions of whether O-O techniques are just hype have been replaced by questions of how to get the benefits with the least amount of pain. Object oriented techniques have been around for some time, but this exploding popularity seems a bit unusual. Why the sudden interest? All kinds of explanations have been offered. In truth, there is probably no single reason. Probably, a combination of factors has finally reached critical mass and things are taking off. Nevertheless, it seems that C++ itself is a major factor in this latest phase of the software revolution. Again, there are probably a number of reasons why, but I want to suggest an answer from a slightly different perspective: C++ has become popular because it makes it easier to design software and program at the same time.

If that comment seems a bit unusual, it is deliberate. What I want to do in this article is take a look at the relationship between programming and software design. For almost 10 years I have felt that the software industry collectively misses a subtle point about the difference between developing a software design and what a software design really is. I think there is a profound lesson in the growing popularity of C++ about what we can do to become better software engineers, if only we see it. This lesson is that programming is not about building software; programming is about designing software.

Years ago I was attending a seminar where the question came up of whether software development is an engineering discipline or not. While I do not remember the resulting discussion, I do remember how it catalyzed my own thinking that the software industry has created some false parallels with hardware engineering while missing some perfectly valid parallels. In essence, I concluded that we are not software engineers because we do not realize what a software design really is. I am even more convinced of that today.

The final goal of any engineering activity is the some type of documentation. When a design effort is complete, the design documentation is turned over to the manufacturing team. This is a completely different group with completely different skills from the design team. If the design documents truly represent a complete design, the manufacturing team can proceed to build the product. In fact, they can proceed to build lots of the product, all without any further intervention of the designers. After reviewing the software development life cycle as I understood it, I concluded that the only software documentation that actually seems to satisfy the criteria of an engineering design is the source code listings.

There are probably enough arguments both for and against this premise to fill numerous articles. This article assumes that final source code is the real software design and then examines some of the consequences of that assumption. I may not be able to prove that this point of view is correct, but I hope to show that it does explain some of the observed facts of the software industry, including the popularity of C++.

There is one consequence of considering code as software design that completely overwhelms all others. It is so important and so obvious that it is a total blind spot for most software organizations. This is the fact that software is cheap to build. It does not qualify as inexpensive; it is so cheap it is almost free. If source code is a software design, then actually building software is done by compilers and linkers. We often refer to the process of compiling and linking a complete software system as "doing a build." The capital investment in software construction equipment is low—all it really takes is a computer, an editor, a compiler, and a linker. Once a build environment is available, then actually doing a software build just takes a little time. Compiling a 50,000 line C++ program may seem to take forever, but how long would it take to build a hardware system that had a design of the same complexity as 50,000 lines of C++?

Another consequence of considering source code as software design is the fact that a software design is relatively easy to create, at least in the mechanical sense. Writing (i.e., designing) a typical software module of 50 to 100 lines of code is usually only a couple of day's effort (getting it fully debugged is another story, but more on that later). It is tempting to ask if there is any other engineering discipline that can produce designs of such complexity as software in such a short time, but first we have to figure out how to measure and compare complexity. Nevertheless, it is obvious that software designs get very large rather quickly.

Given that software designs are relatively easy to turn out, and essentially free to build, an unsurprising revelation is that software designs tend to be incredibly large and complex. This may seem obvious but the magnitude of the problem is often ignored. School projects often end up being several thousand lines of code. There are software products with 10,000 line designs that are given away by their designers. We have long since passed the point where simple software is of much interest. Typical commercial software products have designs that consist of hundreds of thousands of lines. Many software designs run into the millions. Additionally, software designs are almost always constantly evolving. While the current design may only be a few thousand lines of code, many times that may actually have been written over the life of the product.

While there are certainly examples of hardware designs that are arguably as complex as software designs, note two facts about modern hardware. One, complex hardware engineering efforts are not always as free of bugs as software critics would have us believe. Major microprocessors have been shipped with errors in their logic, bridges collapsed, dams broken, airliners fallen out of the sky, and thousands of automobiles and other consumer products have been recalled—all within recent memory and all the result of design errors. Second, complex hardware designs have correspondingly complex and expensive build phases. As a result, the ability to manufacture such systems limits the number of companies that produce truly complex hardware designs. No such limitations exist for software. There are hundreds of software organizations, and thousands of very complex software systems in existence. Both the number and the complexity are growing daily. This means that the software industry is not likely to find solutions to its problems by trying to emulate hardware developers. If anything, as CAD and CAM systems have helped hardware designers to create more and more complex designs, hardware engineering is becoming more and more like software development.

Designing software is an exercise in managing complexity. The complexity exists within the software design itself, within the software organization of the company, and within the industry as a whole. Software design is very similar to systems design. It can span multiple technologies and often involves multiple sub-disciplines. Software specifications tend to be fluid, and change rapidly and often, usually while the design process is still going on. Software development teams also tend to be fluid, likewise often changing in the middle of the design process. In many ways, software bears more resemblance to complex social or organic systems than to hardware. All of this makes software design a difficult and error prone process. None of this is original thinking, but almost 30 years after the software engineering revolution began, software development is still seen as an undisciplined art compared to other engineering professions.

The general consensus is that when real engineers get through with a design, no matter how complex, they are pretty sure it will work. They are also pretty sure it can be built using accepted construction techniques. In order for this to happen, hardware engineers spend a considerable amount of time validating and refining their designs. Consider a bridge design, for example. Before such a design is actually built the engineers do structural analysis; they build computer models and run simulations; they build scale models and test them in wind tunnels or other ways. In short, the designers do everything they could think of to make sure the design is a good design before it is built. The design of new airliner is even worse; for those, full scale prototypes must be built and test flown to validate the design predictions.

It seems obvious to most people that software designs do not go through the same rigorous engineering as hardware designs. However, if we consider source code as design, we see that software designers actually do a considerable amount of validating and refining their designs. Software designers do not call it engineering, however, we call it testing and debugging. Most people do not consider testing and debugging as real "engineering"; certainly not in the software business. The reason has more to do with the refusal of the software industry to accept code as design than with any real engineering difference. Mock-ups, prototypes, and bread-boards are actually an accepted part of other engineering disciplines. Software designers do not have or use more formal methods of validating their designs because of the simple economics of the software build cycle.

Revelation number two: it is cheaper and simpler to just build the design and test it than to do anything else. We do not care how many builds we do—they cost next to nothing in terms of time and the resources used can be completely reclaimed later if we discard the build. Note that testing is not just concerned with getting the current design correct, it is part of the process of refining the design. Hardware engineers of complex systems often build models (or at least they visually render their designs using computer graphics). This allows them to get a "feel" for the design that is not possible by just reviewing the design itself. Building such a model is both impossible and unnecessary with a software design. We just build the product itself. Even if formal software proofs were as automatic as a compiler, we would still do build/test cycles. Ergo, formal proofs have never been of much practical interest to the software industry.

This is the reality of the software development process today. Ever more complex software designs are being created by an ever increasing number of people and organizations. These designs will be coded in some programming language and then validated and refined via the build/test cycle. The process is error prone and not particularly rigorous to begin with. The fact that a great many software developers do not want to believe that this is the way it works compounds the problem enormously.

Most current software development processes try to segregate the different phases of software design into separate pigeon-holes. The top level design must be completed and frozen before any code is written. Testing and debugging are necessary just to weed out the construction mistakes. In between are the programmers, the construction workers of the software industry. Many believe that if we could just get programmers to quit "hacking" and "build" the designs as given to them (and in the process, make fewer errors) then software development might mature into a true engineering discipline. Not likely to happen as long as the process ignores the engineering and economic realities.

For example, no other modern industry would tolerate a rework rate of over 100% in its manufacturing process. A construction worker who can not build it right the first time, most of the time, is soon out of a job. In software, even the smallest piece of code is likely to be revised or completely rewritten during testing and debugging. We accept this sort of refinement during a creative process like design, not as part of a manufacturing process. No one expects an engineer to create a perfect design the first time. Even if she does, it must still be put through the refinement process just to prove that it was perfect.

If we learn nothing else from Japanese management techniques, we should learn that it is counter-productive to blame the workers for errors in the process. Instead of continuing to force software development to conform to an incorrect process model, we need to revise the process so that it helps rather than hinders efforts to produce better software. This is the litmus test of "software engineering." Engineering is about how you do the process, not about whether the final design document needs a CAD system to produce it.

The overwhelming problem with software development is that everything is part of the design process. Coding is design, testing and debugging are part of design, and what we typically call software design is still part of design. Software may be cheap to build, but it is incredibly expensive to design. Software is so complex that there are plenty of different design aspects and their resulting design views. The problem is that all the different aspects interrelate (just like they do in hardware engineering). It would be nice if top level designers could ignore the details of module algorithm design. Likewise, it would be nice if programmers did not have to worry about top level design issues when designing the internal algorithms of a module. Unfortunately, the aspects of one design layer intrude into the others. The choice of algorithms for a given module can be as important to the overall success of the software system as any of the higher level design aspects. There is no hierarchy of importance among the different aspects of a software design. An incorrect design at the lowest module level can be as fatal as a mistake at the highest level. A software design must be complete and correct in all its aspects, or all software builds based on the design will be erroneous.

In order to deal with the complexity, software is designed in layers. When a programmer is worrying about the detailed design of one module, there are probably hundreds of other modules and thousands of other details that he can not possibly worry about at the same time. For example, there are important aspects of software design that do not fall cleanly into the categories of data structures and algorithms. Ideally, programmers should not have to worry about these other aspects of a design when designing code.

This is not how it works, however, and the reasons start to make sense. The software design is not complete until it has been coded and tested. Testing is a fundamental part of the design validation and refinement process. The high level structural design is not a complete software design; it is just a structural framework for the detailed design. We have very limited capabilities for rigorously validating a high level design. The detailed design will ultimately influence (or should be allowed to influence) the high level design at least as much as other factors. Refining all the aspects of a design is a process that should be happening throughout the design cycle. If any aspect of the design is frozen out of the refinement process, it is hardly surprising that the final design will be poor or even unworkable.

It would be nice if high level software design could be a more rigorous engineering process, but the real world of software systems is not rigorous. Software is too complex and it depends on too many other things. Maybe some hardware does not work quite the way the designers thought it did, or a library routine has an undocumented restriction. These are the kinds of problems that every software project encounters sooner or later. These are the kinds of problems discovered during testing (if we do a good job of testing), for the simple reason that there was no way to discover them earlier. When they are discovered, they force a change in the design. If we are lucky, the design changes are local. More often than not, the changes will ripple through some significant portion of the entire software design (Murphy's Law). When part of the affected design can not change for some reason, then the other parts of the design will have to be weakened to accommodate. This often results is what managers perceive as "hacking," but it is the reality of software development.

For example, I recently worked on a project where a timing dependency was discovered between the internals of module A and another module B. Unfortunately, the internals of module A were hidden behind an abstraction that did not permit any way to incorporate the invocation of module B in its proper sequence. Naturally, by the time the problem was discovered, it was much too late to try to change the abstraction of A. As expected, what happened was an increasingly complex set of "fixes" applied to the internal design of A. Before we finished installing version 1, there was the general feeling that the design was breaking down. Every new fix was likely to break some older fix. This is a normal software development project. Eventually, my colleagues and I argued for a change in the design, but we had to volunteer free overtime in order to get management to agree.

On any software project of typical size, problems like these are guaranteed to come up. Despite all attempts to prevent it, important details will be overlooked. This is the difference between craft and engineering. Experience can lead us in the right direction. This is craft. Experience will only take us so far into uncharted territory. Then we must take what we started with and make it better through a controlled process of refinement. This is engineering.

As just a small point, all programmers know that writing the software design documents after the code instead of before, produces much more accurate documents. The reason is now obvious. Only the final design, as reflected in code, is the only one refined during the build/test cycle. The probability of the initial design being unchanged during this cycle is inversely related to the number of modules and number of programmers on a project. It rapidly becomes indistinguishable from zero.

In software engineering, we desperately need good design at all levels. In particular, we need good top level design. The better the early design, the easier detailed design will be. Designers should use anything that helps. Structure charts, Booch diagrams, state tables, PDL, etc.—if it helps, then use it. We must keep in mind, however, that these tools and notations are not a software design. Eventually, we have to create the real software design, and it will be in some programming language. Therefore, we should not be afraid to code our designs as we derive them. We simply must be willing to refine them as necessary.

There is as yet no design notation equally suited for use in both top level design and detailed design. Ultimately, the design will end up coded in some programming language. This means that top level design notations have to be translated into the target programming language before detailed design can begin. This translation step takes time and introduces errors. Rather than translate from a notation that may not map cleanly into the programming language of choice, programmers often go back to the requirements and redo the top level design, coding it as they go. This, too, is part of the reality of software development.

It is probably better to let the original designers write the original code, rather than have someone else translate a language independent design later. What we need is a unified design notation suitable for all levels of design. In other words, we need a programming language that is also suitable for capturing high level design concepts. This is where C++ comes in. C++ is a programming language suitable for real world projects that is also a more expressive software design language. C++ allows us to directly express high level information about design components. This makes it easier to produce the design, and easier to refine it later. With its stronger type checking, it also helps the process of detecting design errors. This results in a more robust design, in essence a better engineered design.

Ultimately, a software design must be represented in some programming language, and then validated and refined via a build/test cycle. Any pretense otherwise is just silliness. Consider what software development tools and techniques have gained popularity. Structured programming was considered a breakthrough in its time. Pascal popularized it and in turn became popular. Object oriented design is the new rage and C++ is at the heart of it. Now think about what has not worked. CASE tools? Popular, yes; universal, no. Structure charts? Same thing. Likewise, Warner-Orr diagrams, Booch diagrams, object diagrams, you name it. Each has its strengths, and a single fundamental weakness—it really isn't a software design. In fact the only software design notation that can be called widespread is PDL, and what does that look like.

This says that the collective subconscious of the software industry instinctively knows that improvements in programming techniques and real world programming languages in particular are overwhelmingly more important than anything else in the software business. It also says that programmers are interested in design. When more expressive programming languages become available, software developers will adopt them.

Also consider how the process of software development is changing. Once upon a time we had the waterfall process. Now we talk of spiral development and rapid prototyping. While such techniques are often justified with terms like "risk abatement" and "shortened product delivery times," they are really just excuses to start coding earlier in the life cycle. This is good. This allows the build/test cycle to start validating and refining the design earlier. It also means that it is more likely that the software designers that developed the top level design are still around to do the detailed design.

As noted above—engineering is more about how you do the process than it is about what the final product looks like. We in the software business are close to being engineers, but we need a couple of perceptual changes. Programming and the build/test cycle are central to the process of engineering software. We need to manage them as such. The economics of the build/test cycle, plus the fact that a software system can represent practically anything, makes it very unlikely that we will find any general purpose methods for validating a software design. We can improve this process, but we can not escape it.

One final point: the goal of any engineering design project is the production of some documentation. Obviously, the actual design documents are the most important, but they are not the only ones that must be produced. Someone is eventually expected to use the software. It is also likely that the system will have to be modified and enhanced at a later time. This means that auxiliary documentation is as important for a software project as it is for a hardware project. Ignoring for now users manuals, installation guides, and other documents not directly associated with the design process, there are still two important needs that must be solved with auxiliary design documents.

The first use of auxiliary documentation is to capture important information from the problem space that did not make it directly into the design. Software design involves inventing software concepts to model concepts in a problem space. This process requires developing an understanding of the problem space concepts. Usually this understanding will include information that does not directly end up being modeled in the software space, but which nevertheless helped the designer determine what the essential concepts were, and how best to model them. This information should be captured somewhere in case the model needs to be changed at a later time.

The second important need for auxiliary documentation is to document those aspects of the design that are difficult to extract directly from the design itself. These can include both high level and low level aspects. Many of these aspects are best depicted graphically. This makes them hard to include as comments in the source code. This is not an argument for a graphical software design notation instead of a programming language. This is no different from the need for textual descriptions to accompany the graphical design documents of hardware disciplines. Never forget that the source code determines what the actual design really is, not the auxiliary documentation. Ideally, software tools would be available that post processed a source code design and generated the auxiliary documentation. That may be too much to expect. The next best thing might be some tools that let programmers (or technical writers) extract specific information from the source code that can then be documented in some other way. Undoubtedly, keeping such documentation up to date manually is difficult. This is another argument for the need for more expressive programming languages. It is also an argument for keeping such auxiliary documentation to a minimum and keeping it as informal as possible until as late in the project as possible. Again, we could use some better tools, otherwise we end up falling back on pencil, paper, and chalk boards.

To summarize:

- Real software runs on computers. It is a sequence of ones and zeros that is stored on some magnetic media. It is not a program listing in C++ (or any other programming language).

- A program listing is a document that represents a software design. Compilers and linkers actually build software designs.

- Real software is incredibly cheap to build, and getting cheaper all the time as computers get faster.

- Real software is incredibly expensive to design. This is true because software is incredibly complex and because practically all the steps of a software project are part of the design process.

- Programming is a design activity—a good software design process recognizes this and does not hesitate to code when coding makes sense.

- Coding actually makes sense more often than believed. Often the process of rendering the design in code will reveal oversights and the need for additional design effort. The earlier this occurs, the better the design will be.

- Since software is so cheap to build, formal engineering validation methods are not of much use in real world software development. It is easier and cheaper to just build the design and test it than to try to prove it.

- Testing and debugging are design activities—they are the software equivalent of the design validation and refinement processes of other engineering disciplines. A good software design process recognizes this and does not try to short change the steps.

- There are other design activities—call them top level design, module design, structural design, architectural design, or whatever. A good software design process recognizes this and deliberately includes the steps.

- All design activities interact. A good software design process recognizes this and allows the design to change, sometimes radically, as various design steps reveal the need.

- Many different software design notations are potentially useful—as auxiliary documentation and as tools to help facilitate the design process. They are not a software design.

- Software development is still more a craft than an engineering discipline. This is primarily because of a lack of rigor in the critical processes of validating and improving a design.

- Ultimately, real advances in software development depend upon advances in programming techniques, which in turn mean advances in programming languages. C++ is such an advance. It has exploded in popularity because it is a mainstream programming language that directly supports better software design.

- C++ is a step in the right direction, but still more advances are needed.

Afterword

As I look back on what I wrote almost 10 years ago, I am struck by several points. The first (and most relevant to this book) is that today I am even more convinced of the fundamental truth of the key points that I tried to make than I was then. My conviction is supported by a number of popular developments in the ensuing years that have reinforced many of the points. The most obvious (and perhaps least important) is the popularity of object oriented programming languages. There are now many OO programming languages besides C++. In addition, there are OO design notations such as the UML. My contention that OO programming languages have gained popularity because they allow more expressive designs to be captured directly in code seems rather passé now.

The concept of refactoring—re-structuring a code base to make it more robust, reusable, etc.—also parallels my contention that all aspects of a design should be flexible and allowed to change as the design is validated. Refactoring simply provides a process and a set of guidelines on how to go about improving a design that has demonstrated some weaknesses.

Finally, there is the whole concept of Agile Development. While eXtreme Programming is the best known of these new approaches, they all have in common the recognition that the source code is the most important product of a software development effort.

On the other hand, there are a number of points—some of which I touched on in the article—that have grown in importance to me in the ensuing years. The first is the importance of architecture, or top level design. In the article I made the point that architecture is just one part of design, and needs to remain fluid as the build/test cycle validates the design. This is fundamentally true, but in retrospect, I think it was a little naïve of me. While the build/test cycle may reveal problems in an architecture, more problems are usually revealed by changing requirements. Designing software "in the large" is tough, and neither new programming languages like Java or C#, nor graphical notations such as UML, are of much help to people who do not know how to do it well. Furthermore, once a project has built a significant amount of code around an architecture, fundamentally changing that architecture is often tantamount to scrapping the project and starting over, which means it doesn't happen. Even projects and organizations that fundamentally accept the concept of refactoring are often still reluctant to tackle something that looks like a complete re-write. This means that getting it right the first time (or at least close) is important, and getting more so as projects get larger. Fortunately, this is the area that software design patterns are helping to address.

One of the other areas that I feels needs more emphasis is auxiliary documentation, especially architecture documentation. While the source code may be the design, trying to figure out the architecture from the source code can be a daunting experience. In the article I expressed the hope that software tools might emerge to help software developers automatically maintain auxiliary documentation from the source code. I have pretty much given up on that idea. A good object oriented architecture can usually be described in a few diagrams and a few dozen pages of text. Those diagrams (and text) must concentrate on the key classes and relationships in the design however. Unfortunately, I see no real hope that software tools are ever going to be smart enough to extract those important aspects from the mass of detail in the source code. That means people are going to have to write and maintain such documentation. I still think it is better to write it after the source code, or at least at the same time, than to try to write it before.

Finally, I remarked at the end of the article that C++ was an advance in programming—and hence software design—art, but that still more advances were needed. Given that I see a total lack of any real advances in programming art in the languages that have risen to challenge C++'s popularity, I feel this is even more true today than it was when I first wrote it.

—Jack Reeves, January 1, 2002

Index

A

A (abstractness) metric, 432, 456
Abbott, Edwin A., 331
Abstract classes
    in class diagrams, 250–251
    for Open/Closed Principle, 430
ABSTRACT SERVER pattern, 496–497
AbstractDbGatewayTest class, 536
Abstractions
    in CoffeeMaker, 265–266, 270–279
    in Dependency-Inversion Principle,
        154, 156–159
    metrics for, 432
    in Open/Closed Principle, 123–124,
        128–131, 430
    in payroll system, 360–363
    for repetition reduction, 106
    in Stable Abstractions Principle,
        431–435
Abstractness (A) metric, 432, 456
AbstractTransactions class
    class allocation in, 458, 464
    metrics for, 465
Accept method
    Assembly, 553–554
    ErnieModem, 550
    HayesModem, 550
    Modem, 544, 548
    PiecePart, 555
    ZoomModem, 551
Acceptance tests
    in extreme programming, 15–16
    purpose of, 36–37
Actions in state diagrams, 184
Activations in sequence diagrams, 183, 226
ACTIVE OBJECT pattern, 299, 305–310
Active objects
    in object diagrams, 213–217

in sequence diagrams, 240
ActiveObjectEngine class, 305–308, 310
Actors in use cases, 222
Acyclic Dependencies Principle (ADP),
    420–426
ACYCLIC VISITOR pattern, 548–552
ADAPTER pattern, 498
    class-form of, 498–499
    for modem problem, 499–505
Add method
    Assembly, 554, 572
    CompositeShape, 468
    Frame, 59–62
    Game, 64, 74, 88, 90, 93
    GameTest, 68, 70–71
    PersistentSet, 146
    Set, 145
    TransactionContainer, 669
    TreeMap, 179–180, 182–184
    TreeMapNode, 180
AddAction method
    PayrollPresenterTest, 659
    TransactionContainer, 668–669
AddClassification method, 635
AddCommand method, 306
AddCommissionedEmployee class, 371,
    386
AddCommissionedEmployeeTransaction
    class, 352
AddEmployee method
    AddEmployeePresenter, 648, 650
    AddEmployeePresenterTest, 644
    AddEmployeeWindowTest, 652–653,
        657
    Blah, 607–610
    InMemoryPayrollDatabase, 606
    PayrollDatabase, 368, 605
    in SqlPayrollDatabase, 608, 614–616,
        618–620, 622–624

D

G